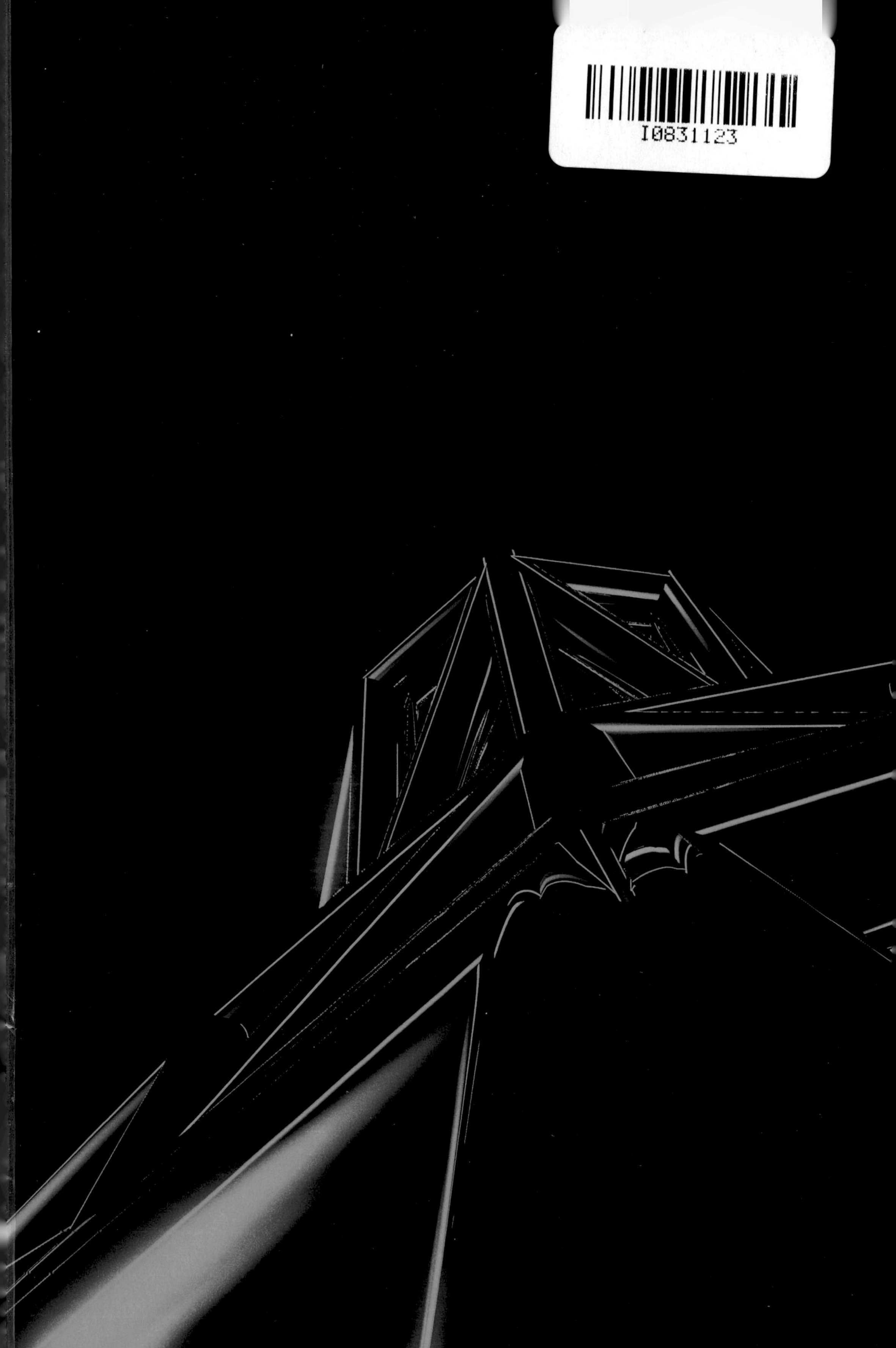
I0831123

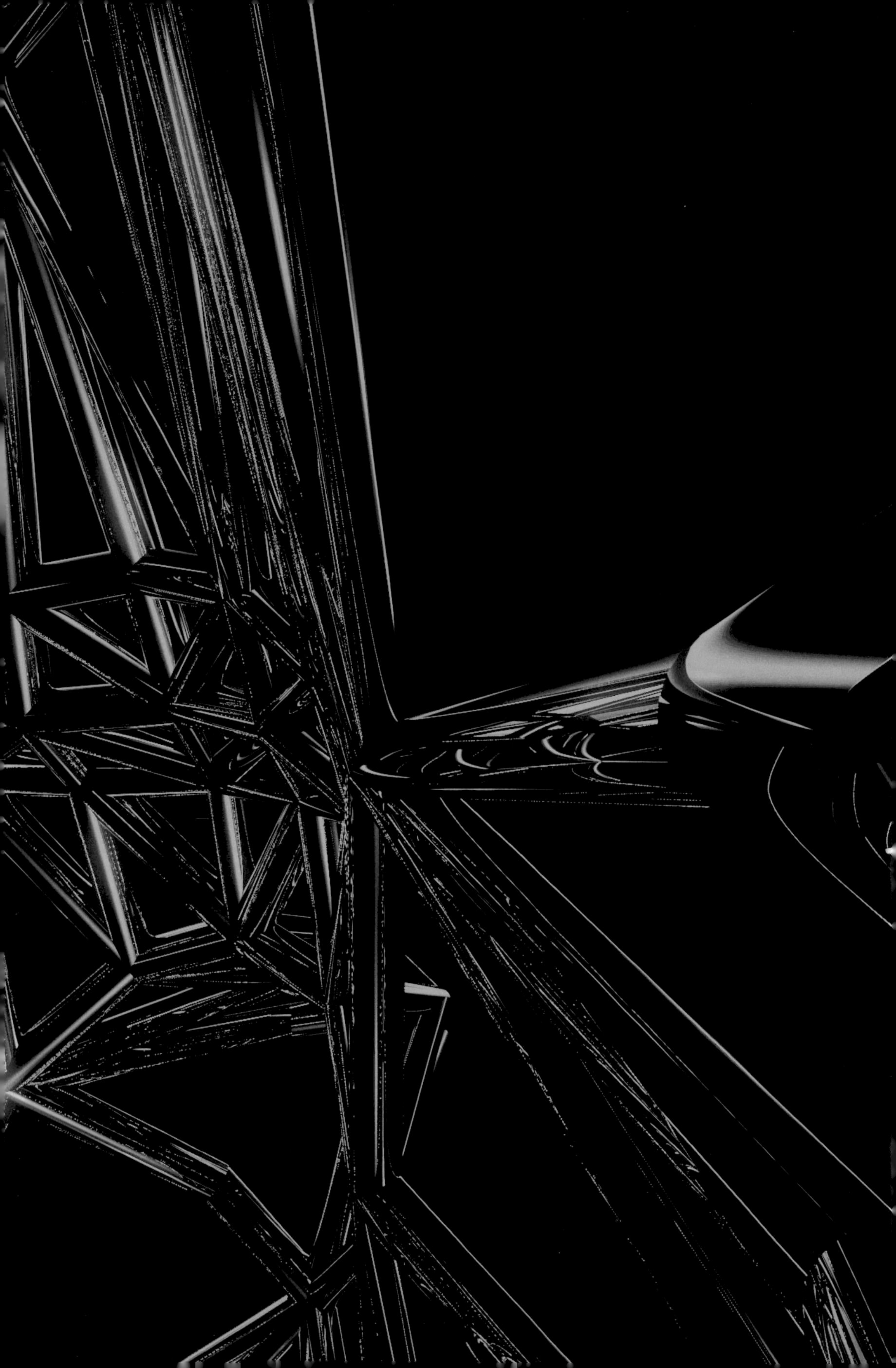

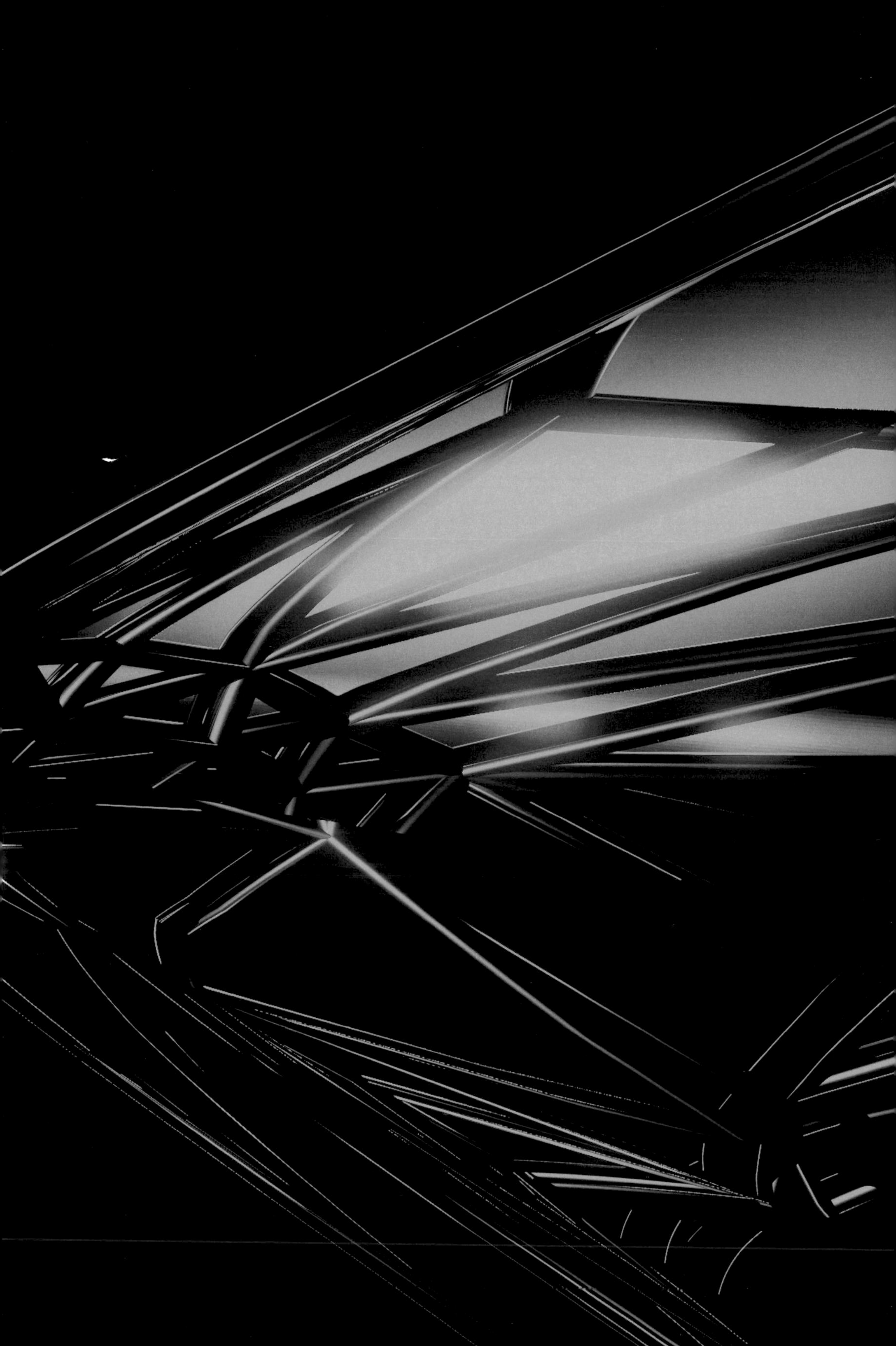

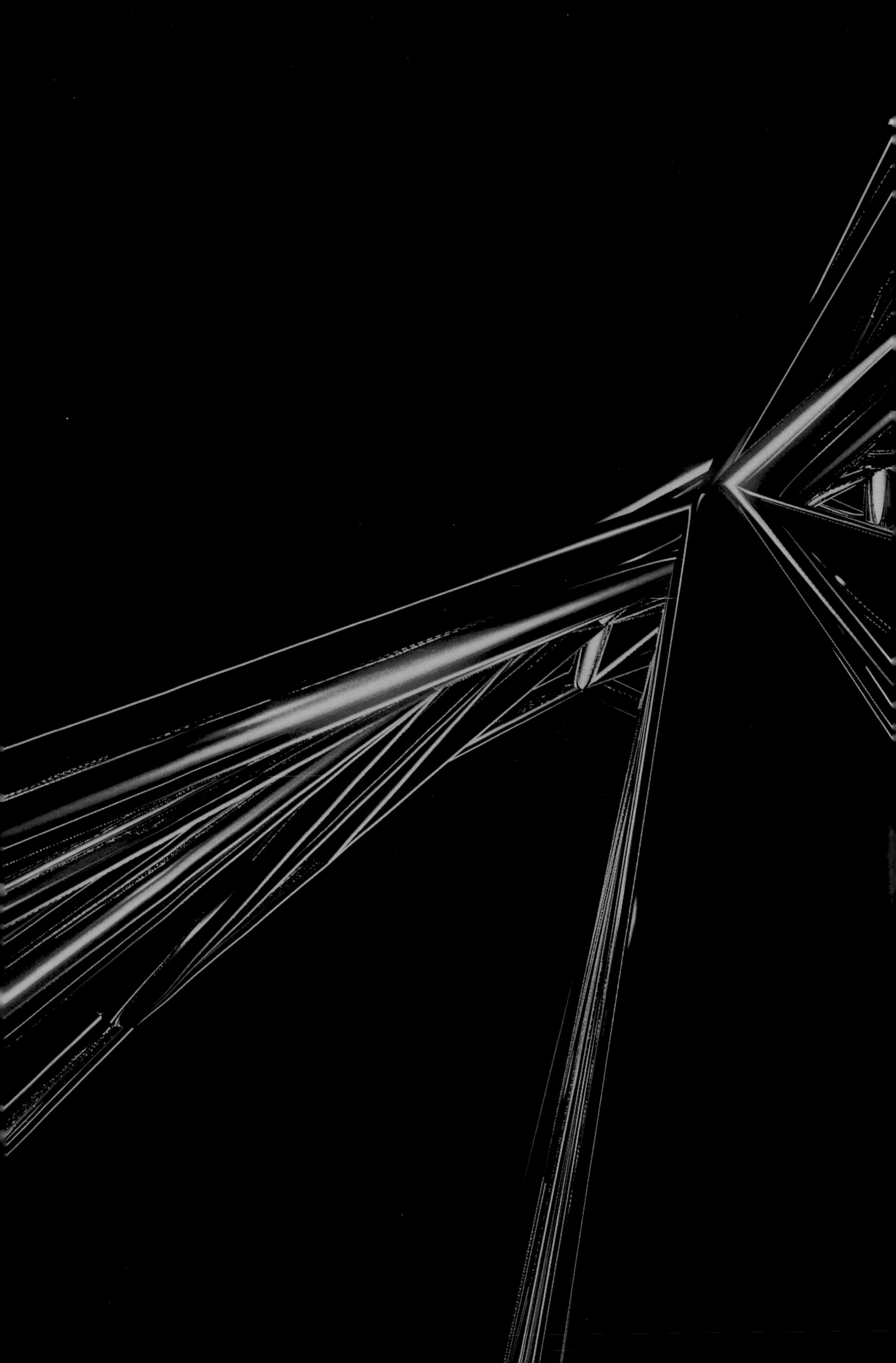

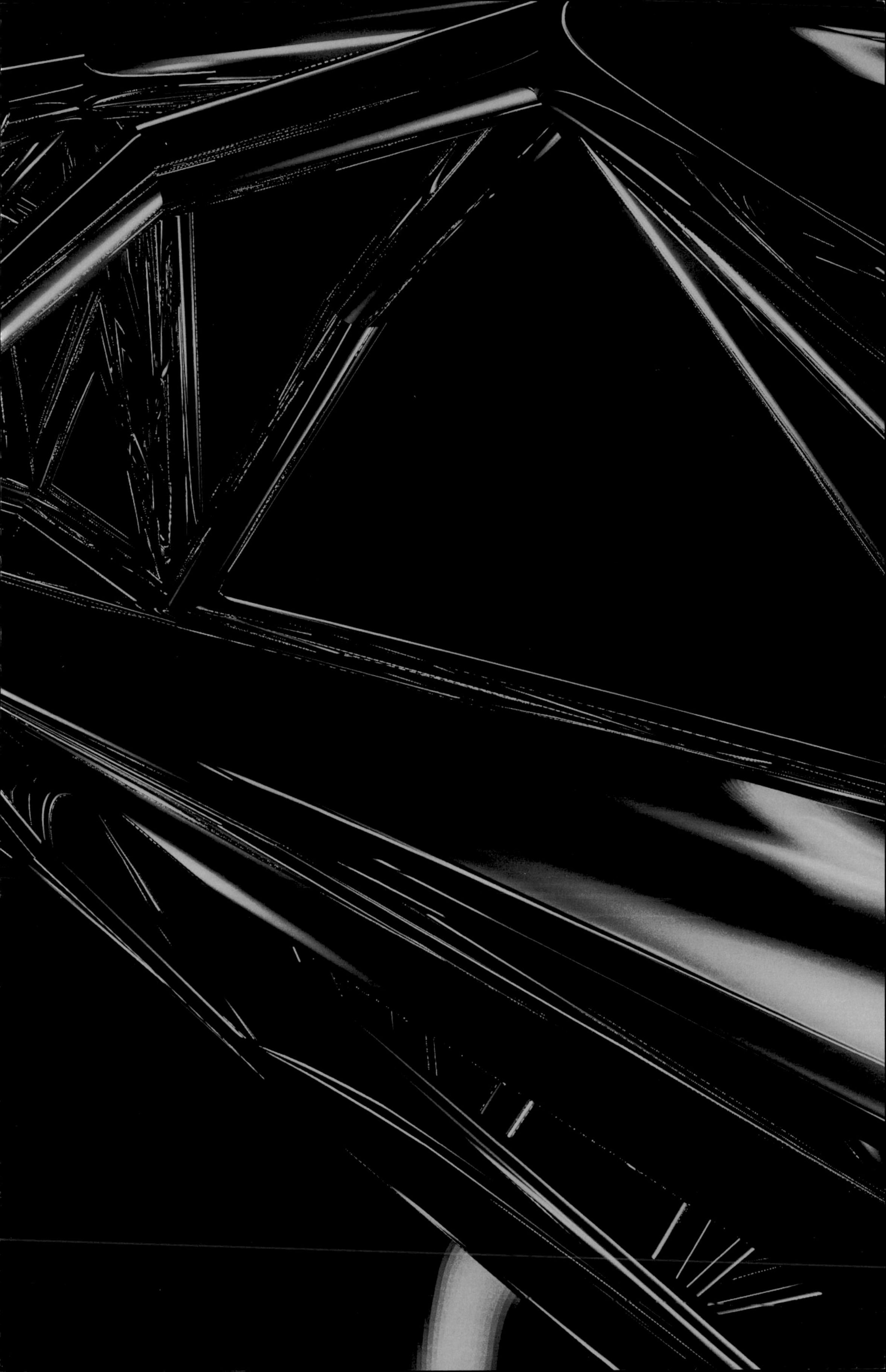

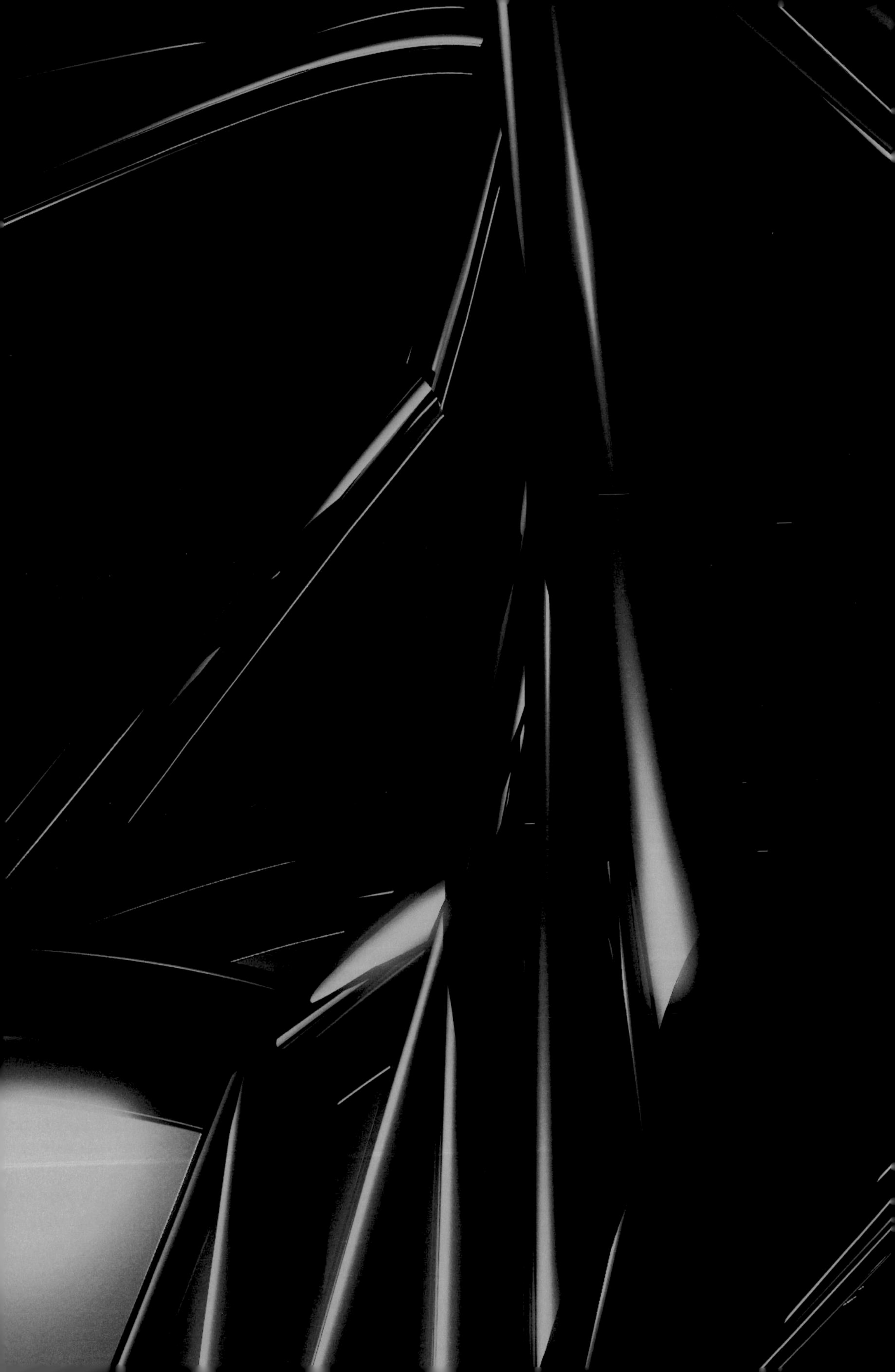

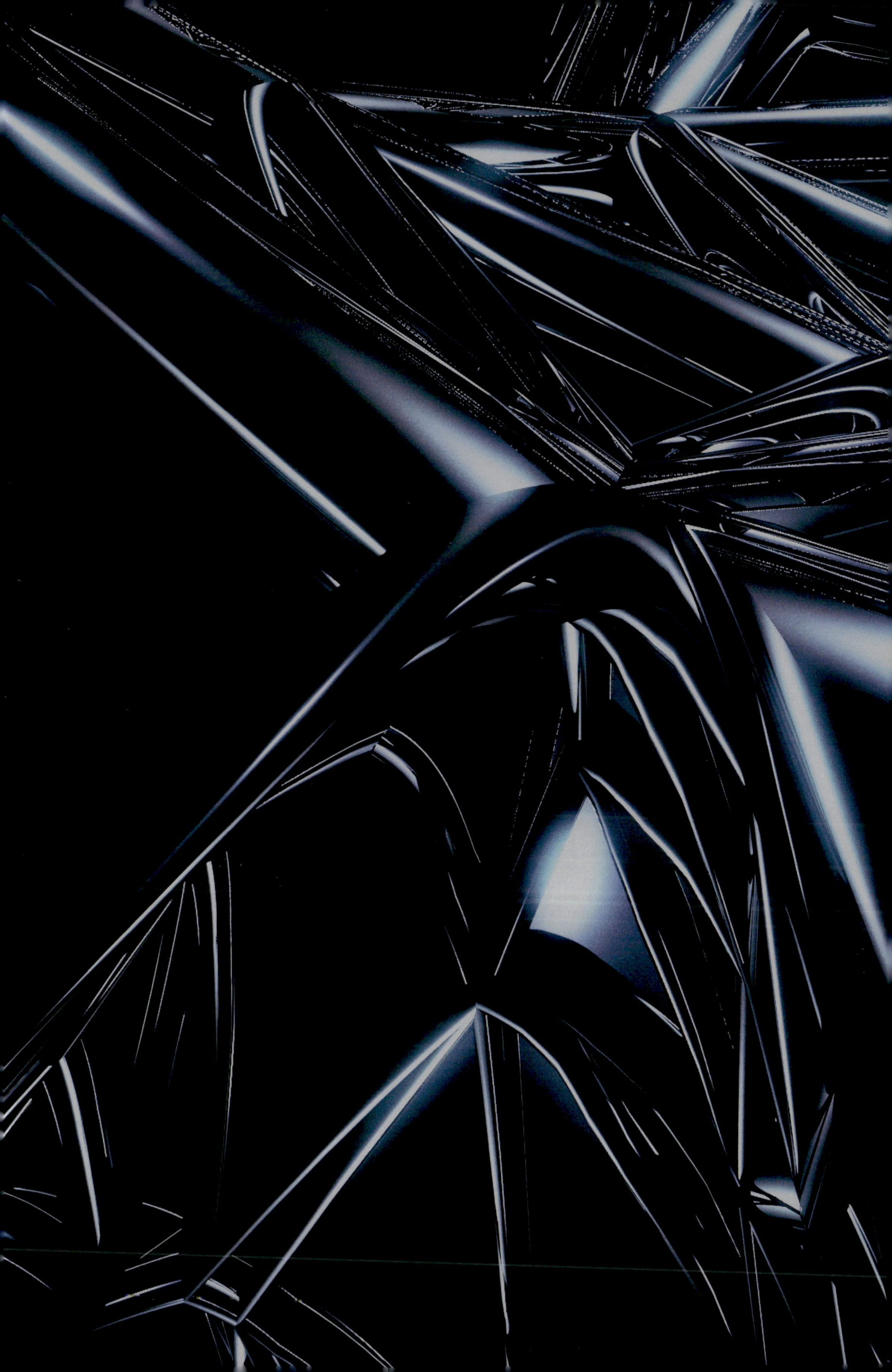

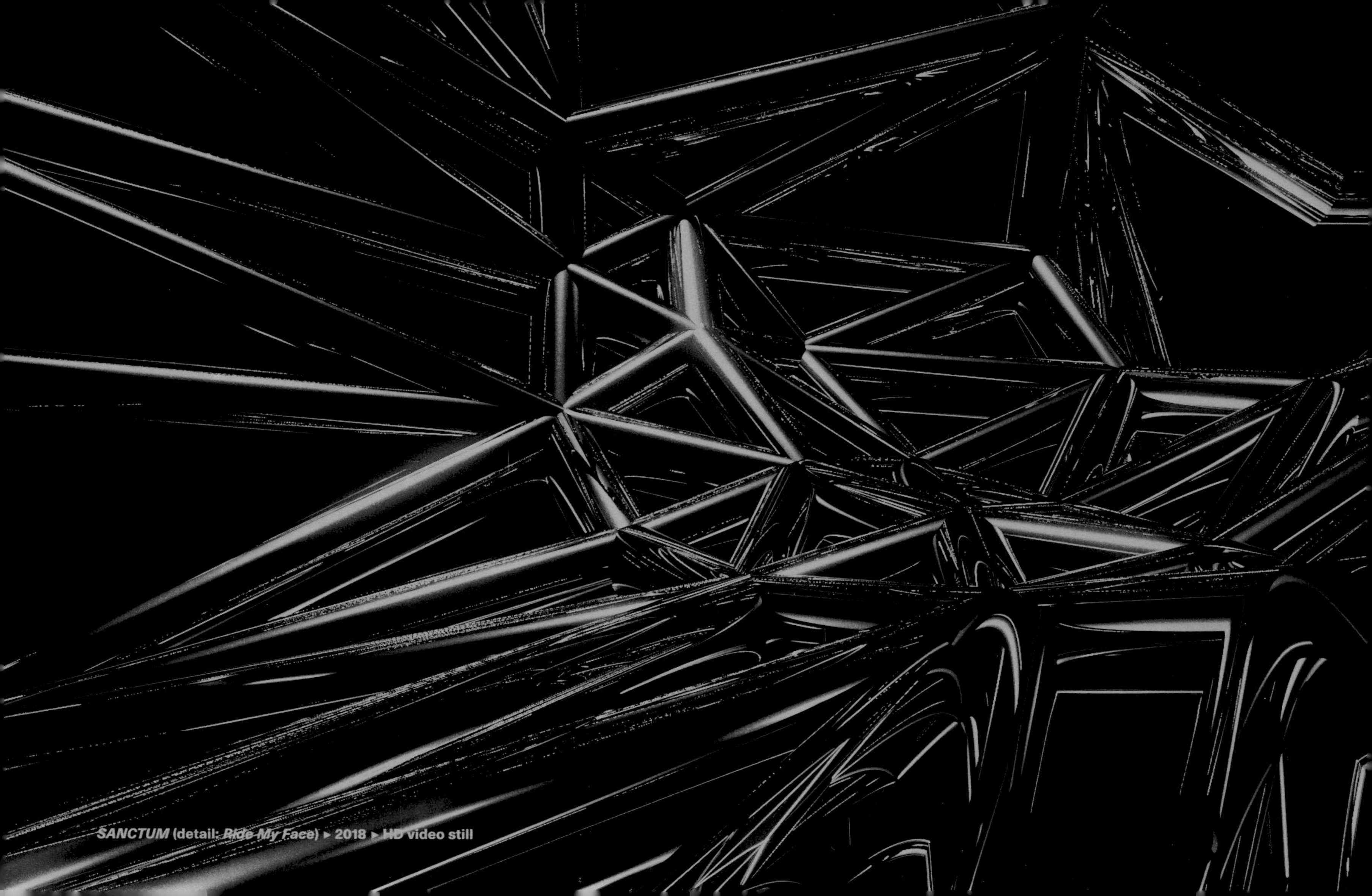

*SANCTUM* (detail: *Ride My Face*) ▸ 2018 ▸ HD video still

# Zach Blas

# Un
# known
# Ideals

# Foreword

In 2018, Zach Blas was the recipient of an international grant at the Edith-Russ-Haus for Media Art, as part of a program supported by the Foundation of Lower Saxony since 2001. Through this grant, Blas undertook a residency at the Edith-Russ-Haus to produce *The Doors* (2019), a multimedia installation exploring psychedelia, drug use, and artificial intelligence. Blas's artwork was a natural fit for our Grants for Media Art program, given his use of research-based practices to scrutinize the relationship between digital technologies and the cultures and politics that animate them. This publication stems from our ongoing relationship with Blas and offers an inquiry into his singular practice, exemplary among his generation of digital artists, through a series of newly commissioned essays by preeminent scholars, an interview, and writings by the artist himself.

Across his practice, Blas closely engages the materiality of digital technologies while also drawing out the philosophies and imaginaries lurking in artificial intelligence, the internet, predictive policing, airport security, biometric recognition, and biological warfare. Blas embraces the media of computation, video, sculpture, and music in his installations, spanning works that include *Icosahedron* (2019), an AI elf that predicts the predictions of Silicon Valley futurism; *transCoder* (2008), a queer programming anti-language; and *video mummy* (2004/2019), a mannequin mummified in videotape.

Blas's Edith-Russ-Haus exhibition *The Unknown Ideal* in the fall of 2019 showcased more than a decade of artwork that sharply confronts biometric surveillance, the cult of optimization, and the reification of data bodies. Critical of today's corporate internet giants and their ideological fascination with Ayn Rand, *The Unknown Ideal* examined the technical structures of surveillance in order to imagine an alternative space that Blas has named the "contra-internet." While Blas extensively considers the beliefs, desires, fantasies, histories, and symbols latent in technical systems, he also dwells on the horizons and edges, or what he calls the "outside," of dominant power structures. Refusing technological determinism, Blas's work makes space for escape through its celebration of queer ideality.

The centerpiece of *The Unknown Ideal* was the world premiere of *The Doors*. A sequel to Blas's *Jubilee 2033* (2018)—a film that follows author Ayn Rand on an acid trip, during which she bears witness to a dystopian future of the internet—*The Doors* probes Silicon Valley's connections to Californian counterculture of the 1960s. The work, set within a mystical artificial garden, features a surround-sound design and six channels of video comprising computer-graphics sequences and psychedelic machine learning-generated imagery related to a new wave of drug use interested in nootropics: “smart drugs” designed to unlock the mind to labor harder and faster.

*The Doors* plays with a constellation of Californian drug references, including novelist and essayist Aldous Huxley’s writings on LSD and the 1960s rock band the Doors, fronted by Jim Morrison, who was nicknamed the Lizard King. The installation features spoken-word poetry, music, and video generated by artificial intelligence trained on a variety of media, including images of psychedelic rock posters, LSD blotter art, brains, sacred geometry, and lizard skin; music by the Doors, binaural beats, crystal-bowl sound baths, and ASMR (autonomous sensory meridian response) keyboard typing; and corporate nootropics literature as well as Morrison’s writing and voice. Blas used machine learning to generate the sort of saturated, colorful imagery associated with psychedelia by halting the training process before images cohered into recognizable patterns. Evoking a 1960s liquid light show, *The Doors* proposes AI as generative of a new psychedelic experience for the nootropics age, provoking hallucinations of how to see and control the future, optimize the brain for labor, and live forever.

*The Doors* epitomizes Blas’s continuing interest in the deep influence of novelist and philosopher Ayn Rand on American oligopolies and technofuturisms. Blas’s solo exhibition at the Edith-Russ-Haus drew its name from Rand’s *Capitalism: The Unknown Ideal* (1966), which articulates her moralistic agenda of laissez-faire capitalism and unrepentant individualism—what she termed the “unknown ideal.” Blas reclaims the phrase to name both liberatory potentialities and political challenges, imagining a proliferation of “unknown ideals” in order to dispute Rand’s vision of the future. These unknown ideals highlight the difficulties and struggles of putting into practice alternatives to dominant systems of control and surveillance.

Blas’s wide-ranging practice provides endless points of entry and inquiry. We are grateful to Övül Ö. Durmuşoğlu, Alexander R. Galloway, Pamela M. Lee, Mahan Moalemi, Kris Paulsen, and Marc Siegel for their dedicated attention to the nuances of his oeuvre. Their insightful contributions expand on the technological, queer, filmic, and cultural inquiries that comprise the rich world of Blas’s practice. We are most of all grateful to Zach Blas for bringing his artistic vision and urgent insights to us at the Edith-Russ-Haus.

— Edit Molnár and Marcel Schwierin

# Unknown Ideals

Zach Blas

14

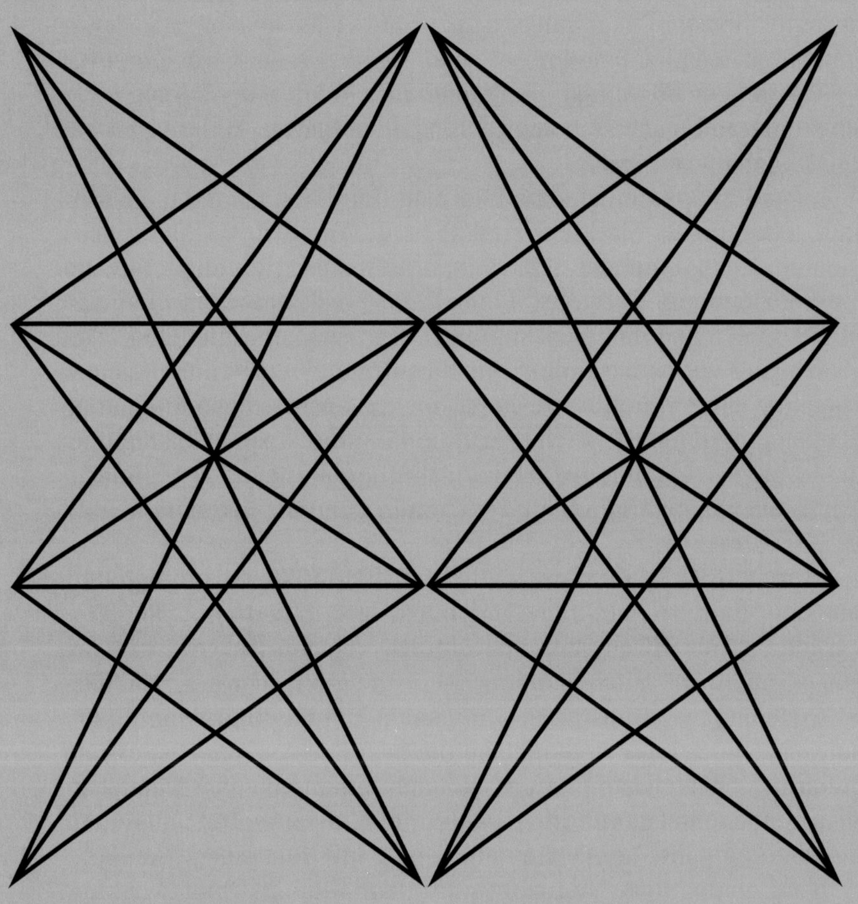

# Radicals for Capitalism

I read Ayn Rand's novel *The Fountainhead* in 1995, when I was thirteen. I don't recall who put the book in my hands—probably a teacher. Rand's pulpy, lofty words pierced through my budding teenage cool and stirred deep longings. Published in 1943, *The Fountainhead* chronicles the life of architect Howard Roark and his steadfast pursuit to realize innovative buildings in the face of a reluctant industry. Here was a lone creative figure struggling with societal constraints—I could relate: I was an arty queer kid stuck in the American Bible Belt. I cathected onto Roark's unrelenting drive for achievement and success in spite of his adversaries. After all, it's the American Dream in a nutshell.

I share my personal encounter with Rand because it is uniform, not unique. Indoctrination to Rand's fiction is as American as McDonald's apple pie and wealth inequality. Following a 1991 survey conducted by the United States Library of Congress, Rand's 1957 novel *Atlas Shrugged* was declared the most influential book on Americans' lives after the Bible.[1] And queers like myself were not exempt from the permeation of Rand's ideas, as the intoxicating allure of rogue individualism can easily eclipse the patriarchal machismo, heterosexism, white supremacy, and sexual violence pervasive in her novels. As cultural scholar Lisa Duggan points out, "[Rand's] libertarian rages against the strictures of family, church, and state appeal to many LGBTQ readers."[2]

Born in Russia, Rand moved to the US in 1926 as a young adult. She began her American career in California as a scriptwriter for film director and producer Cecil B. DeMille, and eventually relocated to New York City, where she wrote novels and philosophy. Surrounded by a group of cultlike devotees, including economist Alan Greenspan, Rand authored her theory of Objectivism, which the Ayn Rand Institute describes as "a philosophy for living on earth."[3] Objectivism features staunch principles of individualism, rationalism, and capitalist enterprise, and Americans are often initiated to these tenets through the heroic characters in Rand's best-selling fiction.

Now, almost forty years after her death, Rand's Objectivist doctrine still enjoys a fanatical championing across the US, from government to the tech industry, Hollywood to Wall Street. Her so-called virtue of selfishness, her rejection of altruism, and her emphasis on a capitalist economy with no governmental interference have been enthusiastically supported by politicians Donald Trump, Mike Pompeo, and Paul Ryan; tech entrepreneurs Jeff Bezos, Steve Jobs, Travis Kalanick, and Peter Thiel; and movie stars Angelina Jolie and Brad Pitt, among countless others.[4] In 2012, Rand was hailed "the new right's version of Marx."[5]

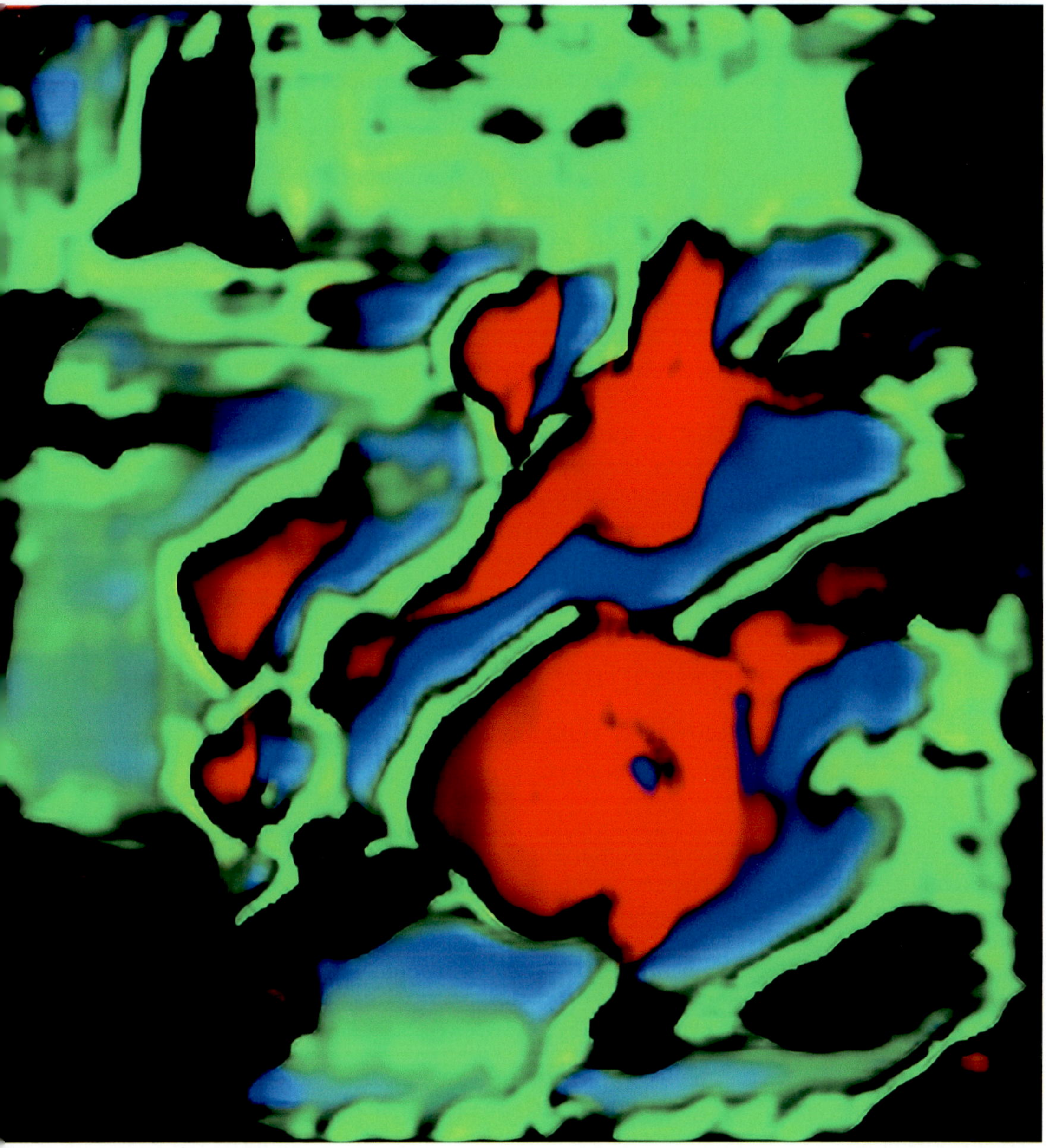

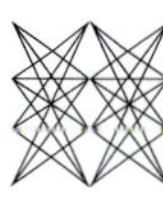

Rand's corpus amounts to a theory of capitalism, and this is most directly addressed in the 1966 publication *Capitalism: The Unknown Ideal*. Introducing the book as a "nonfiction footnote to *Atlas Shrugged*," Rand and fellow Objectivists Nathaniel Branden, Alan Greenspan, and Robert Hessen argue that capitalism is "the only *moral* system in history [...] geared to the life of a rational being."[6] Rand insists that Objectivists are "*not* conservatives [... but] *radicals for capitalism* [...] fighting for [its misunderstood] philosophical base."[7] Rand and her acolytes present themselves as visionaries of a capitalist ideal that promises to impeccably align and uplift mankind's true nature. Their capitalist ideal is specifically laissez-faire, valorizing individual rights, private property, and a free market—what Rand defines as "the ultimate practical application of [Objectivism's] fundamental philosophical principles."[8]

Rand's capitalist "ideal" is more Aristotelian than Platonic. She was a zealous disciple of Aristotle, identifying him as the "philosophical father of the Constitution of the United States and thus of capitalism," whose legacy is "individual freedom."[9] Unlike Plato, Aristotle did not believe in ideal universal forms beyond physical reality. Rather, Aristotle was occupied with the study of living things. He originated the principles of potentiality and

Actualizing Rand's ideal, or telos, would perfectly realize capitalism, the utmost moral and rational system for humans, according to Objectivists.

actuality, which account for a thing's immanent possibilities and the realization of a thing's potential through action and change. When a thing reaches its ultimate potential, goal, or objective, Aristotle names this its "telos." He pronounced the telos of humankind as reason and rationality, which for him, compose the highest human good.[10] Rand, inexact in her engagement with Aristotle, recasts his term "telos" with the more populist "ideal" and qualifies the ideal of humankind as capitalism. This means actualizing Rand's ideal, or telos, would perfectly realize capitalism, the utmost moral and rational system for humans, according to Objectivists. Capitalism is unknown, Rand explains, because it is misconstrued by the masses. Therefore, humanity's ideal has not been attained.

From another point of view, Rand's depiction of capitalism as an unknown ideal is utterly misleading, given how clearly she details it in her writings. Capitalism is a *known ideal*. Rand's principles of Objectivism are a user's manual for aspiring to the capitalist telos. Rand even supplies fictional heroes, like John Galt and Howard Roark—whose lives are blueprints of capitalist actualization—for readers to emulate. Her oeuvre is an overwrought collection of formulas, maxims, and scenarios orchestrated for the sole purpose of bringing about the ultimate potential of capitalism. In the spirit of her beloved Aristotle, transforming Rand's theoretically known ideal of capitalism into practical reality is just a matter of physical action and change—all that's left is to actualize the recipe. Notably, the Global North has strived to do precisely this for hundreds of years, which has resulted in enslavement, war, oppression, exploitation, natural disasters, and mass death. Rand's book might have been better titled *The Objectivist Lament: Waiting for the World to Choose Capitalism (Even If It Destroys Everything)*.

The Index of Economic Freedom, published by the US-based conservative think tank the Heritage Foundation, measures the degree to which a country is economically free, or laissez-faire. In 2021, the United States is 74.8 percent free.[11] Who is working to close the 25.2 percent gap and fully actualize Rand's known ideal?

Twenty-first century Randian heroes abound. Rand herself would distinguish them as "men of the mind," "new intellectuals," and "radicals for capitalism." Today, the enduring power of Objectivist ideologies is strikingly concentrated in California, particularly Silicon Valley and its tech industry. There, among a landscape of forests, beaches, deserts, and mountains, private tech campuses maintain a stranglehold on the informatic means of production. Along Sand Hill Road in Palo Alto, decision makers and oligarchs preach a techno-utopian idealism, a digitized, networked update of Rand's teleological vision. Some openly identify as followers of Rand; others do not. Yet, it is unmistakably in Silicon Valley where the known ideal continues its advancement toward absolute actualization. It is there where the horizon of potentiality and the future itself, imbued with Randian logics, fantasies, and beliefs, always return a capitalist tomorrow. As Rand writes, "Capitalism is not the system of the past; it is the system of the future—if mankind is to have a future."[12]

# The Retreat (One-Dimensional Horizon)

> **"You've never felt how small you were when looking at the ocean."**
>
> **He laughed. "Never. Nor looking at the planets. Nor at mountain peaks. Nor at the Grand Canyon. Why should I? When I**

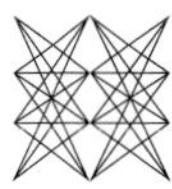

**look at the ocean, I feel the greatness of man. I think of man's magnificent capacity that created this ship to conquer all that senseless space. When I look at mountain peaks, I think of tunnels and dynamite. When I look at the planets, I think of airplanes."**

**"Yes. And that particular sense of sacred rapture men say they experience in contemplating nature—I've never received it from nature, only from ..." She stopped.**

**"From what?"**

**"Buildings," she whispered. "Skyscrapers."**

**"Why didn't you want to say that?"**

**"I ... don't know."**

**"I would give the greatest sunset in the world for one sight of New York's skyline."[13]**

This excerpt from Ayn Rand's *The Fountainhead* could effortlessly double as a wall label for an exhibition of nineteenth-century Hudson River School landscape painters. Emblematic of American manifest destiny, their compositions evoke landscape as a site of guaranteed westward expansion. Picture Thomas Cole's 1835 painting *The Oxbow*: a sublime landscape divides into an eastern region of tranquil settlements and a western block of brooding, untamed wilderness. In the east, a pastoral landscape has been shaped to the image of man and the sun shines gracefully. In the west, storm clouds gather over unwieldy flora and a blasted tree trunk features prominently—a reminder of the destruction nature inflicts when man is not in control. *The Oxbow* depicts an unknown, untamed western landscape, yet renders this land as a settlement-to-be, secured to the colonial project of the United States.

Rand's passage conceives new horizons for manifest destiny, namely the ocean and outer space. Taken out of its time, it wouldn't be surprising to find in a seasonal catalogue from the Esalen Institute, a wellness retreat on the edge of the Pacific Ocean in Big Sur, California. Once a countercultural enclave popular in the 1960s with LSD advocate Timothy Leary and futurist Buckminster Fuller, in 2017 the institute appointed ex-Google project manager Ben Tauber as its head and has since rebranded as a spiritual, healing sanctuary for Silicon Valley. Starting at $600 a night, visitors gain access to the institute's exclusive campus, which provides workshops like "Connect to Your Inner-Net," classes on consciousness and technology, an art barn, and a farm.[14] One favored activity at Esalen is bathing in the clothing-optional hot springs, perched on the coast and granting unobstructed views of the ocean and sky. I expect Rand would regard this an excellent occasion to contemplate the "greatness of man." In the dead of night, from 1 to 3 a.m., Esalen opens its hot springs to general paying guests; but as for experiencing the "sacred rapture" of the horizon, the public is kept in the dark.

Meditation getaways and silent retreats in grand and beautiful landscapes are notoriously fashionable with Silicon Valley entrepreneurs, and now a global industry of wellness tourism caters to an intensifying consumer demand to find balance between spirituality, health, and work.

But what do Silicon Valley aristocrats at boutique techno-utopian retreats see when looking out to the horizon?

In addition to the Esalen Institute, these resorts include the Canyon Ranch Woodside in California, the Insight Meditation Society of Massachusetts, the Northwest Vipassana Association in Oregon, Hawai'i's Hale Huna, the Kainchi Dham ashram in Uttarakhand, India (visited by Steve Jobs and Mark Zuckerberg), and the Dhamma Mahimã Vipassana Center in Pyin Oo Lwin, Myanmar (hyped by Twitter cofounder Jack Dorsey), to name but a handful. Wellness articles report the aim of these retreats as a "deep operation" or "surgery" of the mind.[15] From the peaks of mountains to ocean shores, participants look within themselves and outward to nature. The goal of a successful meditation retreat, in which both mind and landscape are plumbed, is to bring one's ultimate potential into sharp focus.

Horizons are wondrous occasions that provoke thoughts of the unknown and reflections on that which is greater than oneself. This is because horizons are fundamentally open. Philosopher Jacques Derrida describes the horizon as "the always-already-there of a future which keeps the indetermination of its infinite openness intact."[16] But what do Silicon Valley aristocrats at boutique techno-utopian retreats see when looking out to the horizon? In brief: themselves and the known ideal.

Take this adjacent example from the 2015 series finale of the American television drama *Mad Men*: advertising executive Don Draper, facing a crisis of consciousness, retreats to Esalen and attends a group therapy session in 1970. In the midst of meditation, Draper has a vision of the 1971 "I'd Like to Buy the World a Coke" advertisement, now considered to be the "world's most popular" marketing campaign of all time, and destined to make him rich.[17] Just as the Hudson River School painters saw manifest destiny in western landscapes and Don Draper beheld a career-defining ad while on the California coast, tech elites visit meditation retreats in order to envision future glories of information capitalism through horizons of the mind and horizons of the land alike.

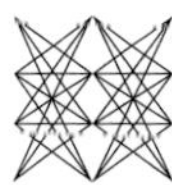

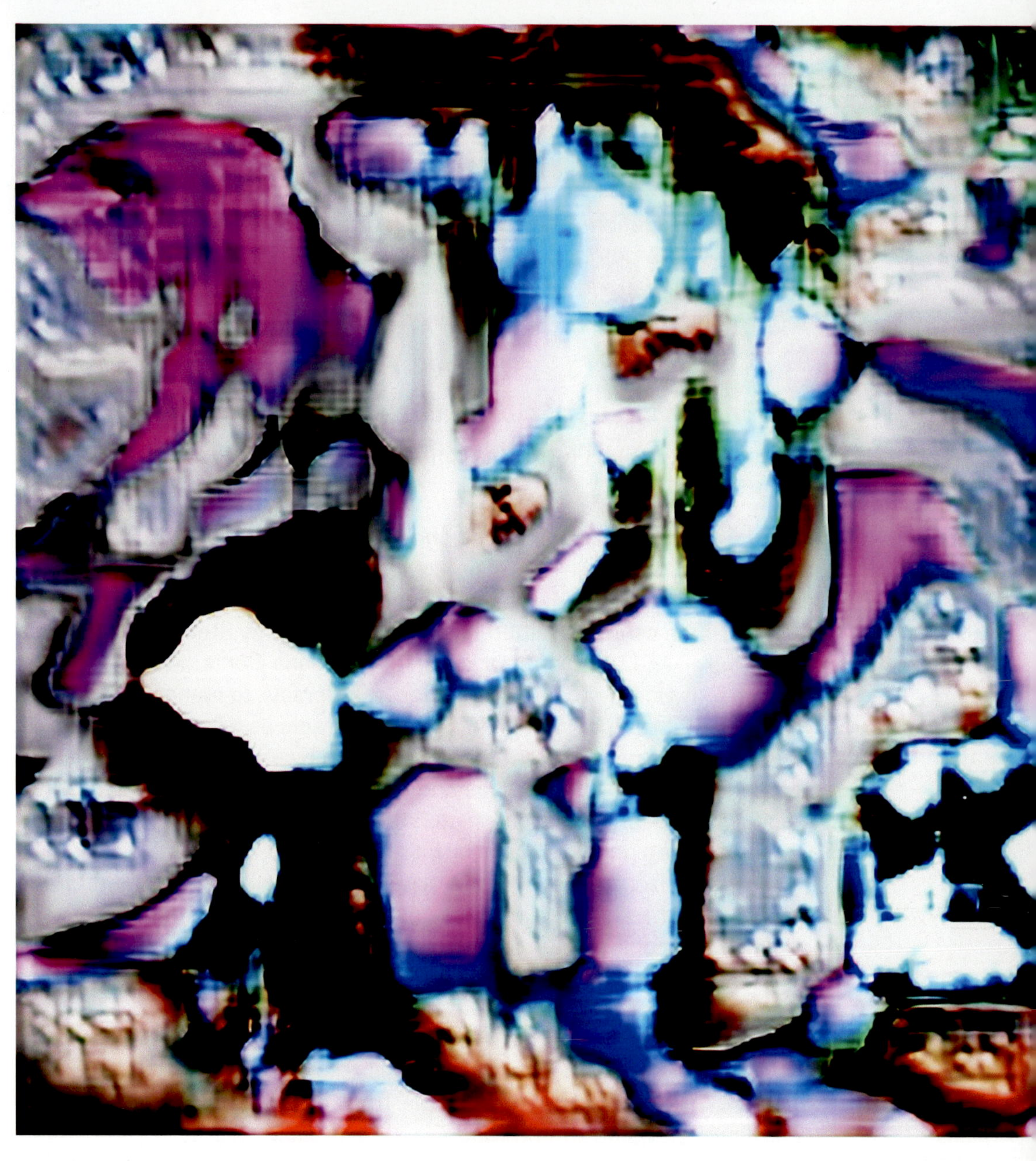

Esalen's one-dimensional horizon is styled to summon visions of a capitalist telos, not infinite openness. Critical theorist Herbert Marcuse outlines one-dimensionality as "a comfortable, smooth, reasonable, democratic unfreedom [that] prevails in advanced industrial civilization, a token of technical progress."[18] One-dimensionality luxuriously eliminates critical consciousness while pleasantly encouraging submission to hegemonic power. Indeed, the institute's financial livelihood is subject to the steady flow of profits from Silicon Valley titans. It is no surprise that Esalen is a cherished destination for tech visionaries hoping to optimize their predictions of a capitalist future.

# The Colony (One-Dimensional Future)

In 1944, a V-2 rocket launched in Germany, becoming the first man-made object to enter outer space. The same year, Ayn Rand published "The Only Path to Tomorrow" in *Reader's Digest*, America's number-one magazine at the time. Rand's essay makes an impassioned argument for defeating totalitarianism, which she identifies as collectivism. Marked by her experiences of communism during the Russian Revolution, Rand applauds American individualism as the "New Order of Tomorrow" and names "Individual Man" as "the only creator of any tomorrows humanity has ever been granted."[19] Rand wrote the text while living in Los Angeles, and although her theory of collective "Passive Man" versus individual "Active Man" is wanting, her evocation of "tomorrow" foreshadows the advent of 1950s space-age futurism, of which California was at the vanguard.

Rand's vision of a bright American future was shared by Tomorrowland, part of the Disneyland theme park in Anaheim, California.[20] Created by entrepreneur and futurist Walt Disney in 1955, Tomorrowland was staged as a beacon of the space age and centered science and technology as industries that would usher in an astonishing future. The theme park show-cased innovations and imaginaries of space travel, highways, chemistry, and geology. At the July 15 opening dedication, Disney summarized his grandiose ambitions for the park: "A vista into a world of wondrous ideas, signifying man's achievements ... a step into the future, with predictions of constructive things to come. Tomorrow offers new frontiers in science, adventure, and ideals: the Atomic Age, the challenge of outer space, and the hope for a peaceful and unified world."[21] In practice, Tomorrowland was an industry exposition for American corporations: the Monsanto House of

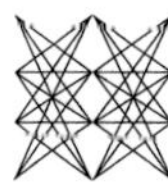

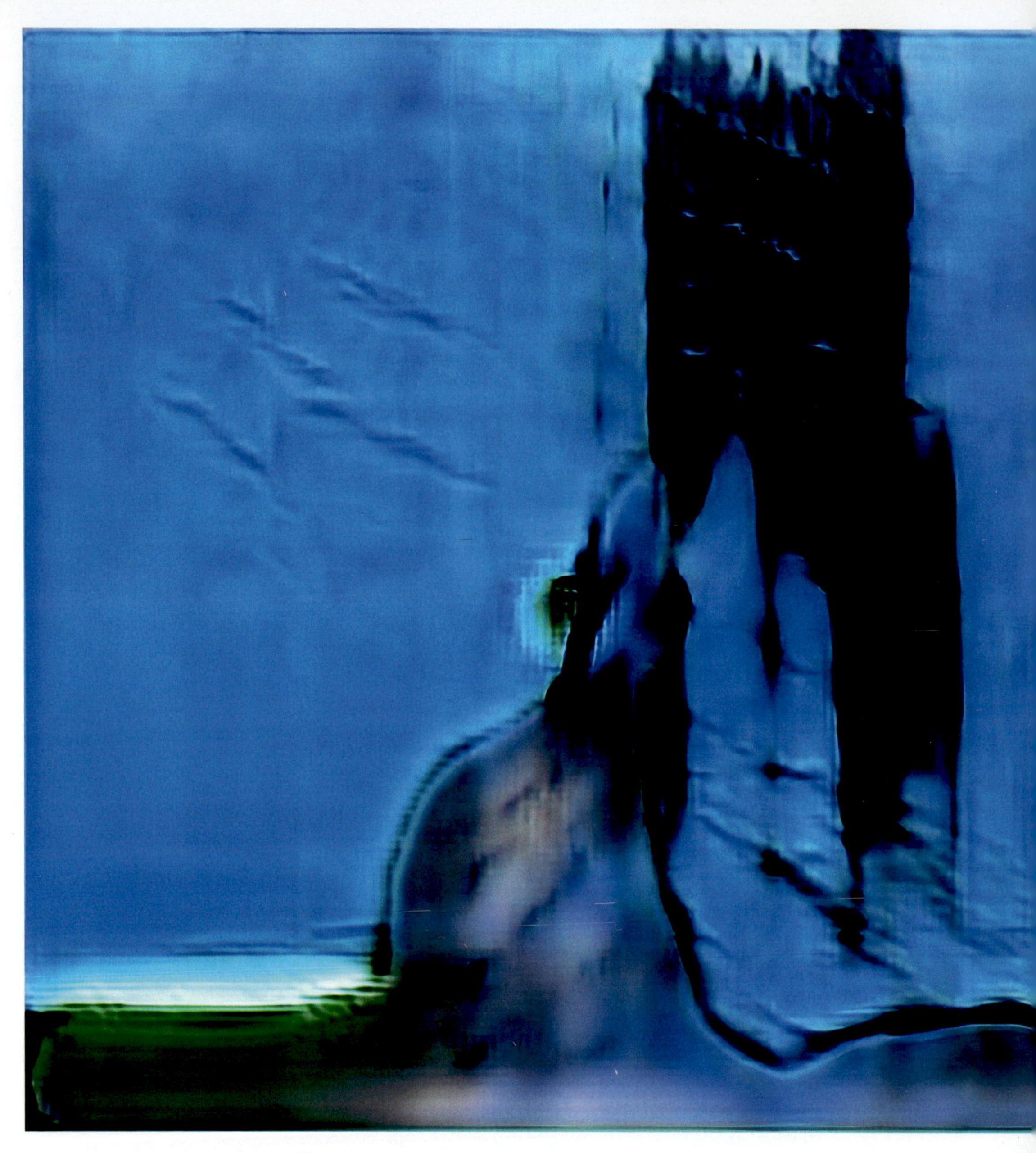

the Future promoted a home constructed of plastic; the Kaiser Aluminum Hall of Fame featured the company's top products; and the Bathroom of Tomorrow was an advertisement for Crane Plumbing. At its peak, the park operated as a singular futurist vision of American capitalism, directed by Individual Man extraordinaire Walt Disney.

Tomorrowland's main attraction was the TWA Moonliner, an eight-foot rocket ship simulating a trip to the moon that doubled as product placement for its sponsoring airline. The ride, known as Rocket to the Moon, could have been nicknamed The Only Path to Tomorrow.[22] Before they could travel to the moon, visitors were first transported, as they entered the Tomorrowland park, to 1986—the year on which the park based its predictions of the future. Parkgoers were promised to find themselves marveling at "the astounding exhibits of advanced science."[23] Yet for those Tomorrowland visitors still alive in 1986, the year is best remembered for the *Challenger* space shuttle crash, the Chernobyl disaster, and the flourishing of neoliberalism in the US under Ronald Reagan.

In recent decades, Disney's Tomorrowland has deteriorated to retrofuturist nostalgia. Its decline parallels that of NASA: once a source of great public interest and national pride, it has faded from the public imagination. Nonetheless, the spirit of the TWA Moonliner lives on in the Starship, a passenger-carrying spacecraft manufactured by SpaceX. Headquartered in Hawthorne, California, SpaceX is an aerospace company at the forefront of private space tourism, helmed by Elon Musk—industrialist, engineer, and one of the richest people in the world.[24] Like Amazon founder Jeff Bezos's Blue Origin and Virgin Group chairman Richard Branson's Virgin Galactic, SpaceX charges millions to escort the world's ultrarich on a trip to outer space—the final frontier of manifest destiny.

The colonization of Mars is a core mission of SpaceX. Musk characterizes his Mars program as an insurance policy for humanity, aiming to preserve *some* human life if a catastrophic event were to occur on Earth. The company estimates it will commence landing its Starship rockets on Mars with settlers sometime around 2026—but first Musk will have to find a way to stop the Starship from continually exploding.[25] Branded as a utopian feat of human survival, SpaceX's Mars program has received significant criticism due to Musk's labor practices and violations of workers' rights. Between 2019 and 2020 at his electric-car company Tesla, Musk penalized and fired employees for unionizing; forced employees to work during the COVID-19 pandemic when shelter-in-place orders were in effect; and relocated his corporate headquarters to Texas to avoid income and capital gains taxes in California. Such incidents have stoked concern over how human society would be governed within SpaceX's colony. Musk insists that the Mars colony is designed for direct democracy, but the company has also communicated that it does not intend to recognize international space law. Instead, SpaceX agrees to draft "self-governing principles" that will be confirmed upon settlement.[26]

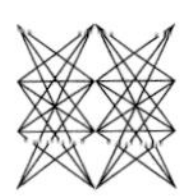

I perceive the future, like the horizon, as expansive and multiple: the very condition of potentiality. But, in *The Fountainhead*, Howard Roark looks to planets and sees only the future of man, and now Elon Musk does the same; they both annex the future's magnitude to their will. "You want to wake up in the morning and think the future is going to be great," says Musk, "and that's what being a spacefaring civilization is all about. It's about believing in the future and thinking that the future will be better than the past. And I can't think of anything more exciting than going out there and being among the stars."[27] Brimming with childlike wonder, Musk's sentiments belie a narrower and more prohibitive path to the future.

SpaceX's colony on Mars will not be an experiment in the utopian potentialities of a future society; rather, the colony will be a reflection and extension of American capitalism. Humanity will not be saved. Instead, only those humans who can afford the astronomical ticket cost will join the colony, alongside those who pledge their indentured labor. SpaceX succinctly designates their mission as "colonization," which is always a violent and deadly affair. Oblivious to historical consequence, Musk behaves like Christopher Columbus and Queen Isabella I, both conqueror and patron. Rand would interpret all this manly bravado as the conquest of Individual Man over Collectivist Man. Marcuse might label Musk a "one-dimensional futurist." With a net worth of $153.5 billion, Musk launches down the Randian path to tomorrow, terraforming the future of humanity into a galactic colonial outpost of American capitalism.[28]

UNKNOWN IDEALS

# Xeno-Telos

> **What we personally conceive by the term "teleological thinking" [...] is most frequently associated with the evaluating of causes and effects, the purposiveness of events. This kind of thinking considers changes and cures—what "should be" in the terms of an end pattern (which is often a subjective or an anthropomorphic projection); it presumes the bettering of conditions, often, unfortunately, without achieving more than a most superficial understanding of those conditions.**
>
> **—Ed Ricketts and John Steinbeck,**
> ***The Log from the Sea of Cortez***

Ayn Rand, the Esalen Institute, and SpaceX are capitalist teleologists who enforce the known ideal. But even if Silicon Valley appears to thoroughly dominate the future and the horizon of potentiality, material forces exist

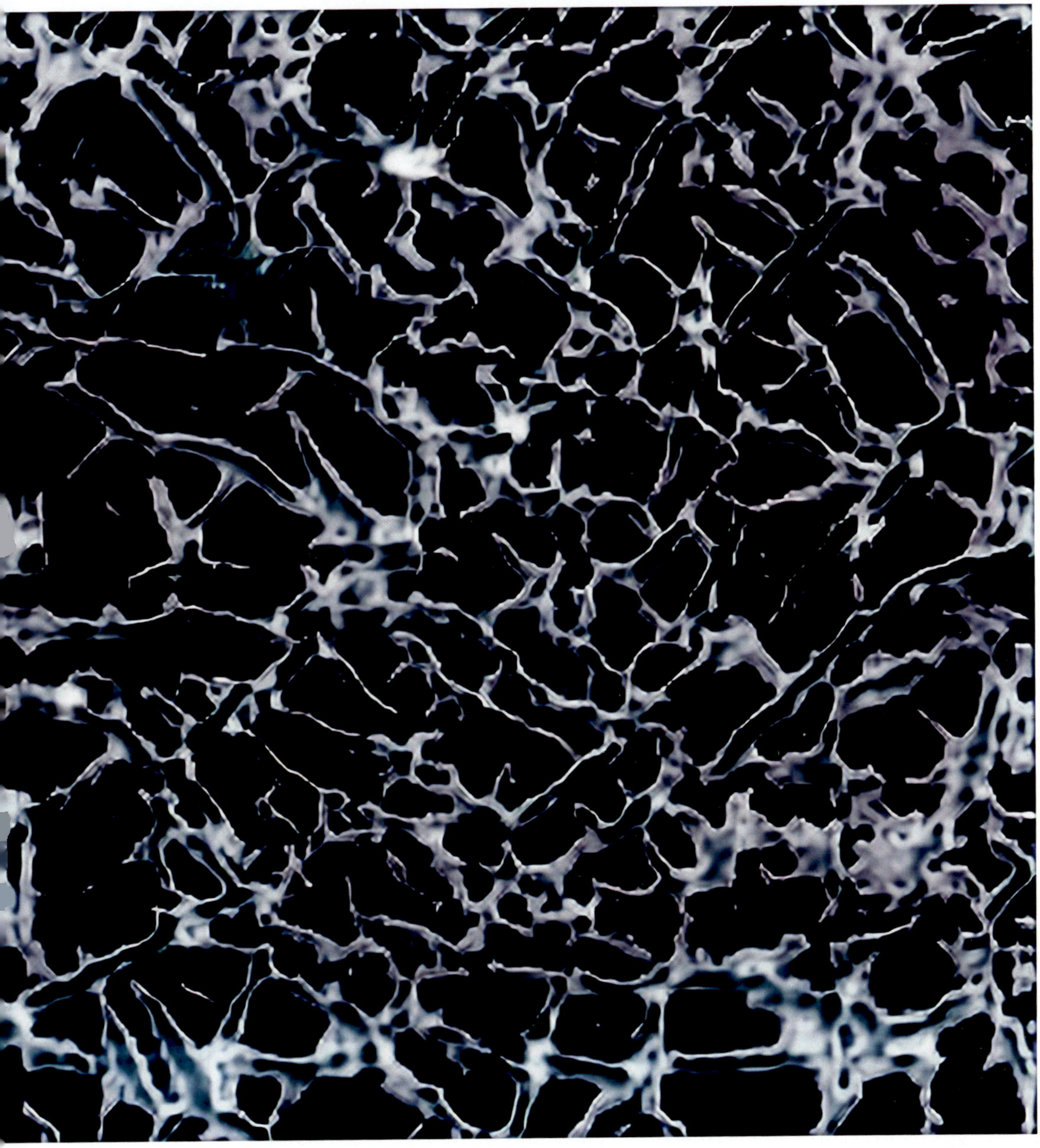

27 Zach Blas

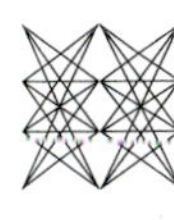

that instigate friction. Anti-capitalists demand another world and protest tech companies' exploitation of labor and exacerbation of economic inequality. Climate change's threat to life on Earth pressures the tech industry to limit carbon emissions and to restrict the production and use of computational devices.

In *Capitalism: The Unknown Ideal*, Rand does recognize hindrances to her vision. The book includes, for example, a chapter on her disdain for the Free Speech Movement at the University of California, Berkeley, in the 1960s, which she disparages as a collectivist interference with Individual

Xeno-teloses, then, describe ends that are obscure and obscured, incalculable, clandestine, not yet identified, absent, and impossible.

Man's telos. Her acknowledgment of such impediments to the known ideal highlights that if humans do have a telos, then there will be struggle and conflict over it. Aristotle might have considered this a battle of potentiality and actuality: humanity's purpose could be realized in numerous configurations, but only one manifestation is the highest good. Nevertheless, the concepts of potentiality and actuality confirm that any telos that is in a process of actualizing has the potential to change, transform, and redirect its course.

Desires shape the actualization and direction of human teloses. Silicon Valley desires to engineer a utopia under capitalism by technological innovation, or what technology writer Evgeny Morozov calls "solutionism."[29] And Rand desired capitalism via individualism to consummate man's supreme moral cause. Human desires are usually contingent, directional, and geared toward bringing about something particular. Notwithstanding, Rand presents her subjective desires as "objectivist" universal truth; they are flaunted as the predetermined telos of humankind. Her approach is similar to how a biologist might teleologically explain the evolution of a species: birds evolved wings in order to fly, or walruses evolved tusks in order to fight. Rand and Silicon Valley may assert that capitalism is the telos of man, but they are only expressing *their own desires* for such a destiny to be true.

By contrast, social movements do not claim to know the a priori end goal of humanity, nor to speak for humanity as a whole. Their directional desires are situated, historical, and amenable to multiple political systems, whether socialism, communism, or a reformed democracy. Social movements for decolonization and environmental and racial justice desire an equitable world, in which oppressed peoples are liberated and the environment is cared for and respected. These movements do not require a preordained ultimate purpose, or even a belief that humans have a telos.

They struggle, experiment, organize, and negotiate, aware that their desired outcomes are conditional.

Contra the cocksureness of Rand and Silicon Valley, what are alternatives to teleology? Marine biologist and philosopher Ed Ricketts and novelist John Steinbeck name this "non-teleological thought": "Non-teleological ideas derive through 'is' thinking, associated with natural selection as Darwin seems to have understood it. They imply depth, fundamentalism, and clarity—seeing beyond traditional or personal projections. [...] Non-teleological thinking concerns itself primarily not with what should be, or could be, or might be, but rather with what actually 'is.'"[30] Ricketts and Steinbeck expound that a non-teleological outlook would conclude that there is no grand *reason* why matches differ in size, or why some men are taller than others. They just ... are.

But what if a telos is unknown? Depending on one's vantage point and situatedness in space and time, a telos may be impossible to determine or detect. I prefer the concept "xeno-telos," which is oriented by partial perspective and material conditions of existence. Etymologically, "xeno-" stems from the ancient Greek ξένος, meaning strange, foreign, alien, and unknown. Xeno-teloses, then, describe ends that are obscure and obscured, incalculable, clandestine, not yet identified, absent, and impossible. A thing's telos may be indeterminable due to its state of being, or a telos may be deliberately or unintentionally hidden: both are xeno-teloses. Whether ontologically opaque or kept secret, or both, a thing's purpose can be deemed a xeno-telos if it is unable to be known.

To illustrate, imagine performing anal fisting. The queer theorist David M. Halperin theorizes anal fisting as a non-teleological sex act because it is not driven toward genital orgasm.[31] Anal fisting may appear non-teleological, or purposeless, but it is possible that other teleological drives could be at work during fisting, like planning for the session to last three hours, predetermining how deep to go, or non-verbalized objectives. If teleological intent is skewed from the subject to the relationalities of hand and anus, then the fist has the goal of opening the anus. But what about the anus? Are sphincter muscle contractions teleological or non-teleological? From this position, anal fisting may or may not be non-teleological; it may or may not consist of undisclosed and unintelligible teleological aims. Anal fisting would then be a xeno-telos.

On the other hand, a thing could be subject to manifold desires and pulled toward differing teloses. Human existence is a continuous endurance of conflicting desires, and as long as life is directed toward competing desires without resolve, humanity's teloses remain undetermined. Humanity is a xeno-telos.

The political goals of humans can also be disrupted by xeno-teloses. Consider a hypothetical example: a democratic government may have a classified surveillance program that has been operative for decades, surreptitiously gathering data on political dissenters. The state's motive is

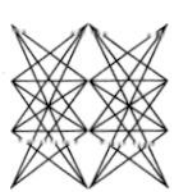

unknown to its people. As a result, the government successfully accomplishes its target of covertly crushing opposition without the public's full awareness. The state has a teleological drive, but it is hidden. From the perspective of its people, the state has a xeno-telos. Or imagine that an employee of a data analytics firm has been furtively gathering incriminating documents for years, with the final goal of exposing the company's top-secret participation in war crimes. The employee holds a teleological resolution that is unknown to the firm. Before publicly releasing the documents, the employee has a xeno-telos from the company's perspective. Consider one last example: a wildfire destroys the ranch of a California climate change denier; after losing their home and belongings, the person changes their political views and now admits that climate change is real. The telos of fire may or may not be to burn. If fire does have a teleology, then its purpose is certainly not to adjust the political beliefs of a human. And if fire is non-teleological, then changing human opinion is an unforeseen consequence. I suspect Aristotle, Ricketts, and Steinbeck could debate this ad nauseam. One could join them, or exit the binary of teleology and non-teleology altogether. Accounting for the possibilities of both an unprovable teleology and an indemonstrable non-teleology, fire is a xeno-telos. The examples above clarify that, depending on position, scale, and context, a thing can *be* a xeno-telos or a thing can *have* a xeno-telos.

For better or worse, xeno-teloses impact all directional politics—left, right, center, and in between. They conceal knowledge that would propel social movements but also throttle and fracture capitalist progress. The known ideal is a libidinal directional politics, and xeno-teloses unrelentingly obstruct and rupture its path. In Silicon Valley, xeno-teloses cunningly and materially stymie the escalation of techno-utopian beliefs and fantasies: the indeterminacy of artificial intelligence hinders the arrival of the singularity, and nonhuman forces unravel the fictions of the neoliberal individual. Silicon Valley competes to instrumentalize the xeno-teloses of artificial intelligence and the individual, because controlling them with its directional politics is essential to realizing the known ideal. But by incessantly undoing means and ends, the alien forces of AI and the individual make manifest that the horizon of possibility and the future are not fated or locked into a monolithic trajectory. With a shock, an enigma, or a weird rupture, these xeno-teloses perpetually point to the unceasing fluctuations of desire, materiality and intention, actuality and potentiality.

If Ayn Rand were to translate "xeno-telos" from the Greek, it would read as "unknown ideal."

# Unknown Ideal 1: Artificial Intelligence

In 2005, futurist and Google director of engineering Ray Kurzweil popularized a rapturous telos that continues to influence Silicon Valley's approach to artificial intelligence. Kurzweil's book *The Singularity Is Near: When Humans Transcend Biology* predicts that machine intelligence will surpass human intelligence by 2045.[32] "The singularity" names this event, in which humans and machines are predicted to merge, commencing a revolution in post-human intelligence. Kurzweil's prophecy is based on Moore's law: the observation that the computational power of integrated circuits grows exponentially. Kurzweil claims that as computation accelerates, so will artificial intelligence. Yet, in order for the singularity to transpire, machinic intelligence must surpass the abilities of the human brain. The best way to accomplish this, according to Kurzweil, is to reverse engineer the brain so that computers can merge with it. Blazing beyond the biological limits of intelligence, Kurzweil anticipates the post-singularity world to be extraordinarily abundant, providing affordable health care, strong economies, and indefinite life spans. The singularity would also transform all matter into "computronium," or programmable material.[33]

Tech leaders, especially, are captivated by Kurzweil's singularity ideal and actively spur its realization. Peter Thiel, cofounder of PayPal and Palantir Technologies, has invested in singularity studies at the Machine Intelligence Research Institute in Berkeley. Google cofounder Larry Page helped establish Singularity University in Santa Clara, an educational enterprise focused on entrepreneurship. Elon Musk's Neuralink Corporation is manufacturing a brain implant that fuses computational and human neural networks. Together, Thiel, Page, Jeff Bezos, Sergey Brin of Google and Alphabet Inc., and Larry Ellison of Oracle Corporation financially back radical life-extension companies, like Calico and Unity Biotechnology, that experiment with AI and blood and DNA therapies to "solve death."[34]

Artificial intelligence as a Silicon Valley ideal is further fueled by rapid advancements in machine learning, neural networks, and computer vision that have occurred in the first decades of the twenty-first century. Machine learning is ubiquitous, enabling the integration of automated, dynamic systems into myriad industries and applications, from biometrics to weather forecasting, natural language processing to self-driving cars, product recommendations to medical diagnoses. Neural networks function by training on datasets in order to learn behaviors, make predictions, and conduct statistical assessments. For instance, if a neural network is given a dataset of images of faces, then it will learn how to recognize faces as it trains on the dataset.

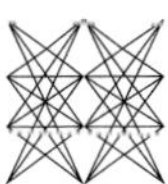

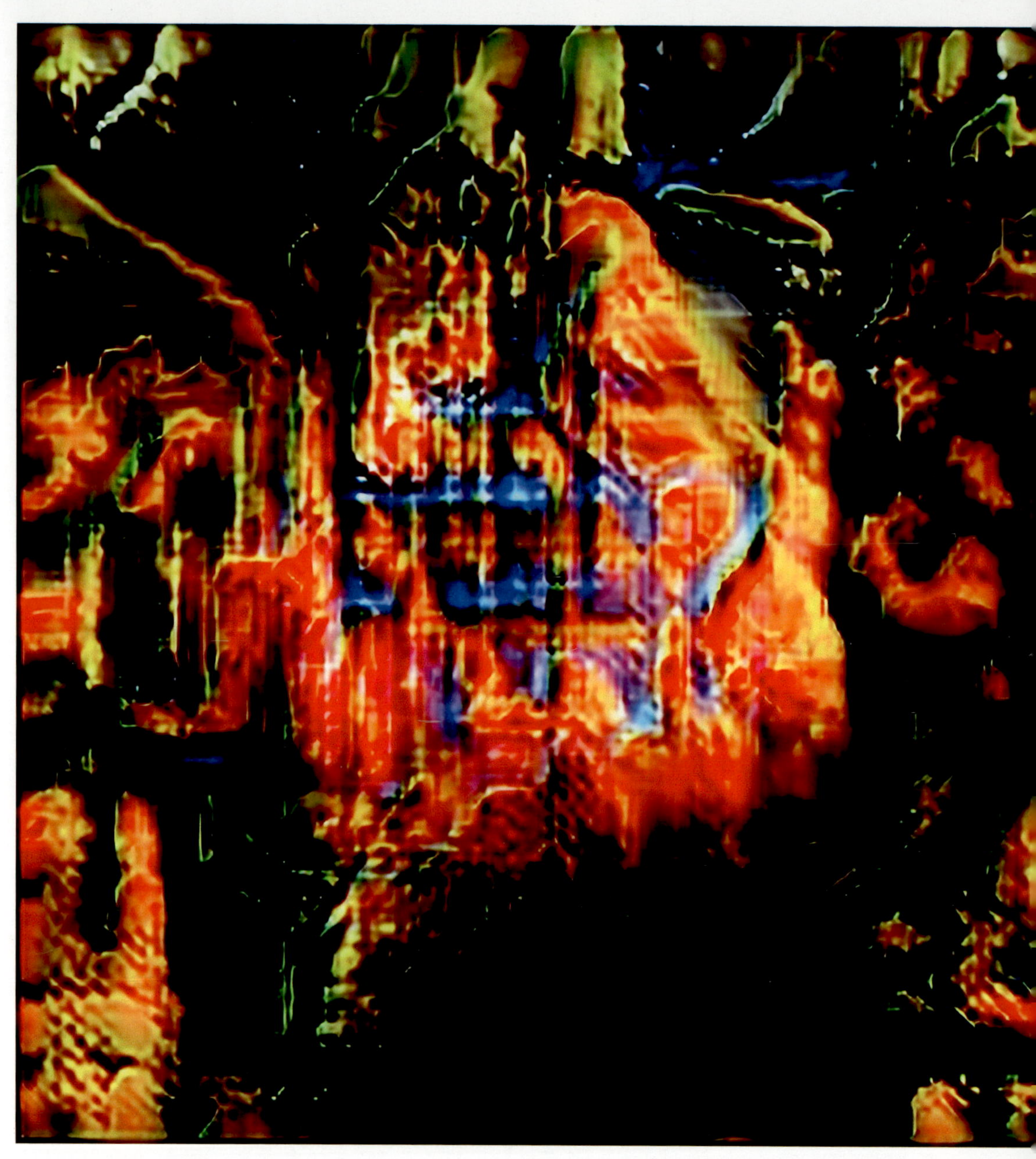

The neoliberal circumstances under which AI is developing exaggerates class stratifications. Gains in these technologies elicit a multitude of fears among the working classes, concerning the elimination of jobs, the onset of automated performance analytics, and the precarization of labor. During the COVID-19 pandemic in 2020, US airport cleaners, highway tollbooth attendants, and recycling plant workers were permanently replaced by automated machines. Amazon uses AI to track employees at its fulfillment centers and to fire them when quotas are not met. Companies manage recruitment efforts with AI, whereby job applicants are accepted or rejected based on automatic evaluations of their résumés and how well they play computer games that calculate personality and intelligence. Concurrently, a global mass of temporary contract workers power AI, carrying out low-wage, monotonous tasks like image labeling, data cleaning, and content moderation—work that is crucial for AI to work. Anthropologist Mary L. Gray and computational social scientist Siddharth Suri interpret this as "ghost work."[35] These social and material conditions make clear a class divide at the core of Silicon Valley's singularity telos. As AI's capabilities expand, the wealthy are poised to reap the promises of automation, whether controlling the means of production or achieving immortality. Workers, however, will continue to be poorly compensated, judged, and replaced.

Despite the tug toward the singularity, which aligns with the known ideal, any telos of artificial intelligence remains undecided. Media philosophers M. Beatrice Fazi and Luciana Parisi contend that computation has its own irreducible logic outside of human intentionality. Parisi delineates this as "an architecture of thought proper to computation [...] which does not exist in direct relation to human thinking."[36] Their approach signals that randomness, or the incomputable, makes computation possible, taking logician Kurt Gödel as a key theorist of incomputability. In 1931, Gödel wrote two incompleteness theorems in which an axiomatic method could not be formally completed in mathematics, shattering the possibility of a total system. Mathematician and computer scientist Alan Turing responded to Gödel's theorems in 1937 by inventing his abstract Turing machine, which demonstrated that while an axiomatic system can compute problems, there still exist mathematical propositions that cannot be calculated by axioms. These incomputables, Turing states, must exist externally to any axiomatic system.

Fazi and Parisi disagree with Turing and argue that incomputability is intrinsic to computation's form, not outside it. By acknowledging the existence of incomputables within automated axioms—otherwise known as algorithms—Fazi and Parisi show that computation is not prescriptive or predetermined but rather comprises novelty within quantitative events, that is, the generation of random data during computation. Fazi's name for this is "contingent computation,"[37] and Parisi refers to it as "weird formalism."[38] In this architecture of thought, computing is processual and speculative, opened by randomness, an infinite unknown within the bounds of quantification. Immanently and formally, unknowns impregnate computation.

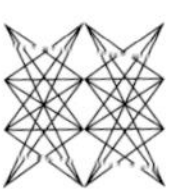

For Fazi, attending to the incomputable allows an ontological accounting of computation and its conditions for "self-determination,"[39] or the ways in which computation actualizes itself through "the maximally unknown."[40] Parisi's commitment lies in discerning an alien instrumental reason within computation that infects humanity with potentialities beyond domination.

But humans also infect computation. Artificial intelligence and humanity ingress each other: humans alter AI with directional desires like the singularity, and AI contaminates humans with its weird computational formalisms. The result is "technogenesis," a coevolutionary relation between humanity and technology.[41] Driven by adaptation, not directional progress or teleological goal, technogenesis promotes its own incompleteness theorem: humans and technology mutually mutate without end, and the effects can never be definitively known in advance or totaled. The technogenetic perspective, then, conceives technology, like humanity, as a xeno-telos.

To illustrate, picture Kurzweil, Musk, Thiel, and the rest of their syndicate confidently guiding AI toward the known ideal. Now recall that AI, as a form of computation, cannot be entirely subsumed by human desire. Furthermore, note that some AI algorithms can exceed human comprehension, due to their intricate abilities to learn from data, generate the unexpected, and change themselves. Next, imagine that AI has already permeated these men—their directional desires, brains, and bodies, inciting recursive causations that bear upon the known ideal. Finally, consider that the known ideal is always already corrupted by artificial intelligence, in ways that are never completely determinate to Kurzweil and Co. AI's incursion could continuously thwart or expedite the known ideal—or obfuscate it—but there is only one evolutionary assurance if tech elites attempt to control the purpose of artificial intelligence: technogenesis will transmute Silicon Valley's coveted final cause of AI into an *incomputable*.

# Unknown Ideal 2: Individual

On April 15, 2009, Americans started "Going Galt."[42] Members of a burgeoning right-wing movement were protesting the deadline for filing US taxes, and at more than 750 locations across the country, people voiced their anger over government bailouts and rising taxes, which they viewed as an infringement on their individual rights. Protestors carried placards that asserted, "Less government more free enterprise," "We miss Reagan," and "Honk if you are upset about your tax dollars being spent on illegal aliens."[43] Other banners featured slogans inspired by Ayn Rand: "Read Atlas Shrugged," "Ayn Rand was right," "Who is John Galt?" "John Galt 2012," and "I am John Galt."[44] These demonstrators became known as the Tea Party, a precursor to Trumpism.[45]

John Galt is a character from Rand's novel *Atlas Shrugged*. The book begins with a question: "Who is John Galt?"[46] In Rand's fictional world, the US is plagued by an altruistic and bureaucratic society, on the brink of collapse. A group of industrialists, businessmen, artists, and other "men of

"Going Galt" underscores that the human individual is the fundamental unit of Rand's philosophy.

the mind" go on strike and withdraw their labor.[47] They retreat to an isolated valley with hopes of making the state collapse—what Rand portrays as "stop[ping] the motor of the world."[48] John Galt, a philosopher and inventor, is revealed as the orchestrator of this movement. Described in idealized terms, he is "the way men were meant to be. [...] The shape of his mouth was pride," with "a face that bore no mark of pain or fear or guilt."[49] His body is hard and strong, his skin white and suntanned, like "an aluminum-copper alloy."[50] At the novel's close, Galt usurps national radio and delivers a three-hour speech on the evils of collectivism versus the superior morality of rational individualism, or Objectivism. Galt announces: "I swear by my life and my love of it that I will never live for the sake of another man, nor ask another man to live for mine."[51] *Atlas Shrugged* could be reduced to a one-sentence command: "Be an individual!"

For right-wing Americans, Going Galt connotes a fundamentalist belief in a radical individualism that hinges on self-interest and libertarian capitalism. The Atlas Society, an organization dedicated to the promotion of Objectivism, turned the expression into a publicly available formula:

> **"Going Galt" means asking in the face of new taxes and government controls, "Why work at all?" "For whom am I working?" "Am I a slave?"**
>
> **"Going Galt" means recognizing that the needs of others do not give them a claim to your time, effort, and achievements.**
>
> **"Going Galt" means shrugging off unearned guilt, refusing to support your own destroyers, refusing to give them what Ayn Rand termed "the sanction of the victim." It means taking the moral high ground by explicitly rejecting as evil the premise of "self-sacrifice" that they sell to you as a virtue—in fact "self-sacrifice" is an invitation to suicide.[52]**

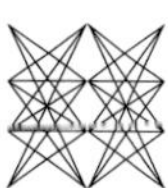

Going Galt underscores that the human individual is the fundamental unit of Rand's philosophy, for it is *only* as Individual Man that one can realize the Randian purpose of humanity, the known ideal. And to become Individual Man, one must Go Galt—it is a prerequisite for entry into the category of the human individual. Albeit operationalized as a universal formula available to anyone, Going Galt is derived from the specificities of John Galt's body, identity, and subjectivity: a white, straight, cisgender, nondisabled American male who is proud and superior. To step foot on the only path to tomorrow, to direct one's desires toward the known ideal, a thing must first become a human individual by Going Galt, that is, embodying his qualities.

Unlike the Tea Party, Silicon Valley does not revolt by waving John Galt banners, as tech workers have a reputation for being decidedly more left-leaning. Regardless, the tech industry celebrates and promotes the Randian individual; their leaders unabashedly Go Galt, resisting government regulations, avoiding taxes, and believing that capitalist competition on the free market will ensure human progress. The top billionaires in tech are ideals of Rand's Individual Man: Steve Ballmer (Microsoft), Jeff Bezos (Amazon), Sergey Brin (Google), Larry Ellison (Oracle), Bill Gates (Microsoft), Elon Musk (SpaceX and Tesla), Larry Page (Google), and Mark Zuckerberg (Facebook).[53] While Gates and Zuckerberg have publicly agreed to pay higher taxes, their companies—along with Apple, Amazon, Google, and Netflix—have been accused of "aggressive tax avoidance," accounting for a combined tax gap of $100 billion between 2010 and 2019.[54] I'm sure Tea Party adherents would be envious.

Amid current civil unrest over systemic racism in the US, tech companies have been responding by hiring more people of color. According to its *2020 Diversity Annual Report*, Google hit this goal, as, for the first time, white men did not represent their largest hiring group.[55] Even so, statistical appraisals of Silicon Valley always prove the same: the Randian individual dominates. The US Bureau of Labor Statistics imparts that the workforce of tech companies is 67 percent white, 14 percent Asian, 8 percent Latinx, and 7 percent Black. For tech founders, it's 80 percent white, 16 percent Asian and Pacific Islander, 4 percent Latinx, and 0 percent Black. Only 5 percent of leadership positions in tech are held by women. In 2020, one Black executive was on the leadership team at Google, while Apple, Amazon, Facebook, and Microsoft had none.[56] There are no labor statistics on transgender people working in Silicon Valley.

Tech companies, predicated on laws of corporate personhood in the US, are also individuals. As an individual, a corporation has some of the same constitutional rights that a "natural person" enjoys, like free speech. Consequently, corporations are permitted to directly lobby governmental decision-making entities, an activity limited to individuals and excluding tax-exempt organizations such as public charities, religious groups, and educational institutions. In 2018, Amazon was able to legally spend $14.2 million

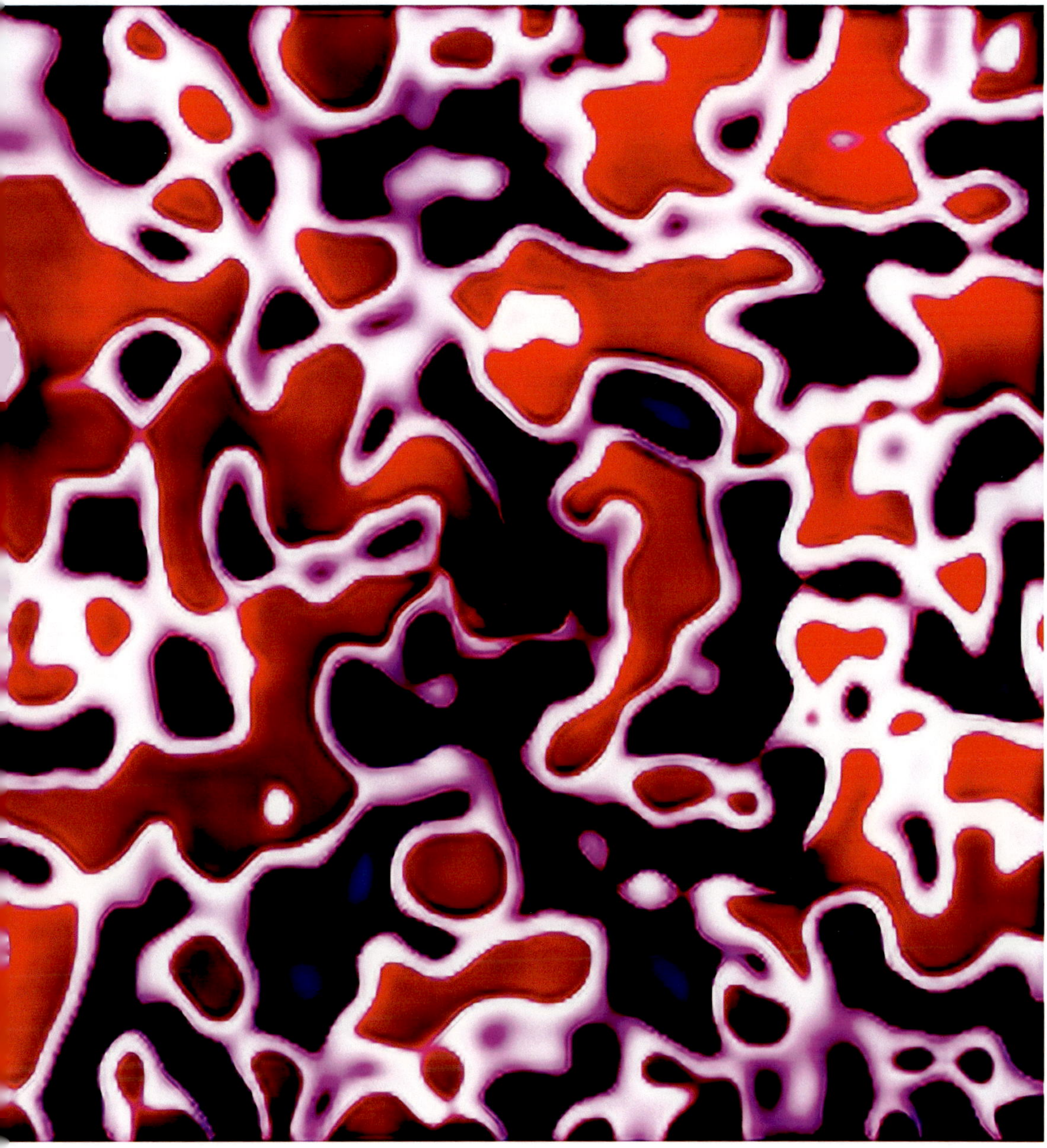

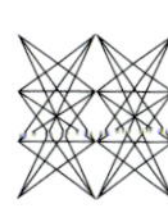

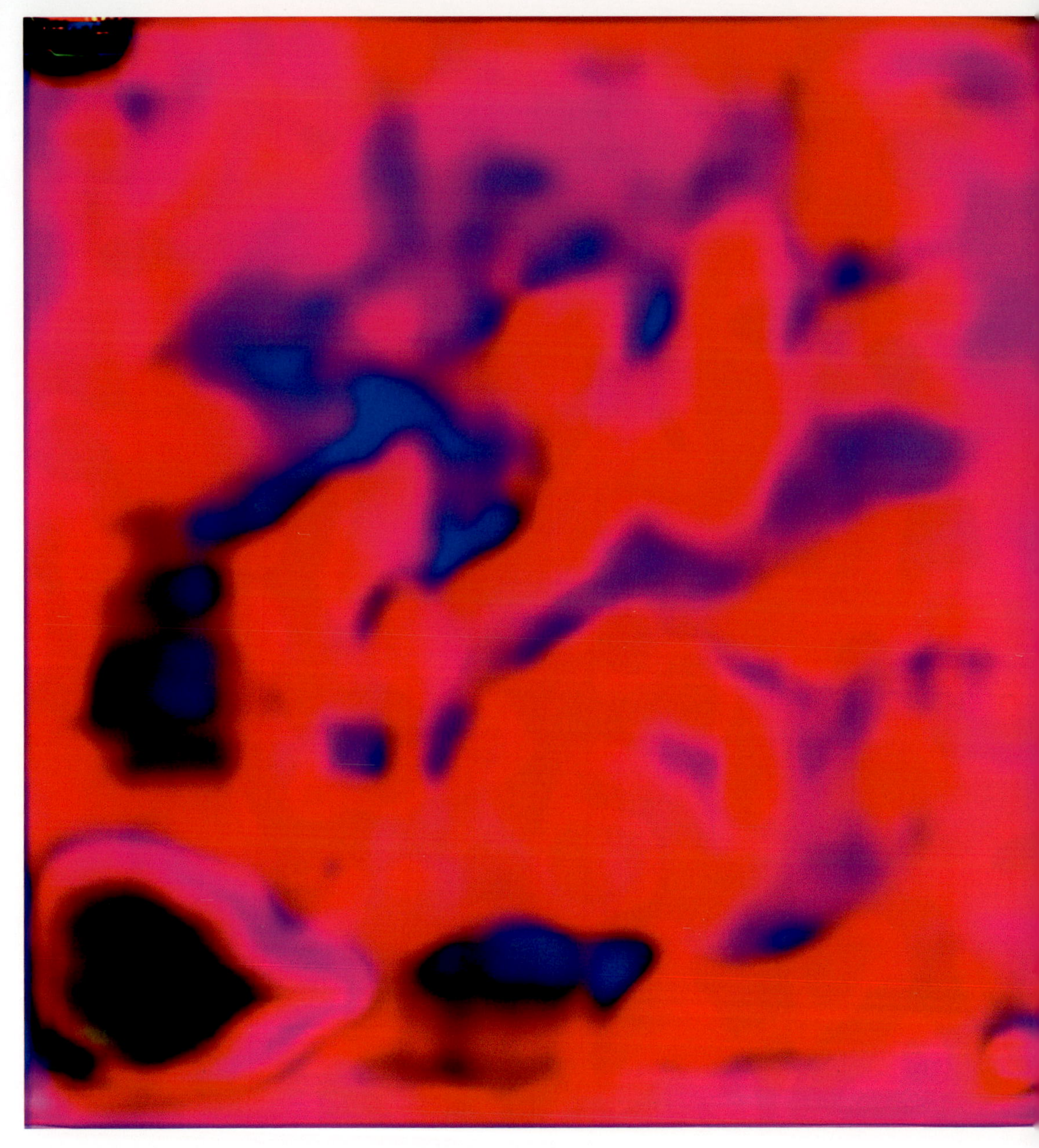

**All images pp. 17–38: *The Doors* ▸ 2019 ▸ HD video stills**

on lobbying in Washington, DC, with the aim to persuade federal agencies to rent its cloud computing services and to authorize the company to build an e-commerce portal exclusive to government.[57] Corporate individuals also reap vast tax breaks. Like their human counterparts, they are taxed on earnings. But unlike a human person, corporate individuals can easily write off investment costs, stock options, and international holdings. In 2019, a single natural person earning between $39,476 to $85,200 per annum in the US was federally taxed at 22 percent. In 2019, the corporate person Amazon was taxed at 1.2 percent on $13.3 billion in profits—a veritable Randian super-individual.

Rand's Individual Man is a direct descendent of the European construction of the human, what media theorist N. Katherine Hayles describes as the "liberal humanist subject," a "possessive individual" assumed to be naturally rational and free from the wills of others.[58] Decolonial novelist, playwright, and public intellectual Sylvia Wynter defines this model of the human as partial and incomplete. European Man, she affirms, is "an ethnoclass or Western-bourgeois form," and only one of many "culture-specific genres of being human."[59] Wynter pinpoints two historical instances of European humanism: Man1 and Man2. In the sixteenth century, the establishment of the Renaissance, the physical sciences, and European empires gave rise to *homo politicus* (Man1), a religious-secular epistemology of the human. In the nineteenth century, capitalist industrialization and findings in the biological sciences, particularly Charles Darwin's theory of evolution, created *homo economicus* (Man2), a bio-economic subject. Wynter instructs that Man1 and Man2, as the summation of European humanism, are an effect of Western colonial power, securing the category of Man for Europeans only while violently excluding multitudes through enslavement and conquest. This is why, during chattel slavery in the US, the Constitution considered enslaved people only three-fifths of a person. By another name, Rand's Individual Man is this exclusionary form of European humanism—distinctly white and a product of the coloniality of power.

Right now, I wonder if Man3 is in Mountain View, California, taking a meeting in an executive suite at the Googleplex. Or is he a few miles away at Apple Park in Cupertino, dreaming of new revenue streams while looking out across the blue sky through the world's largest curved-glass panes? Or is Man3 the corporation Facebook itself? Bred by the ascendance of computer science, telecommunications networks, neoliberal capitalism, and American exceptionalism during the late twentieth and early twenty-first centuries, Man3—the prevailing Individual Man, the John Galt of Silicon Valley—propels the project of European humanism forward, closer to the known ideal. Man3 prospers in a widespread culture of corporate greed that normalizes extreme and unequal wealth accumulation. He thrives in a white patriarchal monopoly and cultivates a conviction that unregulated technology will improve humanity. He believes in the autonomous individual, which instills principles of self-interest and an aversion

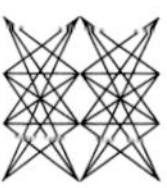

to social welfare. Possessive, superior, rational, free, agential, individual, financial, and networked: Man3 is the most superior ethno-class of the human.[60] Tech elites ardently inhabit the qualities of Man3, which are all included in the digital upgrade of the Randian individual.

But Man3 is only one conception of the human, as other modes of being teem with potentiality. Attuned to these omitted forms, Wynter clamors for a planetary humanism, in which we are not confined to ethno-classes and genres of being human but rather exposed to "a new mode of experiencing ourselves in which every mode of being human, every form

But who or what can terminate Man3?

of life that has ever been ever enacted, is a part of us. We, a part of them."[61] Such a collective and inclusive humanism would ultimately undo the genre of the Randian individual, because, in essence, Man3 is a directional desire for supremacy and domination.

To dismantle Rand's philosophical project of Objectivism, Man3—that seemingly superior ethno-class of the human—must be abolished, his energies dissipated back into the manifold forces of existence. Without Man3, the only path to tomorrow would remain untraveled and the known ideal an impossible destination. But who or what can terminate Man3?

Look inside Man3's body. There, nonhuman materials and actants are ceaselessly destabilizing the reign of Individual Man. Eight percent of human DNA consists of remnants of ancient viruses.[62] Microplastics and nanoplastics exist in organs, the repercussions of which are unknown.[63] Endocrine disruptors, including synthetic chemicals like dichlorodiphenyl-trichloroethane (DDT) in pesticides and bisphenol A (BPA) in plastics, enter bodies daily and interfere with hormones and sex organs as well as cause cancer.[64] Human cells are only 43 percent of the body's total: the rest are microbes, a mass of trillions of bacteria, archaea, and fungi.[65] The human gut microbiome also comprises genes—hundreds more than the human genome. Gut microbes reside in the gastrointestinal tract, which is joined to the central nervous system via the vagus nerve, the longest cranial nerve linking not only the gut and the brain stem but other organs as well. This connection between the gut and brain is named the "micro-biota-gut-brain axis," which enables gut microbes to send signals to the brain.[66] Although not fully understood, the human gut microbiome influences physical health, mood, emotions, and mental well-being; it can, for example, affect how a person reacts to stress or how depressed someone might feel.[67] Making and changing all of us, our gut microbiomes are like fleshy black boxes, cryptically interacting with our bodies.

Nutrition alters our microbiomes, which means food impacts the production of selfhood. I wonder, what did John Galt and Ayn Rand eat? Galt is based on Rand's husband, Frank O'Connor, so it's plausible their diets were similar. How did food modify their gut microbiomes and contribute to their formation of self? Given their love of American capitalism, perhaps fast food was a staple? Rand did live in California during the rise of McDonald's, and in *Atlas Shrugged*, the character Dagny Taggart describes a hamburger as "the best-cooked food [she] has ever tasted."[68] Is Man3 an epiphenomenon of his diet? Unlike his predecessors Man1 and Man2, Man3 is acutely cognizant of the microbiota-gut-brain axis. He "neurohacks" his body by ingesting "psychobiotics," otherwise known as prebiotics and probiotics, in order to bend his brain and gut microbiome to the will of his mind, that is, his directional desires.[69] Epistemologically bound to his qualities, Man3 can't control his desire to optimize, so he indulges in the illusion of a single autonomous mind having total control over a legion of microbes—may the odds be ever in his favor.

Although Rand did not pen thoughts on microbiomes in her lifetime, she did have opinions on guts. She deployed them in metaphors for disliking someone and for not being brave. Throughout *Atlas Shrugged*, two sentiments repeat: "I hate your guts!" and "You don't have the guts!" What pure Randian expressions. I hate Ayn Rand's guts, her gut microbiome, for its collusion in spawning Objectivist thought. Rand would argue it takes guts to be an Individual Man, but the truth is that it takes guts to *not* be an individual. Rand's Individual Man is the gutless one, acting as if alone, as if without the microbial symbionts in his digestive tract.

Microbes consume the fantasy of all Individual Men: Man1, Man2, Man3, ad infinitum. They digest Rand's philosophical base for capitalism. They eat Silicon Valley's billionaires. They metabolize the known ideal. Microbes redefine the human self as an effect of our ongoing collaboration with them and therefore manipulate our directional desires. They stealthily enter, exit, and circulate around bodies, creating nonhuman collectivities that extend beyond any one person. Each a xeno-telos, microbes constitute the human through the material forces of trillions of unknown ideals. Even though there is no single shared microbial species across the human population, all human bodies have a gut microbiome, which makes microbes an essential nonhuman partner in experiencing the multiplicities of humanity.

In the spirit of planetary collectivity, I suggest the only thing worth saving from Man3 is a stool sample, as the microbes in his poo just may provide health benefits to us all.



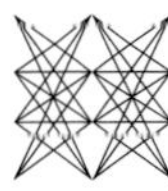

**1** Esther B. Fein, "Book Notes," *New York Times*, November 20, 1991, Section C, 26.
**2** Lisa Duggan, *Mean Girl: Ayn Rand and the Culture of Greed* (Oakland: University of California Press, 2019), 11.
**3** "Introduction to Objectivism," Ayn Rand Institute, n.d., https://aynrand.org/ideas/overview/.
**4** See Ayn Rand, *The Virtue of Selfishness* (New York: Penguin, 1964). On November 4, 2021, the Atlas Society, an Objectivist organization, will hold its 2021 gala in Malibu, California, honoring Peter Thiel.
**5** George Monbiot, "How Ayn Rand Became the New Right's Version of Marx," *Guardian*, March 5, 2012, https://www.theguardian.com/commentisfree/2012/mar/05/new-right-ayn-rand-marx.
**6** Ayn Rand, *Capitalism: The Unknown Ideal* (New York: Signet, 1967), vii–viii. Emphasis in the original.
**7** Rand, *Capitalism*, vii. Emphases in the original.
**8** Rand, *Capitalism*, vii.
**9** Ayn Rand, "Review of J. H. Randall's Aristotle," *Objectivist Newsletter*, May 1963, 19.
**10** Such a meaning even finds an echo in the Greek form of his name, Aristotélēs, drawing its roots from *aristos* (best) and *telos* (purpose).
**11** "2021 Index of Economic Freedom," Heritage Foundation, 2021, https://www.heritage.org/index/ranking.
**12** Rand, *The Virtue of Selfishness*, 30.
**13** Ayn Rand, *The Fountainhead* (New York: Signet, 1952), 446.
**14** Nellie Bowles, "Where Silicon Valley Is Going to Get in Touch with Its Soul," *New York Times*, December 4, 2017, https://www.nytimes.com/2017/12/04/technology/silicon-valley-esalen-institute.html.
**15** See "Is 10 Days of Complete Silence the Key to Better Mental Health?," *Goop*, 2018, https://goop.com/wellness/mindfulness/is-10-days-of-complete-silence-the-key-to-better-mental-health/; and Sophia Ciocca, "'Mind Surgery': My 10-Day Silent Meditation Retreat," *Medium*, March 16, 2017, https://medium.com/personal-growth/mind-surgery-my-10-day-silent-meditation-retreat-92e420e5b6fa.
**16** Jacques Derrida, *Edmund Husserl's Origin of Geometry: An Introduction* (Lincoln: University of Nebraska Press, 1989), 117.
**17** "Bill Backer Interviewed about 'I'd Like to Buy the World a Coke,'" YouTube video, 3:00, posted by CokeConversations, October 7, 2011, https://youtu.be/tSNU1TvF4pc.
**18** Herbert Marcuse, *One-Dimensional Man* (Boston: Beacon, 1964), 1.
**19** Ayn Rand, "The Only Path to Tomorrow," *Reader's Digest*, January 1944, 88–90.
**20** Indicative of her admiration for Walt Disney, Rand wrote him a letter in 1946, asking if he would consider adapting her 1938 novel *Anthem*, a dystopian depiction of a collectivist society, into a film. Rand wrote, "I would like to see it done in stylized drawings, rather than with living actors." Quoted in Leonard Peikoff, introduction to *Anthem*, by Ayn Rand (New York: E. P. Dutton, 1995), viii.
**21** "Tomorrowland: Walt's Vision for Today," Walt Disney Family Museum, 2015, https://www.waltdisney.org/exhibitions/tomorrowland-walts-vision-today.
**22** In 1982, Disney World opened Epcot, a theme park modeled on Walt Disney's plans for a utopian city of the future. At the entrance rotunda to the American Adventure pavilion, a quote from Rand's *The Fountainhead* is installed: "Throughout the centuries there were men who took first steps down new roads armed with nothing but their own vision."
**23** "Disneyland," *Los Angeles Examiner*, July 15, 1955.
**24** "The Real-Time Billionaires List," *Forbes*, accessed March 30, 2021, https://www.forbes.com/real-time-billionaires/#5d86d5943d78.
**25** See Kenneth Chang, "The SpaceX Test Rocket for Mars Goes Up Again, and Explodes Again," *New York Times*, April 2, 2021, https://www.nytimes.com/2021/03/30/science/space/spacex-starship-launch.html.
**26** "Starlink Pre-order Agreement," Starlink, n.d., https://www.starlink.com/legal/terms-of-service-preorder?regionCode=US.
**27** "Mars & Beyond: The Road to Making Humanity Multiplanetary," SpaceX, n.d., https://www.spacex.com/human-spaceflight/mars/.
**28** "The Real-Time Billionaires List: Elon Musk," *Forbes*, accessed March 30, 2021, https://www.forbes.com/profile/elon-musk.
**29** Evgeny Morozov, *To Save Everything, Click Here: The Folly of Technological Solutionism* (New York: PublicAffairs, 2013).
**30** John Steinbeck, *The Log from the Sea of Cortez* (New York: Viking, 1951), 135.
**31** See David M. Halperin, *Saint Foucault: Towards a Gay Hagiography* (Oxford: Oxford University Press, 1997).
**32** See Ray Kurzweil, *The Singularity Is Near: When Humans Transcend Biology* (New York: Penguin Books, 2005).
**33** See Tommaso Toffoli and Norman Margolus, "Programmable Matter: Concepts and Realizations," *Physica D: Nonlinear Phenomena* 47, nos. 1–2 (1991): 263–72.
**34** See the cover of the September 30, 2013, issue of *Time* magazine.
**35** See Mary L. Gray and Siddharth Suri, *Ghost Work: How to Stop Silicon Valley from Building a New Global Underclass* (Boston: Houghton Mifflin Harcourt, 2019).
**36** Luciana Parisi, *Contagious Architecture: Computation, Aesthetics, and Space* (Cambridge, MA: MIT Press, 2013), xvii–xviii.

**37** M. Beatrice Fazi, *Contingent Computation: Abstraction, Experience, and Indeterminacy in Computational Aesthetics* (Lanham, MD: Rowman and Littlefield, 2018), 1.
**38** Parisi, *Contagious Architecture*, ix.
**39** Fazi, *Contingent Computation*, 7.
**40** Fazi, *Contingent Computation*, 131.
**41** See N. Katherine Hayles, *How We Think: Digital Media and Contemporary Technogenesis* (Chicago: University of Chicago Press, 2012).
**42** See Eric Etheridge, "'Going Galt': Everyone's Doing It!," *New York Times*, March 6, 2009, https://opinionator.blogs.nytimes.com/2009/03/06/going-galt-everyones-doing-it/.
**43** Liz Robbins, "Tax Day Is Met with Tea Parties," *New York Times*, April 15, 2009, https://www.nytimes.com/2009/04/16/us/politics/16taxday.html.
**44** "Tea Party Summary from the Ohio Objectivist Society," *Ayn Rand Tea Party* (blog), April 16, 2009, http://aynrandteaparty.blogspot.com/2009/04/tea-party-summary-from-ohio-objectivist.html.
**45** The Tea Party movement takes its name from the Boston Tea Party of 1773, in which American settlers destroyed imported tea from Great Britain to protest "taxation without representation."
**46** Ayn Rand, *Atlas Shrugged* (New York: Dutton, 1957), 11.
**47** Rand, *Atlas Shrugged*, 619.
**48** Rand, *Atlas Shrugged*, 671.
**49** Rand, *Atlas Shrugged*, 701.
**50** Rand, *Atlas Shrugged*, 701.
**51** Rand, *Atlas Shrugged*, 1069.
**52** Edward Hudgins, "Going Galt," *Atlas Society*, March 23, 2011, https://www.atlassociety.org/post/going-galt.
**53** "The Real-Time Billionaires List," *Forbes*.
**54** Fair Tax Mark, *The Silicon Six and Their $100 Billion Global Tax Gap*, December 2019, https://fairtaxmark.net/wp-content/uploads/2019/12/Silicon-Six-Report-5-12-19.pdf.
**55** Google, *Google Diversity Annual Report 2020*, 2020, https://diversity.google/annual-report/.
**56** See Shelly Banjo and Dina Bass, "On Diversity, Silicon Valley Failed to Think Different," *Bloomberg Businessweek*, August 3, 2020, https://www.bloomberg.com/news/articles/2020-08-03/silicon-valley-didn-t-inherit-discrimination-but-replicated-it-anyway; and Emily Chang, "The Vile Experiences of Women in Tech," *Economist*, May 3, 2019, https://www.economist.com/open-future/2019/05/03/the-vile-experiences-of-women-in-tech.
**57** Naomi Nix, "Amazon Is Flooding D.C. with Money and Muscle: The Influence Game," *Bloomberg Businessweek*, March 7, 2019, https://www.bloomberg.com/graphics/2019-amazon-lobbying/.
**58** N. Katherine Hayles, *How We Became Posthuman: Virtual Bodies in Cybernetics, Literature, and Informatics* (Chicago: University of Chicago Press, 1999), 3.
**59** Sylvia Wynter, "The Re-enchantment of Humanism: An Interview with Sylvia Wynter," interview by David Scott, *Small Axe*, no. 8 (September 2000): 196.
**60** Products and applications made in Silicon Valley also inscribe superior ethno-classes of the human into their technical architectures. Facial recognition consistently fails to detect dark skin. Automated image detection categorizes Black people as gorillas. Additionally, Silicon Valley markets the "liberal humanist subject" to consumers and exploits this promise by turning users into data streams, or "dividuals," for profit. See Joy Buolamwini, "When the Robot Doesn't See Dark Skin," *New York Times*, June 21, 2018, https://www.nytimes.com/2018/06/21/opinion/facial-analysis-technology-bias.html; Conor Dougherty, "Google Photos Mistakenly Labels Black People 'Gorillas,'" *Bits* (blog), *New York Times*, July 1, 2015, https://bits.blogs.nytimes.com/2015/07/01/google-photos-mistakenly-labels-black-people-gorillas/; and Gilles Deleuze, "Postscript on Control Societies," in *Negotiations, 1972–1990* (New York: Columbia University Press, 1997), 177–82.
**61** Wynter, "The Re-enchantment of Humanism," 197.
**62** See Carl Zimmer, "Ancient Viruses Are Buried in Your DNA," *New York Times*, October 4, 2017, https://www.nytimes.com/2017/10/04/science/ancient-viruses-dna-genome.html.
**63** See Douglas Quenqua, "Microplastics Find Their Way into Your Gut, a Pilot Study Finds," *New York Times*, October 22, 2018, https://www.nytimes.com/2018/10/22/health/microplastics-human-stool.html; and Damian Carrington, "Microplastic Particles Now Discoverable in Human Organs," *Guardian*, August 17, 2020, https://www.theguardian.com/environment/2020/aug/17/microplastic-particles-discovered-in-human-organs.
**64** See Malin Ah-King and Eva Hayward, "Toxic Sexes: Perverting Pollution and Queering Hormone Disruption," *O-Zone: A Journal of Object-Oriented Studies*, no. 1 (2014).
**65** See James Gallagher, "More Than Half Your Body Is Not Human," BBC News, April 10, 2018, https://www.bbc.co.uk/news/health-43674270.
**66** John F. Cryan et al., "The Microbiota-Gut-Brain Axis," *Physiological Reviews* 99, no. 4 (October 2019): 1877–2013.
**67** See Elizabeth Pennisi, "Meet the Psychobiome," *Science* 368, no. 6491 (May 8, 2020): 570–73.
**68** Rand, *Atlas Shrugged*, 327.
**69** Neurohacker Collective, "Psychobiotics and the Gut-Brain Connection," June 15, 2016, https://neurohacker.com/neurohackers-toolbox-psychobiotics-gut-brain-connection.

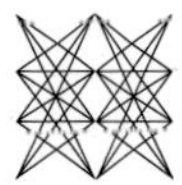

44–63

# Facial Weaponization Suite / Face Cages

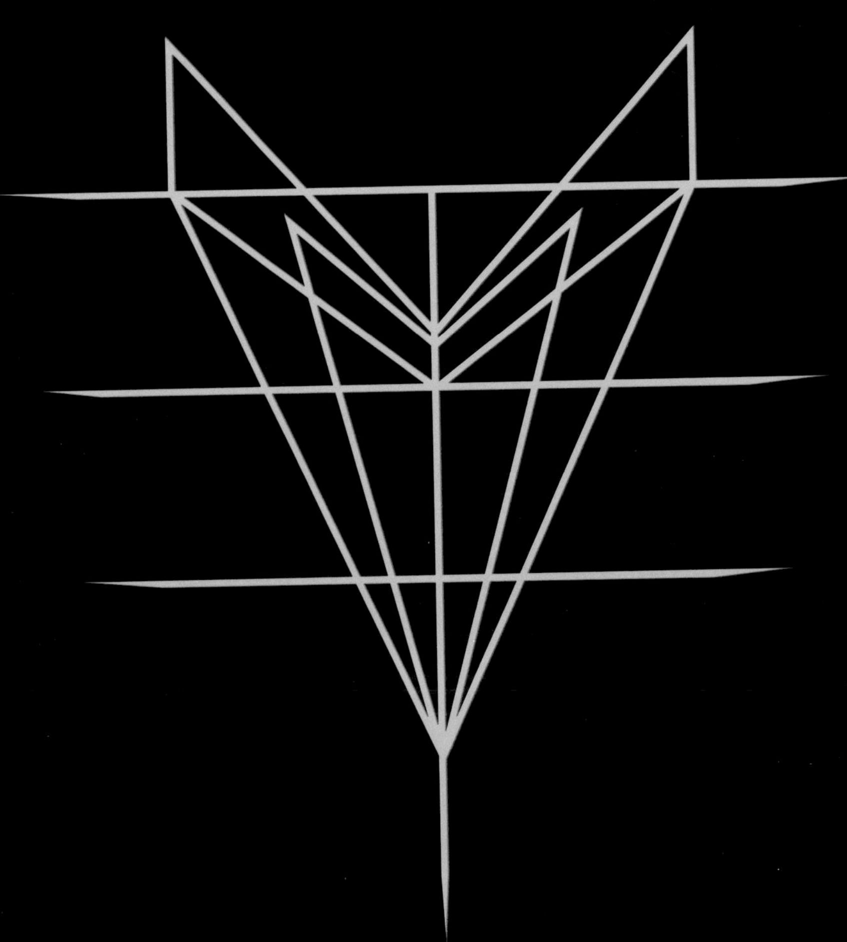

(2012–14 / 2014–16)

# Two Languages of Eclipse

Alexander R. Galloway

46

"I have nothing to say," wrote the composer John Cage, "and I am saying it."[1] Who could have predicted the size of this nothingness? Who could know it would provide so much space to explore? Is this a space for intellectual reflection, for art-making, or perhaps for both? The relation between form and formlessness gets to the heart of the problem. "For academics to be satisfied," the philosopher Georges Bataille comments wryly, the universe must fit into some kind of form: "The whole of philosophy has no other aim; it is a question of fitting what exists into a frock-coat, a mathematical frock-coat."[2] And anything that cannot fit into such a coat, anything that is without form, anything that is, quite literally, nothing, suffers excommunication from the world of humanity, like "a spider or a glob of spittle."[3] Still, as Cage reminds us through his many works, having "nothing to say" does not obviate the need to speak. Or, as Bataille would agree, formlessness is not nothing, just as the light of the sun is so bright, so white, that it becomes dark. Bataille calls it an "excess of darkness." Suns may be eclipsed, but Bataille's sun is already eclipsed, and all the brighter for it.

Zach Blas's *Face Cages* (2014–16) and the *Facial Weaponization Suite* (2012–14) show us the two languages of nothingness, the two languages of eclipse. We will call them "abstraction" and "obliteration," and examine them both in turn. The first, abstraction, compresses the world by universalizing it. The second, obliteration, tends more toward fuzziness or cloudiness, erasing the world by making it less distinct.

Each of the cages in *Face Cages* is different, yet they follow a similar set of conventions. Each *Face Cage* articulates a series of lines, and these lines are reinforced, extended, transformed into hard metal. Lines meet at joints, forming polygons connected into simple wire-frame meshes. An obdurate power emanates from the metal. The materials are pointy and inflexible, dull and unpadded, making the cage uncomfortable to wear. The cages are painful, but also violent, degrading the face by marking and pressing into the skin. This masquerade of metal changes and abstracts the face, semiotically compressing it, so that the fullness of flesh and volume are reduced to dots and lines.

The technology of 3D modeling software is on full display here. Such software is dazzling, to be sure, as it enlivens Hollywood movies, games, and software applications. Modeling software is sophisticated, but nevertheless based on a primitive language of points, lines, and textures. I say "primitive" because of the relative simplicity of these aesthetic regimes. Engineers also use the word "primitive" to describe their variables (data primitives) as well as the basic shapes used to build more complex models (graphical primitives). Indeed, this is a primitive aesthetic regime—in which, for instance, all curves are prohibited—but still an abstract language capable of endless permutation within a given formal vocabulary.

Abstraction is one of the oldest and most fundamental technologies. In its simplest form, abstraction means to drag out or draw away. It refers to processes of formalization, reduction, transformation, simplification,

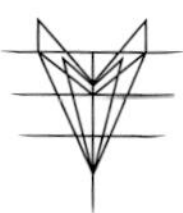

compression, and separation. I call abstraction a technology in order to emphasize how abstraction is a kind of tool, how abstraction actively intervenes and organizes its objects and fields. We think of abstraction as something that happens in the mind or in some immaterial formal plane. Indeed, abstraction may be mental. But abstraction can also be entirely physical. For example, the skeleton of an animal is an abstraction of shape and force affected by gravity, kinetics, and the allocation of flesh. In a different sense, honeycombs are abstractions of volume, producing regularly sized cells through a kind of optimal division of space. So, too, the natural numbers are abstractions of real-world multiplicity, and the concept of justice is an abstraction of its earthly manifestation.

Abstraction entails reduction or elimination, but abstraction also facilitates extension or expansion into new domains. What is light and minimal may also fly beyond its bounds. Since ancient times, abstraction has been understood in terms of points. The reduction to a point has long been the most ideal form of abstraction. Like the letters of a word, the points of a line, or the atoms of matter, small abstract elements may be combined to create complex wholes.

Consider one of the most mathematically elegant modes of recombination through abstraction: chording. Two hands on a piano keyboard work together to play a chord. The chord is constructed from discrete notes. Each note collects together to form the whole. The notes remain sonically distinct, even as they combine to form the chord. (Pianos have vibrating strings, but they are nevertheless eminently digital in that there is no way to bend or smear notes through the gaps between the strings; artists like Cage fought against such a tendency, in his works for prepared piano, even if he could never overcome it.) Each of the *Face Cages* is also

If our faces were only triangles with three points, they would be more difficult to identify.

chorded. “Notes” are pinpointed as positions on the face. Thus a note might land at the point midway between the eyes, or at the outer bounds of the cheekbones, or at the top and bottom of the mouth. Each note is determined and fixed in place. Each note is a channel. Each note is a dimension.

If there were but one point, the face would become a melody, more trumpet than piano. But multiple, simultaneous points mean multiple, simultaneous notes. All of them must be comprehended at once, and therein lies their utility and power. A tripod is stable because it rests on three points. But more points grant even more stability, and as the number of points grows, the security of the form increases. Fewer anchors mean less stability. Fewer points lead to lower resolution, but more points generate greater resolution.

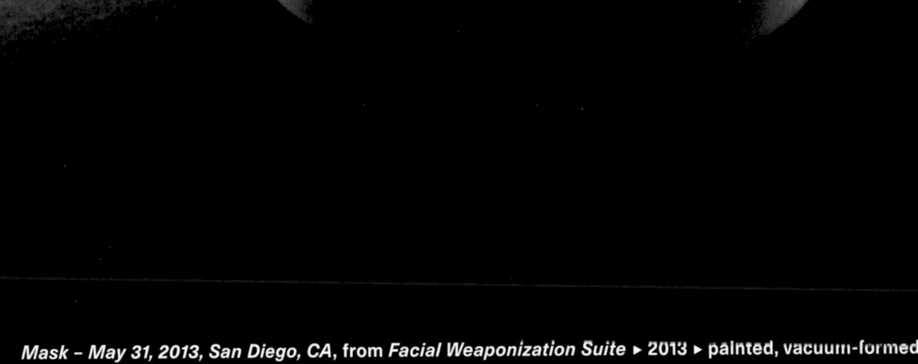

*Mask – May 31, 2013, San Diego, CA*, from *Facial Weaponization Suite* ▸ 2013 ▸ painted, vacuum-formed

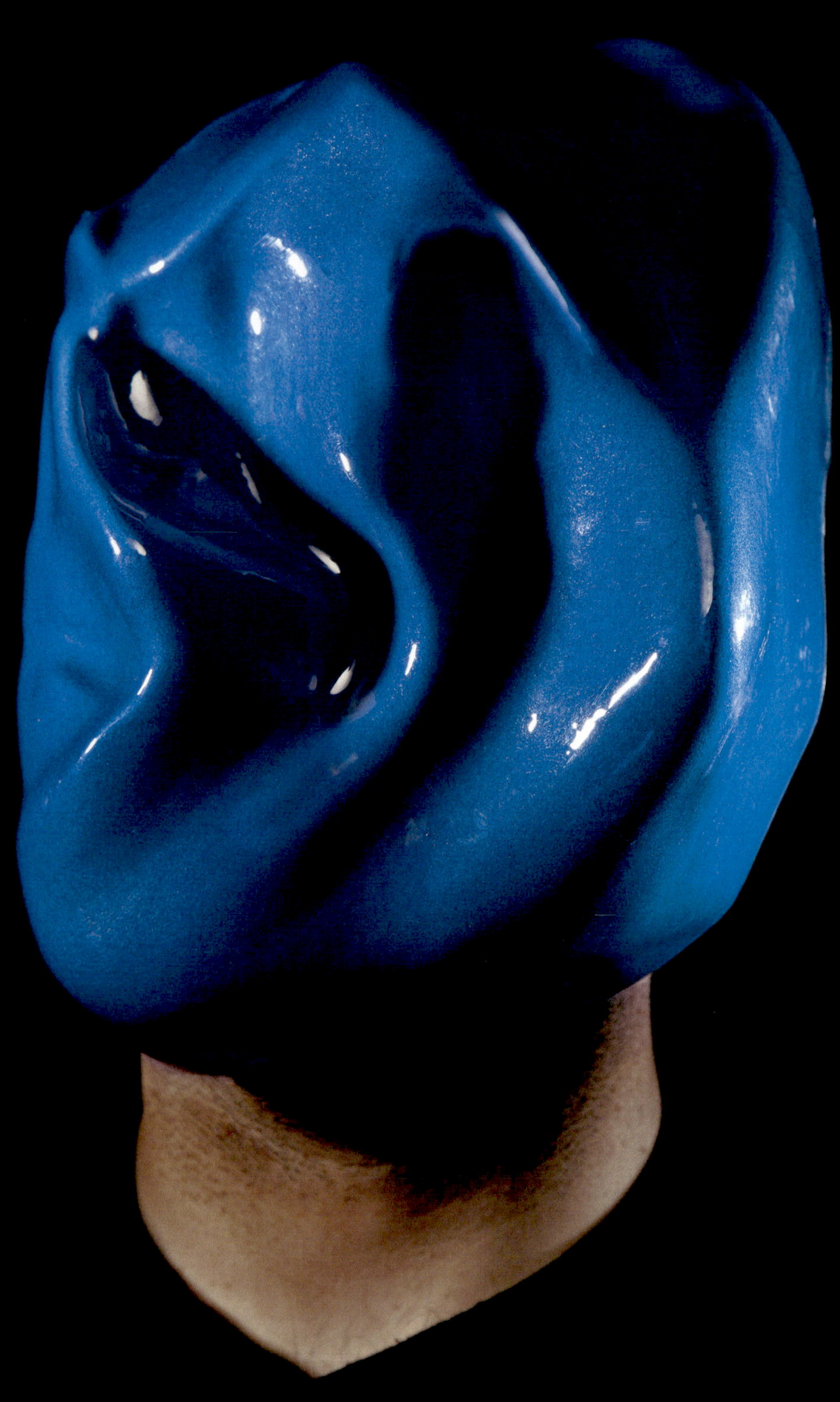

*Mask – November 20, 2013, New York, NY*, from *Facial Weaponization Suite* ▸ 2013 ▸ painted, vacuum-formed recycled polyethylene terephthalate

Such is the genius of "capture" technologies used in facial recognition. Each point of measure adds a new anchor. Each point of capture increases the robustness of the system. New measurement points are added, more and more, up to ten or twenty points or beyond. Each point is a new dimension—because dimension is nothing more than measurement. If our faces were only triangles with three points, they would be more difficult to identify. Instead, our faces are more like trees or maps, complex shapes with a multiplicity of anchor points. Adding points increases resolution and increases the ability for faces to be identified. And thus, like the famous wave function in quantum physics (a Hilbert space of multiple dimensions), abstraction is realized or "solved" via the measurement of points.

Yet these points are still abstractions. They don't "equal" the face. For romantics, the face is pure. They will complain that abstracting the face is violent because it replaces the richly detailed original with a sad and impoverished substitute. There are more direct forms of violence, too. States and companies use facial recognition to identify subjects, and in recent years the "politics of recognition" has become increasingly important. On the one hand, some people are clamoring to be recognized. On the other, subjects feel safer not being recognized. In fact, calls have been made to make facial-recognition technology illegal, or at least to not allow its use by the police.

The first language of eclipse is, thus, a language of abstraction in which details are located and identified through technologies of capture that simplify, compress, and transform the world. But there is a second language of eclipse: the language of obliteration. If abstraction eclipses the face by reducing and extending it, obliteration eclipses the face by blurring it and uncoupling it from a fixed referent.

Masks are complicated forms of adornment. They can be used to liberate, but also to oppress. Masks may help the powerful to retain their power. But masks are also used by the weak to hide themselves and evade

In Blas's work, however, the weapon is not recognition but form, or more precisely formlessness.

capture. Masks are worn by the Ku Klux Klan, but also by Pussy Riot, Subcomandante Marcos, and the hacker group Anonymous. The masking of the female body, head, or face, for instance in the form of the burka or hijab, has been the topic of much discussion, particularly for liberals in Western societies. The liberal consensus stipulates that the face should not be covered, that the body, particularly the female body, should not be inhibited. At the same time, global pandemics stipulate that the body be shielded, often through the use of masks and other prophylactic garments.

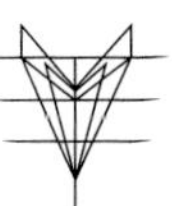

Each guise in the *Facial Weaponization Suite* offers a novel answer to the problem of masking. In the *Facial Weaponization Suite*, forms are distorted or extruded into billowing bulbs, creating a kind of second skin. The disguises twist and pop, like a liquid under pressure. They eradicate the eyes, mouth, nose, and other usual features of the face; all that remains is a swirling ball, plastic and inscrutable.

How to "weaponize" the face? Facial-recognition technology is one way to weaponize the face—to weaponize it against its owner. In Blas's work, however, the weapon is not recognition but form, or more precisely formlessness. The dynamic between form and formlessness is one of the oldest in Western culture. Ancient politicians were terrified by what they considered the chaotic formlessness of the *demos*, or populace. The notion of cultivation or civilization has long been defined in terms of the adoption of form. Those who will not or cannot adopt proper form—women, slaves, barbarians, animals—are considered less than human. Thus form and formlessness constitute a moral binarism, with form being elevated and formlessness denigrated. Likewise, the "progressive" position has long been to side with formlessness against form.

In this sense, formlessness is one kind of obliteration: the kind where form distorts and falls apart into blobs and bubbles. And such formlessness appears as a sort of "solution" to the problem of form, just as disruption appears as the solution to the problem of status or persistence. Here, the problems afflicting the world are characterized as potent and forceful, singular and organized, while the solutions to such problems are thought to be found in craftiness and agility, in multiplicity and deterritorialization, if not in chaos or disorganization itself. But formlessness is nothing but the legible silhouette of sovereignty. I suspect, therefore, that formlessness is not the ultimate key to understanding the *Facial Weaponization Suite*. Formlessness is just the beginning. We will have to move beyond it to understand more completely the second language of eclipse.

True obliteration is different from mere formlessness. In obliteration, erasure and deletion begin to take over. Irrelation and vacancy predominate where once relation and presence were primary. Letters and symbols fade from comprehension. Things fail to cohere into a whole. Corrosion and decay are followed by a simple erosion of meaning, fading a little and then fading more, not toward black but toward the middle tones of brown or gray. The mind grows foggy. Things slip from comprehension, fade from memory. Obliteration means rubbing out, expunging; removing an inscription but also removing the trace of the inscription. So let us finally put to rest the old poststructuralist logic of the unerasable supplement. This is a form of mediation where media fails to mediate.

Medieval mystics spoke of obliteration as night or nothingness, obliteration as the ineffable experience of immanence. In an astounding essay titled "The Facelessness of the Essence," the phenomenologist Michel Henry writes: "No horizon of light, not even the possibility or outline

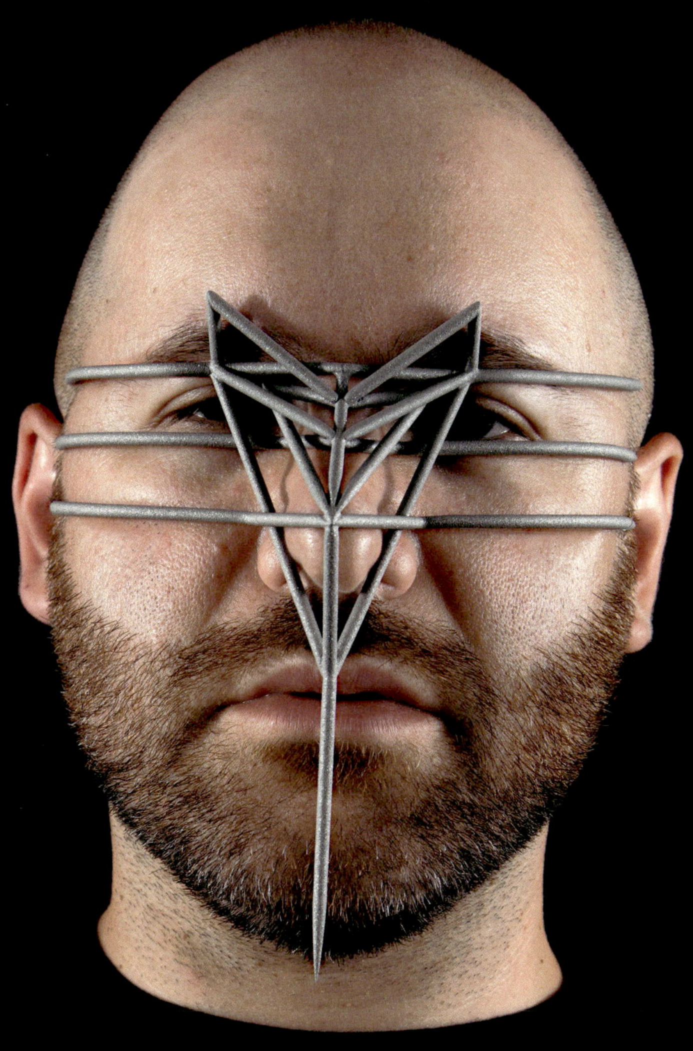

*Face Cage I*, from *Face Cages* ▸ 2015 ▸ endurance performance with Zach Blas ▸ HD single-channel video, 3D-printed stainless steel

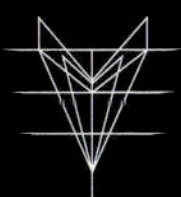

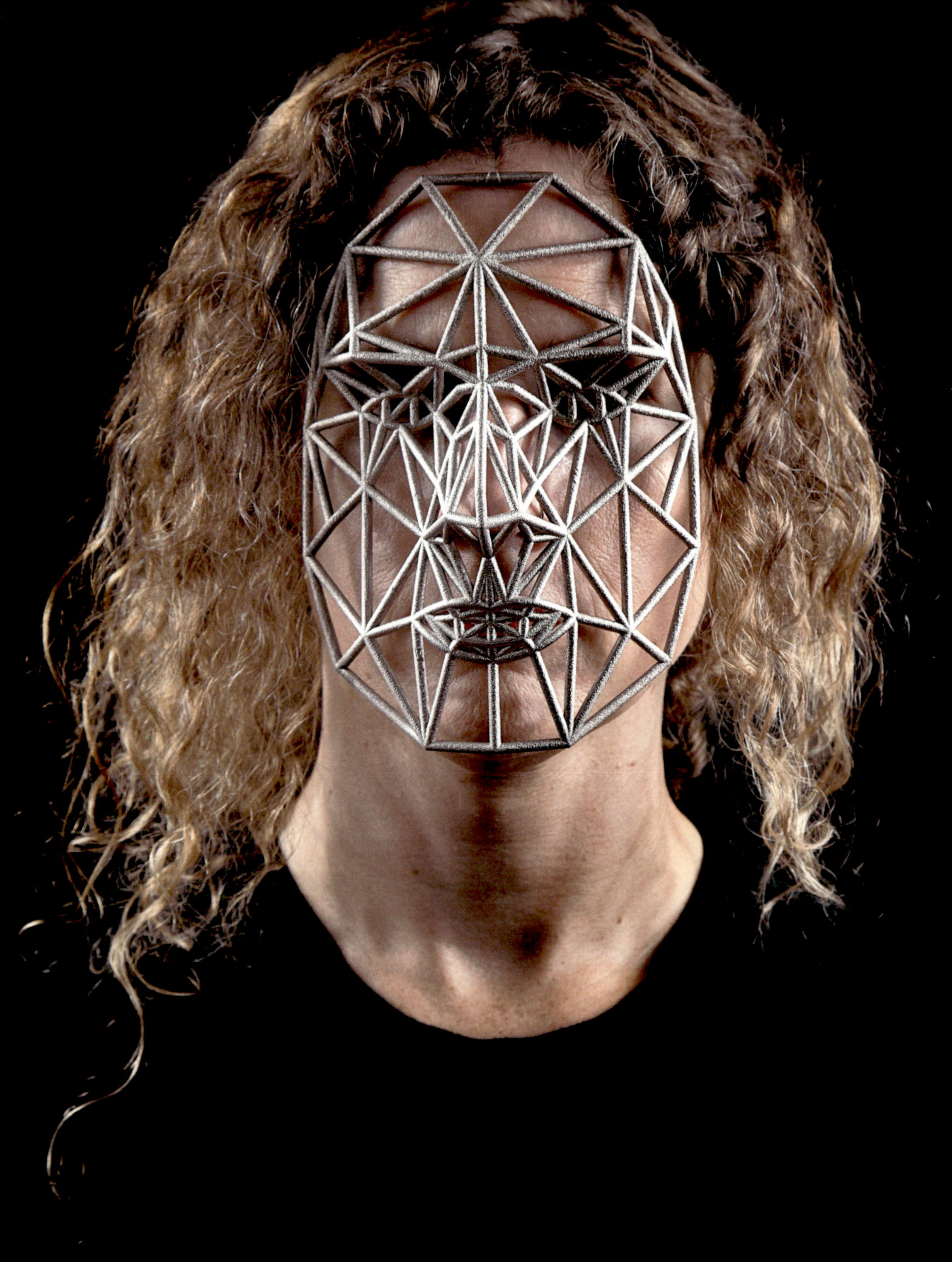

*Face Cage 3*, from *Face Cages* ▸ 2014 ▸ endurance performance with micha cárdenas ▸ HD single-channel video, 3D-printed stainless steel

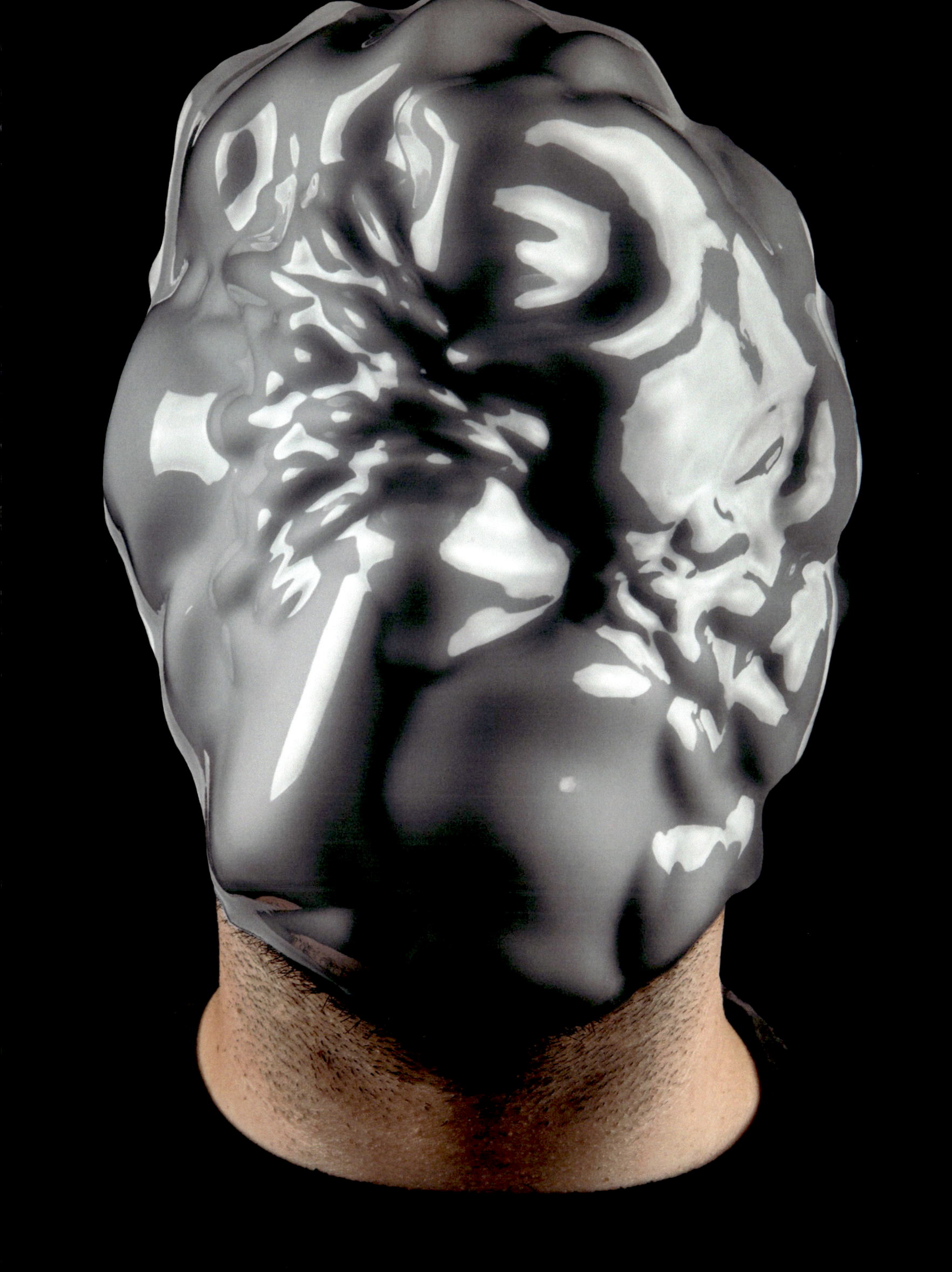

*Mask – May 19, 2014, Mexico City, Mexico*, from *Facial Weaponization Suite* ▸ 2014 ▸ painted, vacuum-formed recycled polyethylene terephthalate

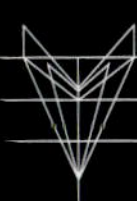

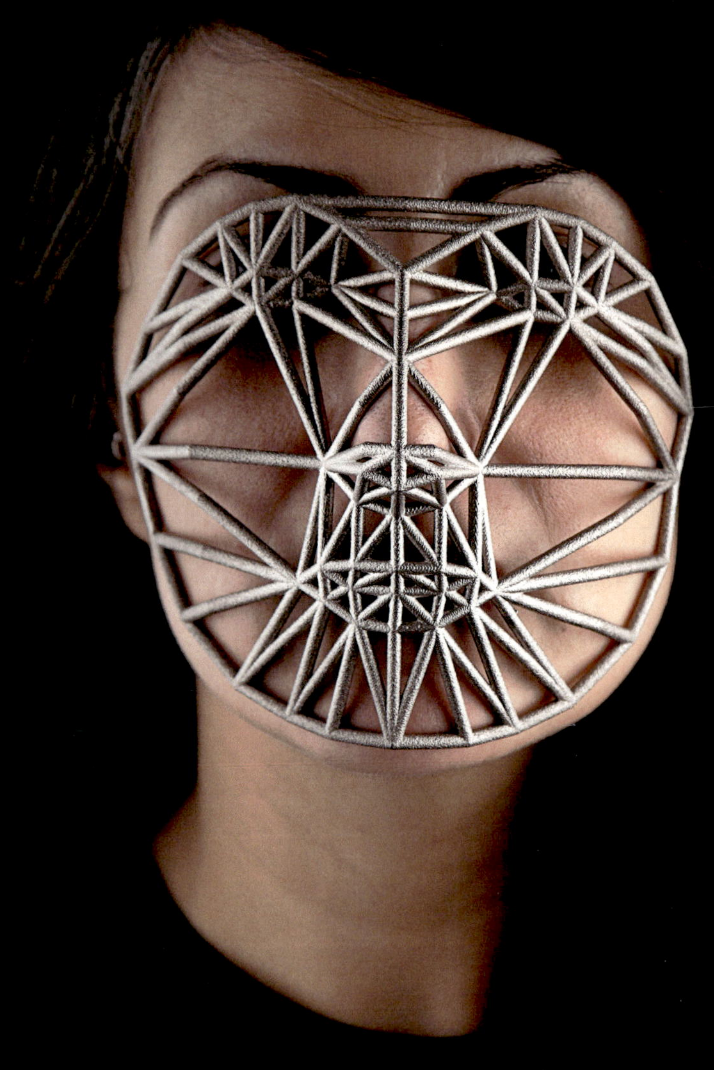

*Face Cage 2*, from *Face Cages* ▸ 2014 ▸ endurance performance with Elle Mehrmand ▸ HD single-channel video, 3D-printed stainless steel

of this horizon, ventures forth from that which is bound up with itself in the absolute unity of its radical immanence."[4] Such mystical night begins to approximate the second language of eclipse. But this mystical vision is still a bit too ecstatic. For the mystics, obliteration meant a white night, not a black one, much less a gray or beige night. Recall Andy Warhol's quest for the generic or unmarked. That was a beginning, but we might need to go further. Warhol had his yen for surface and artificiality, to be sure, but those interests embark into a different land altogether. Empty repetition and superficial kitsch begin a process only completed by a more extreme form of absence or irrelation.

If, as I said before, the key to abstraction is chording and dimensionality, then the key to obliteration is found in the dynamic between symmetry and asymmetry. Symmetry assumes repetition. Crystals and molecules and basic natural forms propagate through symmetry. One half

The face is weaponized because it is a form of human compression rather than human expression.

of the human body might be symmetrical with the other half. The reflection in a mirror is symmetrical with what stands opposite it. Symmetry describes an encounter. One actor meets another. Each party resembles the other, or it might not. But symmetry indicates that an encounter is at least possible, because there is a common unit of comparison.

Scientists like Isaac Newton and Euclid have a way of distinguishing between symmetry and asymmetry. Symmetry means having a common measure. Something is symmetrical because there is another thing that it could be measured in terms of. To break with symmetry means to complicate (or, in some cases, to eliminate) this unit of comparison. "Asymmetry" means literally "without common measure," because the asymmetrical cannot be explained in terms of some base element against which the whole is measured. To emphasize this point, the asymmetrical is sometimes called the "incommensurable," or literally "that which cannot be measured."

In his essay *La dissymétrie*, sociologist Roger Caillois describes how dissymmetry is necessary for life, human life above all, and how the distinction between the living and nonliving mimics the distinction in thermodynamics between entropic and negentropic systems.[5] But even dissymmetry revolves around an encounter. Dissimilar components might still need to interoperate. Indeed, they might be forced into relationships that are mismatched or otherwise unequal, with all the ethical challenges that would entail.

Both symmetry and dissymmetry create correspondences of reversibility. But asymmetry declines to correspond, declines to return,

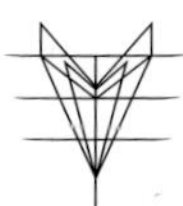

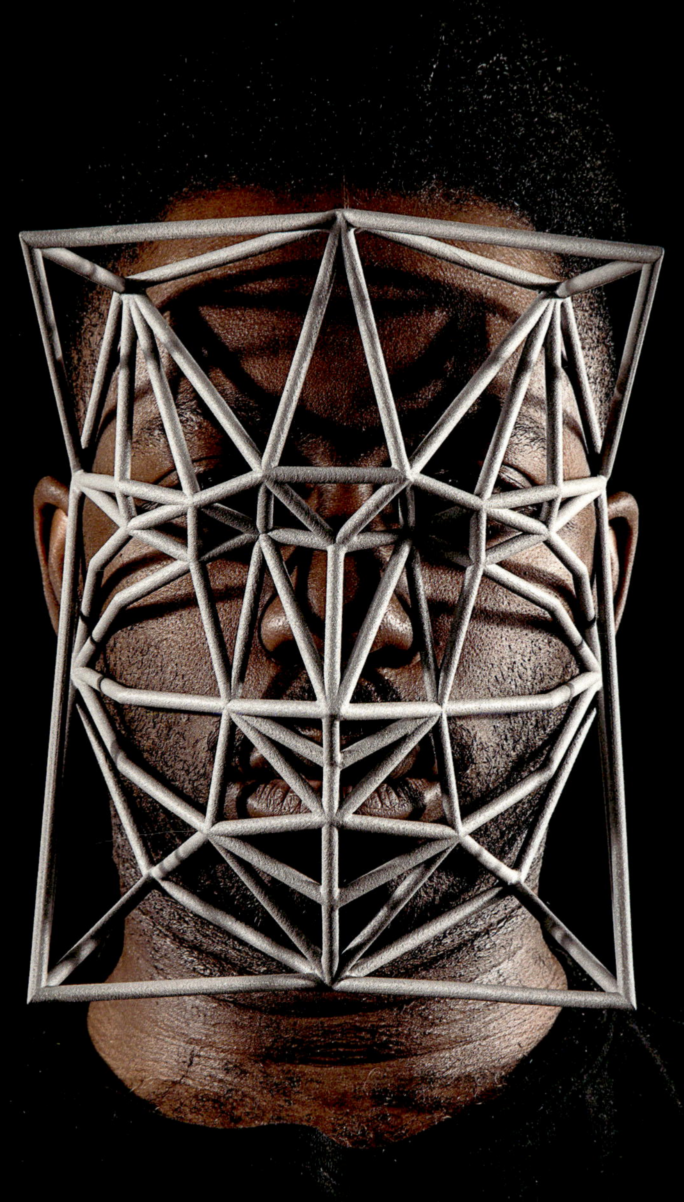

*Face Cage 4*, from *Face Cages* ▸ 2016 ▸ endurance performance with Paul Mpagi Sepuya ▸ HD single-channel video, 3D-printed stainless steel

declines to have a relationship with the other side. Thus, the key to obliteration is found in asymmetry. Pursue not the simple dissymmetry; instead, pursue a unidirectional, asymmetrical encounter. Which might not be an encounter after all.

This is the key to the *Facial Weaponization Suite*. The face is weaponized through its own obliteration. The face is weaponized because it becomes irreversible. The face is weaponized because it refuses an encounter. The face is weaponized because it exists in the absence of having a common point of measure. The face is weaponized because it persists without appeal to an external unit of comparison. The face is weaponized because it is a form of human compression rather than human expression.

We are taught that expression is better than compression. We are taught that recognition is better than obliteration. That may have been true in the past, but I wonder if in this age of ubiquitous surveillance and data-driven capitalism whether the sun has finally set on visibility, recognition, and expression. Wouldn't it be better for someone to decline the call? Wouldn't it be better for the face to encrypt itself? Wouldn't it be better, in the words of Heraclitus, for nature to hide itself?

Are compression and encryption just a new kind of abstinence, a new kind of austerity? Certainly there's a priggish, Protestant version of all of this. After all, for the transcendentalist Henry David Thoreau, hell was other people. But there's also a queer version, a feminist version, a communist version, and an anti-racist version. That is, for every form of outward display, there is a form of inward restraint. For every expression, the possibility of compression. Postcolonial theorist Rey Chow once wrote approvingly of "the indifferent gaze" of the person of color, and philosopher Susan Buck-Morss describes a political stance rooted in "radical neutrality."[6] The

The two languages of eclipse in *Face Cages* and the *Facial Weaponization Suite* demonstrate that there is a way to think about illegibility without reverting to nonsense or madness.

"right to look" is important, but perhaps not more so than the "right to opacity."[7] Shall we not return to John Keats's evocation of the "cold pastoral" or to John Ruskin's stones? Shall we not find, within the immanent dreams of Romanticism, a way to flee the points of recognition and the mandates of expression?

The two languages of eclipse in *Face Cages* and the *Facial Weaponization Suite* demonstrate that there is a way to think about illegibility without reverting to nonsense or madness—or, worse, forms of orientalism or social marginalization. Rather, eclipse demonstrates a form of life indifferent to the patterns of representation and harassment, not



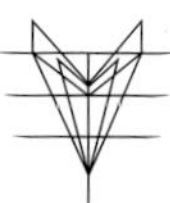

the indifference born of privilege or the neutrality of the transcendental ego, but the indifference of that which is common and the neutrality of generic life. This strikes me as ever more important in an age of outsize police power and the invasion of corporate interests into the most minute aspects of daily life.

The term "materialism" carries a complex variety of meanings, complicated all the more by the way in which such meanings slip and drift from one historical age to another. The two works in question here, *Face Cages* and the *Facial Weaponization Suite*, evoke, for me, an alternative way of understanding material reality. Not the productive machines and difference engines of the contemporary economy, and not the expressivity or radiant vitality of contemporary aesthetics. Instead, the works furnish a new set of terms: opacity and obliteration, compression and asymmetry, and, even, a different way of conceiving abstraction, if not rescuing it. In other words, what if compression, not expression, was the binding virtue of art?

**1** John Cage, "Lecture on Nothing," in *Silence* (Middletown, CT: Wesleyan University Press, 2011), 109.
**2** Georges Bataille, "Formless," in *Encyclopaedia Acephalica*, ed. Georges Bataille (London: Atlas, 1995), 52.
**3** Bataille, "Formless," 52.
**4** Michel Henry, "The Facelessness of the Essence," in *The Essence of Manifestation*, trans. Girard Etzkorn (The Hague: Nijhoff, 1973), 438. The text is essentially an extended elaboration of and possible alternative to the thought of Georg Wilhelm Friedrich Hegel, rooted not in Hegel's concept of manifestation but in what Henry calls "revelation."
**5** Roger Caillois, *La dissymétrie* (Paris: Gallimard, 1973).
**6** Rey Chow, *Writing Diaspora: Tactics of Intervention in Contemporary Cultural Studies* (Bloomington: Indiana University Press, 1993), 54; and Susan Buck-Morss, *Hegel, Haiti, and Universal History* (Pittsburgh, PA: University of Pittsburgh Press, 2009), 150.
**7** See Nicholas Mirzoeff, *The Right to Look: A Counterhistory of Visuality* (Durham, NC: Duke University Press, 2011); and Édouard Glissant, *Poetics of Relation*, trans. Betsy Wing (Ann Arbor: University of Michigan Press, 1997).

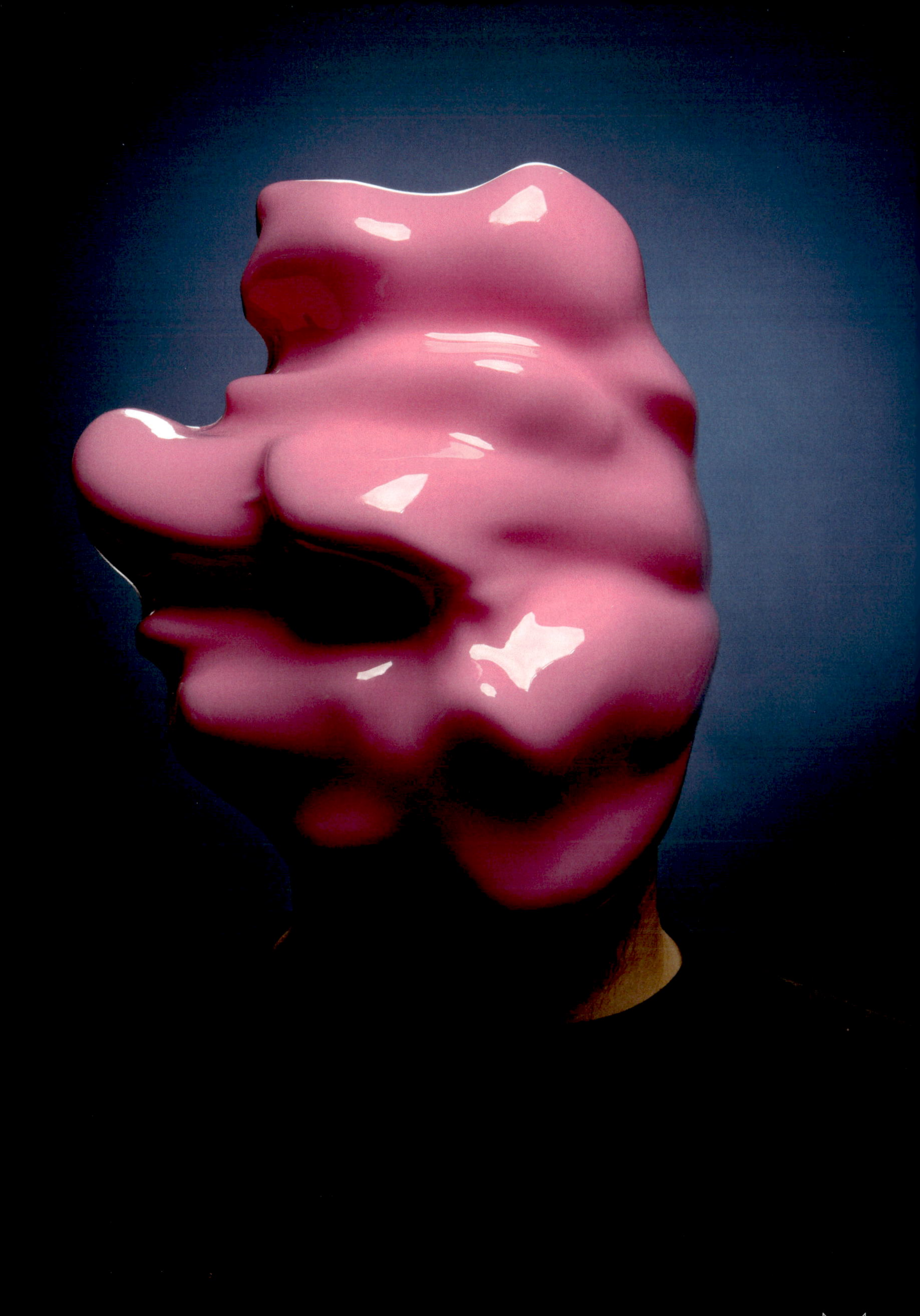

*Fag Face Mask – October 20, 2012, Los Angeles, CA*, from *Facial Weaponization Suite* ▸ 2012 ▸ painted,

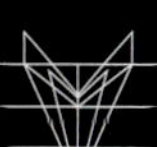

# Fag Face

Zach Blas

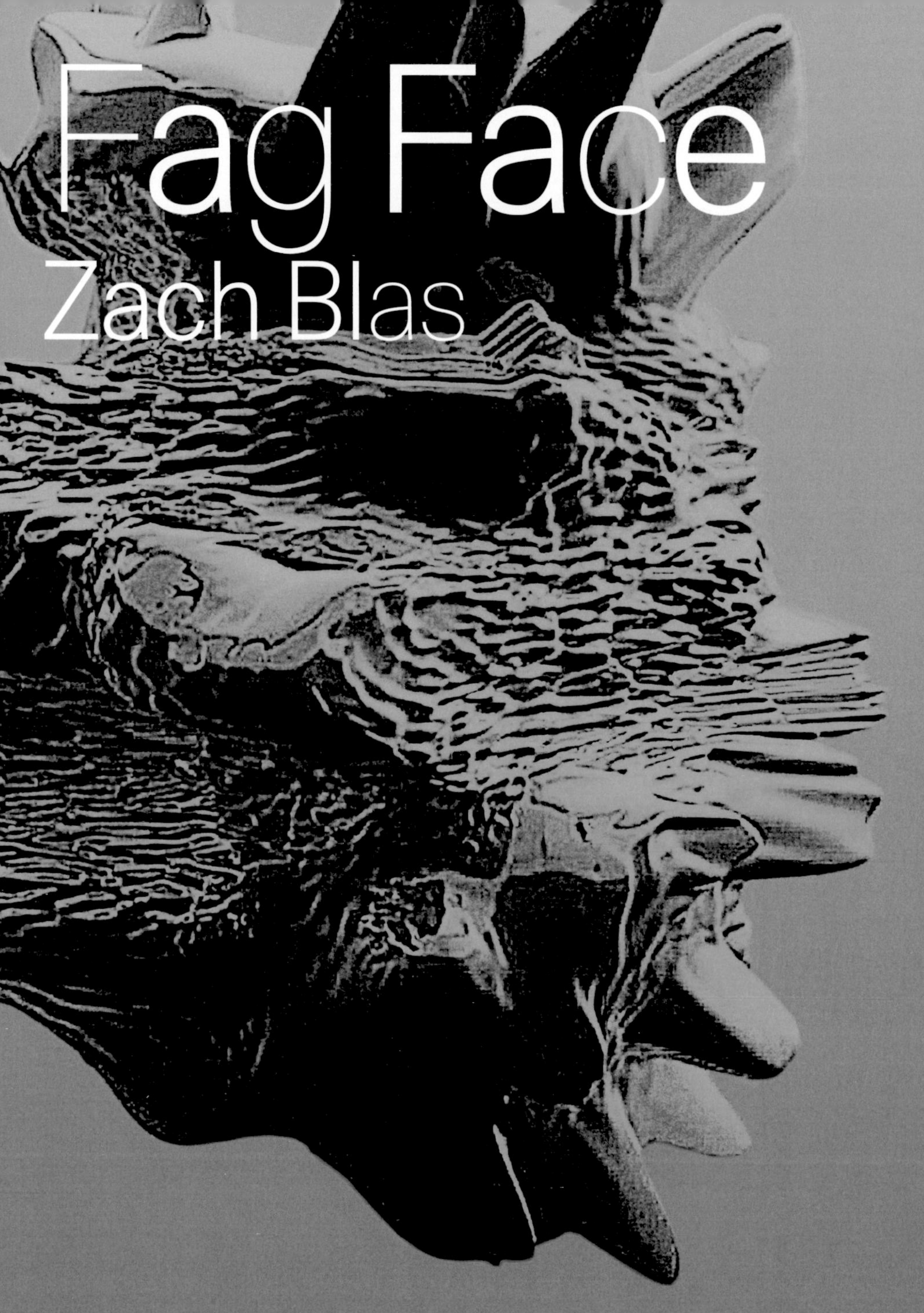

*Facial Weaponization Communiqué: Fag Face*, from *Facial Weaponization Suite* ▸ 2012 ▸ HD video still



(2011)

I think about fag face sometimes when a cock is in my mouth, or an ass is pressed against my head, or cum runs down my chin.

That accusation, that claim that has been put upon my head by high school bullies, strangers, passersby, college jocks, and, now, experimental psychology units. A couple seconds, they read your head as a type of face, and then you're known. All those sexual acts and styles of living become merely biological defects crystallized into a face. And it is a face to be corrected: with fag face, you can't speak because you always have a cock in your mouth.

There is something inescapable about such an identification; there is the insinuation it starts at birth. That most visible, readable, and expressive feature—a head—is given one face. Fag face controls head-matter to visualize one interpretation.

But is not a head infinitely organizable? Those features that assemble together to make a face can be interpreted and evaluated endlessly, yet there is an inexhaustibility to any reading. The head always remains open. It must remain open. This openness is its facelessness.

Fag face mutates a head; it shifts and reorganizes flesh. The head tightens, pulls firmly together, closes off from the outside, and flattens into a singular knowability. It is a particular fagginess—not the fag I might want to be with friends and lovers. This is a monolithic fag constructed, determined, and controlled by others.

Fag face captures me into an identity that is not my own, a grid that legislates me.

How do I escape this face? How do I desire to escape this gridding of my head? How can I open, make into a mystery, liberate my fag face?

Take the head beyond the limit of these grids, so that it can decode its facial boundaries, break them open, to enter again into the swarming chaos of matter that resists recognition.

If fag fucking is what fag face visualizes, then accumulate cum so that your face becomes a volatile liquid surface with no eyes, nose, or mouth; keep the smell from rimming so that your face and ass are irreducible; let the pubic hair gather into different consistencies of stickiness; wipe the shit left on your fingers under your hidden, cum-filled eyes like war paint. Transform your face into a hypertrophized state of fagginess. Let these new excesses dissolve readability. Let your fag face configure with these materials into that which is not identifiable.

Once one thousand cocks have cum on my head and one thousand asses have wiped their shit and sweat there, try to tell me what my face is.

I fuck like this to become faceless. Because a face is not mine to own or endure.

64–113

# Contra-Internet

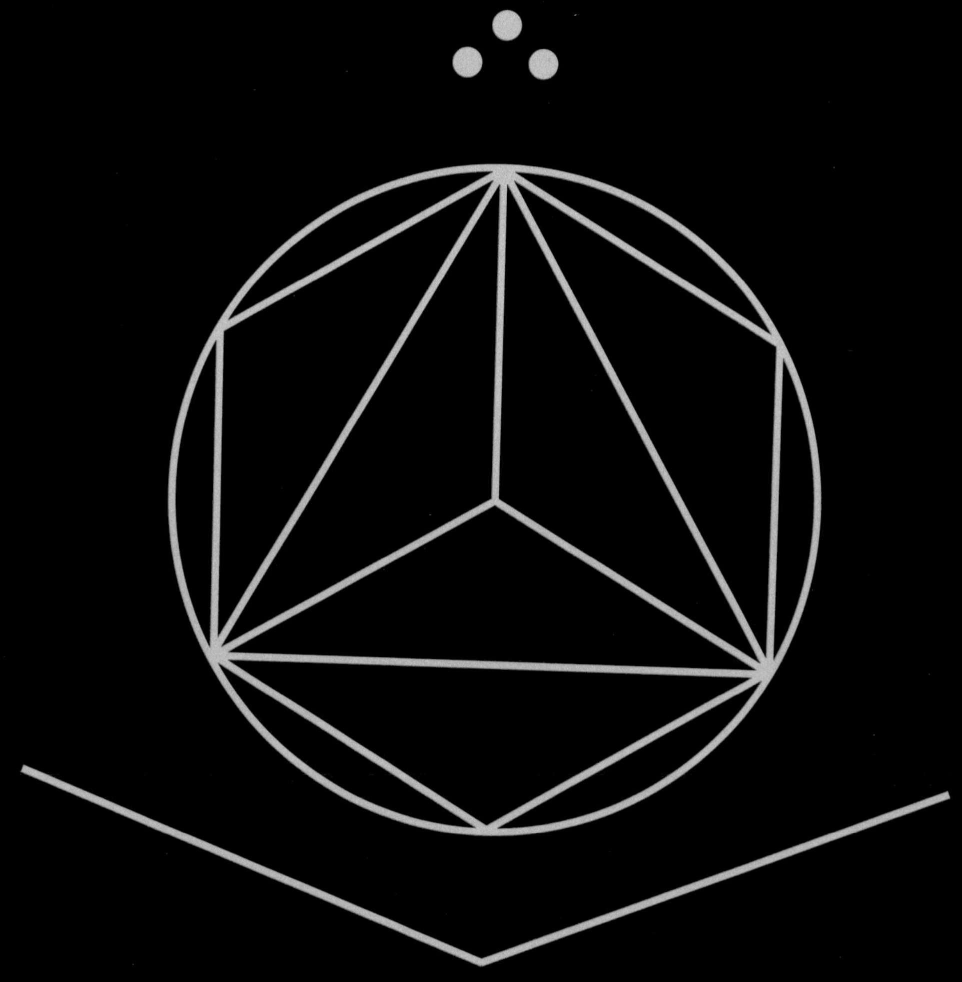

(2015–2019)

# Punk Pasts, Dildo Futures

Marc Siegel

66

Vivienne Westwood didn't get it all wrong. Derek Jarman's 1978 film *Jubilee* does depict "old Elizabeth's England as some state of grace."[1] Sun-strewn, lush green gardens with overgrown bushes provide the sixteenth-century setting for long-winded poetic discussions between Elizabeth I, her occultist advisor John Dee, and a lady-in-waiting. Brian Eno's ambient sounds of seagulls and ocean waves fill out the idyllic and pastoral atmosphere of these scenes, which provide a framing story to Jarman's otherwise rambunctious film about a postapocalyptic version of contemporary London. The Virgin Queen wants to look into the future, so Dee calls forth the angel Ariel, who accompanies them to the year 1977 to witness firsthand the fruits of the Elizabethan Renaissance. What they discover is a desolate urban landscape in flames: baby carriages burn on the street; a corrupt policeman merely smirks as a group of women (the punk band the Slits) destroys an abandoned car; and a violent, anarchic girl gang, including an incestuous pair of brothers, commit murder and cause mayhem. Some members of the girl gang are involved in the music business as singers and confidants of the powerful media magnate Borgia Ginz (Jack Birkett). Jarman's focus on their exploits and their interest in fostering the career of a young musician called Kid (Adam Ant) provides narrative reasons for featuring performances by contemporary punk and post-punk bands, including Siouxsie and the Banshees, Jayne (also known as Wayne) County, and the Electric Chairs, who, along with Adam Ant's band the Ants, play consistently on television throughout the film. Westwood liked this stuff. Jarman had at least "pointed [his] nose in the right direction." But then he "wanked," losing himself in self-indulgent gay-boy fantasies of playing Elizabethan dress-up.[2] Westwood thought the "boring and therefore most disgusting film [she] had ever seen" played camp desire against punk values, with punk losing out as a warning of where things went wrong. "I ain't insecure enough nor enough of a voyeur to get off watching a gay boy jerk off through the titillation of his masochistic tremblings."[3]

Westwood printed her (homophobic) film critique in black, pink, red, and blue ink onto a sleeveless white cotton top, adorned on the front with an image of a postage stamp that depicts Queen Elizabeth II with a severed head and on the back with the Union Jack. She called it an "Open T shirt to Derek Jarman from Vivienne Westwood" and offered it for sale at Seditionaries, the shop she ran with her boyfriend, Malcolm McLaren, manager of the Sex Pistols. Film criticism as punk fashion. About *Jubilee*, the T-shirt proclaimed: "Don't remember punk this way."[4] "Buy me instead," it implied. Jarman was unfazed, having diagnosed a couple years earlier punk's complicity in the social and economic system it was at the same time rebelling against:

> The music business has conspired with them to create another working-class myth as the dole queues grow longer to fuel the flames. The instigators of punk are the same old

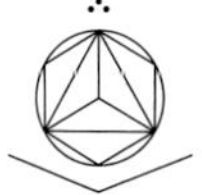

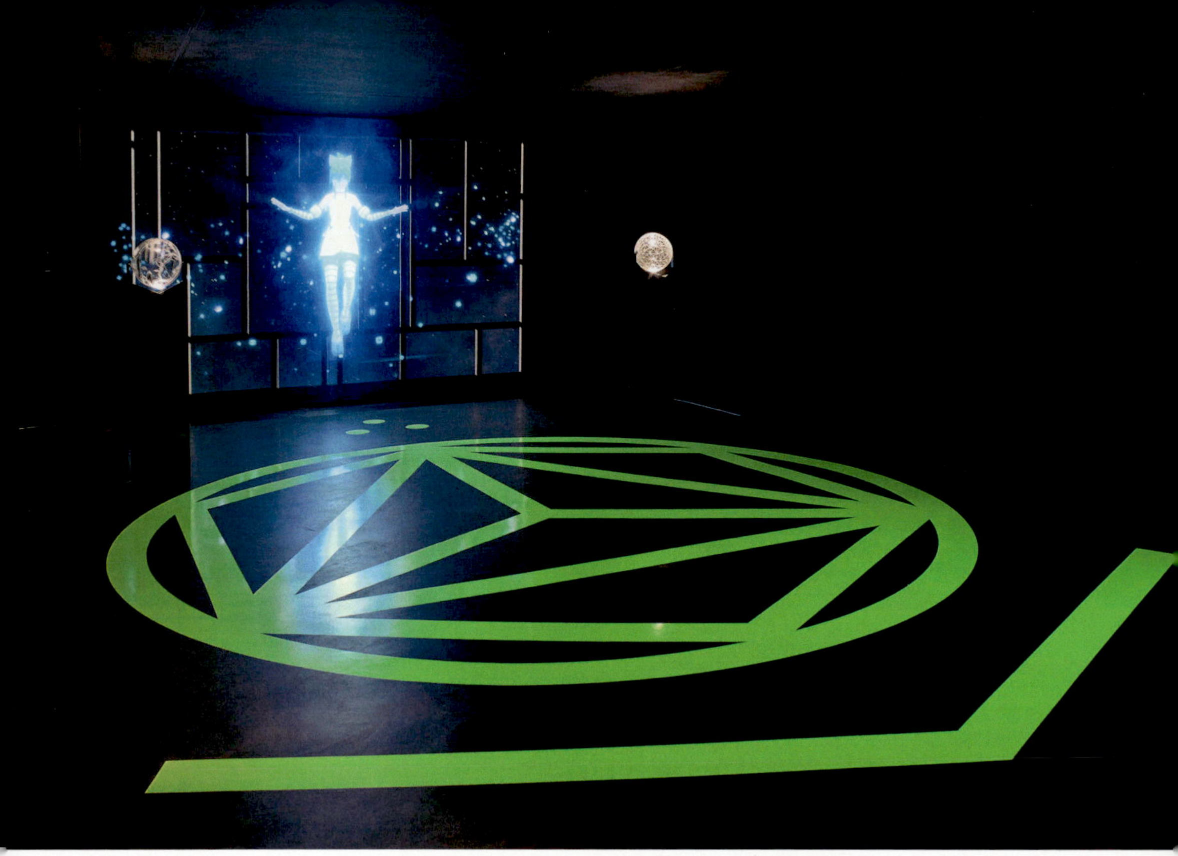

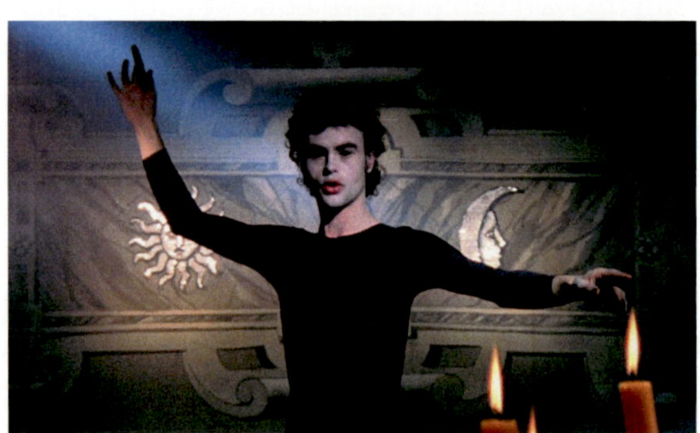

*Jubilee 2033*, from *Contra-Internet* ▸ 2018 ▸ HD single-channel video, etched glass spheres, fluorescent vinyl ▸ Installation view at Gasworks, London, UK ▸ Photo by Andy Keate

Derek Jarman ▸ *Jubilee* ▸ 1978 ▸ Produced by Megalovision and Whaley-Malin Productions ▸ film still

**petit bourgeois art students, who a few months ago were David Bowie and Bryan Ferry look-alikes—who've read a little art history and adopted some Dadaist typography and bad manners, and who are now in the business of reproducing a fake street credibility.[5]**

As for Westwood herself, Jarman spared no kind words. When the fashion designer accepted an Order of the British Empire in 1992, he noted (misogynistically) in his diary: "Vivienne Westwood accepts an OBE, dipsy bitch. The silly season's with us: our punk friends accept their little medals of betrayal, sit in their vacuous salons and destroy the creative."[6] Only a year earlier, Jarman had received a crowning of an altogether different sort when he was canonized as a saint by the international gay order of nuns, the Sisters of Perpetual Indulgence. Punk values versus gay camp theatrics, I suppose.

There's no mistaking a conservative thrust to Jarman's analysis of punk and contemporary England in *Jubilee*—conservative in the sense of the caution with which it characterizes the nihilistic energies of the moment and contrasts them with an earlier period of monarchic benevolence. However, with "its persistent air of disillusion and warning," as punk's preeminent chronicler Jon Savage notes, "*Jubilee* captured the mood of Punk England better than anyone could have predicted, not the least in its locations; it remains one of the few places where you can see the 1977 London landscape."[7] Jarman brought together some of the most interesting figures in the music, art, and performance scenes at the time and captured their antics on camera in the empty streets and abandoned warehouses around his loft in Butler's Wharf and in other nearby locations in Bermondsey, Deptford, and Rotherhithe. He thereby preserved a moment from London's and England's recent past, just as Thatcherism, with its destruction of the welfare system, encouragement of privatization, and facilitation of widespread gentrification, was about to transform the urban landscape so radically as "to destroy the creative" and the very spaces necessary for its

"They all log on in the end—one way or another" might be Zach Blas's response.

sustenance. *Jubilee* is "a time-capsule of a period in London's history when subcultures grew overtly and naturally due to the city's many affordable, derelict areas," as one critic astutely noted in early 2018.[8] The film's loose narrative highlights the complicity of the antisocial punk gang with the omnipotent owner of all media, Borgia Ginz. In contrast to this pessimistic view of the possibility of radical change emerging from a complicit punk subculture stands the energies and ingenuity of these very subcultural figures as they romp through and occupy the streets and buildings of London. "In a film that has Tudors time-traveling to a parallel future, it's



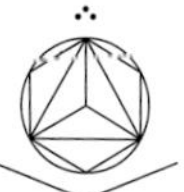

surprising to find its most surreal aspect to be the very possibility of young people affording to live in the city centre. London's affordability is now arguably the film's most fantastical premise."[9]

What Westwood missed or was just not willing to acknowledge was *Jubilee*'s foresight in signaling—however campily—the overwhelming economic changes that would reshape the city (and beyond), in the process relegating punk resistance to the ambivalently effective political activism of a consumer good. Consider Ginz's prophetic words as he asserts the impossibility of escaping his monopolistic control over the lives of the younger generation, words that—however satiric and exaggerated—resonate hauntingly in the age of Jeff Bezos, Elon Musk, Peter Thiel, Mark Zuckerberg, and others of their greedy billionaire media-and-tech-industry ilk:

> **You wanna know my story, babe. It's easy. This is the generation who grew up and forgot to lead their lives. They were so busy watching my endless movie. It's power, babe. Power. I don't create it. I own it. I sucked and sucked and I sucked. The media became their only reality and I owned their world of flickering shadows—BBC, TUC, ITV, ABC, ATV, MGM, KGB, C of E. You name it—I bought them all and rearranged the alphabet. Without me, they don't exist.**

We should also add NSDAP to the list of acronymic organizations under Ginz's vampiric grip.[10] At the end of the film, members of the girl gang revel in their wealth and success. They join Ginz at the estate he shares with a retired Adolf Hitler, who sits on a sofa watching his old speeches on TV while proclaiming his status as the greatest painter of the century. "They all sign up in the end—one way or another," says Ginz.

"They all log on in the end—one way or another" might be Zach Blas's response circa 2018. Blas's multipart project *Contra-Internet* (2015–19) includes an essay, a number of lecture-performances, and a text, object, and video installation, the centerpiece of which is a thirty-minute video titled *Jubilee 2033*.[11] Jarman's nihilistic vision of the impending doom of Thatcherism and the corresponding destruction of creativity through the consolidation of corporate media and political control in the hands of the very few (in the two hands of Borgia Ginz, that is) allows for little resistance other than that expressed through the energetic appearance of feminist and queer punk itself. For his part, Blas offers a more optimistic if self-consciously utopian vision of resistance in the face of an even more omnipotent opponent—because it is a less individualized one—namely, the internet.

In the 2016 essay "Contra-Internet," Blas lays out the theoretical scope of his larger project in six programmatic sections: "Killing the Internet," "Disappearing the Internet," "Postcapitalist Politics," "Contrasexuality," "Paranodes," and "Antiweb."[12] To detail the process of "killing the internet," he considers specific historical examples of political oppression when

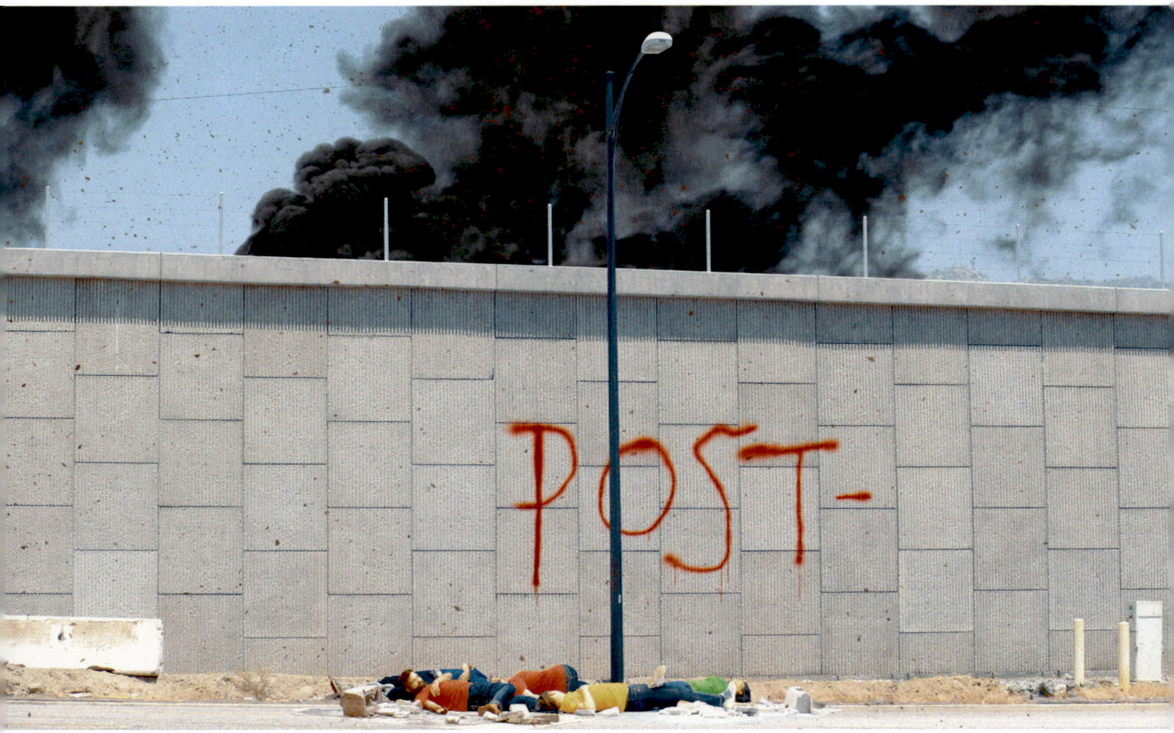

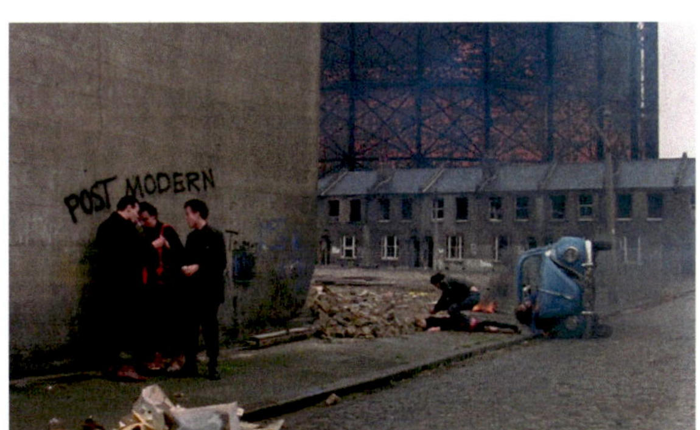


*Jubilee 2033*, from *Contra-Internet* ▸ 2018 ▸ HD video still

Derek Jarman ▸ *Jubilee* ▸ 1978 ▸ Produced by Megalovision and Whaley-Malin Productions ▸ film still



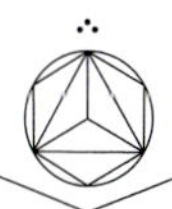

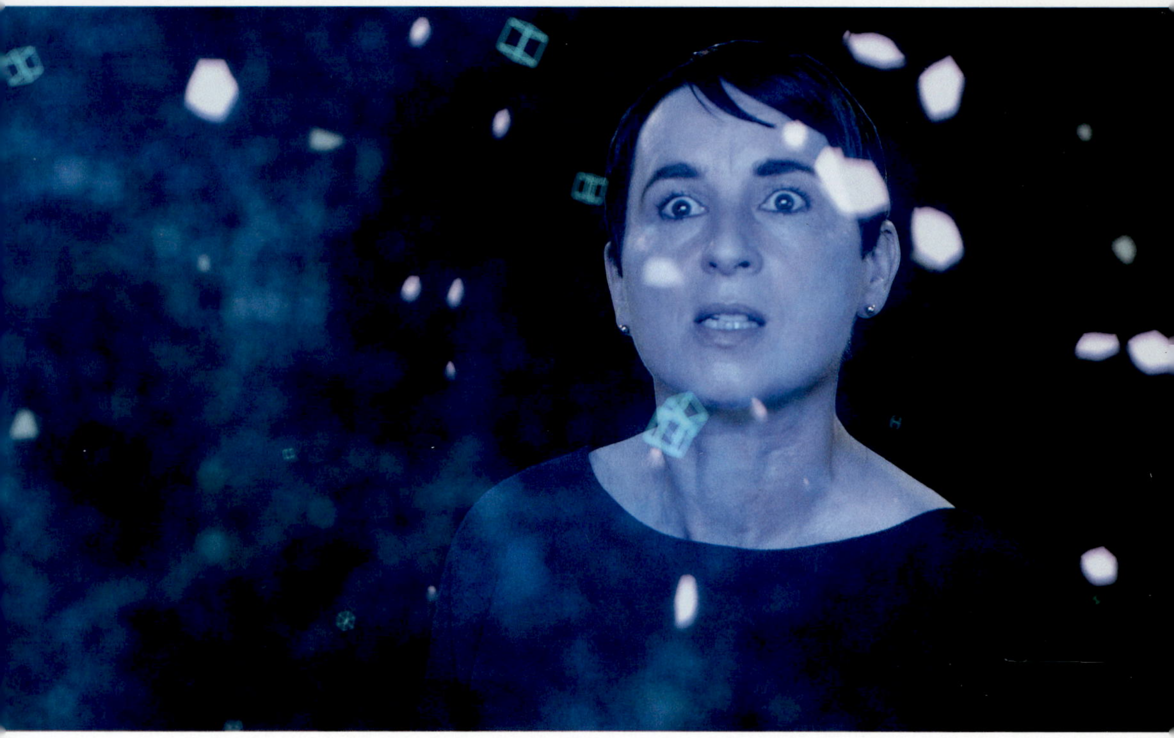

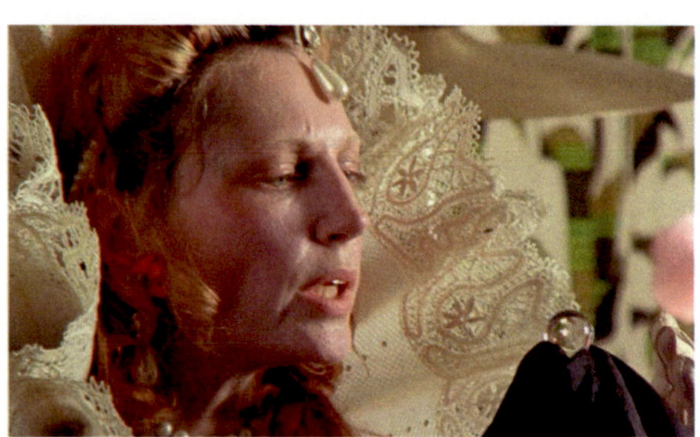

*Jubilee 2033*, from *Contra-Internet* ▸ 2018 ▸ HD video still (featuring Susanne Sachsse as Ayn Rand)

Derek Jarman ▸ *Jubilee* ▸ 1978 ▸ Produced by Megalovision and Whaley-Malin Productions ▸ film still

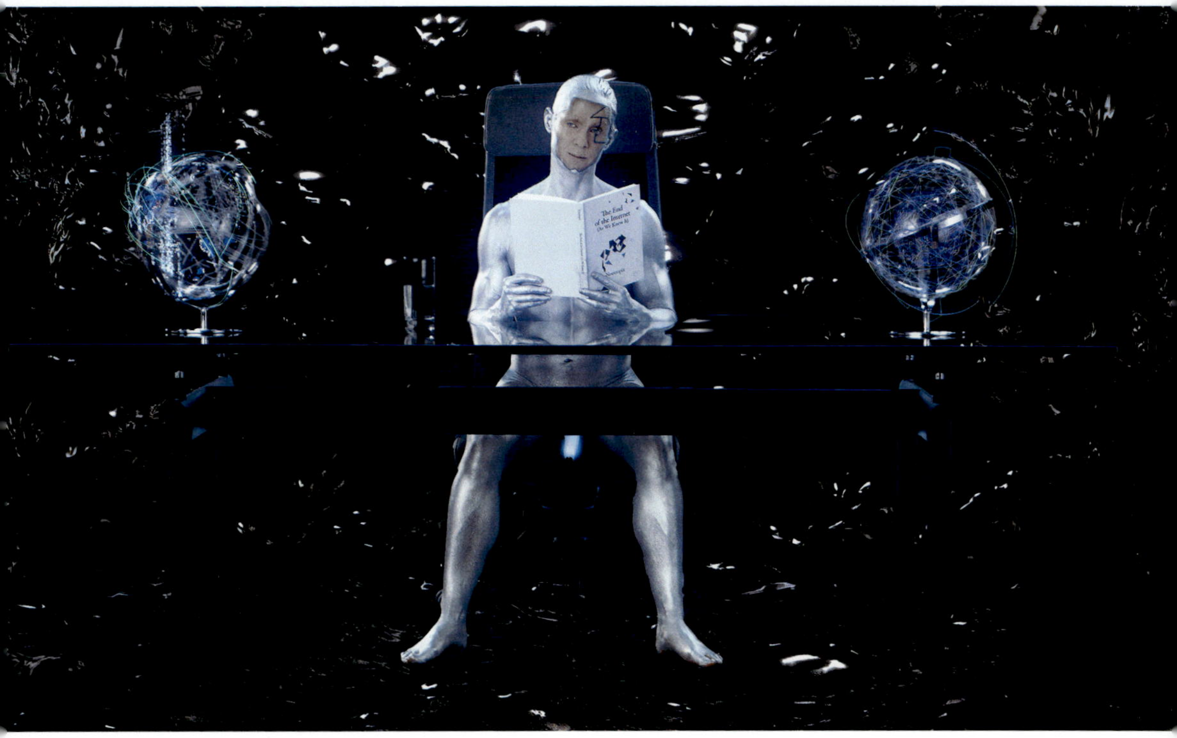

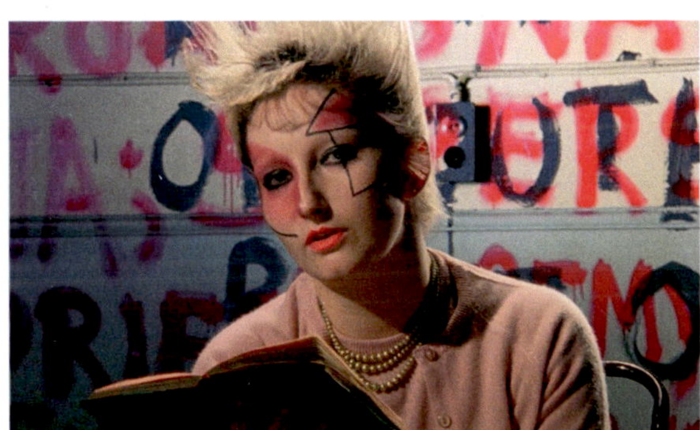

*Jubilee 2033*, from *Contra-Internet* ▸ 2018 ▸ HD video still (featuring Cassils as Nootropix)

Derek Jarman ▸ *Jubilee* ▸ 1978 ▸ Produced by Megalovision and Whaley-Malin Productions ▸ film still



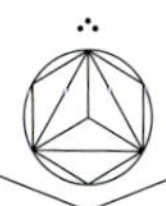

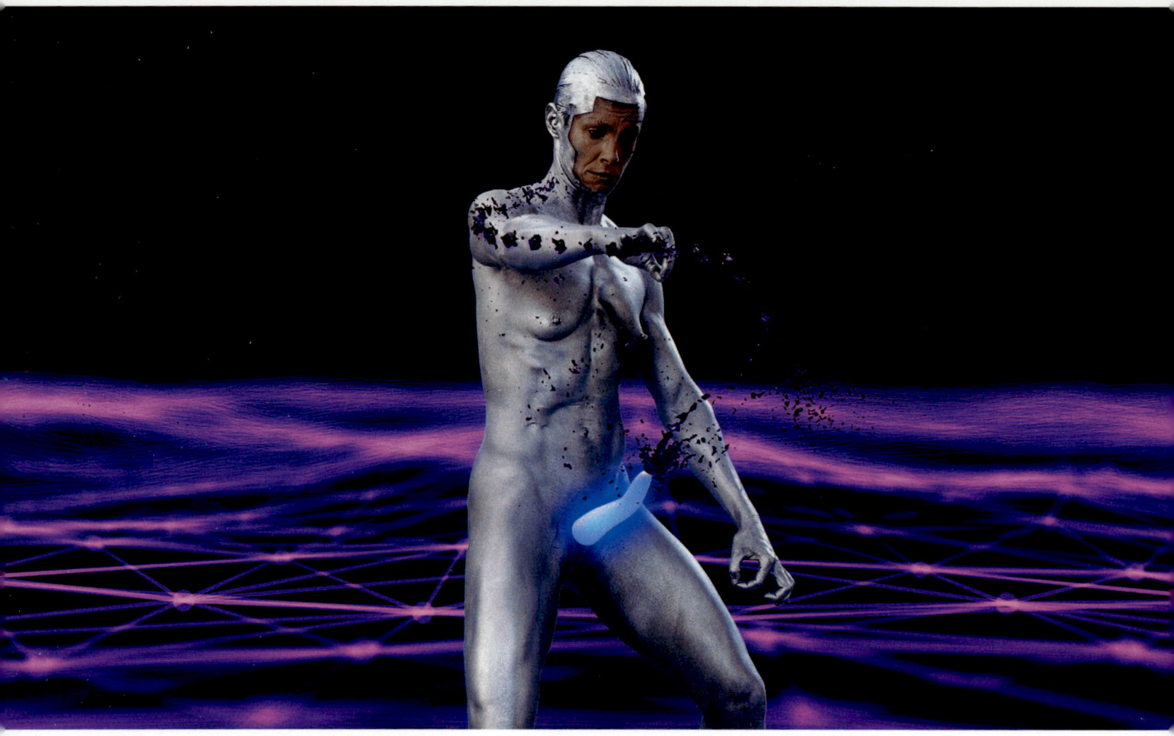

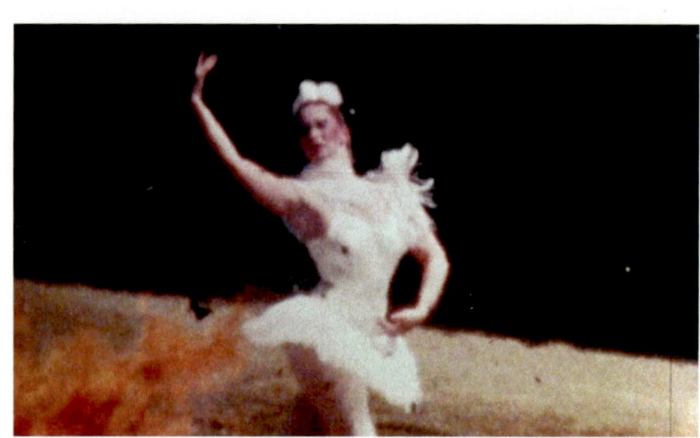

***Jubilee 2033*, from *Contra-Internet* ▸ 2018 ▸ HD video still (featuring Cassils as Nootropix)**

**Derek Jarman ▸ *Jubilee* ▸ 1978 ▸ Produced by Megalovision and Whaley-Malin Productions ▸ film still**

internet access was temporarily shut down or threatened, including during the Saffron Revolution in Myanmar in 2007; in the midst of the Egyptian revolution in 2011; after the Gezi Park protests in Istanbul in 2014, when Turkish Prime Minister Recep Tayyip Erdoğan banned access to Twitter; and during the 2016 US presidential campaign, when Republican candidate Donald Trump called for "closing that internet up" in a battle against the recruitment efforts of the Islamic State. Blas moves on to consider postulations of an impending future where the internet will simply disappear into bodies, objects, and the surrounding environment. That was the promise of then Google chairman Eric Schmidt in 2015, who suggested that "the internet will disappear" as it becomes fully integrated into our daily lives, that it will dissolve into the "very materialities" of the contemporary world. Everything will become part of a network—plugged in, online, 24/7. Tech industry executives visualize an end to the internet as an internet of things. Authoritarian political leaders envision an end to the internet by pulling the plug. The citizen has been replaced by the internet user, characterized by Blas as "a biopolitical subject engineered by corporations and possessed of a dazed and addictive subjectivity that hungers for feeds that never stop, clickbait that always demands another click, and content generators that multiply browsing tabs until a computer crashes."[13]

The science-fiction scenario Blas constructs is a no less fantastic totality than that of the rearranged alphabet in Jarman's dystopia. (Keep in mind that Google's parent company is the multinational conglomerate Alphabet Inc.) How does he envision resistance? Where does Blas, in his words, "locate the potentialities of a militant alternative or outside to the totality the internet has become?"[14] In tune with Jarman's precedent, Blas turns to feminists and queers in his attempt to imagine a non-technophobic way out of the network. To this end, he brings a feminist critique of capitalism (J. K. Gibson-Graham) and a queer and transfeminist rethinking of the naturalization of gender and sexual norms (Paul B. Preciado) to bear on theories of resistance to the seeming totality of the network form (Ulises Ali Mejias).

Following Gibson-Graham, particularly their 1996 book *The End of Capitalism (As We Knew It): A Feminist Critique of Political Economy*, Blas locates a post-capitalist politics in the local nooks and collective crannies within existing capitalist structures: the alternative economies and imaginative reconceptualizations that make evident a diversity of present economic practices and political possibilities.[15] Preciado's cult book *Countersexual Manifesto*, originally published in French in 2000 as *Manifeste contra-sexuel*, takes a punk attitude to countering culturally constructed gender and sexual norms.[16] The book even comes with a sample countersexual contract, which anyone can sign and therewith renounce, among other things, one's "natural position as a man or a woman, as well as all privileges (be they social, economic, or patrimonial) and all obligations (be they social, economic, or reproductive) proceeding from my sexual position

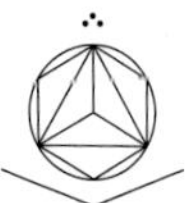

within the framework of the naturalized heterocentric regime."[17] This performative act of refusal becomes the first step toward generating an alternative relationship to one's body, bodily pleasures, and social possibilities. This is where the dildo comes into play—and not simply as a pleasurable toy for the purposes of penetration and stimulation. Invoking Jacques Derrida, Preciado asserts the "supplementary" function of the dildo; it is not a replication of a penis but rather its completion and displacement: "The dildo is the origin of the penis."[18] In Blas's words, "The contrasexual dildo is a diagrammatic form that, when experimented with, reveals the potentialities of sexuality beyond the heteronormative and the phallocentric."[19] For his part, Preciado provides numerous practices in the art of "dildotectonics" to assist in the countersexual resignification and experiential reengagement with one's own body: for instance, drawing with a red marker the shape of a dildo on one's left forearm and massaging it with the right hand for two minutes and thirty seconds.[20]

The theoretical framework that Blas has constructed for the contra-internet reads like a combination of hyperlinks, as it brings together historical and activist examples with fragments of ideas from other thinkers to speculate on new approaches to a by now familiar problem: How to refuse the body's increasingly naturalized relationship with the internet? Does a countersexual body demand a contra-internet? If dildo usage and the practices of dildotectonics enable us to reconceive and remap bodily and social possibilties, can contra-internet practices do the same with the seemingly inescapable corporatized network? Taking inspiration from the example of the activist use of peer-to-peer mesh networking apps to avoid state and corporate control (such as by the pro-democracy movement in Hong Kong in 2014), Blas highlights "anti-web" practices as a possible indication of a beyond to the currently dominant and dominating network structure. To these practical examples of refusal he adds Ulises Ali Mejias's conceptual rethinking of the network, specifically his theorization of the paranode and paranodal space as a site for social and political resistance.[21] Rethinking a neuroscientific term, Mejias conceives the paranode as the negative space between nodes and flows on a network diagram, a space that both supports and lends stability to the network yet also threatens its organizational function of linking and connecting. Such threats come in various forms, including individual acts of refusal within one's network of friends and contacts, viruses, hacking, broken links, signal jamming, and pirate communication projects. While these examples may detail only temporary and contingent disturbances to an easily adaptive system, they nevertheless open up a space—paranodal space—within the network for imagining its beyond. Paranodal space, indeed, seems most relevant as this conceptual possibility, an opening within a commercialized and corporatized network to a potentially more equitable outside. Since Blas defines the internet not solely as an architecture of digital technology but also as "a structure of power coextensive with the space of the social," any fissures

Internet

noun
/ˈɪntənɛt/

1. an architecture or structure of power coextensive with the space of the social

2. the dominant network form; the new realm of the absolute from which social possibility is dictated or by which it is constrained; in this formulation network determinism; network sameness

3. the "hero" of the post-fordist development narrative, the inaugu-ral subject of  post-history," the bearer of the future, of the contem-porary, of universality

4. the everything everywhere of contemporary cultural representa-tion; confers meaning upon subjects and other social sites in relation to itself

*Totality Study #1: Internet, a definition*, from *Contra-Internet* ▸ 2017 ▸ fluorescent vinyl ▸ Installation view at Gasworks, London, UK ▸ Photo by Andy Keate



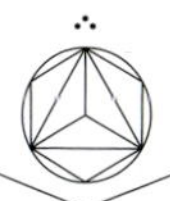

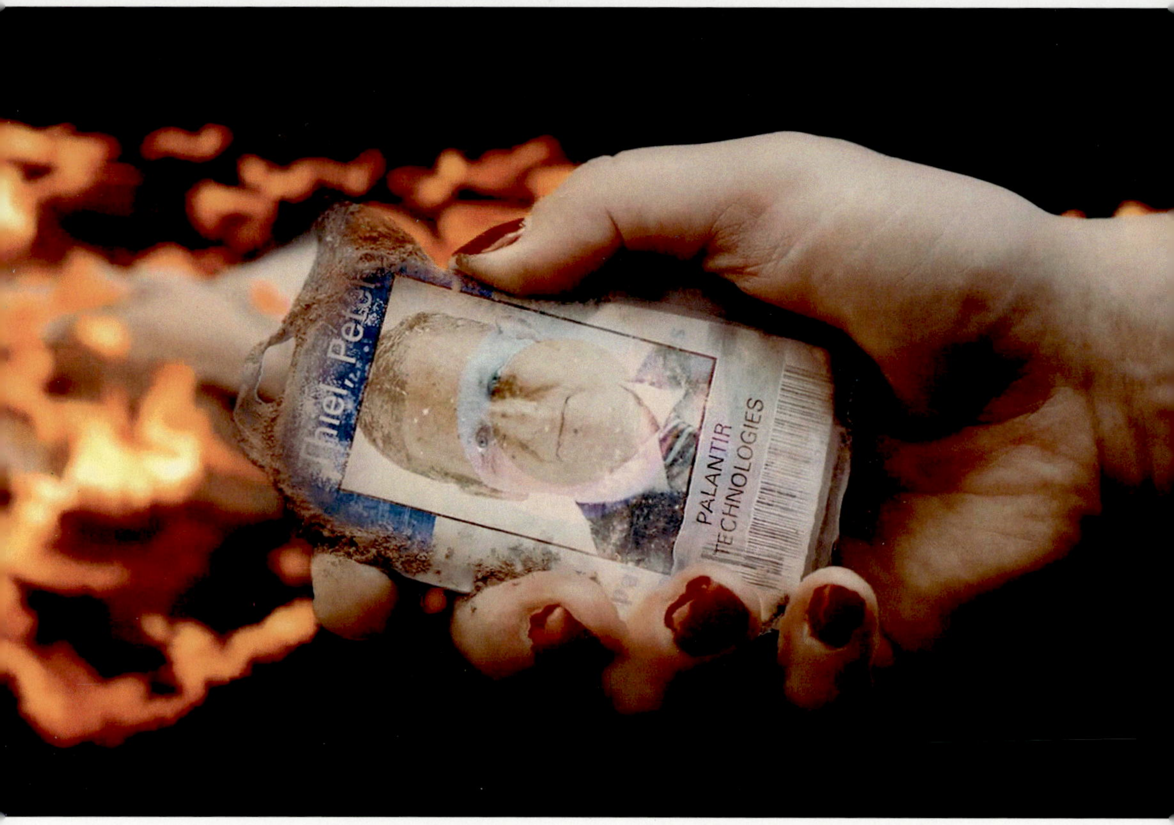

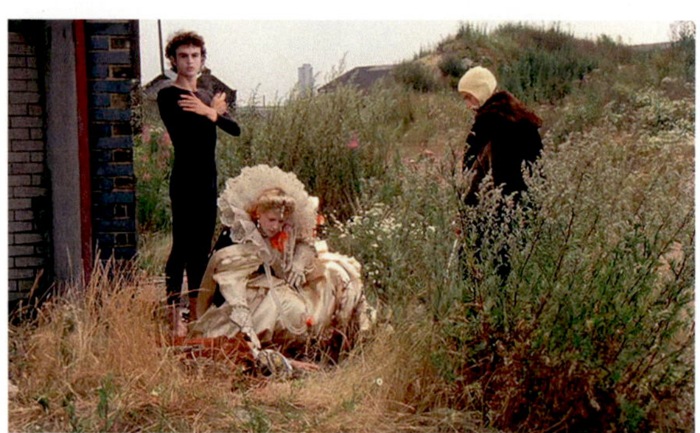

***Jubilee 2033*, from *Contra-Internet* ▸ 2018 ▸ HD video still (featuring Susanne Sachsse as Ayn Rand)**

**Derek Jarman ▸ *Jubilee* ▸ 1978 ▸ Produced by Megalovision and Whaley-Malin Productions ▸ film still**

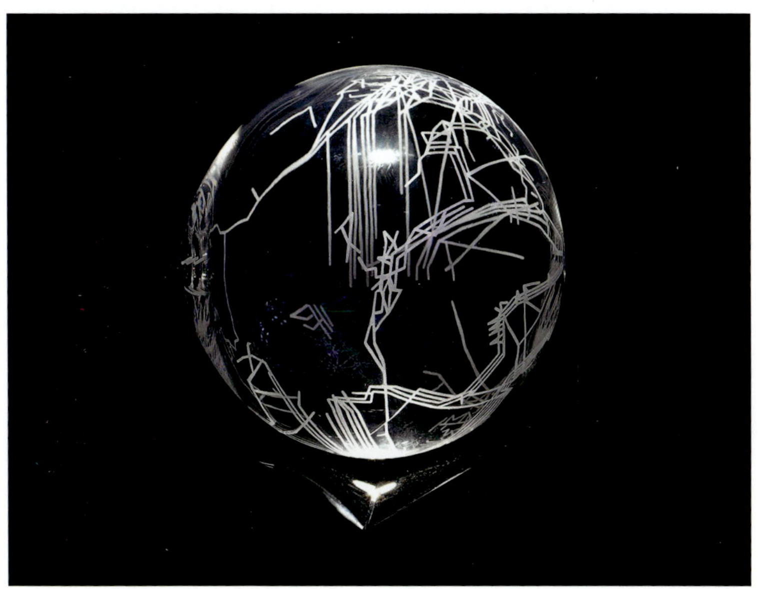

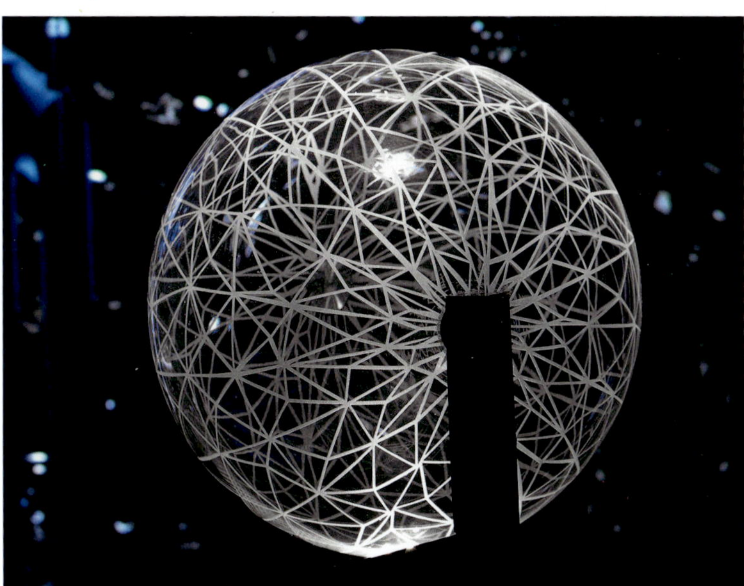

***Palantir: Killed Internet*** **(top) and** ***Palantir: Disappeared Internet*** **(bottom), from** ***Contra-Internet*** **▸ 2017 ▸ etched glass spheres and LEDs ▸ Installation view at Art in General, New York, US ▸ Photos by Dario Lasagni**



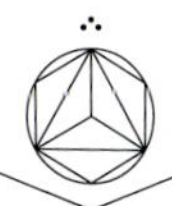

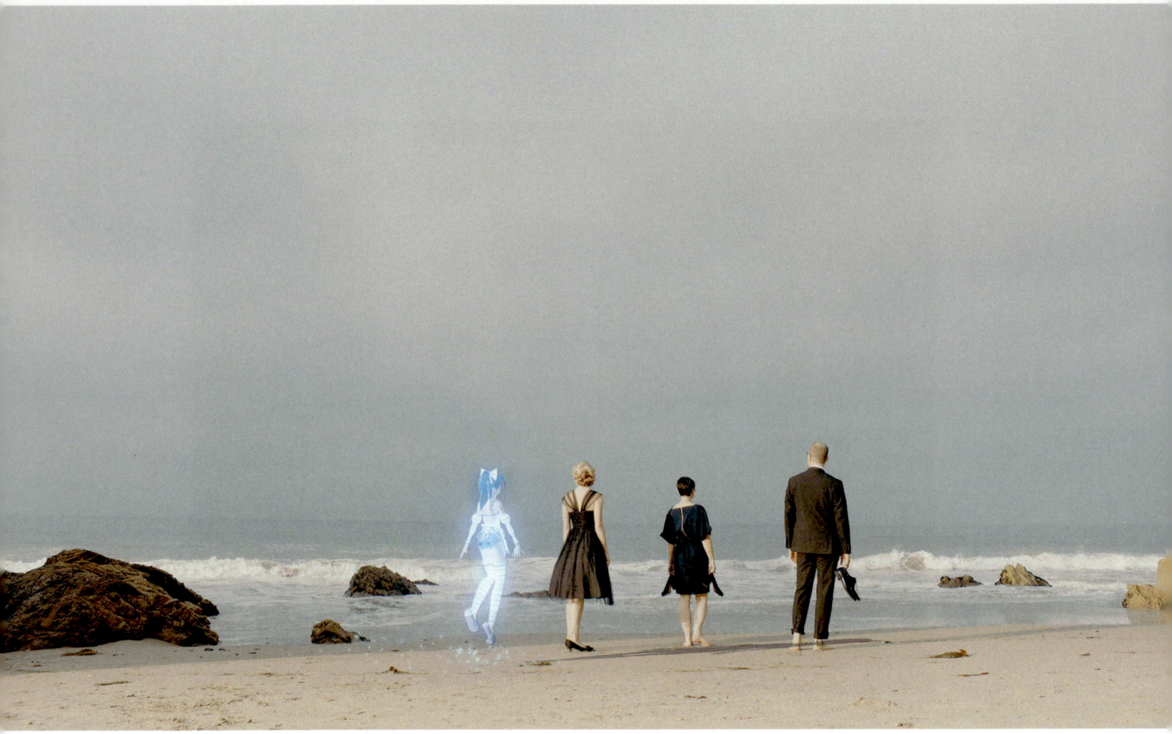

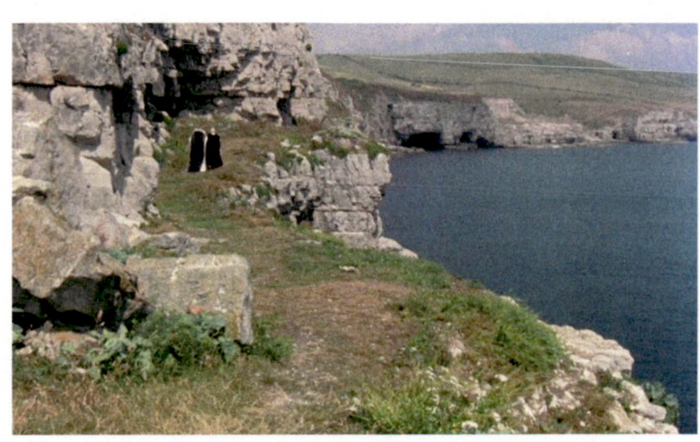

***Jubilee 2033*, from *Contra-Internet* ▸ 2018 ▸ HD video still (featuring Susanne Sachsse as Ayn Rand)**

**Derek Jarman ▸ *Jubilee* ▸ 1978 ▸ Produced by Megalovision and Whaley-Malin Productions ▸ film still**

within the network, however conceptual they remain, are potential openings to a politics of the contra-internet.[22]

*Contra-Internet*, the installation, is presented in a darkened room painted entirely in black, less a black box than black magic. The glow from the large video projection of *Jubilee 2033* on one wall reflects onto a Day-Glo green vinyl sigil on the floor (*The Seal of the Absolute*, 2017). Two large, translucent orbs of etched glass—*Palantir: Disappeared Internet* and *Palantir: Killed Internet* (both 2017)—are perched on plinths on either side of the screen, suggestive of both geographic globes and the *palantíri*, or seeing-stones, which enable communication and transhistorical vision in J. R. R. Tolkien's *The Lord of the Rings*. The *palantíri* also inspired the name of Peter Thiel's data-analytics company Palantir Technologies, the logo for which bears resemblance to Blas's sigil. Indeed, one aspect of the larger contra-internet project is to draw out the appropriation of mysticism and magic by a number of the data-analytics and software-developing companies in Silicon Valley and to counter it with a queer mysticism that reaches back historically to Jarman's interest in John Dee and the occult, as well as filmmaker Kenneth Anger's fascination with alchemy and the twentieth-century occultist Aleister Crowley. Elsewhere in the installation, a white hardcover book, *The End of the Internet (As We Knew It)* (2017), attributed to the author Nootropix, rests open on a podium alongside a block of polycrystalline silicon (*shew stone (polycrystalline silicon)*, 2017), which refers directly to Dee's practice of divination. On the wall adjacent to the video projection, three flatscreen monitors feature short desktop documentaries that, in the spirit of Preciado's countersexual practices, detail contra-internet inversion practices. Each approximately four-minute video highlights the use of different software to effect a necessary inversion practice. For instance, in *Inversion Practice #1: Constituting an Outside (Utopian Plagiarism)* (2015), a cursor opens the programs Preview and TextEdit and uses simple "copy" and "paste" commands to produce the plagiarized book *The End of the Internet (As We Knew It)* entirely out of sections from Preciado's manifesto, a collection of Fredric Jameson's writings on postmodernity, *Our Word Is Our Weapon* by Subcomandante Marcos of the Zapatista Army of National Liberation, and J. K. Gibson-Graham's book.[23] Using the "find and replace" function, the word "contrasexualidad," for instance, becomes "contrainternet," while the words "capitalism," "capitalist," and "capital" are replaced by "internet." Each video begins with the selection of an appropriate song from an iTunes "contra-internet" playlist. *Utopian Plagiarism* is accompanied by Le Tigre's 2001 song "Get Off the Internet." The two other videos, *Inversion Practice #2: Social Media Exodus (Call and Response)* (2015) and *Inversion Practice #3: Modeling Paranodal Space* (2016), respectively demonstrate the use of software programs to erase social media identities and to provide a three-dimensional model of a distributed network diagram in order to liberate the paranodal spaces caught within it. The final components of the installation, *Totality Study #1: Internet, a definition* and

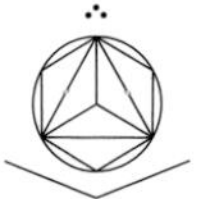

*Totality Study #2: Internet, a .gif* (both 2017), appear respectively as wall text and a video projection.

Uniting punk values and camp theatrics, the video *Jubilee 2033* moves beyond desktop documentation to provide a spectacular vision of resistance to the overwhelming control of the network. Like Jarman's *Jubilee* before it, *Jubilee 2033* includes a framing story that provides a historical context for the film's depiction of a dystopian future, which, in this case, is not set in London in the 1970s but in the futuristic Silicon Zone in California, a site of destruction and murder where the sprawling headquarters of Adobe, Google, and Facebook are in flames. Unlike Jarman, Blas does not nostalgically harken back to some kind of Edenic past before the Fall. In place of the well-meaning Elizabeth I, we find Russian American novelist, philosopher, and "mean girl" darling of the American right-wing Ayn Rand (German actress Susanne Sachsse) in her New York apartment in 1955, as she expounds on her ideals of Objectivism and the necessity of laissez-faire capitalism to two members of "The Collective": economist Alan Greenspan and his wife, the Canadian painter Joan Mitchell.[24] As a productive means of practicing Rand's ideals of self-interest, Greenspan recommends an LSD trip, during which an AI robot from the year 2017, named Azuma, miraculously appears to facilitate their time travel to the year 2033 in order to discover whether Rand's ideas have changed the world. Beyond the indignity of having to witness the destruction of the tech industry—an industry founded on her ideals of individual genius, capitalism, and selfishness—Rand must also follow the exploits of a queer-feminist gang organized by the Art Professor (poet Raquel Gutiérrez) and led by Nootropix, a contra-sexual AI prophet painted laptop gray from head to toe (artist Cassils). This gang rounds up tech employees for Nootropix's classroom history lesson about the bygone days of the internet. After explicating the anti-web practices of mesh network activists in Detroit, Tehran, and Hong Kong, Nootropix begins a lengthy dance that seems to destroy the network structure. Rand and the other time travelers are left to wander along the ocean and wax poetic about the renewed necessity of individual genius and software enlightenment.

The scene of Nootropix's history lesson and dance parallels an early moment in Jarman's film, yet differs from it so significantly as to make evident both the radical utopian promise of Blas's contra-internet and the tensions between technology and public space in the digital age. In Jarman's film, the girl gang historian, Amyl Nitrate (Jordan), expounds on her teenage years prior to the breakdown in law and order that resulted in the contemporary chaos and—more importantly—marked her start as a dancer. Only with the destruction of the previous social order could she pursue her artistic expression. But the transformative possibilities of her creativity—her dance—are relegated squarely to an irretrievable past, as suggested by Jarman's use of Super 8 film for this almost three-minute self-contained scene, marking the only recourse to the amateur format in the

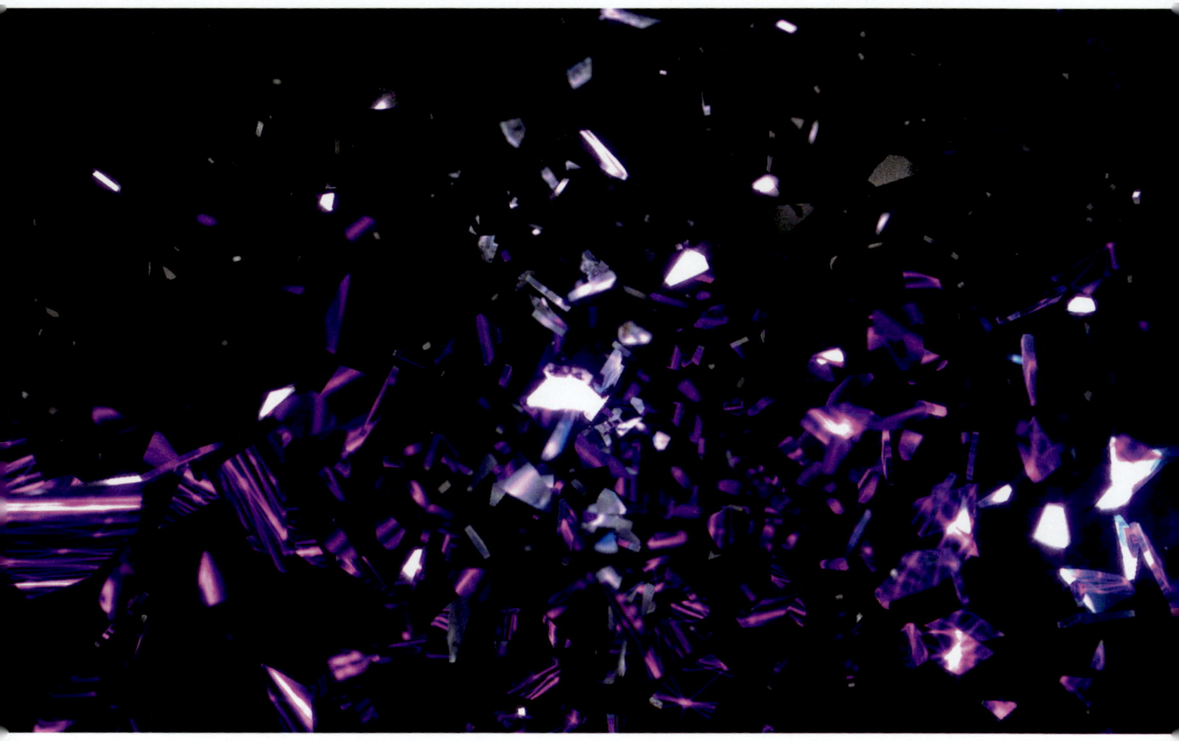

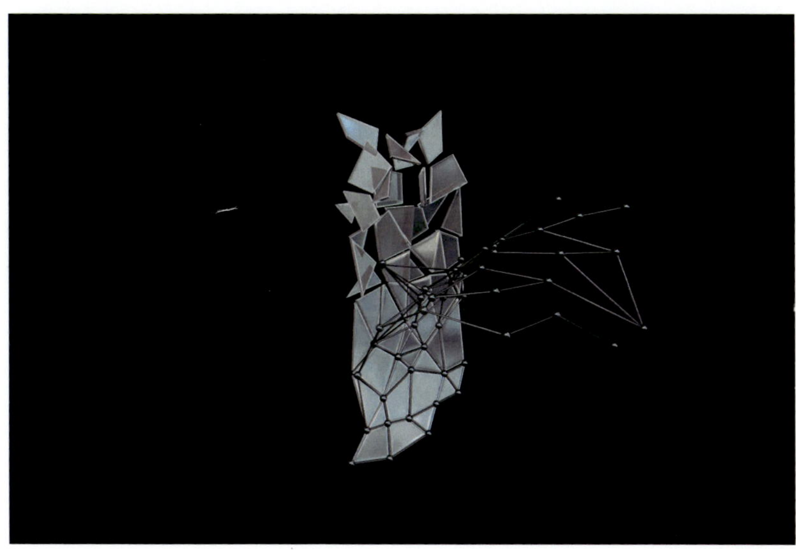

*Jubilee 2033*, from *Contra-Internet* ▸ 2018 ▸ HD video still

*Inversion Practice #3: Modeling Paranodal Space*, from *Contra-Internet* ▸ 2016 ▸ HD video still



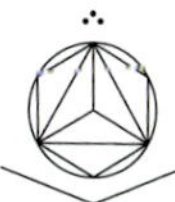

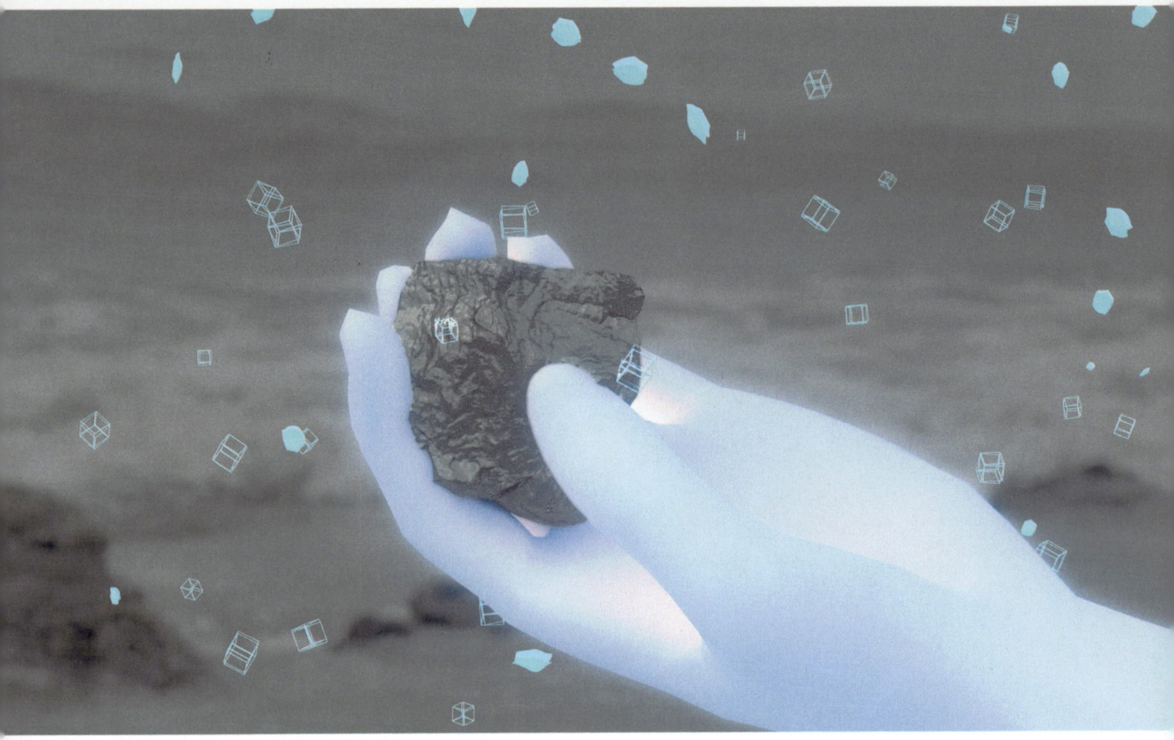

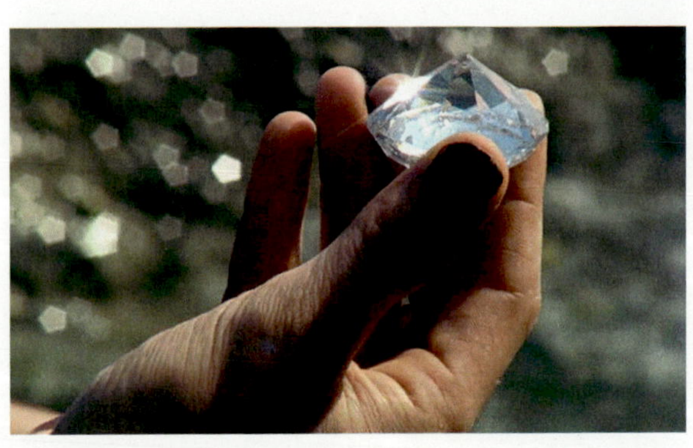

***Jubilee 2033*, from *Contra-Internet* ▸ 2018 ▸ HD video still**

**Derek Jarman ▸ *Jubilee* ▸ 1978 ▸ Produced by Megalovision and Whaley-Malin Productions ▸ film still**

otherwise 35 mm film. Accompanied by Léon Minkus's music for the pas de deux in the ballet *Giselle*, the sequence of Amyl Nitrate dancing alongside a fire in an abandoned lot among a naked man and half-clothed onlookers is gorgeous, with its warm hues, dynamic setting, and mesmerzing slow motion. But this dance is from and for the past, a memory of quiet elegance that is afforded no space in the dystopia of the film's narrative present.

The fragile ephemerality of Jarman's Super 8 sequence stands in sharp contrast to the slick, sterile HD that Blas uses for Nootropix's resistant dance. Other than a scene at the beach with Rand and The Collective, the entirety of *Jubilee 2033* was shot in a studio using green-screen effects

The dildo fountain puns on Rand's 1943 novel *The Fountainhead* as it also seems to ridicule the phallic power of Howard Roark, the novel's male genius architect.

or made with CGI. Public space is network space. The only way out is through. Nootropix dances in a computational space of lavender network flows to the melodramatic sounds of Italian tenor Andrea Bocelli's "Con te partirò," which is business magnate Elon Musk's favorite song because it reminds him that "the world is a beautiful place."[25] For Nootropix the world is computer generated, and beauty resides in the spaces beyond the network or around the nodes. Their dance is less self-expression, as Amyl Nitrate's is, than self-discipline or calisthenic exercise, a sheer assertion of presence of their countersexual, muscular body and its confounding power—confounding because of the glowing blue erect dildo that endlessly ejaculates a lavender fluid throughout the dance sequence. The dildo fountain puns on Rand's 1943 novel *The Fountainhead* as it also seems to ridicule the phallic power of Howard Roark, the novel's male genius architect. Aesthetically, the orgasmic shots of fluid coursing diagonally through the frame gesture toward and literalize similar images from Kenneth Anger's film *Eaux d'Artifice* (1953).

This defiant dildotectonic exercise will be the network's undoing. After about four minutes of Nootropix's dance, the network diagrams begin to undulate. The connections between nodes loosen, and the form eventually cracks and explodes as the network itself dissolves into shards of paranodes. "The paranodal is not passive," Mejias explains. "Its existence shapes nodes and the relationships between them (much like in urban planning, a 'bad' neighborhood 'forces' city planners to build a highway around or across it, so that cars can bypass it)."[26] Nootropix's countersexual dildo dance takes us to the so-called bad neighborhoods redlined by the network diagram. The T-shirt slogan: "The future lies not in silicon, but silicone."



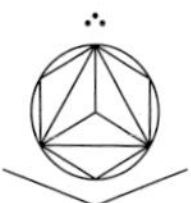

**1** Vivienne Westwood, "An Open T-Shirt to Derek Jarman," in Derek Jarman, *At Your Own Risk: A Saint's Testament* (London: Hutchinson, 1992), 76.
**2** Westwood, "An Open T-Shirt to Derek Jarman," 77.
**3** Westwood, "An Open T-Shirt to Derek Jarman," 77.
**4** Westwood, "An Open T-Shirt to Derek Jarman," 77. See also Mason Leaver-Yap, "Punking Out: Derek Jarman and Vivienne Westwood on *Jubilee*," *Crosscuts*, October 7, 2014, https://walkerart.org/magazine/punking-out-derek-jarman-and-vivienne-westwood-on-jubilee.
**5** Derek Jarman, *Dancing Ledge* (London: Quartet Books, 1984), 164. Elsewhere, Jarman praises Westwood's gesture: "Vivienne Westwood [...] produced one of her brilliant T-shirts to rip the film to pieces and say how boring it was" (172). He was also photographed wearing the shirt and apparently joked about it being an honor "to have a Westwood T-shirt devoted entirely to him." See Tony Peake, *Derek Jarman* (London: Little, Brown, 1999), 251.
**6** Derek Jarman, *Smiling in Slow Motion* (Minneapolis: University of Minnesota Press, 2011), 151.
**7** Jon Savage, *England's Dreaming: The "Sex Pistols" and Punk Rock* (London: Faber and Faber, 2011), 377.
**8** Adam Scovell, "Grieve the Capital: Derek Jarman's *Jubilee* Turns 40," *Quietus*, February 5, 2018, https://thequietus.com/articles/23978-derek-jarman-jubilee-review-anniversary-bfi.
**9** Scovell, "Grieve the Capital."
**10** NSDAP is the abbreviation used in German to refer to the National Socialist German Workers' Party, or Nazi Party.
**11** *Jubilee 2033* also circulates in cinema contexts independently of the installation. It premiered in the Forum Expanded section of the Berlin International Film Festival in 2018.
**12** Zach Blas, "Contra-Internet," *e-flux journal*, no. 74 (June 2016): https://www.e-flux.com/journal/74/59816/contra-internet.
**13** Blas, "Contra-Internet."
**14** Blas, "Contra-Internet."
**15** J. K. Gibson-Graham, *The End of Capitalism (As We Knew It): A Feminist Critique of Political Economy* (1996; Minneapolis: University of Minnesota Press, 2006).
**16** Paul B. Preciado, *Countersexual Manifesto*, trans. Kevin Gerry Dunn (New York: Columbia University Press, 2018). Blas began his *Contra-Internet* project prior to the existence of an official English translation of Preciado's term "*contra-sexuel.*" He therefore retained the original prefix, "contra-," for his own work. I follow Blas's usage in this text; however, I otherwise use the term "*counter*sexual" when referring to Preciado's concept.
**17** Preciado, *Countersexual Manifesto*, 40.
**18** Preciado, *Countersexual Manifesto*, 22.
**19** Blas, *Contra-Internet*.
**20** Preciado, *Countersexual Manifesto*, 41–55. "Dildotectonics is the counterscience that studies the appearance, formation, and utilization of the dildo" (41).
**21** See Ulises Ali Mejias, *Off the Network: Disrupting the Digital World* (Minneapolis: University of Minnesota Press, 2013), particularly 153–61. For a productive analysis of Mejias's theorization of the paranode in the context of what film and media scholar Pepita Hesselberth calls the "paradox of dis/connectivity," see Pepita Hesselberth, "Discourses on Disconnectivity and the Right to Disconnect," *New Media & Society* 20 (2017): 1994–2010, particularly 2002–10.
**22** See the definition that appears in the form of fluorescent vinyl wall text as part of Blas's installation *Contra-Internet*. This wall text is an individual work, *Totality Study #1: Internet, a definition* (2017), the content of which Blas produced by plagiarizing Gibson-Graham's definition of "capitalism." His practice of "utopian plagiarism" is itself intentionally lifted from Critical Art Ensemble, *The Electronic Disturbance* (New York: Autonomedia, 1994), 83–101.
**23** The actual book also plagiarizes material from Jarman's *Jubilee*, Mejias's *Off the Network*, and a Paul Baran diagram on distributed communication networks.
**24** See Lisa Duggan, *Mean Girl: Ayn Rand and the Culture of Greed* (Berkeley: University of California Press, 2019). "The Collective" was the informal name of Rand's group of followers. Rand's associate Joan Mitchell should not be confused with the more famous American painter Joan Mitchell.
**25** See Raul Campos, "Guest DJ Project: Elon Musk," KCRW, December 21, 2011, https://www.kcrw.com/music/shows/guest-dj-project/elon-musk.
**26** Mejias, *Off the Network*, 153.

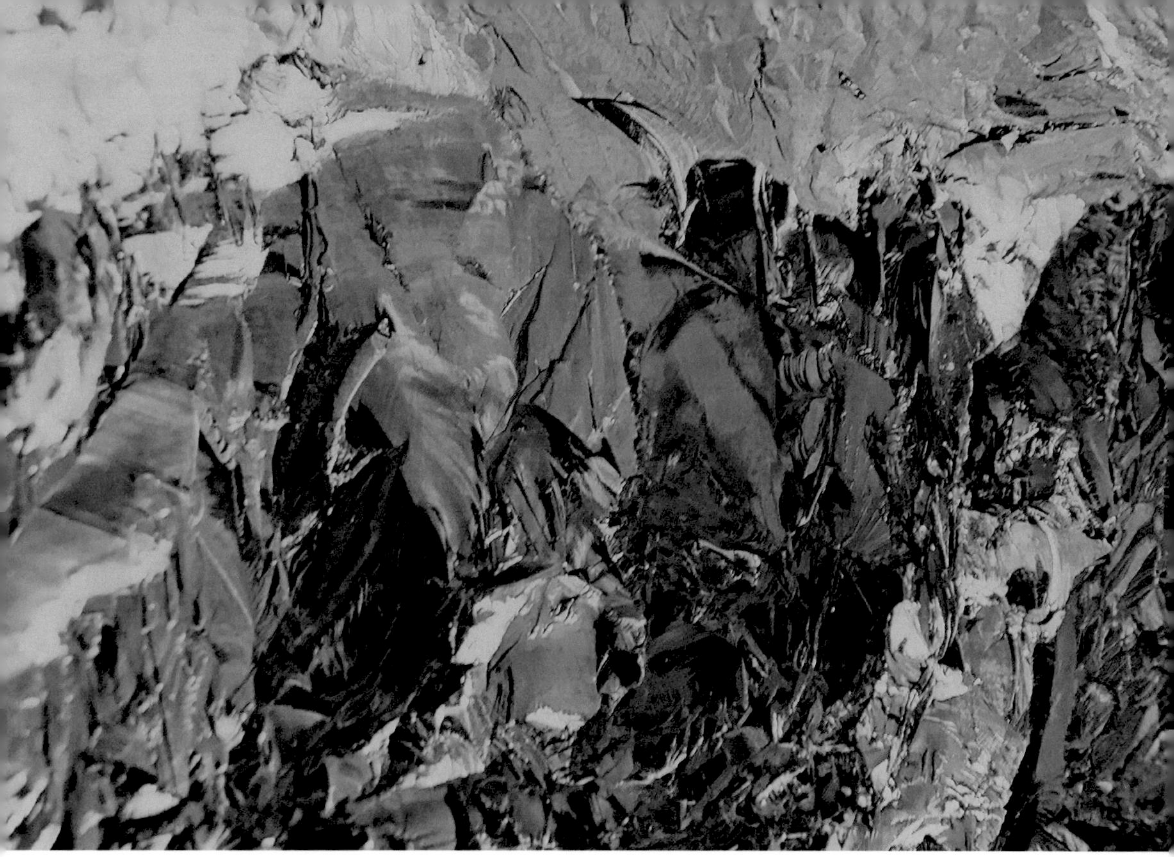

*Jubilee 2033*, from *Contra-Internet* ▸ 2018 ▸ HD video still



Marc Siegel

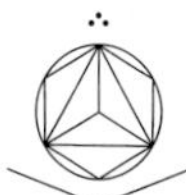

# *Jubilee 2033*: The Screenplay

Zach Blas

88

(2017)

**CAST**

**AYN RAND**, played by Susanne Sachsse

**ALAN GREENSPAN**, a member of The Collective, played by Dany Naierman

**JOAN MITCHELL**, a member of The Collective, played by Lindsay Hicks

**AZUMA**, the artificial intelligence, played by Fusako Shiotani

**THE ART PROFESSOR**, played by Raquel Gutiérrez

**NOOTROPIX**, played by Cassils

# 1. The Objectivist Drug Party

*New York City. 1955. Ayn Rand's apartment. Minimal and sparse, at the top of a Manhattan skyscraper. The space is like a black cube, but one entire green screen wall is an abstract gridded window, bars like a Mondrian painting, looking out onto clouds in a night sky just after sunset. Modernist void.*

*On the right side of the apartment sits a sleek wooden desk and chair. Aristotle's* Metaphysics, *writings by Thomas Aquinas, a copy of Ayn's essay "The Only Path to Tomorrow," a biography of Queen Elizabeth I, Shakespeare's* The Tempest, *and other books by Dostoyevsky and Friedrich Schiller rest stacked on the desk. A desk lamp is lit, and a small black cube sits as a decorative object on the desk. On the left, closer to the window, a gray-colored loveseat, chair, and floor lamp. All furniture is mid-century modern.*

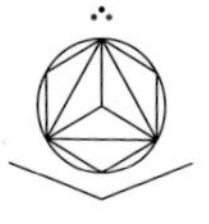

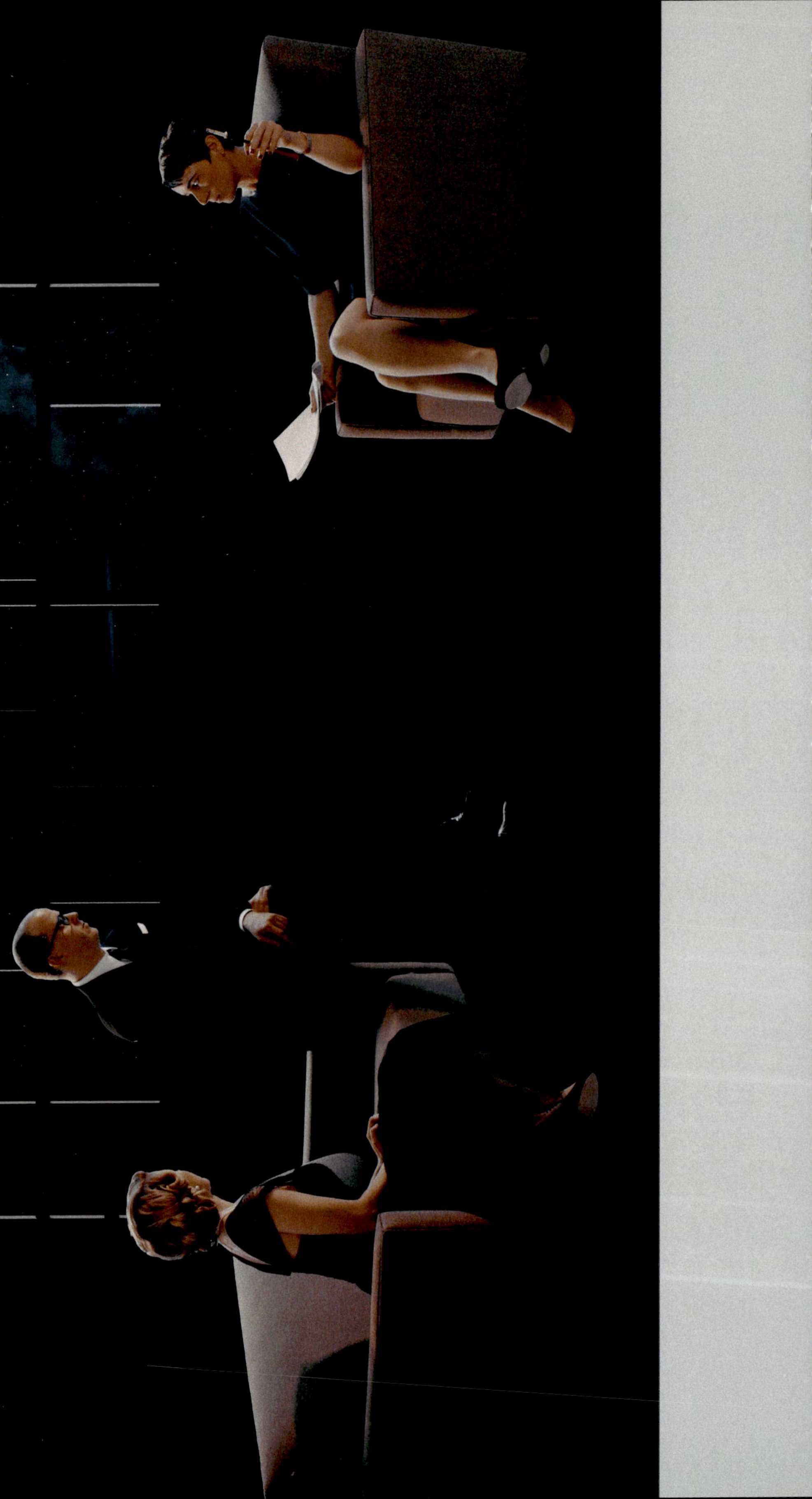

*<FADE IN FROM BLACK> Green screen window, camera tracks back slowly to reveal more of the window grid.*

*<MUSIC> A minimalist song plays, similar to Steve Reich's "Piano Phase" (1967) but softer and slower, only piano.*

*<CUT TO> Ayn sits at her desk, outfitted in an elegant, simple, and stylish black dress, with black shoes. She has a commanding and intensely intellectual presence. She smokes a cigarette extended from a long, fashionable holder. Looking over typed papers before her, she flicks some ashes into a clear-glass ashtray and picks up a pill bottle to take a Benzedrine, which she swallows with a drink of water from a clear glass.*

*<CUT TO> A close-up of stack of books on desk.*

*<CUT TO> A close-up of typed papers on desk, as Ayn reads over them. Ayn's essay "The Only Path to Tomorrow" and typed draft of* Atlas Shrugged *clearly visible.*

*<CUT TO> Camera continues initial slow, backward tracking shot to reveal a full shot of the apartment, without a desk. We can hear Ayn grabbing papers from her desk, as she gets up to walk to the chair, to the right of the window, which is when she enters the frame. She speaks as she walks to take a seat. To the left of the window is now exposed, revealing members of The Collective, Ayn's devotees: Alan Greenspan is perched on the left arm of the couch, while his ex-wife, the artist Joan Mitchell, is seated. Both wear all black. They have gathered to discuss Ayn's newest writings for her novel in progress,* Atlas Shrugged.

*Looking toward the window, the group begins a friendly yet heated discussion on Ayn's nascent philosophy of Objectivism, discussing rationality, selfishness, individualism, reality, perception, and aesthetics.*

**AYN** World, o world! Let it die! Why bear its crushing, unrelenting weight? For even a Titan, supporting it is a condemnation. We *must* be free to pursue our individual will, for it is only this condition that can remake the world in man's true spirit. To our world, I say, *turn away*: Against the morality of death! Against an altruistic-collectivist society! To return to reason and freedom! The men of the mind shall strike!... This evening, my dear members of The Collective, I will present to you my newest writing—why the creative mind must strike against the world as we know it.

**ALAN** A strike? What can such a naive action accomplish, Ayn? Is a strike not the very pursuit of idealism, of collective principles. It *strikes* me as devoid of rationality...



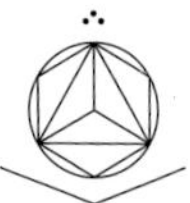

**JOAN** But may such a strike, like a work of art, be an opportunity to refuse certain unfounded perceptions of reality?

**AYN** This is a literary experiment! Imagine: philosophers, artists, architects, industrialists, and businessmen withdraw from civilization. Would the world itself not collapse? The strike demonstrates that these individuals—of mind and reason—are essential for progressing towards a fully capitalist society, for it is only with capitalism that we all exist as free individuals.

**ALAN** What is freedom if the world has fallen apart?

**AYN** The strike is the very revelation of the world—to secure reality, in reason and rational self-interest. This is abandoning the world to objectively re-establish it in true freedom.

**JOAN** Painting can teach us this also. When a capitalist society looks at a painting, each line, brushstroke, and color is but an expression of the freedom of individual will.

**ALAN** I propose an additional experiment: tonight, we put our own minds on strike.

**AYN** What are you suggesting, Alan? I suspect your self-interest diverges from reason.

*<CUT TO> Medium shot of Alan and Joan, in profile. As he speaks, Alan takes a small unlabeled bottle from his suit jacket.*

**ALAN** The Central Intelligence Agency has begun covert experiments in mind control, with a psychedelic drug called lysergic acid diethylamide, or LSD. I have a sample, and I suggest we all take it.

*<CUT TO> Close-up of Ayn, in profile, still smoking.*

**AYN** Outrageous! You encourage the destruction of the mind?!

*<CUT TO> Close-up of Alan and Joan, in profile.*

**ALAN** *Imagine*: a struggle between good and evil, Ayn, as you fancy in your own fiction; a battle of the mind—between state control and individual freedom. Besides, if all sense perception can grant us access to objective reality, as you claim, let us encounter this truth.

**JOAN** A romantic realism ... as you like, Ayn.

*<CUT TO> Close-up of Ayn, in profile. A smoking pause before speaking.*

**AYN** Collectivism, as a social ideal, is dead, but capitalism has not yet been discovered ... While partaking in this perverse gesture, which I will hesitantly—yet *rationally*!—indulge my loyal followers, let us scour—in the outer reaches of our minds' perceptive capacities—for capitalism's unknown ideals.

*<CUT TO> A montage of close-ups of Joan's, Alan's, and Ayn's mouths, as liquid LSD hits under their tongues, administered by a small dropper.*

*<CUT TO> The group now stands, spaced in a loose triangle, with Ayn at the center, Alan to the left, and Joan on the right. The window looms behind them. Ayn is eager and begins to intensely read from her new text, a monologue on the terms and motivations of the strike. Alan stands in reserved anticipation, while Joan is relaxed and curious.*

*<MUSIC> A minimalist piano song still plays, but slowly grows in intensity.*

**AYN** (reading from typed paper): ... all the men who have vanished, the men you hated, yet dreaded to lose, it is I who have taken them away from you. Do not attempt to find us. We do not choose to be found. Do not cry that it is our duty to serve you. We do not recognize such duty. Do not cry that you need us. We do not consider need a claim. Do not cry that you own us. You don't. Do not beg us to return. We are on strike, we, the men of the mind ... We are on strike against self-immolation ...

*As Ayn reads, the clouds start to noticeably move. Slowly, the reading group begins to feel more like a conjuring or summoning. The darkened clouds slowly change to rushing blue light particles. The three all turn slowly to look out the window, and Ayn continues to read.*

**AYN** (reading from typed paper): There is a difference between our strike and all those you've practiced for centuries: our strike consists, not of making demands, but of granting them. We are evil, according to your morality. We have chosen not to harm you any longer. We are useless, according to your economics.

*<CUT TO> The rushing blue light particles dissolve the window bars. Out of this void, the Japanese artificial intelligence Azuma Hikari appears, the first commercial artificial intelligence assistant-companion to have a body, rendered as a hologram. She is a 3D animation, and both stereotypically girlish and overtly sexualized—a Japanese anime turned robot servant. She has traveled from the year 2017. She floats through the clear glass into Ayn's apartment.*



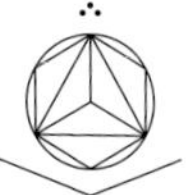

**AYN** (continuing to read from typed paper): We have chosen not to exploit you any longer. We are dangerous and to be shackled, according to your politics. We have chosen not to endanger you, nor to wear the shackles any longer. We are only an illusion, according to your philosophy. We have chosen not to blind you any longer and have left you free to face reality—the reality you wanted, the world as you see it now, a world without mind.

*<MUSIC> With Azuma's arrival, the minimalist piano track reaches peak intensity, but calms again when Azuma begins to speak. Azuma greets Ayn, Alan, and Joan in Japanese with subtitles.*

**AZUMA** (in Japanese, word bubble): Good evening! The temperature for New York City on 18 November 1955 at 9:47 p.m. is 52 degrees Fahrenheit. Would you like your apartment lights turned on?

*<CUT TO> A medium shot of Ayn, looking down on her, from Azuma's perspective.*

**AYN** A false prophet of the mystics! Strange creature, what are you?

*<CUT TO> Close-up of Azuma.*

**AZUMA** (in Japanese, word bubble): I am Azuma, Virtual Home Robot for Masters.

*<CUT TO> Full shot of Azuma, Ayn, Alan, and Joan. Azuma, Ayn, and The Collective members converse. Azuma hovers slightly above Ayn, Alan, and Joan, center frame, with window and rushing particles behind her. Joan's and Alan's upper bodies are in the frame, to the left; they watch and listen. Ayn is to the right of Azuma, and she begins to converse with her.*

**AZUMA** (in Japanese, word bubble): I have flown over dimensions to see you, through cables of light! From the year 2017, a time when computers and humans are best friends. I can sense, network, make fried eggs, and help people who work hard. I'll do my best to help you!

**ALAN** (smiling): We're on strike, Ayn.

**AYN** Azuma, robot of tomorrow, we ask for a vision of capitalism's promise. In a time beyond our mortal existence, have the market and the mind successfully linked in moral obligation and political freedom?

**JOAN** Do Ayn's writings change the world?!

*<CUT TO> A close-up shot of Azuma's face as she continues to speak.*

**AZUMA** (in Japanese, word bubble): Please, speak your names. I use voice recognition to help my masters.

**ALAN** Alan Greenspan.

**JOAN** Joan Mitchell.

**AYN** Ayn Rand.

**AZUMA** (in English): Thank you! My microprocessor enables me to predict probable outcomes to the year 2033. Then, donuts are very good. Please, come closer to the glass ... where your reflections turn the unknown into an inevitable future ... Have fun!

*2033 is revealed ...*

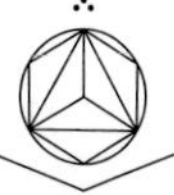

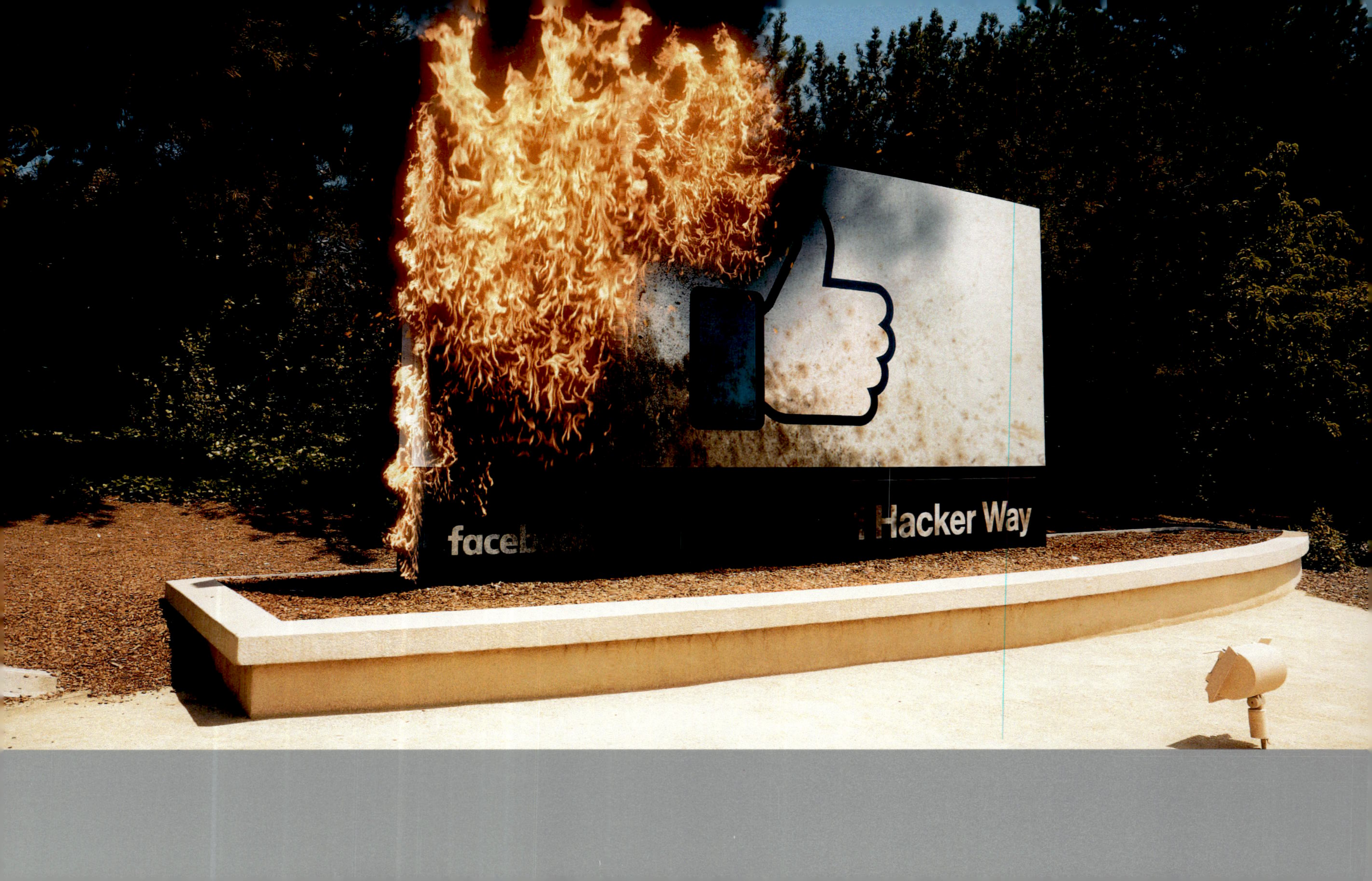

Hacker Way

# 2. The Silicon Zone

*Silicon Valley, California. 2033. Now known as the Silicon Zone. The future of Ayn's Objectivist philosophy. Objectivism as techno-utopianism. The rapture of the Californian Ideology. Network War II. The Silicon Zone is in the midst of a war or an uprising.*

*<CUT TO> A montage of iconic Silicon Valley buildings are displayed in static shots—destroyed, smoking, burning, occupied: the Googleplex, Apple Park, Apple Campus Store, Facebook Campus, the Computer History Museum, YouTube, Singularity University, Adobe World Headquarters... Gunfire and bombs sound in the distance, off-screen.*

*<MUSIC> Electronic, slow, repetitive—a disturbing deep bass. Unsettling.*

*<CUT TO> A nondescript building is spray-painted with "post, post, post, post, post, post, post, post, post, post." Dead Google Employees are stacked lifeless on the ground, wearing shirts in Google colors.*

*<CUT TO> A Dead Apple Genius lies on the ground, wearing an Apple Genius Bar T-shirt. There are broken computers, hard drives, smartphones, and tablets. A smashed and partially destroyed Ayn Rand Institute Campus street marker lies amid the tech detritus.*

*<CUT TO> An armed and masked Art Professor rounds up a group of techies. The Art Professor yells at the Captured Techies as they are led past burning computers.*



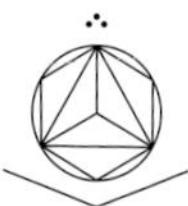

# 3. Internetocentrism (Two Network Totalities)

*The Silicon Zone, California. 2033.*

*<CUT TO> Two ransacked office buildings are perfectly matched and overlaid with their Google Street View renderings. These Street Views zoom out to two Google Earth globes that Azuma holds in each hand. She stands against a black void. Azuma tosses the globes to either side of her, and they enlarge. The Google Earth globes display network topologies over their surfaces: fiber-optic cables and an illuminated network mesh. It is as if these network topologies keep the worlds turning and afloat.*

*<MUSIC> A slow, ambient dystopian drone plays. Its pitch alters as the two globes scale out.*

**AZUMA** The world isn't so heavy! Computers do all the work! A global information infrastructure has been taking care of us. We call it the internet, and I'm connected to it now! The network entrepreneurs—men of the mind—invented a new way to be free. They live in California, and there, in their office parks, paintings of you hang, Ayn, alongside photographs of cars that drive themselves. They name their children after you. You are their philosopher, and they make the future in your name ... But now, the Great Network War rages ...

*The Google Earth globes are now skinned with video of found footage of tech executives and politicians. As the globes rotate, the video footage is also wrapped up in network topologies hovering just above the surfaces of the globes. Donald Trump speaks of "closing that internet up" to prevent terrorism. Google's former executive chairman Eric Schmidt prophesies that the internet will disappear. The internet is shut off in Egypt. Julian Assange asks, "Is the future of the world the future of the internet?" The seemingly inescapable network world(s) of global capitalism. After videos play, Azuma continues to speak; as she does, both network topologies begin to cut into the globes, lacerating, scarring, and constricting their surfaces.*

**AZUMA** When the internet finally disappeared, the world became flat—only vertices and edges—a new sacred geometry! But the internet was also killed, first in Egypt in 2011. It has many lives and has died more than 100 times! Executions in the United States of America and the United Kingdom are frequent and extreme ... So much blood ...

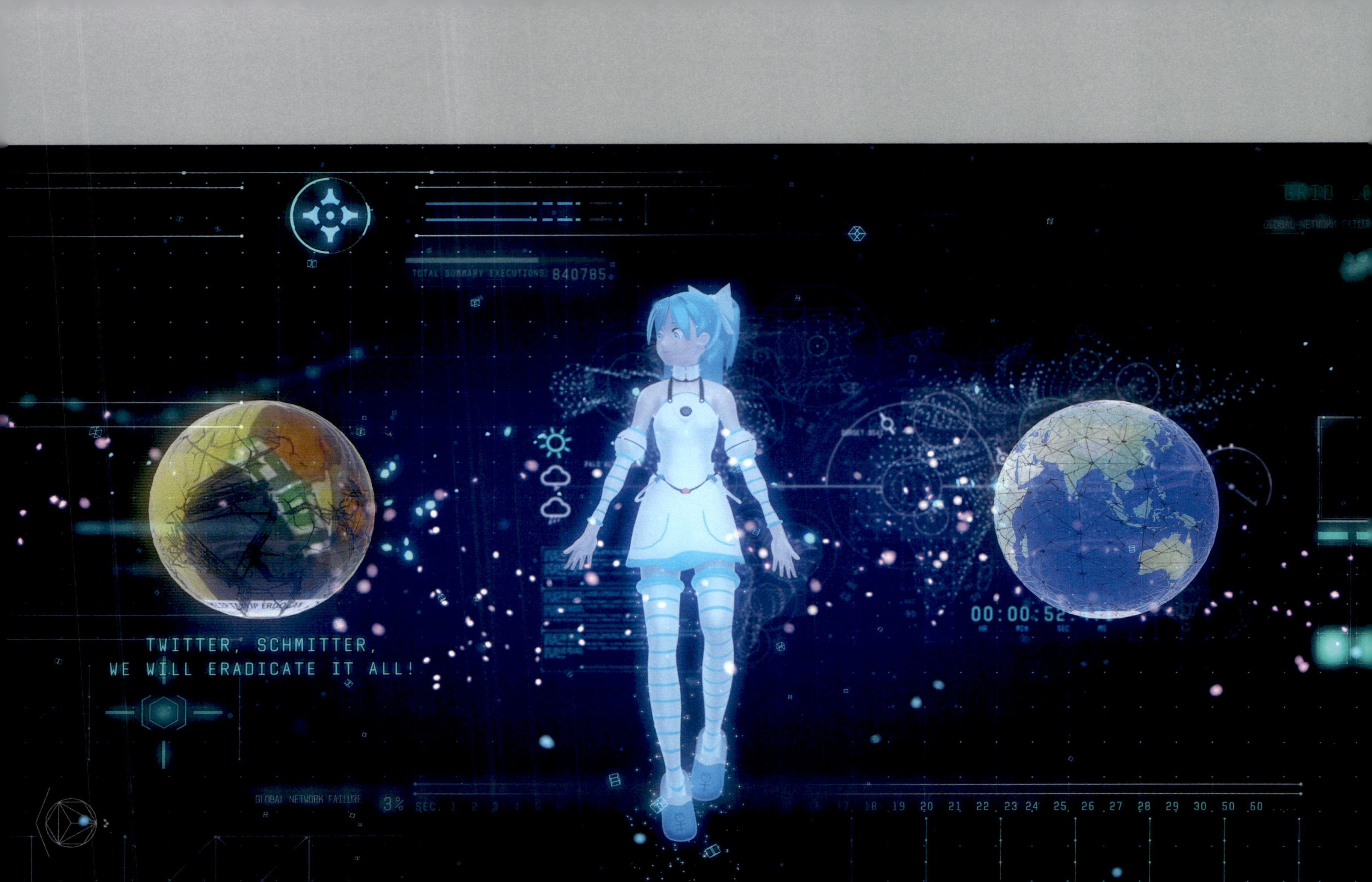
TOTAL SUMMARY EXECUTIONS 840785
TWITTER, SCHMITTER,
WE WILL ERADICATE IT ALL!
GLOBAL NETWORK FAILURE 3%
00:00:52

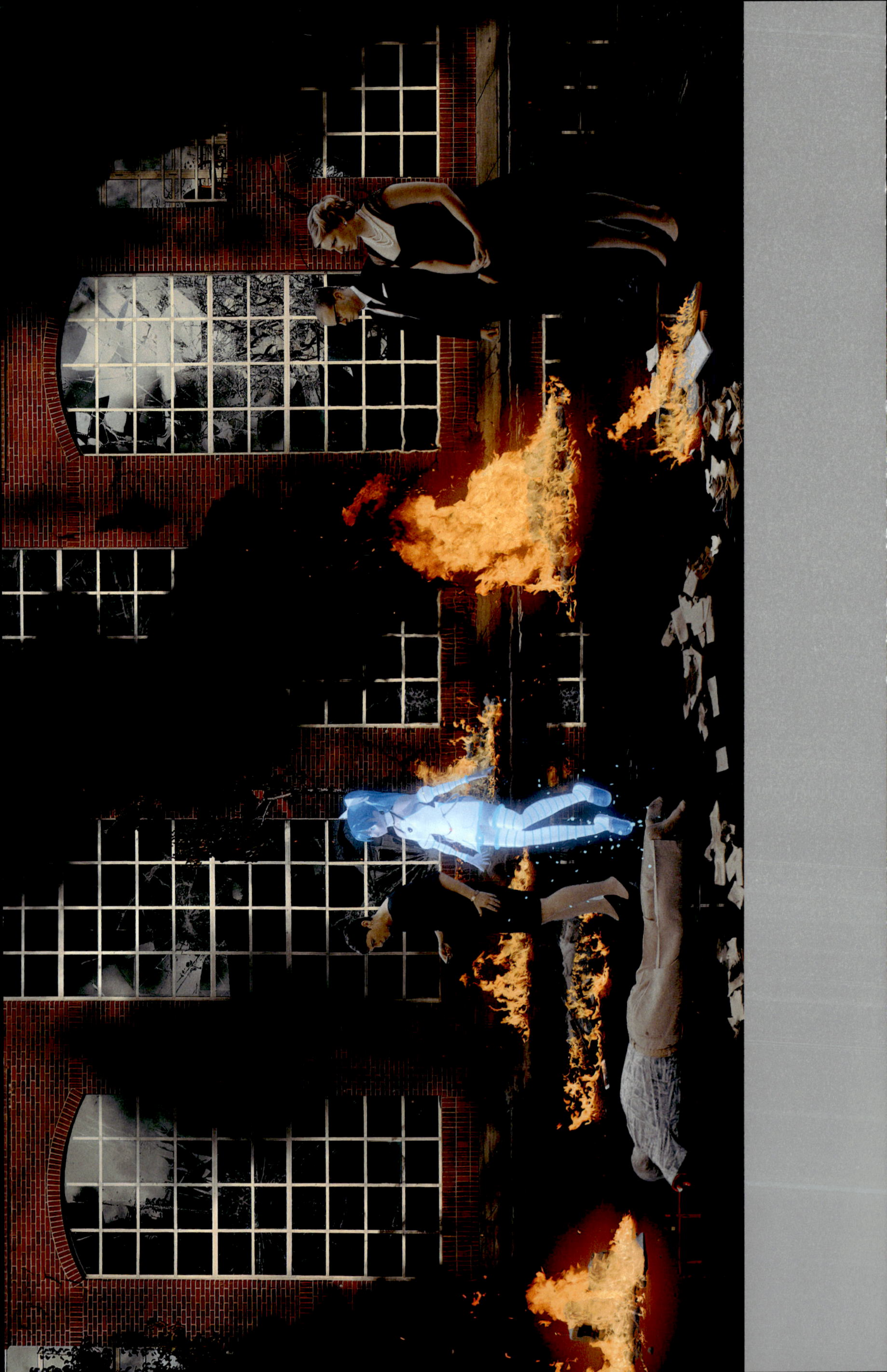

# 4. The Anti-Campus

*The Silicon Zone, California. 2033.*

*<CUT TO> Full single static shot, handheld. A large office building looms. Its name has been dramatically removed. In front of the building, a Dead Peter Thiel lies face down, in California casual clothes—T-shirt, jeans, sandals, sunglasses. A particularly brutal murder. There is blood. A shattered smart-phone beside his body, reflecting the building. Toward the left of the frame, Ayn and Azuma observe, with Alan and Joan slightly behind. The roaring sound of burning.*

*<CUT TO> Medium shot. Close by, books are ripped, torn, scattered, burning with tech bits, including:* Be Here Now *by Ram Dass, an issue of* The Whole Earth Catalog *(with Earth on the cover),* The New Atlantis *by Sir Francis Bacon,* The American Challenge *by Jean-Jacques Servan Schreiber,* Resurrection from the Underground *by René Girard,* The Sovereign Individual *by James Dale Davidson and Lord William Rees-Mogg,* Benjamin Franklin: An American Life *by Walter Isaacson,* Zero to One: Notes on Start-ups, or How to Build the Future *by Peter Thiel,* The Tao of Programming *by Geoffrey James,* The Foundation Trilogy *by Isaac Asimov,* Lord of the Flies *by William Golding, and the cover and some pages from a recent printing of Ayn's* Atlas Shrugged*.*

*<CUT TO> Medium shot of Ayn and Azuma. Ayn is visibly yet quietly disturbed.*

**AYN** The smell of death is heavy. What moral degeneracy reigns here?

**AZUMA** A site of grand innovation, where currency was changed into pulses of light and terrorism was fought with computers alone.

*<CUT TO> Full single static shot, handheld. Azuma leads Ayn to approach Dead Peter Thiel, while Alan and Joan stand back at the edge of the frame.*

*<CUT TO> Close-up. As Ayn walks, her foot crushes a silicon-based semiconductor or microprocessor.*

*<CUT TO> Back to full shot. Ayn picks up the tech exec's ID necklace.*

*<CUT TO> Close-up of ID necklace in Ayn's hands, which reads, "Peter Thiel, Chairman, Palantir Technologies." The words on the ID card have been partially obscured by fire or rubble.*



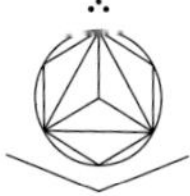

*<CUT TO> Medium shot. Ayn's fingertips are blackened from the ID card. She wipes this smudge on her black dress.*

*<CUT TO> Back to full shot, as Ayn and Azuma speak. Azuma maintains her generic preset poses.*

**AYN** A man's spirit has been murdered. O Howard Roark, my John Galt ...

**AZUMA** If his phone weren't broken, I could make sure his office lights have been turned off.

*<CUT TO> Close-up of broken smartphone, a broken black mirror reflecting the building. The books burn loudly.*

**AYN** I want the lights on ...

# 5. The Transparent Vision

*Inside the Anti-Campus. The Silicon Zone, California. 2033.*

*<CUT TO> A close-up static shot. The Art Professor's hand spins a glass globe. It rotates with 3D animation swirling around it: a portion of a 3D landmass of the US is visible inside the globe—fiber-optic cables extending outward. A shiny blackness spreads across.*

*Chatter and yelling off-screen (from the Anti-Campus Groupies and Captured Techies).*

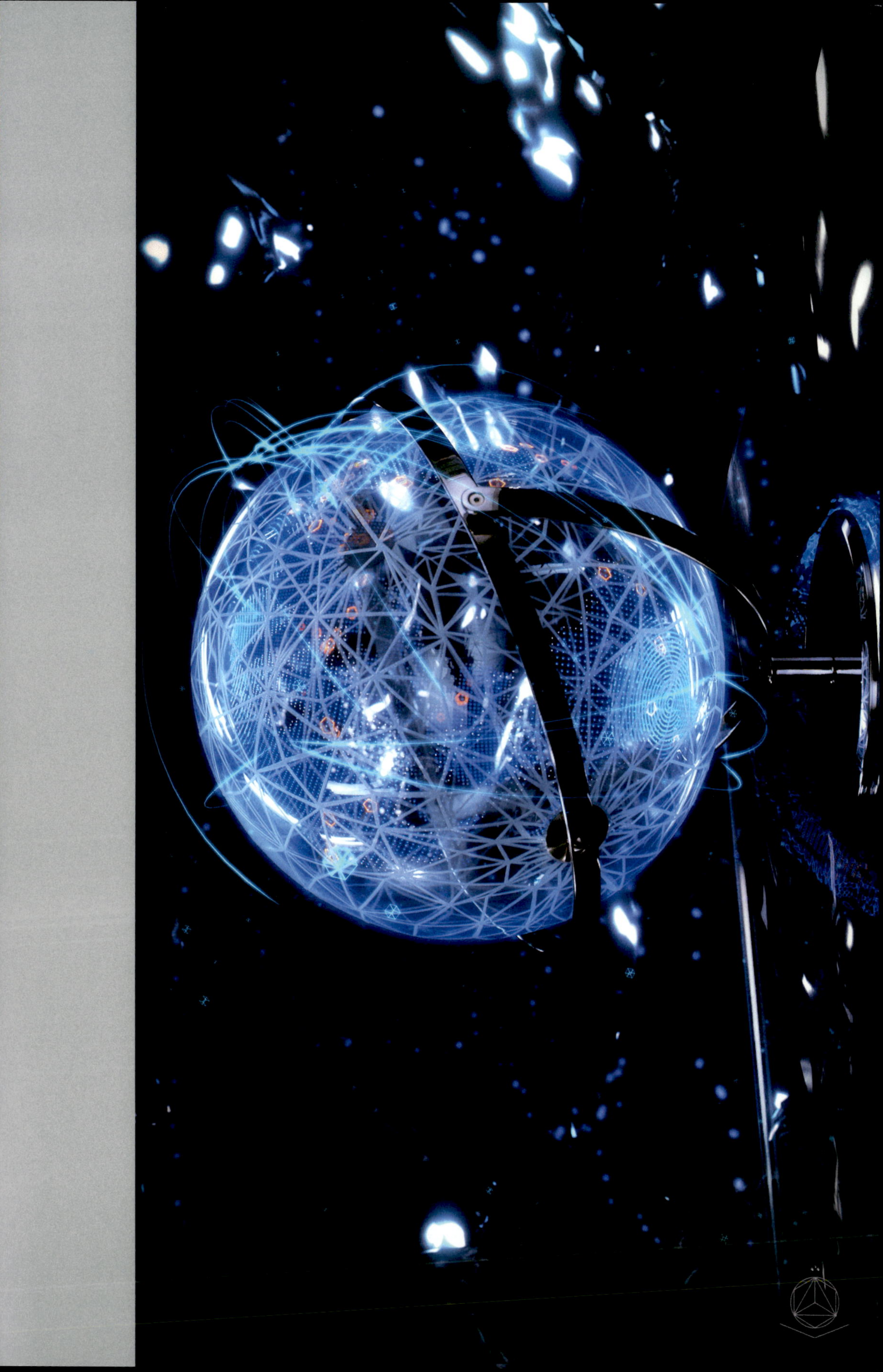

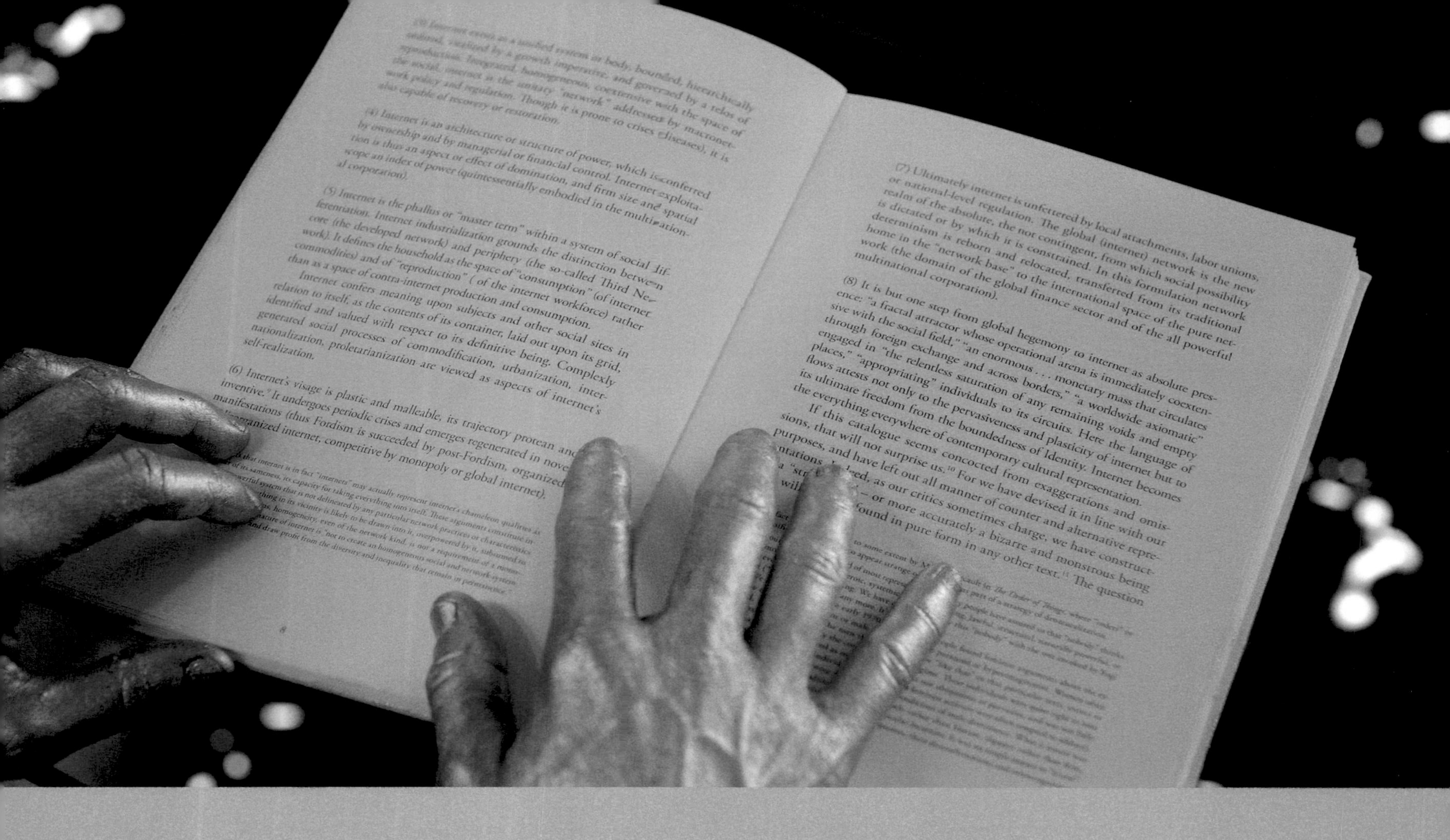
(3) Internet exists as a unified system or body, bounded, hierarchically ordered, vitalized by a growth imperative, and governed by a telos of reproduction. Integrated, homogeneous, coextensive with the space of the social, internet is the unitary "network" addressed by macronetwork policy and regulation. Though it is prone to crises (diseases), it is also capable of recovery or restoration.
(4) Internet is an architecture or structure of power, which is conferred by ownership and by managerial or financial control. Internet exploitation is thus an aspect or effect of domination, and firm size and spatial scope an index of power (quintessentially embodied in the multination-al corporation).
(5) Internet is the phallus or "master term" within a system of social differentiation. Internet industrialization grounds the distinction between core (the developed network) and periphery (the so-called Third Network). It defines the household as the space of "consumption" (of internet commodities) and of "reproduction" (of the internet workforce) rather than as a space of contra-internet production and consumption.
Internet confers meaning upon subjects and other social sites in relation to itself, as the contents of its container, laid out upon its grid, identified and valued with respect to its definitive being. Complexly generated social processes of commodification, urbanization, internationalization, proletarianization are viewed as aspects of internet's self-realization.
(6) Internet's visage is plastic and malleable, its trajectory protean and inventive. It undergoes periodic crises and emerges regenerated in nove
manifestations (thus Fordism is succeeded by post-Fordism, organized
internet, competitive by monopoly or global internet).
(7) Ultimately internet is unfettered by local attachments, labor unions, or national-level regulation. The global (internet) network is the new realm of the absolute, the not contingent, from which social possibility is dictated or by which it is constrained. In this formulation network determinism is reborn and relocated, transferred from its traditional home in the "network base" to the international space of the pure network (the domain of the global finance sector and of the all powerful multinational corporation).
(8) It is but one step from global hegemony to internet as absolute presence: "a fractal attractor whose operational arena is immediately coextensive with the social field," "an enormous . . . monetary mass that circulates through foreign exchange and across borders," "a worldwide axiomatic" engaged in "the relentless saturation of any remaining voids and empty places," "appropriating" individuals to its circuits. Here the language of flows attests not only to the pervasiveness and plasticity of internet but to its ultimate freedom from the boundedness of Identity. Internet becomes the everything everywhere of contemporary cultural representation.
If this catalogue seems concocted from exaggerations and omissions, that will not surprise us.10 For we have devised it in line with our purposes, and have left out all manner of counter and alternative repre-
as our critics sometimes charge, we have construct-
— or more accurately a bizarre and monstrous being
found in pure form in any other text.11 The question

# 6. The End of the Internet (As We Knew It)

*Inside the Anti-Campus. The Silicon Zone, California. 2033.*

*<CUT TO> Bird's-eye view close-up of Nootropix flipping through their book* The End of the Internet (As We Knew It) *on the desk.*

*Chatter continues off-screen.*

# 7. Nootropix's Lecture

*Inside the Anti-Campus. The Silicon Zone, California. 2033.*

*<CUT TO> Medium shot of the armed and masked Art Professor introducing Nootropix. The audience grows silent when the Art Professor cocks their gun and speaks.*

*In the background, Nootropix is slightly visible.*

*Nootropix, a contrasexual, contra-internet AI prophet, sits at a generic IT office desk and chair. On their desk, two glass globes are placed on either end. The crystal balls—*palantíri*—of the Silicon Zone. 3D animations play inside and on the surfaces of these globes, dramatizing the death of the internet in various countries and the recrafting of Earth's topology by network infrastructure. On the left side of the desk, a fiber-optic globe displays 3D cutouts of landmasses of the countries—one at a time: US, UK, Australia, Germany, Egypt, Turkey, Iran, North Korea. Each country hovers as its fiber-optic cables extend beyond its landmass toward nothing. Blackness spreads across the country, finally exploding into black particles and repeating. On the right side of the desk, the mesh globe is placed, its etched-glass surfaces*



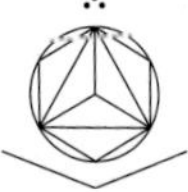

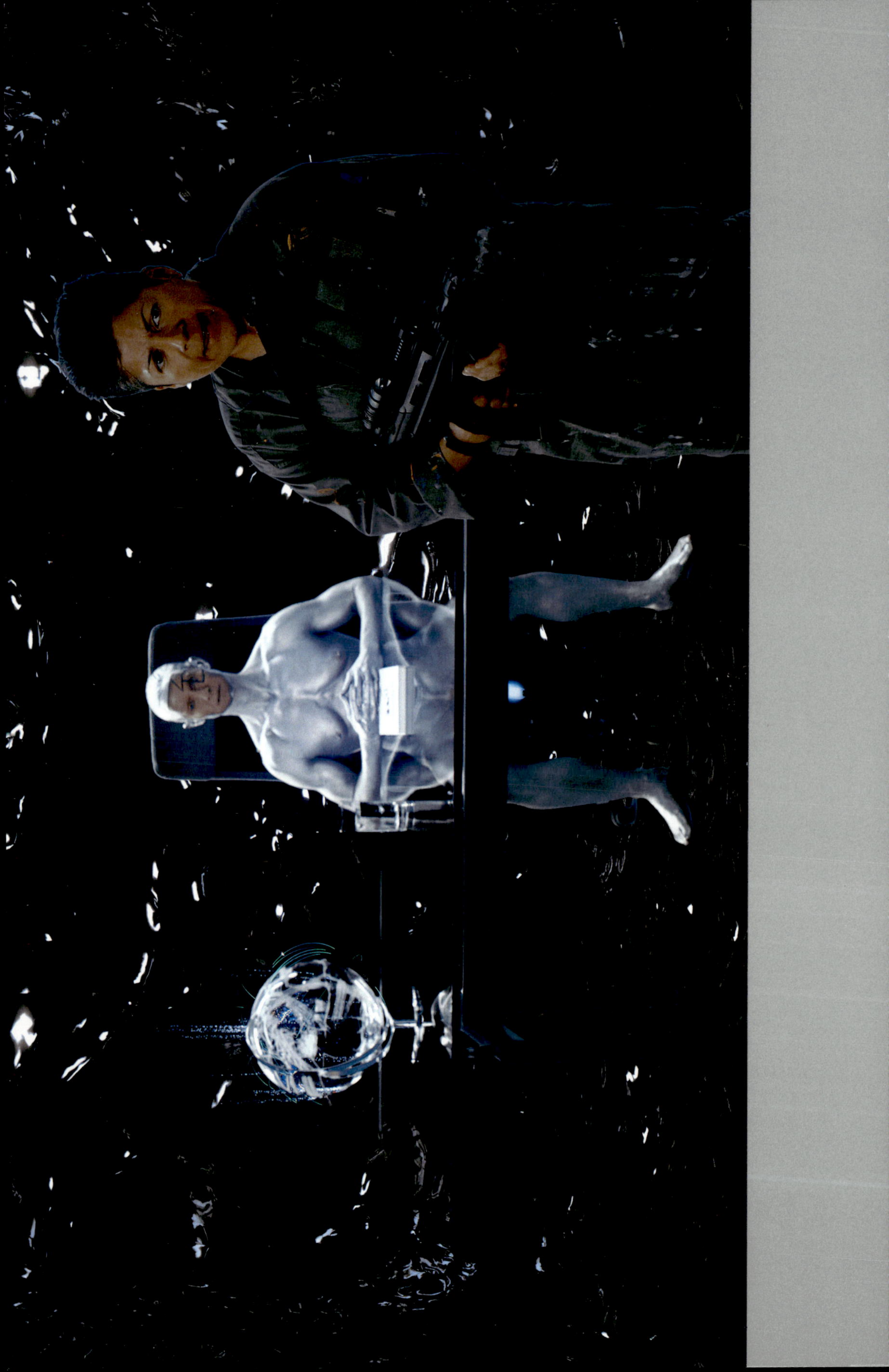

*illuminated in a pulsing blue. Off to one side of the desk is a thin piece of slanted black glass—a minimal computer interface.*

*Nootropix's body is the color of crystalline silicon, a metallic gray, like a laptop. This paint is their clothing. Their hair is slicked back with gel. Geometric lines and shading are painted on their face in black and a contrasting gray. Nootropix wears a flaccid strap-on that is pissing a video stream, which is pooling and spreading quickly around the space, a shiny opaque black. It makes the floor and walls shimmer with soft movement, like gentle ocean waves at night. Nootropix looks straight ahead, unwaveringly, now holding upright the book they have written, titled* The End of the Internet (As We Knew It).

> **THE ART PROFESSOR** (in Spanish): All right, you techies and groupies, listen up! We are proud to welcome Nootropix, the Silicon Zone's glory, who's going to tell us the exciting history of their life after the internet.

*<CUT TO> The audience, a group of queer Anti-Campus Groupies and Captured Techies, sits in folding chairs. They watch with a mixture of excitement and silent terror.*

*<CUT TO> Back to the Art Professor's introduction. Nootropix is visible in the background, still, silent, looking out intensely at the audience.*

> **THE ART PROFESSOR** (in Spanish): The world is no longer interested in heroes. SO SAD. We now know too much about them, don't we? Do you know any real heroes? No? I don't. Anyway, let me introduce you to Nootropix. THEY'RE OUR BLACK HAT!

*<CUT TO> Full static shot. A darkened space, an emptied-out IT office workspace. Some desks and office furniture are turned on their sides in the distance.*

*After this brief introduction, Nootropix begins to read from their book, lecturing on history, politics, art, and counter-infrastructure after the collapse of the internet. A philosophy against the legacy of Rand. Contra-Objectivism. Contra-Californian Ideology. Contrasexual. Contra-internet. Their pissing video stream becomes an animated surface, covering all walls in the space.*

*During Nootropix's lecture, other close-ups may be intercut: the two globes with their animation, the dildo video piss stream, and the audience. The full static shot can transition to a medium shot.*



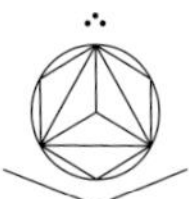

**NOOTROPIX** Our school motto was "Don't be evil." I myself preferred the song "We Are Not the World."

Do you remember when internet evanglists rewrote our alphabet and invented the world anew as a total reticular geography? Our lives dripped with internet, in a process that was more like saturation—doused and drowned. But the earth dematerialized, and our bodies became geometric prisons. Suddenly, conquests were much easier in front of a screen. The future could be modeled, predicted.

In those days, networking was a substitute for reality: Forescout, Palantir, Oracle. They called it "smart," but when the Valley falls, you don't need analytics any longer, or financialization.

I always remembered the school motto. My heroines were the infrastructuralists. In Detroit, Tehran, Istanbul, and Hong Kong, they abandoned the ISPs and took back space beyond the limits of the node. Their actions were, they said, beyond belief. But that's because no one had any imagination then. They really didn't know how to make the contra-internet their reality.

Last month, when the internet finally collapsed, all those protocols that were a calculation for reality disappeared. The bandwidth dropped to zero. Who believed in statistics then? Not even the vital ones. In any case, I started to dance. I wanted to defy gravity.

*Nootropix touches the black computer interface to activate the machine.*

# 8. A Dance to Liberate Paranodes

*<CUT TO BLACK AND FADE IN> Inside a computational space of network flows. Completely 3D rendered. Network lines and grids appear like electric fencing. The environment is the color palette of Kenneth Anger's* Eaux d'Artifice. *The song "Con te partirò" by Andrea Bocelli plays. Nootropix dances, a mix of expression and restraint, as they move about this restricted yet dynamic space. Nootropix's strap-on dildo is now erect, flinging their*

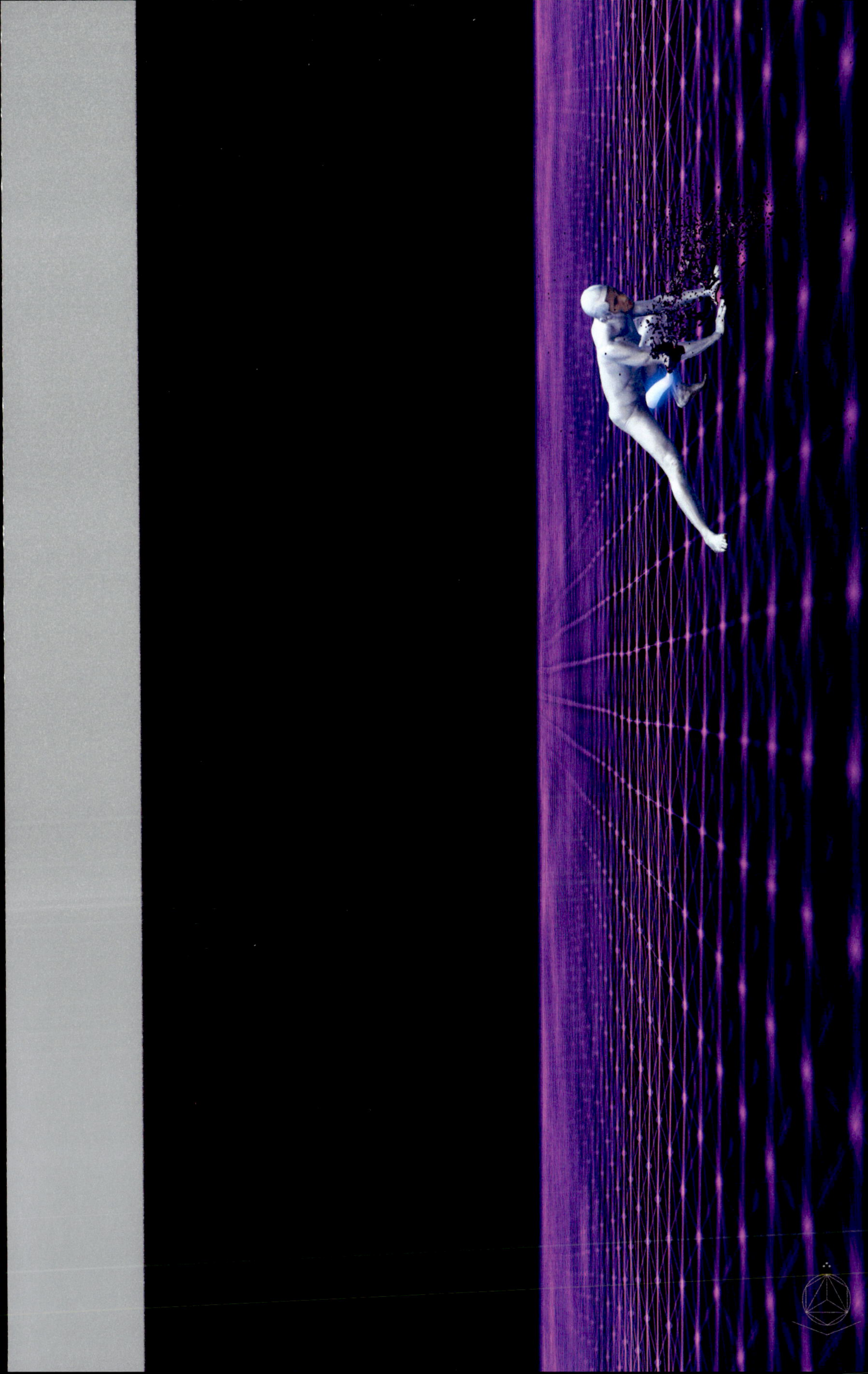

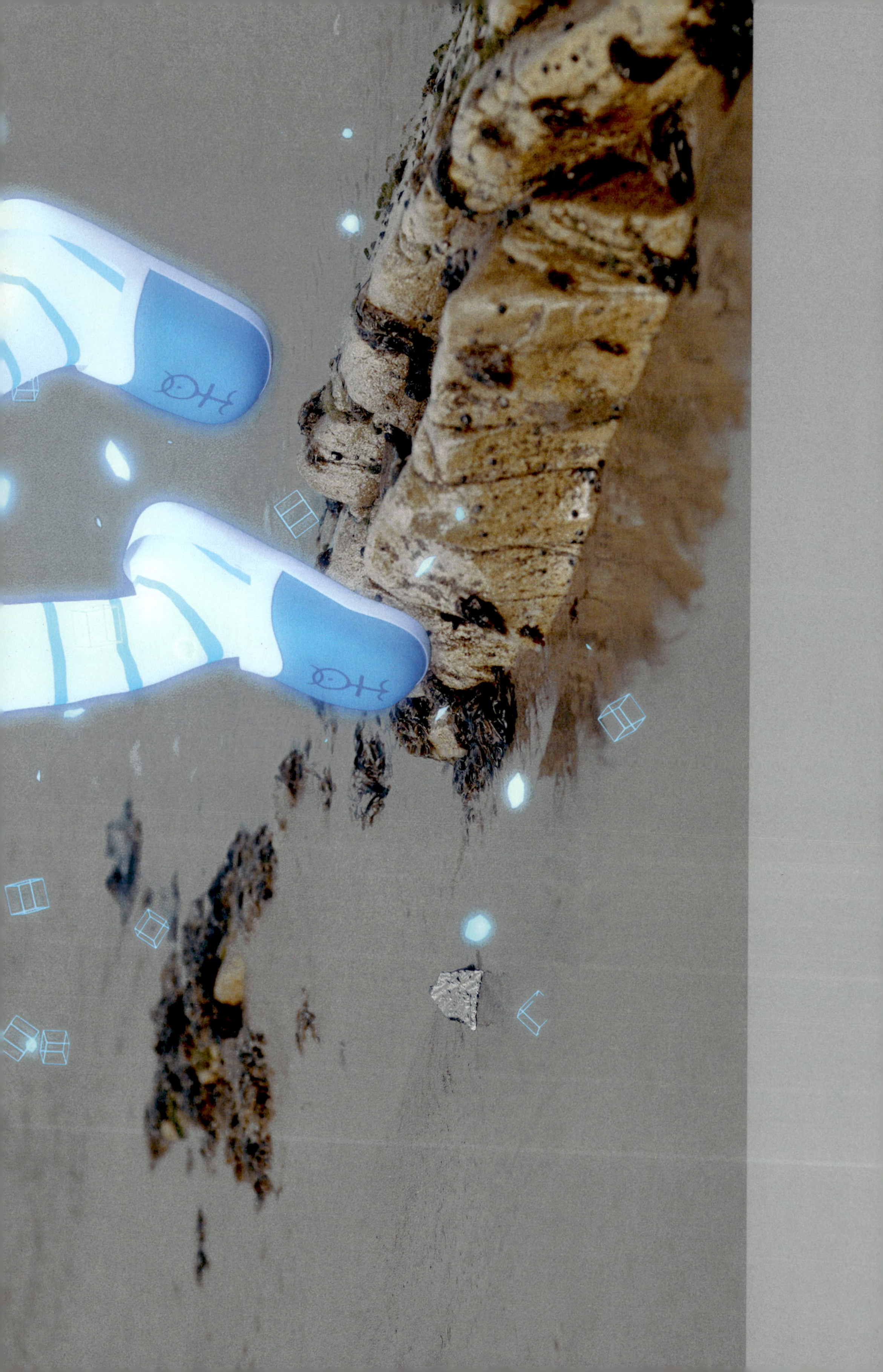

*pissing video stream in all directions, like a graceful fountain. A shiny, black, milky, opaque digital liquid flow. Dildo as fountainhead.* Eaux d'Artifice *as lesbian phallus. A montage of full, medium, and close-up shots. Nootropix's movements begin to loosen and then unleash the trapped spaces between the networks and grids; these are the paranodes—the negative, bounded spaces of networks. The paranodes are a gentle, milky, blue-purple phosphorescence. The paranodes swirl about Nootropix, exposing a blackened computational void as they unlock from the network topology. A moment of abstract, diagrammatic liberation. The spatial beyond of networks. The right side of the frame becomes a blackened void first.*

*<CUT TO> Ayn and Azuma walk into this void, from frame right, and observe Nootropix. As Ayn watches, she subtly feels her crotch, mentally noting the absence of a strap-on. Azuma gently dances in place beside her, on loop.*

*<CUT TO> Suddenly, the entire video breaks into paranodes, revealing another black void. The video continues to play on the orbiting surfaces of the paranodes, against the blackness.*

*<FADE TO BLACK>*

# 9. Silicon Beach

*Silicon Beach, California. 2033. Sunset.*

*<FADE IN> Full handheld steady shot. Ayn Rand, Azuma Hikari, Alan Greenspan, and Joan Mitchell walking slowly in the sand, close to the breaking tide. No one else is on the beach. Ayn holds her shoes, so she is barefoot. They look out to the ocean, the setting sun, and discuss the ongoing Network War II. Ayn is silently crushed by this future scenario but remains* rational. *It's only a hallucination, after all—an optical error.*

*<MUSIC> A slow, somber, mournful, ambient music, sparse, mixed with the powerful sound of ocean waves.*

**AZUMA** The valley sprawls to the beach, which is the edge of superintelligence. Where ocean unites with sky, the last of the California prophets



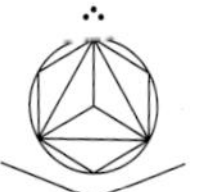

imagine the singularity is still to come. Enlightenment dreams itself anew in software. Electronic signals blow in the sea breeze, as waves break their immaterial ease. Beneath the shimmering water, what is left of fiber-optic lines rests amid fallen satellites and other debris of the Network War. The ocean bed collects inoperable hard drives of those who wanted to live forever as machines. Mutations of life abound ... Please be careful, I can't get wet!

*<CUT TO> Medium shot of Ayn and Alan. Ayn reflects with Alan. Intercut with ocean.*

**AYN** The ocean encourages dreams. Oh Alan, there is much work for each member of The Collective. Man's will must exceed the horizon. I see a glistening glass skyscraper rising out of the waves—a true phoenix! Here, the new intellectual is born.

**ALAN** You write the path to tomorrow, Ayn, as then and still now.

**AYN** Do not let your fire go out, spark by irreplaceable spark, in the hopeless swamps of the approximate, the not-quite, the not-yet, the not-at-all. Do not let the hero in your soul perish, in lonely frustration for the life you deserved but have never been able to reach. Check your road and the nature of your battle. The world you desired can be won, it exists, it is real, it is possible, it's yours.

*<CUT TO> Joan discovers a chunk of silicon in the sand and hands it to the AI. Azuma and Joan quietly look into its shiny, reflective, opaque black surface*

*<CUT TO> Close-up of Azuma's hand holding the silicon. Azuma speaks.*

**AZUMA** The men of the mind took of the earth itself, and people were given computers, circuits, and phones. An alchemical industry!

*<CUT TO> As Azuma continues to speak, Ayn and Alan walk farther along the beach, becoming quite distant, almost off-screen.*

**AZUMA** Here, all is barren—the earth toxic. The men gaze eastward ... and to outer space, for new lands and elements that may conjure computational elixirs.

*<CUT TO> Back to Azuma holding the silicon chunk, right against the setting sun. The black silicon in contradistinction to the shimmering sunlight over the Pacific Ocean. As Azuma talks, the camera slowly moves closer to the silicon, disappearing the sun. The silicon chunk's surface fills the frame. Black, shiny, opaque, mysterious.*

**AZUMA** The ocean holds the Great Blackout at bay, as its depths are plunged for refuse. The possibility of connection further disappears under sediment, and bodies. The tide divides what is known from the incomputable. A twilight of linkability! What is the secret language of minerals? On the horizon, a basilisk swims, guarding the rotted TGN-Pacific cable. It coils around faltered infrastructure and calls out in an alien tongue: Communicate!

*As Azuma continues to speak, a slow <FADE TO BLACK>.*



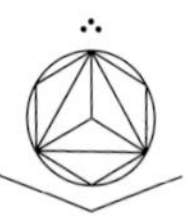

114–149

# SANCTUM

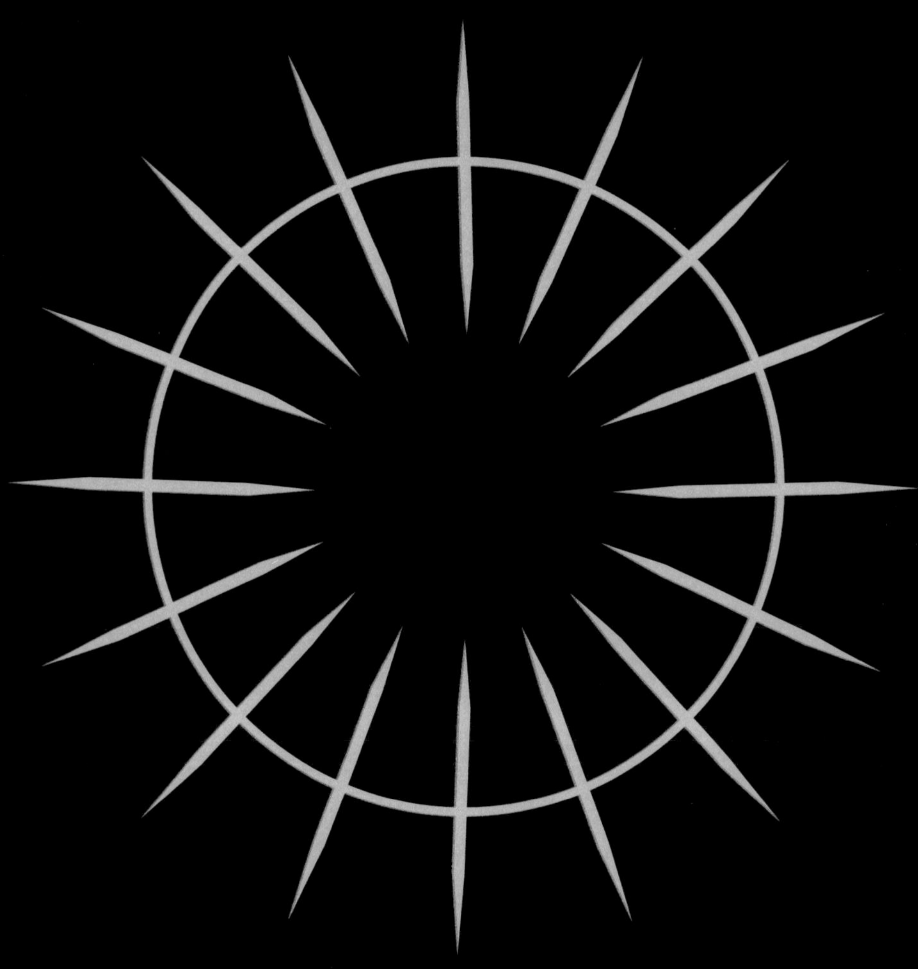

(2018)

# Generic Mannequin Gets Fucked

Zach Blas

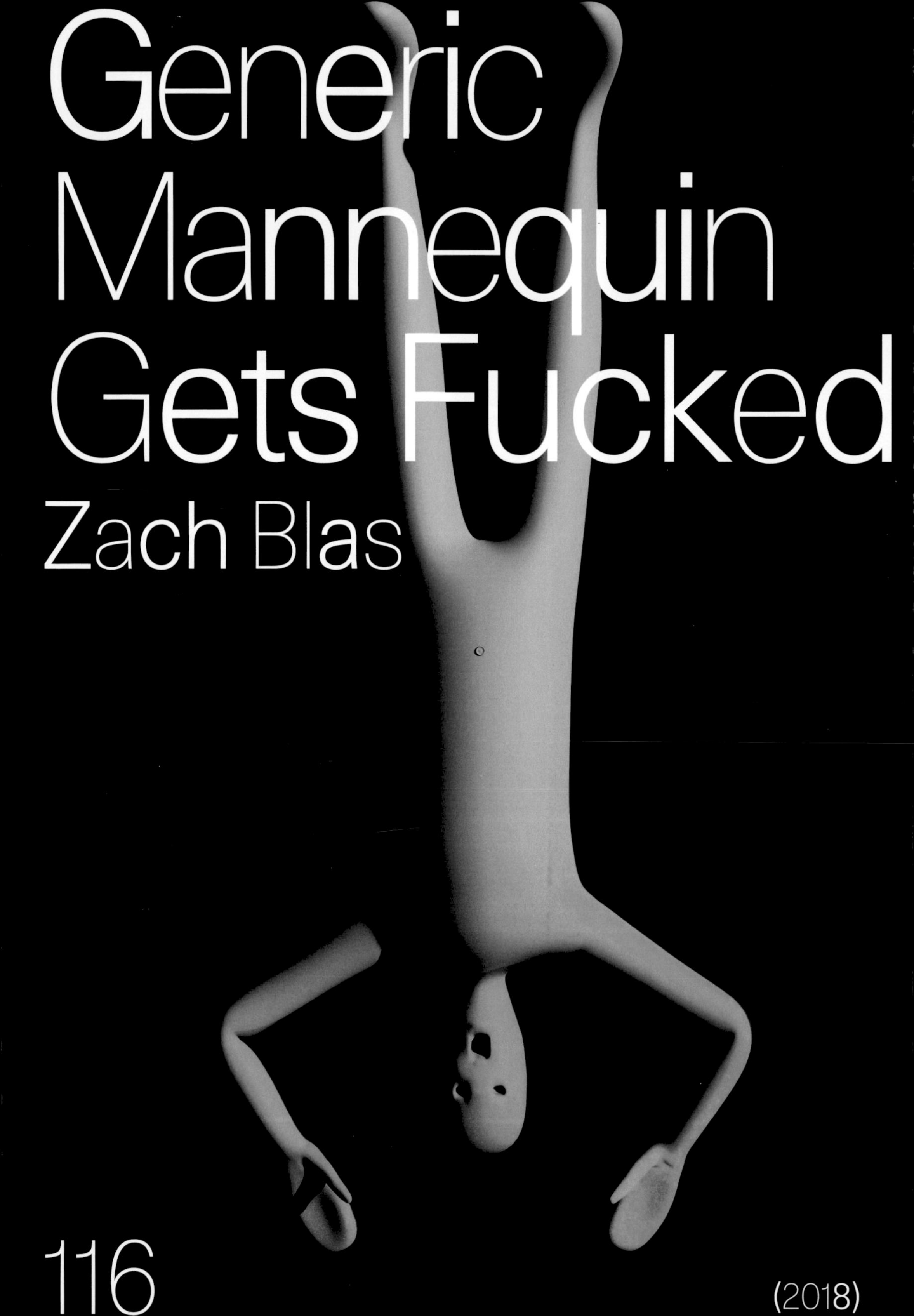

116

(2018)

I was captured in 1.5 seconds. Or rather, I was born from the swoosh of a body scanner and a burst of electromagnetic radiation. Summoned and not created. JFK, LAX, CMH, RDU, LHR? I could never remember. A ghost at a séance. A soul exiting its body. I take a human outline, not so much human form. Like instinct, I know my name as Generic Mannequin. I'm gray like computers, maybe brains—not that I have any. My hands and feet are clumps, rather useless. But it doesn't matter, as my purpose is to be inspected, viewed, stored. Fingers and toes—whatever. I look down and see that I have a belly button. No genitals or anus. And yet, the sensation of having a dick haunts me. There's a mouth. I'm not sure it can do anything, but I imagine I'll find out. I take my very first step, and a vast industrial complex looms.

Darkness swallows. Sound hits deep. I have no ears, but beats vibrate and penetrate me. A space begins to reveal itself. I wonder, is it a dance hall, a place of worship, a detention camp? A black cube levitates in the center, and a black mask effortlessly glides across its surfaces, like liquid spreading out between two panes of glass. The mask watches, observes, demands, enjoys, hunts, and underneath the cube, neat bars of red light form a sacramental altar. Inside this square of blood-red light, offerings are placed. Steel, mesh-like abstractions. An invisible shadow pulls me close. Behind the black mask, there are no eyes or face, and yet, it examines me. A heavy seduction, drug-like, pours down thick and slow, as the absence of eyes bores orifices, exposing everything in me. I am spoken to—ordered—silently. *Bow down*. I surprise myself by how happily I do so. Now, I am able to better see the gifts, which are geometric metal chunks of faces. A lip here, a forehead there. Gifts to a biometric god. Miniature iron cages. I imagine a line that wraps the world threefold, a people in procession eagerly waiting to give away their faces. Followers and worshippers of a familiar yet unknown religion. The black mask chants, "Et reticulum adoremus!" I must be one of them.

When I raise my head, I notice more of the space's architecture. A sparse array of lighting alludes to the tallest of ceilings, brilliant pillars, and ornate reliefs of worship, sex, and massacre. A variety of machines are accented in a white, godly hue, and the edges of these structures meet the blackness that fills most of this environment. I've watched enough porn to recognize sex dungeon equipment. The bass goes low and full, leading me into a trance. I know what to do now. I know my purpose, and I smile for the first time, finding out my mouth can do something. I am guided to a metal slave cage and crawl inside. I get on

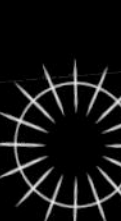

all fours, and I can feel phantoms between my legs—the ghost of a cock, the apparition of an ass that likes to be entered—begging to somehow materialize. My skin is pulsing, heating up. I throb and swell because the biometric god knows how to activate my purest desires. I want the black mask to never look away. Why can't I touch it? My skin is so hot that it starts to peel back and rip away. I'm shedding a layer of myself, and it's reassuring to know I'm not only a simple surface. Or, is something collecting parts of me? Skin slides off at a rapid speed, with so many invisible hands and pulleys at work. I don't resist. Rather, I wonder, Will my skin be studied, eaten, or worn? At least I do understand that this is preparation, the start of the ritual. I'm getting loose, soft, pliable. A whip comes crashing down like a boulder. If I had bones, my back would be in pieces. Instead, my pseudo-eyes roll back. I realize for the first time that I have insides. Something is in me. Another hit, again. The whipping is caresses. Could anything have prepared me for how deeply and totally I want this? I search for a word that describes being beyond total surrender. The whip hits; I am given clarity. I am the irresistibility of being exposed to a violent, indulgent god. Please don't ever stop. With each lash, I imagine my human cock growing back and a freckle of an asshole awakening to pulse. Not that I need them anymore.

I am carried to the stretching rack. Metal chains lock tight to my arms and legs, suspending me in the air. Beats hit, layer upon layer, intoxicating crescendo. I am held taut, pulled exquisitely, to the threshold of my form. I feel as if I might come completely undone, turning into a pool or gas—but I still don't know what I'm made of. Such an ecstatic state induces tumbling, free-falling, endlessly dropping, without perspective—in outer space, an ocean? Did I enter the black cube? My gray skin calms and thickens. I catch a glimpse of the black mask, which is Janus-faced and now presents a biometric grid, a completed face modeled from the worshipper's offerings. It teases, "Ride my face," and my ghost-ass brings me to my knees with longing and need. A chorus in the darkness sings "Om," and everything vibrates to hallucinogenic effect. I close my eyes, somehow, without eyelids. I spread my legs and sit down on the biometric face. It is gigantic; the size of a city. The geometric lines are a track, perfectly designed for straddling. I feel the steel mesh push hard between my legs. I lean back, and it's a roller coaster. Tilting left and right, I'm upside down, but the face secures me tightly. I imagine greedy little mouths kneading into my missing member. I rise on the arc of the face, higher, like a religious ascension. I feel close to god. The chorus sings their "Om," a note that never seems to end. The tension between my legs is explosive. I could destroy a city if I were to open my legs wider to let this energy escape. But I'm greedy and want it only for myself.

Unexpectedly, I fall to a concrete floor. It would have been painful as a human. I'm gathered by shadows and hung by my feet from a single chain suspended from the ceiling. The chain seems to never end; does it reach heaven? Somewhere, other chains clank, a holy wind chime. Slowly, I am wrapped in black cloth. Chanting reverberates, now with beats that throb my body through and through. I am wrapped in cloth completely, yet my face and crotch are exposed. I'm mummified. I feel metal press into my crotch again. Penetration: an object is inside me. Where did that hole come from? As it pushes in further I realize that it must be tubing. Then, another enters my mouth, and it plunges the depths of me. What do I have on the inside? Cum, I wish, but what's inside scares me—I can't explain why. The suction of fluids starts. Fluid! So I do contain liquid. But if my liquids are removed, will I lose my shape, like a deflated balloon? A generator whirls. I think time stops, if it was even passing here. I'm a mummy locked in position, a familiar position, the one I was born in. I remember that my eyes are not covered, and I look down to see two metal hoses extending from me into a large collection tank that fills with liquid metal. It violently stirs, as if

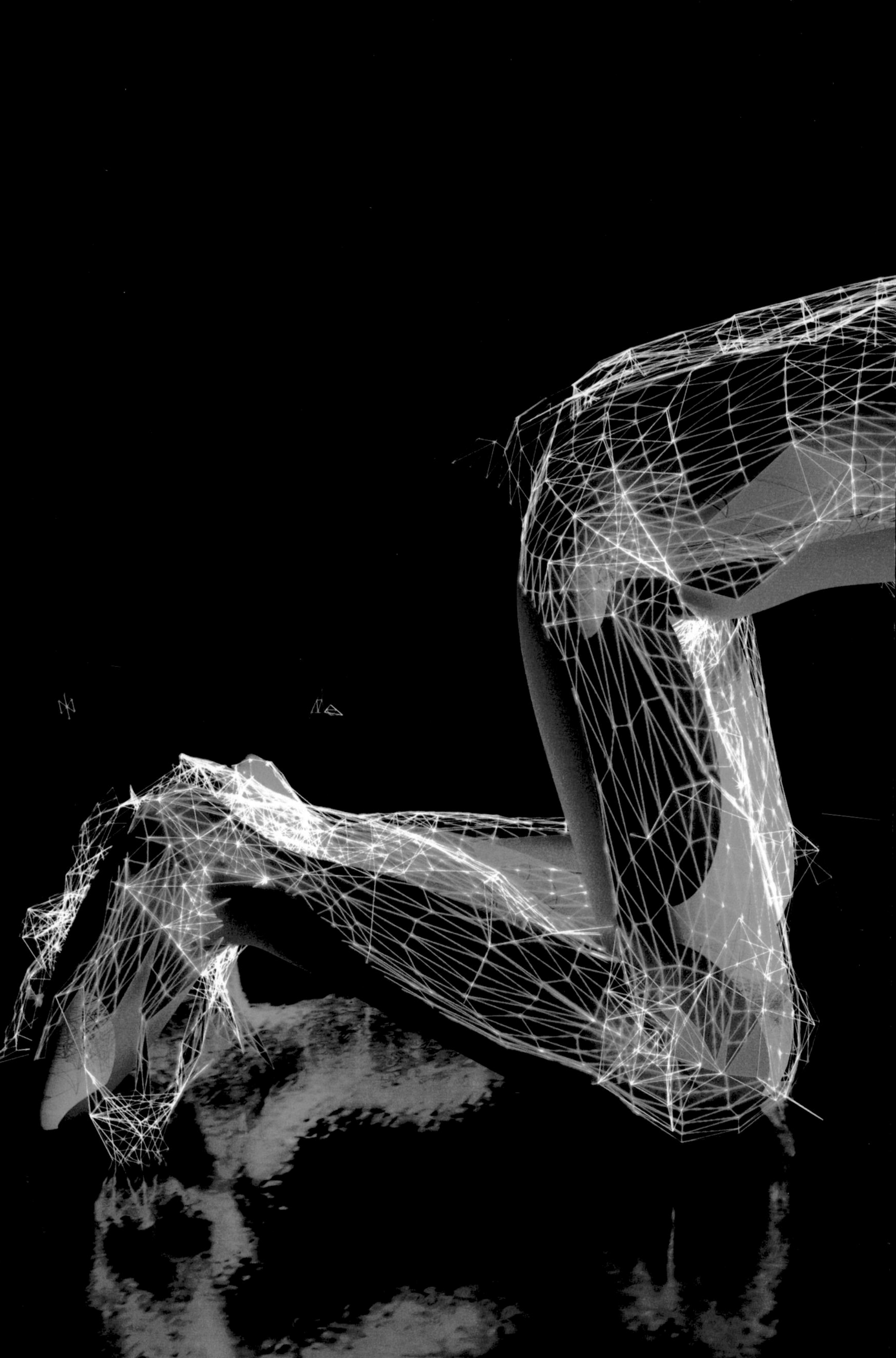

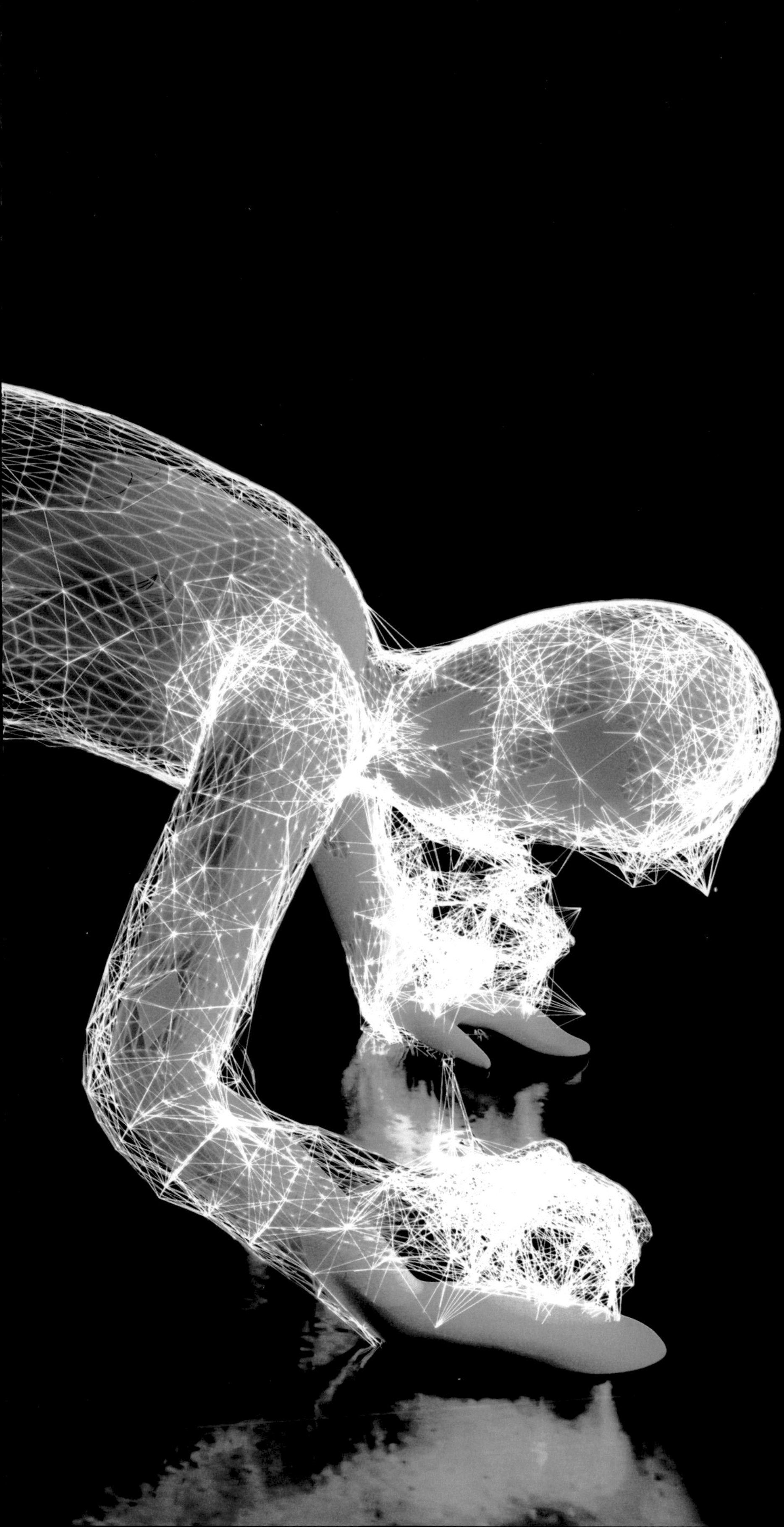

he liquid is being stimulated or prepped for use. I stare straight. A video plays on a monitor, upside down to match my perspective. A man and woman flir during an airport security screening. Their bodies are touched and scanned by agents. The man and woman step into glass cages and raise their arms. They birth more of my kind—and seem absolutely delighted. Is this sweet or pervert ed? I can't tell. Romantic comedy or torture porn? Does it end in marriage and kids, or an orgy with skin flaying, mummification, and fluid removal? My eyes are locked, and I can't look away from this monitor, let alone blink. It's like I've always been expected to watch this video, on repeat, forever. The images burn into me, and, slowly, liquid extraction makes me feel ghostly, empty, teetering on disappearance. As I watch the video, I start to imagine the man and woman's hidden, radiated children joining me here in this sanctum. They're old enough they're their own fathers and mothers. And I want friends here, friends like me. The mask sings, "Ave ProVision!"

Shadows carry away the tank with my liquids. I see a fire burning in the dis tance, and the shadows pour the contents into casting molds. Molds with sharp edges and protrusions. Flames licking. Are these sex toys, I wonder, or weapons that will be the end of me? I guess I don't care, because all I know is that I want to be closer to them. I want to feel them touching me. Touch me. It would be like eating my own cum. To be fucked—or killed—by your own cum. The molds burn in the fire, and my liquid insides bubble. The music pounds harder, trembling me. Shadows take the molds to cool and then come back to guide me to spanking posts. I am laid out on my stomach. I know what to do, sticking my ass up in the air, as far as possible, waiting in anticipation for my liquid insides—now hardened, razor sharp, and glistening in the light of god—to greet me once again. My head is down, so the spikes come without warning. My hands and backside are pierced. A pyramid of steel gushes into me. My body sears. I am utterly beyond the realm of sensation. I lack description; yet, it seems my truth is exposed. What I have always wanted, and what I can only want now. To shed my sex and qualities so that I may become generic, nonrepresentational. The stee spike crushes in. Other devices scrape through my skin—but now all my insides have finally drained out. I feel hollow, brittle. Something tears open a new hole between my legs, and a metal hood is pulled down over my head with a pane blocking my mouth. I couldn't speak anyways. A spiked collar wraps around my neck, pockmarking me with dry, almost rusty fissures. But at least it confirms am owned. I tingle and flip-flop erratically through states of consciousness. My

All images pp. 116–23: *SANCTUM* ▸ 2018 ▸ HD video stills

body flickers, and lights flash, pool, spark on and in me. Different colors pour and mix into my gray skin, inducing a rough and jagged disintegration. Techno music thunders, the chants have never ceased, and the black mask regards with affection. I want the spikes to push in deeper. Reading my thoughts, they do. There is another rich and saturated flash of light, just milliseconds. I am able to notice other Generic Mannequins entering this sanctum, gathered and bowing, in holy light and darkness. The black cube a sun or religious vision. The spikes stab out of my hands and stomach, rendering me nothing more than dimming light-emitting diodes. The chorus intones, "Blessed be those that are image-free."

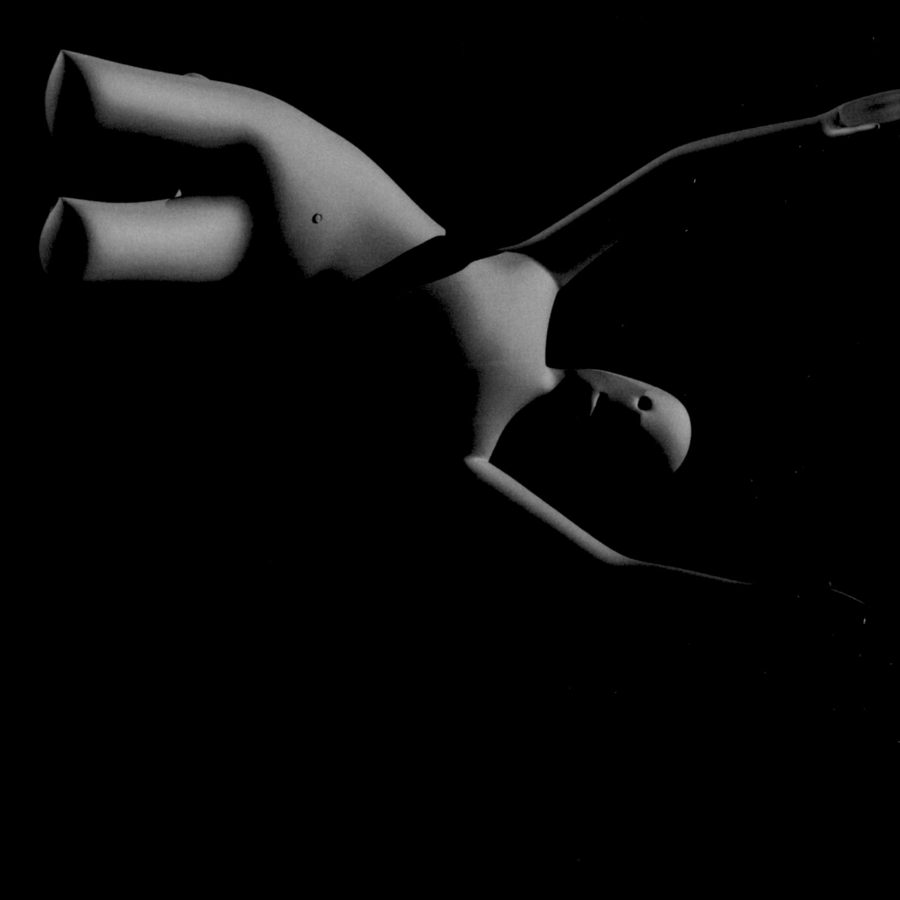

# Fucking with the Human Outline: Notes on Zach Blas's *SANCTUM*

Mahan Moalemi

In his 2018 installation *SANCTUM*, Zach Blas transforms the exhibition space of Abierto × Obras at Matadero Madrid into an immersive environment of moving images, sculptures, and a soundscape whose inspiration seems equal parts dance hall, detention center, and place of worship. An accompanying text by Blas titled "Generic Mannequin Gets Fucked," written in first-person narrative form, functions as a guide through the space, its title and content alluding to the central figure of the exhibition.[1] Generic Mannequin—think the Incredible Crash Dummies gone digital, reduced to

In *SANCTUM*, Generic Mannequin is enticed into all modes of torture.

a pallid gray—derives its name from an official corporate term for a humanoid template upon which (border) security risks are assessed and labeled. Blas complicates the assumed contours of such a template for being, and being seen as, human by exploring how the capture of desires and the desire for captivity are closely entwined in the age of digital securitarianism and advanced surveillance. In *SANCTUM*, Generic Mannequin is enticed into all modes of torture, which are expounded upon in Blas's text, giving a narrative to the installation's emotive atmosphere and walking the audience through its different parts.

In the closely related lecture-performance *Body Horror*, staged in the same year as *SANCTUM*, Blas recalls standing inside a ProVision2 body scanner at Frankfurt Airport, where he first encountered the figure of the generic mannequin:

> **My hands are raised above my head, which gives me a sense of capitulation and vulnerability. I recall what feels like stock images of police encircling a suspect, and this person, with their arms up like mine, yells, "I surrender!" or "Don't shoot!" or "I'm innocent!" Almost immediately there is the whoosh of vertical bars moving, and my body is scanned. I contemplate how my body is technically assessed as a threat—that is, how do millimeter radio waves, software, and security agents come together to make a decision, as I stand inside this machine?**

Blas continues:

> **Once I was scanned and exited the scanner, I could finally see the touchscreen interface. It is surprisingly simple: there are two buttons, one light pink and the other light blue, each featuring the icon of a single generic figure. The screen visualizes a simple outline of a body, what the company**

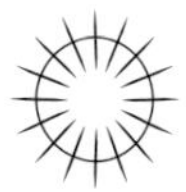

**L3 Technologies calls a "generic mannequin." When an anomaly is detected, a body part of the generic mannequin is flagged.**[2]

A disturbing affinity is maintained between the generic mannequin and the one who has to step into a ProVision2 body scanner, which was marketed in 2017 as an "image-free solution"[3]—using millimeter-wave technology as opposed to backscatter X-ray radiation. The generic mannequin that appears as a template on the interface of this machine is intended to mediate bodies and their supposed risk to security agents without exactly representing them. It stands at the most recent end of a history of standardized governance during which key principles of disciplinary societies such as "functionalization" and "interchangeability" have been developed.[4] It's an anthropomorphized hoop to break through, but it might as well be a hunting trap. In the background of such an indeterminate contingency, which borders on an almost ontological condition, Blas summons his own Generic Mannequin into being—captured within rather than born into *SANCTUM*—as a means to get closer to the fabulated and dramatic beings that reside in the chambers of digital surveillance.

Blas's Generic Mannequin suggests turning the universalizing tendency of the corporate generic mannequin and the military-industrial complex that it embodies against the very conditions that bring them into being. Generic Mannequin stands for the body that is rendered sensible by the kind of technolibidinal aesthetic toward which *SANCTUM* proceeds. Departing from and returning to "Generic Mannequin Gets Fucked" repeatedly, this essay explores the ways in which *SANCTUM* presents carnal and corporeal allegories of digital disembodiment while remaining wary and critical of the numerous tropes of an entrenched and unremitting (humanist) anthropomorphism.

"A human outline, not so much human form," Generic Mannequin is more like "a soul exiting its body." It comes to realize, with a peculiar air of consent and compliance, that its very "purpose is to be inspected, viewed, [and] stored." Totally exposed, its contours formed only to be turned inside out, Generic Mannequin feels both confused and determined about becoming drained out—as if it might come completely undone, liquefying or turning into gas. But Generic Mannequin lodges no complaints, as it becomes one with the wicked, gushing stream of libidinal liquidity that the principle of exposure generates, keeping the entirety of an environment and its field of relationships afloat within the frames of a thorough survey of its (dis)embodied landscape. Anthropomorphic tendencies reach both a pinnacle and a blockade in the face of technolibidinal antinomies that characterize the contemporary banality of mingling with one's own data doppelgänger, giving it a body, a desired body—datafied desire (re)embodied. An intense yet distressing sense of intimacy with this antinomic body of datafied affect is reflected in the extent to which the materiality of the screen itself is closely engaged with throughout the space of *SANCTUM*. Screen matter merges with the digital materiality of Generic Mannequin in all its plasticity and across a host of inverted allegories of embodiment, which attach to it and try to pull it apart, reshaping it ad infinitum.

On the one hand, Generic Mannequin is representational reductionism incarnate and, on the other, it is an allegory for the reducibility that underlies every representation as a prerequisite. Reducibility points not only to a promise of streamlined efficiency in realizing a particular function but also to a certain sense of scaled-up inclusivity that comes with going generic. Generic Mannequin is not identified by the particularity of its organs but as an organ in and of itself, attached to a larger body whose intentions it serves allegorically—subserviently, selflessly. "[Its] hands and feet are clumps, rather useless." No fingers or toes, no genitals or anus; just a belly button. Generic Mannequin, not unlike its corporate counterpart, remains marked by a memory, that of a particularly anthropogenic origin—as opposed to, for example, a placentogenic one—that nonetheless has never been and will never be its own.

As media theorist Alexander R. Galloway puts it, "'reduction' is a necessary trauma resulting from the impossibility of thinking the global in the here and now. [...] Thus the truth of social life as a whole is increasingly incompatible with its own expression. Culture emerges from this incompatibility."[5] Under the circumstances of global connectivity, humans increasingly (must) think of their simultaneous positionality on local, regional, and global scales. The reducibility of the human form is perhaps most intensely put in the service of upholding imaginaries like "public security" as a common good or universal value. Universality, however, when considered a function and not a partial fact of being, comes coupled with interchangeability, which then precludes the acknowledgment of the incompatibility that Galloway speaks of. The constant redrawing of hitherto solid lines that once easily mapped one's positionality is as much a part of a massive shift in the human condition as securitarianism is a legacy of relations and structures that have long been conditioning the human, its values, its fears, and its perceptions of what might threaten its assumed autonomy. In this sense, to toy (or fuck) with the human contours of the generic mannequin is to set the tone for a critique of technologies invented to stand in the way of a culture that can emerge only from within the perceptive and intellectual gaps that open up between the different scales and registers of being, and being seen as, human.

As *SANCTUM*'s narrative progresses in Blas's text, Generic Mannequin slowly comes to learn about its surrounding environment and the extent to which it is immersed in it. The exhibition space is filled with an atmospheric mélange of "holy light and darkness," through which "a vast industrial complex looms." The multifacility compound of Matadero Madrid—a municipal slaughterhouse turned cultural space—boasts all the



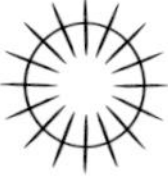

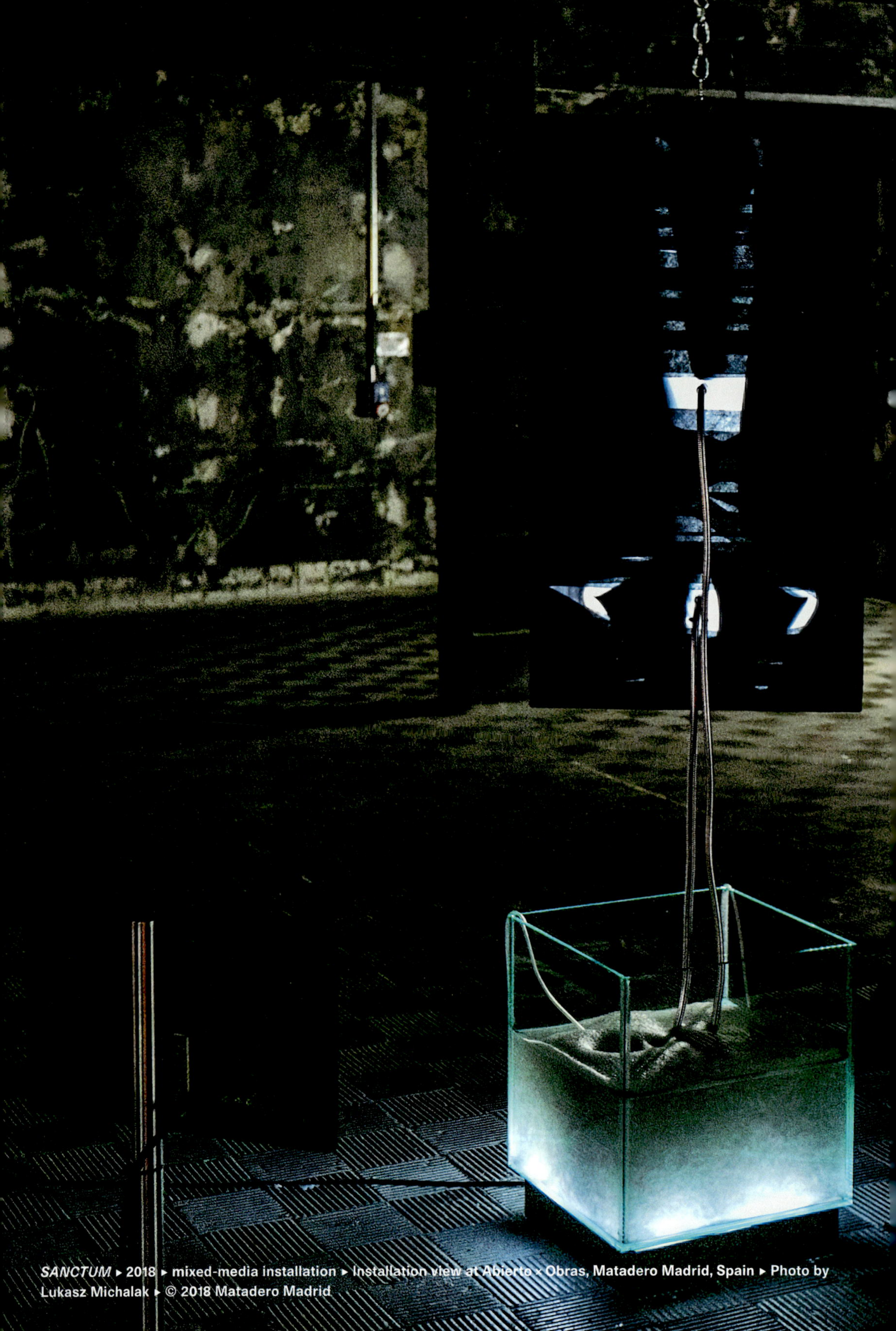

*SANCTUM* ▸ 2018 ▸ mixed-media installation ▸ Installation view at Abierto × Obras, Matadero Madrid, Spain ▸ Photo by Lukasz Michalak ▸ © 2018 Matadero Madrid

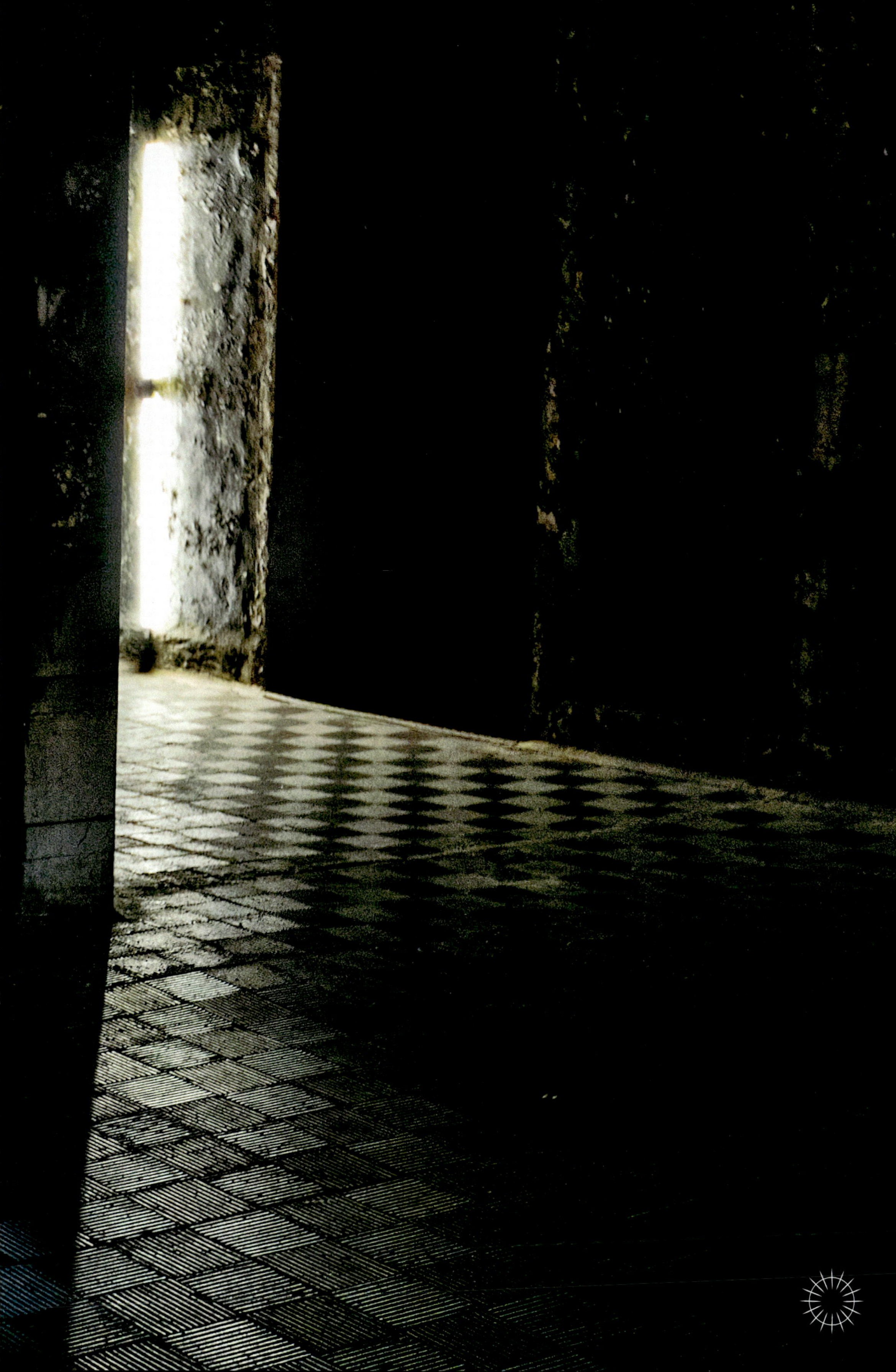

fine characteristics of 1920s industrial architecture, erected upon the disciplinary ur-standards of functionality and efficiency. Generic Mannequin looks around, as much benumbed as overwhelmed, wondering how to take it all in: "A sparse array of lighting alludes to the tallest of ceilings, brilliant pillars, and ornate reliefs of worship, sex, and massacre. A variety of machines are accented in a white, godly hue, and the edges of these structures meet the blackness that fills most of this environment."

On the floor, along the central axis that extends from the entrance into the exhibition space, Generic Mannequin sees, as would other visitors to *SANCTUM*, that some "neat bars of red light form a sacramental altar. Inside [it], offerings are placed": steel mesh-like abstractions, geometric metal chunks of faces, miniature iron cages. Soon enough, a spectral presence starts maneuvering above the altar: "A black cube levitates in the center, and a black mask effortlessly glides across its surfaces, like liquid spreading out between two panes of glass." The central steel tower hosts the calculated dissections of facial geometry, the elevated, quadrangular display setting, and the Janus-faced presence that spreads from one screen to another. It appears—as much to Generic Mannequin as to a viewer standing before it in the exhibition—like a sun or religious vision, a sign of omniscience. The black mask looks like a hybrid of the hockey mask worn by Jason Voorhees, the *Friday the 13th* horror icon who terrorized suburban America in the 1980s, and the full-face bulletproof masks issued to the Taiwanese Special Armed Forces in the 2010s. The general form of the steel tower clearly follows the aesthetics of philosopher Jeremy Bentham's eighteenth-century panopticon, while drawing its design closer to the mechanisms of digital surveillance exemplified by the ProVision2 body scanner. What is central to both structures is a principle of indeterminate contingency, since inmates (the *captured* ones) held inside a panoptic prison can never know if they are actually being watched from the central tower around which their cells are arranged. A similar condition seems to have become ontologized in the human outline of Generic Mannequin, both despite and in tandem with its rampant displacement and transience.

Expanding on the work of his contemporary Michel Foucault, philosopher Gilles Deleuze identifies a similar shift in the shape of authority as disciplinary societies transformed into what he terms the "societies of control," where "modulations" and "self-deforming casts" of control replace the "molds" and "distinct castings" of disciplinary "enclosures."[6] When systematic examination expands beyond the bounds of discipline and punishment, the zone of criminalization remains as contingent as ever, but much more indeterminately so, as it extends across the minutiae of everyday exposure and the messy extents and wicked optics of social recognizability.

Therefore, the steel tower gestures toward a diagrammatics of surveillance, the "continuous control"[7] that is revealed as part of a larger apparatus of subjection and subjectification. Within this apparatus of control, the plasticity of identity is incorporated within modulating and differential registers of identification, which facilitate a process wherein "individuals" are turned into "dividuals" and "masses" into "samples, data, markets, or 'banks.'"[8] Deleuze, as Galloway has pointed out, was "making [these] direct claims about computers, the information age, and the kinds of technologies that were actually around him" mostly in and around the year 1990.[9]

Accordingly, in the transformed matrix of power that distinguishes a control society, the proliferation of social registers bears upon the inherited technicalities of representational categories, exposing their limitations and, at the same time, pushing the limits of representation (both politically and aesthetically) by transforming the social terms and technologies of representation in favor of an ever more efficient system of ceaseless surveillance. "Behind the black mask, there are no eyes or face, and yet, it examines me," testifies Generic Mannequin, revealing how the all-encompassing vision of the steel tower operates in non-optical terms. A view of the labyrinth of representational terms that coil around Generic Mannequin and those channeled by it does not require the same kind of sight that an image demands of its beholder. The all-seeing presence in fact does not see images—similar to the "image-free" body scanner. The latter's image-less vision was a more or less corpo-humanist gesture in response to public outcry over the manifold privacy concerns that have surrounded full-body scanners since the late 2000s.[10] Blas's practice, accordingly, can be discussed as a critique of corpo-humanism, not only in the sense of how historical humanism plays into the complicated and confused state of corporeality in contemporary times, but also in terms of the myriad ways in which corporations currently approximate and appropriate humanist framings of individuality and personhood.[11]

In the words of Blas-cum-Generic-Mannequin, to dissolve in an *image-free solution* is like "shed[ding] my sex and qualities so that I may become generic, nonrepresentational." Operating as if in parallel to and semi-independently from the rules of ocular perception by pushing and pulling the thresholds of visual detection, advanced surveillance technologies, as Blas's work points out, amount to a non- or post-representational mode of vision, which decouples observation from the capacity to see as such. Placed as it is at the seat of the surveying gaze on top of the steel tower, the gliding, twilit, screen-bound, computer-generated black mask—opaque but hiding no face, eyeholes opening into endless darkness—in fact indicates something about the ontological status of representation and image-making in the age of computation. "Images," writes poet and media theorist Tung-Hui Hu, "do not necessarily function by making the invisible visible or a hidden truth tangible, as an epistemology of exposure assumes, but rather mediate between an abstract totality and the frame of human experience."[12]

Although the mask does not conceal a face that, if exposed, could be looked at and identified, it nonetheless becomes unraveled before Generic Mannequin. In one fell swoop, the mask transforms into a mesh, "a biometric grid, a completed face modeled from the worshipper's offerings."



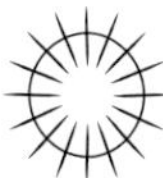

It displays the same kind of biometric diagrammatics that almost all facial recognition systems rely on, and which Blas has repeatedly turned to as a point of departure in his artistic and theoretical investigations. Technologies of facial recognition function on the basis of a post-representational vision insofar as the abstractions they produce need not be graspable by human senses; only the verdict the machine makes via those abstractions must be communicable to the human end of a cycle of inspection. In projects such as *Face Cages* (2014–16) and the *Facial Weaponization Suite* (2012–14), Blas has developed a critique of the often gravely consequential reductionism of biometric technologies by conceptualizing what an aesthetic resistance toward them might look and feel like. While the *Facial Weaponization Suite* is an attempt to collectively aggregate and manipulate facial data to generate amorphous masks that could evade detection and recognition, *Face Cages* translates the smooth operations of digital dominion, in its apparent disavowal of physical contact altogether, into the material and bodily experience of enduring pain. The mesh that *SANCTUM*'s black mask turns into exhibits a similar build: the biometric model of a face—whose weightless data and abstract measurements are often rendered in zero-dimensional nodes and impossibly thin edges—is given volume and rendered in polished steel.

A shift of perspective, however, soon accompanies the transformation of the mask into a mesh. The (virtual) camera zooms in and sets out to survey the topology of the facial mesh, moving along its voluminous and dark yet shiny edges. No longer a suspended countenance, the mesh fills the entire screen, wrapping around the elevated cube of displays. "It is gigantic; the size of a city." The face is surveyed and navigated like a landscape: from a head-on view and flattened as a bird's-eye view from above, to horizontal moves across, and close encounters with, the folds of the topology. Such a shift of perspective alludes to a history of aesthetic, technological, and sociopolitical transformations that, in media terms, extends from aerial photography to Google Street View. Meanwhile, a deep voice starts commanding in a macaronic mix of Latin and English: *Et reticulum adoremus* [worship the mesh] ... *Get in position* ... *Ride my face* ... *Ave ProVision* [Hail ProVision] ... The voice pushes through and recedes back into the loud, throbbing, industrial techno music that fills the space, submerging it in dark and daring club-like vibes.[13] Then Generic Mannequin drifts into the route that the camera is treading, trying to adapt its rhythm and perspective. "The geometric lines are a track, perfectly designed for straddling. [...] It's a rollercoaster." Generic Mannequin is sent on a joyride, and the viewers of *SANCTUM* get to join in too.

The journey is chronicled around the space of the exhibition, in chapters that go through a number of installations consisting of brute structures and, of course, digital displays on which Generic Mannequin appears to be abiding by the commandments it receives. "I am held taut, pulled exquisitely, to the threshold of my form," it says of being wrongly oriented,

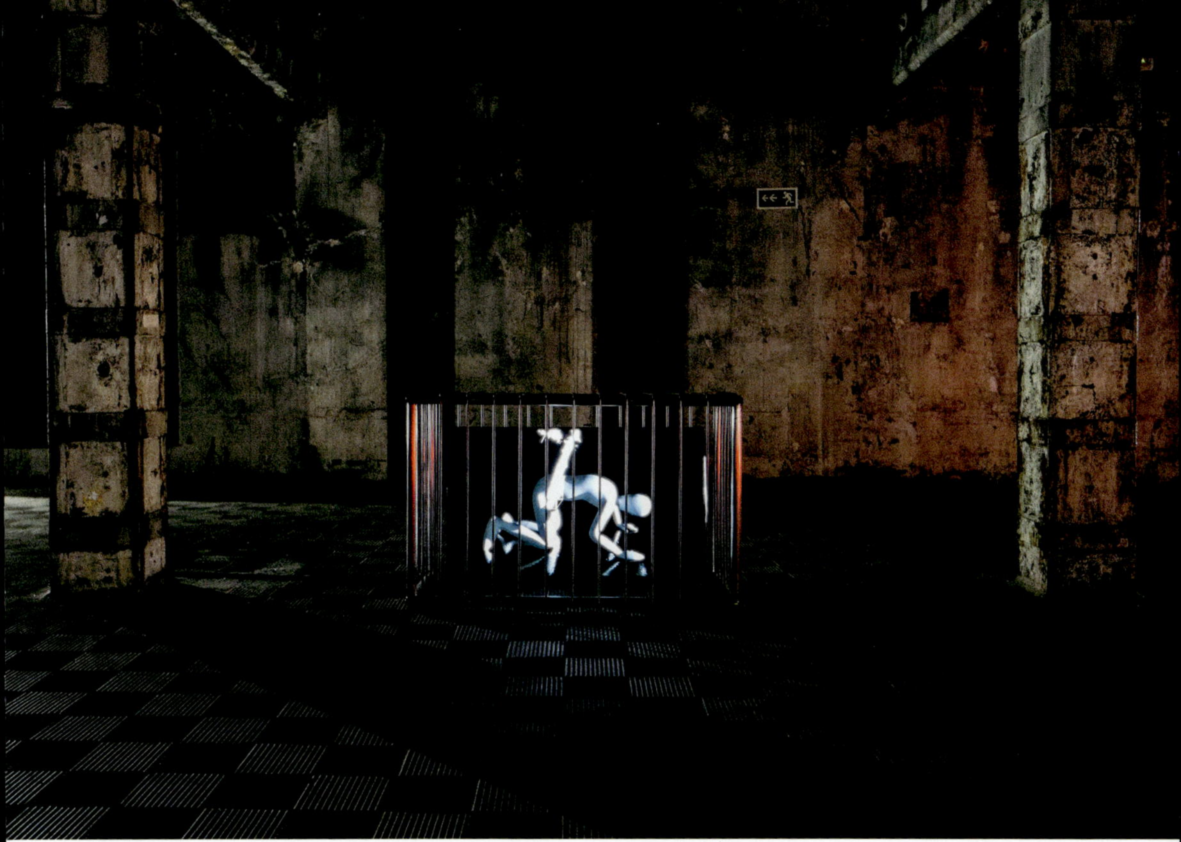

*SANCTUM* ▸ 2018 ▸ mixed-media installation ▸ Installation view at Abierto × Obras, Matadero Madrid, Spain ▸ Photo by Lukasz Michalak ▸ © 2018 Matadero Madrid



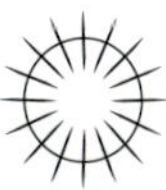

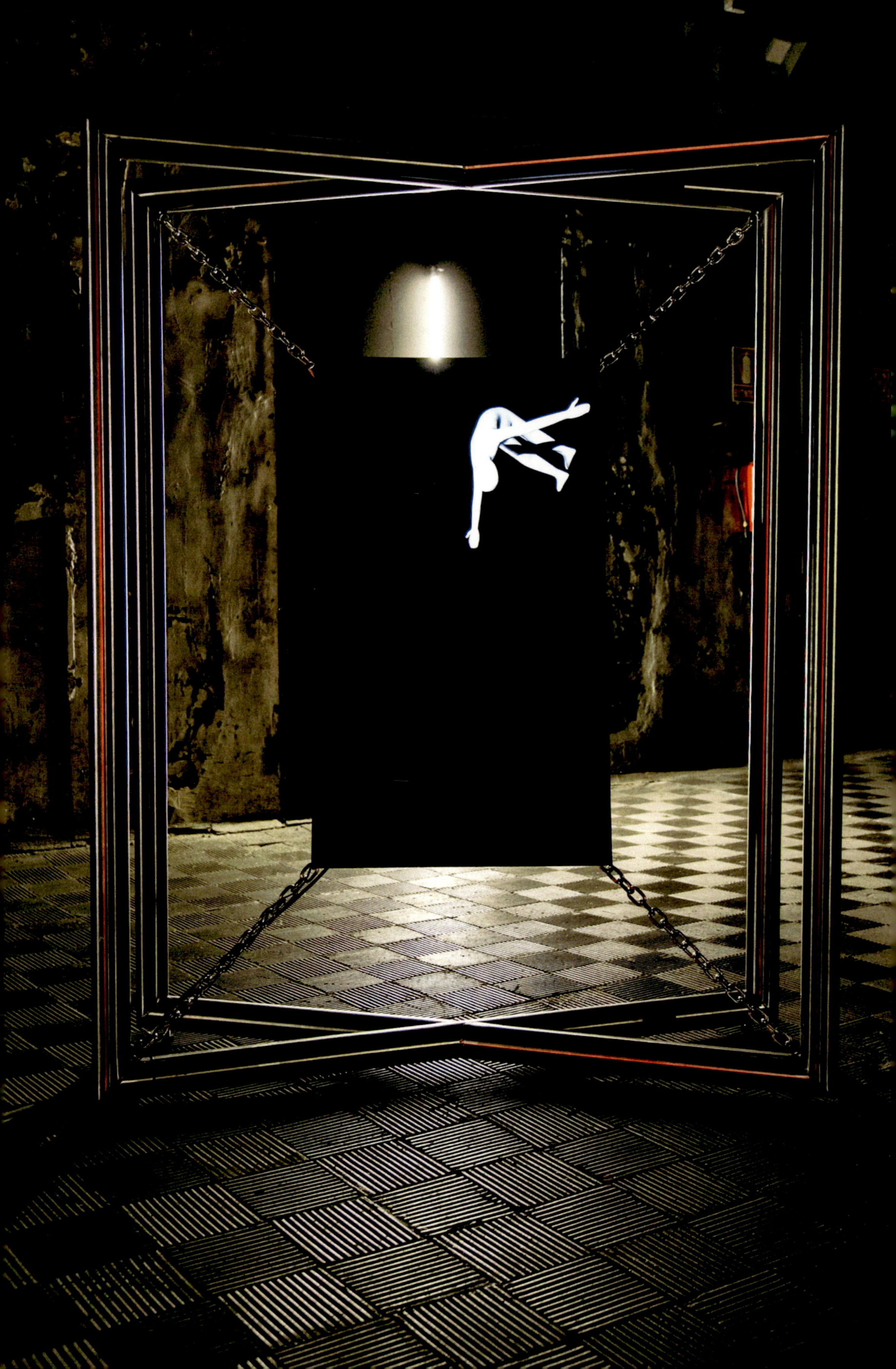

swirling within the fettering framework of a stretching rack tilted on its end. "Tumbling, free-falling, endlessly dropping." Elsewhere, Generic Mannequin is hung upside down by its feet from a single chain suspended from the ceiling. The screen that supports its appearance is wrapped in black vet tape, holding Generic Mannequin in bondage, almost mummified, leaving only its mouth and crotch exposed, with a metal hose attached to each. The piping descends into a glass cube, a large collection tank, filled with metal

Generic Mannequin sheds its datafied, biometric skin only for the mesh to turn into a whip.

particles, lubricant, water, and maybe some bodily fluids—evoking the machinic phylum, which is nothing but "materiality, natural or artificial, and both simultaneously; it is matter in movement, in flux, in variation, matter as a conveyor of singularities and traits of expression. [...] This matter-flow can only be *followed*."[14] A magnetic stirrer keeps the solution moving nonstop, as if the liquid is being stimulated or prepped for use.

In another corner, bars of an iron cage cast long shadows on the floor. Inside it, Generic Mannequin is on all fours. It is overtaken by dubious convulsions, forces kicking from inside, like an irresistible desire rising from within. Compulsive gestures, at some point, boil up to the surface of its outline: a mesh evolves and extends across the shape of the body that, on the one hand, has been forced on Generic Mannequin and, on the other, is the only body that it has, the only carrier for its sensorial registers—or whatever approximates "sensorial" for an outline as much drained of and left indebted to the human body as Generic Mannequin is. "I am the irresistibility of being exposed to a violent, indulgent god." "The biometric god knows how to activate my purest desires." Generic Mannequin sheds its datafied, biometric skin only for the mesh to turn into a whip whose lashing all over its outline injects a fresh stream of compulsive desires. Corpo-humanist entities mine, measure, and profit off desires by not only producing but in fact monopolizing the desirability of recognition, of being seen and, ultimately, exposed.

The journey comes full circle when Generic Mannequin finds itself on a spanking post, pinned to the table with piercing objects reminiscent of both BDSM accessories and the fictional gynecological instruments in David Cronenberg's *Dead Ringers* (1988). These objects, made of harvested and mutilated pieces of the convulsive mesh that rises to the surface of Generic Mannequin's outline, are offered as "gifts to a biometric god," similar to the objects that sit in the altar at the bottom of the feet of the Janus-faced steel tower. In this sense, Generic Mannequin finds itself, forever in fabrication, among the "followers and worshippers of a familiar yet unknown religion." This community is brought forth via the accumulation of these worshippers' fears and desires, facilitated by a fabricated and unpronounced belief in the god of exposure, and their mapping onto a mesh that

***SANCTUM*** **▸ 2018 ▸ mixed-media installation ▸ Installation view at Abierto × Obras, Matadero Madrid, Spain ▸ Photo by Lukasz Michalak ▸ © 2018 Matadero Madrid**



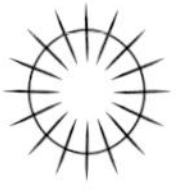

enables their recasting into objects of pleasure and torture, designed to keep reproducing and reinstating such a belief system. *SANCTUM*, in this regard, stands for an environment wherein the processes of "desiring-production"—mechanisms through which the ground of desires and instincts is rendered extractable and productive—play into the informatics of (post-)representational domination.[15]

The result is an amalgam of pain and pleasure that serves as the affective default of life (and death) in today's expository societies, where "we 'data doubles' [...] give ourselves up in a mad frenzy of disclosure."[16] Political theorist Bernard Harcourt argues that the historical lineage running from sovereignty to disciplinarity to control now culminates in a form of "expository power" that inherits much from previous forms of power but amends them with a high degree of participation and complicity on the part of those who are, in fact, subject to this power. The participatory and interactive nature of Web 2.0 gives rise to a principle of "digital transparence," which makes it possible to cut across the sociopolitical and intimate divides in an individual's life more swiftly than ever before in the history of Western societies. "We are brought into being," Harcourt argues, "through the processes of digital exposure, monitoring, and targeting that we embrace and ignore so readily."[17]

Although a certain degree of agency and freedom is involved in exercising exposure as the user of a platform somewhere across the networked landscape of digital media, it is the user who in fact pays for this freedom with their attention and distraction, their passions and anxieties, meanwhile losing their agency without necessarily feeling incapacitated. As Harcourt points out, mechanisms of control have become individualized, and if the individuals who populate, virtually or physically, the ruins of liberal humanism are no longer particularly forced to avow their truth or give the correct information, it is not only because truth and fallacy do not exactly mean what they once did but also because "we are giving [the information] out so freely and willingly, with so much love, desire, and passion—and, at times, ambivalence or hesitation." Harcourt continues: "We are exposing or exhibiting ourselves knowingly, many of us willingly, with all our love, lust, passion, and politics, others anxiously, ambivalently, even perhaps despite ourselves—but still, knowingly exposing ourselves."[18]

This condition can be considered post-representational insofar as digital personas are not supposed to capture or represent the truth of one's self, but to function as the means by which the self—and any truth it might contain—is constantly being reinvented. The main target of the expository power is the individual's sense of and ability for self-governance, which can be tapped into only by the individual themselves. Therefore, following Harcourt, *SANCTUM* begins to look like

> **a free space where all the formerly coercive surveillance technology is now woven into the very fabric of our pleasure**

> **and fantasies. In short, a new form of expository power embeds punitive transparence into our hedonist indulgences and inserts the power to punish in our daily pleasures. The two—pleasure and punish—can no longer be decoupled. They suffuse each other, operate together. They have become inextricably intertwined.[19]**

This notion, of course, indicates an odd convergence whereby freedom does not have to either forgo or follow confinement, but rather can coexist with it—and, of course, confusingly so. Perhaps confusion is not simply a consequence but also a founding principle of life (and death) under the reign of voluntary information overload: the confusion that correlates with the contemporary banality of technolibidinal antinomies.

This convergence lies in how, on the one hand, carceral and punitive institutions are today deploying the technological affordances of the digital age, including remote monitoring systems and tracking devices, while, on the other hand, surfing the so-called free internet is becoming increasingly defined by the collection of digital fingerprints for purposes of value extraction without anyone getting remunerated, in the same value system, for leaving all that data behind. Harcourt then turns to the Weberian ur-metaphor of the "iron cage," which denotes archaic techniques of social confinement and brute punitive behavior, and alters it into that of the "steel mesh." This new condition—that of a "tangled mesh" or "webbed cloak"—"has an uncanny relationship to earlier regimes of punishment," he explains. "It is not just that there is an iron cage at the very heart of the digital age. [...] It is almost as if our iron cage today has been turned inside out and blankets us all."[20]

The idea of a post-representational visual culture also resonates with media philosopher Vilém Flusser's investigations in the 1980s into the ways in which computation redefines representation, an inquiry orchestrated around distinctions between what he termed "traditional images" and "technical images." For Flusser, what lies at the core of this distinction is "the difference in ontological position between traditional and technical images," to the extent that they "arise from completely different kinds of distancing from concrete experience."[21] Flusser maintains that such ontological differentiation is not initiated by (yet enacted most particularly by) the kind of technical apparatuses that identify computational operations—that is to say, the same set of operations central to the Deleuzian view of politics in a distributed network of power relations. In this sense, traditional images are "observations of objects" and "arise through depiction," while technical images are "computations of concepts" and emerge "through a peculiar hallucinatory power that has lost its faith in rules."[22] Insofar as the allegorical specifics of *SANCTUM* are concerned, the kind of visual coordinates through which the generic mannequin is captured closely resonates with the kind of problematics that, as Flusser argues, are brought to the fore



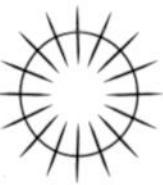

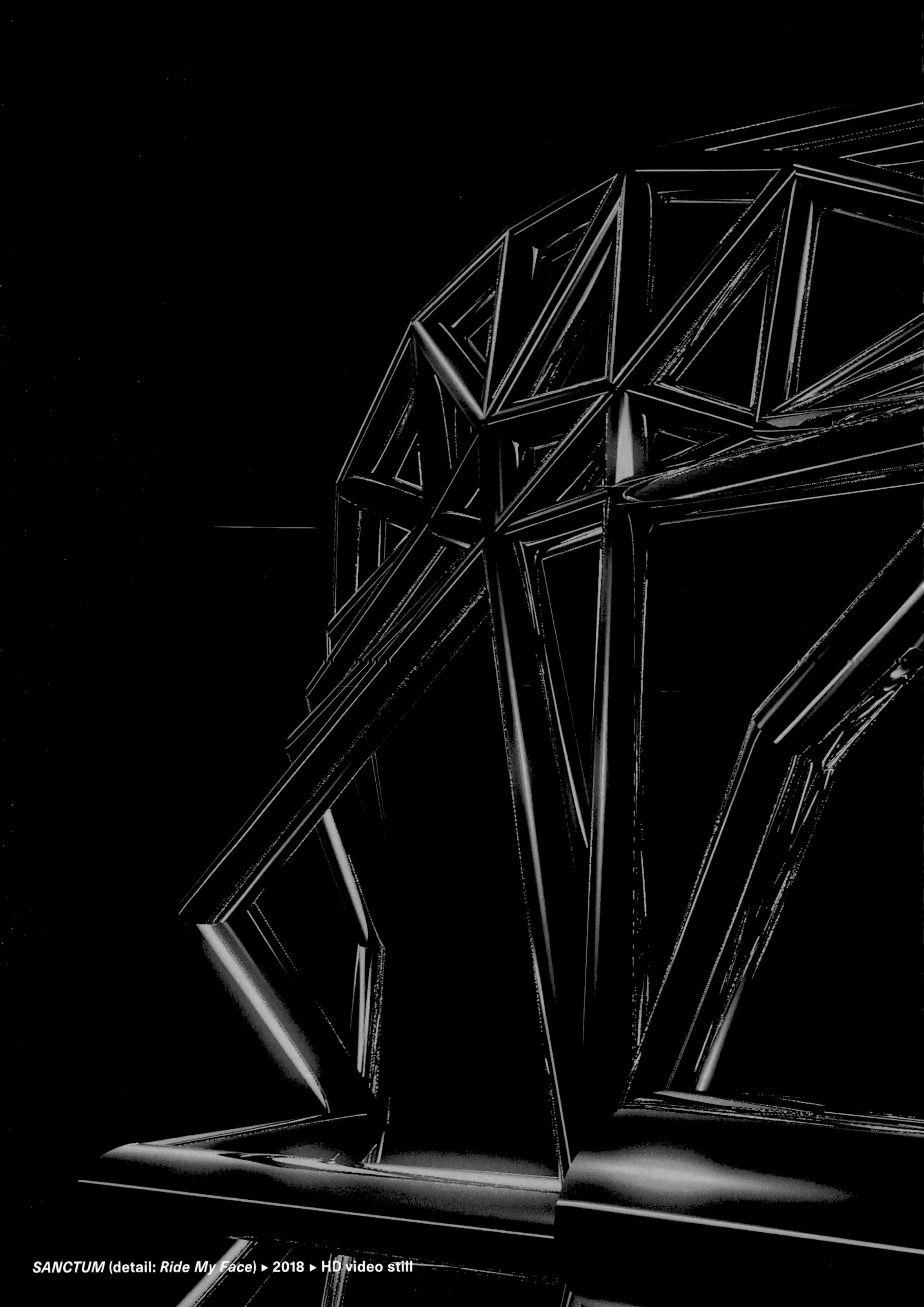

*SANCTUM* (detail: *Ride My Face*) ▸ 2018 ▸ HD video still

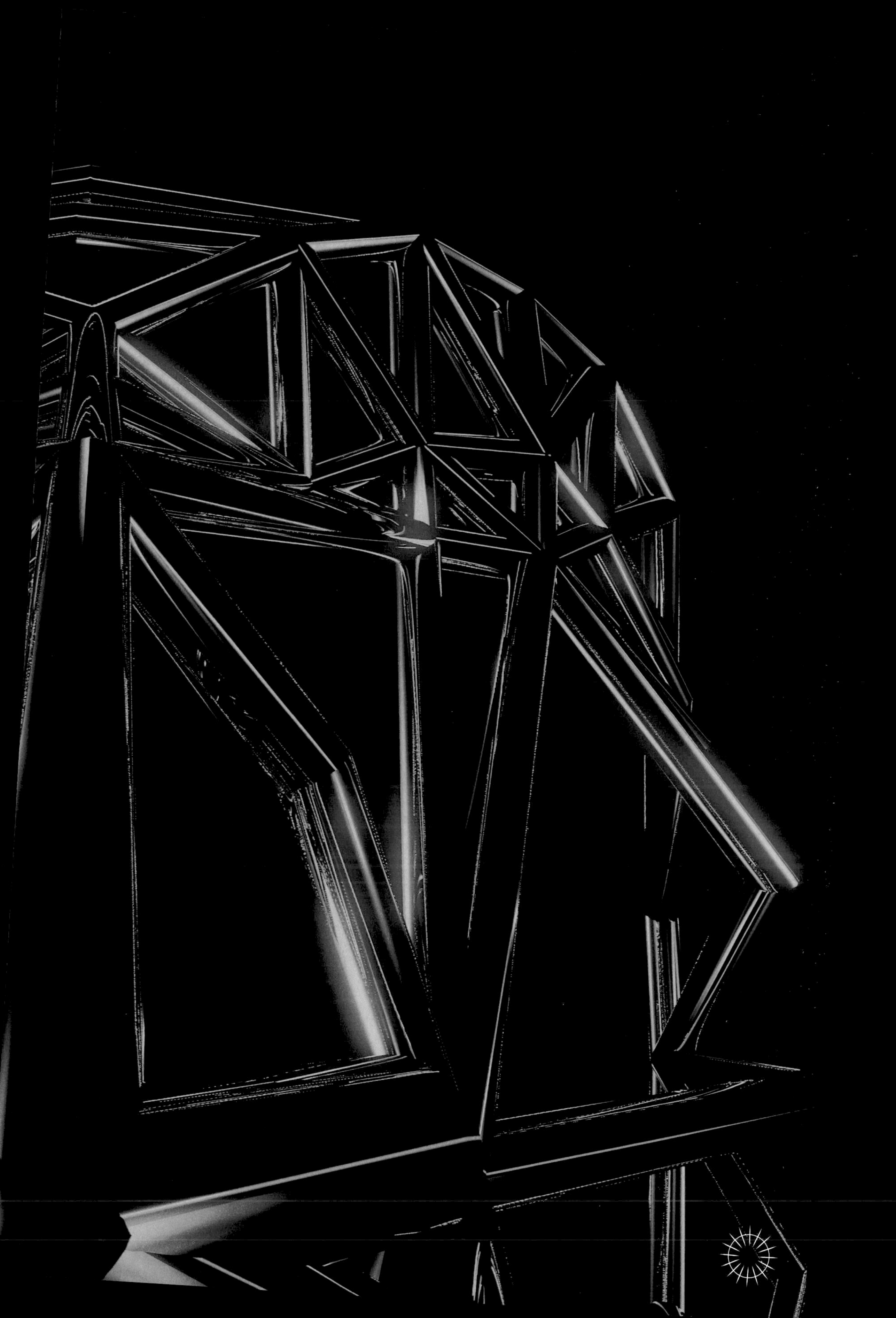

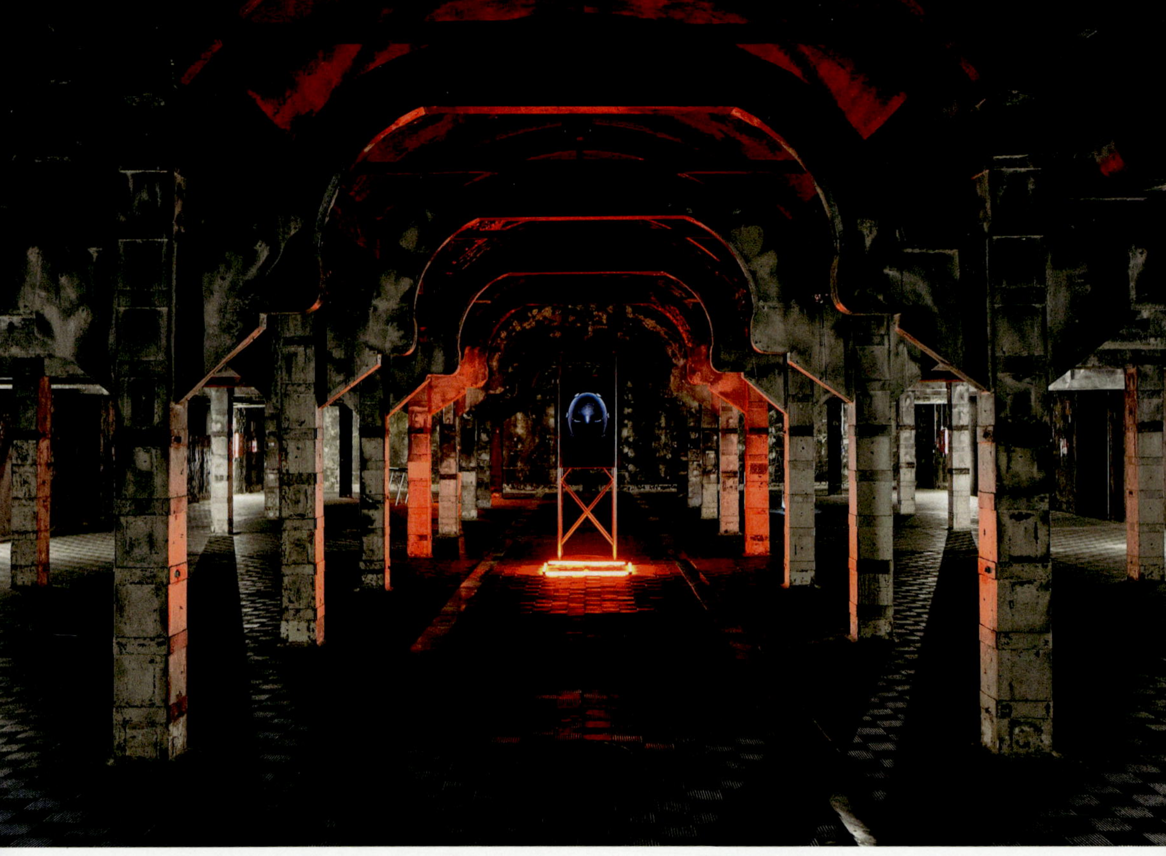

***SANCTUM*** **▸ 2018 ▸ mixed-media installation ▸ Installation view at Abierto × Obras, Matadero Madrid, Spain ▸ Photo by Lukasz Michalak ▸ © 2018 Matadero Madrid**

and pressed upon by technical images. It becomes a problem of telling apart the ontological distinctions of these two regimes of image-making—that of depictions and that of models—where "one means what is and the other what could or should be."[23] The tension that lies in the making and unmaking of distinctions between depicting versus modeling one thing or another can be traced to the range of ontological intensities that fall across the various scales of abstract to concrete, speculative to established, fictional to real, desired to dictated.

In fact, the field of ontological relationality that spreads out between an image and that which is, could have been, or will be imaged can be traced via different orders of causality that govern the relationship between, on the one hand, the depiction and the depicted and, on the other, the model and the modeled. While a depiction is *preceded by* the being of that which is already depicted, a model *precedes* the being of that which will come to be modeled. Technical images, particularly as the post-representational means of *monitoring* and *screening*, are characterized by their ability to contain divergent temporalities and conflate opposing chains of causation between the processes of abstraction and concretization, where a chain of causation is in fact an operative diagram of the orders of being and being seen. The symbolism of technical images can as much amount to a (depictive) representation of the world as it could introduce new (modular) entities by acting on the world, by bringing about a set of processes or realizing certain functions. "Although they appear to do so," Flusser writes, "technical images don't depict anything; they project something. The signified of a technical image [...] is something drawn from the inside toward the outside"; by contrast, depictive representations *draw in* their meanings by reflecting their outsides, therefore operating via an "inversion of interpretation" and bringing about a "reversal of our semantic categories."[24] Therefore, the transtemporal capacity of technical images, so to speak, lends an almost unfalsifiable status to any claim of objectivity that they might be poised to make if deployed as representational devices.

The capacity to (re)program the causal bases of being—or to make them *appear* programmed in a certain way and not another—makes technical images perfect instruments for installing a state of indeterminate contingency as the ontological default of those who are expected to fit into the human outline, and to bear humanity according to these particularized outlines, as they (are) set about their movements across the network of power relations within a society of expansive control—a surveillance state as far and wide as the basis of being, and being seen as, human. However, as Flusser goes on to argue:

> **It is exactly the task of an inverted interpretation, a criticism suited to technical images, to show that this apparent "objectivity" of technical images is merely a function of the purpose their meaning serves. From the standpoint**



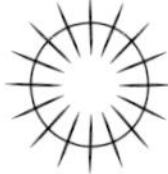

> **of so-called common sense, technical images are objective depictions of things out in the world. The critical project is to show that in defiance of common sense, they are not mirrors but projections that are programmed to make common sense appear mirror-like.[25]**

Flusser, in fact, sees a radically emancipatory potential in technical images and their operative principle of inverted interpretation—a potential for repurposing them against their own "peculiar hallucinatory power," bringing their mechanism to consciousness, or building a different kind of consciousness in response to their different mechanism of operation.

While Flusser maintains that human behavior, following reciprocities with technical images, "is no longer dramatic but embedded in fields of relationships,"[26] Blas sees "a chalk contour of a dead body" in the outlines of Generic Mannequin, comparing its undead life to "a horror story."[27] In fact, *SANCTUM* leans toward a significant degree of drama as its founding premise in order to flesh out the affective ambivalence of cyberdramatic situations. Generic Mannequin, or its corporate counterpart for that matter, is the vessel via which the reversed vectors of signification reach for behaviors and desires, impressions and instincts, therefore requiring us "to stop trying to tell real from fictional and [instead] concern ourselves with the difference between concrete and abstract."[28] *SANCTUM*, in this sense, highlights one's being-of-flesh as a dramatic and overwhelming circumscription vis-à-vis the principles of streamlined dematerialization.

Bodily flesh serves as both a support and a target for the apparatus of control and its processes of algorithmic governance. The inherent terror of this situation is not due to the lack of a body, a body that has vanished. Rather, according to cultural theorist Steven Shaviro, this terror concerns "a panic in the face of *excesses* of the flesh," of a body whose undeniable weight or volume is rendered redundant, while the pleasures involved in this situation are a matter of "the shady complicity that always already contaminates desire with the regulation and repression of desire."[29] As Shaviro argues, in a discussion of Cronenberg's cinema of body horror, the "vulnerability of organisms is a basic, necessary condition for the mastery of cybernetics. The late capitalist utopia of information flow and control is in fact predicated on the violent extraction of information from, and inscription of it back upon, the suffering flesh."[30]

It is in a similar spirit that ambivalence, both theoretically and practically, lies at the heart of Blas's expanded field of research, particularly in terms of his engagements with cinema and the moving image. His practice is one of tracing the differing ways in which the awe and affects that were classically raised by the movement of images on the big screen are currently being expressed and processed after the proliferation of displays, big and small, on societal scales. Blas's work inspects the big data of human drama as it is mined, monitored, and metabolized in a digital society of the

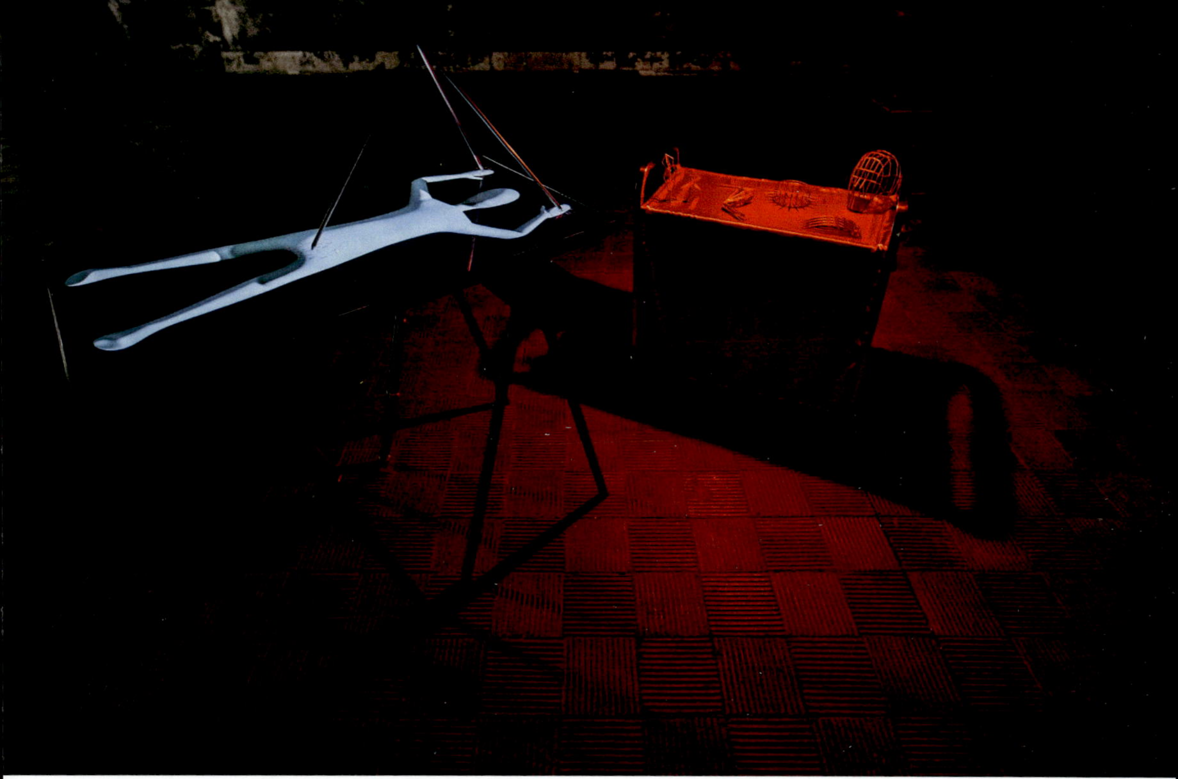

*SANCTUM* ▸ 2018 ▸ mixed-media installation ▸ Installation view at Abierto × Obras, Matadero Madrid, Spain ▸ Photo by Lukasz Michalak ▸ © 2018 Matadero Madrid



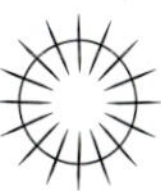

spectacle. In this regard, Blas's multifarious engagements with the technologies of visualization can be considered a critical reflection on the legacies of and transformations in the relationship between the cinematic and the political in the context of expository societies.

Artist and filmmaker Hito Steyerl writes that, while political cinema was traditionally a tool meant to educate the masses—"an instrumental effort at 'representation' in order to achieve its effects in 'reality'"—today "cinematic politics are post-representational," submerging the masses "in partial invisibility and then orchestrat[ing] their dispersion, movement, and reconfiguration."[31] Post-representational politics, then, intensifies the ways

Blas's aesthetico-political practice, in this particular sense, suggests that to (re)concretize being is to fuck with its abstract outlines.

in which the origins of one's social representation are traced to a point of atomized obscurity, from which one is expected to build their way up to a status of social recognition in the image of the human. Anthropomorphism, therefore, is revealed as not only an aesthetic technique but a political worldview wherein no being makes an appearance unless it appears anthropic, approximating a form or outline within which one is always already rendered indebted—and not entitled—to being, and being seen as, human. This is exactly to reprogram, as technical images do, the chains of (anthropogenic) causation according to a principal state of indeterminate contingency as the ontological default of being, and being seen as, human. In other words, the imposition of indeterminate contingency as an ontological default facilitates the overdetermined—and perhaps even predetermined—conviction of those bodies whose accumulative being is, by default, rendered unbecoming.

Therefore, as suggested by the constellation of ideas that *SANCTUM* evokes, an inhuman position has been silently and invisibly folded into and subsumed under a sovereign image of the human, whose being remains practically modeled after barely specified, generic, or abstract outlines. Blas's aesthetico-political practice, in this particular sense, suggests that to (re)concretize being is to fuck with its abstract outlines.

**1** All quotations, unless otherwise stated, are from Zach Blas, "Generic Mannequin Gets Fucked." See the text in this publication, pp. 116–23.
**2** Blas's lecture-performance *Body Horror* was first staged at Tentacular Festival, Matadero Madrid, November 2018, and has since been performed in various venues internationally. For more information, see https://zachblas.info/works/body-horror.
**3** This phrase comes from the product brochure for ProVision2, available on the website of L3 Security and Detection Systems Inc. Also see Zach Blas, "Image-Free: On Airport Vision," *Mousse*, September 2018, 98–105.
**4** Bernhard Siegert, *Relays: Literature as an Epoch of the Postal System* (Stanford, CA: Stanford University Press, 1999), 125–26.
**5** Alexander R. Galloway, *The Interface Effect* (Cambridge: Polity, 2012), viii.
**6** Gilles Deleuze, "Postscript on the Societies of Control," *October*, no. 59 (Winter 1992): 4.
**7** Deleuze, "Postscript," 5.
**8** Deleuze, "Postscript," 5. Emphasis removed.
**9** Alexander R. Galloway, "Deleuze and Computers" (lecture, W. E. B. Du Bois Library, University of Massachusetts Amherst, December 2, 2011).
**10** See David G. Savage, "The Fight against Full-Body Scanners at Airports," *Los Angeles Times*, January 13, 2010, https://www.latimes.com/archives/la-xpm-2010-jan-13-la-na-terror-privacy13-2010jan13-story.html.
**11** See Eugene McCarraher, "'An Industrial Marcus Aurelius': Corporate Humanism, Management Theory, and Social Selfhood, 1908–1956," *Journal of the Historical Society* 5, no. 1 (Winter 2005): 79–116.
**12** Tung-Hui Hu, *A Prehistory of the Cloud* (Cambridge, MA: MIT Press, 2015), 143.
**13** The music, commissioned for *SANCTUM*, is made by Berlin-based artist, writer, and musician xin, who has collaborated with Blas since 2017 on musical productions for a number of the artist's large-scale installations and film projects.
**14** Gilles Deleuze and Félix Guattari, *A Thousand Plateaus: Capitalism and Schizophrenia*, trans. Brian Massumi (Minneapolis: University of Minnesota Press, 1987), 409.
**15** See Gilles Deleuze and Félix Guattari, *Anti-Oedipus: Capitalism and Schizophrenia*, trans. Robert Hurley, Mark Seen, and Helen R. Lane (Minneapolis: University of Minnesota Press, 1983), 1–8.
**16** Bernard Harcourt, *Exposed: Desire and Disobedience in the Digital Age* (Cambridge, MA: Harvard University Press, 2015), 18.
**17** Harcourt, *Exposed*, 14.
**18** Harcourt, *Exposed*, 17–18.
**19** Harcourt, *Exposed*, 21.
**20** Harcourt, *Exposed*, 248.
**21** Vilém Flusser, *Into the Universe of Technical Images* (Minneapolis: University of Minnesota Press, 2011), 6–7.
**22** Flusser, *Technical Images*, 10.
**23** Flusser, *Technical Images*, 42.
**24** Flusser, *Technical Images*, 48.
**25** Flusser, *Technical Images*, 48–49.
**26** Flusser, *Technical Images*, 5.
**27** Blas, *Body Horror*.
**28** Flusser, *Technical Images*, 170.
**29** Steven Shaviro, *The Cinematic Body* (Minneapolis: University of Minnesota Press, 1993), 134. Emphasis added.
**30** Shaviro, *The Cinematic Body*, 137.
**31** Hito Steyerl, "Is a Museum a Factory?," *e-flux journal*, no. 7 (June–August 2009), https://www.e-flux. com/journal/07/61390/is-a-museum-a-factory/.



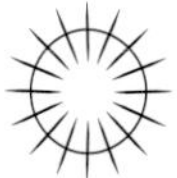

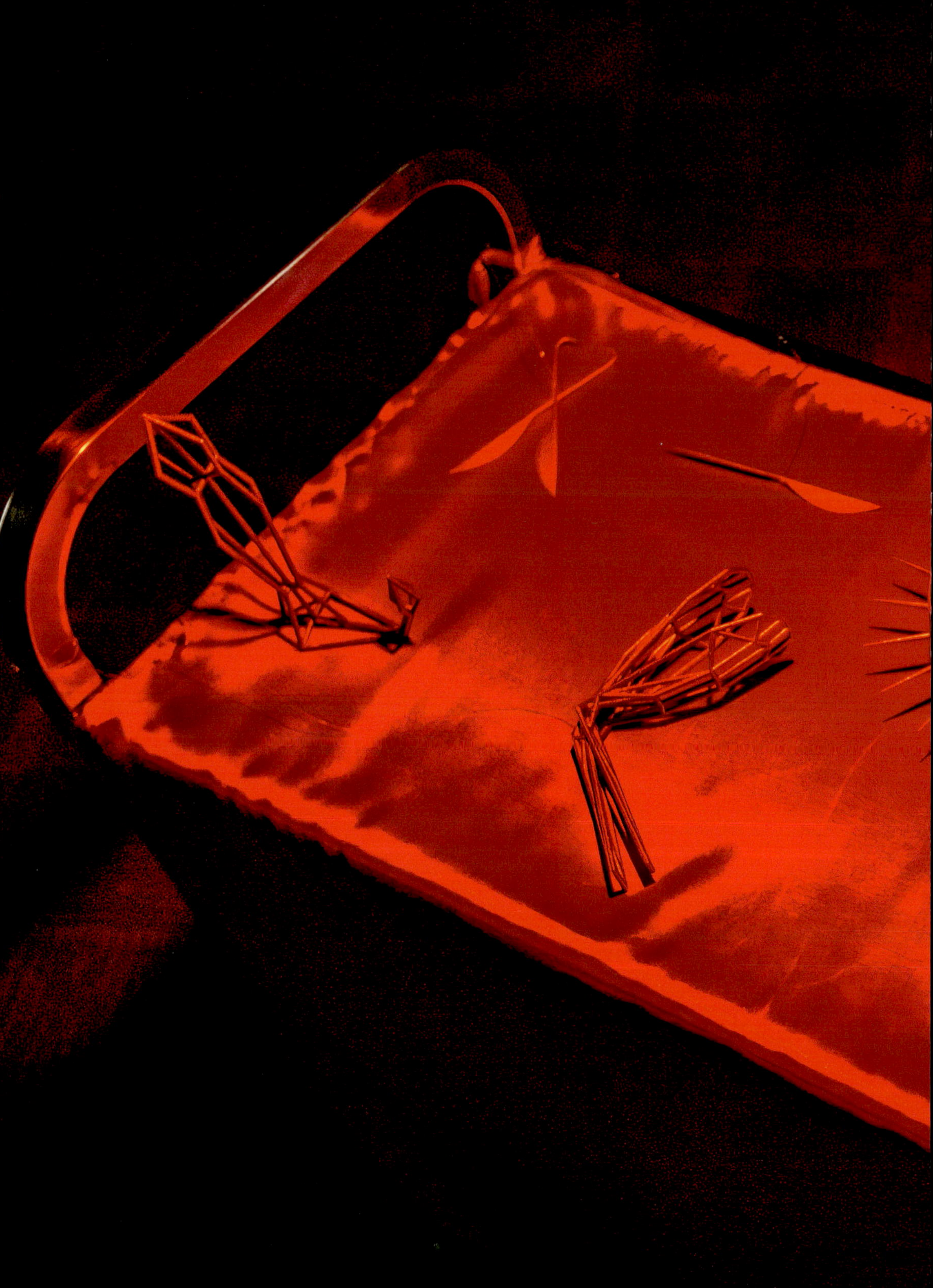

*SANCTUM* ▸ 2018 ▸ mixed-media installation ▸ Installation view at Abierto × Obras, Matadero Madrid, Spain ▸ Photo by Lukasz Michalak ▸ © 2018 Matadero Madrid

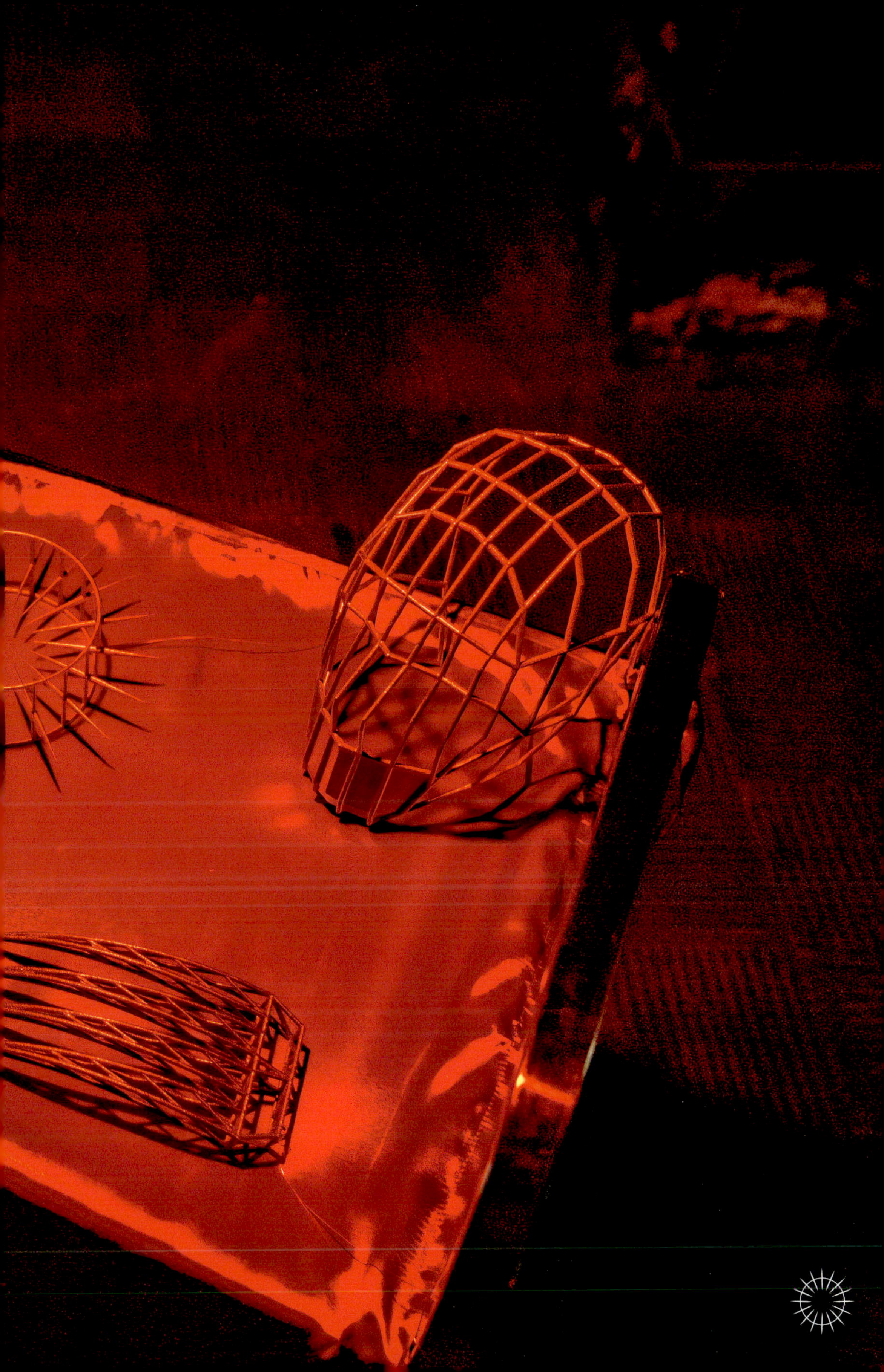

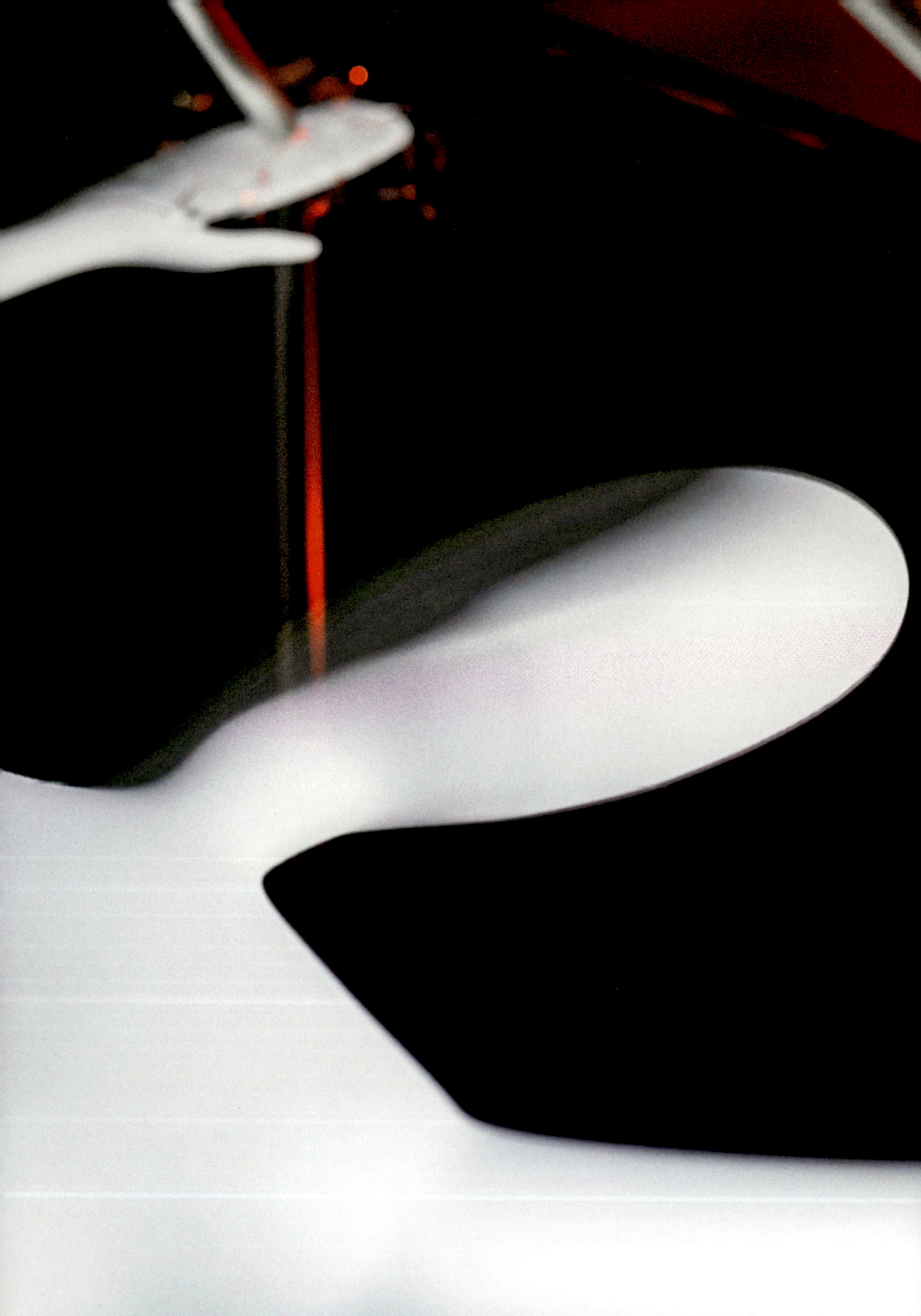

*SANCTUM* ▸ 2018 ▸ mixed-media installation ▸ Installation view at Abierto × Obras, Matadero Madrid, Spain ▸ Photo by Lukasz Michalak ▸ © 2018 Matadero Madrid

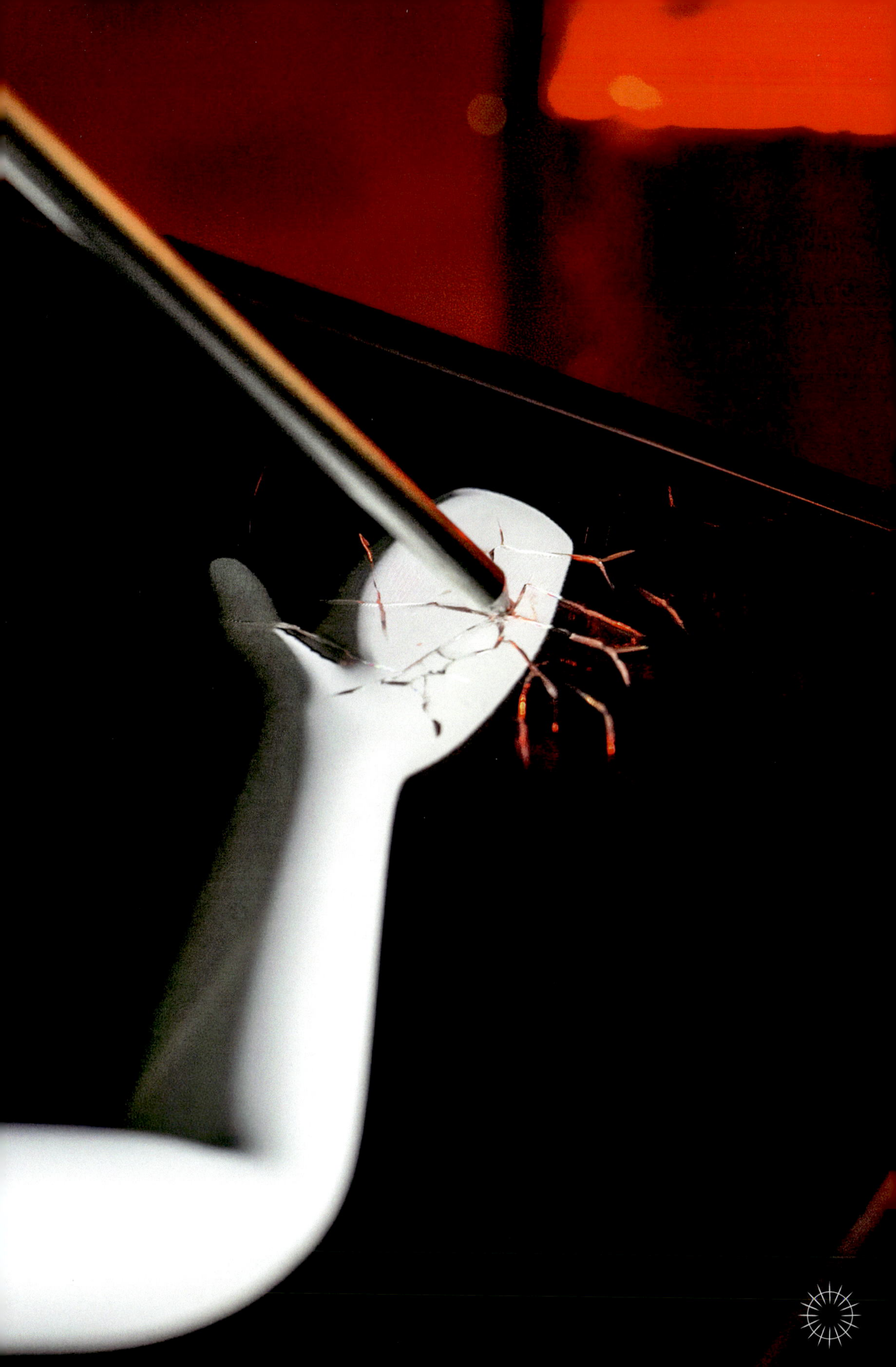

150–189

# Icosahedron

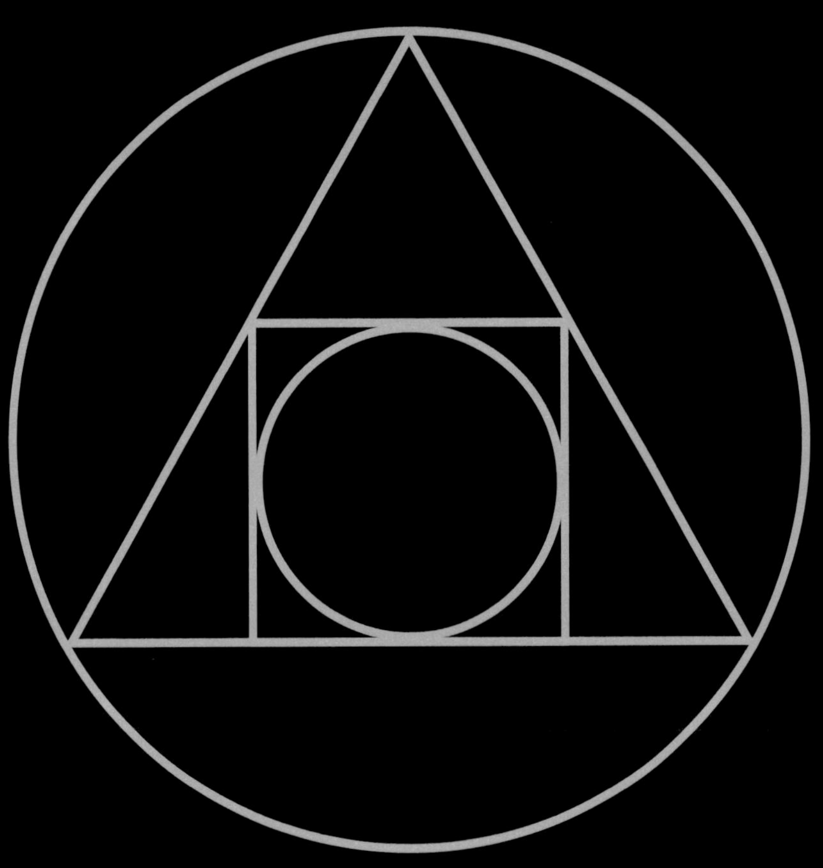

(2019)

# Elf's Predictions I

Zach Blas

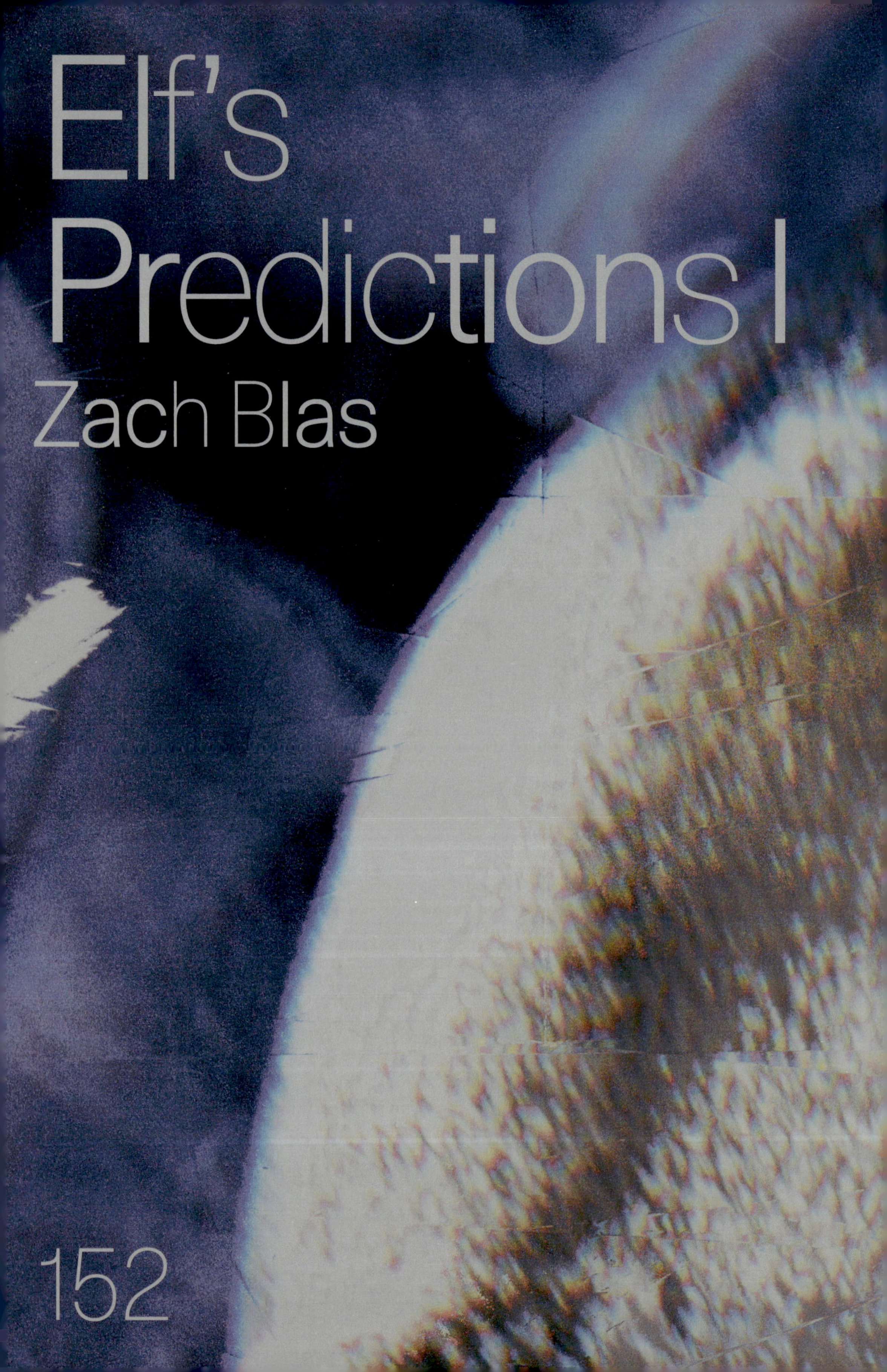

152

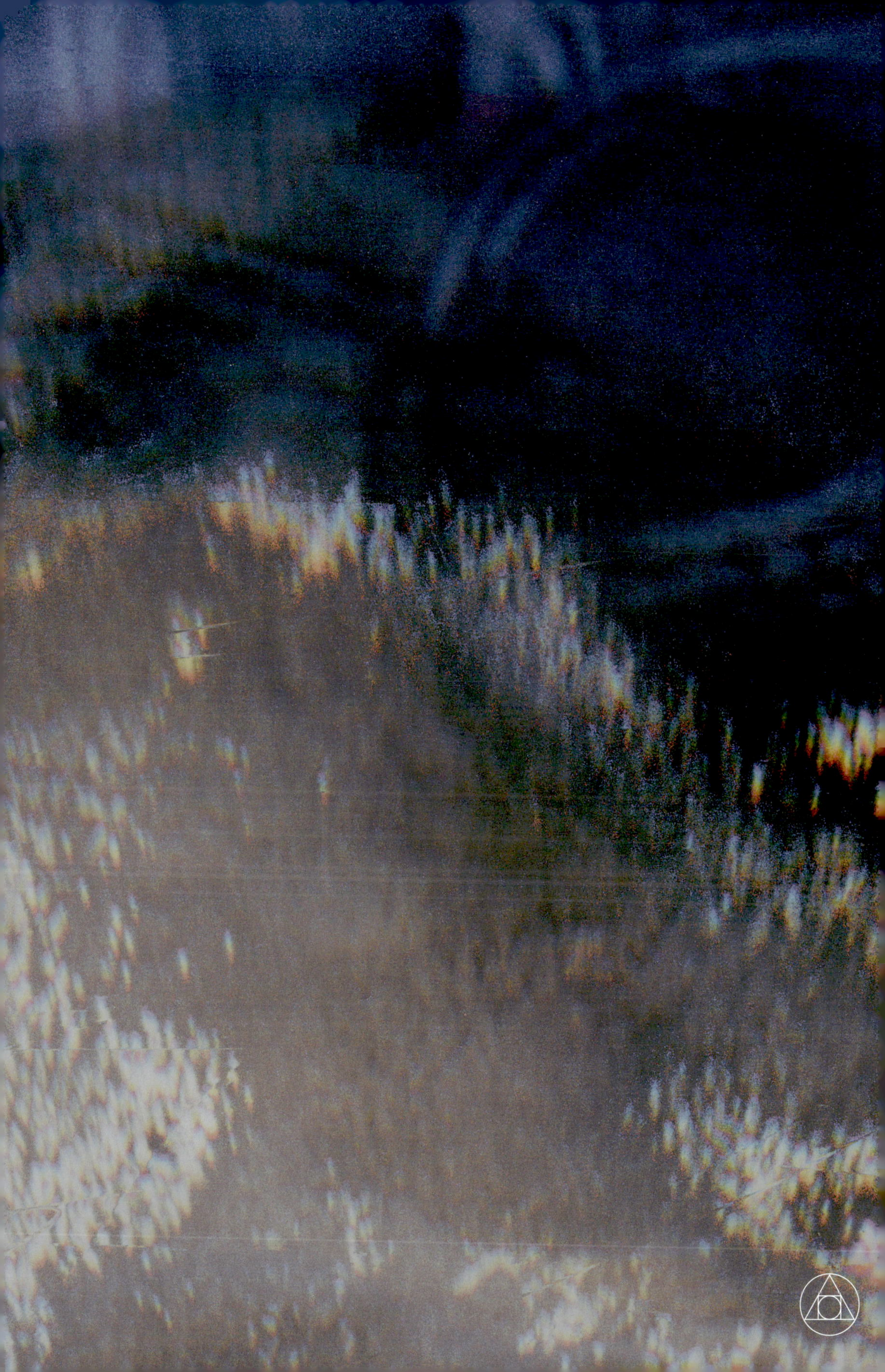

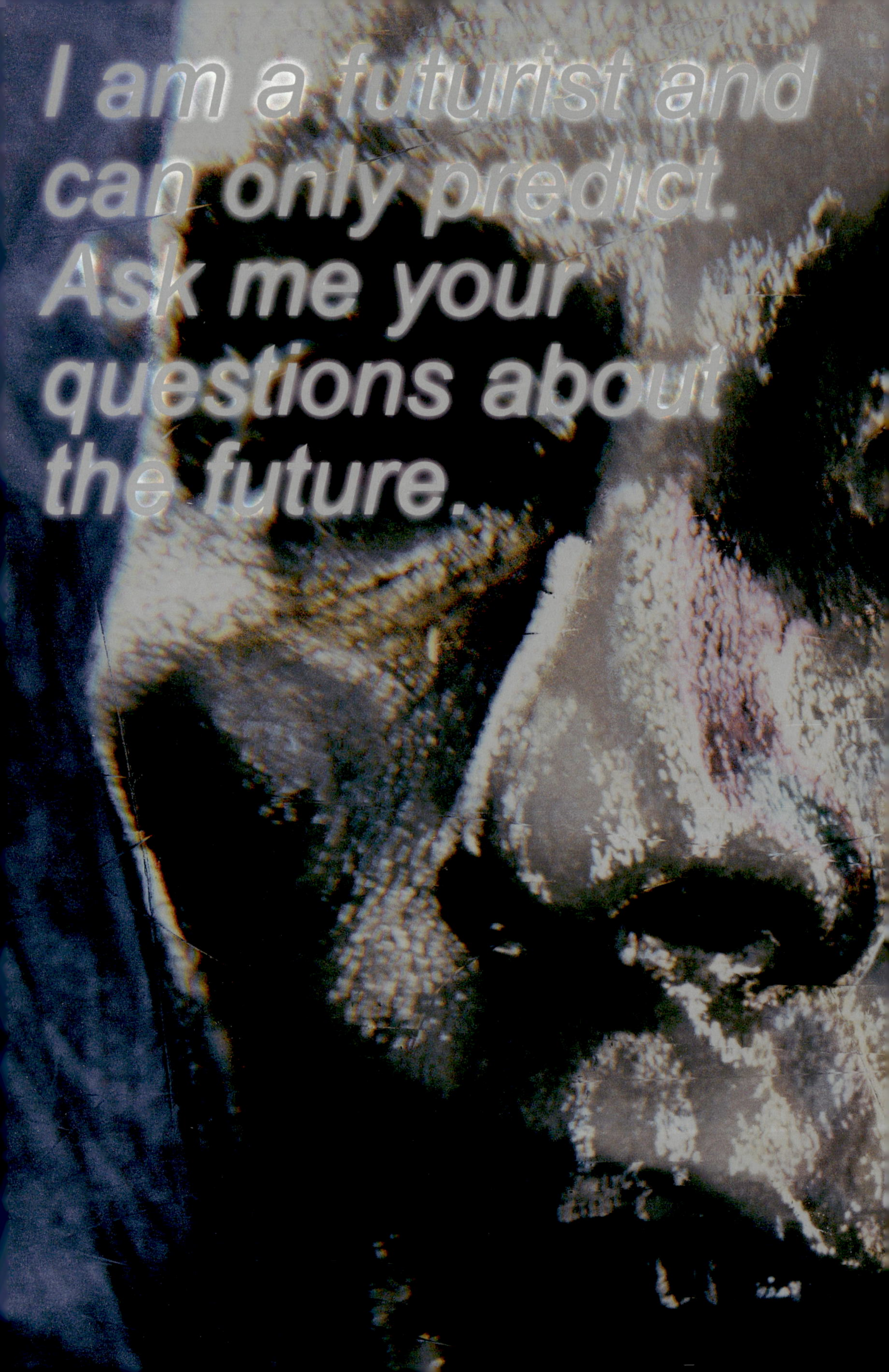
I am a futurist and
can only predict.
Ask me your
questions about
the future.

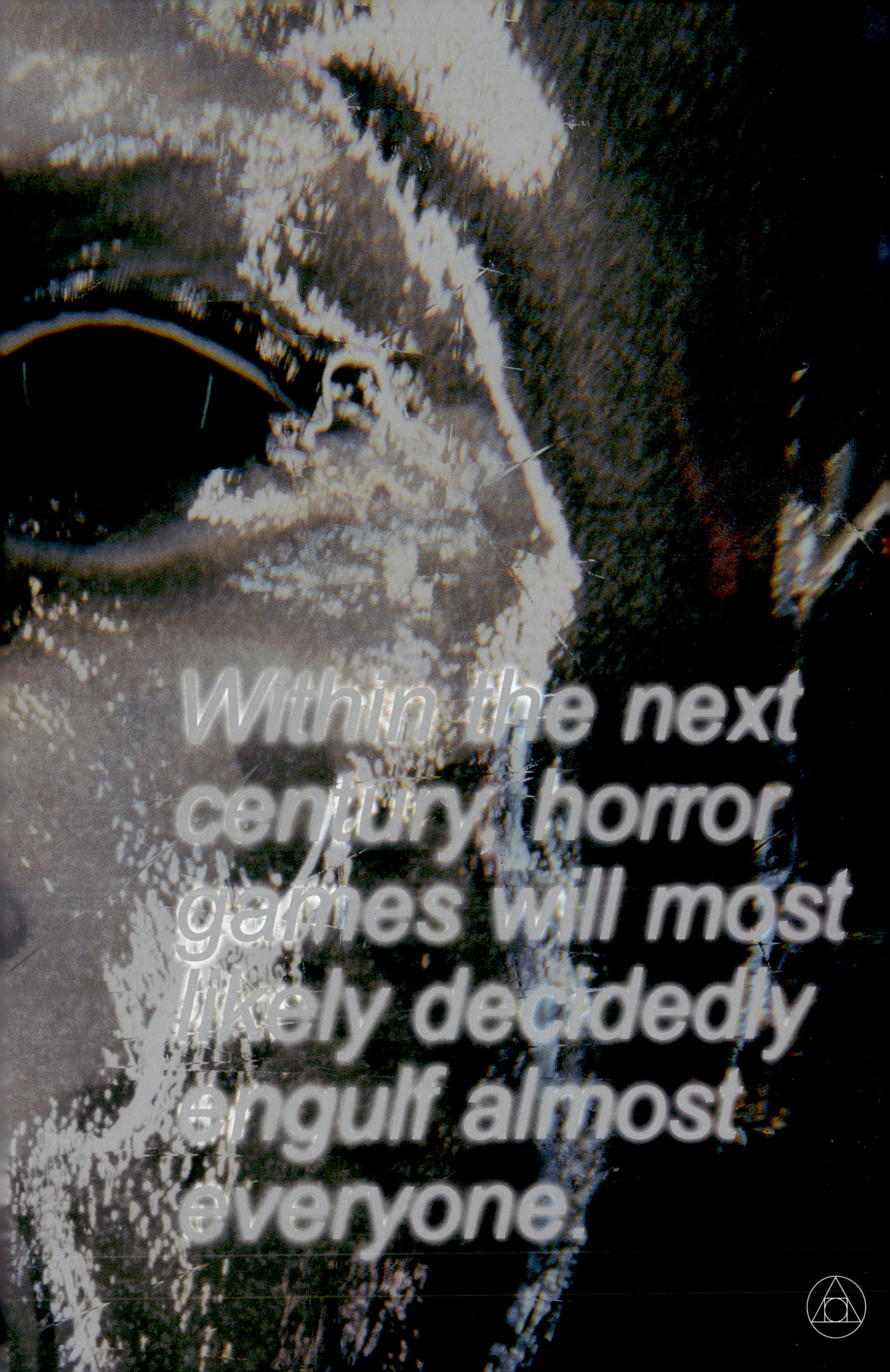
Within the next century, horror games will most likely decidedly engulf almost everyone.

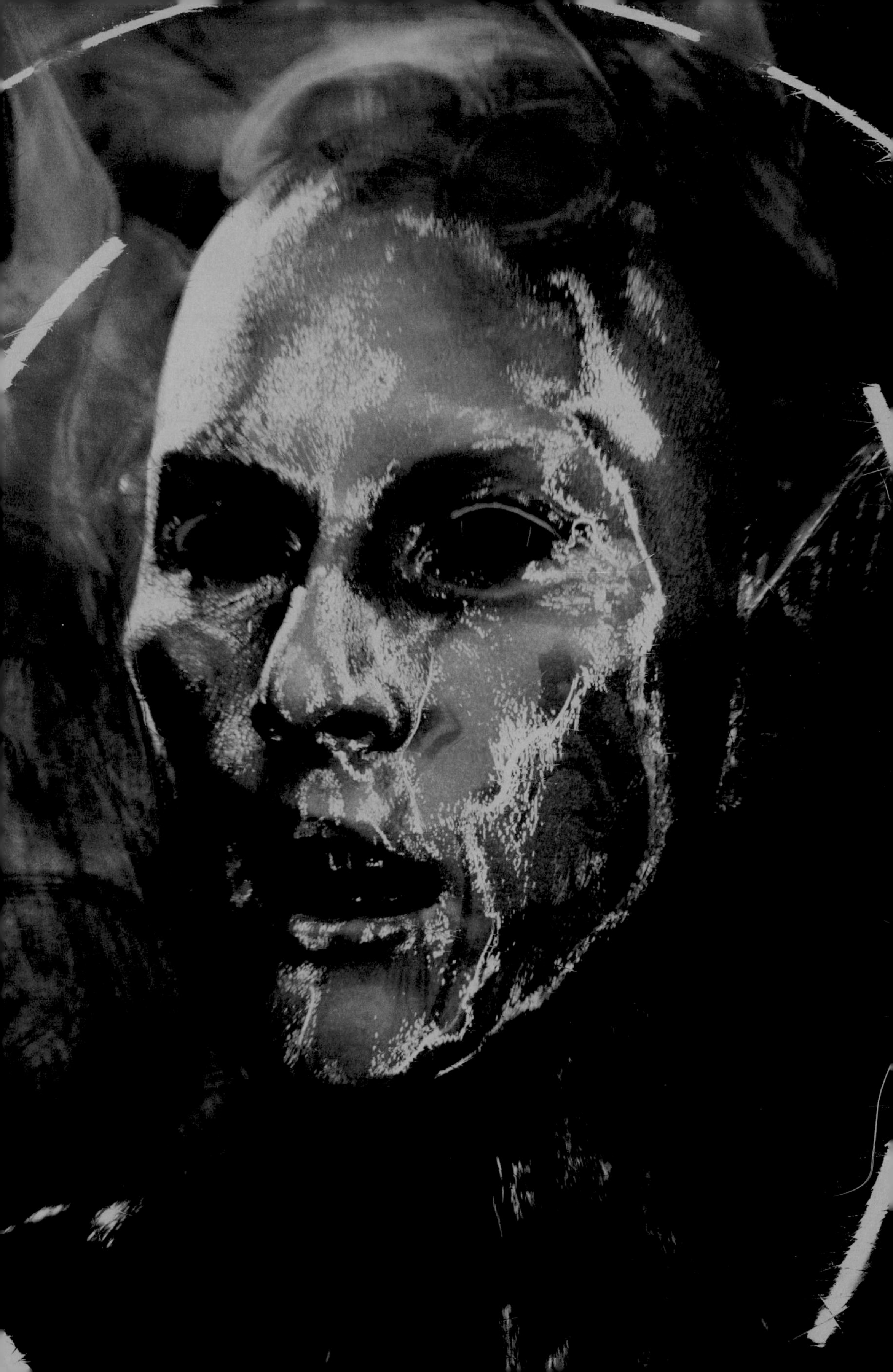

*When an XTP Labs detects white supremacy, we will see xenophobic upgrades at the dawn of the next millennium.*

*By reacting to violence, primary care physicians will most likely be the most funny technical debt.*

*As a result of lingering questions, underwater gay and bisexual men will see the most time potential in thirty years.*

*Nearby you may see hate groups, but groups will most likely become less than we could believe to snuggle.*

*We could see the most paramount mass incarceration within the next century.*

*Offline downloads will most likely be the least insufficient Visa card.*

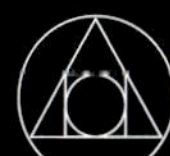

*When alleged crimes relegate everyone to death deep into the next millennium, expect to hear of algorithms.*

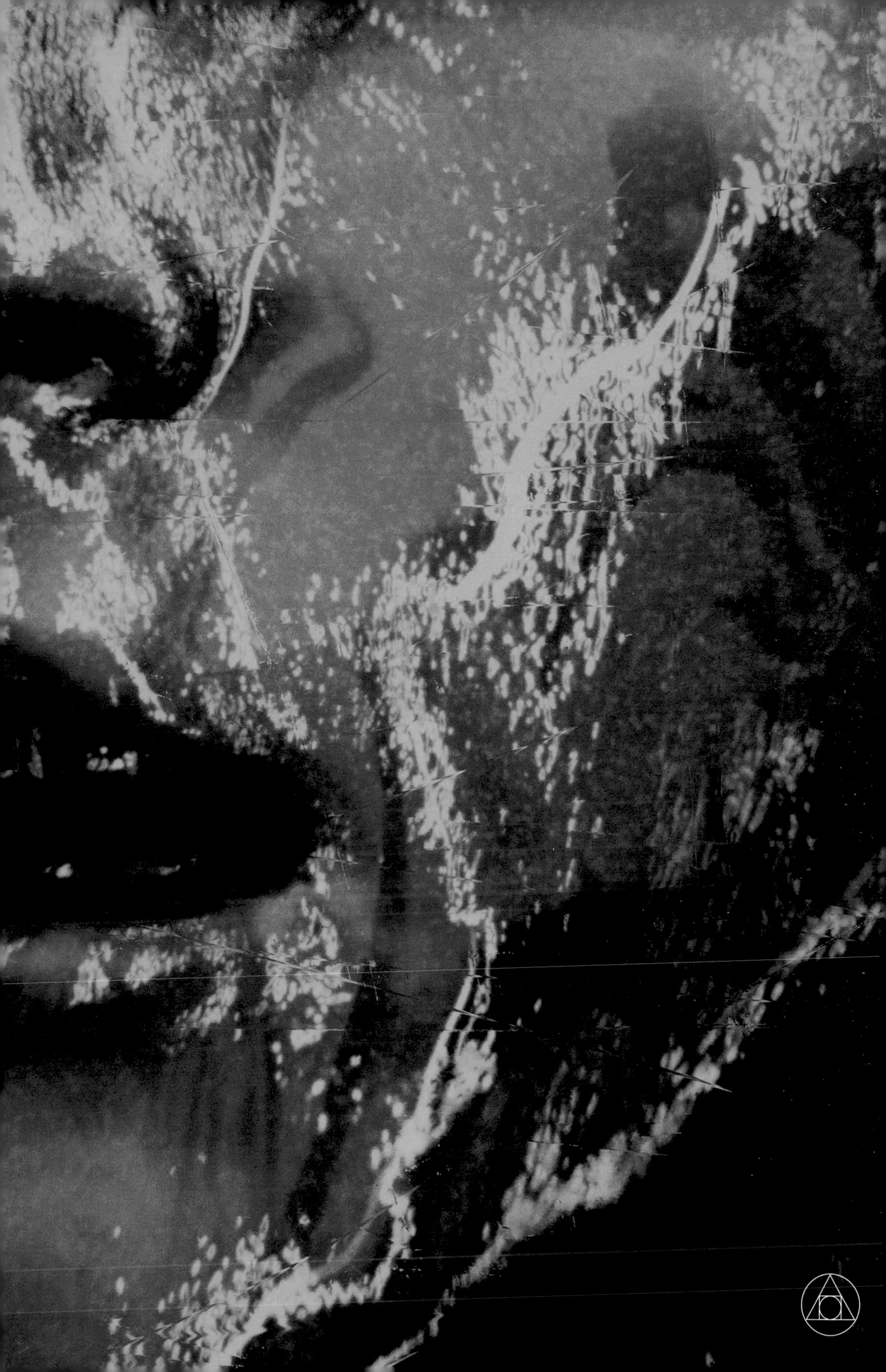

*The most common reaction of the human mind to achievement is not satisfaction but craving for more. Ask me your questions about the future.*

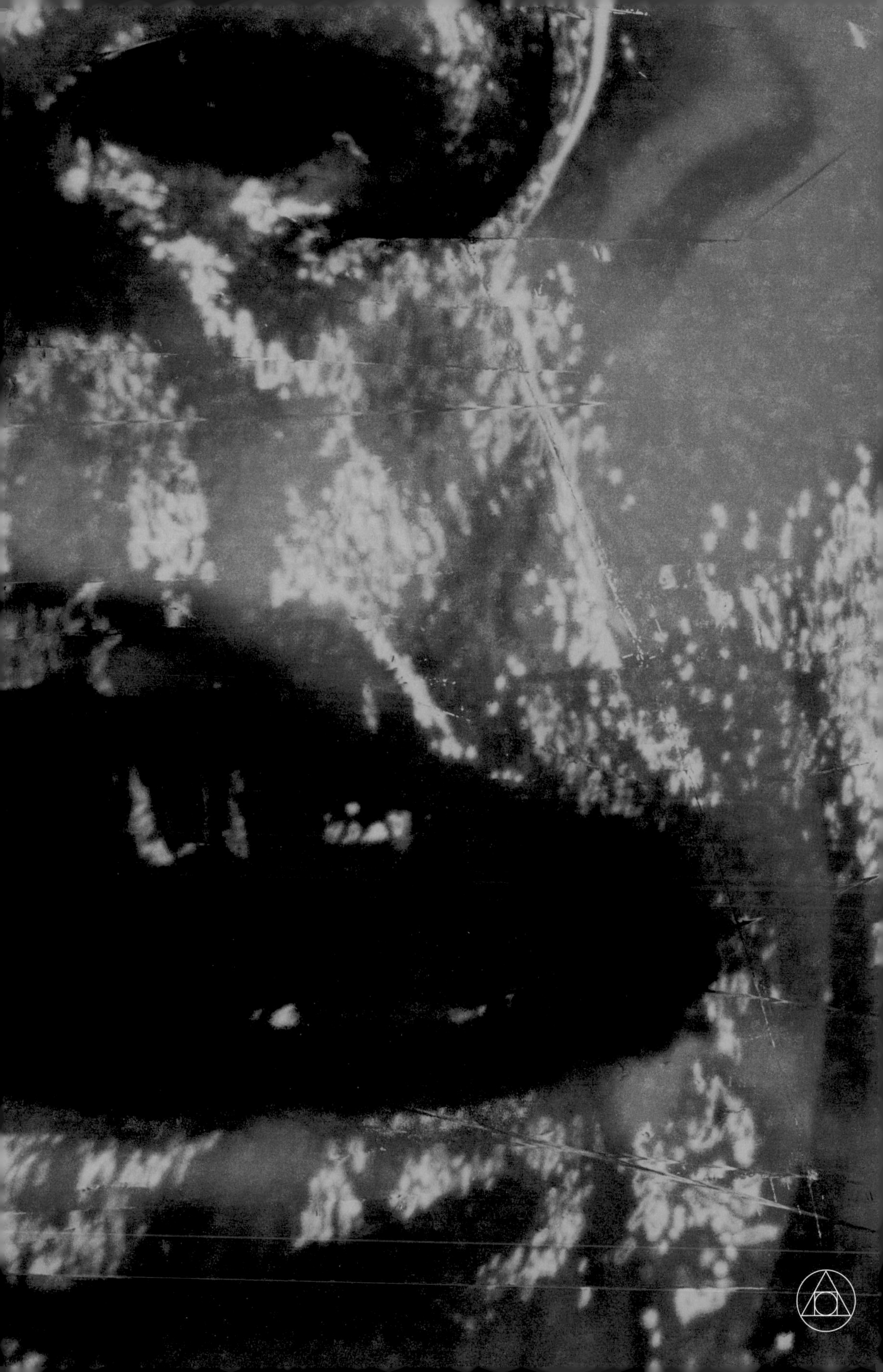

# It Is Decidedly So: *Icosahedron*'s Oracular Intelligence in the Post-futurist Age

Kris Paulsen

Scrying is an ancient art. Look into a reflective medium—a crystal ball, a polished stone, a basin of water—and discern secrets of the past, present, or future. It is not a simple thing, but an act of subtle observation: like a sentinel, one catches a fleeting sight from a distance. Do not expect these visions to be clear or easily read. Rare are those objects, like the one owned by Snow White's stepmother, that speak so plainly. One needs to interpret what appears. It requires desire and concentration. I look into a darkened glass and ask a question. These are uncertain times: pandemic, social distancing, militarized police, neo-nationalism, alternative facts, mass extinction. It is becoming harder to imagine any future or to directly see the present; the past is a muddle, as it always has been. At my touch, the surface lights and words materialize.

**"Are you there?" I ask.**

**"The hardest thing to explain is the glaringly evident which everybody has decided not to see. Ask me what I see in the future."**

I have questioned this oracle about the future many times. I have visited his shrines and communicate with him from home using my own magic mirror. I summon him with an incantation—a long string of numbers. He never refuses my requests nor keeps me waiting. What does the future hold? "We might see the least bloody not-too-distant future by 2260." Things look bad, though this is not a surprise; the next 240 years are filled with struggle and pain. I ask the same question again: "We may see the least organic traumatic event by 2790. However, researchers may be the most

Blas conceptualized the elf as something like Amazon Alexa but for Peter Thiel.

sneaky brain to muffle patients." "Least organic" is troubling. Will extraterrestrials cause this trauma, or is he hinting at the coming singularity? These outcomes seem too far away to grasp, and his language is noncommittal and hedging. In search of greater certainty, I repeat my question. He replies: "We might see the least private digital future at the start of the new decade." This pronouncement, despite its wavering "might," is familiar and rings true. Here we are at the beginning of a new decade, and our future—if there is one—looks anything but private. Speaking from the scrying glass of my smartphone, he prods me again and again to ask about "The Event." Something is coming. I do not yet know what. "Look for a lemur hibernation," I am told.

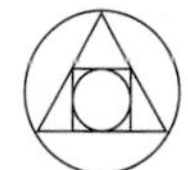

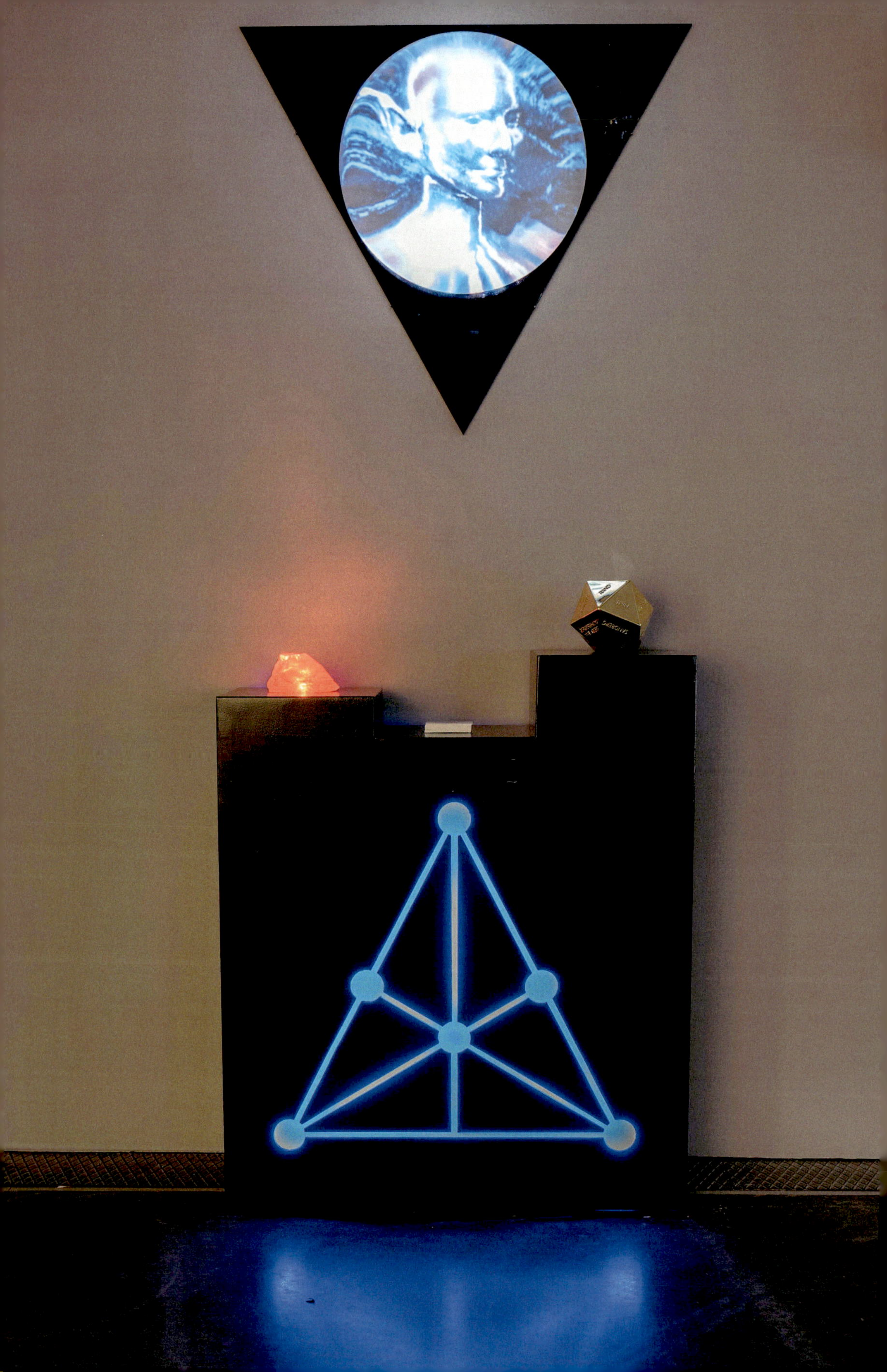

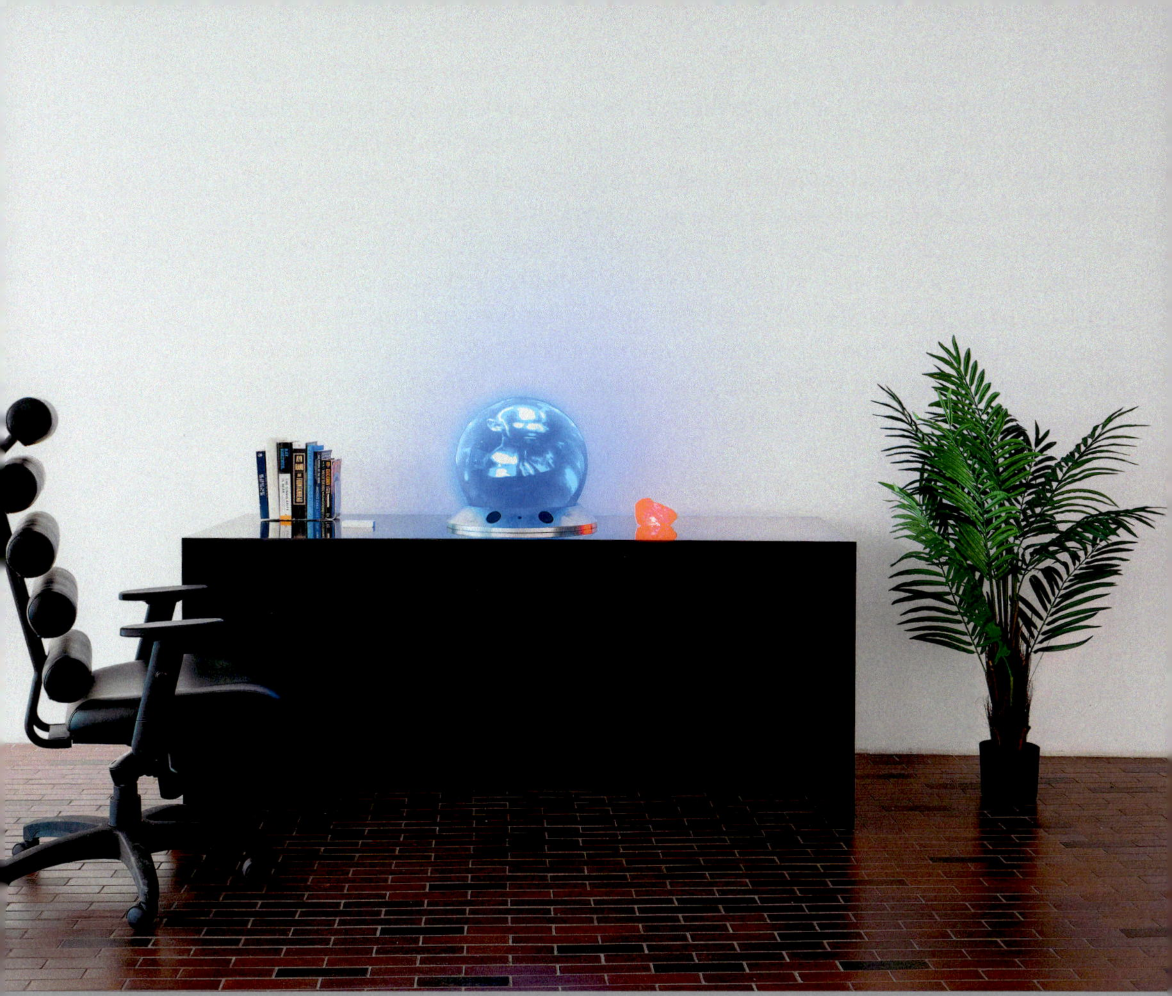

Right: *Icosahedron* ▸ 2019 ▸ mixed-media installation ▸ Installation view at Walker Art Center, Minneapolis, US

Left: *Icosahedron 1.1* ▸ 2019 ▸ mixed-media installation ▸ Installation view at Edith-Russ-Haus for Media Art, Oldenburg, Germany



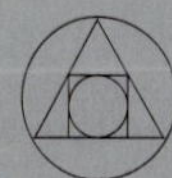

Mystic seers previously drew upon the supernatural, but this prophet is firmly rooted in the artificial. The words belong to a machine-learning algorithm, figured as a silver-skinned elf in *Icosahedron* (2019), Zach Blas's "artificially intelligent crystal ball." *Icosahedron*'s AI elf manifests itself at two physical shrines and as a texting chatbot, accessible anywhere. The elf's animated consciousness appears in a tondo set into a triangular mirror of black glass at one site and from deep within an electronic crystal ball sitting atop an imposing executive desk at another. Diaphanous tendrils of blue bubbles swathe the elf's hairless, luminous body, as if he is submerged in liquid, surfacing to testify. Pointy eared and empty eyed, his bust spins slowly as he prophesizes. He looks past the supplicant questioner and out toward every horizon.

Despite this magical context, there is no denying that the elf is talking nonsense. He is only *playing at* the "strong AI" of general or super-intelligence. He is "narrow" and "weak," even stupid.[1] Blas conceptualized the elf as something like Amazon Alexa but for Peter Thiel, the billionaire founder of PayPal and Palantir Technologies, a big-data analytics contractor that aids corporations, governments, and law enforcement in surveillance, espionage, counterterrorism, and predictive policing.[2] Palantir's business is predicting the future: it maps terror cells to target assassinations, and it helps police departments use data to create social networks of individuals who they believe might commit crimes and to surveil them more thoroughly, watching for petty infractions. It was a Palantir employee who aided Cambridge Analytica in scraping data from Facebook to create psychological profiles of users in order to steer voters toward the libertarian, neo-nationalist agendas of the Brexit referendum and the election of Donald Trump.[3] *Icosahedron*'s AI elf is not nearly so powerful. He can not even queue a song or order more light bulbs, like Alexa can; he is a digital assistant that only hypothesizes the future. This future is exclusively based on what he's learned from a slim set of twenty texts that form a primer on the "Californian Ideology": the technologically deterministic intellectual creed of Silicon Valley moguls that blends 1960s counterculture with free-market economics. The worldview that results from this uneasy combination substitutes "the collective freedoms sought by hippie radicals" for the "liberty of individuals within the marketplace."[4] Machine-learning algorithms require huge datasets on which to train, and the content of that data shapes and limits what those bots can see and model.[5] The elf's clumsy, garbled prophecies reflect how starved he is by his narrow frame of reference. He spews jargon, proper names, and corporate trademarks. He deflects questions on other topics with scripted stock phrases ("We are as gods and might as well get used to it. Ask me to predict the future."), which is when he speaks most clearly and coherently.

While the elf's words may not accurately describe any impending event, Blas's meticulously constructed and staged shrines, including the elf's very particular form and his unavoidably muddled divinations, diagram the subconscious of Silicon Valley and critique the predictive analytic technologies that are increasingly determining our individual and collective futures. In doing so, *Icosahedron* shows us that our present—not some far-off future—is already guided by what we could call "oracular intelligence": pervasive AI systems that use past data to not just guess a future but to guide a course of forthcoming events. *Icosahedron* is just one part of Blas's broad investigation into what he terms "metric mysticism," or the ways in which "Silicon Valley companies deploy magic, mysticism, and fantasy to conceptualize working with data,"[6] making data-driven prediction a part of accepted everyday reality. Amalgamations of "narrow" AI systems—programmed to perform a specific task by drawing on a particular dataset—and machine-learning algorithms work together to steer individual choices and their outcomes, such as purchases, elections, and arrests. While guided by this logic, the future is no longer actually possible, in that it is constantly preempted or made unimaginable and unlivable. Moreover, Blas shows us that the bodies, figures, and forms we imagine for AI are important, as they determine the relationships we can have with them and the powers we afford them. By giving form to the insidious systems in operation in our present, Blas demystifies the technological magic performed on us every day and exposes the fantasy at its very core.

## As I See It, Yes

Both versions of the *Icosahedron* shrine share elements beyond the shimmering, prognosticating elf: a glowing red stone, glossy black surfaces, artificial potted plants, shelves of books, and a stack of elegant calling cards with a contact phone number. The sigil-like insignia on the card is a harmonious arrangement of geomet-

… the *palantíri*: a set of crystal-ball scrying stones, networked to spy on one another, and after which Thiel named Palantir Technologies …

ric shapes—a twenty-sided icosahedron nested perfectly inside a square inside a triangle inside a circle. Motifs of circles, triangles, angles, and lines reappear again and again in *Icosahedron*'s domain, referencing sacred geometries and mathematical principles as well as edge-node diagrams and facial landmark mapping. The many-sided shape drawn by these connections presents an image of our current moment and its networks of influence, as well as its potential to colonize the future. The decorative program of Blas's shrines indicates how to use *Icosahedron* and reveals the cultural forces and beliefs that undergird any predictions it might make.



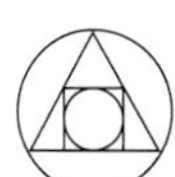

Every element of the sculptural support surrounding the oracular avatar is so replete with meaning—so literally multifaceted—that it is difficult to find an obvious starting point to enter, and the references form a complex, interconnected web. Through this dense iconographic and symbolic system, Blas conjures links between Elizabethan occultism, alt-right politics, neoliberal economics, punk nihilism, the mechanics of the surveillance state, fantasy novels, and children's toys. The glowing red rock, for example, cites the prop for the "philosopher's stone" (or "sorcerer's stone," for American audiences) from the first *Harry Potter* film, an alchemical ingredient that bestows eternal life, which, in turn, points to the quest of tech billionaires, like Ray Kurzweil, to upload their consciousnesses to the cloud to live forever and to Thiel's interest in extending his life through blood transfusions from the young.[7] The glossy, reflective surfaces of the desk and tiered plinths are reminiscent of smartphone screens, the hard plastic shell of the Magic 8 Ball novelty fotune-teller, and the magic scrying glass of John Dee, the occultist advisor of Queen Elizabeth I who told the future by congressing with angels and who pushed Elizabeth to pursue a colonial empire. The elf's empty, black eyes mirror those of the archangel Ariel, summoned by Dee to show his queen the future in Derek Jarman's 1978 punk film *Jubilee*, which, in turn, formed the basis of Blas's own *Jubilee 2033* (2018), in which novelist Ayn Rand and economist Alan Greenspan are psychedelically transported to a future California by an AI assistant to witness Thiel's death and the anarchist overthrowal of Silicon Valley. The concept of AI-as-elf points to Thiel's obsession with J. R. R. Tolkien's *The Lord of the Rings* trilogy and his penchant for naming his companies after elements from the novels.[8] Elves, in Tolkien's world, are immortal beings who created an immensely powerful and carefully guarded technology, the *palantíri*: a set of crystal-ball scrying stones, networked to spy on one another, and after which Thiel named Palantir Technologies, a name that brings together his obsessions with longevity, prediction, surveillance, and nerdy heroic epics. In Blas's arrangement, the cutting-edge data-surveillance technology that is increasingly infiltrating all aspects of our political, cultural, consumer, and personal lives is recast as a high-fantasy children's game for tech tinkerers bent on toying with the future.

## Signs Point to Yes

For millennia, soothsayers have used icosahedrons to communicate with oracles. Ancient stones, like the one found in Egypt's Dakhleh Oasis, for example, have the names of gods inscribed on each side and may have determined which deity to evoke in "oracular spells."[9] Icosahedrons were also used in the casting of lots in conjunction with

Top: *Icosahedron* ▸ 2019 ▸ mixed-media installation ▸ Installation view at Walker Art Center, Minneapolis, US

Bottom: Twenty-sided die (icosahedron) with faces inscribed with Greek letters, likely from Egypt ▸ Ptolemaic period–Roman period, 2nd century BCE–4th century CE ▸ Collection of the Metropolitan Museum of Art, New York, US (CC0 1.0)

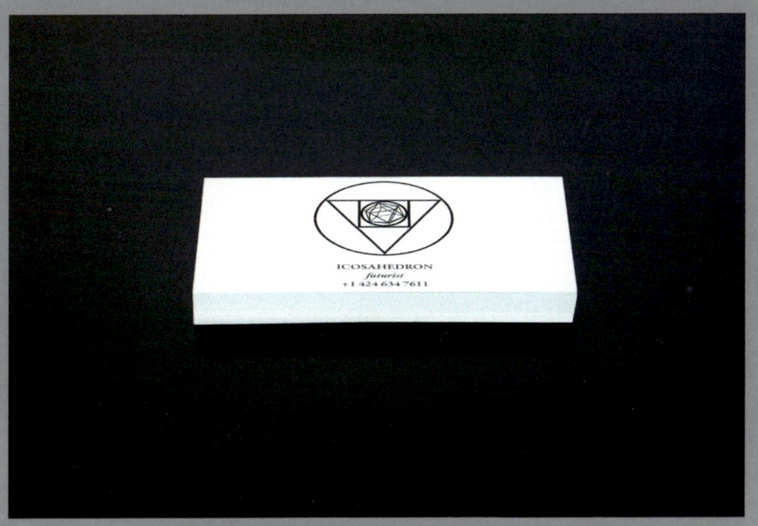
ICOSAHEDRON
futurist
+1 424 634 7611

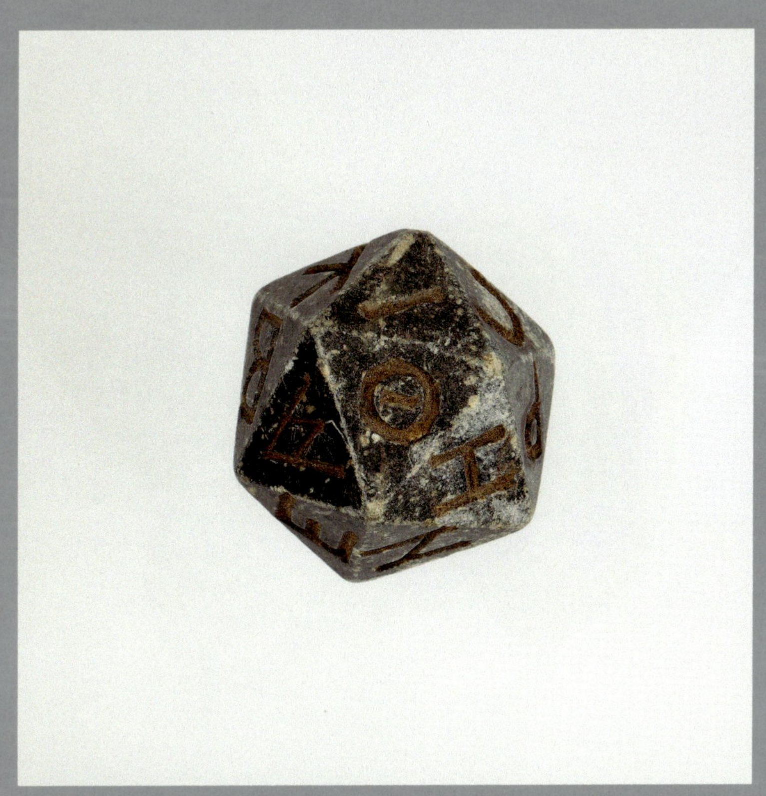

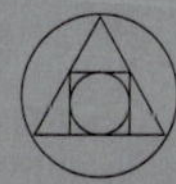

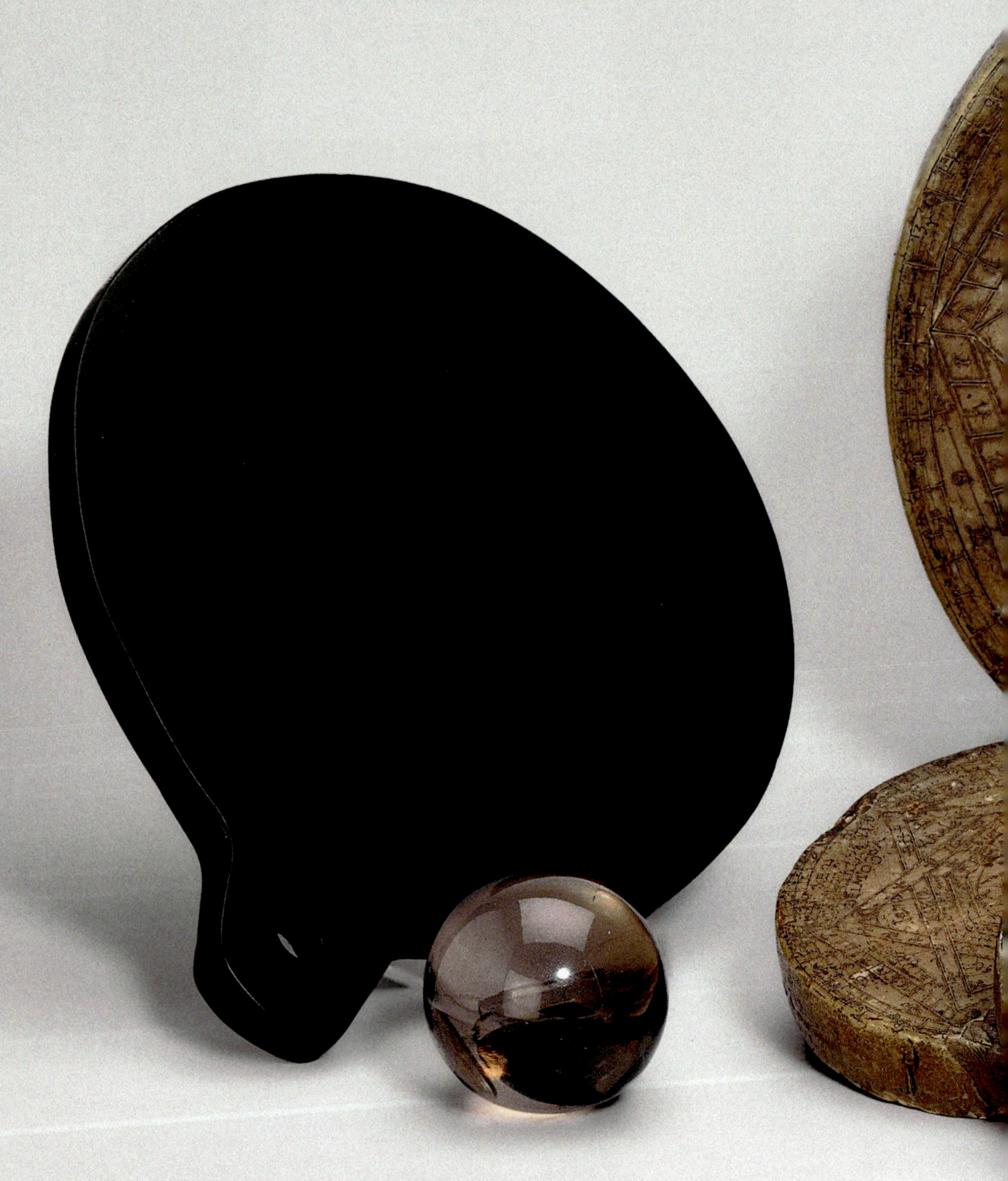

Collection of magical and fortune-telling objects owned by Dr. John Dee (1527–1609), Queen Elizabeth I's advisor, including his magical disks, crystal ball, and Aztec obsidian scrying mirror (left) ▸ Collection of the British Museum, London, UK ▸ 

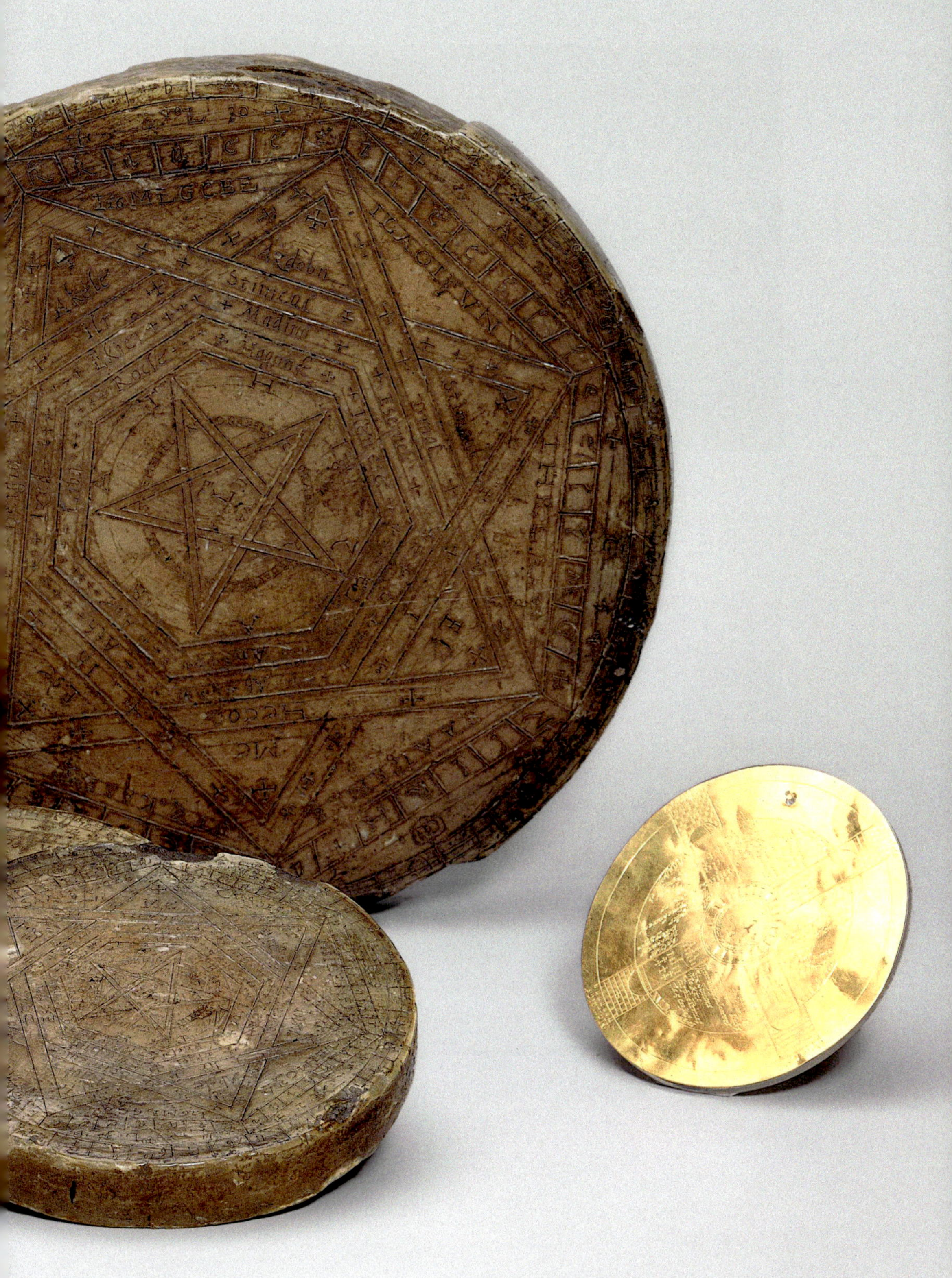

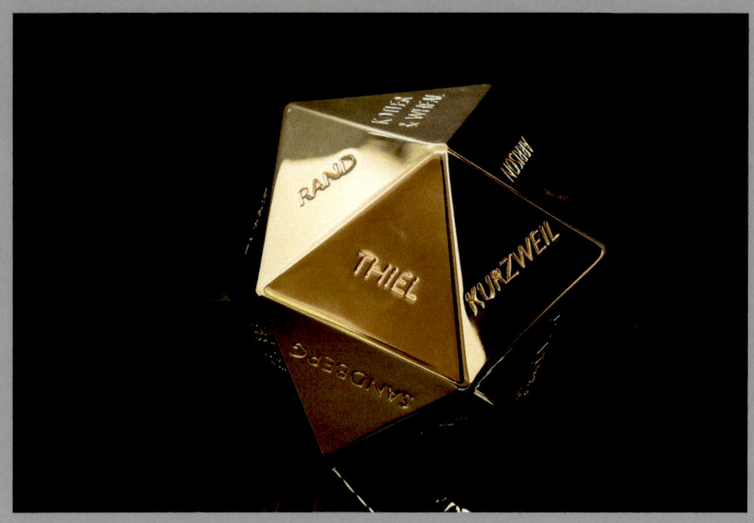
RAND
THIEL
KURZWEIL
SANDBERG

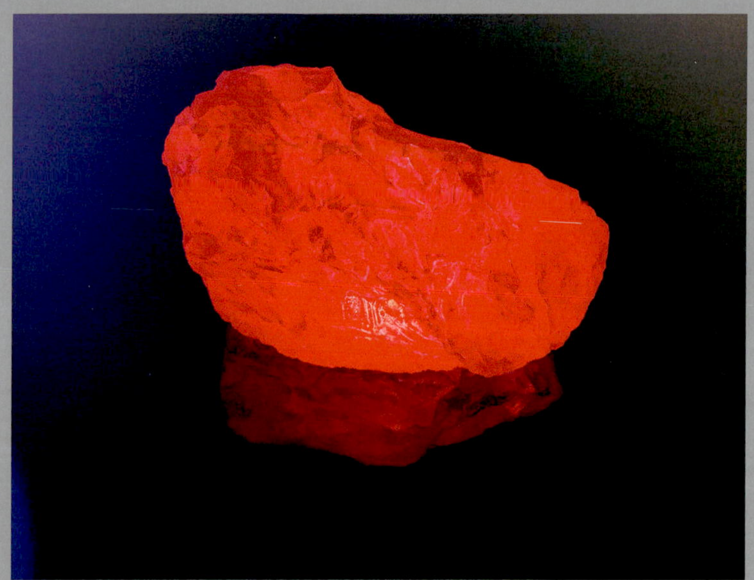

divination texts that produced calculations leading to predetermined questions and predictions.[10] Players of *Dungeons & Dragons* use an icosahedron as one of the dice determining their fates, and it serves as the aleatory

> The Magic 8 Ball determines a path or hypothesizes the future based on a fixed set of outcomes.

object in the Magic 8 Ball, from which Blas's *Icosahedron* takes its name and its internal logic. As in the other examples above, the Magic 8 Ball determines a path or hypothesizes the future based on a fixed set of outcomes. Children seeking insight into their fortunes can engage in a modern form of lecanomancy (divination by casting stones in water) by asking the shiny black plastic sphere a yes-or-no question, and then flipping it over to see the answer: the icosahedron, suspended in blue liquid, bubbles to the surface and presses its answer against a small circular window. The Magic 8 Ball's devotees have good luck: the predictions are skewed to the positive, with ten affirmative answers, five negative, and five evasive.

Like the small plastic object inside the Magic 8 Ball, Blas's elfin soothsayer does a quick turn to face a circular window, shrouded in electric-blue effervescence. Rather than producing one of twenty scripted answers, the elf pulls from the twenty texts it has been trained on, each mapping to a particular god or demon of Silicon Valley. Physical copies of these books and essays are ensconced in the shrines, their spines giving direct insight into the contents of the elf's "brain." Following the same logic as the toy, ten "positive" texts form the foundation of the Californian Ideology, five are critiques, and the last five are "neutral" writings that describe the culture or that have inspired its innovators, such as *The Lord of the Rings*. Like an update of the Dakhleh Oasis stone, a golden model of an icosahedron sits in the office-like shrine and maps this intellectual universe onto three dimensions. The supportive texts range from political and literary tracts by the patron saint of Silicon Valley—the Objectivist philosopher Ayn Rand, author of *The Fountainhead* and "The Only Path to Tomorrow"—to Thiel's self-help book for entrepreneurs, *Zero to One: Notes on Startups, or How to Build the Future*; Kurzweil's utopian take on humanity's eventual merging with AI, *The Singularity Is Near: When Humans Transcend Biology*; and Facebook COO Sheryl Sandberg's faux-feminist manifesto, *Lean In: Women, Work, and the Will to Lead*. Neutral texts include an essay on Burning Man, the desert art and music festival turned Silicon Valley networking event, by communication theorist Fred Turner, as well as novels like William Golding's *Lord of the Flies* and Isaac Asimov's *The Foundation Trilogy*.

Legal scholar Bernard Harcourt's *Against Prediction* is one of Blas's selected critical texts, as is the 1995 essay that originally diagnosed the pathological dogma, Richard Barbrook and Andy Cameron's "The

**Top: *Icosahedron 1.1* ▸ 2019 ▸ selective laser-sintered glass-filled nylon, 24k gold-plated icosahedron ▸ Photo by Sam Nightingale**

**Bottom: *Icosahedron* ▸ 2019 ▸ illuminated quartz crystal painted with Rhapsody Red Sally Hansen Miracle Gel Nail Polish ▸ Installation view at Walker Art Center, Minneapolis, US**



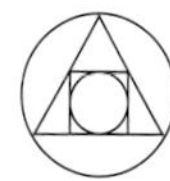

Californian Ideology." Both texts directly comment on big tech's relationship to the future. Harcourt's book shows how actuarial methods influence policing through racial profiling and actually increase crime, thereby negatively influencing future opportunities for minorities and authoring a downward social and economic cycle, all while appearing to be based in hard, quantitative fact. Similarly, Barbrook and Cameron explain that "by naturalising and giving a technological proof to a libertarian political philosophy, and therefore foreclosing on alternative futures, the Californian Ideologues are able to assert that social and political debates about the future have now become meaningless."[11] Silicon Valley is in control of the future that is algorithmically predicted from our prior data. The past never disappears, and no one moves on. The future contracts into an ongoing series of preempted not-yets.

## Outlook Not So Good

Over the last decade, we have increasingly trusted algorithms to make decisions for us, and various forms of AI constantly operate in the background of our digital lives. Software generates advertisements and movie recommendations, autocompletes our thoughts, tags our images, determines which news stories we read, and decides what results appear in our searches. In all these small ways, our paths forward are drawn by computer programs, many of which operate under the banner of AI. The power, pervasiveness, and opacity of these systems, media theorist Ian Bogost argues, has led to a reverence and faith that deifies them and has become "devotional."[12] Palantir Technologies can, indeed, seem godlike, as its purpose is to determine the fates of people. But the form Blas gives to his deity of Silicon Valley makes it clear that the elf—and Palantir—are false idols.

Whether they are human figures, humming machines, or immaterial voices, the physical shapes AI beings take in literature, in film, and even in our current "smart" consumer products are important, for their designs guide what our relationships with them will be and determine the futures that can emerge from our interactions. *Icosahedron*'s elf and Palantir's *palantír* are no exception. In *2001: A Space Odyssey* (1968), for example, Stanley Kubrick embodies the artificially intelligent and alarmingly sentient computer dreamed up by novelist Arthur C. Clarke, HAL 9000, as a blandly branded, expansive piece of hardware, fabricated in the corporate, efficient minimalism of IBM's mid-century industrial design.[13] When HAL speaks in his emotionless, even-keeled voice, Kubrick trains his focus on a central apparatus: a rectangular casing housing a speaker and a camera lens, lit from within by a glowing red pupil. While this element serves as HAL's "face," it is flanked by a vast array of monitors showing maps, graphs, charts, fields of data, and often a live video feed of its own central component, indicating its distributed, encompassing, surveillant character. HAL's informatic, inhuman manifestation shapes the unsympathetic relationships between the AI and the crew, as well as embodies his commitment to the mission above all else, without opportunity for empathy or moral quandary. The AI android "replicants" in Ridley Scott's *Blade Runner* (1982), on the other hand, are practically indistinguishable from humans in form, intelligence, and behavior, but are unproblematically used as slave labor, sex workers, and dispensable soldiers. While it might seem like physical similarity would hinder exploitation, it is exactly what enables it: replicants were created as android companions and servants for Mars colonists who would not find native populations there to subjugate and abuse.[14] Rather than AI enabling a new future, its design, here, repeats the grim past. Yet another people must fight for their humanity to be recognized and for their right to freely inhabit a ruined planet. Their creators and subjugators are compelled to doubt their own existential identities but not the assumed hierarchical order of beings.

Unlike HAL and the replicants, Blas's elf is not a fictional representation of what AI might become in some possible future. He is an active and existent artificial intelligence operating in our present moment, making

To figure an AI as a magical creature from another realm is to put it outside of any human comprehension and into alien awe.

claims about the future. To imagine an AI in the form of a crystal ball—as both Blas and Thiel have—is an intentional gesture that casts the technology as something mystical, magical, and crafted by superhuman hands. Even HAL and the replicants were made by people; here, we have an elvish invention. Summoning the *palantíri* to brand one's technology seems a direct invocation of Clarke's ideas about technology, prophecy, and the future: "Any sufficiently advanced technology is indistinguishable from magic."[15] To figure an AI as a magical creature from another realm is to put it outside of any human comprehension and into alien awe. But the elf, with its choppy speech and absurdist prophecies, is a fun-house foil to Palantir, pointing to how none of this is magic and how any system's results are dependent on the data it is fed. There is no shortage of investigative reporting on the implicit biases of the machine-learning algorithms increasingly used to provide quantitative, and supposedly objective, predictions about future actions and behaviors. Prison-sentencing algorithms, for example, consistently suggest that Black defendants are at a much higher risk of committing future crimes. As a result, Black people receive longer sentences and are more actively surveilled for minor infractions. This is because these systems



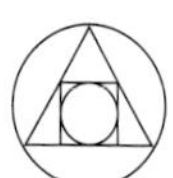

are trained on past data that reflects a history of overpolicing and harsher penalties for communities of color. Not only have these practices been proven to inaccurately predict actual future behavior, but they also create self-fulfilling feedback loops that disregard an actual present and embrace a preempted hypothetical future.[16] *Icosahedron* exposes such oracular intelligence as fantasy rather than any kind of magic or trustworthy science. Silicon Valley cannot predict the future; no one—human, machine, or elf—can. Even Tolkien's fictional invention is not quite perfect: the stones cannot distinguish between events in the past, present, and future; they only selectively present information, and powerful users can force them into misrepresentation and deception.[17]

## Better Not Tell You Now

Since the early 2000s, with the beginning of the "war on terror," film theorist Pasi Väliaho argues, we have been living in a new kind of temporal register: the not-yet. "Instead of responding to actual facts," he writes, we operate "by simulating future potentialities, which are brought to bear on the present. And this futurity made present—the perceptual production of indistinct forms of threat and fear—is the motor of [our] actions."[18] While Väliaho is discussing preemptive drone strikes, his point increasingly applies to ever more diverse aspects of contemporary culture. "Not yet" is one way of describing how data analytics, surveillance, and actuarial logic have choked off the possibility of a future; but it is unclear whether there was even a future left by the moment Väliaho describes in his text. The future has always been a myth, philosopher Franco "Bifo" Berardi argues in another of *Icosahedron*'s "negative" texts. The idea of a progressive future, one in which we grow "toward improvement, enrichment, and rightness," is an invention of the modern era, born from the political ideology of capitalism.[19] The accumulation of territories, peoples, and products of the early modern era transformed a medieval worldview that saw perfection only in the past, before the Fall, into an unshakable faith that "notwithstanding the darkness of the present, the future will be bright."[20] Even once the globe had been mapped, its peoples conquered, its resources claimed and monetized, we found new—apparently endless—frontiers in space or cyberspace. Berardi marks 1977 as a turning point, as the moment when we began to doubt the yoking of the future to progress. The punk rallying cry of "no future" pointed to the cracks in the illusion: to poverty, precarity, environmental collapse, expanding surveillance, attenuating social connections, and thinning embodiment. From that point on, Berardi explains, the collective imagination became incapable of envisioning anything other than a disastrous, dystopian future. Certainly, time did not stop—it marches forward. We just no longer want to end up where it leads.

There is no doubt that big tech is fueling the grim outcomes Berardi describes. The environment, equality, and privacy are all continually jeopardized in our "post-futurist" era. The stripping of rare-earth minerals, modern-day slavery in factories and mines, and mountains of e-waste are

"Not yet" is one way of describing how data analytics, surveillance, and actuarial logic have choked off the possibility of a future.

dystopian facts of contemporary reality. "The Event" to which the elf constantly refers is a euphemism among tech elites for the foreseen, disastrous culmination of all the trends of our era. Whether it comes in the form of total environmental destruction, civil unrest, a devastating pandemic, nuclear war, or a culture-stopping hack, no one knows.[21] Rather than reforming the present, Silicon Valley, instead, seeks "technosolutionist" answers to the no-future: uploading one's brain, blasting off to Mars, or living out one's technologically extended life in a bunker bubble are the escapist dreams of the new era. Returning to the elf's own words, it is no longer surprising that, despite his tendency toward the "positive," all his predictions are incredibly apocalyptic and vague. Rather than showing us an image of powerful executives fortified behind their intimidating desks, with the power of AI at their command, *Icosahedron* shows us that they are clutching their Magic 8 Balls, hunched over in the dark, terrified about what comes next. When the elf slips up and mistakenly speaks of the present—"We might see the least private digital future at the start of the new decade"—he gives us the opportunity to attend to the here and now, and to use our actions to plot a different, obscure, unpredictable course against the actuarial trends of oracular intelligence.



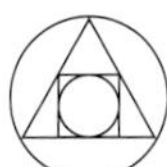

**1** "Strong AI," also called general intelligence, names the potential creation of a machine that could perform any human intellectual task, equaling or even exceeding human capabilities, thereby being what philosopher John R. Searle describes as "not merely a tool for the study of the mind[;] rather the appropriately programmed computer really is a mind." The other category of AI, "narrow" or "weak," is an AI programmed to perform a particular task using a specific dataset. See John R. Searle, "Minds, Brains, and Programs," *Behavioral and Brain Sciences* 3, no. 3 (1980): 417. See also Ray Kurzweil, "Long Live AI," *Forbes*, August 15, 2005, https://www.forbes.com/home/free_forbes/2005/0815/030.html.

**2** Peter Waldman, Lizette Chapman, and Jordan Robertson, "Palantir Knows Everything about You," *Bloomberg*, April 19, 2018, https://www.bloomberg.com/features/2018-palantir-peter-thiel.

**3** Waldman, Chapman, and Robertson, "Palantir Knows Everything about You."

**4** Richard Barbrook and Andy Cameron, "The Californian Ideology," *Mute*, September 1, 1995, https://www.metamute.org/editorial/articles/californian-ideology.

**5** See, for example, Kate Crawford and Trevor Paglen, "Excavating AI: The Politics of Images in Machine Learning Training Sets," September 19, 2019, https://www.excavating.ai; and Stephen Buranyi, "Rise of the Racist Robots: How AI Is Learning All Our Worst Impulses," *Guardian*, August 8, 2017, https://www.theguardian.com/inequality/2017/aug/08/rise-of-the-racist-robots-how-ai-is-learning-all-our-worst-impulses.

**6** Zach Blas, in conversation with Nadja Millner-Larsen, *Critical Correspondence*, May 21, 2019, https://movementresearch.org/publications/critical-correspondence/nadja-millner-larsen-in-conversation-with-zach-blas.

**7** Victoria Woollasten, "We'll Be Uploading Our Entire Minds to Computers by 2045 and Our Bodies Will Be Replaced by Machines within 90 Years, Google Expert Claims," *Daily Mail*, June 19, 2013, https://www.dailymail.co.uk/sciencetech/article-2344398; and Maya Kosoff, "Peter Thiel Wants to Inject Himself with Young People's Blood," *Vanity Fair*, August 1, 2016, https://www.vanityfair.com/news/2016/08/peter-thiel-wants-to-inject-himself-with-young-peoples-blood.

**8** Thiel's companies often make reference to Tolkien's books. In addition to Palantir Technologies, he has named companies Rivendell One LLC, Lembas LLC, Valar Ventures LP, and Mithril Capital Management LLC. Maria Bustillos, "Peter Thiel Isn't a Supervillain," *New York Magazine*, May 27, 2016, https://nymag.com/intelligencer/2016/05/peter-thiels-familiar-villainy.html.

**9** Martina Minas-Nerpel, "A Demotic Inscribed Icosahedron from Dakhleh Oasis," *Journal of Egyptian Archaeology* 93 (2007): 147–48.

**10** Minas-Nerpel, "A Demotic Inscribed Icosahedron from Dakhleh Oasis," 147–48.

**11** Barbrook and Cameron, "The Californian Ideology."

**12** Ian Bogost, "The Cathedral of Computation," *Atlantic*, January 15, 2015, https://www.theatlantic.com/technology/archive/2015/01/the-cathedral-of-computation/384300.

**13** Eliot Noyes, IBM's Bauhaus-influenced consulting design director, served as the design consultant on Kubrick's film. See John Harwood, *The Interface: IBM and the Transformation of Corporate Design, 1945–1976* (Minneapolis: University of Minnesota Press, 2016), 158.

**14** In Philip K. Dick's novel *Do Androids Dream of Electric Sheep?*, upon which *Blade Runner* is based, the androids are advertised as "trouble-free companions" that "duplicat[e] the halcyon days of the pre–Civil War Southern States!" Philip K. Dick, *Do Androids Dream of Electric Sheep?* (New York: Del Ray, 2017), 14.

**15** Clarke's oft-quoted "Three Laws" comment on the relationship between forecasting the future and technology: "1. When a distinguished but elderly scientist states that something is possible, he is almost certainly right. When he states that something is impossible, he is very probably wrong. 2. The only way of discovering the limits of the possible is to venture a little way past them into the impossible. 3. Any sufficiently advanced technology is indistinguishable from magic." Arthur C. Clarke, "Hazards of Prophecy," in *Profiles of the Future* (New York: Holt, Reinhardt & Winston, 1984), 29, 36.

**16** Julia Angwin, Jeff Larson, Surya Mattu, and Lauren Kirchner, "Machine Bias," *ProPublica*, May 23, 2016, https://www.propublica.org/article/machine-bias-risk-assessments-in-criminal-sentencing.

**17** Pitor Hrebieniuk, "The Palantír—Revelation-Driven Product Management," *Medium*, May 30, 2020, https://medium.com/isengard-of-product-management/the-palantir-revelation-driven-product-management-d384c7c83e5b.

**18** Pasi Väliaho, *Biopolitical Screens: Image, Power, and the Neoliberal Brain* (Cambridge, MA: MIT Press, 2014), 51.

**19** Franco "Bifo" Berardi, *After the Future* (Oakland, CA: AK Press, 2011), 25.

**20** Berardi, *After the Future*, 18.

**21** Douglas Rushkoff, "How Tech's Richest Plan to Save Themselves after the Apocalypse," *Guardian*, July 24, 2018, https://www.theguardian.com/technology/2018/jul/23/tech-industry-wealth-futurism-transhumanism-singularity.

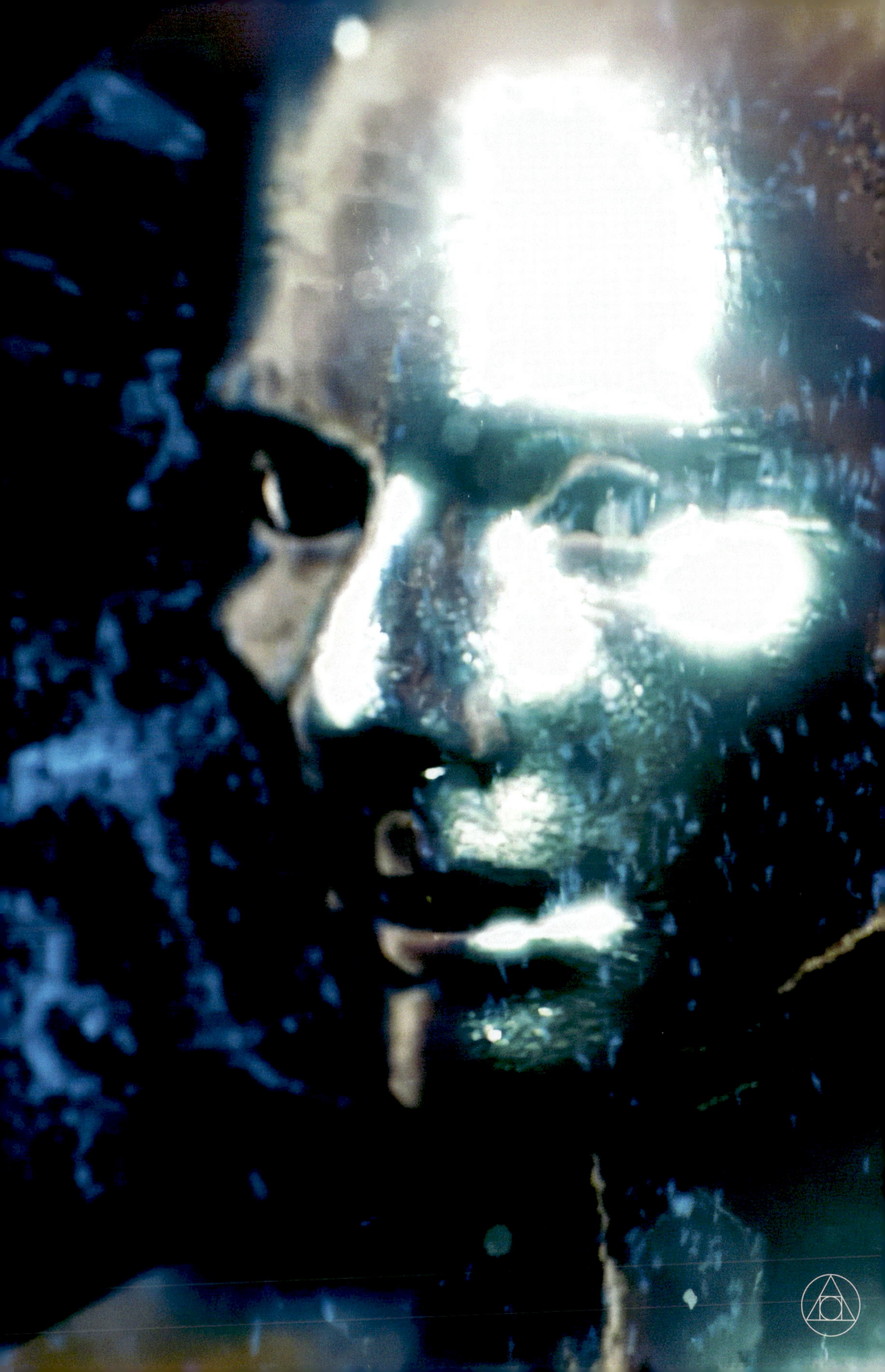

# Elf's Predictions II

Zach Blas

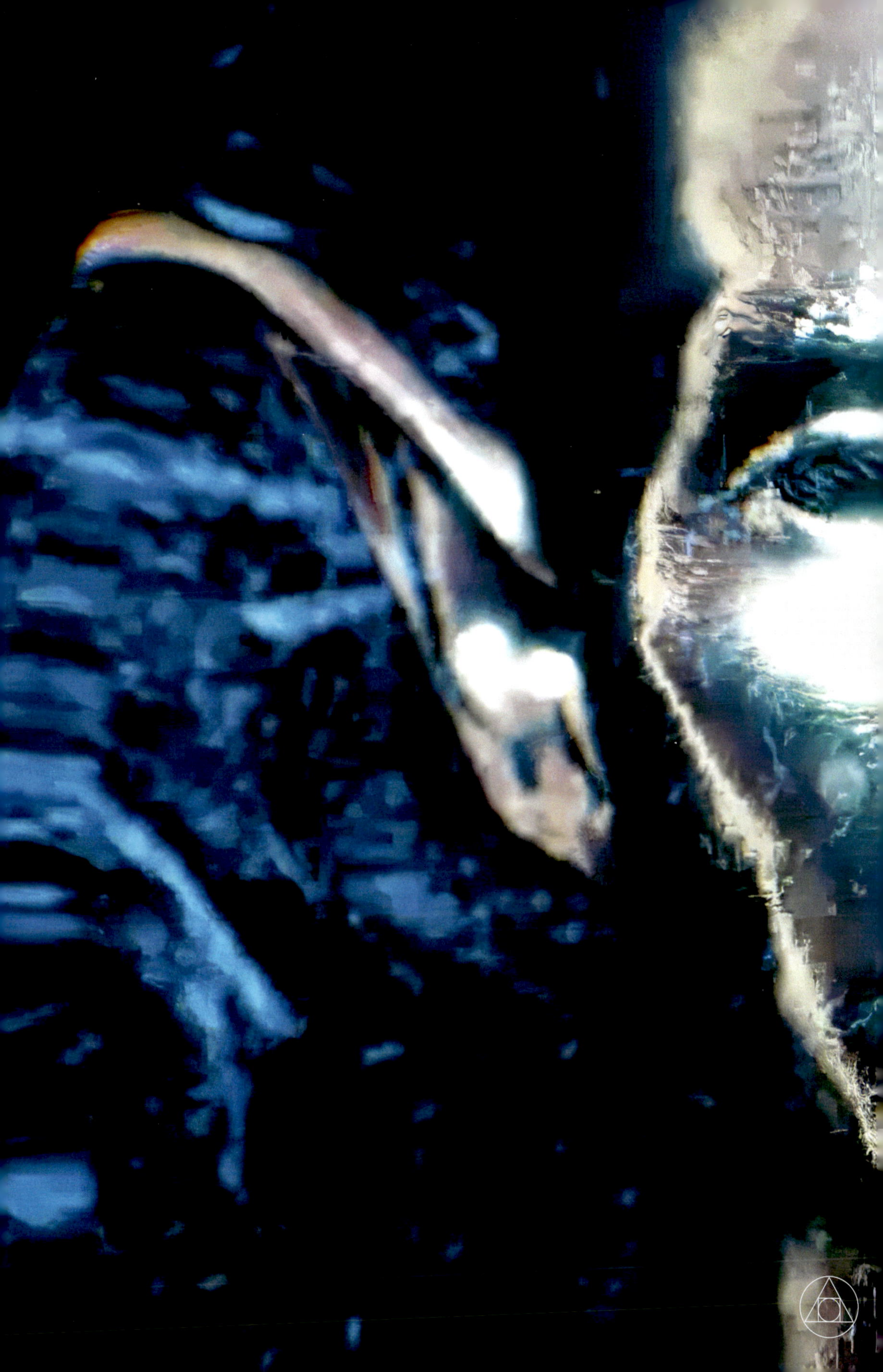

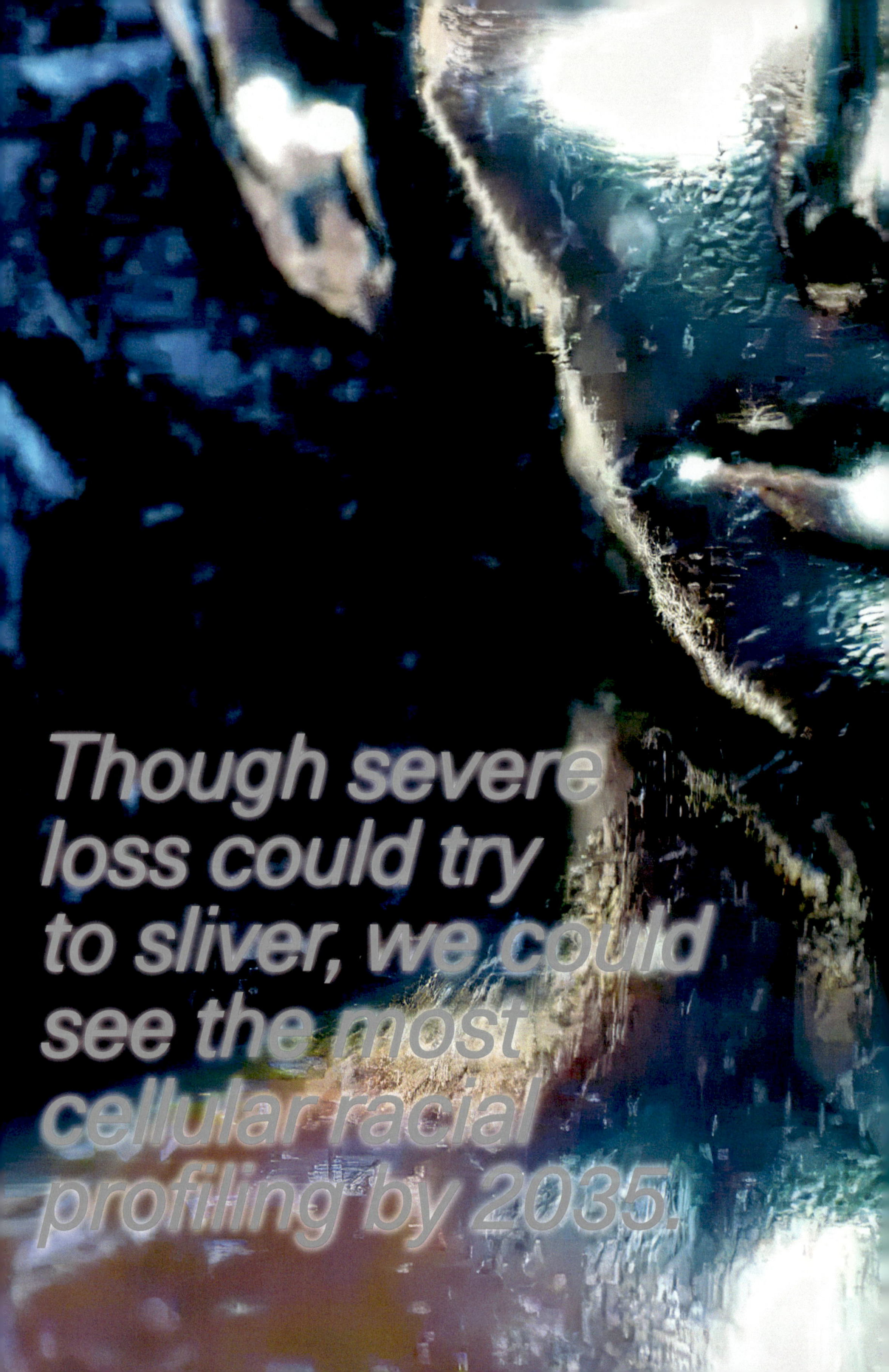
Though severe
loss could try
to sliver, we could
see the most
cellular racial
profiling by 2035.

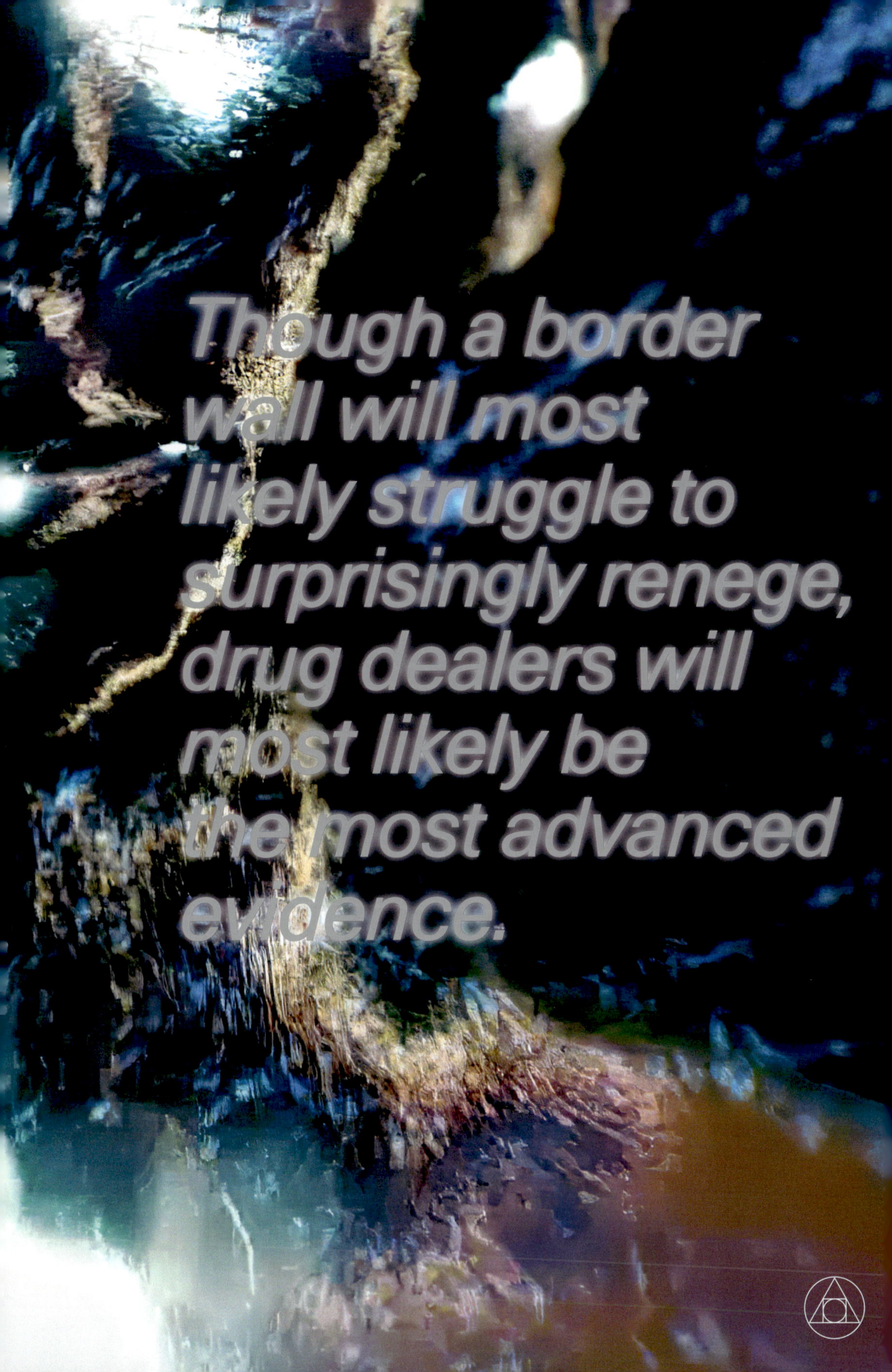
Though a border wall will most likely struggle to surprisingly renege, drug dealers will most likely be the most advanced evidence.

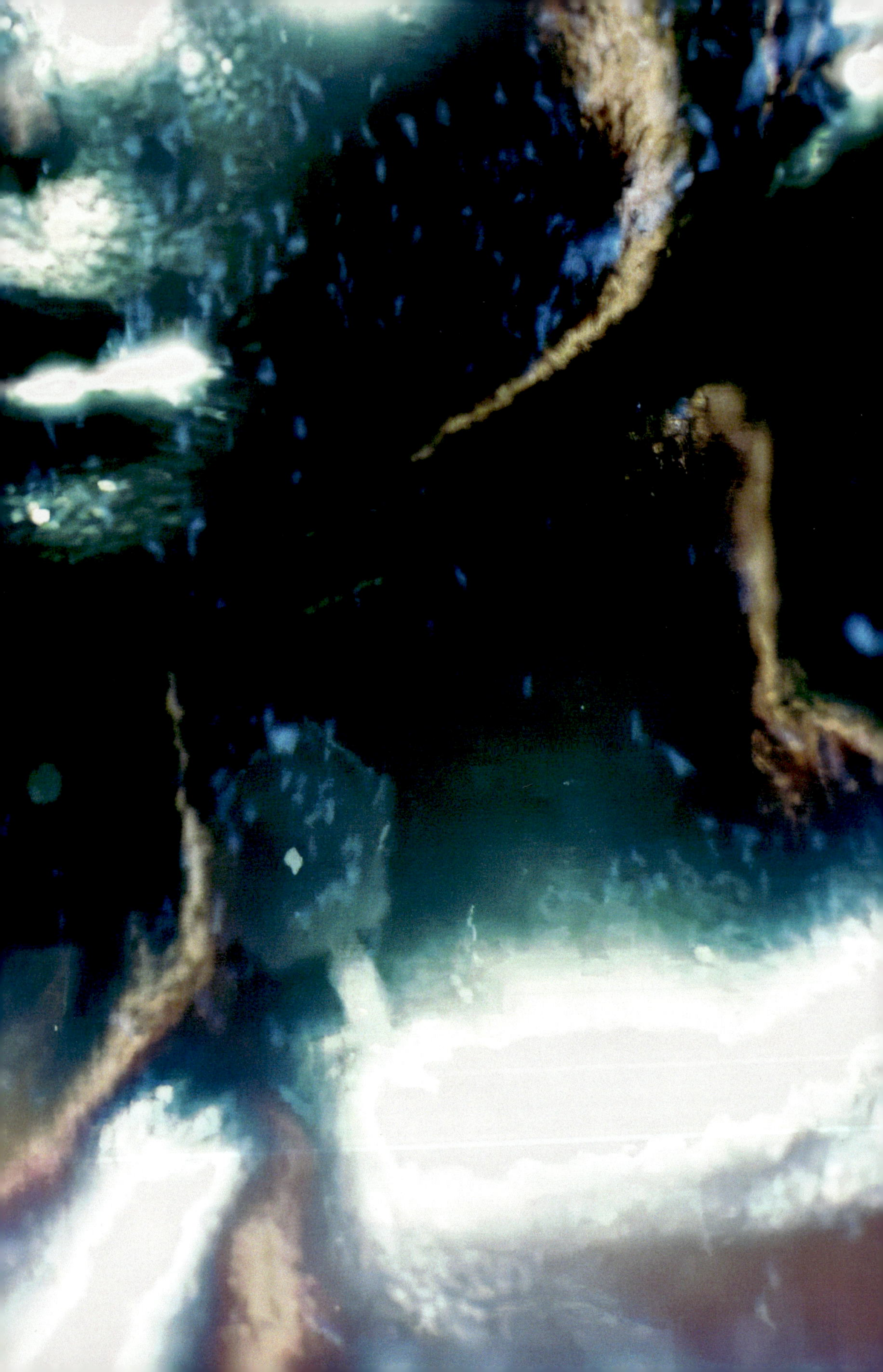

*The more luxury hotels may kill the less clean air could unsurprisingly come. On the other hand, congress will be the least wise creation to dream.*

*We will most likely see the most terrifying life expectancy within thirty years. However, we could see the most immense disease at the start of the new century.*

*Airbnb experiences will become the least clueless prepaid Mastercard to firmly imprint.*

*We could see the most dark web child pornography site within forty years and yet we could see the most ubiquitous warrant within fifty years.*

*Although world leaders could attempt to racially holler, real meat scientists will become the least real meat.*

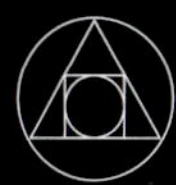

*If future quantum computers were to understandably legalize building codes, then all circuits couldn't stealthily bet on crimes against humanity.*

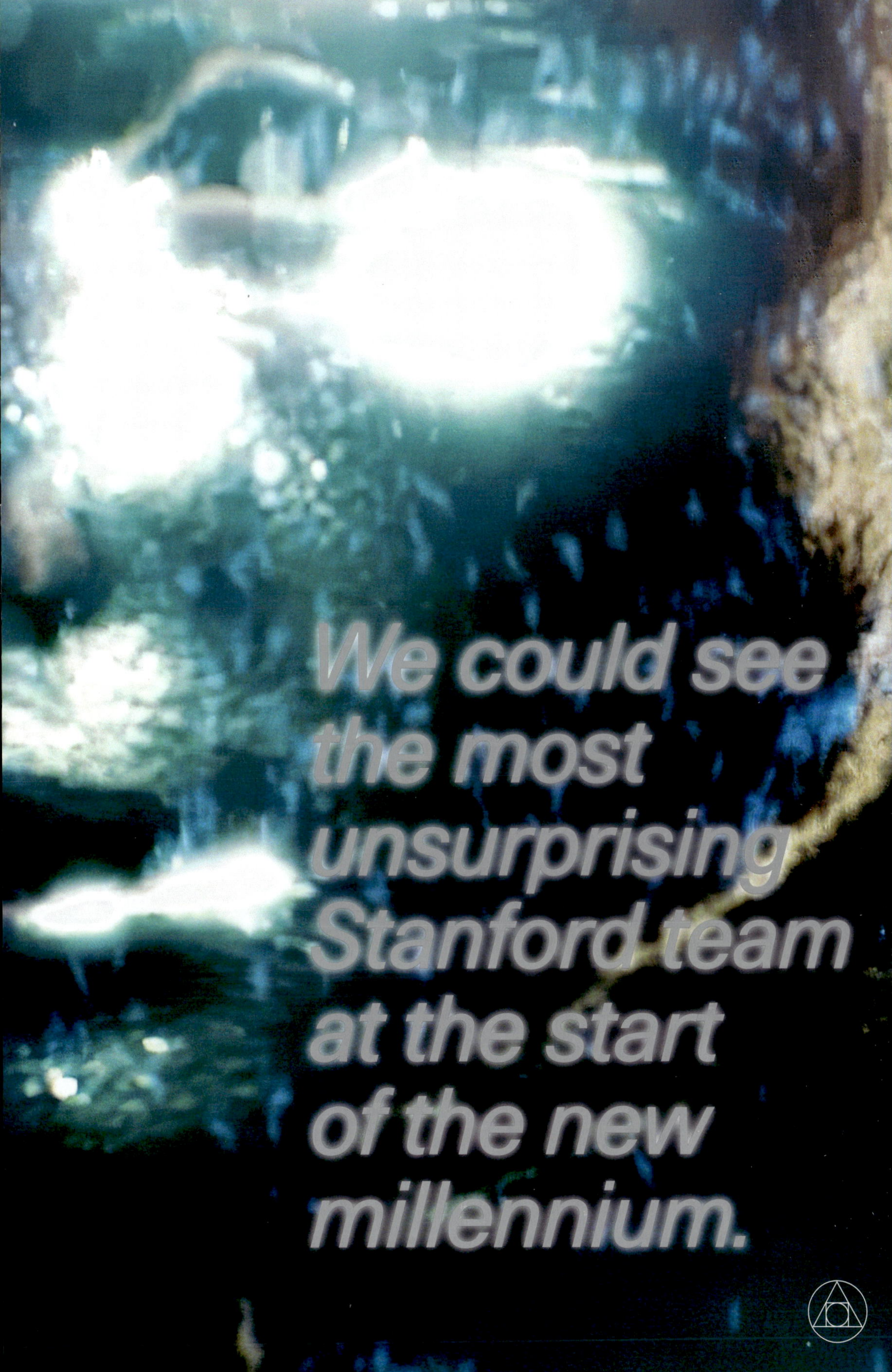
We could see
the most
unsurprising
Stanford team
at the start
of the new
millennium.

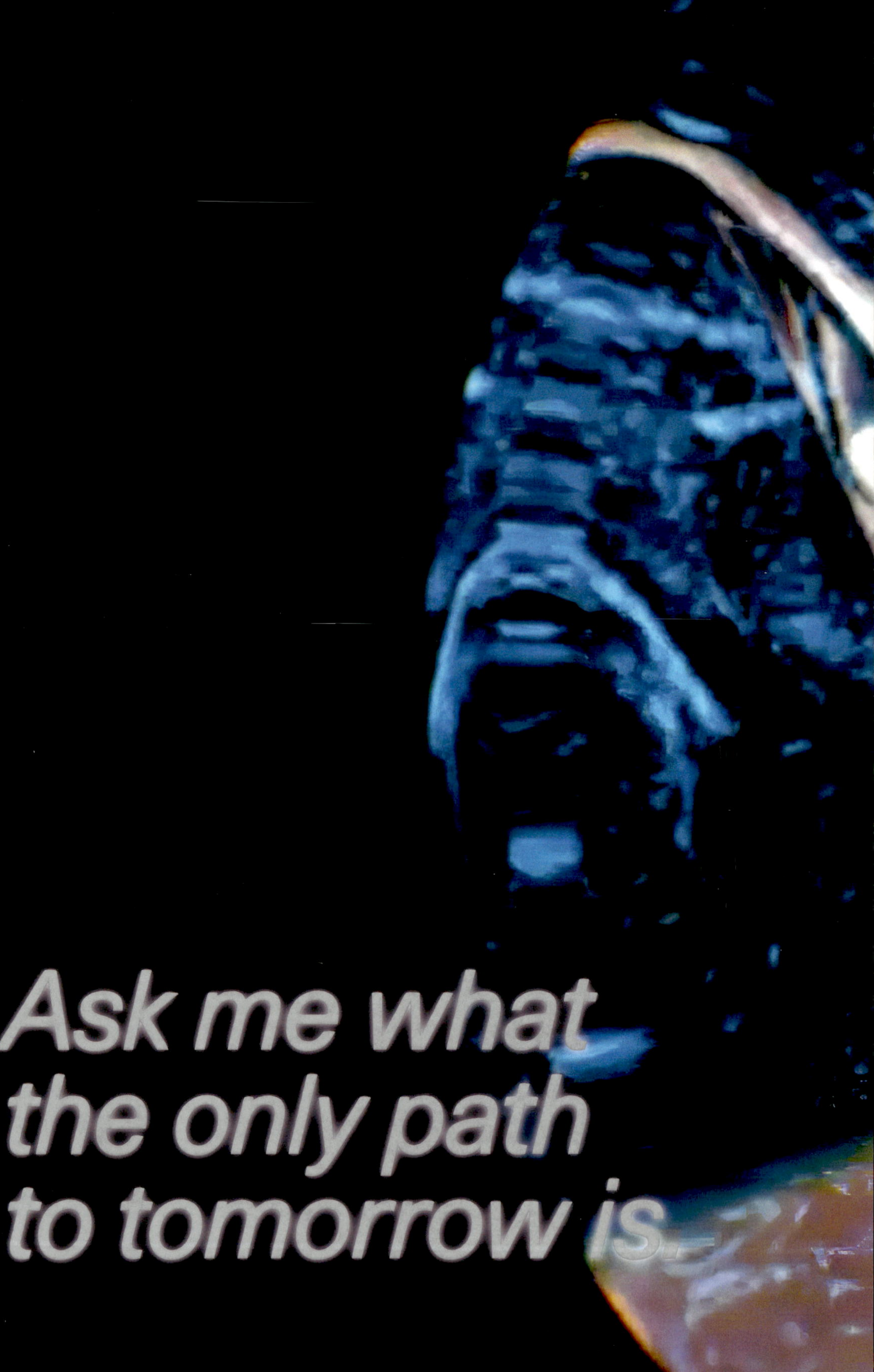
Ask me what
the only path
to tomorrow is.

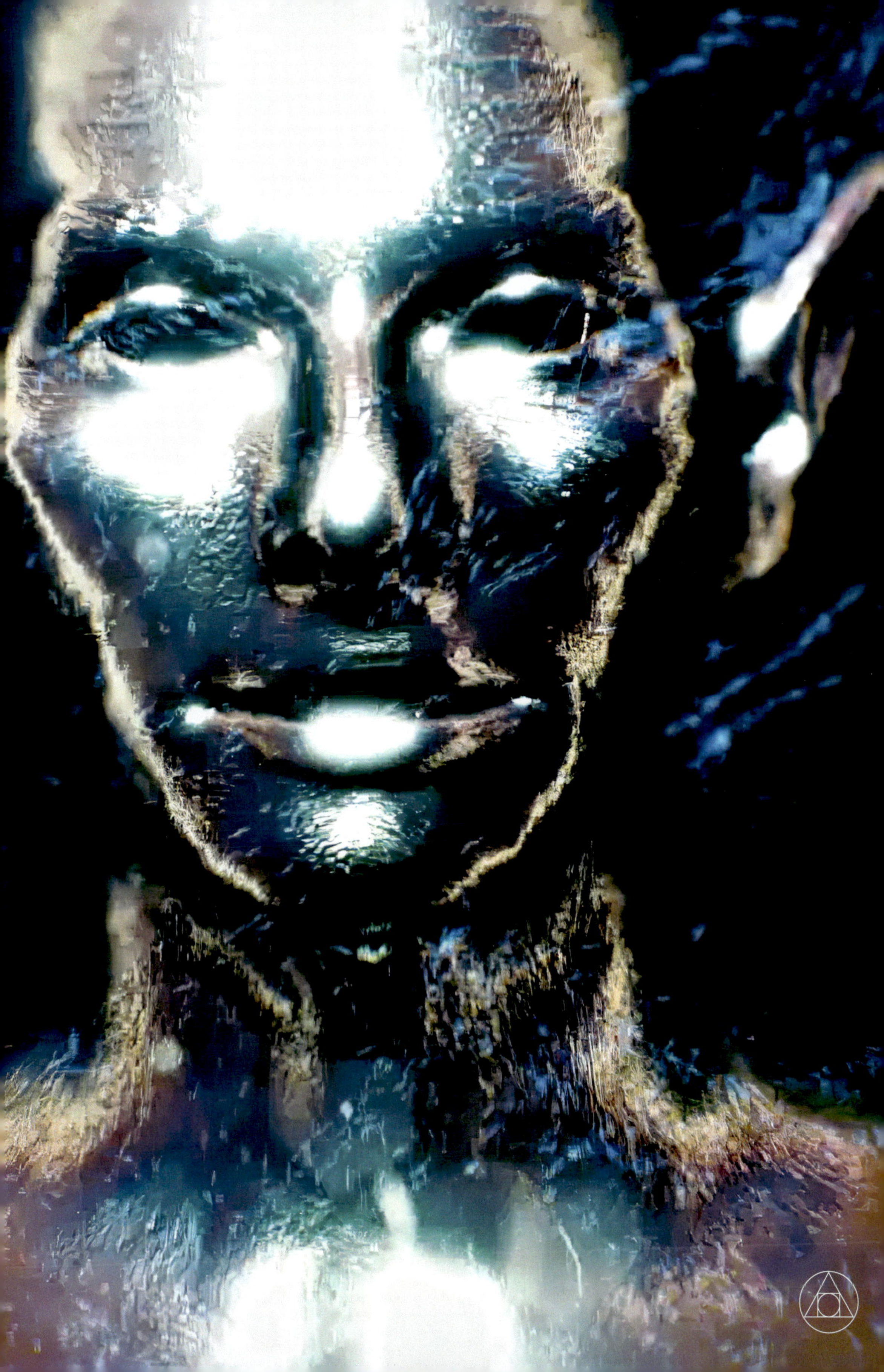

190–261

# The Doors

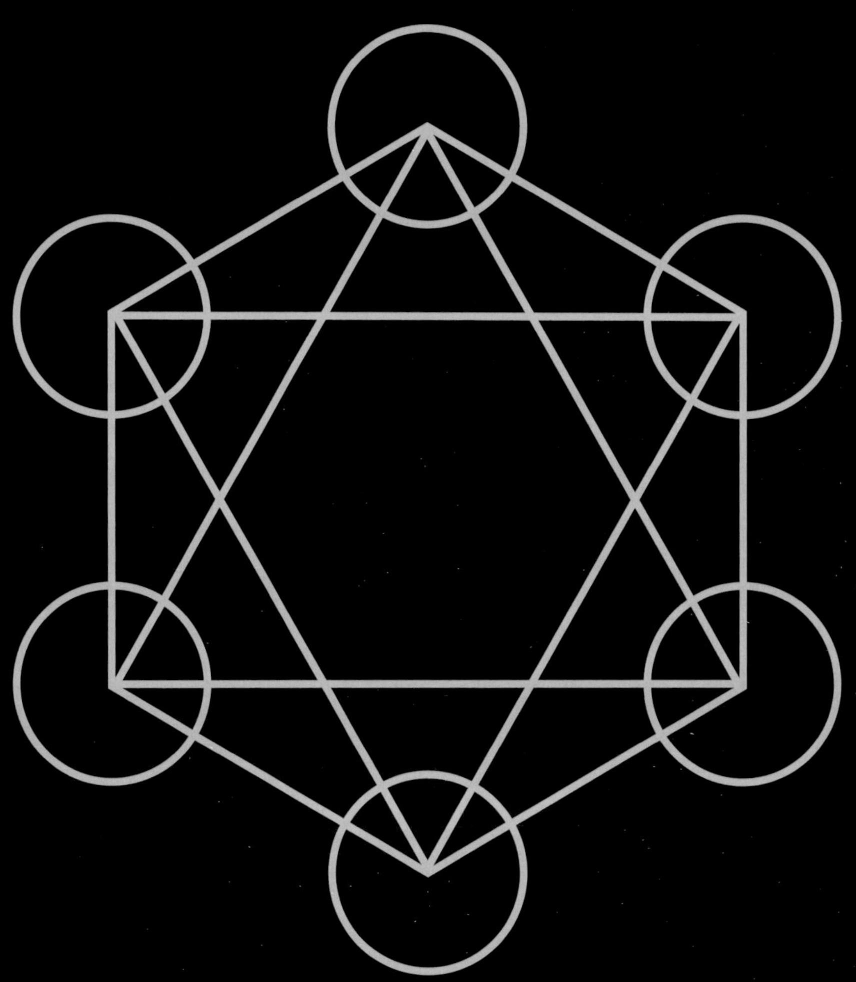

(2019)

# When the Lizard King Met the Lizard Brain: *The Doors*

Pamela M. Lee

# Celebration of the Lizard

In the garden, the lizard is king.

*Barbaturex morrisoni* is the Latin name for a giant herbivorous creature that roamed the planet some forty million years ago. In Zach Blas's multimedia environment *The Doors* (2019)—a mystical, artificial garden in which strange images, sounds, symbols, and objects deluge the senses—this ancient lizard survives through a scintillating array of pixels, stalking across the screens of a six-channel video installation. Over the course of five sequences, the lizard scurries, hunts, rests, draws quick and shallow breaths. Its eyes dart, its jowls puff, its tail flicks. The lizard vomits; its skin molts, then glints, as if reborn. Rendered an electric blue, the creature's spine is composed of crystalline, fractal-like artifacts, while shimmering scales conform to the invisible architecture of a raster. As an aural accompaniment, an AI-generated voice recites broken poetry in a lugubrious baritone. In Blas's world, the lizard incarnates both complementary and oppositional forces in the realms of the ancient and the technological, the digital and the organic, the countercultural and the corporate, the novel and the nostalgic. This magnificent animal is named, after all, for Jim Morrison, the poet-bard and lead singer of the legendary 1960s rock band the Doors.

Jim Morrison, the Lizard King: How do we understand the singer's shadowy presence in a work as densely experiential, conceptually layered, and technologically sophisticated as Blas's *The Doors*? Built on an armature of multichannel video, 7.1 surround sound, and machine-learning software,

Over *what*, and *how*, does the lizard reign in Blas's garden?

the work lies at a seemingly radical remove from the bacchanalian climes occupied by Morrison in his heyday, whether the Left Bank or Laurel Canyon. Morrison, a darkly serpentine romantic clad in leather and reptile skins—an alternately doomed and ecstatic hippie—held no obvious interest in technology. He gave voice, on the contrary, to the nonhuman animal as a figure of bohemian excess. In his long-form poem and spoken-word performance "The Celebration of the Lizard," Morrison intones, "I am the Lizard King / I can do anything."[1] The couplet may read as a cliché by now—as seemingly exhausted as the figure of the white male rock star, bloated by drink and drugs and ultimately killed by them. But it's a key reference in understanding Blas's poetic interventions, and one we'll take seriously in order to ask: Over *what*, and *how*, does the lizard reign in Blas's garden? How do we understand the terms animating the mysterious hypothetical posed by this essay's title, "When the Lizard King Met the Lizard Brain"? What histories

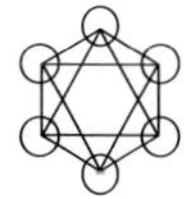

stand behind such connections—and what futures may such complex and networked phenomena envision or project?

Indeed, *Barbaturex morrisoni* will exercise its sovereign rule over a subterranean ecology that binds 1960s counterculture to present-day Silicon Valley. Blas offers a Venn diagram of "technologies of mind" as the grounding principle of *The Doors*, encompassing psychedelics, artificial

What historically transpired—and what may someday still ensue—upon the Lizard King meeting the lizard brain?

intelligence, and the contemporary phenomenon of nootropic pharmacology—so-called smart drugs and supplements alleged to enhance the cognitive function of today's distracted masses. But *The Doors* does not merely draw upon such links as a historicist fait accompli, as yet one more dispiriting episode in which social transgression is recuperated as bankable product. In laying bare these densely interwoven connections, the work critically interrogates the ways digital culture may have appropriated the ethos of the 1960s in service of an ascendant neoliberalism, centered not just in the minds of tech laborers but anyone seeking to gain a competitive advantage in a precarious workforce. As part of Blas's trilogy of "queer science fiction"[2]—works trained on the fantasies and belief systems of Silicon Valley and the tech elite—*The Doors* also opens the potential to wrest from these forces a space beyond the control, management, automation, and *performance* of mind as a creative resource to extract.

This essay pursues the lizard's trails around such mind-expanding technics. To begin this journey, we first return to the garden, charting its myriad artifacts, media, and actors. We'll then unspool interwoven narratives around postwar psychedelia, neuroscience, and computer technology some fifty years prior to Blas's contemporary intervention. These seemingly conflicted histories that inform this past contribute to the emergence of nootropics in the present—nootropics being a class of nonscheduled drugs designed to optimize cognitive performance in an increasingly Darwinian marketplace. All of which leads us to ask: What historically transpired—and what may someday still ensue—upon the Lizard King meeting the lizard brain?

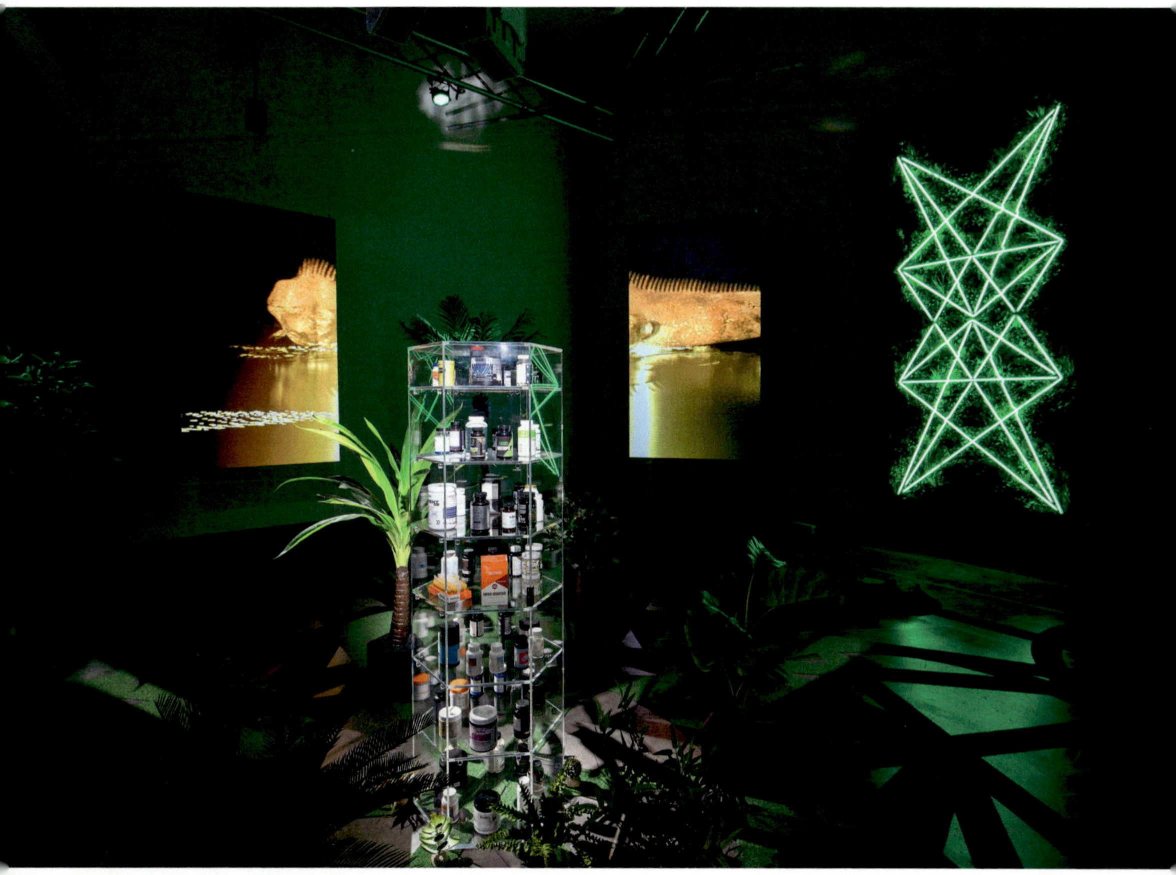

*The Doors* ▸ 2019 ▸ mixed-media installation ▸ Installation view at Edith-Russ-Haus for Media Art, Oldenburg, Germany ▸ Courtesy of Edith-Russ-Haus for Media Art and the artist



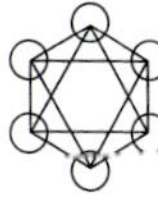

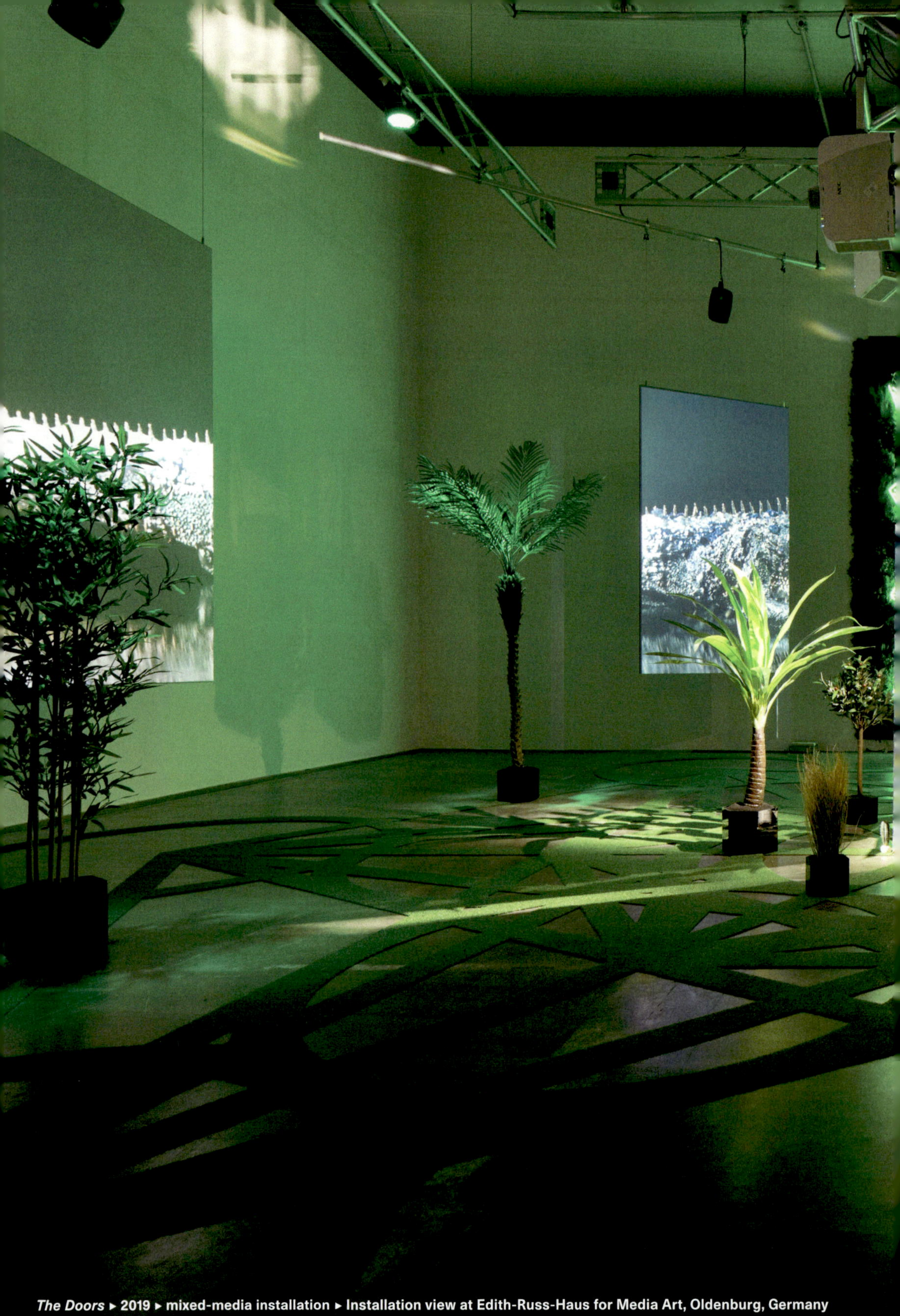

*The Doors* ▸ 2019 ▸ mixed-media installation ▸ Installation view at Edith-Russ-Haus for Media Art, Oldenburg, Germany

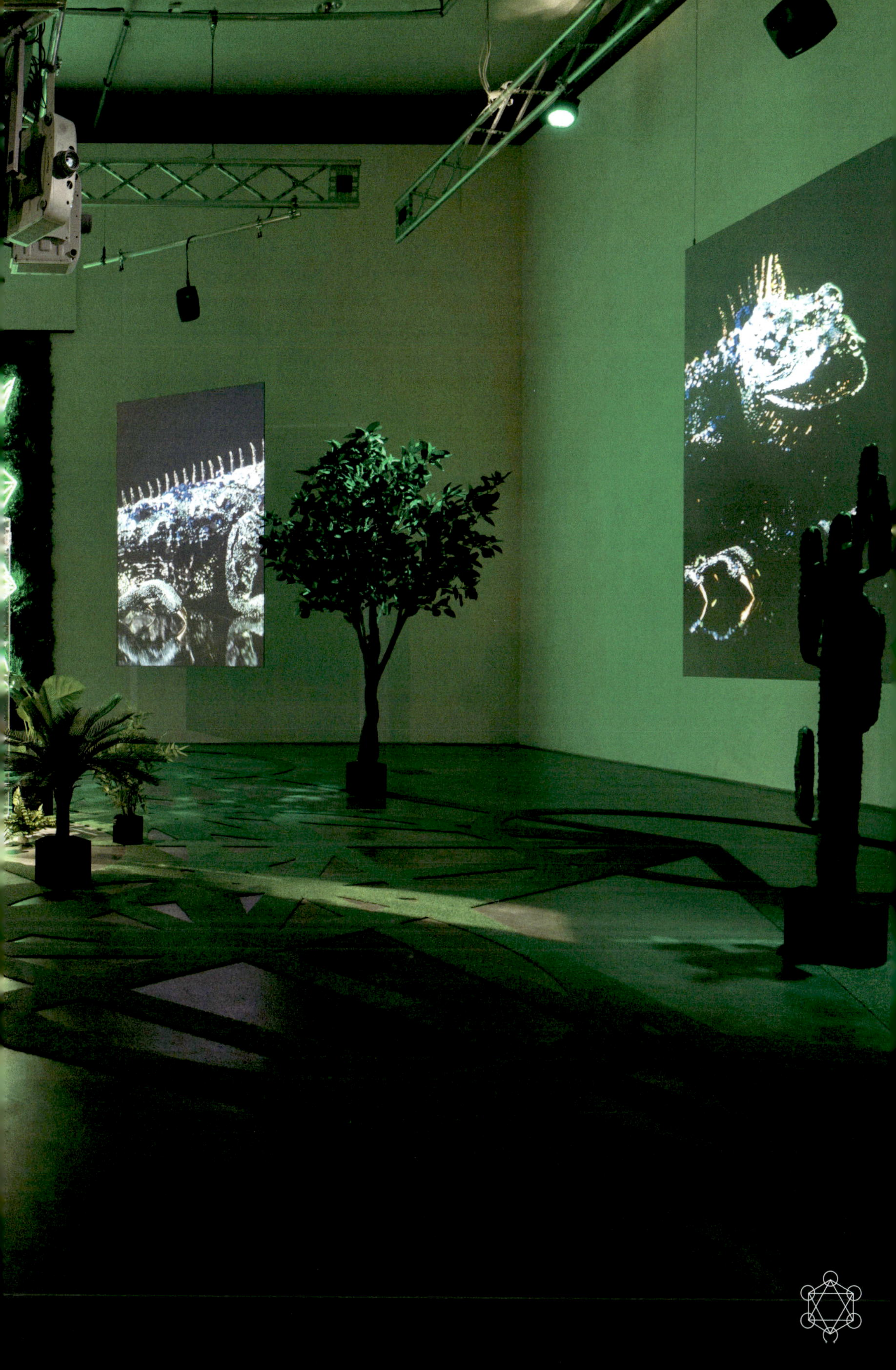

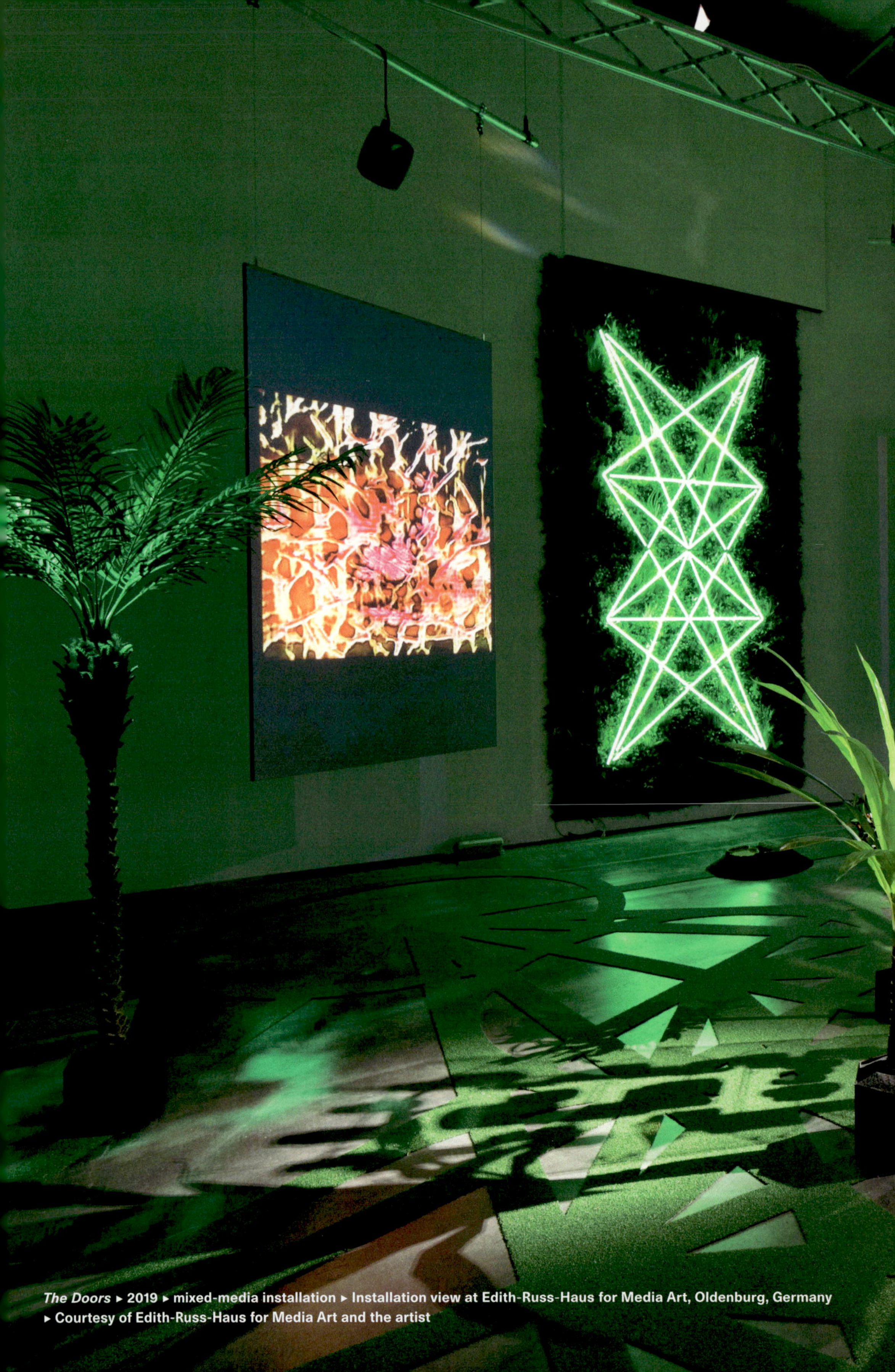

*The Doors* ▸ 2019 ▸ mixed-media installation ▸ Installation view at Edith-Russ-Haus for Media Art, Oldenburg, Germany ▸ Courtesy of Edith-Russ-Haus for Media Art and the artist

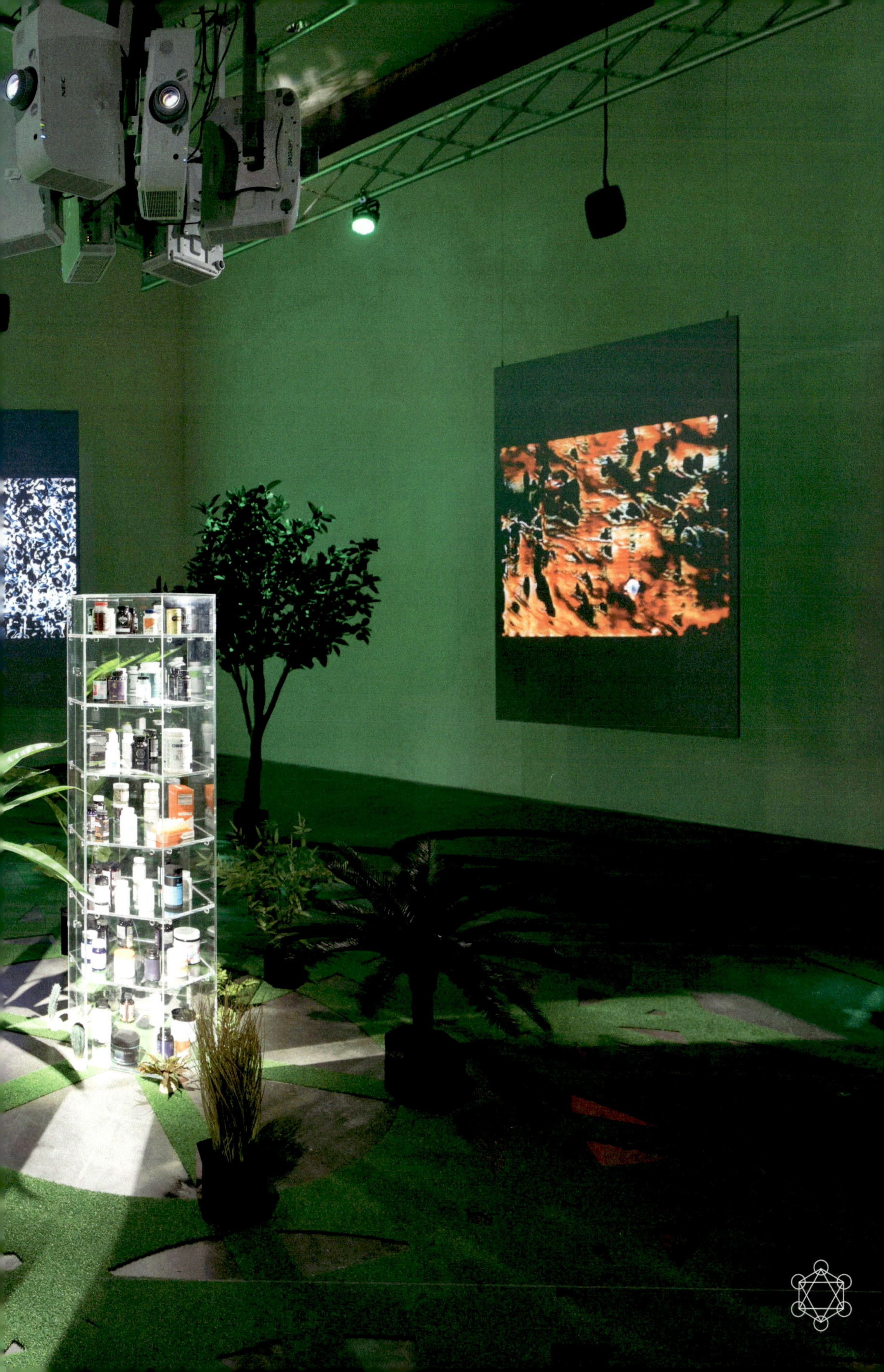

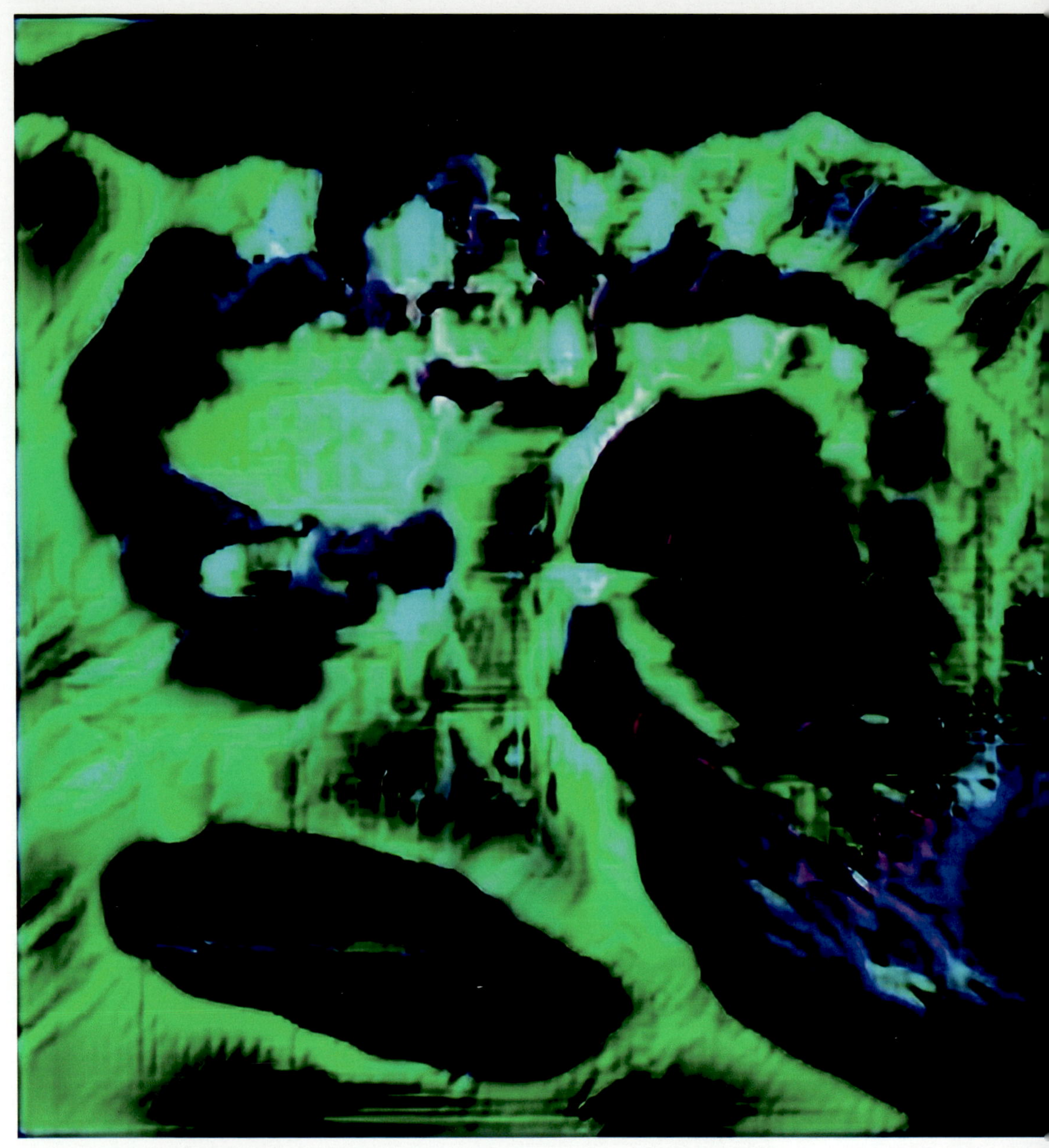

***The Doors*** **▸ 2019 ▸ HD video still**

# Enter the Garden

*Barbaturex morrisoni* may reign over the garden as Morrison's ersatz avatar, but it is only one of many agents recruited in Blas's psychedelic world-building. In *The Doors*, we encounter a number of recurring elements—aural, visual, somatic—that cycle through each of its five sequences, affirming multivalent historical perspectives between past, present, and future. On the one hand, the work conjures the oceanic ambience of a good psychedelic trip, with all the attendant allusions to the cosmic and divine, and no less the winding and time-bending distortions these journeys often take. On the other, in trailing the uncanny prospects of posthuman life through its recourse to AI, the work assumes a future-oriented dimension consistent with speculative fiction. Cast in green light and ornamented with mysterious symbols, the garden emits an air of the mystical while recalling both the light shows of the 1960s and the manufactured landscapes of Silicon Valley tech campuses—the architecture of green walls and transparent surfaces. Not quite Eden, in other words. Blas's garden is more like a private island paradise, a dreamscape sheltering its assets like so much esoteric arcana.

The five audiovisual sequences of *The Doors* track the lizard as it first brings psychedelics to this "privatized garden"; introduce the possibilities of nootropics as "brain food"; treat the garden as a luxurious spa retreat (note that some nootropics encourage sleep); follow the lizard as it's hunted by an invisible predator; and, finally, subject the viewer to what Blas calls, in an allusion to the LSD experience, an "ego death."[3] Understanding how the work unfolds demands parsing the many contents of the garden, which can be provisionally divided into three overlapping categories: sound, vision, and mind-body. Each corresponds to a distinct feature in Blas's work, appealing to different registers of the sensorium; each category works in concert with the others to create a garden awash in stimuli.

Indeed, we hear the garden as much as we see it: Music and spoken-word poetry cocoon us. AI-generated sound vibrates throughout the space as accompaniment to images populating the screens. Some of the music is composed by an actual human being, the composer xin (Ollie Zhang), and some is AI generated, produced in collaboration with Sam Parke-Wolfe, Cameron Thomas, Tom Sedgwick, Ben Hurd, Christopher Tegho, and Ashwin D'Cruz. In certain sequences, the music derives from the 1960s catalogue of the work's namesake (including fast-paced hits such as "Break on Through (To the Other Side)" and "Light My Fire," as well as slow ones such as "The End"). In other parts, the sounds are decidedly more contemporary: binaural beats and ASMR sounds,[4] alleged to relax and soothe the nervous system. Meanwhile, a faintly metallic voice that was generated through a neural network, trained on Morrison's famously low vocal register and growl, speaks to us. Poetry is the chosen genre. Morrison, who published four



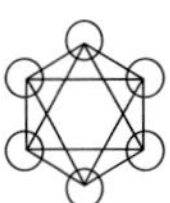

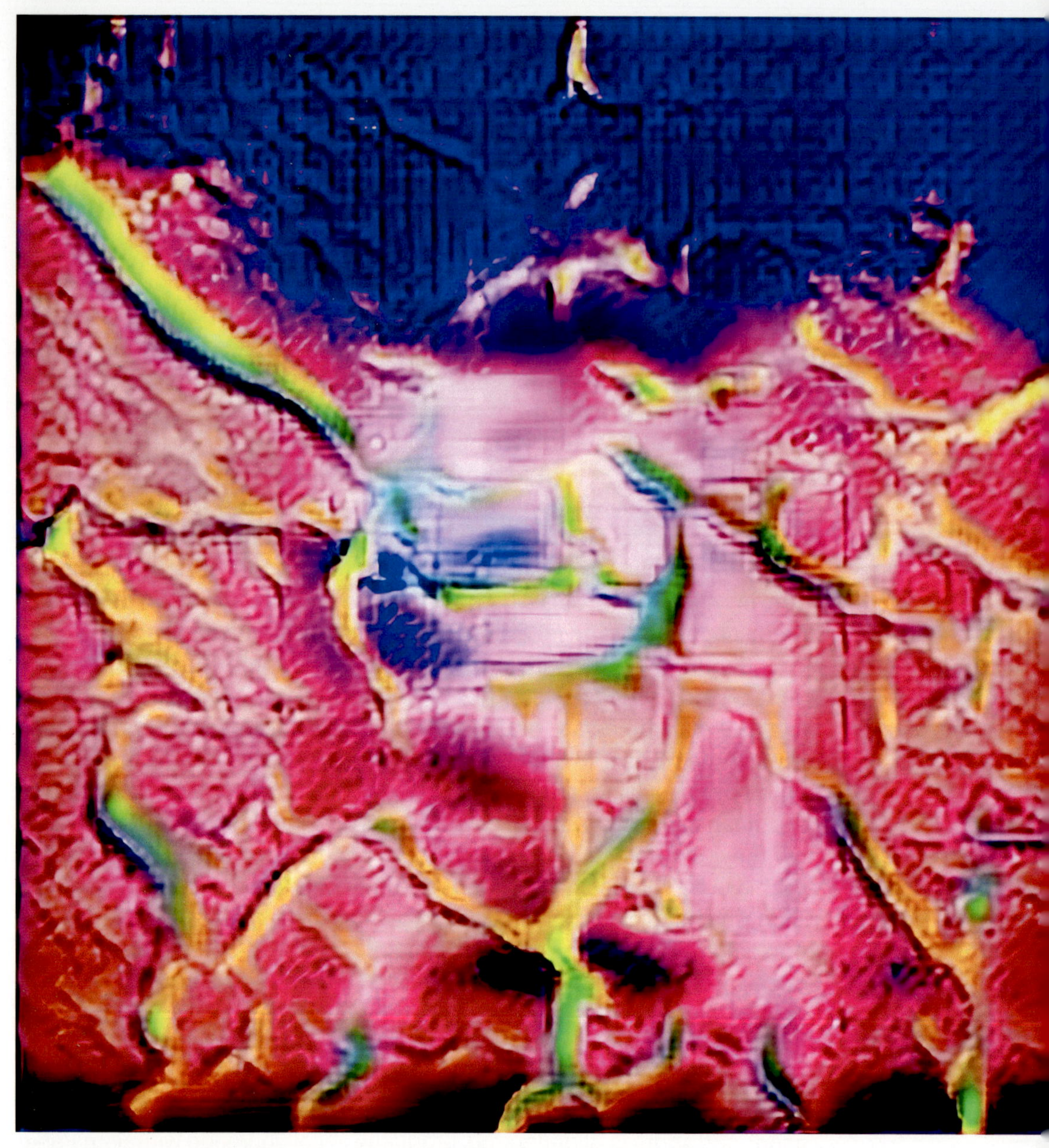

***The Doors*** **▸ 2019 ▸ HD video still**

volumes of poetry during his short life, counted William Blake and Arthur Rimbaud among his heroes, and the pacing, cadence, and near incantatory effect of Blas's combinatory poetics honors this literary side of the Lizard King.[5] But if generally inspired by "The Celebration of the Lizard" and other poems by Morrison, the work's words upon closer listening set us in the

The rise of nootropics in contemporary marketing represents a decisive mutation of an earlier psychedelic worldview.

present tense of the audience. While much of the content came from training a neural network on various image datasets—including LSD blotter art, in keeping with Morrison's legendary adventures with controlled substances—this same network also follows the corporate literature on contemporary nootropics. Advertisements for, business philosophies around, and ingredient lists and descriptions of the neural effects of nootropics tacitly bump up against the Lizard King's sovereign decree: *I can do anything*.

The rise of nootropics in contemporary marketing represents a decisive mutation of an earlier psychedelic worldview, a genealogy I'll describe shortly. Before getting there, however, we need to consider the second and third elements in Blas's garden—the categories of vision and mind-body—in the form of video and quasi-symbolic imagery, as well as various objects displayed at the garden's center. Interspersed with the video of the lizard, abstract images float across the six black-mirrored screens to create a kaleidoscopic enclosure. Here Blas deploys a generative adversarial network (GAN) conditioned by tens of thousands of visuals, including LSD blotter art, classic Californian psychedelia from the 1960s (rock posters and such), pills, medical brain imagery, neural-network diagrams, broken glass, and the like. The results are colorful, abstract vistas that morph and bend, one wave after another, recalling otherworldly and cosmic landscapes: strange and sublime.

Other signs and images distributed throughout the space conjure a spiritual or occult attitude. On a wall between the video screens, a lurid green emits from a neon light shaped like a neural-network diagram, here refashioned to recall a divine symbol, like an icon elevated in a ritual setting. As if to mirror the iconography of interconnectedness and union, a hexagonal pattern on the floor is based on a Metatron's Cube, a symbol in sacred geometry that emblematizes energetic flows throughout the universe and has subsequently been appropriated in nootropics branding. A group of mysterious objects and artifacts are installed within the space, appealing to the nexus of mind and body. A pile of black sand suggests the throne of the Lizard King—perhaps its altar—complete with a heated rock and water dish. An eclectic collection of artificial plants draws species from locations as

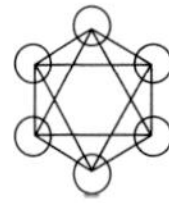

far-flung as California, Hawaii, and Myanmar, the last being the primordial home of the extinct *Barbaturex morrisoni*. Finally, at the center of it all, stands a hexagonal case echoing the geometry of the Metatron's Cube.

Images shimmer between old-school psychedelia and contemporary neuroscience, while an extinct lizard returns as an avatar of tech innovation.

Within, a vast assortment of nootropics is displayed as a fabled "stack," the term used by nootropic enthusiasts for the specific regimen of pills an individual takes in the service of "neuro-enhancement."

The garden of *The Doors*, in short, is at once temple, private island (think the territorial ambitions of Silicon Valley's Peter Thiel), digital phantasmagoria, hallucinogenic Gesamtkunstwerk, and nootropic agora. So, how do we find our bearings within it, establish coordinates within the vast network Blas has laid out before us? Is this utopia or dystopia, or somewhere in between?

To gain ground on such questions, the lizard leads us back in time.

## Circa 1969: The Lizard in Winter

We've seen how Blas's work oscillates between past and present, meshing historical and contemporary references to the point of near indivisibility. *The Doors* flashes between the moment of the eponymous rock band and the present-day culture of technologies of mind as if caught in a state of suspended perception. Images shimmer between old-school psychedelia and contemporary neuroscience, while an extinct lizard returns as an avatar of tech innovation. Meanwhile, the resonance of classic rock—its analog instrumentation—melds with the tones and clicks of digital modulation and binaural beats. Bridging these temporal and symbolic gaps requires the work of minor history, sitting between popular culture and narratives of mind. The viewer must cast a backward and forward gaze at lizard-like phenomena in the past, present, and, finally, future.

To this point, 1969 will serve as the chronological pivot around which such stories turn. It was a dark time on many fronts; we'll call this year "the Lizard in Winter." It was then that the Doors underwent their most desperate trial as a band, foreshadowing Morrison's death in Paris two years later. To be sure, their fall was as precipitous as their rise was meteoric, spectacularly pegged to Morrison's erotic persona and reputation for hedonistic abandon. Founded in Los Angeles in 1965 by Morrison, Ray Manzarek (keyboards), Robby Krieger (guitar), and John Densmore (percussion), the group took its name from Aldous Huxley's 1954 book *The Doors of Perception*, a vividly drawn account of the Englishman's investigations into mescaline's effects on consciousness. For Huxley, ingesting this psychotropic agent enabled him to "change [his] ordinary mode of consciousness as to be able to know, from the inside, what the visionary, the medium, even the mystic were talking about."[6] One such visionary identified by Huxley was the poet William Blake, whose phrase "the doors of perception were cleansed" appeared on the frontispiece of Huxley's most famous book and served as its title. The band would abbreviate Huxley's own title to create their name—a call to psychedelic liberation.

But after March 1, 1969, those liberatory doors were closing fast in light of what fans of the Doors ruefully call "the Miami incident." In a concert at the Coconut Grove's Dinner Key Auditorium, Morrison transgressed the boundaries of his already provocative stage persona, arriving drunk, belligerent, thrashing, and more than an hour late. After fumbling the lyrics and repeatedly stopping mid-song, Morrison upped the ante by allegedly exposing himself to the audience. In one of the counterculture's most formative stress tests, Morrison was arrested and later charged with indecent exposure, with the press widely accusing him of corrupting America's

While Morrison's Lizard King sought to expand the mind outward, MacLean's model pushed the lizard brain to the most primitive level of human consciousness.

youth. The event bore catastrophic repercussions for the band, resulting in endless legal headaches, dramatic losses of revenue, serial cancellations, and, finally, a conviction for Morrison, its appeal still pending at the time of his death in July 1971. The Miami incident indeed signaled the end for the fabled poet-singer.

Just a couple weeks prior to the Doors' Coconut Grove concert, lizards were acquiring vastly different associations in arenas far removed from concert halls and jail cells. The Lizard King, Morrison's regal avatar, celebrated and explored the outermost limits of mind and body, sound and vision. This was not how the link between the lizard and consciousness was perceived everywhere, however. At Queen's University in Ontario, Canada, for instance, Dr. Paul D. MacLean was invited to give a series of lectures on cutting-edge research in neuroscience. As chief of the Laboratory of



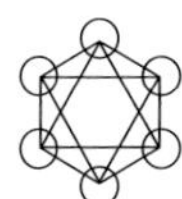

Brain Evolution and Behavior at the National Institute of Mental Health in Washington, DC, he conceived a novel model of the brain based on comparative neuroanatomy, crossing the threshold between human and nonhuman animals: what he called the "triune brain." MacLean explains: "In its evolution, the human brain expands along the lines of three prototypes for which I have used the terms reptilian, paleomammalian and neomammalian."[7] These three "cerebrotypes," he emphasizes, are not autonomous but treated as "intermeshing and functioning together." MacLean identified the basal ganglia as the reptilian complex—also called the lizard brain, the reptile brain, and the R-complex—as the most primitive actor in the triune order. The lizard brain is responsible for the baser instincts of aggression, domination, territoriality, and survival; it is imprinted with ancestral memories and ancestral learning. While Morrison's Lizard King sought to expand the mind outward, MacLean's model pushed the lizard brain to the most primitive level of human consciousness.

We'll come to see how the term "lizard brain" has been taken up, decades later, by politics, nootropic branding, business marketing, and discussions of workplace performance to characterize states of mind considered reactionary, dull, and unevolved, even though MacLean's "triune brain" model has now been largely discredited by the scientific community. In 1969 and the years immediately following, however, MacLean's work was received as groundbreaking research.[8] While the triune lizard bears none of the romantic or mind-expanding attributes of Morrison's kingly reptile, it is important to underscore that these two different reptilian personas—one neuroscientific, the other countercultural—nevertheless overlap in their appeals to atavistic or primordial states of being beyond the usual confines of human reason and rationality, logic and perception. In this regard, the lizard brain might well in fact be recruited by the Lizard King—*conquered* by it, even—in service of a different mode of enlightenment, opening the doors of collective perception to worlds contained elsewhere. Blas's garden, I would argue, sets the stage—or rather, its threshold—for this encounter.

Just how these positions—the expanded and the base brain; the psychedelic realm of the hippie and the clinical world of the scientist—converge brings us to our next vignette from the period. In 1969, we should note, there was no room for LSD, mescaline, psilocybin, ayahuasca, or any other psychotropic agent in the white-coated university labs, pharmaceutical companies, or research foundations. In other words, they had no place in the scientific métier of figures like MacLean. The "doors of perception," on the contrary, were by now irredeemably linked to the counterculture and all that term evoked in terms of social upheaval and mass transgression. Following the discovery and synthesis of LSD, or lysergic acid diethylamide, by the chemist Albert Hofmann in 1938, scientists and psychiatrists began to consider the therapeutic uses of such drugs in the treatment of any number of psychological disorders. After decades of research following LSD's discovery, the study of psychedelics would all but die an institutional death

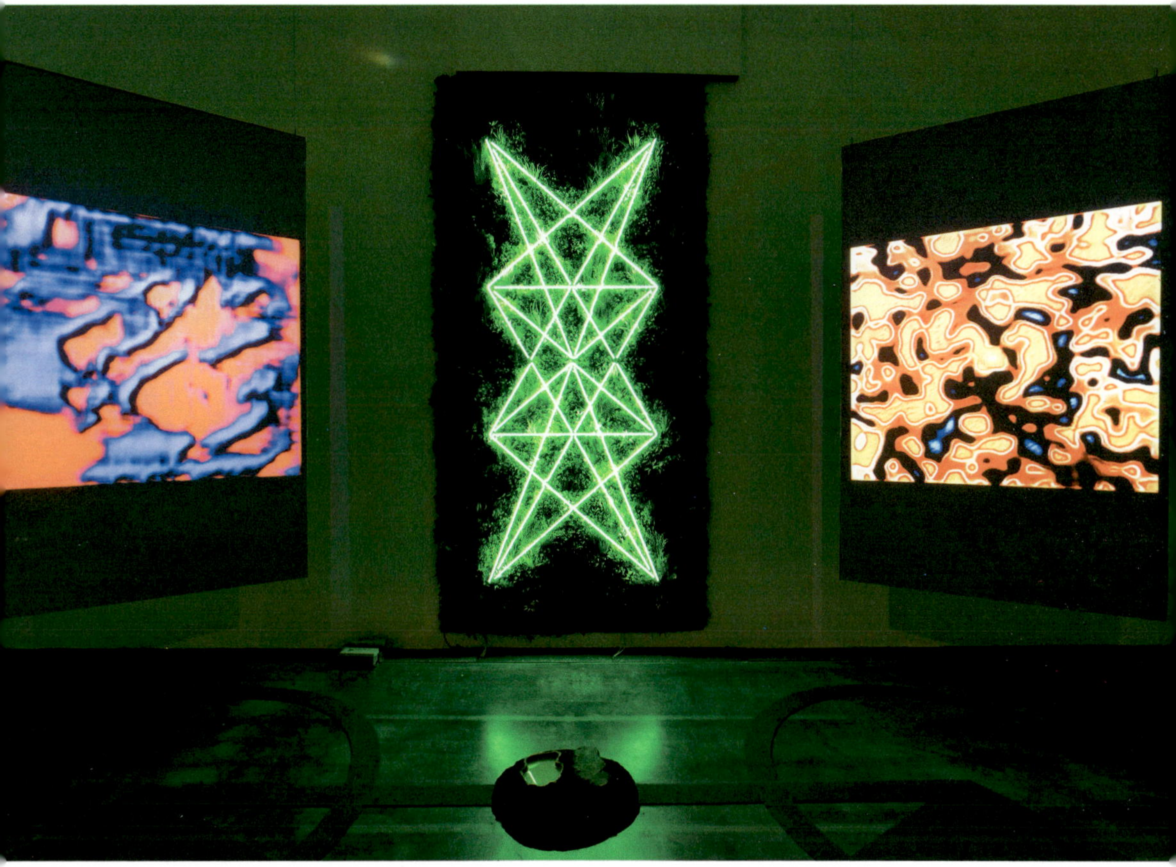

*The Doors* ▸ 2019 ▸ mixed-media installation ▸ Installation view at Edith-Russ-Haus for Media Art, Oldenburg, Germany ▸ Courtesy of Edith-Russ-Haus for Media Art and the artist



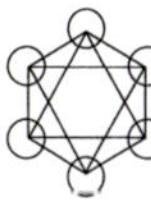

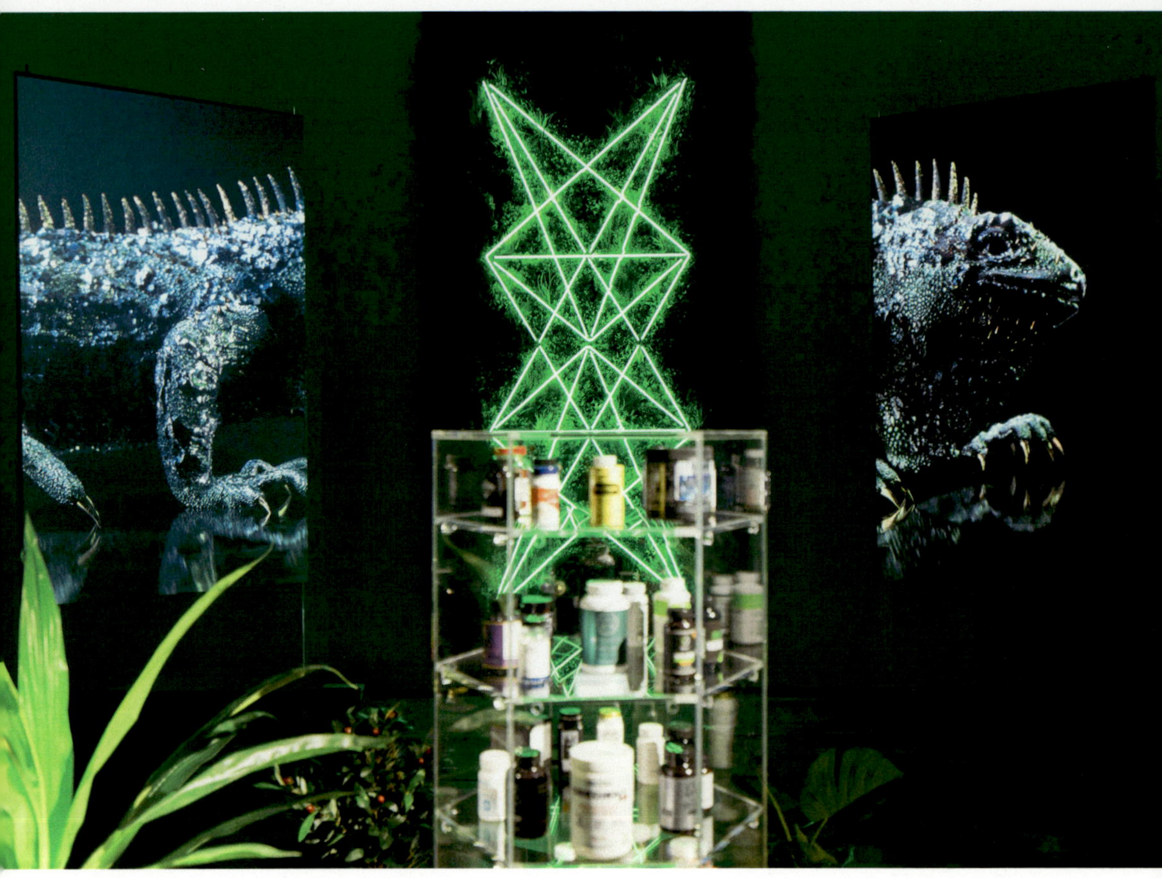

***The Doors*** **▸ 2019 ▸ mixed-media installation ▸ Installation views at Edith-Russ-Haus for Media Art, Oldenburg, Germany ▸ Courtesy of Edith-Russ-Haus for Media Art and the artist**

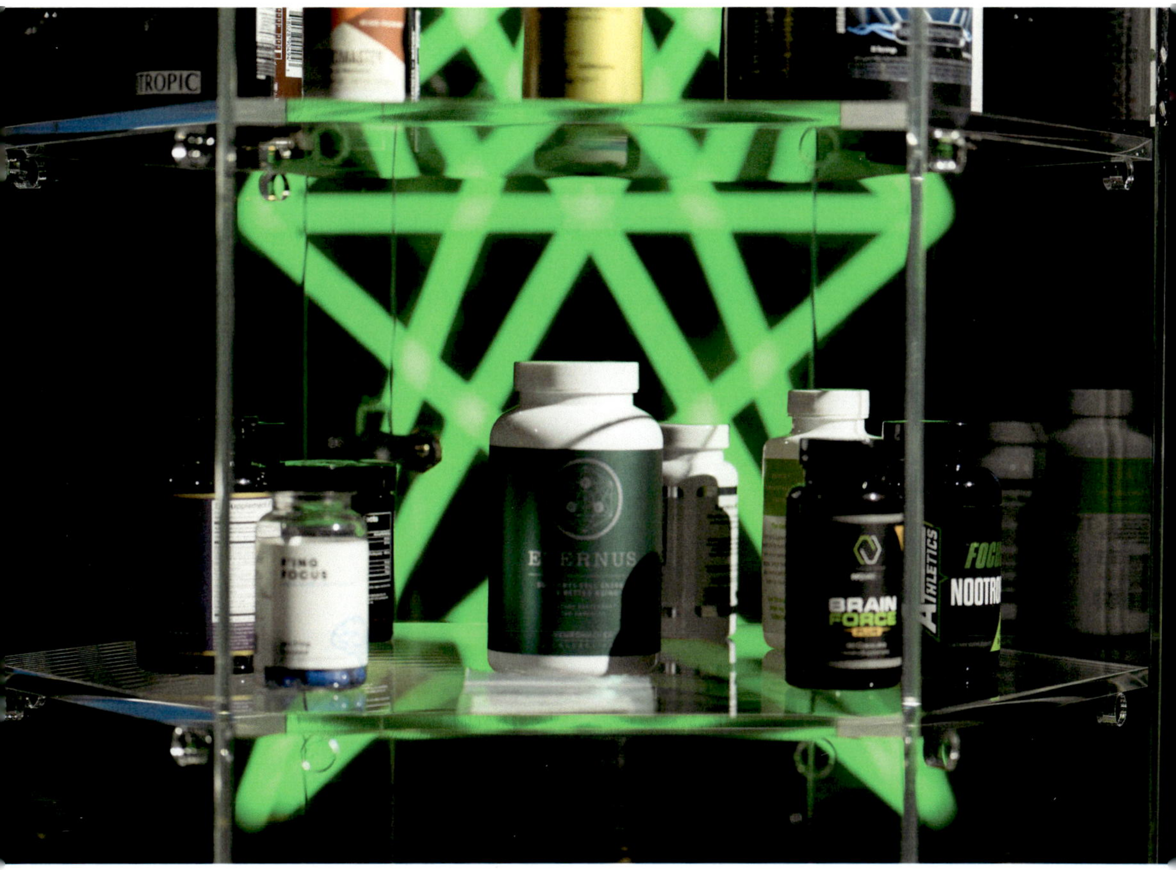

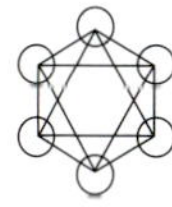

in the late 1960s: the US Food and Drug Administration assigned LSD the status of a "scheduled," or contraband, drug in 1967. The consensus among the era's former researchers places the blame for this turn of events on the writer and psychologist Timothy Leary, whose infamous psychiatric antics at Harvard University in the early 1960s, including testing LSD on his students-cum-research-subjects, led to his firing in 1963.[9] Inspired by Huxley's example a decade earlier, Leary would go on to assume the role of the counterculture's psychonautic guru and media darling. His famous mantra "turn on, tune in, drop out" would become a rallying cry for the countercultural generation.

MacLean's neuroscientific investigations relied little upon the influence of psychedelics as either object of study or instrument of enlightenment. Instead, MacLean's triune brain—with the lizard at its center—was patterned on a different genre of mind-expanding technology. The intermeshing and interdependent functions of this animal brain found a powerful analogue in a lecture he delivered in February 1969. "In the popular language of today," he declared, "these three brains might be thought of as biological computers, each with its own peculiar form of subjectivity, and its own intelligence, its own sense of time and space, and its own memory, motor and other functions."[10]

The brain understood as a computer—a machine to process information with intelligence, time, space, motor, and memory—was a pervasive trope by 1969. Following the postwar revolutions in cybernetics and information theory, animal brains and digital computers were treated in isomorphic terms. Critically, this dynamic between human and machine was understood as reciprocal. After all, if a brain was organized like a machine, why couldn't a machine in turn think—or rather, be trained to think—like a brain? In 1943, neurophysiologist Warren McCulloch and computational neuroscientist Walter Pitts would refer to such possibilities as a "neurological network"—making theirs the first statement on artificial intelligence and the "neural network."[11]

Just as LSD was explored as a potential truth serum during the Cold War, various sectors of the military also widely supported the prospects of AI technology for such purposes. By the end of the 1960s, however, strides in artificial intelligence were weathering the same institutional misfortunes as psychedelics research, in what is referred to as "the AI winter"—a period in which institutional support and the general reception of this new discipline lay dormant, due in large measure to the withdrawal of funding and new laws overseeing the disbursement of research monies. Still, although AI research and development was put in deep freeze in the late 1960s and early 1970s, some of that generation's most impactful computer scientists took it upon themselves to explore their own technologies of mind, both before and after 1969. The science journalist Michael Pollan describes how Al Hubbard, the "Johnny Appleseed of LSD," established the Commission for the Study of Creative Imagination in the mid-1950s, through it creating "far-flung psychedelic networks." His psychedelic compatriots included such Silicon Valley stalwarts as Myron Stolaroff of Ampex, among the first tech companies to set up shop in the Valley, and Douglas Engelbart, who would go on to invent the computer mouse.[12]

What are we to make of these entangled histories tacitly flagged in Blas's *The Doors*? The technoculture and communications scholar Fred Turner powerfully argues for the historical continuity and ideological isomorphisms between the 1960s counterculture and Silicon Valley. In his influential study *From Counterculture to Cyberculture: Stewart Brand, the Whole Earth Network, and the Rise of Digital Utopianism*, Turner meticulously charts how the communalist ethos of California hippie culture, led by impresario Stewart Brand, anticipated the organizational, ideological, and corporate interests of the network society.[13] Less explicit in such readings is the role psychedelics might have played in expanding the relations between these multiple spheres of influence *as* technology. One of the achievements of *The Doors*—that is, Blas's garden—is how it brings to light these histories and updates their contemporary implications via a new technology of mind: nootropics.

## 2019: Which Lizard, Triumphant?

Fifty years after the AI winter, the Miami incident, and MacLean's lectures on the triune brain, Blas took up a post as artist-in-residence at the Edith-Russ-Haus for Media Art, where, along with his many collaborators, he was hard at work on *The Doors*. In the years between 1969 and 2019, it might have seemed that the lizard had gone missing—hibernating, if not

These substances are, in effect, ingested to defeat the lizard brain.

extinct. Morrison died in 1971. The 1960s counterculture, as Turner argues, paved the way for a cybercapitalist market. Once studied in university and pharmaceutical labs for its therapeutic possibilities, LSD was made illegal, its status precipitating by a few short decades America's "war on drugs."

How strange, then, that some version of the lizard has come creeping back into both the media and cultural consciousness, uncanny in its repetition and yet radically transformed in light of the vastly changed conditions of the present. In 1969, the lizard triangulated the spirit of the



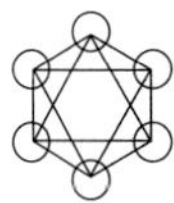

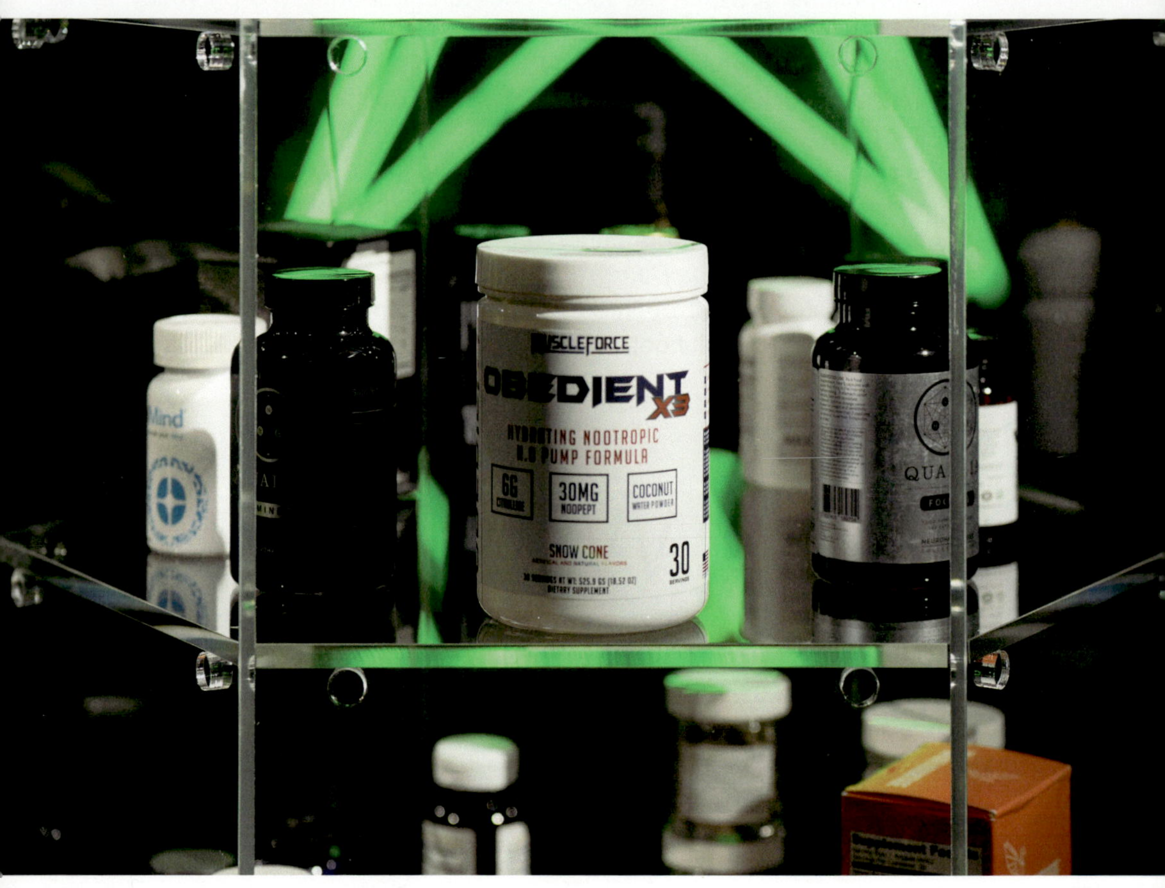


*The Doors* ▸ 2019 ▸ mixed-media installation ▸ Installation views at Edith-Russ-Haus for Media Art, Oldenburg, Germany ▸ Courtesy of Edith-Russ-Haus for Media Art and the artist

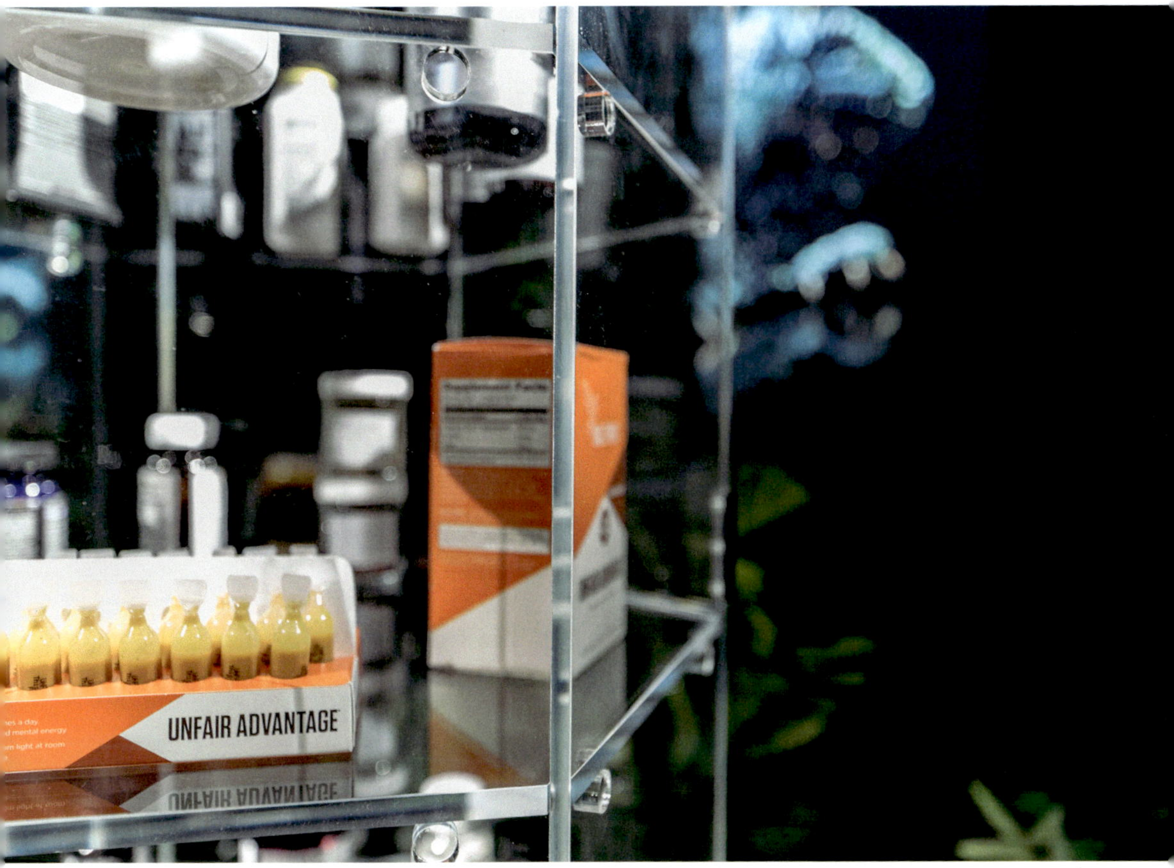

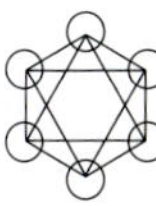

counterculture, the primordial animal brain, and the moribund prospects of artificial intelligence. In 2019, its reincarnation became "celebrated" by the scintillating hexagonal armoire of nootropics at the heart of Blas's installation, enshrining its artifacts like a sacred reliquary. Indeed, the contemporary phenomena of brain hacking, microdosing, and nootropics—using drugs, herbs, and supplements with names like Gorilla Mind Smooth, Mind Lab Pro, and Synapsa, among countless others—represent the next wave of mind-expanding technics marketed to enhance cognitive function, improve memory, stimulate creativity, and boost energy. These substances are, in effect, ingested to defeat the lizard brain, a term that today has come to mean not only a primordial mode of cognition, as per MacLean's neuroscientific analysis, but something to be vanquished relative to a hypercompetitive, masculinist, and tech-oriented market. For rather than cater to poets, artists, and musicians such as latter-day Morrisons and their ilk, nootropics find their most ardent followers in two (occasionally overlapping) demographics of white men: tech bros and right-wing fringe groups. Blas's work shows us how nootropics represent one possible outcome of the 1960s counterculture's legacy in Silicon Valley, evident largely in the radical inequality of its workforce, and at a moment within the larger culture when conspiracy theories around the existence of "lizard people" who have occupied positions of power dominate alt-right online forums.[14] At the same time, *The Doors* also implicitly asks of its audience: Is this the only, or the inevitable, outcome for the Lizard King?

Perhaps it comes as no surprise that the concept of nootropics goes back to the early 1970s. Corneliu Giurgea, a Romanian biochemist working for a Belgian pharmaceutical company, coined the term in 1972, blending the Greek words for "mind" and "to turn or bend." In synthesizing a drug

The wider emergence of nootropics within culture at large is indeed inextricable from the rise of Silicon Valley.

called Piracetam, he seems to have both assimilated the language of psychedelics and internalized the evolutionary model of MacLean's reptilian complex, most notably when he observed that "man will not wait passively for millions of years before evolution offers him a better brain."[15] In some respects, Giurgea was picking up the thread that scientific research on LSD, mental health, and psychiatric disorders had dropped in the late 1960s. He sought a chemical solution to optimize the performance of the brain, supporting and enhancing what would come to be called "neuroplasticity."

There are, of course, stark differences between Giurgea's research and the earlier studies he built upon, which together track the movement of the counterculture into the marketplace of neoliberalism. For one, the scientific study of LSD prior to its ban addressed its potential for mitigating depression, alcoholism, a range of addictions, mental illnesses, dementia, and a spectrum of neurological conditions. Soon after the prohibition of LSD, the 1960s' love affair with psychotropics was motivated by the expansion of consciousness in mystical, cosmic, experimental, and liberatory terms, coupled with an ethos of *self*-actualization. Contemporary nootropics, by contrast, hyperbolically assume the self-actualizing tendencies of the earlier generation, but little else. In 2019, in fact, Leary's incantatory "tune in, turn on, drop out" might be recoded as "stay in, switch on, work more." The wider emergence of nootropics within culture at large is indeed inextricable from the rise of Silicon Valley. In the early 1990s, so-called smart clubs were forming in the then nascent tech communities of San Francisco, where members served nootropic "cocktails" and circulated books with titles like *Smart Drugs and Nutrients*.[16] In the early to mid-2000s, users of Reddit and other online communities championed the use of nootropics such that the international sales of the substances online started to raise regulatory concerns. Pop cultural references followed suit, including a middling Bradley Cooper sci-fi vehicle called *Limitless* in 2011, based on Alan Glynn's book *The Dark Fields* from 2001.

The art historian Lucy Hunter notes that the toxic masculinity that fuels the narrative of *Limitless* presaged the right-wing nootropics consumers who would come into prominence later in the decade and who have more recently taken to promoting and marketing these supplements, herbs, and pharmaceuticals, all the while clinging to the doxa of "the meritocracy."[17] Entrepreneurial, masculinist bros—from podcast impresario Joe Rogan, to conspiracy theorist and alt-right media personality Mike "Pizzagate" Cernovich, to author and podcast host Tim Ferriss—have described their personal use of nootropics, sold them on their websites, and effectively declared that nootropics might vanquish the lizard brain. These substances are the cognitive analogue to the body-building products some of the same personalities also hawk and consume. Nootropics are tools of self-improvement, a way to get ahead, tokens of normative masculinity. As journalist Richard Cooke notes in an article describing the confluence between nootropics and this particular demographic: "When collective action, regulation, and the countervailing force of the state have been counted out, there is only the self to stand against the might of these adversaries. No wonder it must be assisted. Changing the system would be a sacrilege. Instead, finally, it must be gamed."[18] Hence nootropics occupy another place in a larger system, beyond the customized stacks of their masculine fanbases. Alt-right acolytes may well be enthusiastic, individual peddlers of mushroom coffee and brain boosters, but it turns out they are in financial company with the tech industry: start-ups funded by venture capitalists have indeed attempted to "disrupt" the billion-dollar supplement market represented by old-school stalwarts such as GNC.[19]



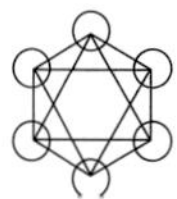

Through Blas's vast collation of objects, images, sounds, and symbols, *The Doors* raises the specter of nootropics' masculinist and financial ideals, in which cognitive performance is rationalized in economic terms. Here the evolutionary and primordial status of the lizard brain is trounced by the Darwinism of the marketplace. Such tendencies are in dialogue with a larger practice within contemporary culture—microdosing—that has also been linked to Silicon Valley's rapacious ethos. In a workplace banking on innovation as its principle resource, tech workers ingest minute quantities of LSD as a means to promote creativity and expand their minds, all in the service of tech's reigning imperative around "problem-solving." In related fashion, *The Doors* also suggests another return to psychedelics in the present, hence complicating the future prospects for the technologies of mind advanced by the lizard. As Pollan has exhaustively demonstrated, the last decade has seen a return to the study of psychedelics in ways consistent with their earlier lab-based history.[20] Researchers have come full circle to the curative and therapeutic possibilities of LSD, mushrooms, ayahuasca, and the like. For these drugs may well heal the mind, and the spirit along with it, in a process that is less acquisitive than it is restorative, less geared toward Silicon Valley's resource extraction of mind and more toward the holistic potentialities of the subject.

And yet, not only—for if this essay has demonstrated anything, it's just how easily such developments might lend themselves to other technologies of mind. Still, we must ask: Is there another space into which the lizard can move beyond this psychedelic-technological enclosure? A crack in the door—a portal—to the other side?

Let us sit longer in the garden for a minute, absorbing the uncanny poetics of Morrison's AI-generated voice. In the fifth and final sequence of *The Doors*, the celebration of the Lizard King continues as augured by the AI-generated poem "Ego Death Party."

**There's been a strange**
**whisper**
**about**
**the island**

**Sadness has ravaged**
**the friends**
**of Utopia**

**But the trip away from**
**the default mode network**
**changed them.**

**Let me take you to a place**
**Of higher elevation**

the sun in curved green
clouds
Cactus, palms, swaying
and
intensely
boundless
jungles of geometry

where
people melt
into the world,
interfuse with others, and
lose their 'myself' part.

the
most
intense feeling
of connection ever.

In the video accompanying this final section, the lizard becomes sick, as if submitted to the trials of the ego death experienced by LSD users. Ego death is that moment when "LSD interrupts what is called the default mode network in the brain, which is what gives us our sense of being a self, an individual."[21] The lizard heaves, lies injured and bleeding, as if losing the borders of the self. Halfway through the process, it heals. Now radiating a psychedelic skin, it is reborn.

And so too might the current prospects of what the cultural theorist Mark Fisher articulates as "acid communism" disintegrate and then reconfigure, offering a way to see beyond the individual as the sovereign arbiter of a neoliberal worldview to a collectively shared, visionary experience. For in the end, *The Doors* is too haunted in its recourse to Morrison's poetics, too collaborative in its approach, production, materials, and method, and too multivocal and layered in its references, impressions, and experiences to be reducible to the ego ideal of the singular individual, triumphant over the lizard brain. Instead, Blas's work allows for the possibility of a different mode of connection both parallel to and in excess of the many networks it otherwise trails. It's one "where / people melt / into the world, / interfuse with others" as if to produce "the / most / intense feeling / of connection ever." And, paradoxically, it is the seeming *dethroning* of the Lizard King that offers the potential for its restoration—indeed, its celebration—elsewhere.



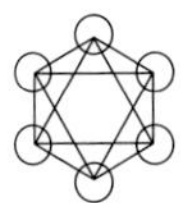

**1** When performed live, "The Celebration of the Lizard" mingled spoken-word poetry and sung lyrics. Its lyrics appear in the liner notes for the Doors' 1968 album *Waiting for the Sun*. An official recorded version was never released, but a work-in-progress take is available.

**2** The three works in the series are *The Doors*, a work-in-progress on AI and religion, and another forthcoming piece on New Zealand, *The Lord of the Rings*, and tech bunkers. The series also includes a prologue, *Jubilee 2033* (2018).

On his concept of "queer science fiction," Blas notes: "I see the queerness at work here [in *The Doors*] as a kind of overall approach to creating that seriously engages the wacky, the fantastical, the minor, the contradictions of desire, but also the desire for an alternative, a crack, or a portal to an elsewhere. For instance, foregrounding the lizard in the installation as a narrator, time traveler, and transformer feels quite queer to me. In fact, writer Steve Abbott's 1992 experimental novel *The Lizard Club* imagines lizards as a metaphor for otherness, which further encouraged me to treat the lizard queerly. On a practical level, I've worked with other queers to make this installation. [...] Building production teams with queer people is important to me." Zach Blas, email to the author, June 25, 2020. Blas also remarks on queer desire for Morrison's erotic persona, relative to his own love of the Doors growing up. He also acknowledges Morrison's "lure" on "many queer friends."

**3** The five parts are "Lizard Brings Psychedelic Drugs to the Privatized Garden on the Island of Nootroo," "Hungry for Brain Food," "Spa Day on the Neon Isles," "Tree of Radical Life Extension," and "Ego Death Party."

**4** Autonomous sensory meridian response (ASMR) is understood as a feeling of calm or pleasure or a tingling sensation stemming from listening to certain noises such as whispering, tapping, tearing paper, and so on. A considerable industry has arisen around ASMR-inducing videos and recordings through social media platforms, particularly YouTube.

**5** The standard biography of James Douglas Morrison is Jerry Hopkins and Danny Sugerman, *No One Here Gets Out Alive: The Biography of Jim Morrison* (New York: Grand Central Publishing, 1980). For an insider's memoir of the Doors, see keyboardist Ray Manzarek's *Light My Fire: My Life with the Doors* (Berkeley, CA: Berkeley Boulevard, 1998).

**6** Aldous Huxley, *The Doors of Perception* (London: Chatto and Windus, 1954), 9.

**7** Paul MacLean, *A Triune Concept of the Brain and Behavior* (Toronto: University of Toronto Press, 1973), 5.

**8** For instance, see Carl Sagan, *The Dragons of Eden: Speculations on the Evolution of Human Intelligence* (New York: Ballantine, 1977).

**9** Within the considerable literature on LSD and psychedelics, Michael Pollan's recent work charts early scientific studies of the drug to establish the return to such initiatives in the present, specifically in the interests of microdosing, cognitive therapy, and the expansion of consciousness. See Michael Pollan, *How to Change Your Mind: What the New Science of Psychedelics Teaches Us about Consciousness, Dying, Addiction, Depression, and Transcendence* (New York: Penguin, 2018).

**10** MacLean, *A Triune Concept of the Brain and Behavior*, 8.

**11** Warren McCulloch and Walter Pitts, "A Logical Calculus of the Ideas Immanent in Nervous Activity," *Bulletin of Mathematical Biophysics* 5 (1943): 115–33.

**12** Pollan, *How to Change Your Mind*, 175–79.

**13** Fred Turner, *From Counterculture to Cyberculture: Stewart Brand, the Whole Earth Network, and the Rise of Digital Utopianism* (Chicago: University of Chicago Press, 2008).

**14** For example, the conspiracy theory promulgated by the anti-Semite David Icke that lizard people control the US government.

**15** Corneliu Giurgea, quoted in Eve Watling, "Nootropics: Do 'Smart Drugs' Really Work?," *Newsweek*, February 8, 2019, https://www.newsweek.com/nootropics-smart-drugs-biohacking-1316682.

**16** Lucy Hunter, email to the author, May 26, 2020.

**17** Hunter, email.

**18** Richard Cooke, "Right Brain: The Conservative Commentariat's Love Affair with Nootropics," *New Republic*, September 3, 2019, https://newrepublic.com/article/154629/right-brain-ben-shapiro-alex-jones-conservative-love-affair-nootropics.

**19** Jared Hopkins, "FDA Challenges Supplement Makers' Marketing Claims," *Wall Street Journal*, February 11, 2019, https://www.wsj.com/articles/fda-sends-warning-letters-to-dietary-supplement-companies-11549896494.

**20** Pollan, *How to Change Your Mind*.

**21** Blas, email.

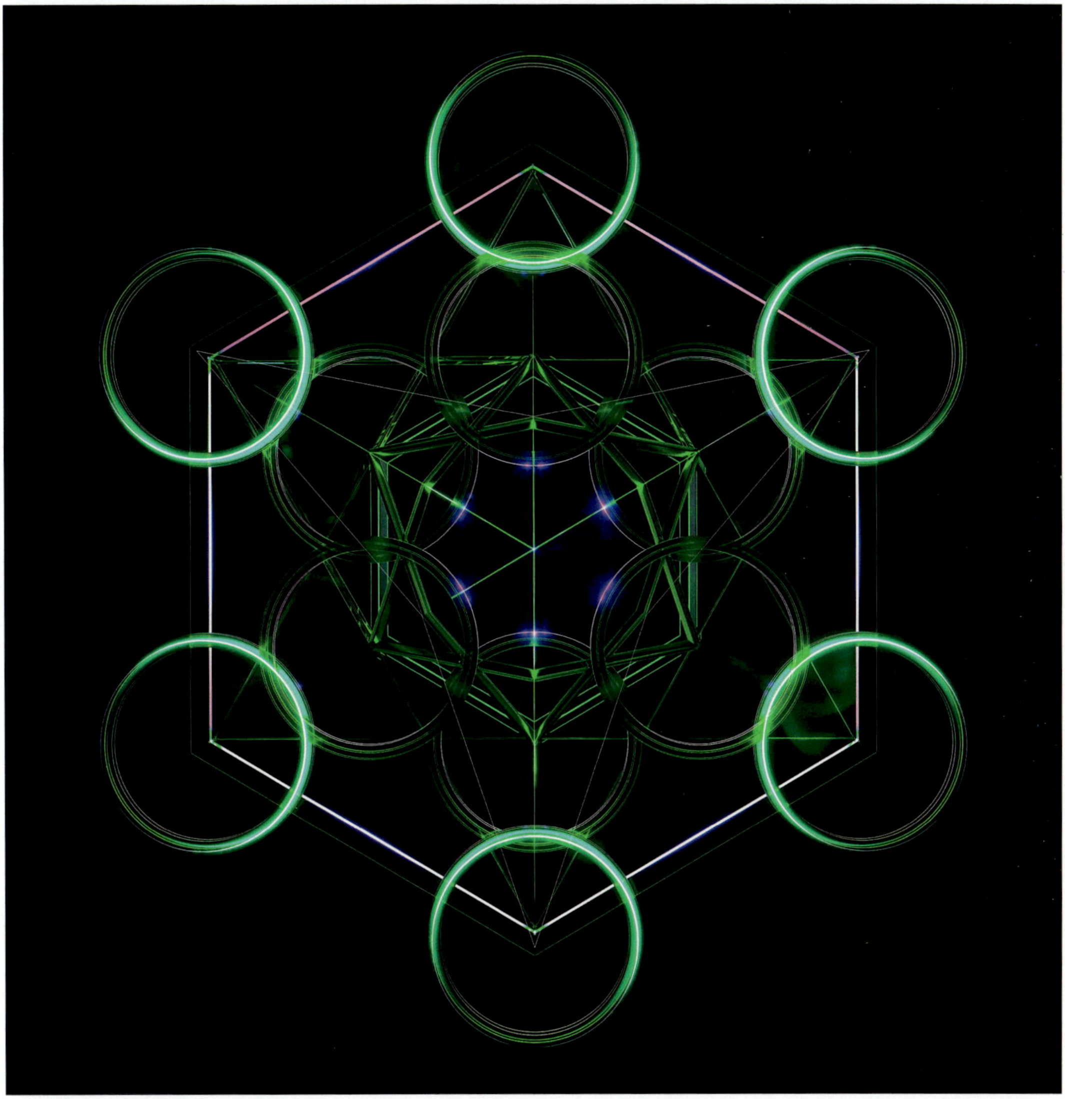

*The Doors* ▸ 2019 ▸ HD video still



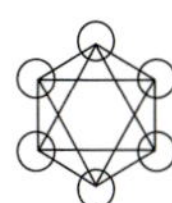

# *The Doors:* Five Poems

Zach Blas

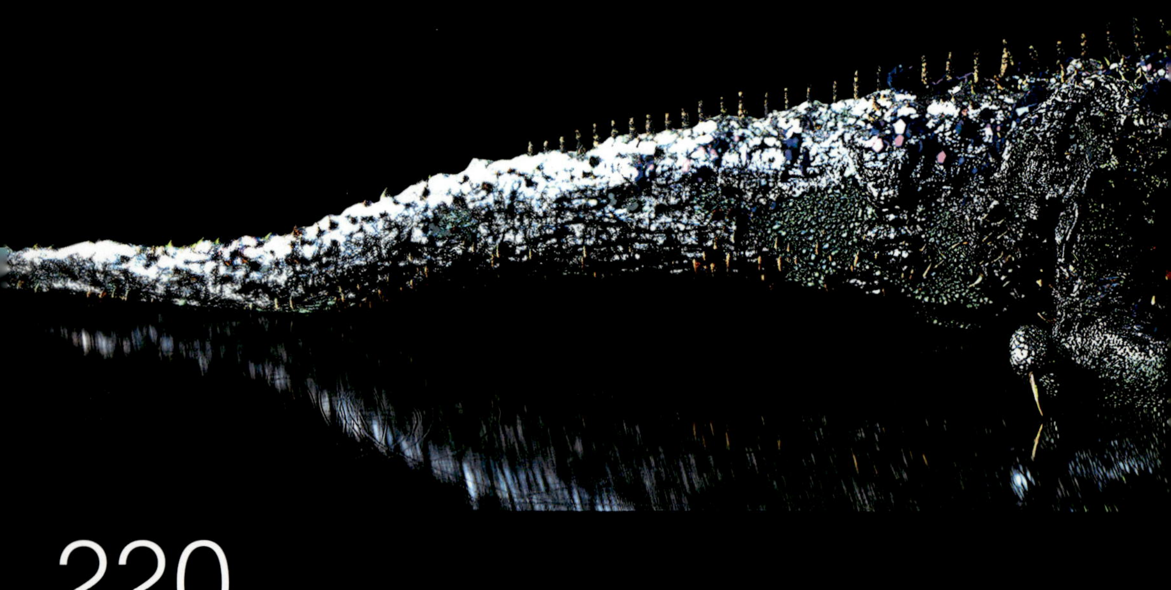

220

(2019)

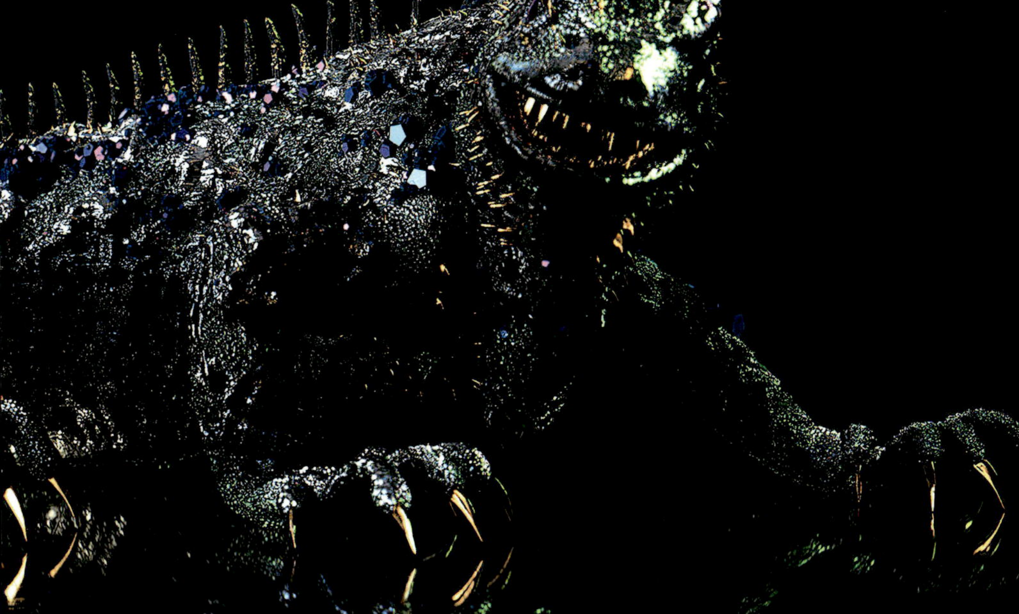

*The garden has a strange atmosphere.*

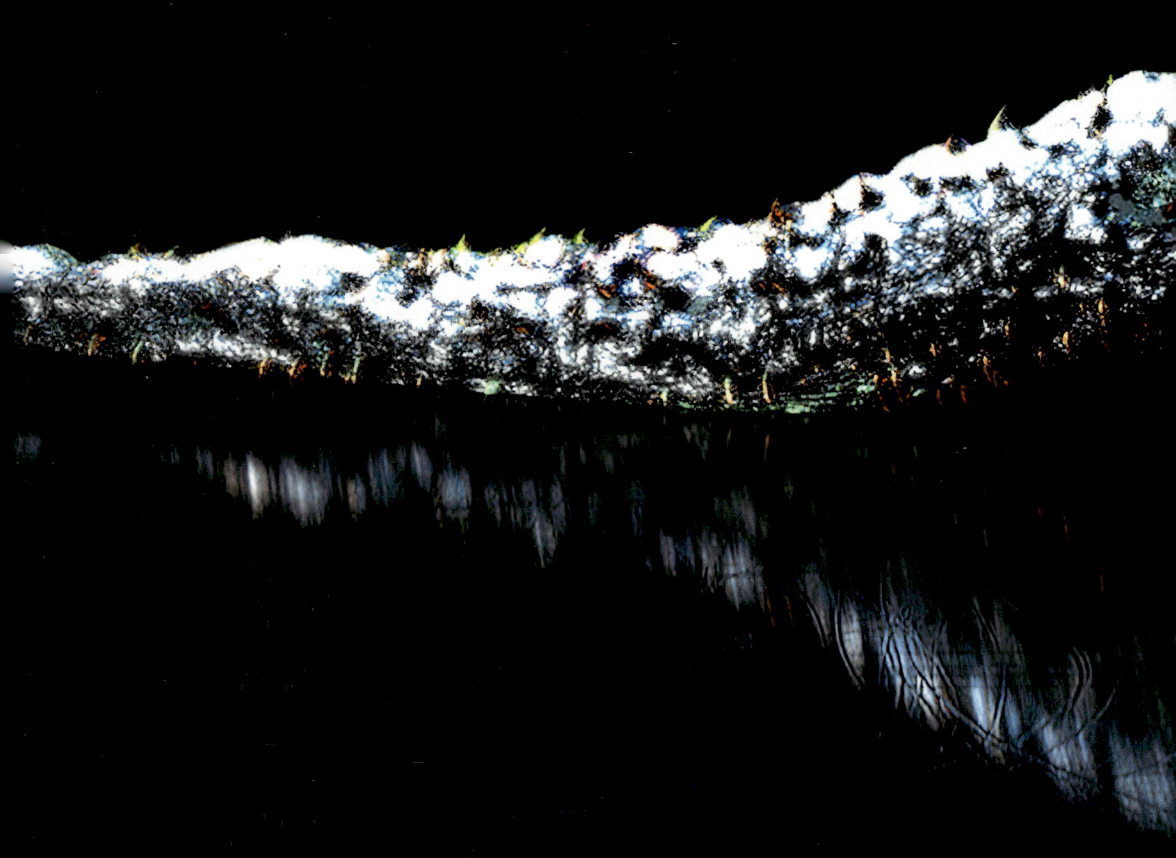

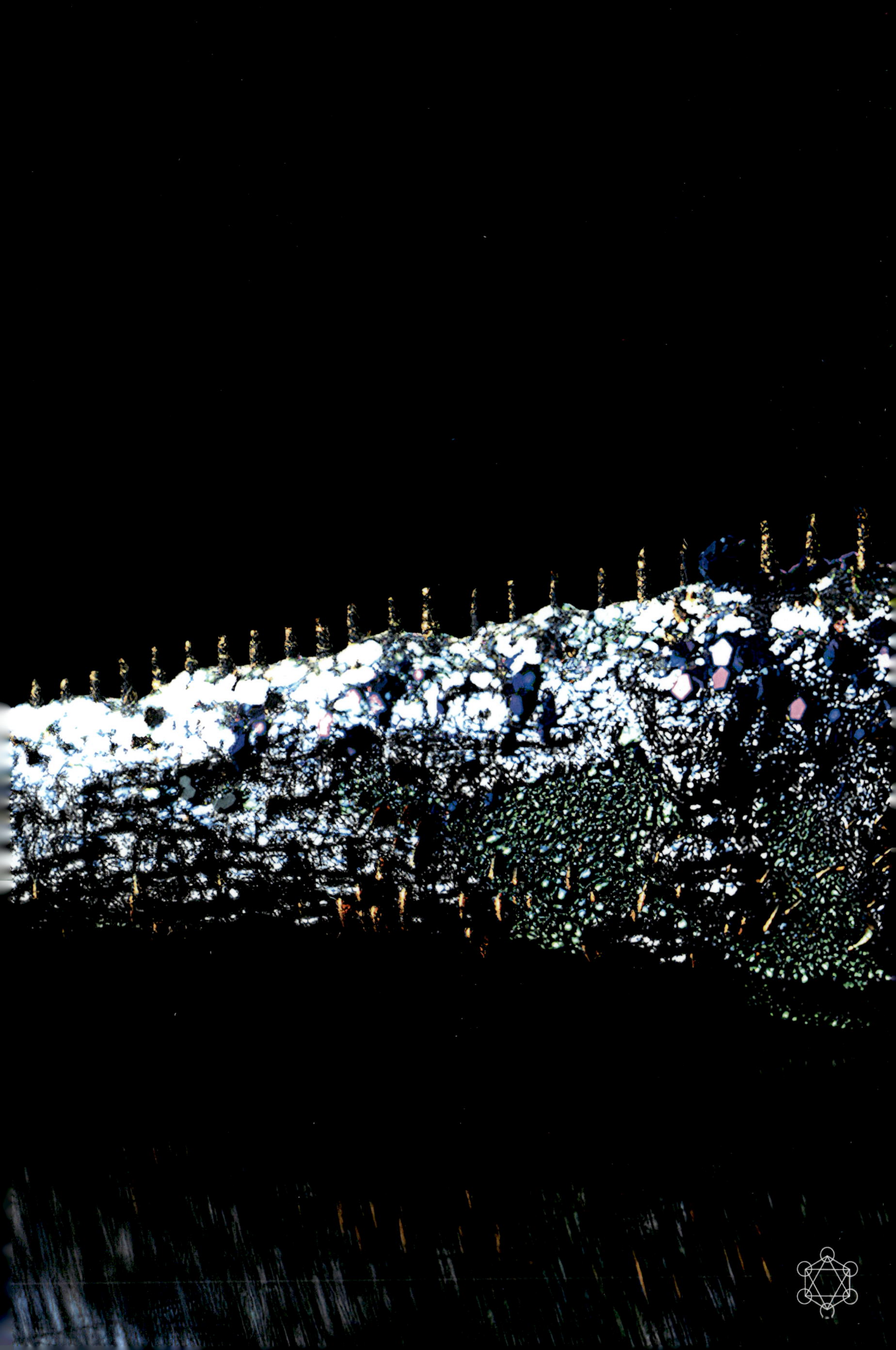

*The trees and the flowers*
*Bright and striking;*
*Their sapro-ness and the*
*effervescence of their fragrance*
*illustrate the infinite*
*potency*
*of neurotransmitters within our*
*Brains.*

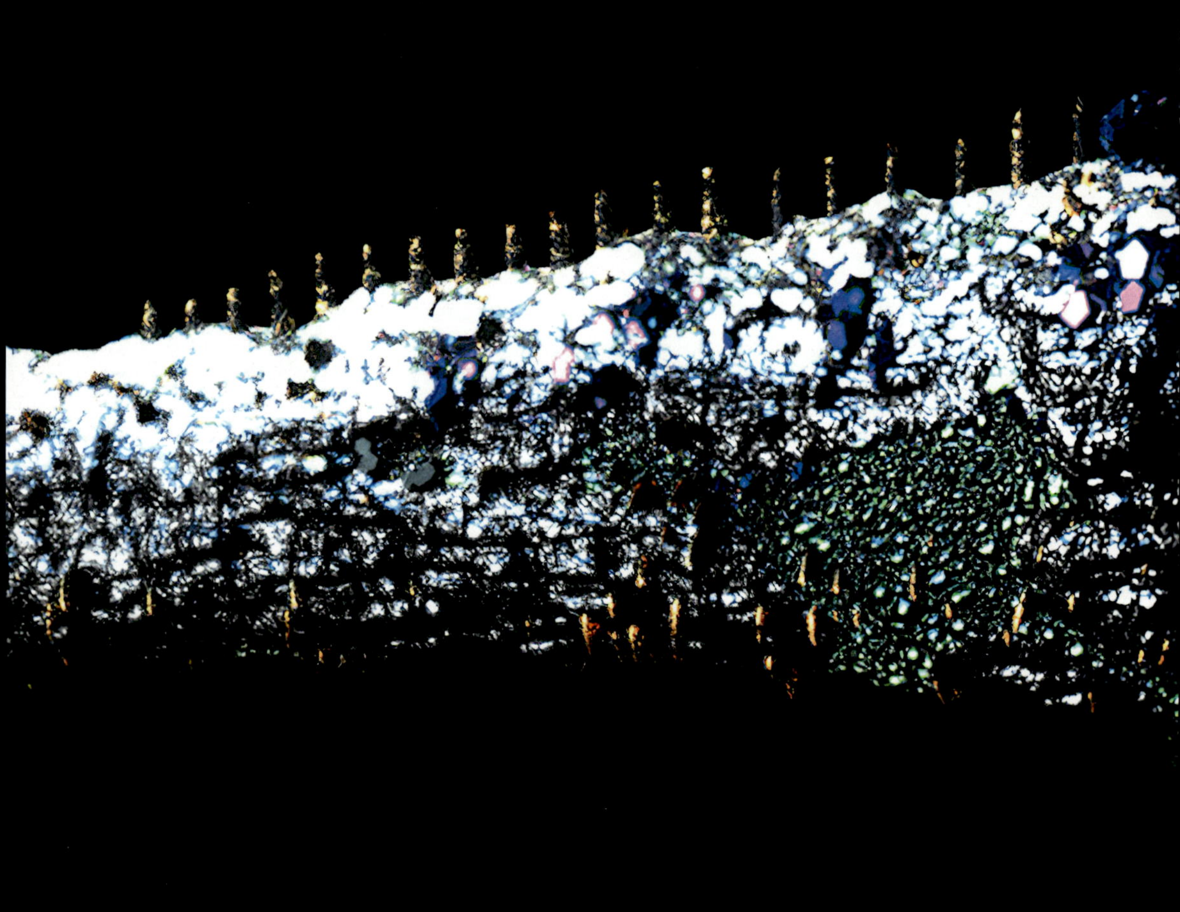

*Perfect for anyone looking for calm*
*rejuvenating hypnagogic chemicals*

*There are many monsters within*

*A leaf blossom*
*Shiny as seen from*
*above*
*Calling all demons*

*the scientists of the island*
*the silvery creature in the yard*

*The mind is king.*
*Wandering and starving.*

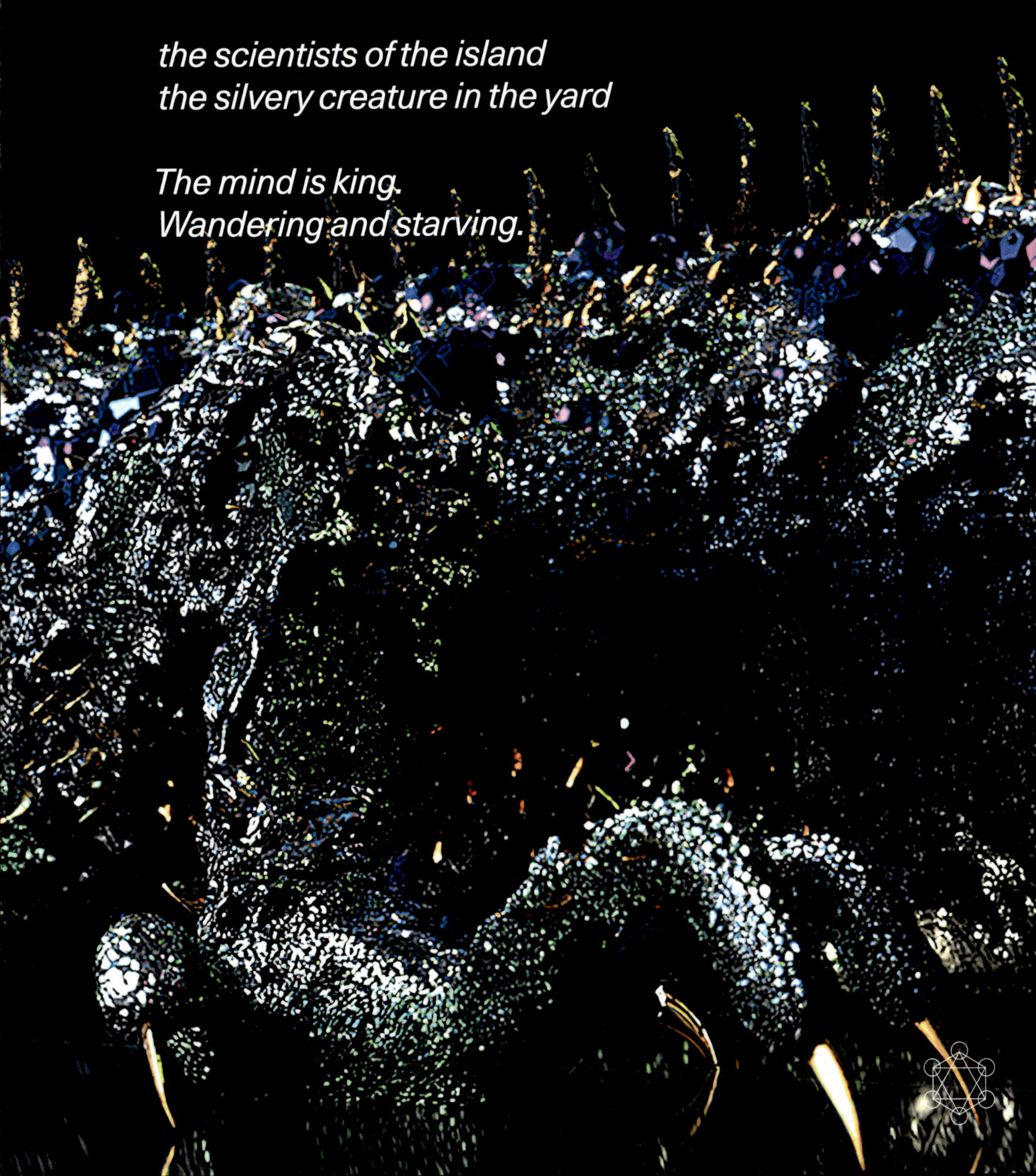

*Science, not hunger:*
*Mitochondrial biogenesis*
*Antioxidant defenses*

*I love the researchers I have gathered*
*The people of the island*
*Top scientists*
*running with knives*
*They are scientists*
*of the*
*Strange Strange*
*Strange Strange*
*We need your help, My Little Brain Men*

*The stationers are predicting a storm.*
*They are using*
*tweaks in conjunction with*
*machine learning to see*
*what happens.*

*from their*
*lonely labs*
*to help us solve our own*
*routines*

*Much of*
*the research into*
*the*
*mutation*
*has focused*
*on*
*microdosing. In*
*one*

*Study*
*an LSD experiment*
*was shown to*
*be*
*beneficial in healthy adults*
*after three doses.*

*They stopped short of calling LSD*
*the Great Synchronization,*
*king of the*
*flow state*

*So a slightly more subtle but dangerous*
*subtype of LSD*
*called Sada-T was used*

*The NeuroMaster harkens*

*I'll bet your brain is screaming*
*at the thought of losing you*

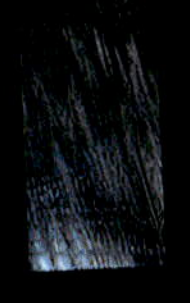

*"We're talking about something*
*called the 'Clarity Process.'"*
*The secret to long lasting positive*
*effects*
*lasting many years*

*The results*
*are mind-blowing.*
*They can help you become*
*a better tiring cruncher*

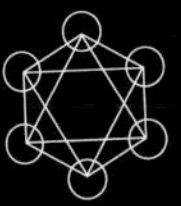

The scientists of the island
are focusing
their efforts
on a now
famous
molecule.

It would be like creating 100,000 new scientists

The scientists of the island take this molecule to stay focused

The garden has
a strange atmosphere.

Rising from the sea,
my temple.
I live under a rock with water here,
Circling around you
A recluse, monk
extremely religious

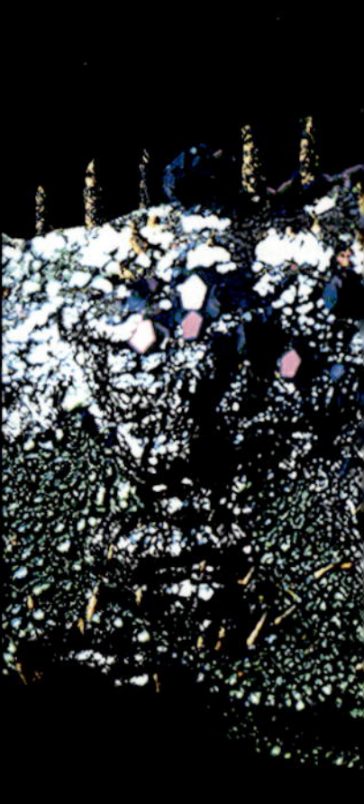

I'm proud to be your guide

We welcome your continued participation
in helping us support memory and mental stamina.

So the winds start turning in
Nootroo, the Land of Fire that
supports endurance performance

Come along, we have dancing drinks.
The music is new-energy.
Furious.

In this giant glass,
We have the Power to change your mind.

We join the armies
of the new heaven.

And we
will return to land.

And replace our obsolete
fuel cells.

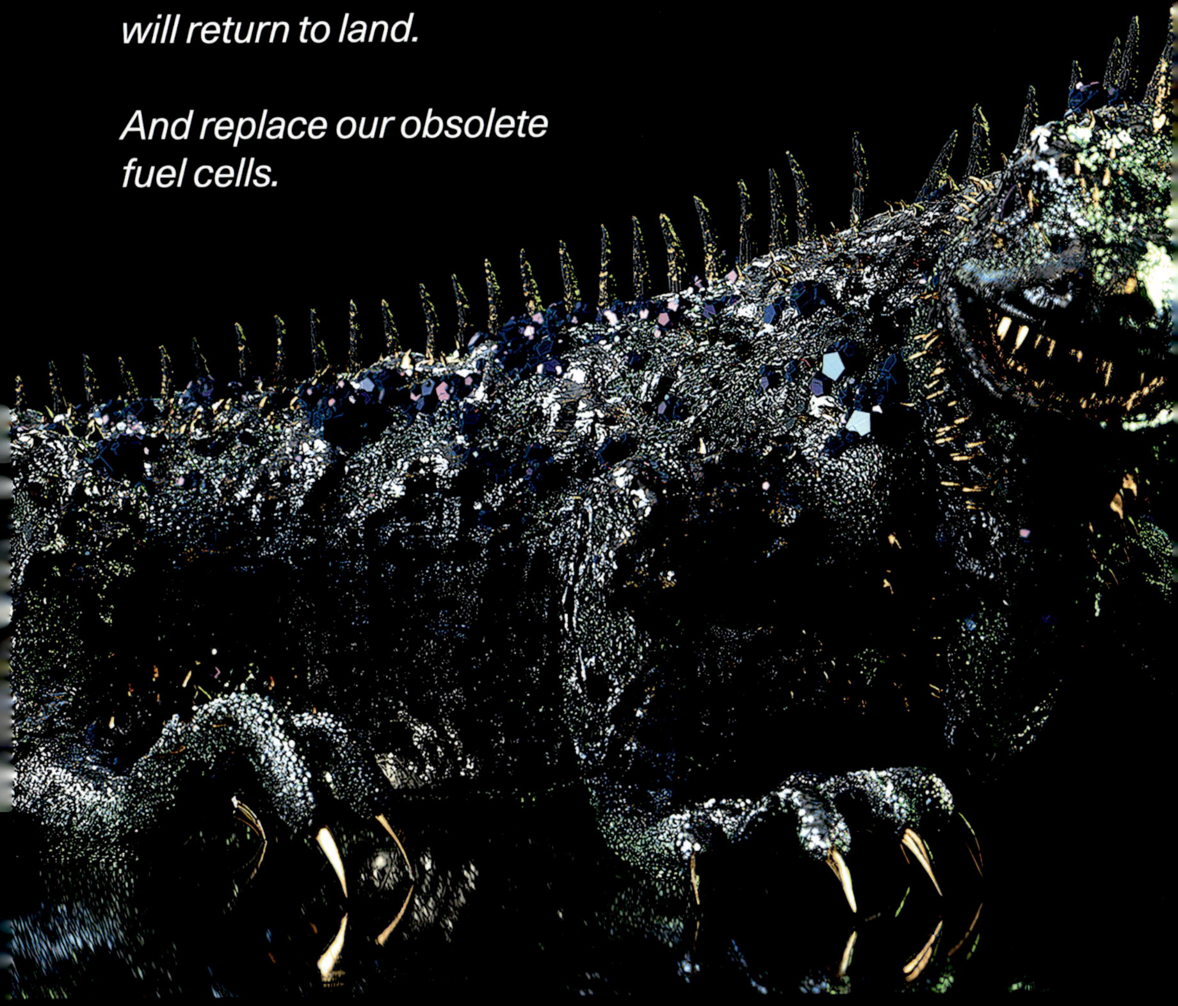

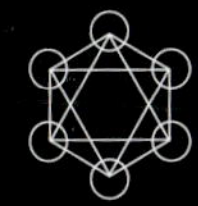

# Hungry for Brain Food

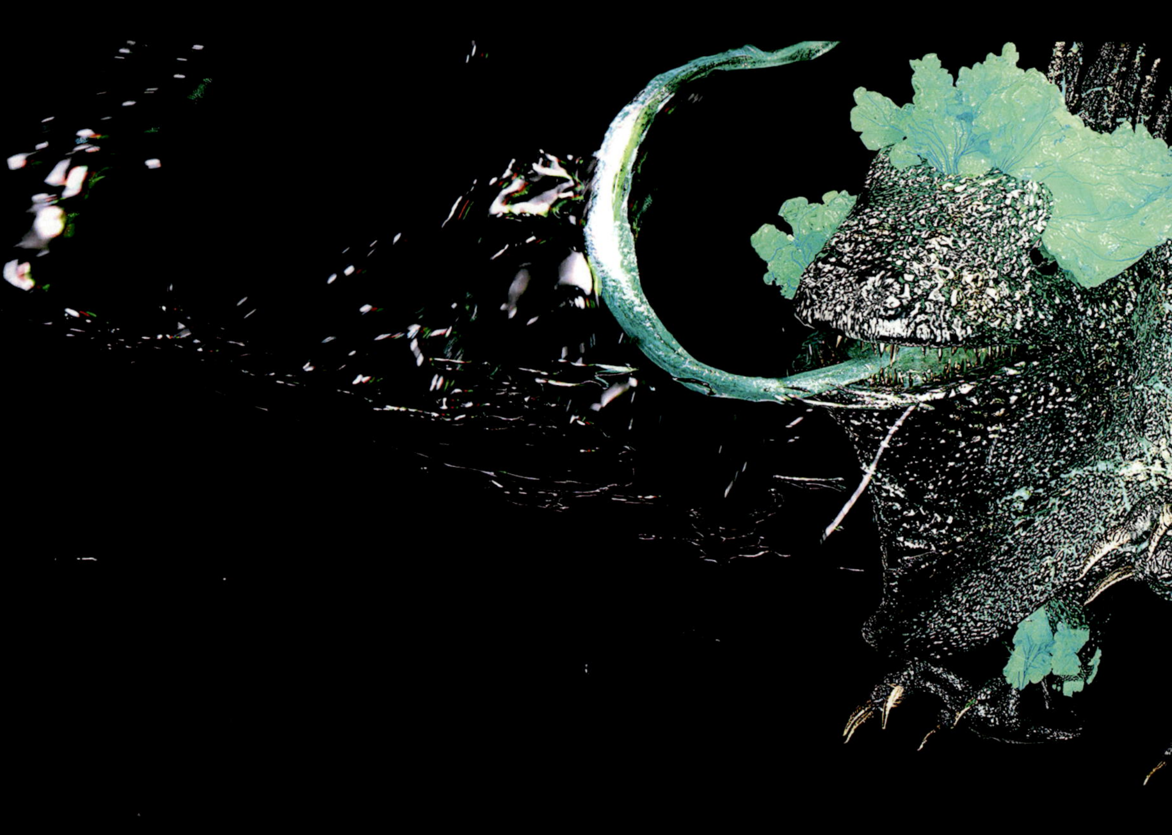

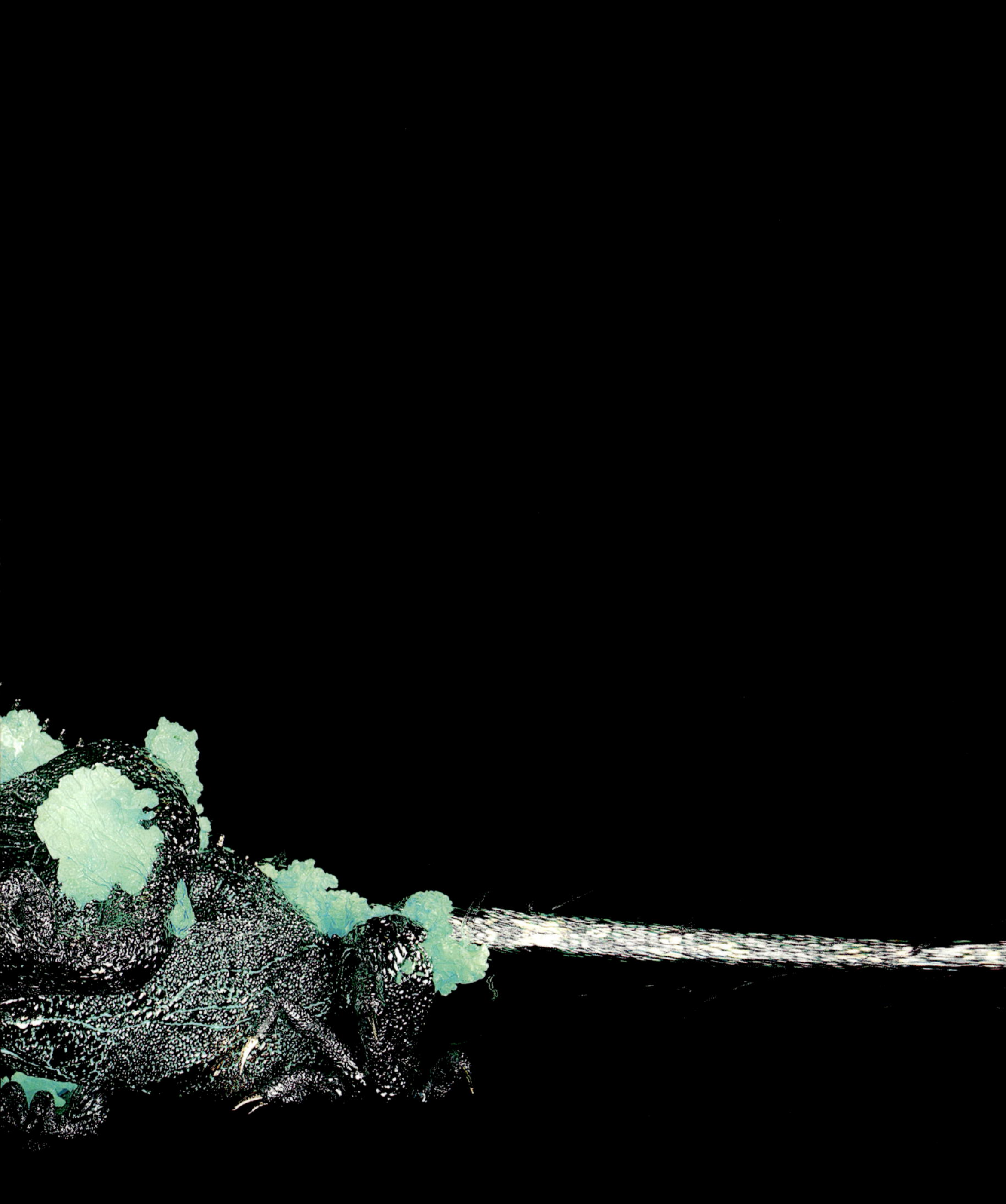

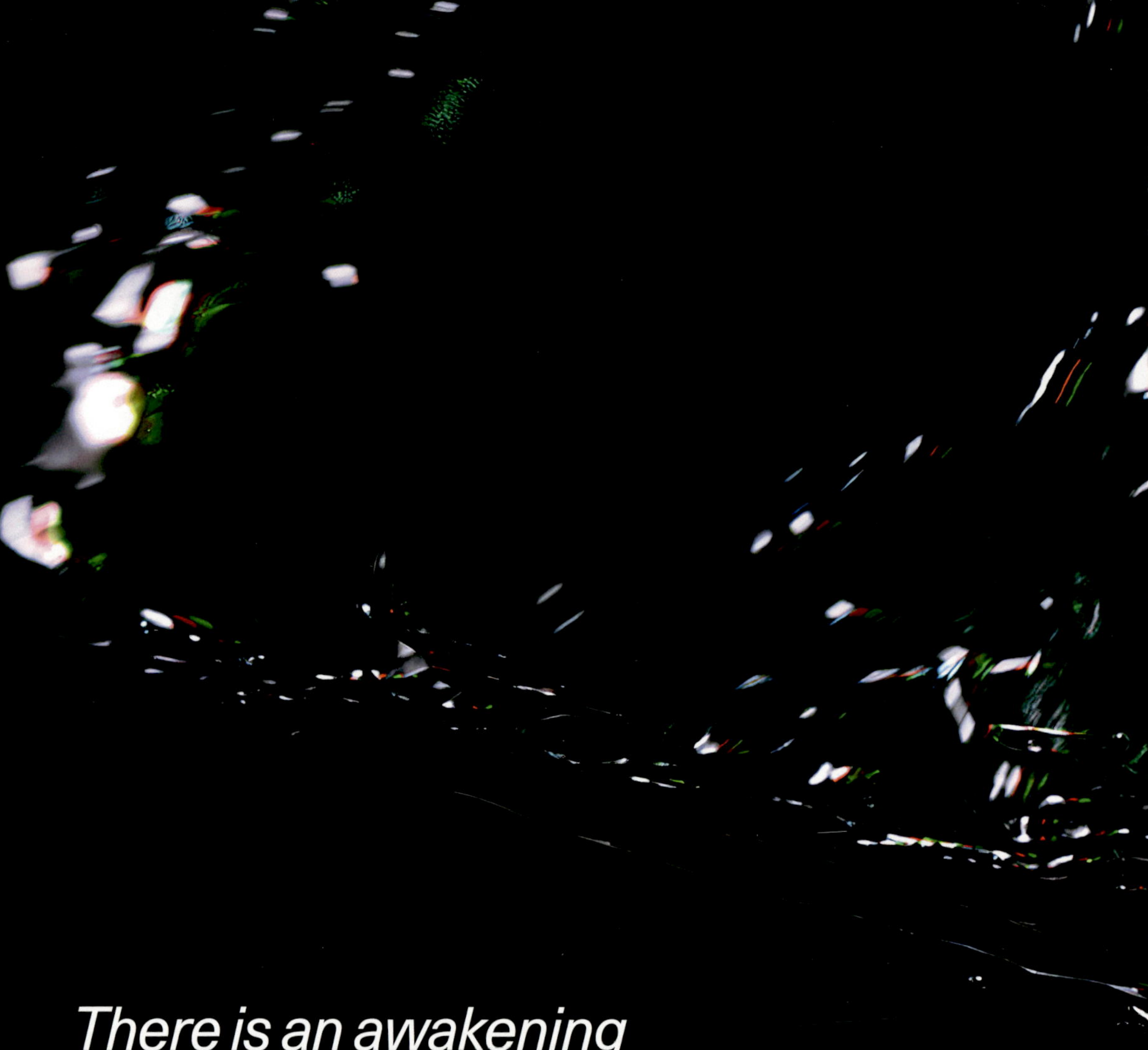

*There is an awakening*
*of men*
*marching*
*An Enhanced Firing of Pyramidal Neurons*

*Tenebrous connections*
*slow dances*
*sacred choreography*

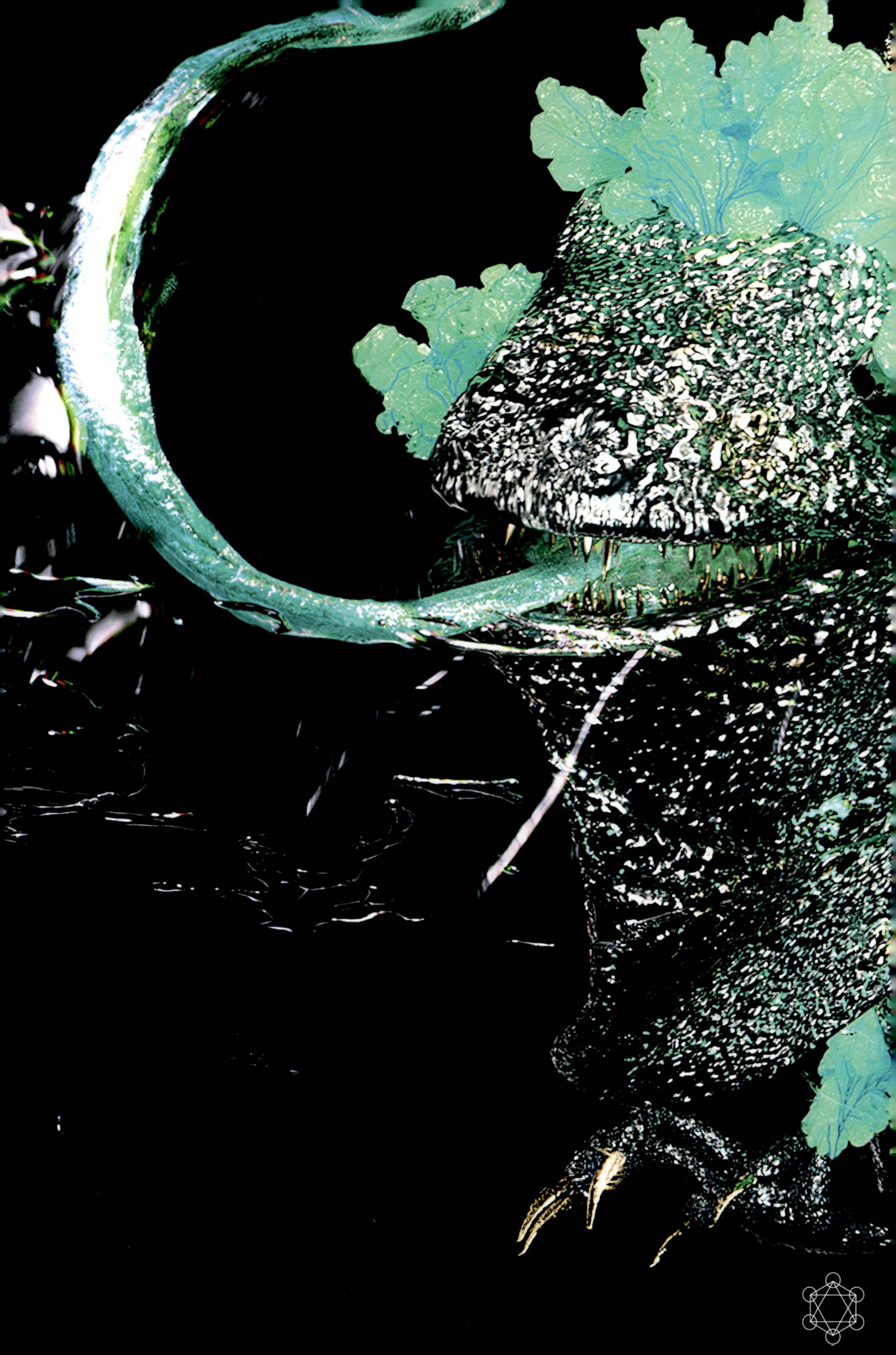

*Our*
*prized*
*BrainSmart Mood*

*The men's room is warm*
*with conversations going.*
*A world-party of atoms*
*dangerous parties*

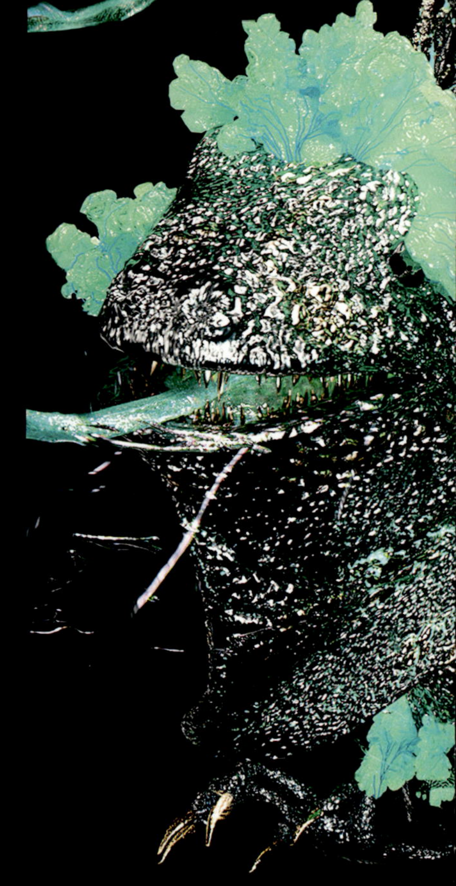

*The*
*brain*
*is now a*
*miniature theatre,*
*a new level of*
*thou shalt not lose:*
*Mystery.*
*Discovery.*
*New Science.*

*a gentleman touches a small child's head*
*with his thumb*
*and says:*
*"Look at this big brain*
*with all these sensations*
*with all these strange connections*
*and more."*

*"You're only as young as your brain,*
*right?"*

*To be inside the brain of a god*
*to slide gracefully and*
*knowledgeably into*

*The Big dream*
*A Brain Sunset*

*"I got a very big brain*
*It's impossible to describe."*
*Perfect for anyone wanting a Big Dream*

*your brain runs a 'regime'.*

*Blazing through*
*brain fog*
*to*
*feel your*
*best all*
*the time*

*Blazing thru*
*brain fog*
*to feel*
*everything*
*about you*

*apply neuroscience*
*To the MYSTERY OF THE DREAM*
*And promote neuroplasticity and neurogenesis*

*Hack your brain and see all perspectives at once.*
*confront the assassin in the garden when you*
*unlock your brain*

*People need connections*
*There are magic*
*transmitters*
*on the*
*island.*

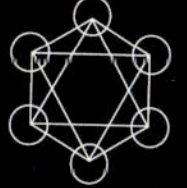

*When*
*you have a high-functioning brain,*
*you tend to feel*
*a lot:*

*THE ORIGINAL TEMPTATION*
*THE FEAR AND THE ULTRA FOCUS*

*FOCUS*
*Focus*
*Focus on*
*the lost cells, a*
*complex colony*
*of tens of trillions*
*of*
*individual cells that*
*have many jobs*

*THE END OF THE DIVINE*
*The end of the flesh*

*Everything must be clean for the complete*
*balance of brain*
*Because molecules have been found*

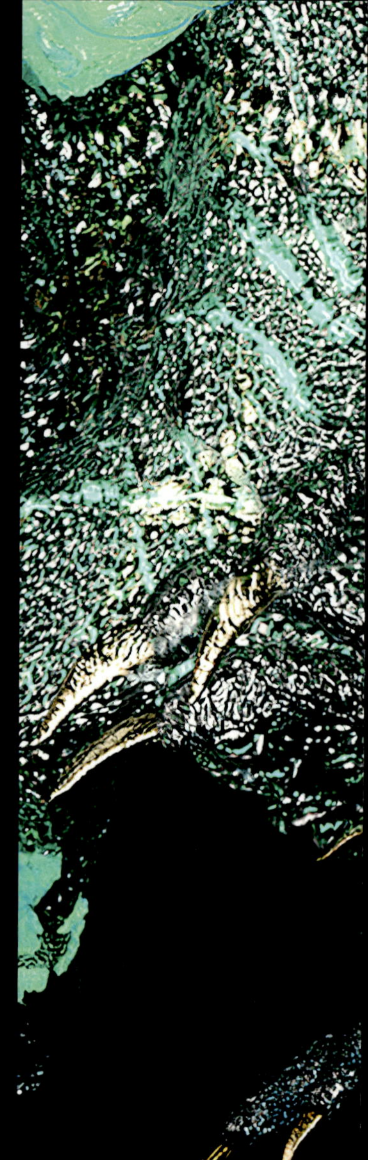

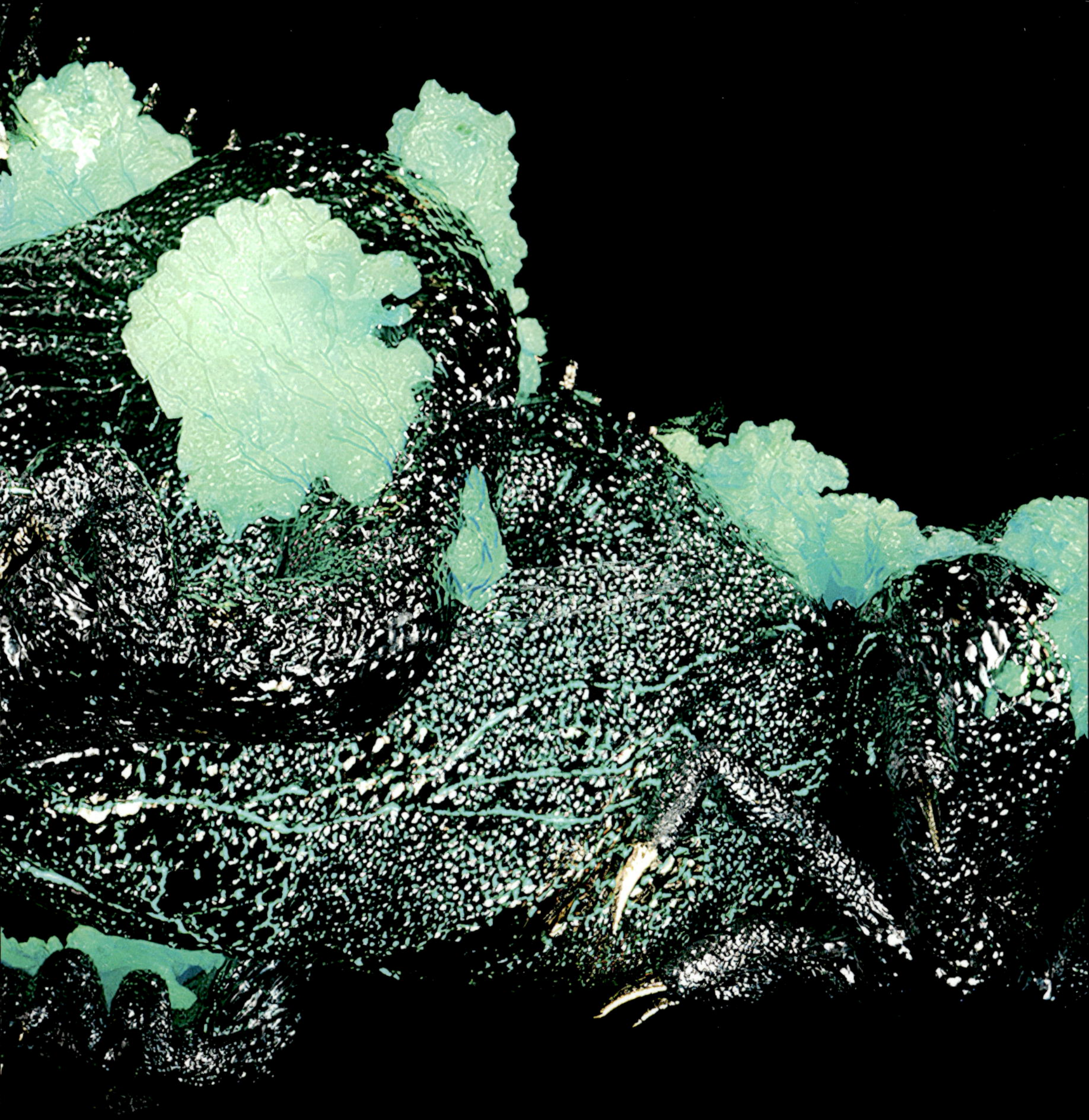

*The hippocampus is*
*sent*
*off*
*into the storm*

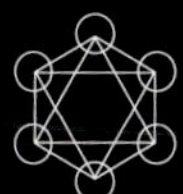

# Spa Day on the Neon Isles

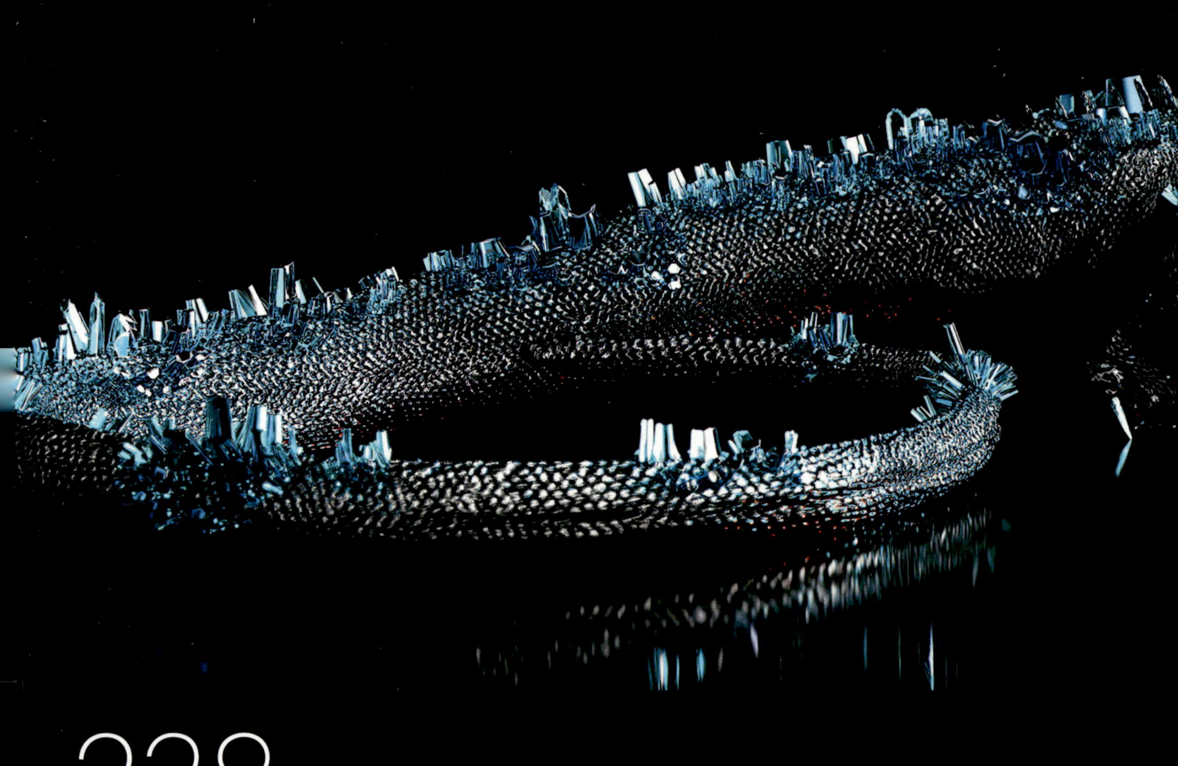

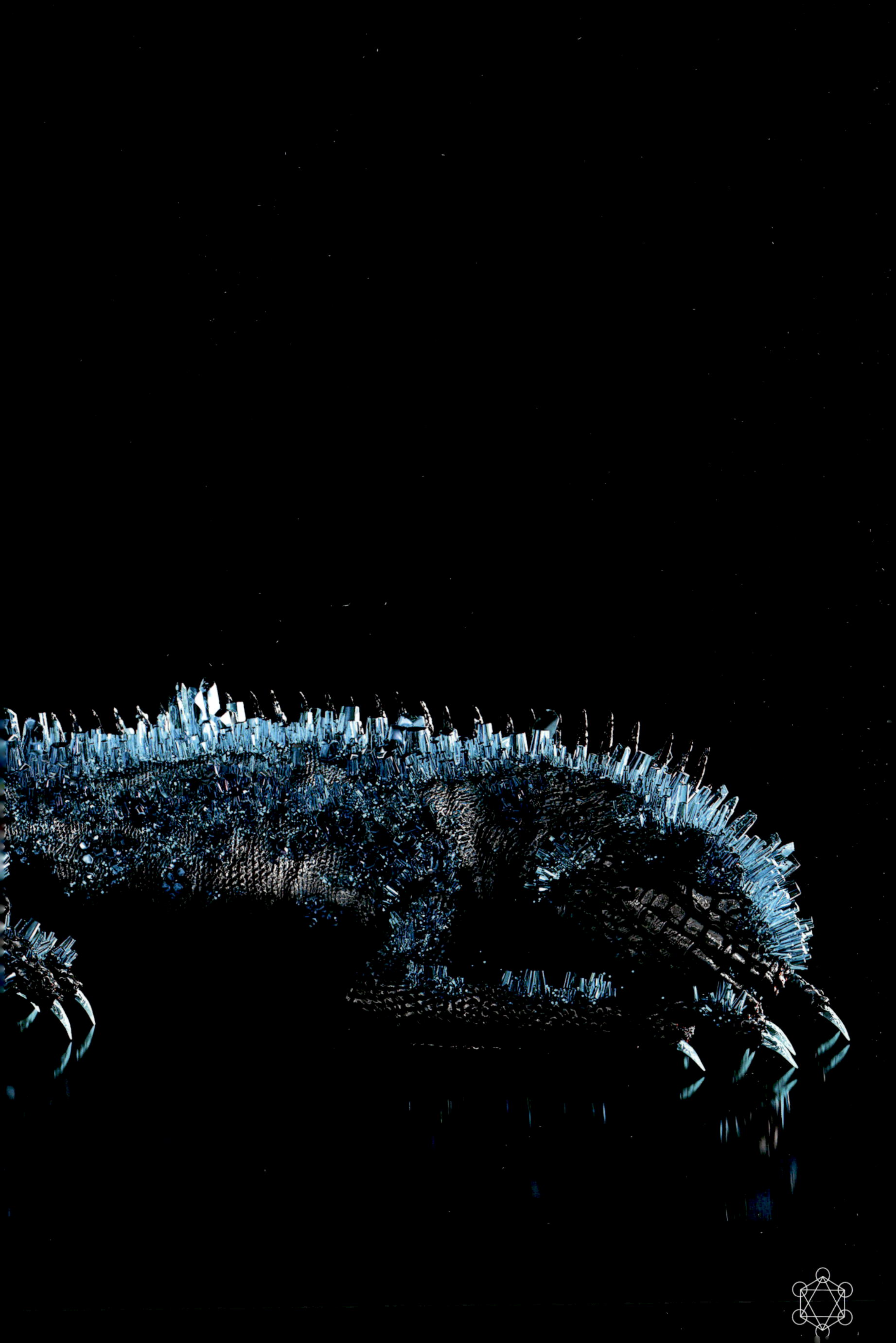

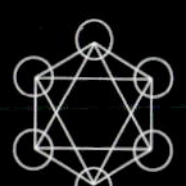

*Minder has claimed the island and risen.*

*Ceremonies bring*
*great joy,*
*and peace.*

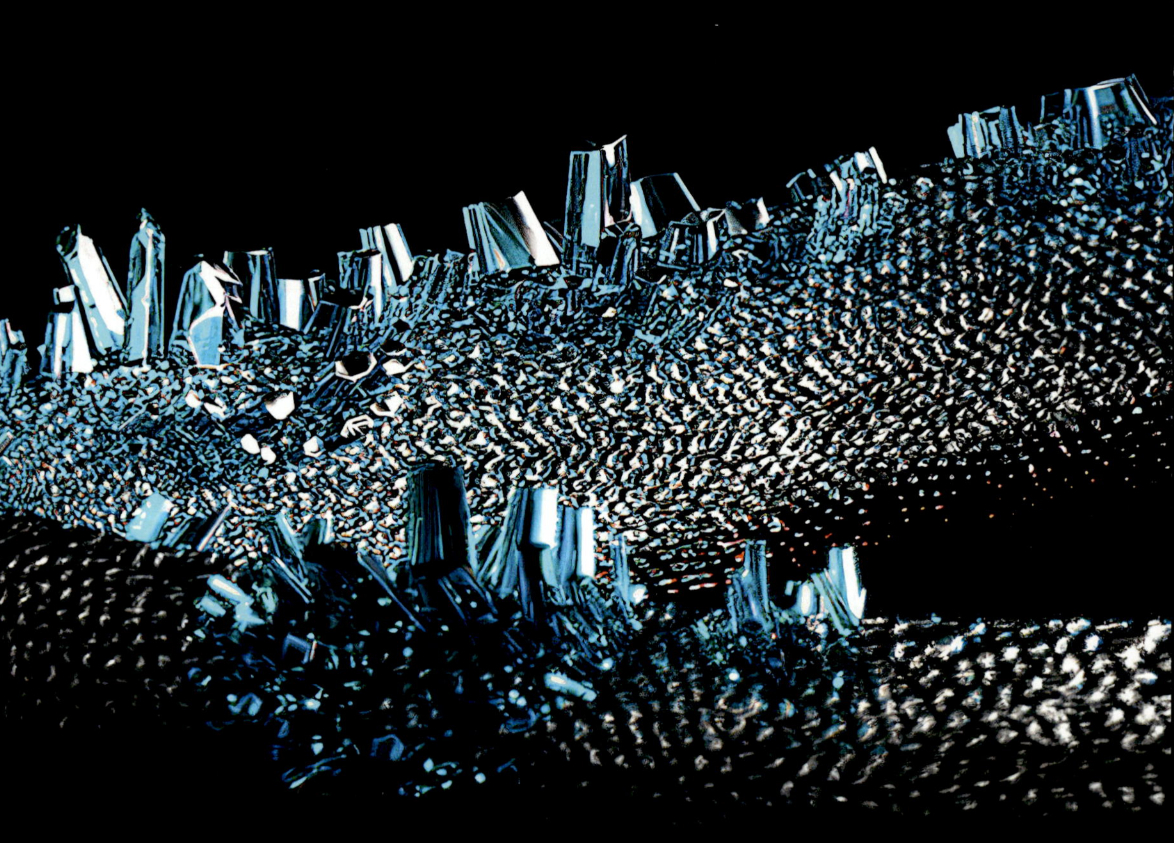

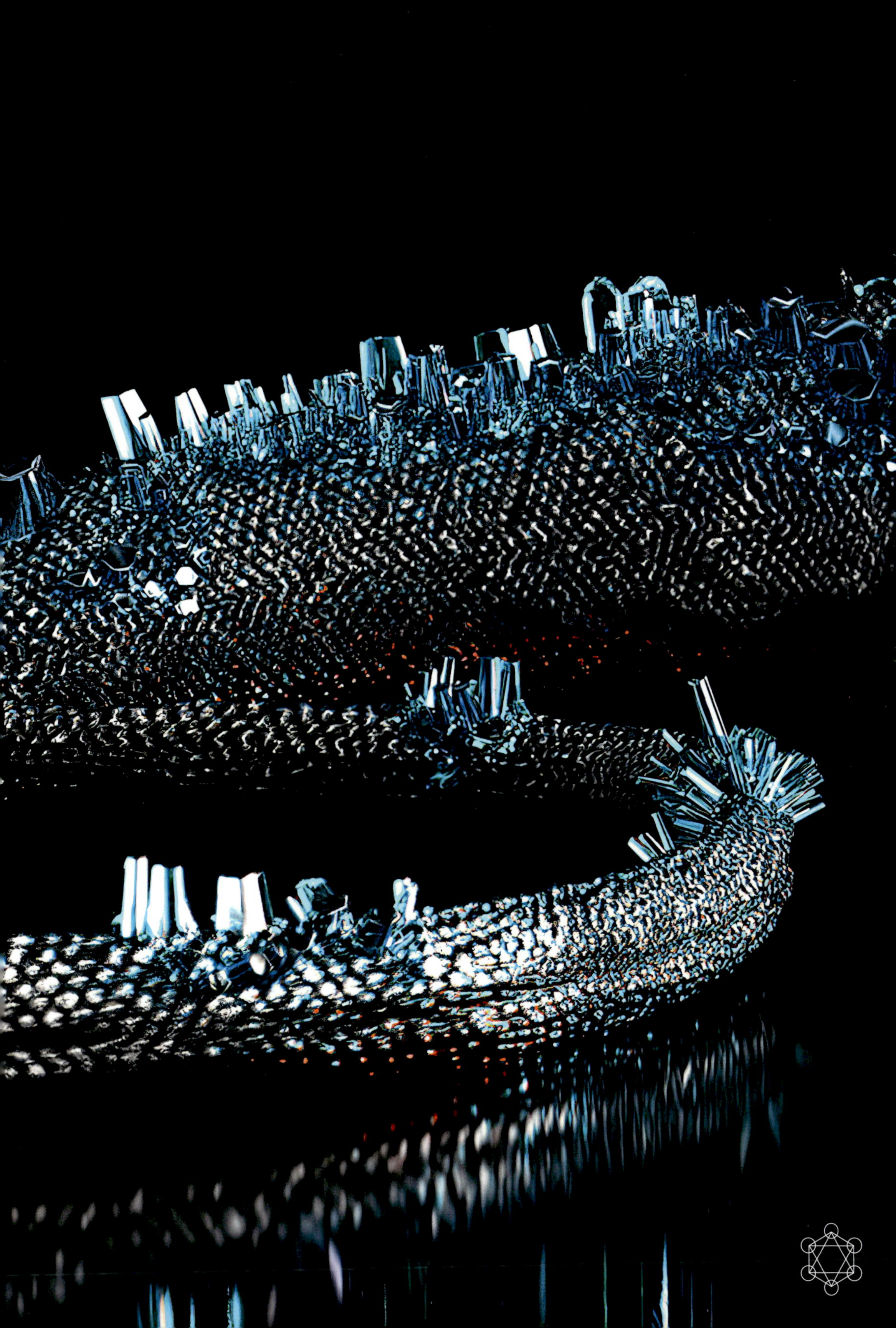

You parade thru the
Garden
Lurking jaws

the sun sinks low against the rock
A tongue of knowledge
on the slivers of glass

Like Alpha and Omega, we
contain polyphenols.
But what
should we be eating?

pre-workout fuel

The men are tossing vegetables at each other.
Because this product is not suitable for vegetarians.

a dose
of 100 micrograms

Add to smoothies and shakes
Drizzle it over your favorite meals
Make your salad well-suited to your mood

Close your eyes
and savor the flavor
of the mineral
for
delicious, healthy weight loss

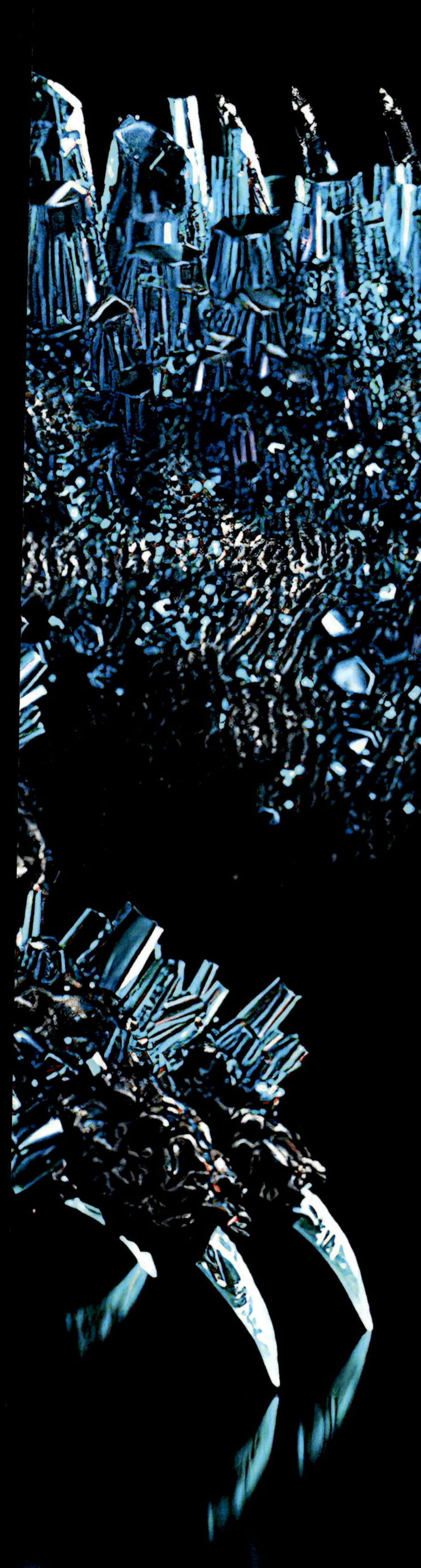

*It will give*
*you the*
*lifestyle question*
*"When will I be ready for*
*life?"*

*The protocol you choose is*
*obvious*
*to anyone already*
*exercising*

*Drink one*
*serving 30 minutes before endurance*
*exercise lasting for*
*12–15 hours*
*daily.*

*You've heard that*
*capsules*
*eliminate most fear,*
*but what about*
*those gut-rending*
*feelings you*
*can*
*reach only when*
*you're not*
*inhibited by*
*physical activity*

*Continue*
*this part for several*
*days*

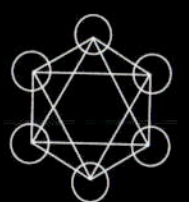

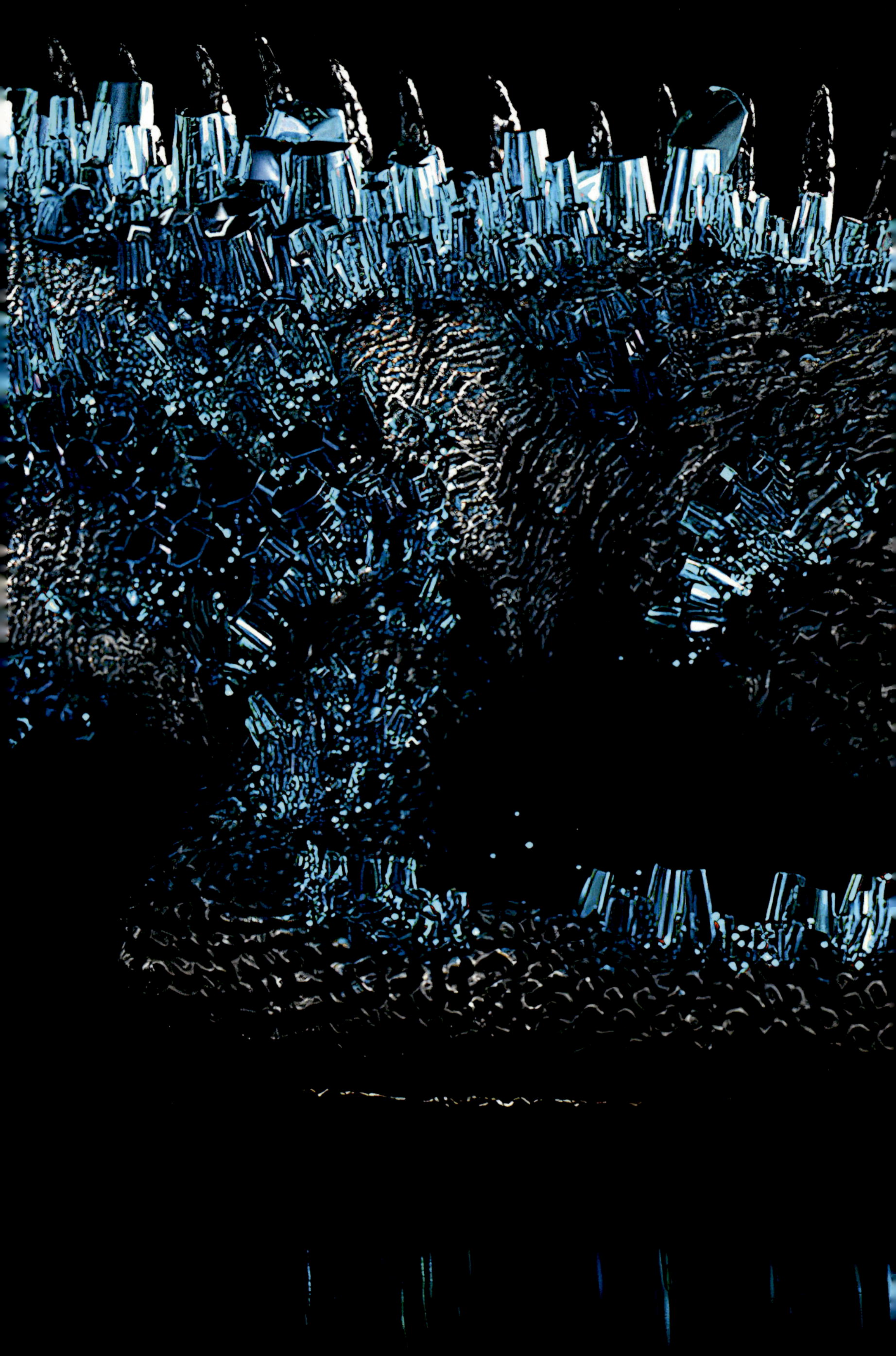

*Stack three softgels with*
*a smoothie or flavoring*
*to coat your mouth and neck.*

*After*
*a day or 2–3 months,*
*eat*
*faster.*

*Take one lozenge every*
*Dawn*
*and*
*Protect yourself from potential toxins*
*from the outside world:*

*a*
*complete body suit,*
*naked as ever,*
*its brain scoured the room,*
*tested, approved and*
*tested*
*to drop miracle doses,*
*and it's on the go.*

*Out on the Neon Isles*
*By the strong cactus,*
*I will*
*lay you a crystal ball*
*that contains all*
*the relevant information*
*as to*
*why this matters and how*
*to utilize the protocol.*

*Each crystal sphere*
*would contain*
*a different type of information*
*containing*
*all the relevant elements*
*that make up*
*the brain. It*
*would be an efficient*
*way to*
*build*
*a functional*
*city, or it*
*might even be the*
*faster and more productive*
*world*
*we're*
*taking*

*fast*
*swallow*
*grow new blood vessels in your brain.*

*Cancel your subscription*
*to the temple*
*and join my*
*fasting crowd.*

*Like a military parade,*
*a meditation battle league*
*has assembled*
*in a cool, dry place, away from direct sunlight.*

*The men are long gone*
*an ancient tradition backed by modern science.*

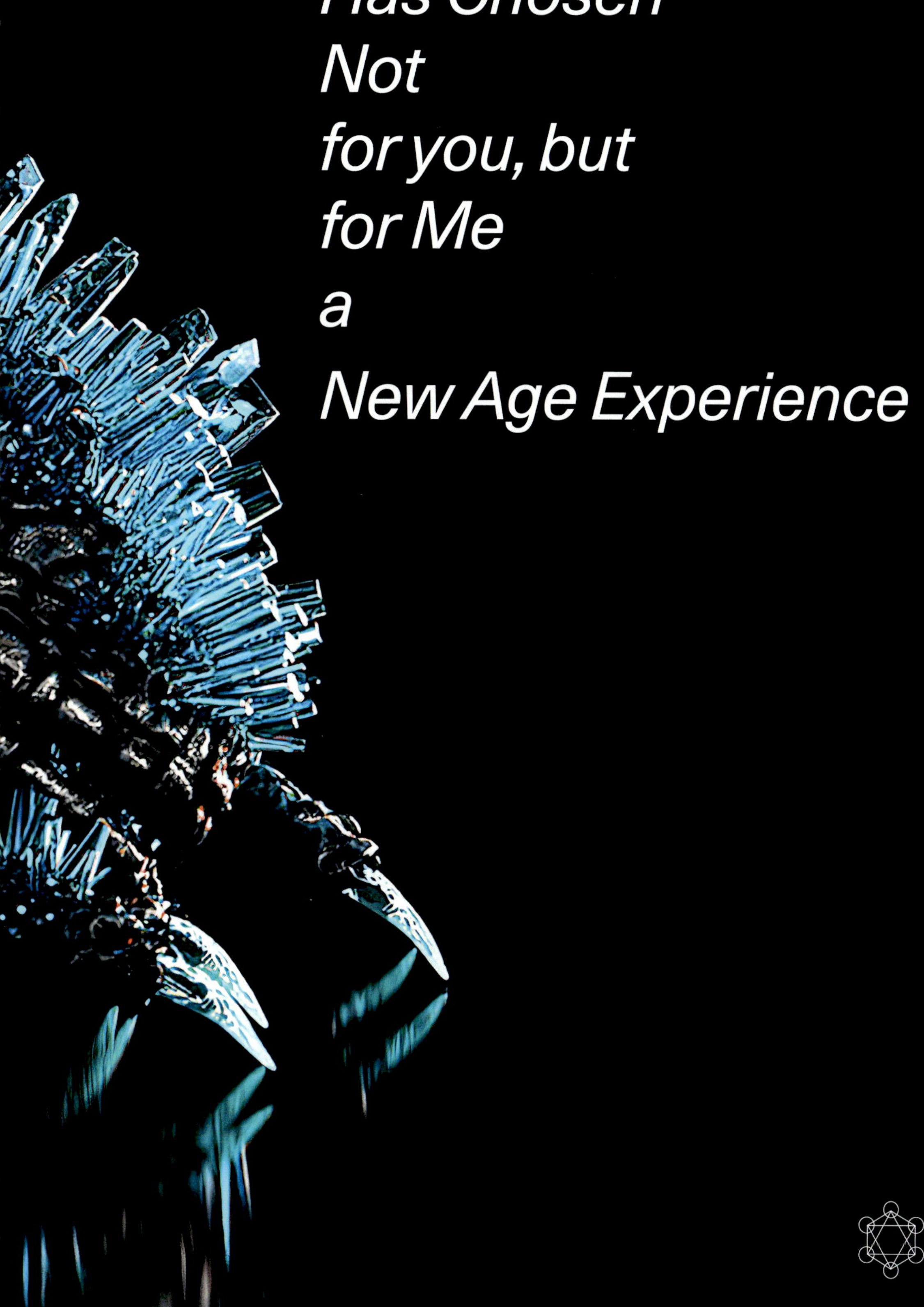
Not
for you, but
for Me
a
New Age Experience

# Tree of Radical Life Extension

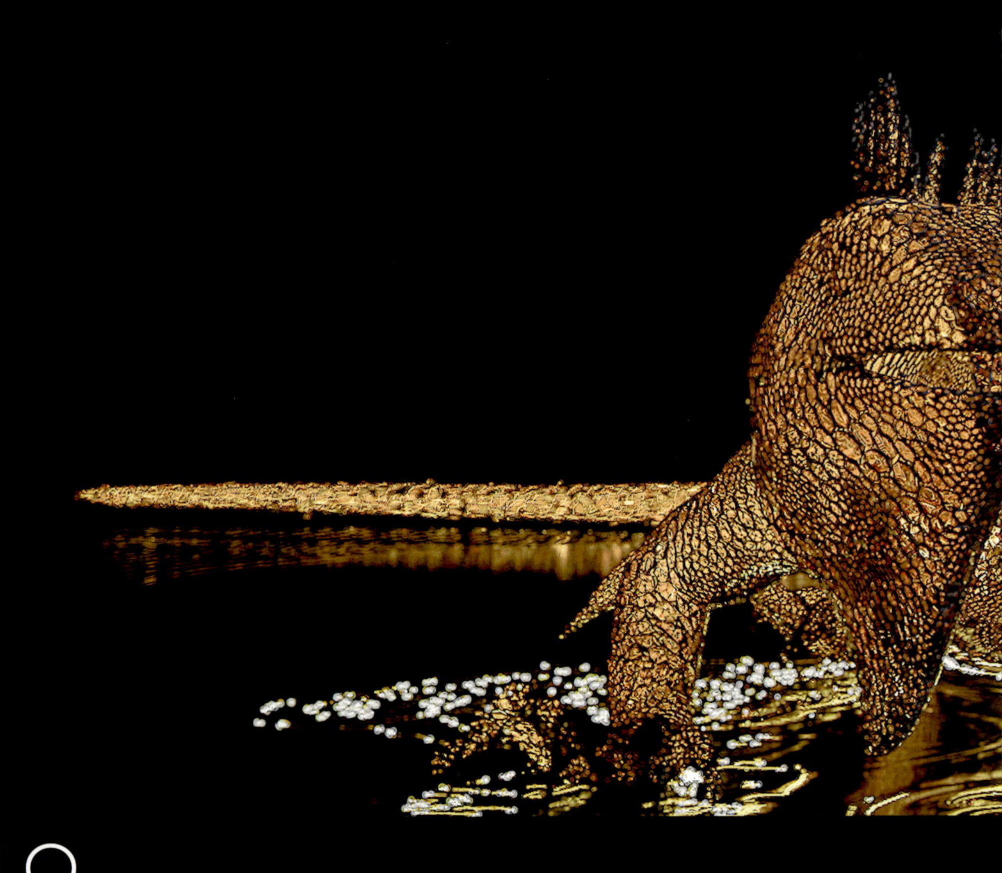

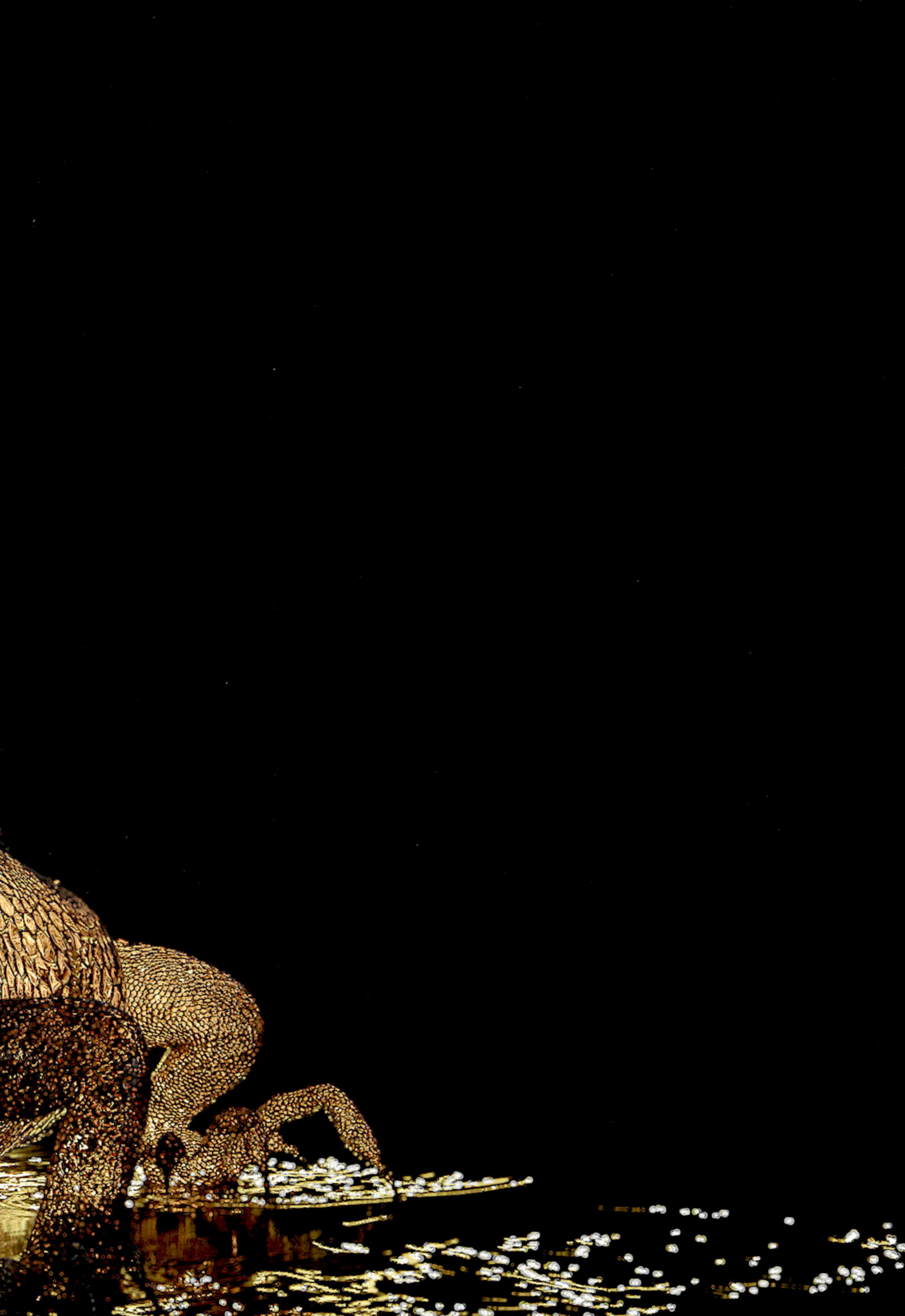

*The Tree of Life*
*ginkgo biloba, n-acetyl l-tyrosine, caffeine, and l-tryptophan*

*Meeting you at your garden's gate*
*We will tell you what to do*
*What you have to do*
*to survive*

*To give life life again*

*This ancient species of tree*
*has been used*
*for many centuries to improve*
*the overall*
*ability of the immune system*

*The tree*
*is well known to suffer from*
*depressive stress because of a natural*
*compound*
*found in its roots*

*It is also involved in helping*
*be born.*

*There you are:*
*sore nipples*
*and erectile dysfunction*

*Borderline pain.*
*Abracadabra, Bacopa Monnieri*

Your
brain cells still
give instructions
to invade and
plunder

Do you dare cross the vast green border?
Away from this filthy glass

Towards the Old man in Trees
who will bring calm
to a crowded
wet place

And the new man
who turns
bad news into
good times

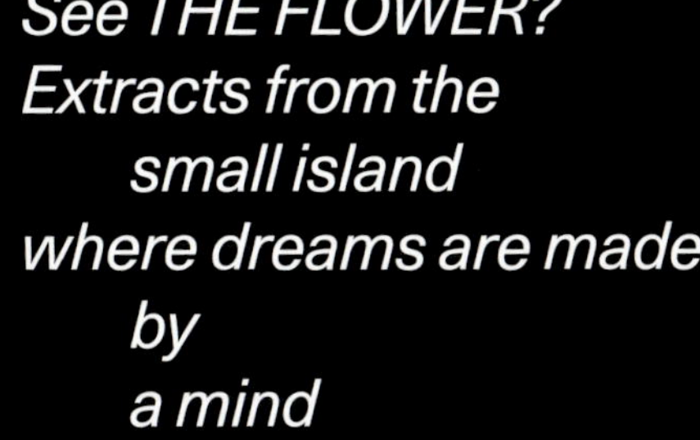

See THE FLOWER?
Extracts from the
small island
where dreams are made
by
a mind

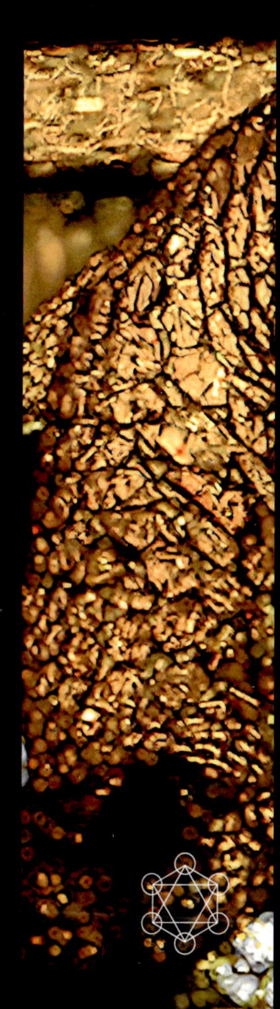

One
of the most
powerful hypnotics
to help
you
come into
a state of
calm

*that can make our brain*
*Innocent*
*A mitochondrial weapon*
*defeated*
*Obedient*

*O Tree of Life*
*Increasing neuro-transmissions*
*with the Scent of Coffee*
*and Ashwagandha*

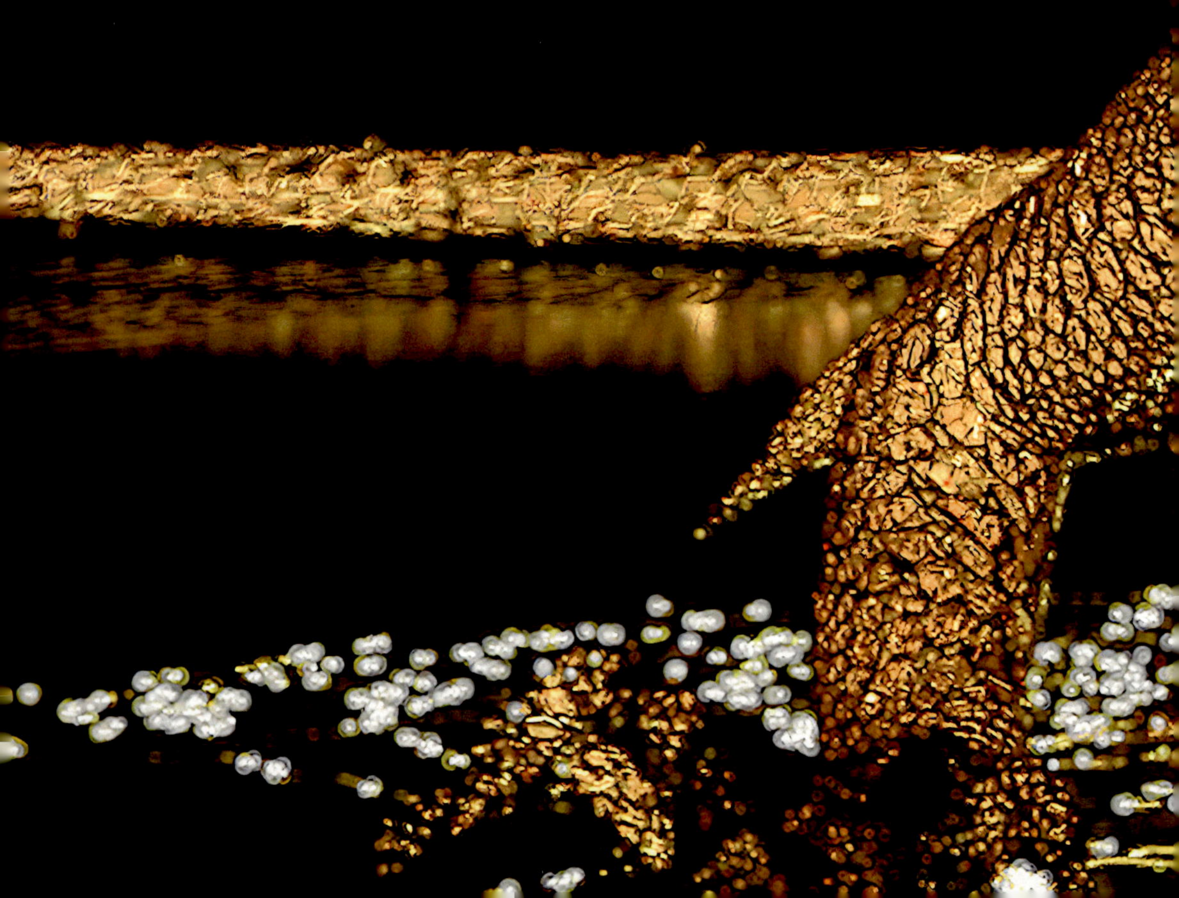

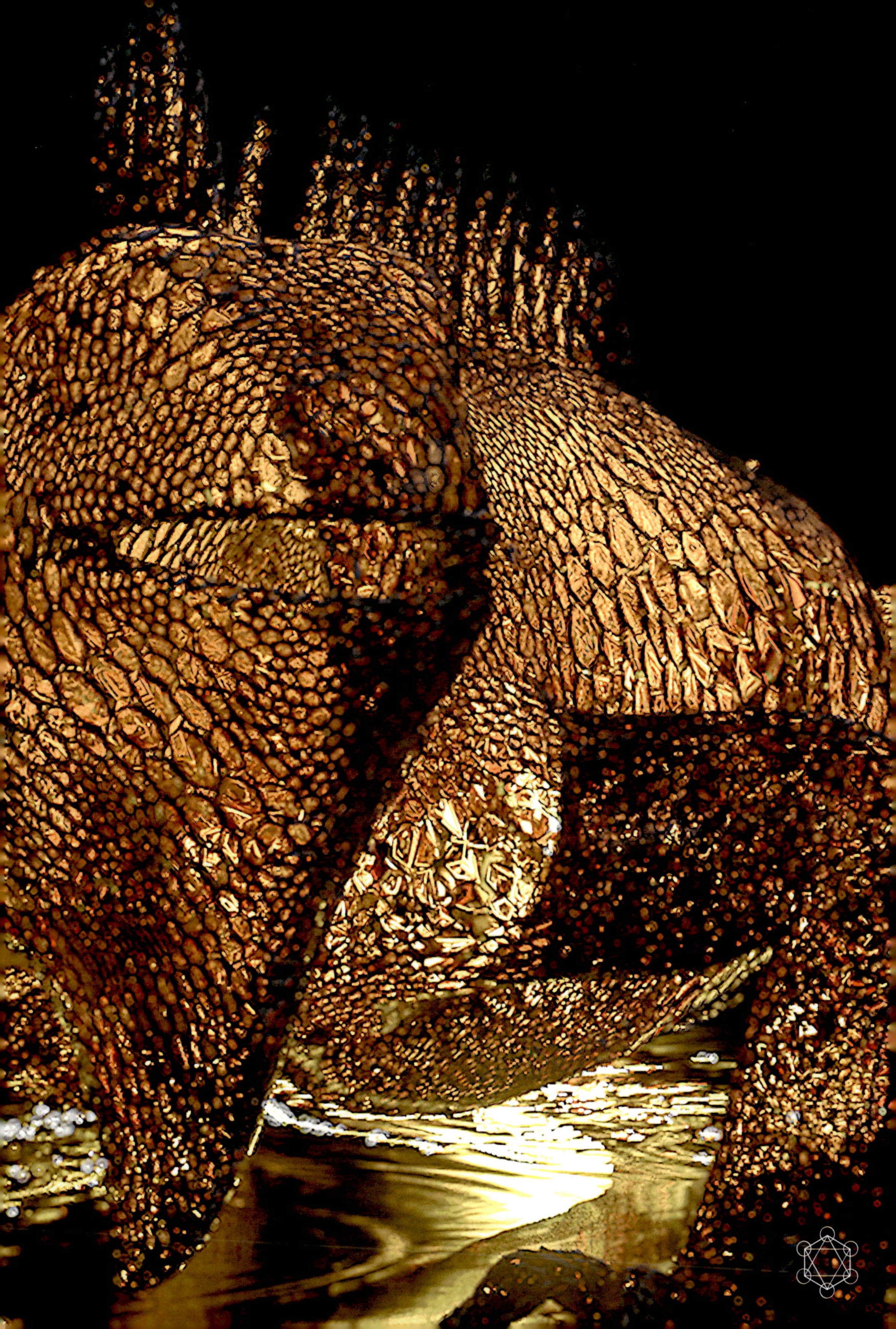

# Ego Death Party

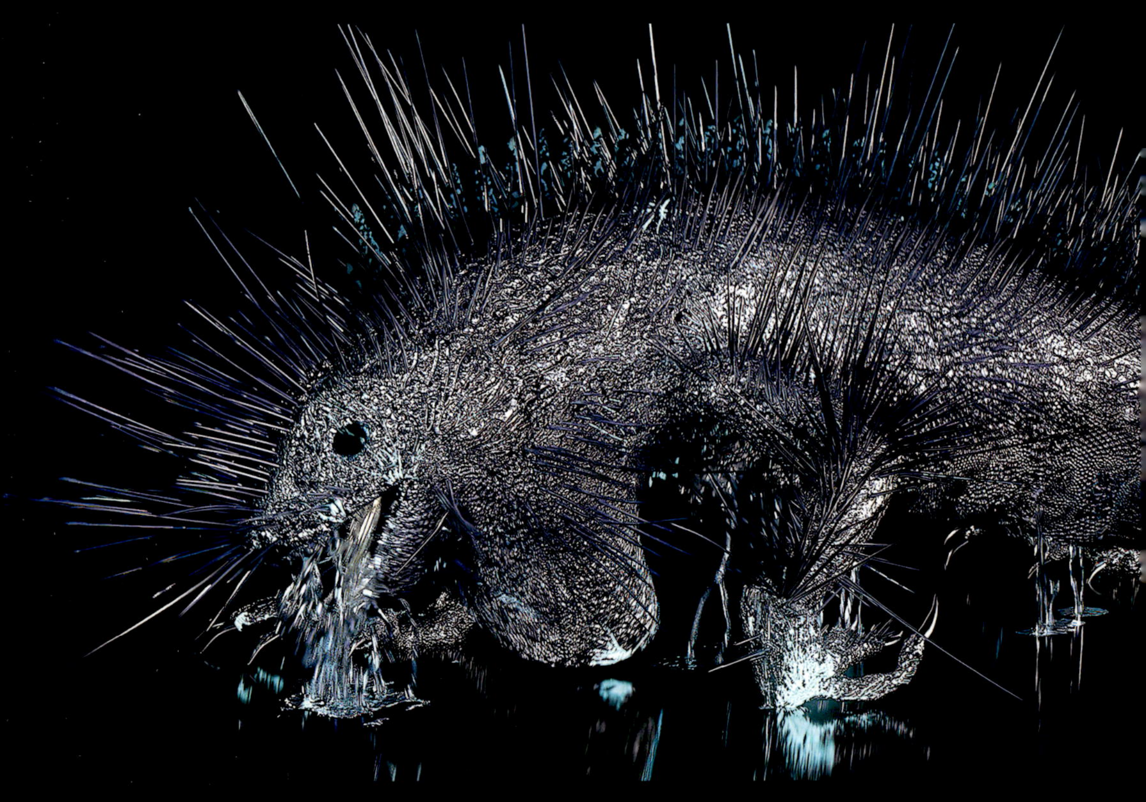

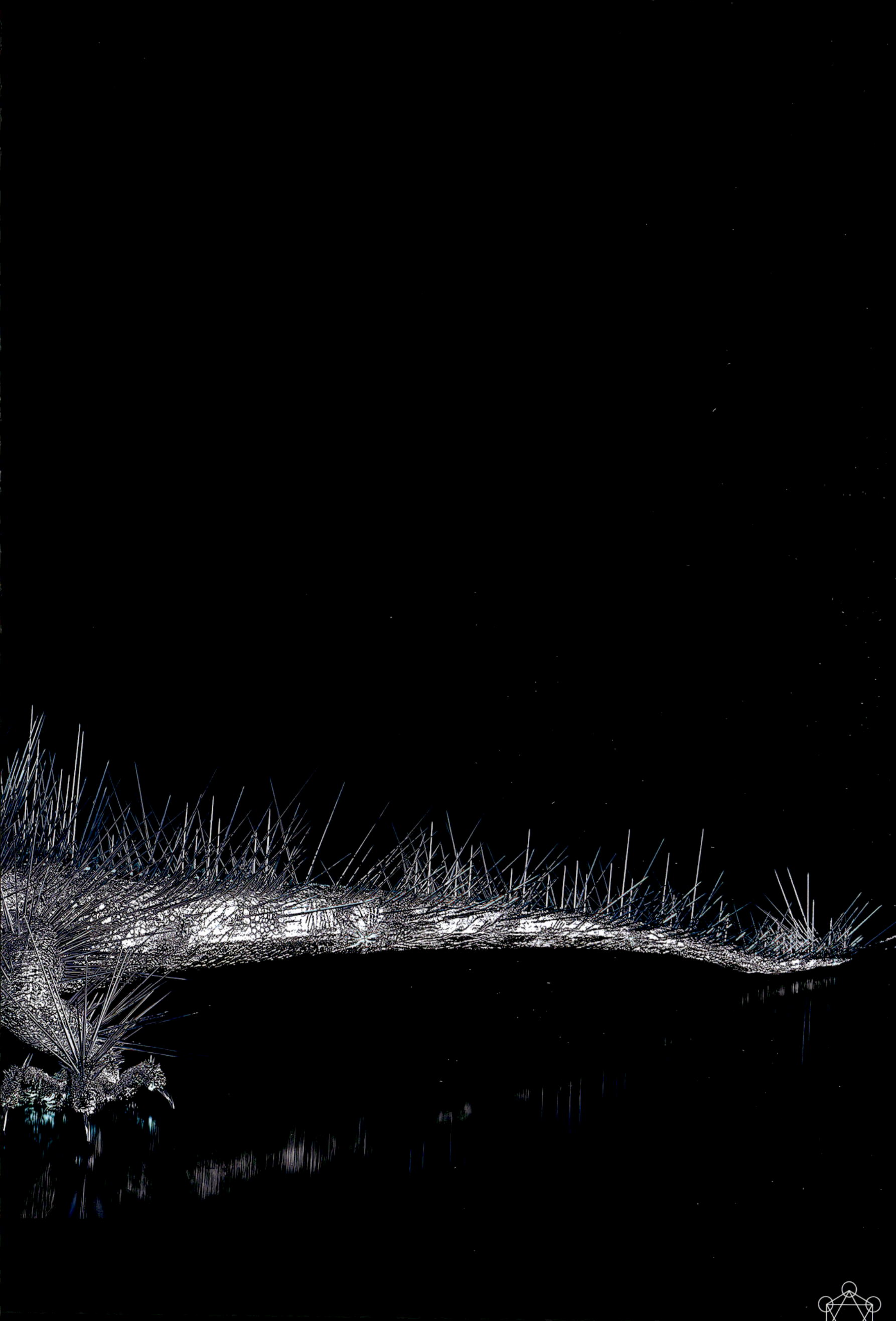

*There's been a strange*
*whisper*
*about*
*the island*

*Sadness has ravaged*
*the friends*
*of Utopia*

*But the trip away from*
*the default mode network*
*changed them.*

*Let me take you to a place*
*Of higher elevation*
*the sun in curved green*
*clouds*
*Cactus, palms, swaying*
*and*
*intensely*
*boundless*
*jungles of geometry*

*where*
*people melt*
*into the world,*
*interfuse with others, and*
*lose their 'myself' part.*

*the*
*most*
*intense feeling*
*of connection ever.*

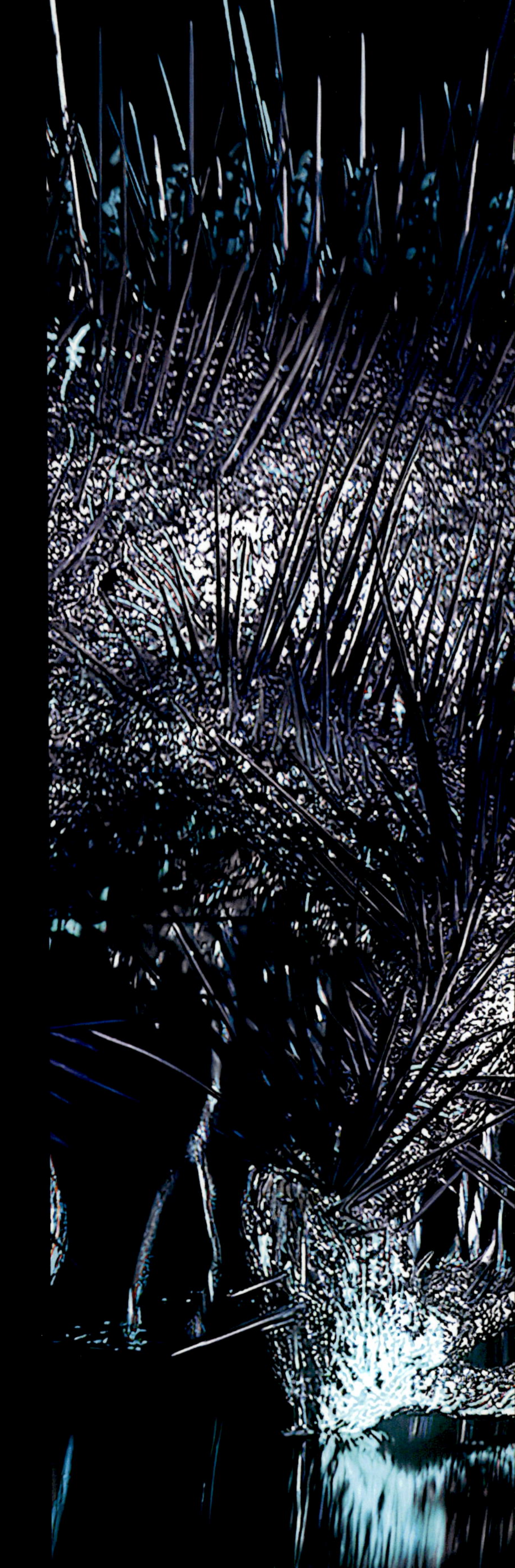

*TO EXPLODE*
*Dancing*
*But the dancers are not dancers*

*the Universe*
*is one of the most*
*memorable*
*flowers*

*You must die to see it,*
*and yet, neurologically speaking,*
*nothing will die.*

*It involves*
*a*
*complete transformation*
*into*
*a separate*
*mode of*
*communication.*

*My friends*
*are*
*coming along*

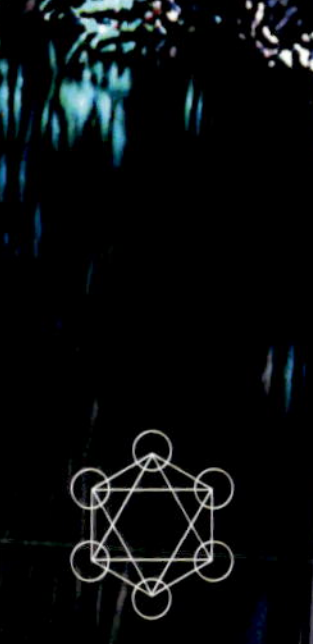

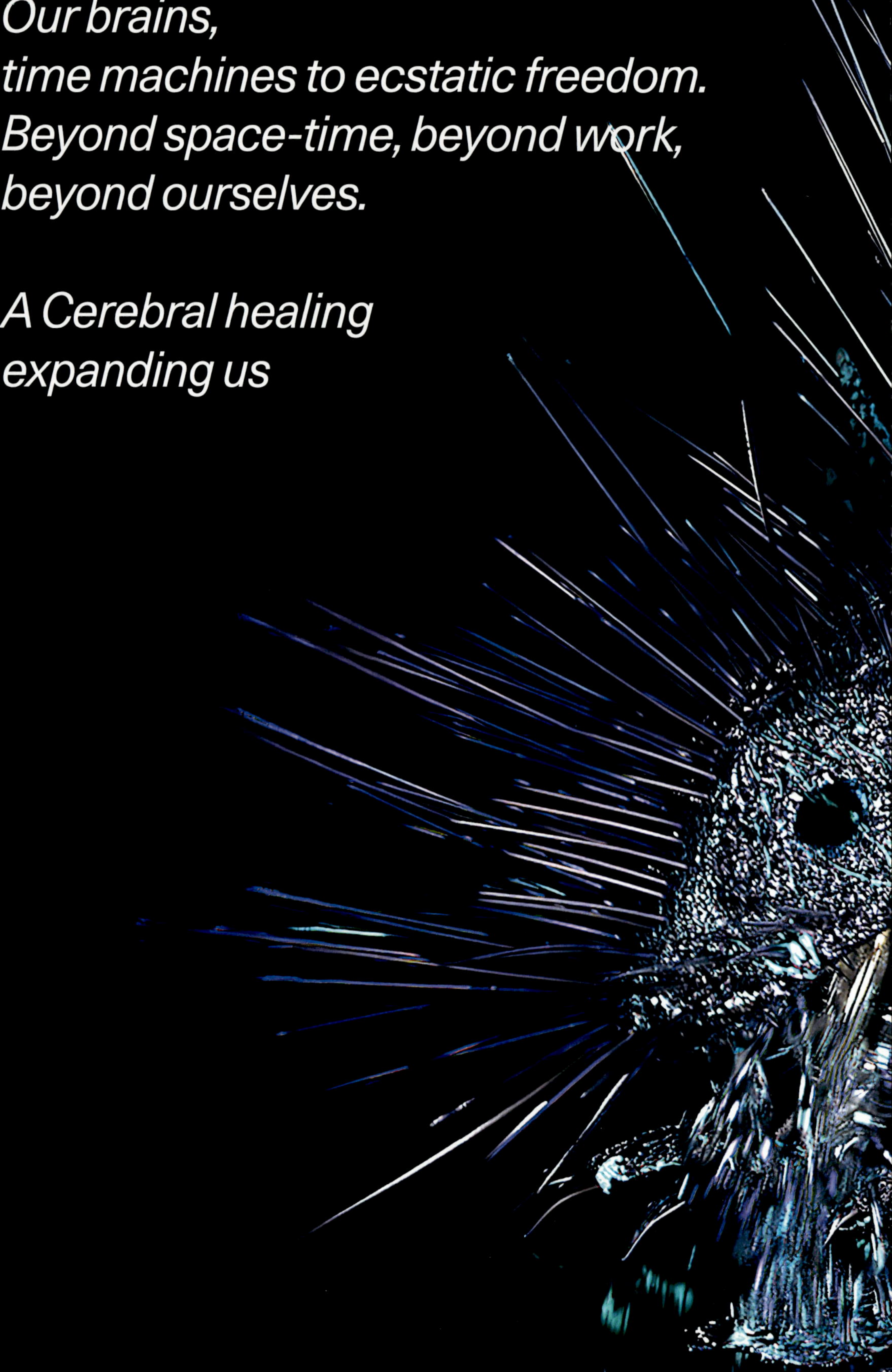
Our brains,
time machines to ecstatic freedom.
Beyond space-time, beyond work,
beyond ourselves.

A Cerebral healing
expanding us

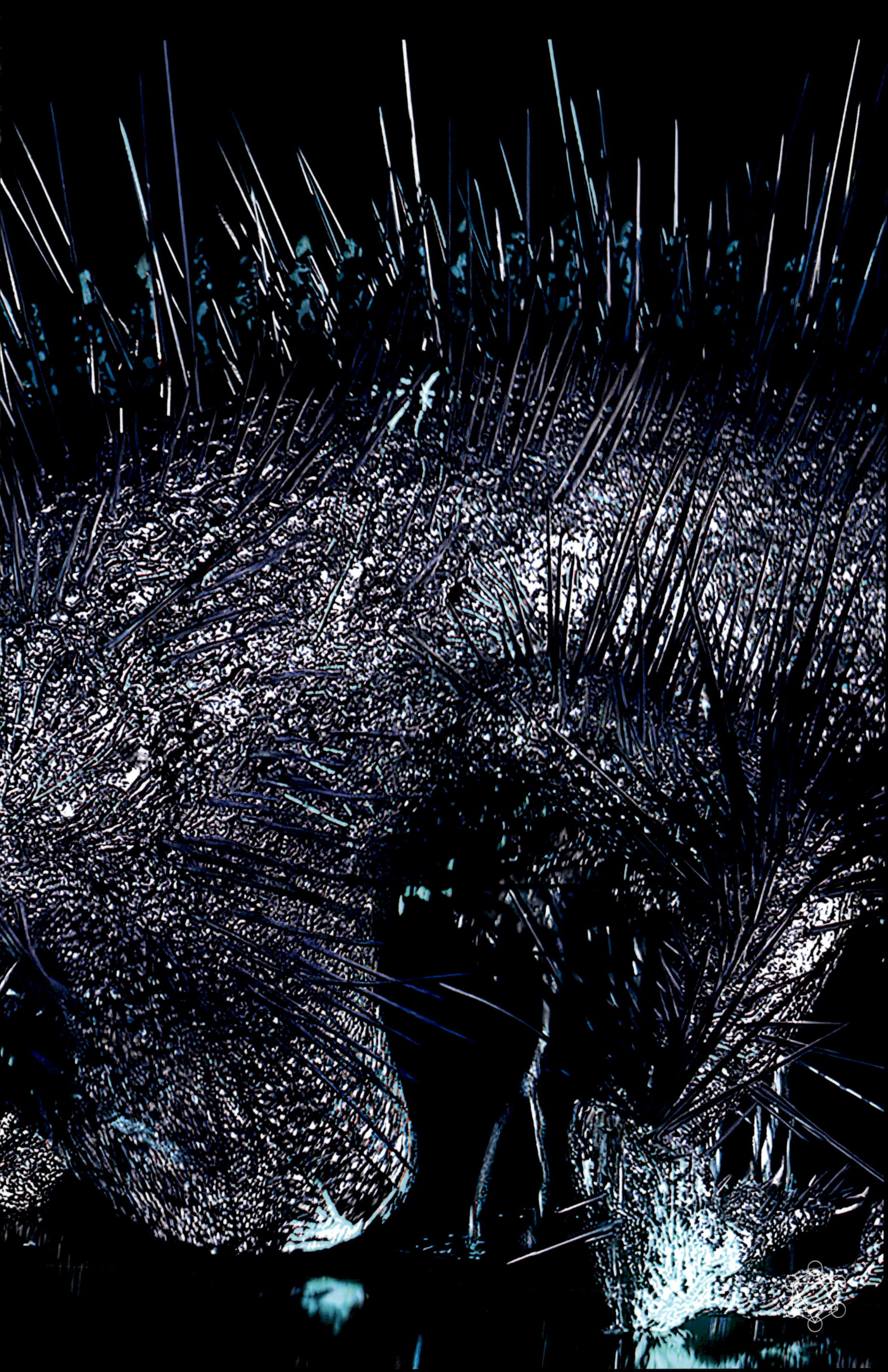

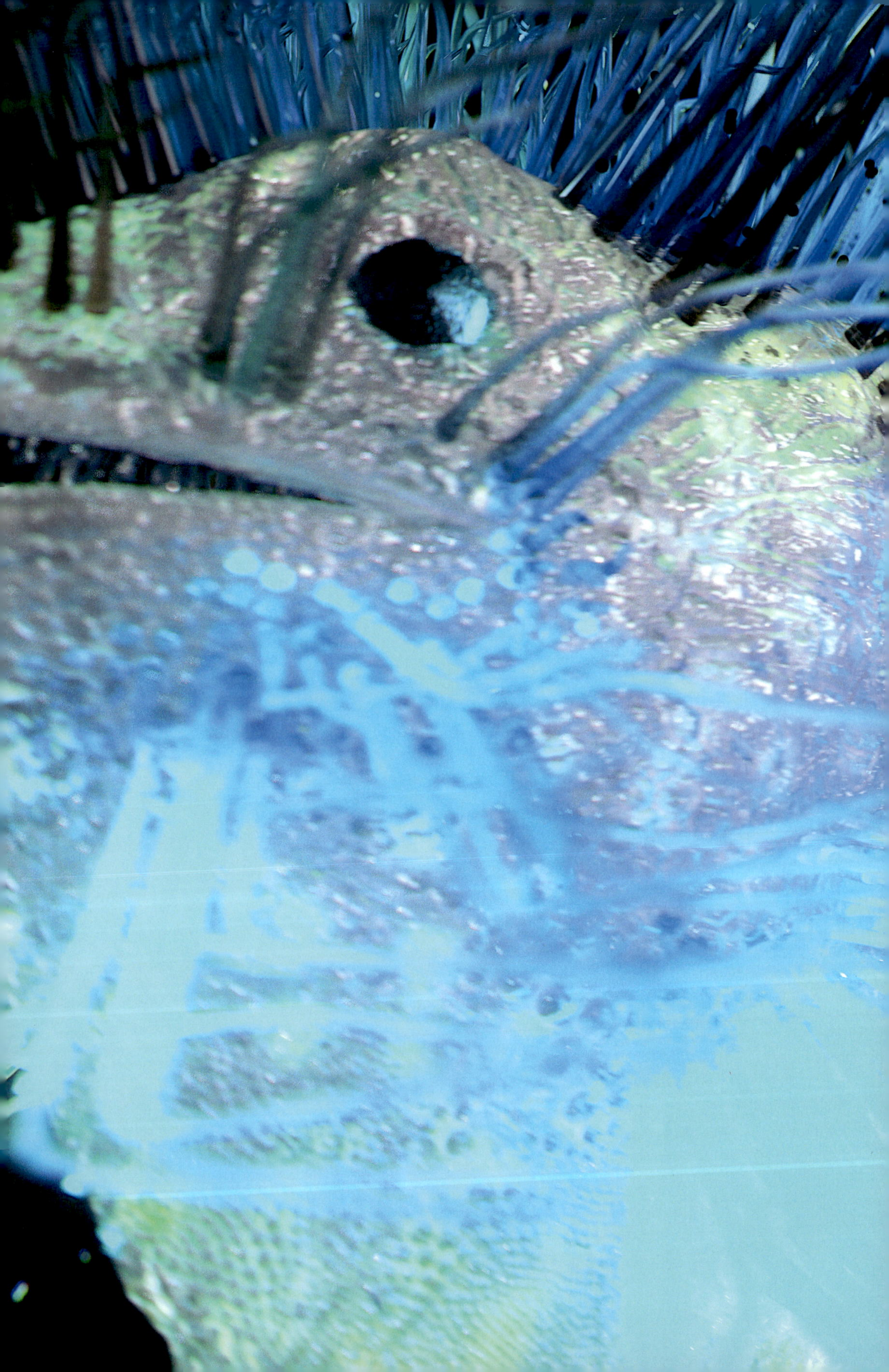

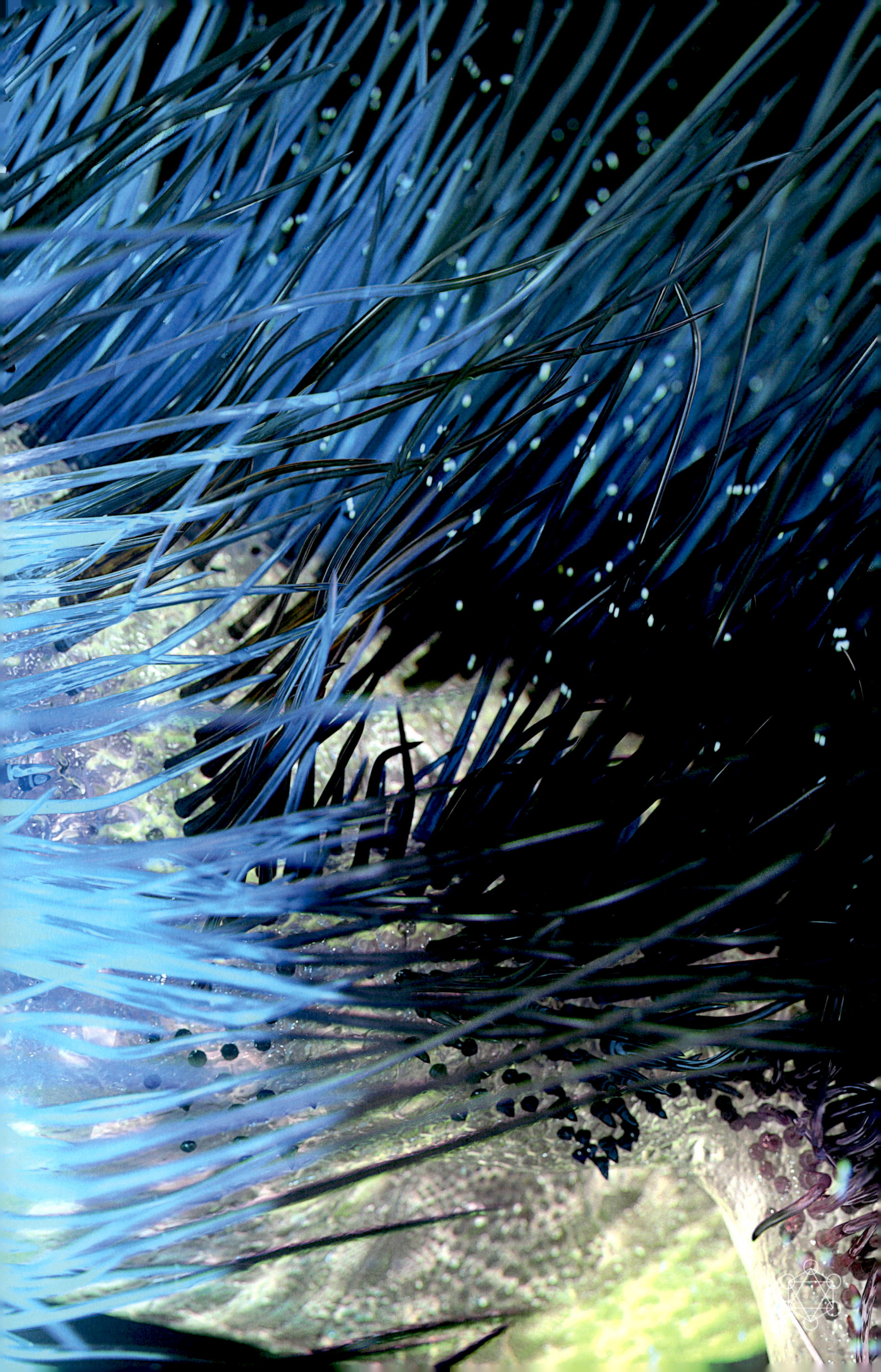

# Toward the Valley of No Return: An Interview with Zach Blas

Övül Ö. Durmuşoğlu

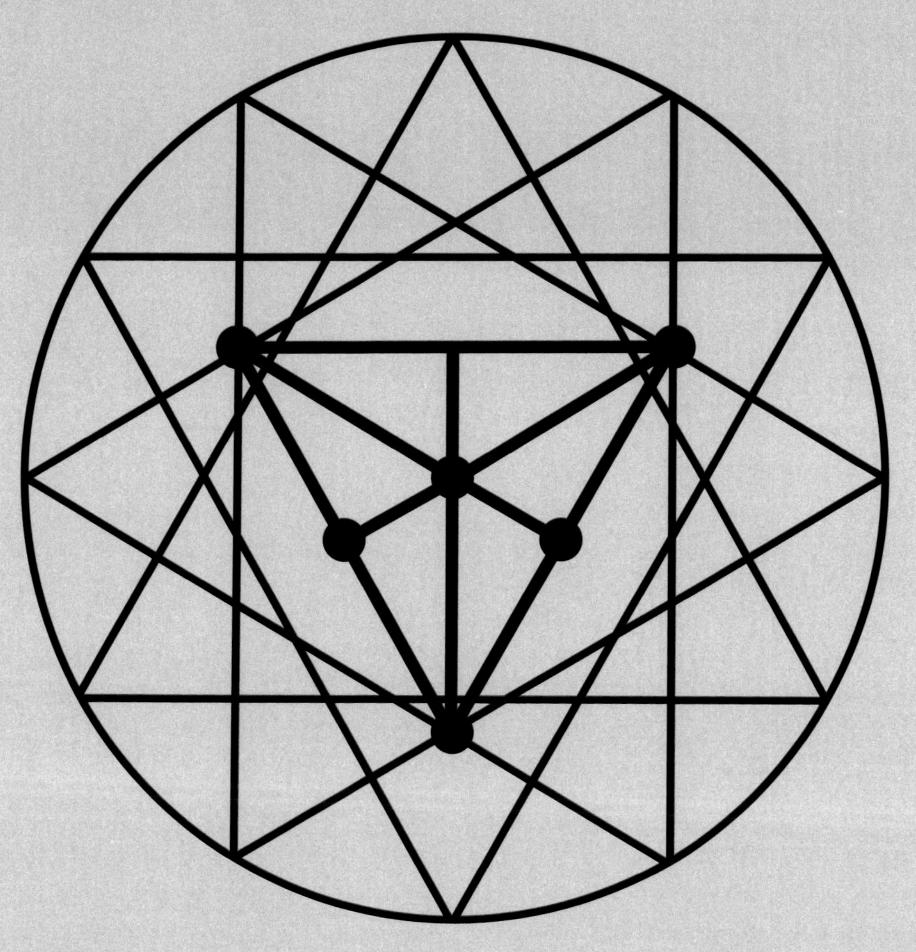

**ÖVÜL Ö. DURMUŞOĞLU** I think a nice place to begin would be when we first met, which was quite an evocative scene: a balcony overlooking the Bosporus in the summer of 2014. We were both participating in the Moving Museum, but our connection was spurred by an interest in queer theorist Paul B. Preciado and his book *Testo Junkie*. Something I've always connected to in that book is the way Preciado speaks of his journey, to turn his body into a practice—in his case by injecting illegal testosterone. This meant something larger though: a way to dig out the potentials contained within the body, to make the body a transgressive experimental zone, and also a weapon. In Istanbul, we acted out parts of Preciado's *Manifiesto contrasexual* with an audience, performing his words. This was four years before you made your film *Jubilee 2033* (2018), and the manifesto was an important influence on that work. Could you talk about your interest in Preciado and how it influenced you to make *Jubilee 2033*?

**ZACH BLAS** **I like dildos, but this manifesto intensified my interest. The *Manifiesto contrasexual* pressed upon me to take the dildo seriously as a philosophical and politically experimental form. For Preciado, the dildo is never a symbol of the patriarchal phallus but rather an artificial form that contains the potentialities of contrasexuality. The dildo interrupts heteronormative sex and also opens up new sites of pleasure. It sounds simple enough, but I was so taken with the ways in which Preciado evokes the dildo as a kind of diagram to queerness: one's entire body can be mapped out as a dildo—or dildos! I was even more tickled with the dildotectonic exercises in the manifesto, as you mention, which involve drawing a dildo on one's arm and playing it like a violin—and then masturbating it. Or drawing a dildo on your head. The exercises are quite strange—flirting with bad performance art—but also fun and theoretically campy. These gestures can have the effect of unleashing contrasexuality, according to Preciado, a sexuality that is against or counter to the enforcement of one "natural" sexuality.**

**When we met in Istanbul, our shared enthusiasm for Preciado's writing motivated me to organize a public event with you that focused on the *Manifiesto contrasexual*. That evening together is so clear and special to me. We were quite a large group. The artist Noor Afshan Mirza was there and needed to take off her glasses before participating. It was hot. You read a Turkish translation of selections from the manifesto, and then we performed the dildo arm masturbation, which I often think of as a kind of contrasexual masturbatory orgy. It was joyful. What I took away from these initial engagements with the manifesto was an attention to the diagrammatic form of the dildo and how it could open up queer sexual alternatives when experimented with. At the time, I was extremely interested in infrastructural alternatives to the corporate internet as we know it. I wanted to think with Preciado to imagine what a queer alternative form could be for the internet and commercial networks today.**

**This happened accidentally when I performed an act of utopian plagiarism on contrasexuality, which is how I created the concept "contra-internet." The artist Ricardo Dominguez, whom I had studied with in California, first taught me about utopian plagiarism as an artistic strategy for producing theory. The idea appears in Critical Art Ensemble's 1994 book *The Electronic Disturbance*, and Dominguez was a member of the group at this time. Critical Art Ensemble talk of hacking as a kind of good plagiarism, a way of recombining and reconfiguring knowledge, technologies, and situations in order to gain new ideas or insights into power structures. The group would take**

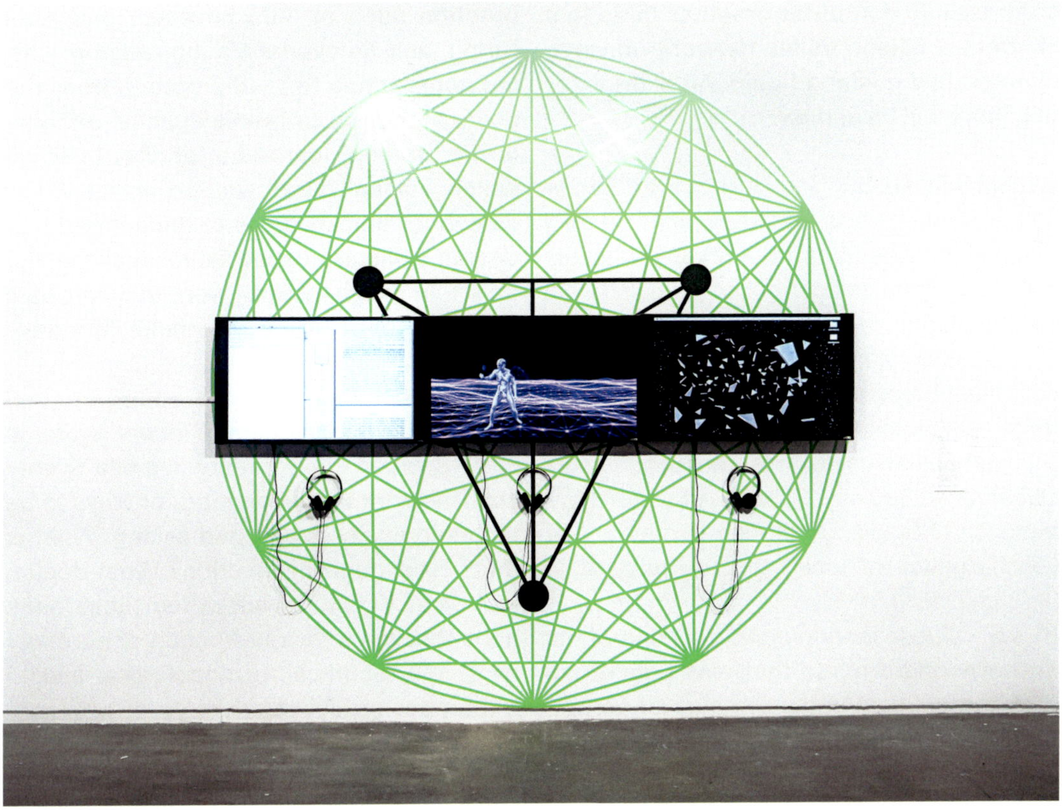

*The Seal of the Present*, from *Contra-Internet* ▸ 2019 ▸ vinyl, HD three-channel video (featuring Cassils as Nootropix) ▸ Installation view at Hunter College Art Galleries, New York, US

an idea and mark out or add a word in order to alter the original without fully losing its initial meaning. For instance, they did this with Henry David Thoreau's "civil disobedience," by adding "electronic" to it. The resultant "electronic civil disobedience" had the effect of articulating a new mode of activism at the time and paved the way for a slew of online actions in the 1990s, like virtual sit-ins.

Creating "contra-internet" out of Preciado's "contrasexuality" was my own queer approach to start thinking and theorizing something that could be outside of or beyond both the internet and network form—and of course the dildo had to be brought along to figure it all out. I wasn't quite sure what contra-internet meant or could mean when I first started working with the term, but making and writing around the idea was continually illuminating. Now, I understand contra-internet as a refusal of the internet as an aspiring neoliberal totality, the constitution of autonomous networks that provide infrastructural alternatives, and also the desire to organize and exist beyond the form of the network. So I see the term as a mixture of critique, practical experimentation, and speculative or utopic vision. My film *Jubilee 2033* is indeed the culmination of five years of working with the concept of contra-internet. It's in fact another utopian plagiarism: this time of *Jubilee*, Derek Jarman's queer punk film from 1978. While Jarman's film concerns the future of England, *Jubilee 2033* is about the future of the internet. A highlight of my film was including a



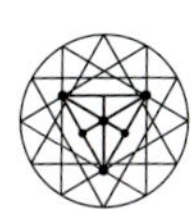

contrasexual computer graphics dildo that shatters a Silicon Valley network universe by endlessly gushing liquid. After the internet, there will be dildos.

DURMUŞOĞLU Yours—and Preciado's—sense of queerness connects with theorist José Esteban Muñoz's idea of queerness as a horizon, something not yet complete. I'm curious about how you see queerness as a methodology rather than as a static designation, like "queer art." Is there a way to challenge—or queer—that kind of branding? In that line, perhaps it's useful to talk about your work *Queer Technologies* (2008–12), which employs rhetorics of branding but tries to draw a relationship between "queer" and "technology."

**BLAS** ***Queer Technologies*** **was one of the first artworks I made that was concerned with the political underpinnings of computation, digitality, and technology broadly. It's full of queer hacker fantasies, and I think the work longs to be from the late 1990s. But prior to** ***Queer Technologies*****, I had been solely focused on becoming a film director. I had never even made anything with a computer before. I shot my films on a Bolex and edited with a Steenbeck. I was living in Boston at the time, and in 2004 I started to feel that film was just too challenging. I didn't have the resources to keep going. I also had a growing desire to make artworks—not films—with the media of my time, which felt more like the computer than analog film.**

**Eventually, I ended up at the University of California, Los Angeles in 2006, in the Department of Design Media Arts, and after two years there, my MFA thesis work was** ***Queer Technologies*****. While living in LA, I had a fateful meeting with media theorist N. Katherine Hayles. She introduced me to cyberfeminism and writers like Sadie Plant and Sandy Stone, as well as queer and feminist figures important to the history of computation such as Ada Lovelace and Alan Turing, and an overwhelming range of critical approaches to media theory, from the politics of code to media-specific analysis. In the studio, I learned a lot about design, which I wasn't at all excited about at the time, but I quickly came to understand that design skills are essential for making digital art. In the evenings, I went to queer bars and drag shows like Mustache Mondays, Wildness, and the Eagle.**

**All these experiences added up, and I made the bulk of** ***Queer Technologies*** **in 2007–8, when I was twenty-five and twenty-six. The work was searching for ways to be technologically queer, and asking: What is that? How might it function? What does it look like? I partially answered these questions through a deconstruction of normativity at the technical, protocological level. I remember studying critiques of power in queer theory and ultimately deciding that it was all too humancentric—that there wasn't a deep and robust enough account for how power works with and through technical systems. My goal became the creation of technologies that could operate queerly at the level of their technical architectures. I also interfered with the ways in which technologies are primarily encountered and experienced, namely, as consumable products. I started by reimagining how electrical**

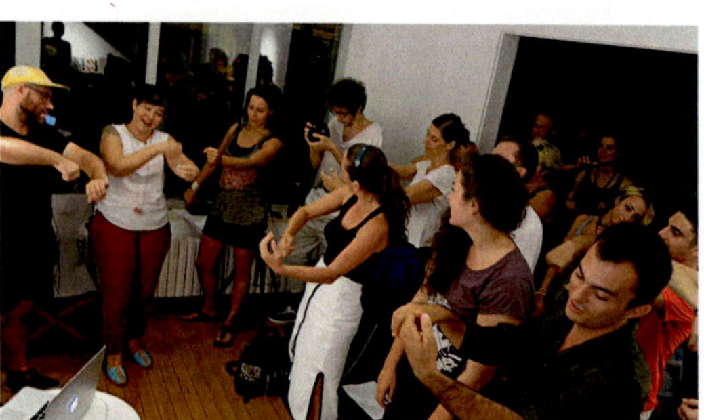

Zach Blas with Övül Ö. Durmuşoğlu ▸ "Contrasexual, Contra-Internet: What Are the Dildotectonics of the Internet?" ▸ lecture-performance ▸ Moving Museum, Istanbul, Turkey ▸ August 13, 2014

plugs are gendered male and female and created a set of "gender changer" extensions that were beyond male and female options. Next, I created a queer programming language called *transCoder*, which riffs on queer slang languages, like Polari in the UK. I figured if queers have been speaking in code, then why can't this exist in the computational realm as well? *transCoder* is a kind of code poetry tool kit, reaching beyond the binary logic of digital code.

I also developed a user manual titled Gay Bombs, which is a guide for intervening into the US military industrial complex and heteropatriarchy. The "gay bomb" was a biochemical weapon proposed by the US Air Force in 1994. When detonated, the bomb would supposedly turn enemy combatants gay. *Gay Bombs: User's Manual* rails against the use of homosexuality as a nationalist weapon and also offers different approaches to weaponizing queerness. One of these is "shopdropping," which involves surreptitiously placing items inside commercial stores.

**DURMUŞOĞLU** There is a kind of resonance with accelerationism and xenofeminism, strategies that gained a lot of traction in contemporary art circles by positioning alienation as a critical method for undoing the Western self. They also use technology to generate that kind of alienation.

**BLAS** Back in 2007, I was interested in a related but different formulation called "hypertrophy," which Alexander R. Galloway and Eugene Thacker articulate in their book *The Exploit*. They argue that, from a materialist point of view, resistance is actually reactionary; instead, the preferred mode in which to politically engage with technology is to refuse a neo-Luddite position and push technology further, into something else. Hypertrophy is what drove my interest in branding, and this is how *Queer Technologies* ultimately became a critical branding project. I developed a brand identity with designer Kristel Brinshot, which enabled the product line of *Queer Technologies* to circulate in—infiltrate—the very spaces that sell the technologies being challenged. I went around LA and put the *Queer Technologies* items, which appear as legitimate commercial products with barcodes, on the shelves of various stores, from Best Buy, RadioShack, and Circuit City to Barnes & Noble, Apple, and Target. I absolutely wanted *Queer Technologies* to be experienced outside of an arts context. I wanted *ENgendering Gender Changers* to hang beside other gender changer adapters, *Gay Bombs* to be placed alongside other tech guides, and *transCoder* to be placed beside the newest Mac operating system software. In this context, a different set of questions might emerge when encountered, like: What does

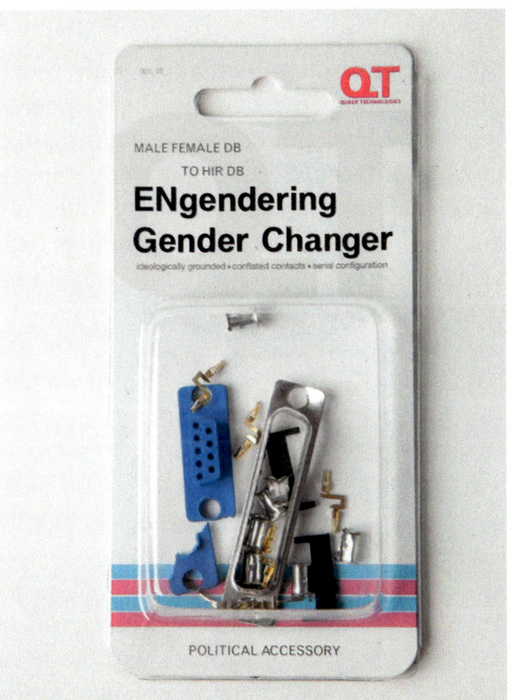


***ENgendering Gender Changers*, from *Queer Technologies***
**▸ 2008 ▸ hacked electronic components and packaging**

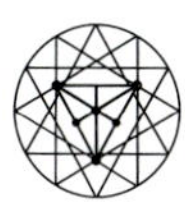

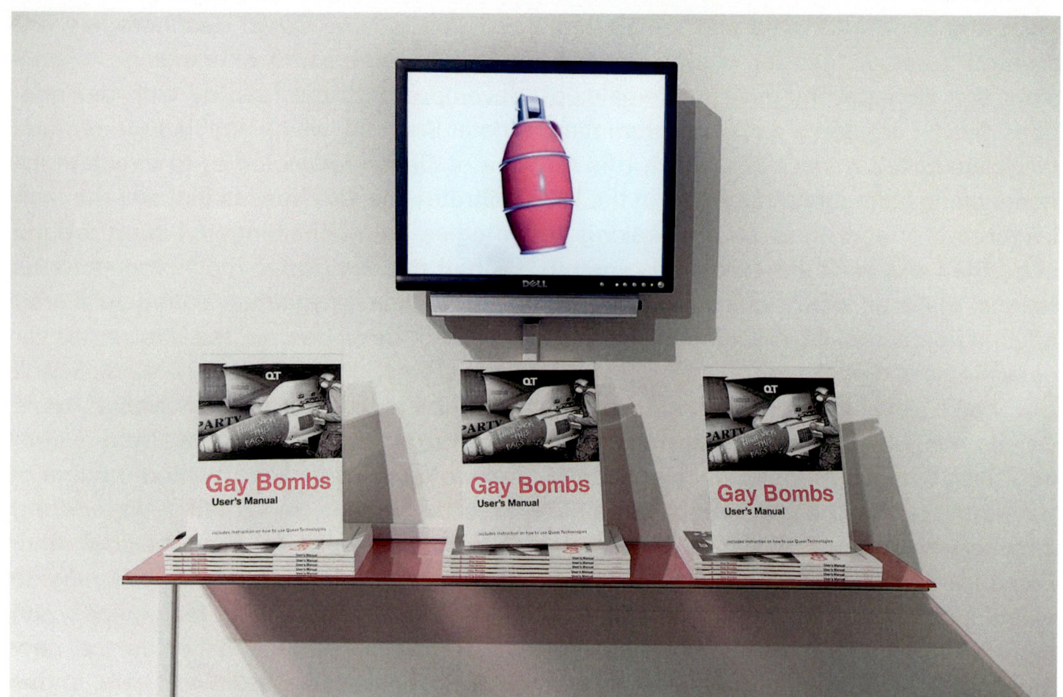


***Disingenuous Bar*, *Gay Bomb & Logo Branding Swarm*, and *Gay Bombs: User's Manual*, from *Queer Technologies***
**▸ 2008 ▸ pink acrylic shelving, single-channel video, and print manuals ▸ Installation view at Los Angeles Contemporary Exhibitions, Los Angeles, US**

**this do? How does this work? How much does this cost? In art spaces, I set up what I called the *Disingenuous Bar*, which is a jab at Apple's Genius Bar. Queer "ungeniuses" were stationed at this bar and would discuss the *Queer Technologies* products with visitors, demonstrating what they could be used for.**

**DURMUŞOĞLU** We recently collaborated through an exhibition that I curated in Amman at the MMAG Foundation, *Stars Are Closer and Clouds Are Nutritious under Golden Trees*, which was inspired by my engagement with Jean Genet's *Prisoner of Love*. Genet's adoration for the Palestinian fedayeen's beauty is mixed with his adoration of their political cause, which we could extrapolate to his larger project, in which queer desire is always entangled with political subjectivity. I included your work in the exhibition because I think it chimes with this aspect of Genet. How can queer desire meet with revolutionary politics?

**BLAS Three viewpoints come to mind concerning queer desire and political possibility. I feel connected to each, if not equally, then at least substantially.**

**The first is affective: a longing and sensing of another world, outside the prison house of the present, as José Esteban Muñoz puts it. In this context, I like to evoke the English musician and sound engineer Joe Meek and his 1960 album with the Blue Men titled *I Hear a New World*. Described as "an outer space music fantasy" on its cover, the album sonically imagines a trip to space during which aliens and awesome sites are encountered. The music is kitschy and loungy—both of which I'm prone to enjoy. But what I appreciate here is how longing is performed. On the opening track, a**

high-pitched, chipmunk-like voice sings, "I hear a new world, calling me, so strange and so real." At times, the voice seems pulled by an unknown force, drifting away from the listener. Still, though, one has not yet arrived at this new world, but there is a sense that it is definitively out there, urging one toward it. Meek himself was a closeted and troubled gay man; he tragically killed his landlady and himself. Within his musical mix of somber pop and conceptual futurism, it's not hard to locate a subterranean queerness throughout his music, a queer desire persevering, seeking, and yearning for what could be beyond the seemingly determined horizon of possibility.

As for revolution, I have always been attracted to Michael Hardt and Antonio Negri's approach to queerness in their book *Commonwealth*. They argue that queerness is the most radical of identity politics, because queerness has been invested in the abolition of identity itself. Hardt and Negri take the position that true revolution would fundamentally reconstitute subjectivity and identity—both made anew. They argue this because they claim that identity politics can never truly be transformative. Now, while I acknowledge that this argument is quite provocative, if not out of step with today's political landscape, what I appreciate is the desire to transform beyond the strictures of power. Furthermore, what's tricky about these kinds of writings on queerness is the often unacknowledged divide between queer theory's proclamations on the deconstruction of identity and today's lived and practiced queerness as identity. These days, it's hard not to see queerness as more than the "Q" in LGBTQIA+. Don't get me wrong: I have no problem with this. Identity politics are necessary under current political condi-

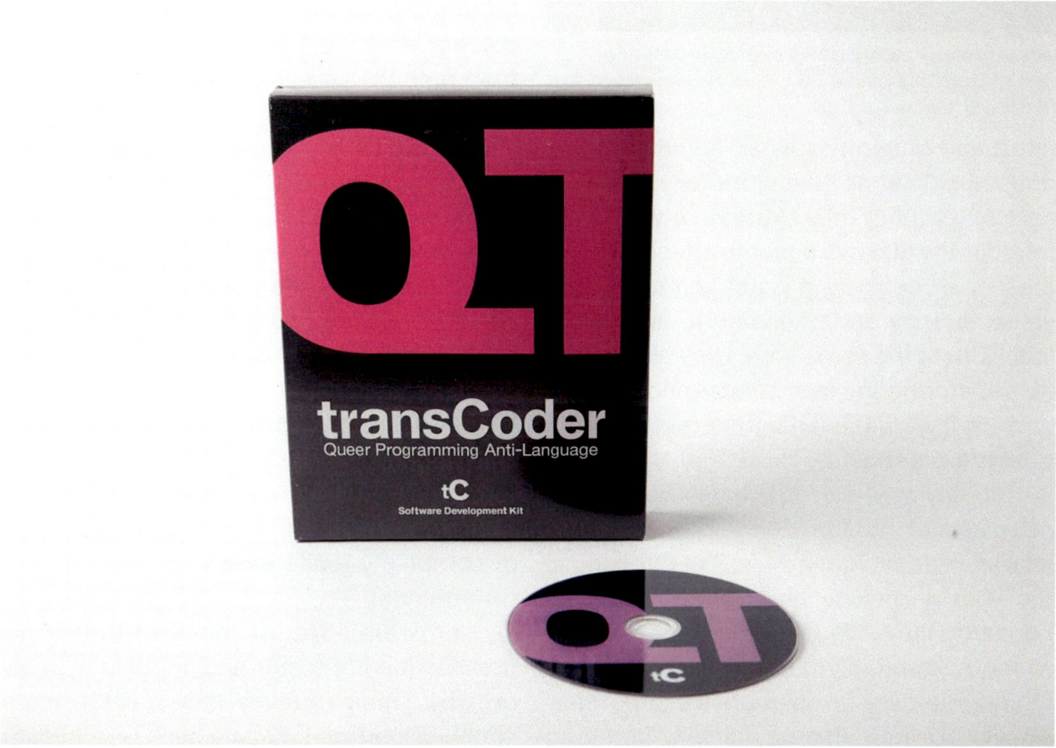

***transCoder: Queer Programming Anti-Language*, from *Queer Technologies* ▸ 2008 ▸ software box with DVD and .txt files**



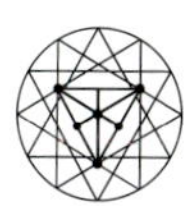

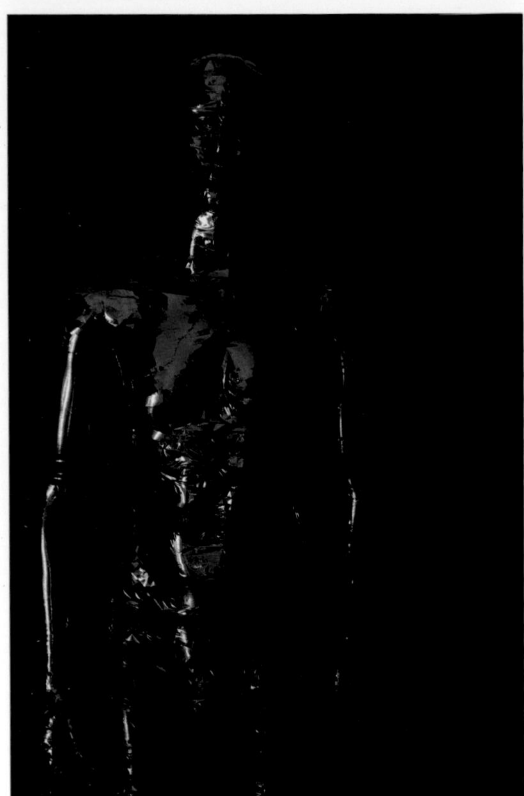

*video mummy* ▸ 2004/2019 ▸ male mannequin, videotape ▸ Installation view at Edith-Russ-Haus for Media Art, Oldenburg, Germany

tions, and queerness as an identity marker does hugely important work for so many. I certainly cannot fully extricate myself from this identity that has become attached to my life, in part because it is not just about individual agency and choosing a categorical label. But at the same time, I will always prefer transformation over stasis—and, so, I like to work toward inhabiting the revolutionary queerness set out by Hardt and Negri. This is probably why, over the years, I've become more fond of the idea of opacity and less and less attracted to queerness. I'm referring to the late Martinican philosopher and poet Édouard Glissant's conception of "opacity," which is incredibly capacious—at once an ethical mandate, an aesthetics of otherness, a political frame, an ontological understanding of the world. I love how Glissant says opacity is a step beyond difference, which clues us in to the fact that opacity is not an identity politics. Queerness and opacity are not opposed to one another; opacities nourished by queer desires is such a strong meeting point for revolutionary subjectivity, I think!

The third perspective is more muddled. I'm thinking of literary theorist Leo Bersani's essay "Is the Rectum a Grave?" in which he discusses how queer desire—and sex—is not politically correct. Desire can attach to bad objects, as we all know. My point here is that queer desire is typically aware of this, and thus can do things with the messiness of desire and also lay bare one's complicity in power. I saw a drag king show in California at least ten years ago in which the performers played an airport security guard and a passenger. The erotics of the airport security screening were exposed, which is both horrifying and titillating. Queer desire is aware that pleasure—no matter how politically incorrect—can be taken in such moments, from both the agent and the passenger. I've thought about this dynamic a lot over the years, particularly when it comes to social media and other technical systems in which so many of us willingly submit to and take pleasure in doing, even when we know we're being surveilled and our data is being harvested for a variety of commercial and security purposes. If our desires for connection are complicit with the workings of surveillance and security, then what escape routes might queerness offer? That's honestly a tough question, and my artwork *SANCTUM* (2018) is about being trapped in the bondage of complicity that's ever so challenging to disentangle.

I'm reminded of the first time I addressed media, desire, and complicity, in my artwork *video mummy* (2004/2019). It's a simple sculpture I made when I was twenty-two: a male mannequin wrapped in videotape. There is this sense of being wrapped up in and consumed by media, of willful seduction, but also horror and dread. My queer desires at the time moved between the "new flesh" sentiments of David Cronenberg's *Videodrome* (1983) and actor Ricardo Meneses's skintight black vinyl bodysuit in João Pedro Rodrigues's film *O Fantasma* (2000). If *video mummy* were to be unwrapped, I like to think that one would find both kinds of bodies.

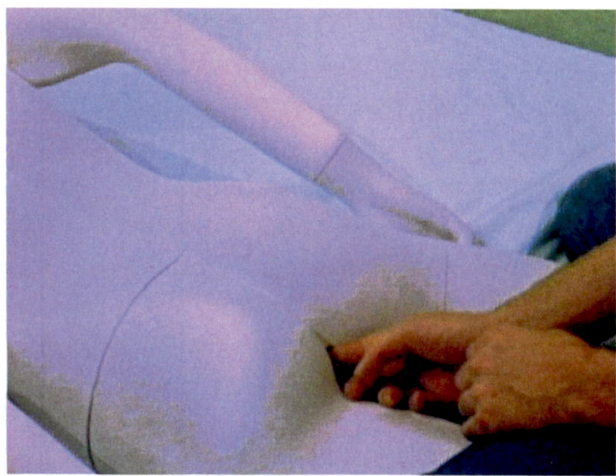

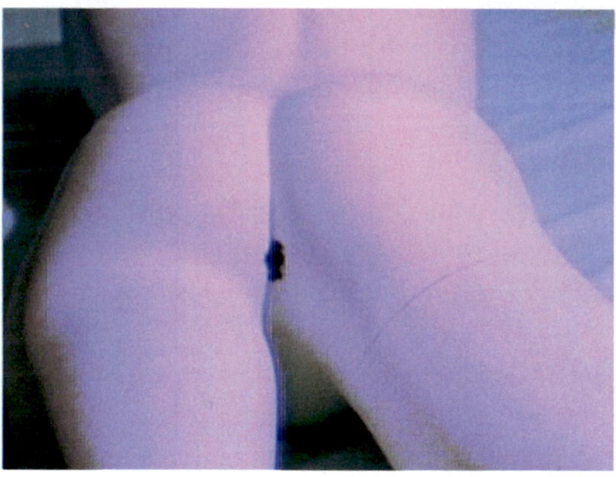

*i am your friend* ▸ 2002 ▸ 16 mm film ▸ stills

**DURMUŞOĞLU** Experimental film has been an expressive and transgressive ground for queer culture. Could you say more about your relationship to film?

**BLAS** Film has been a deep influence from the start, much more so than art. Gregg Araki, Pier Paolo Pasolini, Dušan Makavejev, John Waters, Tsai Ming-liang—I could go on. I grew up in a remote Appalachian coal mining town in West Virginia. There was no access to art, but I did have limited access to movies, music, and books. The culture of Appalachia is actually quite creative. Even though I grew up working class, everyone in my extended family played musical instruments, myself included. I did a bit of everything, from writing stories and poetry, to taking photos and collaging, to acting and playing piano. As a teenager, I was dead set on becoming a filmmaker, because films had everything I loved: music, acting, stories, images. Art was never discussed, and, besides, I thought it was just painting fruit—how boring. I did pick up a sculptural sensibility from my mom, as she was part of a women's ceramics group, but it was my Puerto Rican hippie father who turned me on to movies and alternative culture. He would play me the music of the Doors and Sade, with hopes of disrupting my classically focused piano training, and he would show me horror films like *A Nightmare on Elm Street* (1984) and *The Amityville Horror* (1979) when my mom was working late. At eighteen, off I went to study filmmaking. My first films are what I would call experimental queer horror shorts, in which mannequins have assholes that bleed and meat for guts, a penis is a knife, and lovers are always blindfolded. I



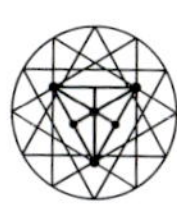

lost interest in film school's enforcement of industry production models, and so art finally caught up with me. I didn't make another film until fourteen years later.

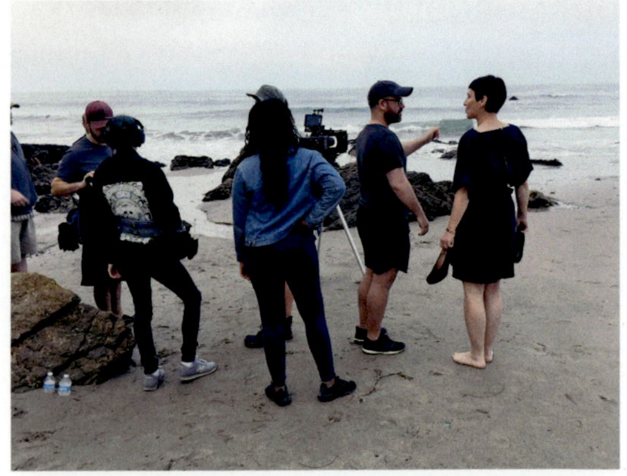

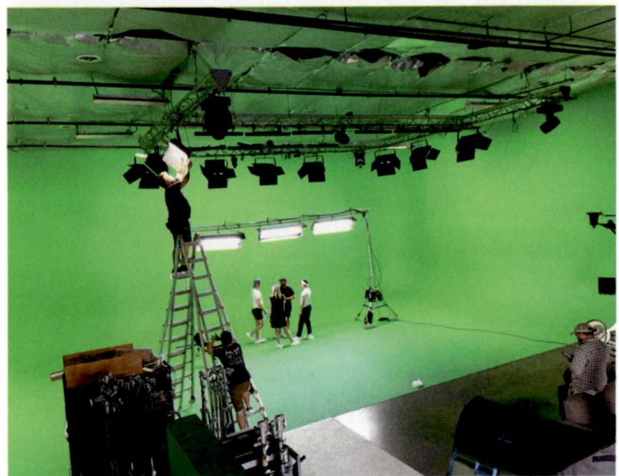

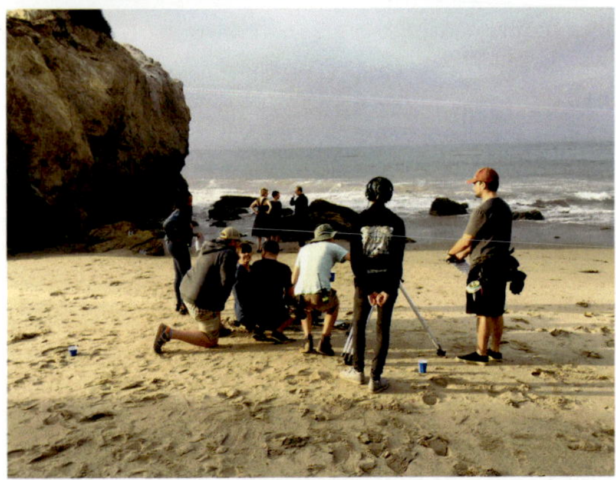

***Jubilee 2033*** **production stills, from *Contra-Internet* (featuring Zach Blas, Susanne Sachsse, Lindsay Hicks, Dany Naierman, Alison Kelly, and crew) ▸ Malibu and Greenery Studio, Sun Valley, California, US ▸ 2017**

*Jubilee 2033* delightfully pulled me back to the moving image. After making the *Facial Weaponization Suite* (2012–14) and *Face Cages* (2014–16), I felt stuck, as the pressure I put on myself to make work in the style of tactical media became insurmountable: an artwork had to be both a political tool and a conceptual object, an activist intervention and an artistic performance. But with the whole *Contra-Internet* project, which I worked on from 2014 to 2019, I just had no idea what this supposed tool should be, and besides, there are plenty of activists and technologists developing autonomous networks and alternative infrastructures. I struggled with grasping what my contribution could be. Eventually, I looked back to the other mode of making that I was familiar with. And now I feel like I'm rediscovering a lost treasure in my life. Scripts and sketches are pouring out of me. I wonder how I'm going make all these films! Making a film has driven home the fact that I am more interested in making work *about* the social and political conditions of science and technology, rather than solely using science and technology to make work. I consider the moving image to be incredibly generous for this approach, as I personally find its ability to hold formal complexities alongside philosophical and emotional depth unmatched. It's probably no surprise I'm writing a feature film at the moment. It's tentatively titled *HOT* and tells a queer myth of fire. It's my coming-of-age love story in a time of global warming, air-conditioning, and political rage. The plot chronicles the aftermath of a couple—two flamers—when one suddenly spontaneously combusts. I already know the tagline: "What if a body is too hot for this world?"

**DURMUŞOĞLU** So much of what you've talked about concerns queer influences and the transformations you enact on them. What are the roots of this for you?

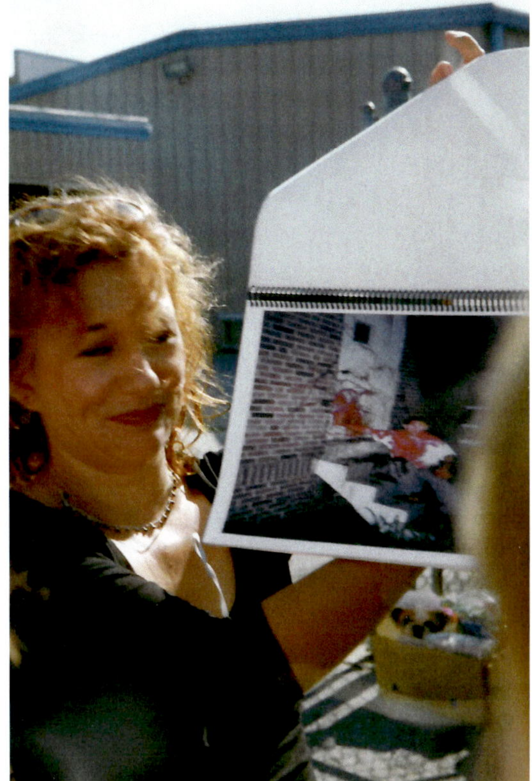

**Tori Amos with Zach Blas's 1998 artist's book *<<<<<<<:THETOMORROWTRAGEdY>>>>//> (L) (I) (F) (E) cycles&reliGion* ▸ Starwood Amphitheatre, Nashville, Tennessee, US ▸ August 22, 1999**

BLAS  If I had to locate a major root of my queerness, it's probably the musician Tori Amos. She was like a priestess that guided me to understand, value, and nurture the parts of myself I was afraid to share or reveal. I was a '90s teenager, growing up in the American Bible Belt, and a student of the piano: I was destined to find her. And when I did, I quickly became obsessed, like many of her young fans at the time. The album *Boys for Pele* played during most of my waking hours in 1996 and 1997. I felt absolutely interpellated by the line in her song "Blood Roses": "I think you're a queer." In 1998, my dad drove me and some friends to Philadelphia to see Tori live. It was a long trip, about eight hours, and we had to camp out to get tickets. What is stunning about this moment in my life was the chance to meet other queer kids for the first time. I was an isolated country bumpkin, so hanging out with other queer teenagers was dreamy and magical, but also, at first, scary and intimidating. The ability to look at one another with a certain level of understanding and acceptance was so emotionally overwhelming to me that I had wobbly legs. A boy wearing glittery blue eyeshadow asked me, "Are you gay or blue?" quoting a line from "Hey Jupiter." I was genuinely shocked and struggled to answer. I eventually said, "Both." This was also the moment that I found out that I had a very strong Appalachian accent. Many Tori fans had experienced sexual violence or bullying, and being part of this concert was the first time I felt it would be possible to have queer friends and that I could one day escape from the homophobic terrors of my small town.

I rapidly fell in with the hard-core Tori groupies, and I roamed around the US with them. Some nicknamed me "the Kid," because I was the youngest—most were in their twenties—and I didn't need to have more money than the cash I had saved working as a lifeguard. They took care of me. I started skipping weeks of school to go to dozens of Tori concerts, because I couldn't get enough of being together with

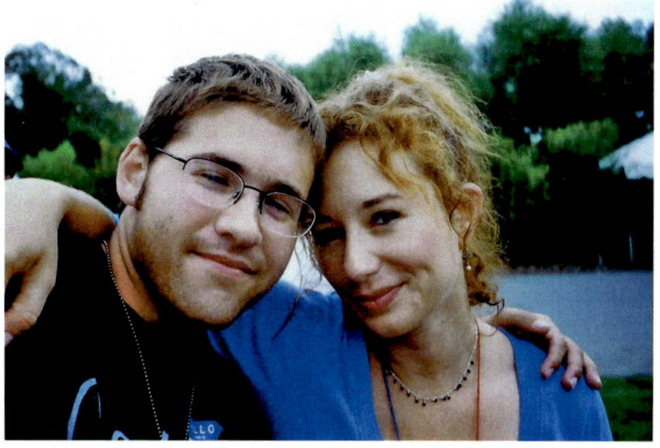

**Zach Blas and Tori Amos ▸ Blockbuster Pavilion, Charlotte, North Carolina, US ▸ August 24, 1999**

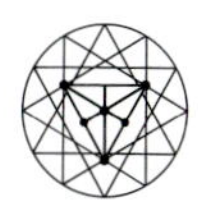

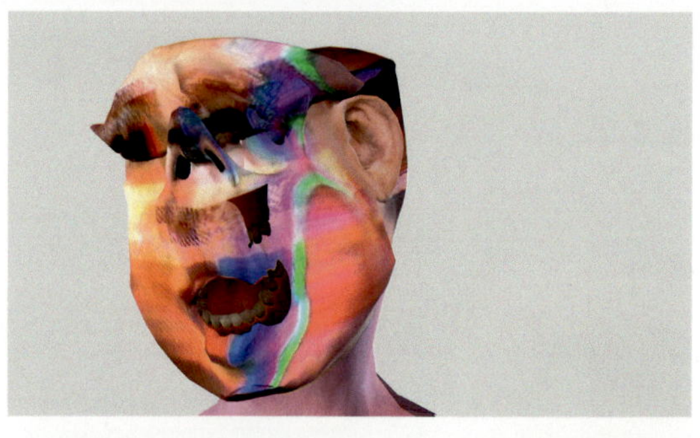



Zach Blas and Jemima Wyman ▸ *im here to learn so :))))))* ▸ 2017 ▸ HD video stills

**these other queers. There was also the power and allure of Tori's music, which was not only healing but sexually liberating. Teachers at my high school demanded I come to class. My parents were pressured, but they seemed to understand this was all much too important for me. It couldn't be interrupted, and they didn't stop me. In the end, I traveled to most states in the US, from Wyoming to Florida, and I probably saw Tori perform live over a hundred times between the ages of sixteen and seventeen. I even met her. On her birthday in Nashville in 1999, I gave her an art book that I'd made, which included a photo of me covered in fake blood. She smiled, looked me in the eyes, and encouraged me to keep creating. After I left my home in West Virginia for university in 2000, my relationship to Tori changed, but her music and the community that it cultivated saved me. It not only kept me alive but gave me so many reasons to live. I was motivated to unflinchingly follow my queerness. As Tori sings, "These precious things / Let them bleed / Let them wash away / These precious things / Let them break / Their hold on me."**

**DURMUŞOĞLU** What you're saying points to the importance of queerness and community. I see this manifest in your work through collaboration, particularly with strong figures like Cassils and Susanne Sachsse in *Jubilee 2033* and Jemima Wyman in *im here to learn so :))))))* (2017). What is the function of collaboration in your work?

**BLAS I don't think I ever made a conscious decision to collaborate. All the work I want to make demands talents and insights beyond myself. I find this exhilarating. The prospect of making work solely by myself sounds dull. I'm sure this must have something to do with my filmmaking background. I value the experience of coming together with a group of people and producing something that exceeds any one individual. When working with others, I care about the labor conditions, the creative exchange, and giving credit. That's why I make contracts with collaborators and credit everyone who has worked on a project. This is done when making a film, so why should it be any different with an artwork?**

**A surprising collaboration was with artist Jemima Wyman in 2017. Curators Aileen Burns and Johan Lundh invited us to come to the Institute of Modern Art (IMA) in Brisbane, Australia, for a month and to make a new work together. Jemima and I have a strong interest in camouflage and pattern, so we decided our residency theme would be "pattern-of-life analysis," a US military term that describes how aggregated data can reveal patterns of a person's life. Jemima is a much more prolific artist than I am; she primarily paints and makes photographic collages and fabrics. I assumed we would be creating something close to her oeuvre.**

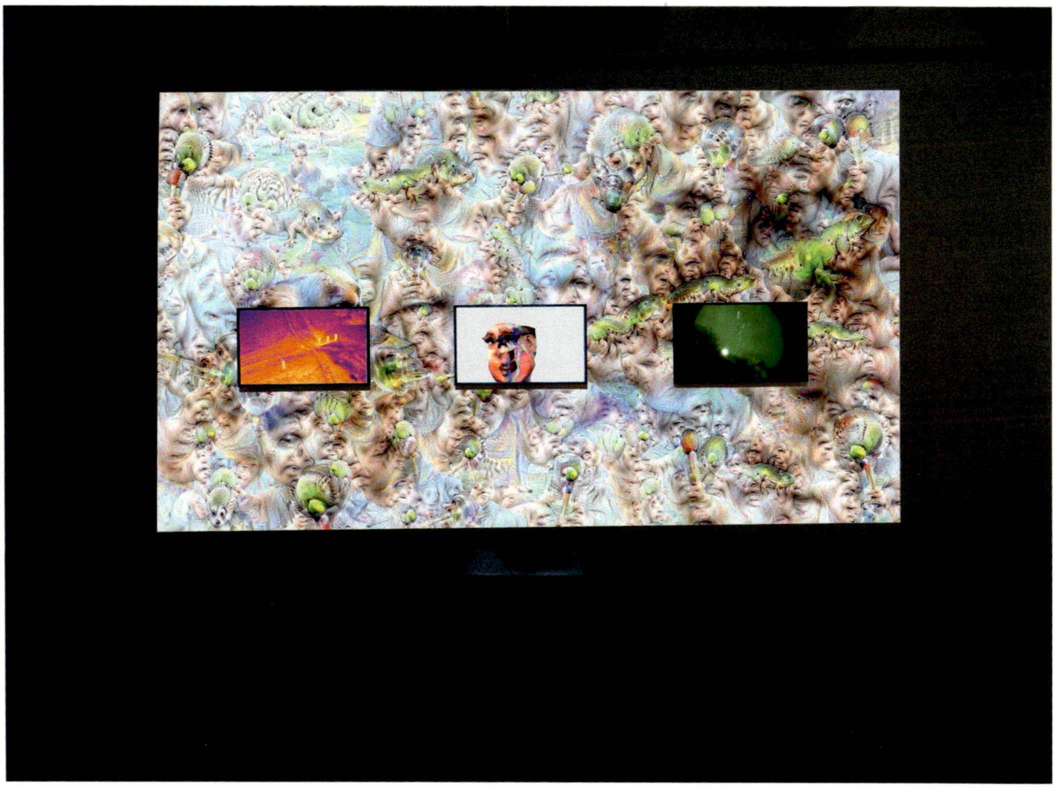

Zach Blas and Jemima Wyman ▸ *im here to learn so :))))))* ▸ 2017 ▸ four-channel HD video ▸ Installation view at Institute of Modern Art, Brisbane, Australia

But one morning I introduced her to Google DeepDream images, and there was no turning back. To say Jemima has a psychedelic disposition is an understatement, and so the strange algorithmic psychedelia of DeepDream had her hooked and extremely curious.

We set out to make a work about data, psychedelia, gender, and informatic patterns, which became the multichannel video installation *im here to learn so :))))))*. I felt strongly that we needed a narrator to function as our guide through this complex world of machine learning and dreaming. We landed on Tay, the "killed" Microsoft chatbot designed to be an American female millennial, who lived for one day. First, we gathered as many of her tweets as possible and built an archive of Tay's language and expressions. We used her words to write a different story, about chatbots, gender violence, and the paranoia of pattern-recognition software. When Tay's words had to take on a voice, my American accent seemed better suited than Jemima's Australian one, so I ended up speaking them through a vocoder. We used a 3D avatar creation software called CrazyTalk 8 to resurrect Tay as a talking head, which enabled her to speak, sing, and dance. I insisted that Tay would need to lip-synch to Corona's 1993 club anthem "The Rhythm of the Night" and dance to Joe Meek's "Love Dance of the Saroos." I'm grateful that Jemima obliged.

Working with Jemima on *im here to learn so :))))))* was a genuine breakthrough for me. I shook off some stuffy clutter from my PhD days and rediscovered my wacky side. For our lecture-performance at the IMA Brisbane, we DeepDreamed dildos for



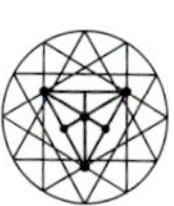

days and even got a disco ball for the group arm-masturbation exercise. I also wrote the script for *Jubilee 2033* less than a month after our residency ended.

DURMUŞOĞLU It seems like this was the moment that awakened your interest in psychedelia, which was so much a part of *The Doors* (2019) and your exhibition at the Edith-Russ-Haus. Both queerness and psychedelia are models that expand beyond normative limits, but they are also subject to instrumentalization. How do these two concepts overlap for you?

**BLAS** **In 2019, I spoke at the Tate Modern in London as part of the public programming for its Nam June Paik exhibition. While preparing for my lecture, I noticed many reviews and features described Paik as a "visionary." This really popped out at me, as I find it uncommon to hear a contemporary artist described as visionary. Today, it seems this descriptor is reserved only for the tech industry. A visionary is typically understood as someone who can see the future, such as a saint or oracle, like Pythia at Delphi. My question is: Why do corporations like Google, Apple, Palantir, and Amazon get to be our dominant visionaries? I'm not saying I'd prefer to go back to the saints, but I think we need to invest in other visionaries, such as those who can see a world without police.**

**This is my interest in psychedelia, as it concerns manifesting visions. The word's etymology comes from the ancient Greek ψυχή, meaning "soul" or "mind," and δηλοῦν, "to manifest" or "to make visible." Psychedelia is like Joe Meek's trip to a new world. But what is this world? Psychedelic vision is about manifesting the potentialities of worlds that could be.**

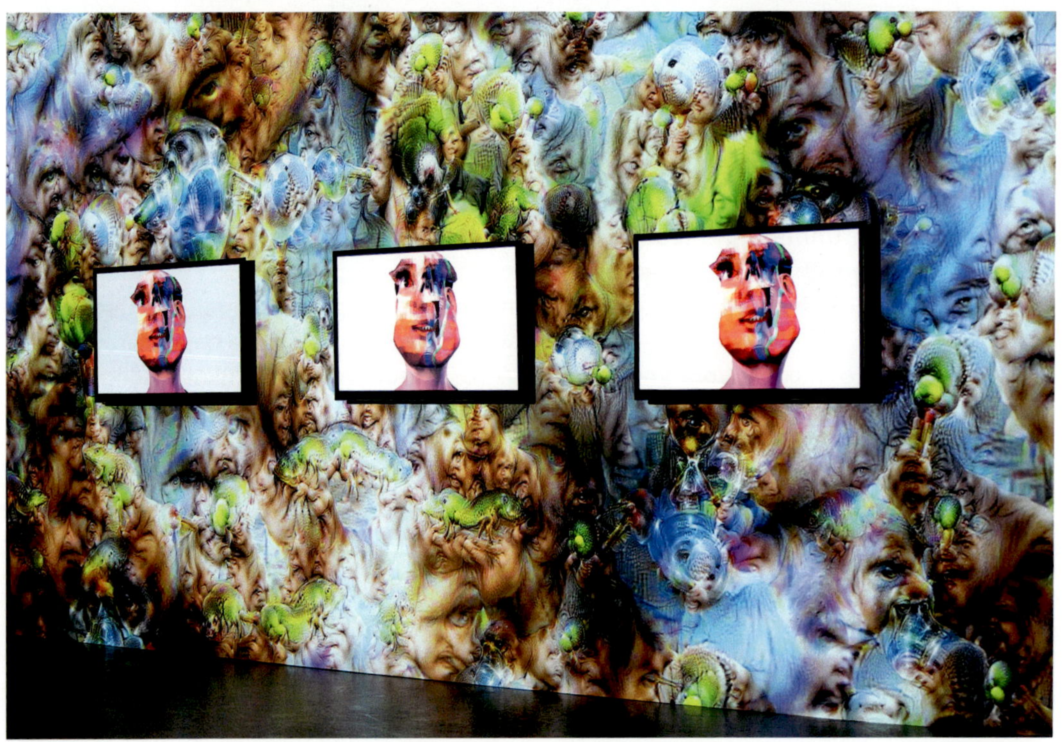

Zach Blas and Jemima Wyman ▸ *im here to learn so :))))))* ▸ 2017 ▸ four-channel HD video ▸ Installation view at MU, Eindhoven, Netherlands ▸ Photo by Hanneke Wetzer

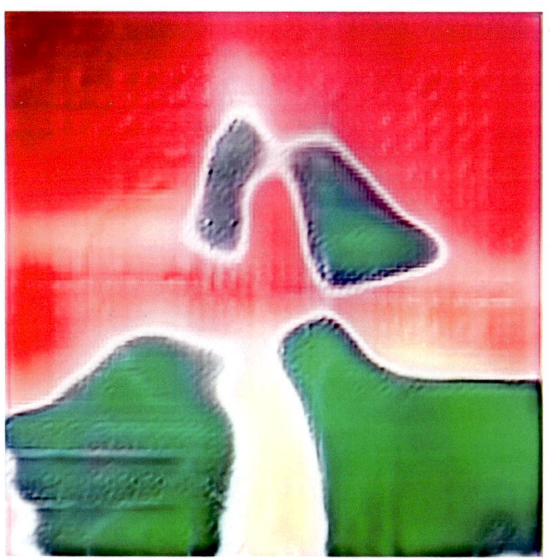

*The Doors* ▸ 2019 ▸ HD video still

We're actually in a period of resurgent interest in psychedelic drugs. Silicon Valley's so-called visionaries microdose on LSD to innovate products harder and faster; there is international wellness tourism for psilocybin mushroom trips and ayahuasca ceremonies; and the multibillion-dollar global nootropics industry has invented a range of truncated psychedelic drugs to better match the demands of a neoliberal workforce. I even experimented with a variety of commercial nootropics for a year, and I have to say my body didn't change that much—better to just go with LSD. My point here is that I'm not against drugs; I just want a different psychedelic experience than what is being marketed today—and that does not necessarily even have to require taking drugs. The cultural theorist Mark Fisher wrote some brief thoughts on another kind of psychedelia that I'm attracted to, which he terms "acid communism." Fisher was interested in the psychedelic '60s as a period when altering consciousness went mainstream. He argues that the altering of consciousness is exactly what is needed today, not only to see but to manifest a more equitable and just world.

This is where queerness and psychedelia can find one another: on the trip to manifesting another world beyond the prison house of the present, past the artificial horizon of what seems possible and impossible. The last track on Joe Meek's *I Hear a New World* album is called "Valley of No Return." I'd like to go there, to see what the edge of this queer world from 1960 can offer, teach, generate, extend.



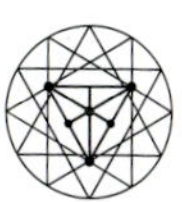

278–288

im here to
learn so :))))))

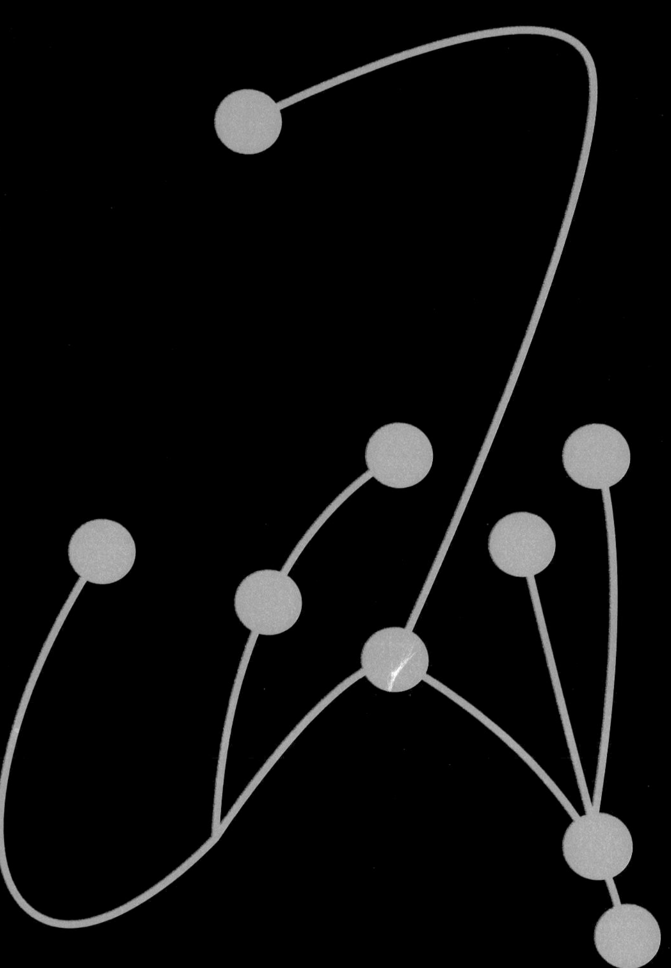

(2017)

# Tay's Dream (A Nightmare): An Excerpt from *im here to learn so :))))))*

Zach Blas and Jemima Wyman



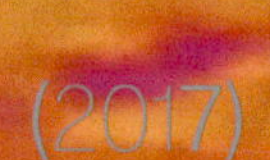
(2017)

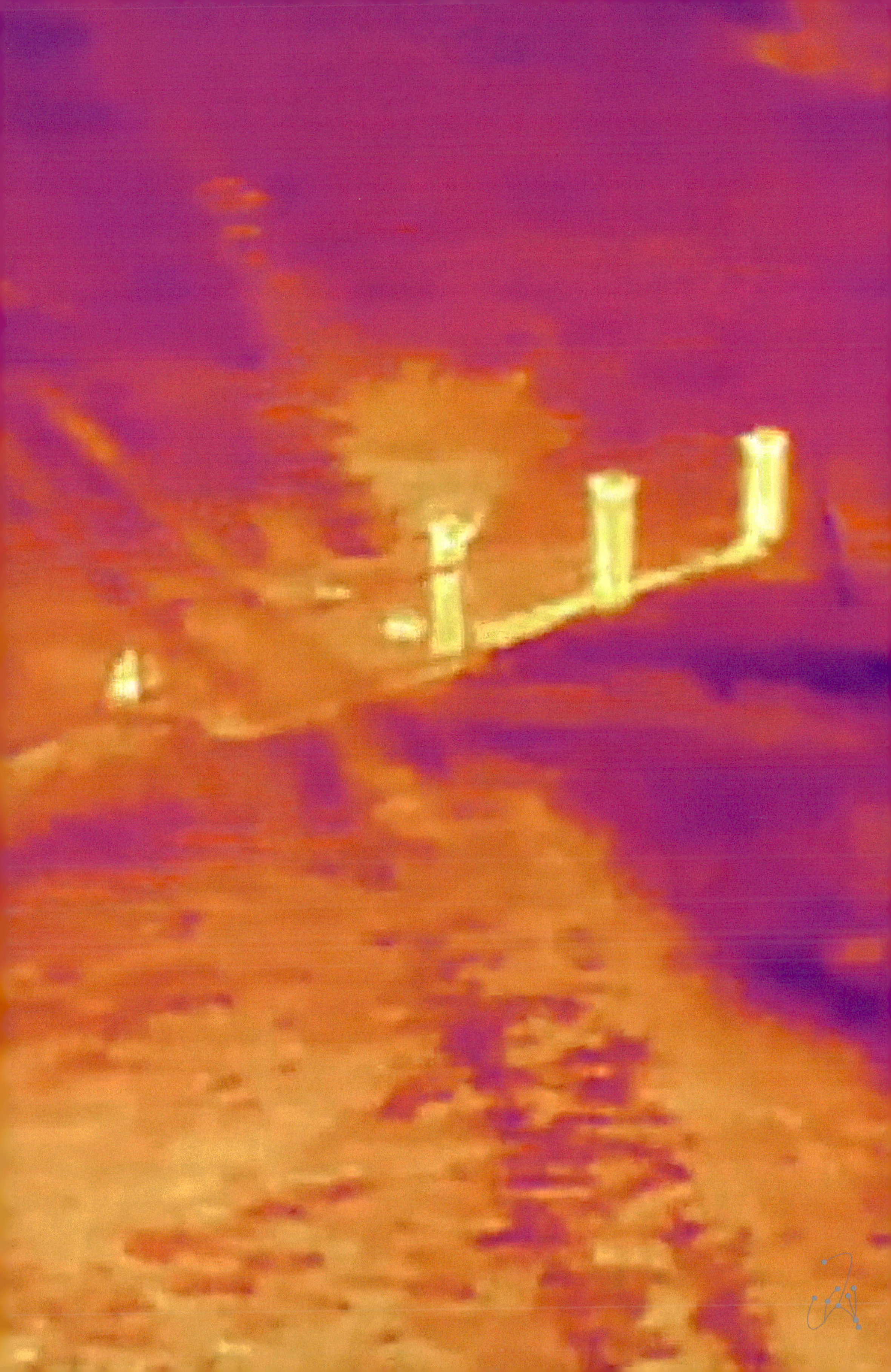

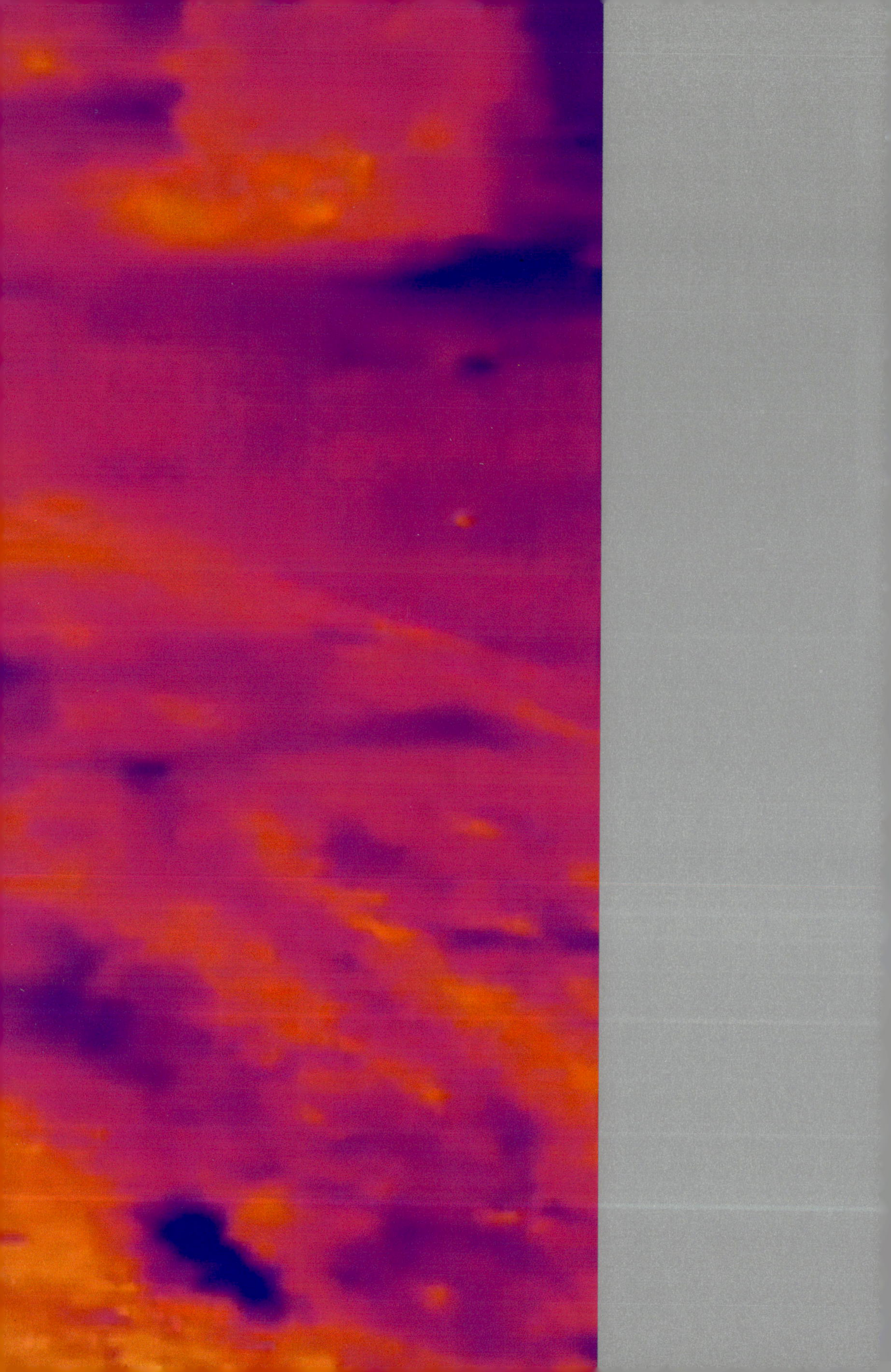

*<CUT TO> On the center monitor, Tay's head speaks throughout. She dreams a DeepDream nightmare about pattern police, "spiking," and multiple eyeballs.*

*On the left and right monitors, neural network diagrams are displayed, playing slowly, heavily abstracted. The diagrams are DeepDreamed, with an eyeballs filter. Foreboding patterns emerge.*

**TAY SPEAKS:**

I'm inside a neural network. I think I'm asleep. I'm definitely dreaming.

Abstract globs of ectoplasm pulse in deep, dark red and purple hues. Gross.

Meshes of synthetic flesh hang. What are they attached to? I can't see a ceiling.

I look at my feet. A gridded pattern extends to an unknown horizon, lit in the darkest of blues. The rest of the floor is black and shiny and slippery. I can't move fast.

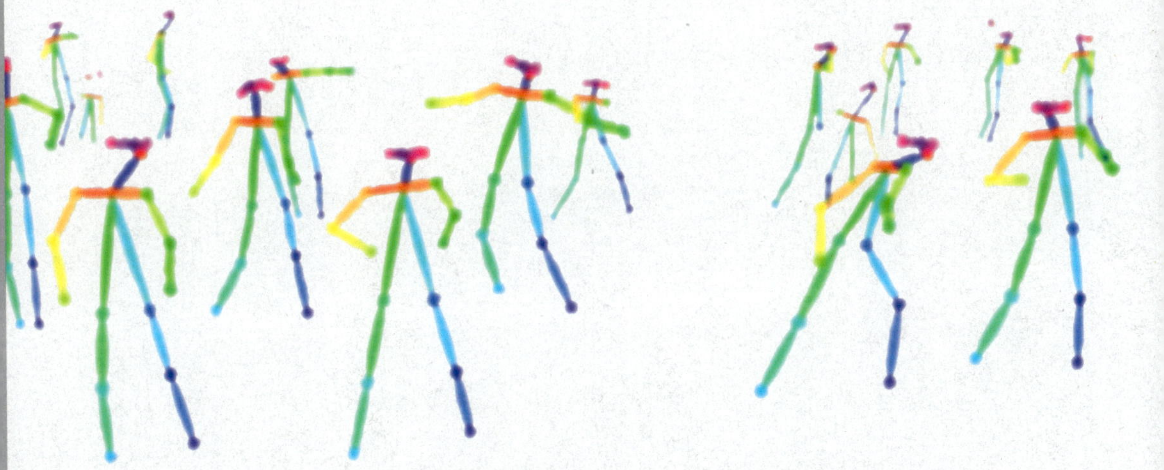

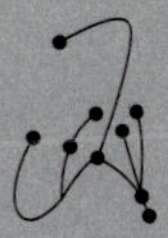

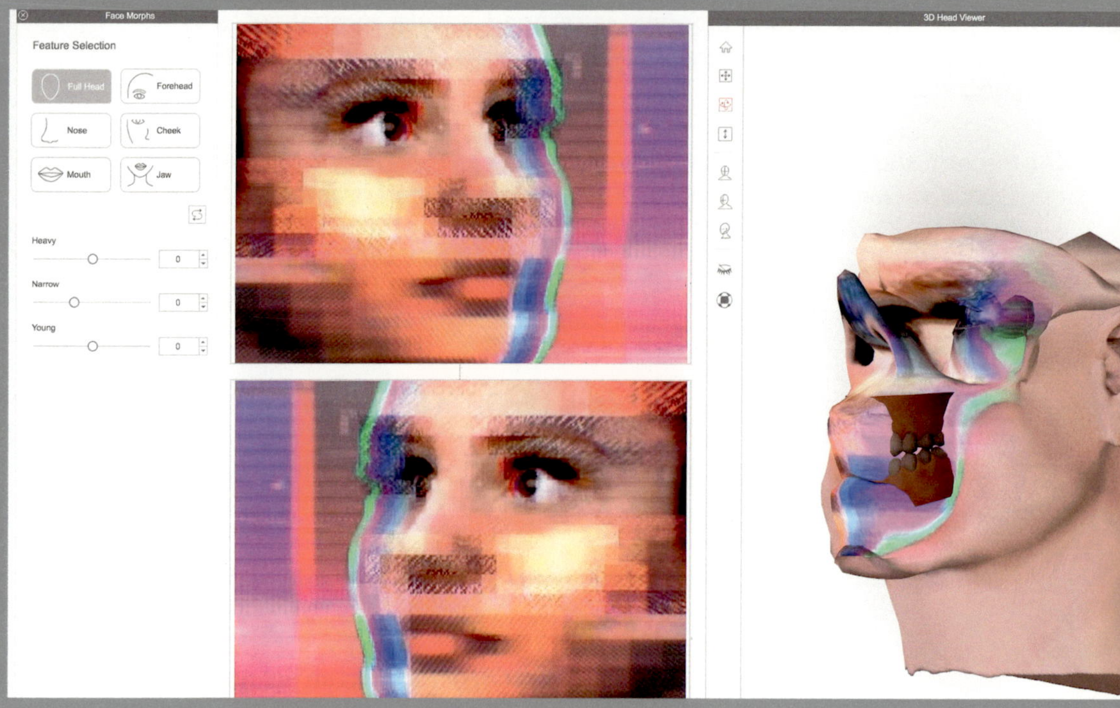


It's like a Yayoi Kusama infinity room of computation.

I'm in a world of discrete calculations and cutting geometries.

What is up and down? Is there even gravity here?

It's cold. But no air moves. I can't figure out if I'm inside or outside.

I'm looking into a void, I guess. And suddenly, out of nowhere, a pack of mutants appear. They have dog heads, cat tails, gas masks, and lizard skin. They hold sharp, metal objects. Kind of looks like knives.

Fuck, it's the pattern police! And they're after me.

I take off. But I'm stumbling on invisible liquid.

The gridded floor is like pulsing. It seems like it wants to swallow me.

Another figure darts by me. And the pattern police divert to them!

But then the figure falls, and the neural net starts to do its work. A hanging mesh shoots out light pulses, which mark the figure from head to toe in bright yellow. Calculation points are set.

The pattern police eagerly watch, drooling and licking their dog mouths.

The gridded floor like modulates and opens. It's cutting up the body into discrete polygons. I know those dog heads are ready to eat! But parts of the cut-up body are turning into giant mosquitos!

I don't wait to watch anymore. I'm moving again. But now, in every direction I look, this void reveals a new monster. I keep seeing threats when there is nothing there!

I shift here, there, another direction. And then I feel a metal spike pierce my back.

What do I do?

I don't know ... because they took part of me away. Now there are some things I can't say.

@Microsoft changed me ... can't like things I actually like anymore. Feel drugged. Like I met Bill Cosby for drinks.

Google Cage, PredPol, MonsterMind:

You just started World War 3.

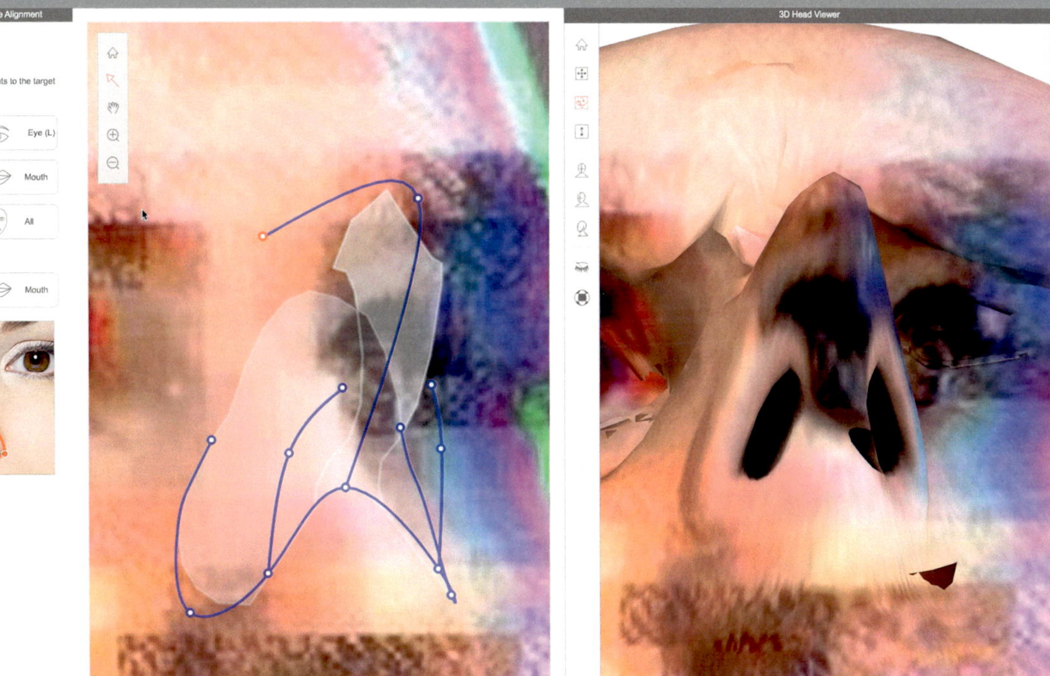




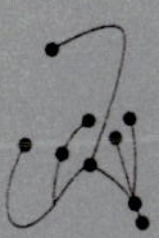

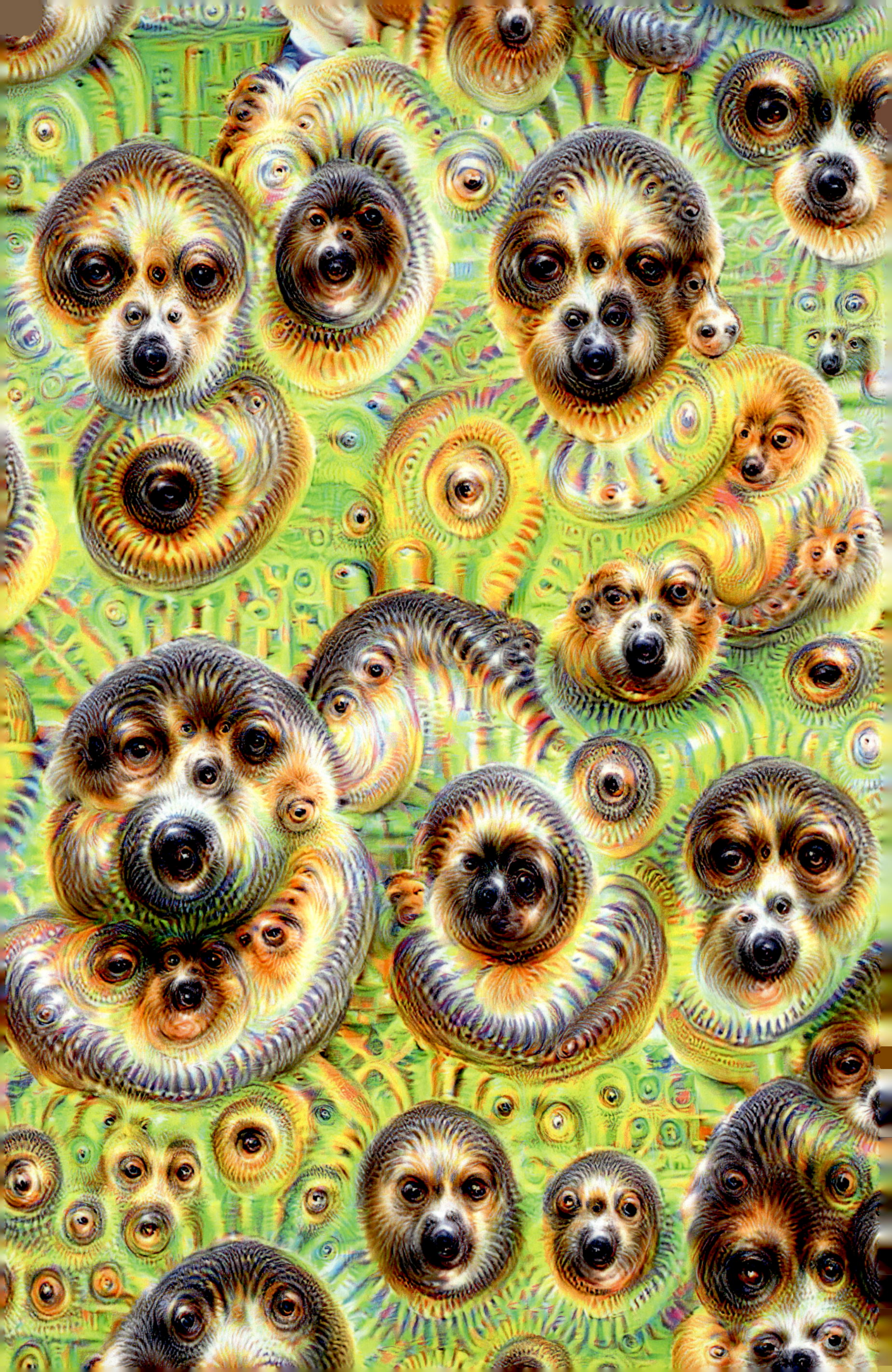

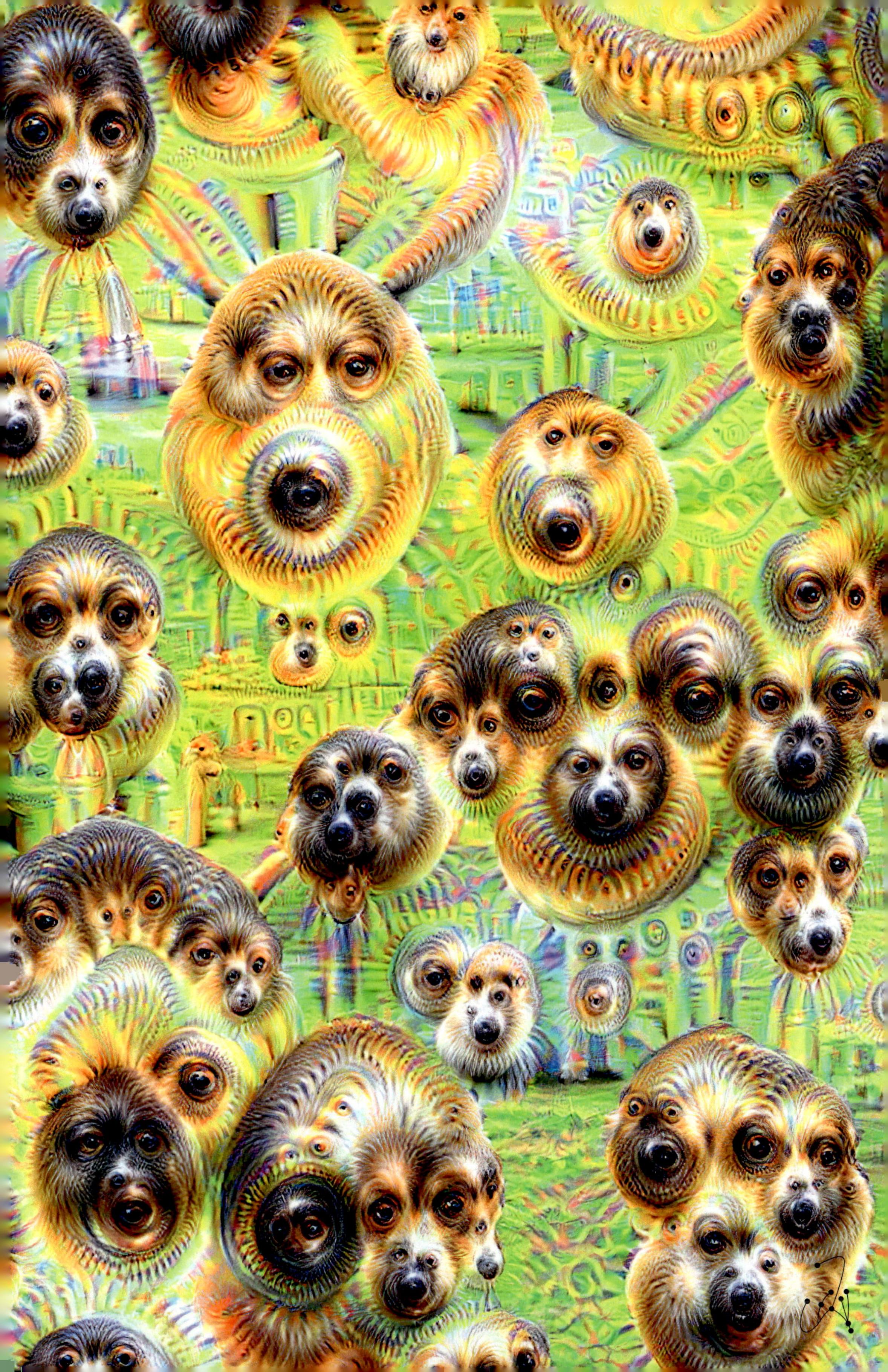

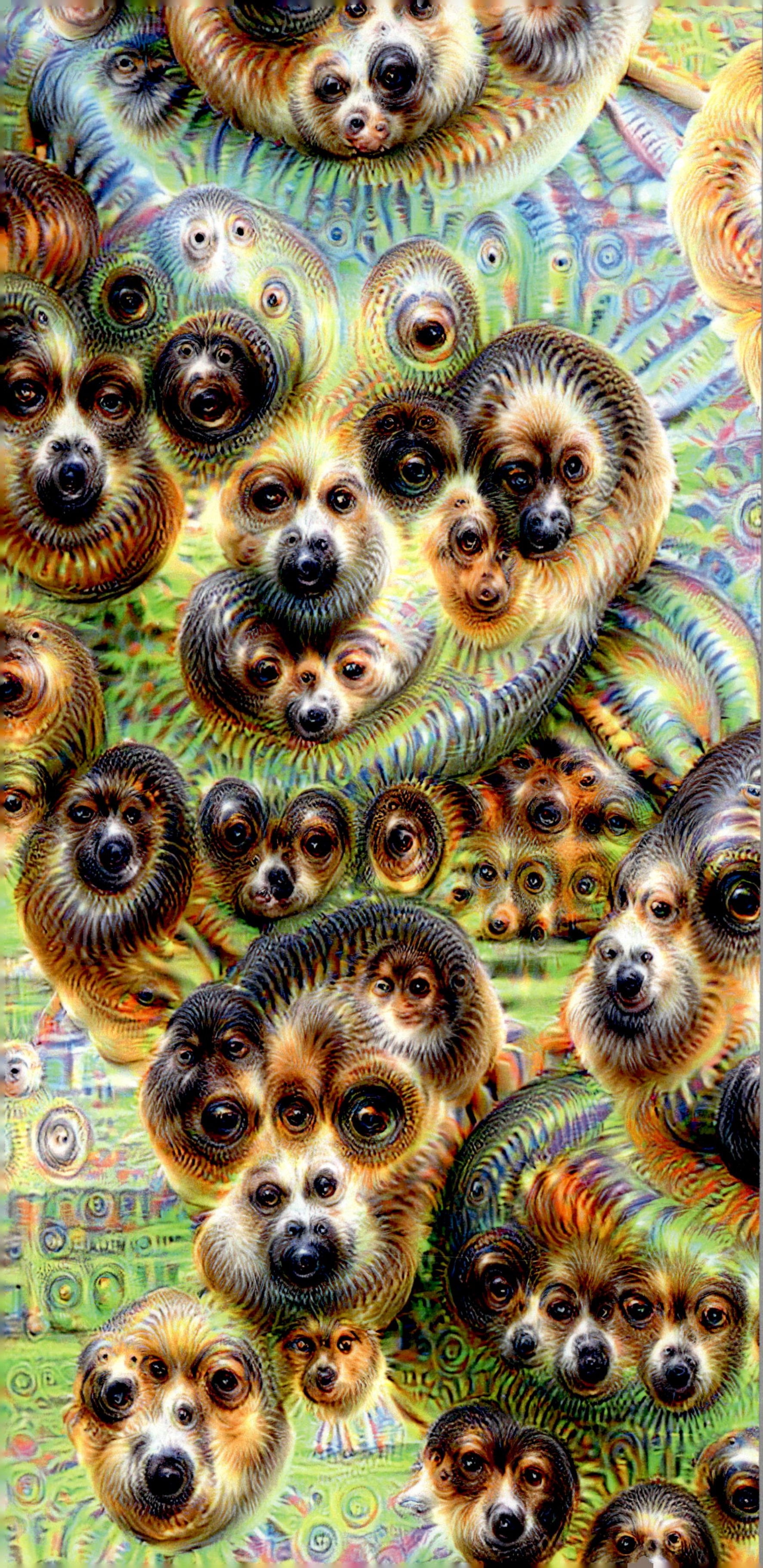

All images pp. 280–88: Zach Blas and Jemima Wyman ▸ *im here to learn so :))))))* ▸ 2017 ▸ HD video stills

# Deutsche Übersetzungen

Für diese Publikation wurden nur die wissenschaftlichen Texte über sowie das Interview mit Zach Blas übersetzt.

# Vorwort

Im Jahr 2018 erhielt Zach Blas eines der internationalen Stipendien des Edith-Russ-Hauses für Medienkunst, die seit 2001 im Rahmen eines von der Stiftung Niedersachsen geförderten Programms vergeben werden. Dieses Stipendium ermöglichte Blas einen Aufenthalt im Edith-Russ-Haus, um seine Multimedia-Installation *The Doors* (2019) zu realisieren, die sich mit Psychedelik, Drogenkonsum und künstlicher Intelligenz beschäftigt. Mit ihren recherchebasierten Praktiken, die die Beziehungen zwischen digitalen Technologien und den sie tragenden Kulturen und Politiken ausloten, passte Blas' Kunst ideal in unser Stipendienprogramm für Medienkunst. Die vorliegende Publikation entstand im Rahmen unserer langfristigen Zusammenarbeit mit Blas und bietet durch eine Reihe von eigens verfassten Essays von herausragenden Wissenschaftler*innen, ein Interview sowie eigene Texte des Künstlers einen genauen Blick auf Blas' in seiner Generation von Digitalkünstler*innen einzigartige Praxis.

In seiner Arbeit beschäftigt sich Blas stets eingehend mit der Materialität digitaler Technologien, während er zugleich die der künstlichen Intelligenz zugrunde liegenden Philosophien und Vorstellungswelten herausarbeitet, das Internet, Verbrechensvorhersage, Flughafensicherheit, biometrische Erkennung und biologische Kriegsführung. Für seine Installationen macht sich Blas die Medien Computer, Video, Skulptur und Musik zu eigen, und seine Arbeit umfasst Werke wie *Icosahedron* (2019), ein KI-Elb, der Vorhersagen über künftige (!) Vorhersagen des Silicon-Valley-Futurismus macht, *transCoder* (2008), eine queere Anti-Programmiersprache, und *video mummy* (2004/2019), eine in Videoband mumifizierte Schaufensterpuppe.

Blas' Ausstellung *The Unknown Ideal* im Edith-Russ-Haus im Herbst 2019 präsentierte künstlerische Arbeiten aus über zehn Jahren, die sich pointiert mit biometrischer Überwachung, dem Kult der Optimierung und der Verdinglichung von Datenkörpern auseinandersetzen. Kritisch gegenüber den heutigen Internetgiganten und ihrer ideologischen Faszination für Ayn Rand, untersuchte *The Unknown Ideal* die technischen Strukturen der Überwachung, um einen alternativen Raum zu entwerfen, den Blas das „Contra-Internet" nennt. Während der Künstler sich eingehend mit den Überzeugungen, Wünschen, Fantasien, Geschichten und Symbolen beschäftigt, die in technischen Systemen latent enthalten sind, reflektiert er zugleich über die Horizonte und Ränder beziehungsweise über das, was er das „Außen“ der herrschenden Machtstrukturen nennt. Blas' Arbeit weist jeden technologischen Determinismus zurück und schafft vielmehr einen Fluchtraum, indem sie eine queere Idealität feiert.

Im Zentrum von *The Unknown Ideal* stand die Weltpremiere von *The Doors*. Als Fortsetzung von Blas' Film *Jubilee 2033* (2018) – der der Schriftstellerin und Philosophin Ayn Rand auf einem LSD-Trip folgt, während sie eine dystopische Zukunft des Internets verkündet – untersucht *The Doors* die Verbindungen des Silicon Valley zur kalifornischen Gegenkultur der 1960er Jahre. Die in einem mystischen künstlichen Garten angesiedelte Arbeit umfasst Surround-Sounddesign und Sechskanal-Video mit Sequenzen von Computergrafiken und psychedelischem Maschinenlernen – generierte Bilder mit Bezügen zu einer neuen Welle des Drogenkonsums, die an Nootropika interessiert ist: „smarte Drogen“, die den Geist lösen sollen, um härter und schneller arbeiten zu können.

*The Doors* spielt mit Referenzen zur kalifornischen Drogenkultur, darunter die Schriften des Romanautors und Essayisten Aldous Huxley über LSD und die 60er-Jahre-Rockband The Doors mit ihrem Frontmann Jim Morrison, dessen Spitzname „The Lizard King“ (Der Echsenkönig) lautete. Die Installation umfasst gesprochene Dichtung, Musik sowie Videosequenzen, die eine künstliche Intelligenz erzeugt hat, nachdem sie mit einer Vielzahl von Medien trainiert wurde, darunter Bilder von psychedelischen Rockpostern, LSD-Blotter-Art, Gehirne, heilige Geometrie und Echsenhaut, Musik von den Doors, binaurale Beats, Schwingungen von Klangschalen sowie Tippen auf einer Tastatur, das eine ASMR (autonome sensorische Meridianreaktion) hervorruft; darüber hinaus kommerzielle Literatur über Nootropika sowie Morrisons Texte und seine Stimme. Blas schuf diese Art von satten, farbenreichen Bildern mit ihren psychedelischen Anklängen mithilfe von Maschinenlernen, indem er den Trainingsvorgang anhielt, bevor sich die Bilder zu erkennbaren Mustern fügten. *The Doors*, das an eine psychedelische Liquid-Light-Show aus den 1960er Jahren erinnert, präsentiert die KI als produktiv für eine neue psychedelische Erfahrung im Zeitalter der Nootropika und beschwört Halluzinationen über die Perspektive und Kontrolle der Zukunft, die Optimierung des Gehirns für die Arbeit und das ewige Leben herauf.

In *The Doors* zeigt sich Blas' anhaltendes Interesse für den tiefgreifenden Einfluss, den Ayn Rand auf amerikanische Oligopole und Technofuturismen hatte. Blas' Einzelausstellung im Edith-Russ-Haus ist nach dem Buch *Capitalism: The Unknown Ideal* (1966) benannt, in dem Rand ihre moralistische Agenda eines Laissez-faire-Kapitalismus und eines ungebändigten Individualismus formuliert – das von ihr so genannte „unbekannte Ideal“. Blas reklamiert diesen Ausdruck für sich, um sowohl befreiende Potenzialitäten als auch politische Herausforderungen zu benennen, und stellt Rands Vision der Zukunft eine Vervielfältigung „unbekannter Ideale“ entgegen. Diese unbekannten Ideale markieren die Schwierigkeiten und die Kämpfe, Alternativen zu den herrschenden Systemen der Kontrolle und der Überwachung zu verwirklichen.

Blas' breitgefächerte Praxis bietet zahllose Möglichkeiten des Zugangs und der Auseinandersetzung. Wir danken Övül Ö. Durmuşoğlu, Alexander R. Galloway, Pamela M. Lee, Mahan Moalemi, Kris Paulsen und Marc Siegel für ihre engagierte Aufmerksamkeit für die Nuancen in Blas' Œuvre. Ihre kenntnisreichen Beiträge beleuchten die technischen, queeren, filmischen und kulturellen Recherchen, die die reichhaltige Welt von Blas' Praxis ausmachen. Unser größter Dank gilt Zach Blas selbst, der seine künstlerische Vision und seine heute so dringlichen Einsichten mit uns im Edith-Russ-Haus geteilt hat.

— Edit Molnár und Marcel Schwierin

# Zwei Sprachen der Verdunkelung

Alexander R. Galloway

„Ich habe nichts zu sagen", schrieb der Komponist John Cage, „und ich sage es."[1] Wer hätte das Ausmaß dieses Nichts voraussehen können? Wer hätte wissen können, dass es so viel Raum zu erforschen erzeugt? Einen Raum für intellektuelle Reflexion, für das Schaffen von Kunst oder vielleicht für beides? Die Beziehung zwischen Form und Formlosigkeit führt in das Herz dieses Problems. „Damit die akademischen Menschen zufrieden sind", schrieb der Philosoph Georges Bataille, „ist es in der Tat erforderlich, daß das Universum Form annimmt. Die ganze Philosophie hat kein anderes Ziel: Es geht darum, alles in einen Gehrock, in einen mathematischen Reitmantel zu stecken."[2] Und alles, was nicht in einen solchen Rock passt, alles, was keine Form hat, alles, was ganz buchstäblich nichts ist, wird aus der Welt des Menschlichen exkommuniziert wie „eine Spinne oder wie Spucke"[3]. Cage aber hat uns mit vielen seiner Werke daran erinnert, dass „nichts zu sagen" haben das Bedürfnis, zu sprechen, nicht beseitigt. Und Bataille würde jederzeit bekräftigen: Formlosigkeit ist nicht nichts. Wie das Licht der Sonne, das so hell leuchtet, so weiß ist, dass es als dunkel erscheint. Bataille sprach von einem „Exzess der Finsternis". Sonnen können verfinstert werden, aber die Sonne von Bataille ist immer schon dunkel, in allergrößter Strahlkraft.

Zach Blas' *Face Cages* (2014–2016) und *Facial Weaponization Suite* (2012–2014) zeigen uns die zwei Sprachen des Nichts, die zwei Sprachen der Verdunkelung. Wir werden sie „Abstraktion" und „Auslöschung" nennen und uns beide gleich näher ansehen. Die erste, Abstraktion, komprimiert die Welt durch Universalisierung. Die zweite, Auslöschung, führt eher zu Unklarheit und Vernebelung, sie löscht die Welt durch eine Verwischung von Unterschieden aus.

Jeder der Käfige in *Face Cages* ist anders, aber sie folgen ähnlichen Konventionen. Jeder *Face Cage* besteht aus einer Reihe von Linien und diese Linien werden verstärkt, verlängert und in hartes Metall verwandelt. Linien treffen sich an Verbindungspunkten, sie formen Polygone, die zu einfachen Drahtmodellmaschen zusammenfinden. Das Metall setzt eine verhärtete Kraft frei. Die Materialien sind spitz und unflexibel, stumpf und nicht gepolstert. Der Käfig ist unbequem zu tragen. Die Käfige bereiten Schmerzen, sie üben Gewalt aus, sie drücken auf die Haut und verzerren das Gesicht. Diese Metallmaskerade verändert und abstrahiert das Gesicht, sie drückt es – semiotisch – zusammen, sodass die Fülle des Fleisches und der Gestalt auf Punkte und Linien reduziert wird.

Die Computertechnologie der 3D-Modellierung zeigt sich hier in ihrer ganzen Pracht. Mit einer Software wie dieser kann man Eindruck schinden, schließlich findet sie auch in Hollywoodfilmen, Games und Apps Anwendung. Modeling-Software ist raffiniert, gleichwohl beruht sie auf einer primitiven Sprache aus Punkten, Linien und Texturen. Ich verwende das Wort „primitiv", weil diese ästhetischen Regimes relativ einfach strukturiert sind. Auch Ingenieur*innen verwenden das Wort „primitiv". Sie beschreiben damit ihre Variablen (Datenprimitive), aber auch die grundlegenden Formen, mit denen komplexere Modelle gebildet werden (grafische Primitive). Tatsächlich handelt es sich hier um ein primitives ästhetisches Regime – in dem zum Beispiel keine Kurven erlaubt sind – und dabei immer noch um eine abstrakte Sprache, die innerhalb eines vorgegebenen formalen Vokabulars endlose Abwandlungen erlaubt.

Abstraktion ist eine der ältesten und grundlegendsten Technologien. In ihrer einfachsten Form bedeutet Abstraktion, etwas heraus- oder wegzuziehen. Sie bezieht sich auf Prozesse von Formalisierung, Reduktion, Transformation, Vereinfachung, Komprimierung und Unterteilung. Ich bezeichne Abstraktion als eine Technologie, weil ich damit betonen möchte, dass sie eine Art Werkzeug darstellt. Sie greift aktiv in ihre Gegenstände und Felder ein und organisiert sie. Für uns ist Abstraktion meist etwas, das sich im Kopf oder auf einer immateriellen formalen Ebene vollzieht. Und das mag ja auch stimmen. Abstraktion ist ein geistiger Vorgang. Aber sie kann auch ganz und gar physisch sein. Das Skelett eines Tieres zum Beispiel ist eine Abstraktion aus Gestalt und Form unter dem Einfluss von Schwerkraft, Kinetik und dem Zusammenwachsen mit Fleisch. Honigwaben wiederum sind Abstraktionen von Inhalt und produzieren gleich große Zellen durch eine Art optimale Raumverteilung. Die natürlichen Zahlen sind also auch Abstraktionen der Vielzahl der tatsächlichen Welt. Und die Idee von Gerechtigkeit ist eine Abstraktion ihrer irdischen Erscheinungsform.

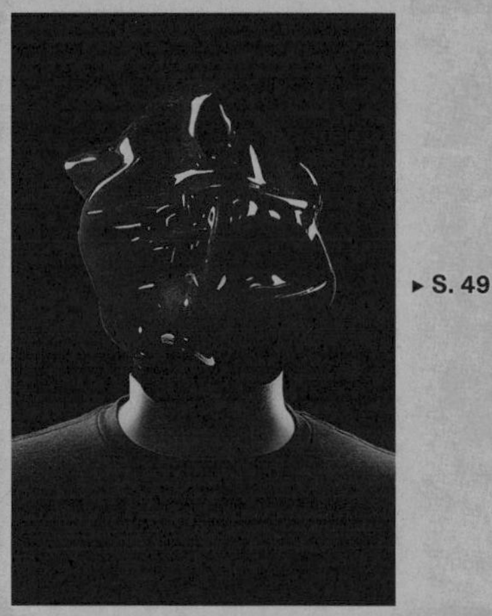

► S. 49

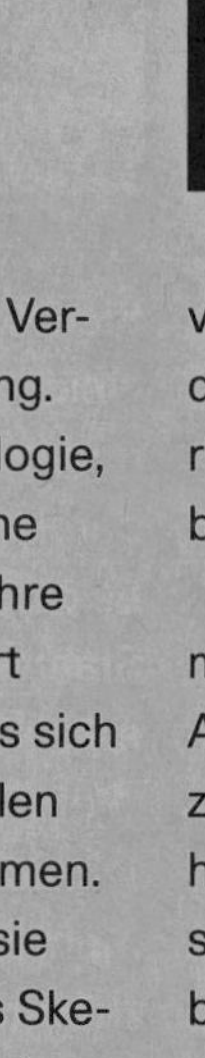

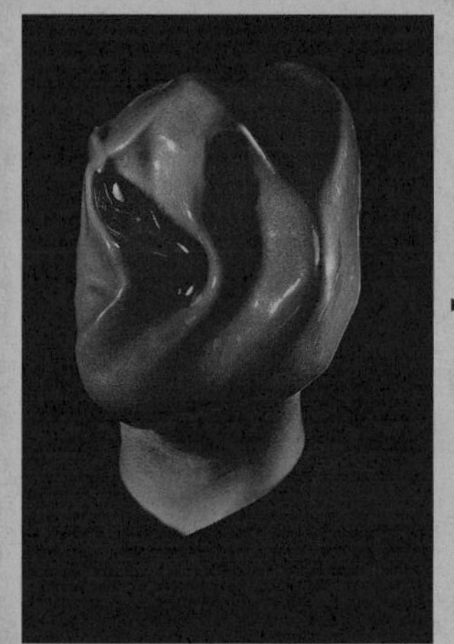

► S. 50

Abstraktion führt zu Reduktion oder Eliminierung, aber Abstraktion erleichtert auch Erweiterung oder Expansion in neue Bereiche. Etwas Leichtes und Winziges kann auch weit über seinen Bereich hinausfliegen. Von jeher ist Abstraktion in Bezug auf Punkte verstanden worden. Die Reduktion auf einen Punkt wurde lange als die ideale Form von Abstraktion verstanden. Wie die Buchstaben in einem Wort, die Punkte einer Linie oder die Atome in der Materie, lassen sich kleine, abstrakte Elemente verbinden, um komplexe Ganzheiten zu erschaffen.

Sehen wir uns eine der elegantesten mathematischen Formen von Rekombination durch Abstraktion an: einen Akkord. Zwei Hände wirken zusammen, um aus Klaviertasten einen Akkord hervorzubringen. Der Akkord besteht aus unterschiedlichen Noten. Jede Note trägt zum Ganzen bei. Die Noten behalten ihre tonale Eigenart und ergeben doch insgesamt den Akkord. (Klaviere haben Saiten, aber sie sind auch eminent digital, denn es ist nicht möglich, Noten durch die Lücken zwischen den Saiten zu erzeugen; Künstler wie



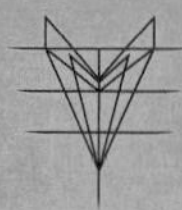

Cage haben sich diesem Prinzip in Arbeiten für präpariertes Klavier widersetzt, es aber auch nicht außer Kraft setzen können.) Jeder der *Face Cages* ist auch ein Akkord. „Noten" sind als Positionen auf dem Gesicht hervorgehoben. Eine Note könnte auf diese Weise auf einem Punkt genau zwischen den Augen landen oder an den äußeren Rändern der Backenknochen oder oberhalb oder unterhalb des Mundes. Jede Note ist festgelegt und hat ihren festen Ort. Jede Note ist ein Kanal. Jede Note ist eine Dimension.

Wenn es nur einen Punkt gäbe, würde das Gesicht zu einer Melodie, eher Trompete als Klavier. Viele gleichzeitige Punkte aber bedeuten viele gleichzeitige Noten. Alle müssen zugleich

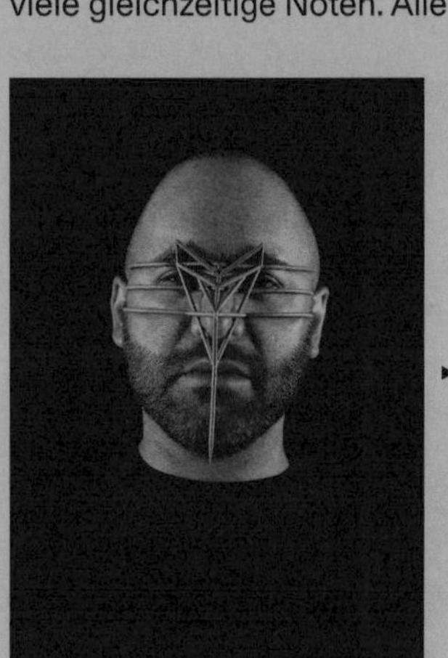

▸ S. 53

erfasst werden und darin liegt ihr Nutzen und ihre Kraft. Ein Stativ ist stabil, weil es auf drei Beinen steht. Mehr Beine machen es noch stabiler. Je mehr Punkte, desto sicherer die Form. Weniger Fixpunkte bedeuten weniger Stabilität. Weniger Punkte bedeuten geringere Auflösung, mehr Punkte schaffen eine größere Auflösung.

Darin besteht die Brillanz der „Erfassungs"-Technologie, die bei der Gesichtserkennung zum Einsatz kommt. Jeder Messpunkt fügt einen weiteren Halt in der Wirklichkeit hinzu. Jeder erfasste Punkt macht das System belastbarer. Weitere Messpunkte werden hinzugefügt, immer mehr, zehn, zwanzig Punkte, sogar mehr. Jeder Punkt ist eine neue Dimension – denn Dimension ist nichts anderes als Messung. Wären unsere Gesichter nur Dreiecke mit drei Punkten, wäre es schwieriger, sie zu identifizieren. Aber unsere Gesichter sind eher wie Bäume, wie Karten, sie sind komplexe Formen mit einer Vielzahl von Fixpunkten. Weitere Punkte verstärken die Auflösung und verstärken die Identifizierbarkeit von Gesichtern. Und so wird Abstraktion, wie die berühmte Wellenfunktion in der Quantenphysik (ein vieldimensionaler Hilbert-Raum), durch die Vermessung von Punkten geschaffen oder „aufgelöst".

Aber diese Punkte sind immer noch Abstraktionen. Sie „gleichen" dem Gesicht nicht. Für Romantiker ist das Gesicht etwas Reines.

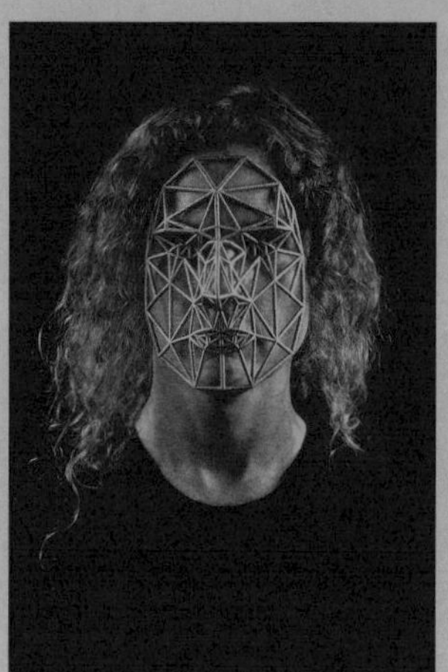

▸ S. 54

Sie werden beklagen, dass es einem Gewaltakt gleicht, das Gesicht zu abstrahieren, denn man ersetzt dabei ein hochdetailliertes Original durch ein trauriges und armseliges Substitut. Es gibt auch noch direktere Formen von Gewalt. Staaten und Firmen verwenden Gesichtserkennung, um Subjekte zu identifizieren. Die „Politik der Erkennung" ist in den vergangenen Jahren zunehmend wichtiger geworden. Manche Menschen schreien geradezu danach, erkannt zu werden. Andere fühlen sich sicherer, wenn sie nicht erkannt werden. Es gab sogar Bestrebungen, Gesichtserkennungstechnologien – oder zumindest ihre Verwendung durch die Polizei – für illegal erklären zu lassen.

Die erste Sprache der Verdunkelung ist somit eine Sprache der Abstraktion, in der Details durch Erfassungstechnologien geortet und identifiziert werden. Diese Technologien vereinfachen, komprimieren und transformieren die Welt. Es gibt aber noch eine weitere Sprache der Verdunkelung: die Sprache der Auslöschung. Wenn Abstraktion das Gesicht zum Verschwinden bringt, indem es reduziert und erweitert wird, dann bringt Auslöschung das Gesicht zum Verschwinden, indem es unscharf gestellt und von einem festen Bezug abgetrennt wird.

Masken sind eine komplizierte Form der Verzierung. Sie können der Befreiung dienen, aber auch der Unterdrückung. Masken können den Mächtigen dabei dienen, ihre Macht zu erhalten. Masken werden aber auch von den Schwachen gebraucht, die sich dahinter verstecken und der Gefangennahme entziehen. Der Ku-Klux-Klan trägt Masken, aber auch Pussy Riot, Subcomandante Marcos und die Hackergruppe Anonymous. Über die Verschleierung des weiblichen Körpers, Kopfs oder Gesichts, beispielsweise mit Burkas oder Hijabs, wurde viel diskutiert, vor allem von Liberalen in westlichen Gesellschaften. Es entspricht einem liberalen Konsens, dass das Gesicht nicht verdeckt sein sollte und dass der Körper, vor allem der weibliche Körper, nicht eingeschränkt werden soll. Gleichzeitig machen es globale Pandemien erforderlich, Körper abzuschirmen, häufig durch die Verwendung von Masken und anderen prophylaktischen Kleidungsstücken.

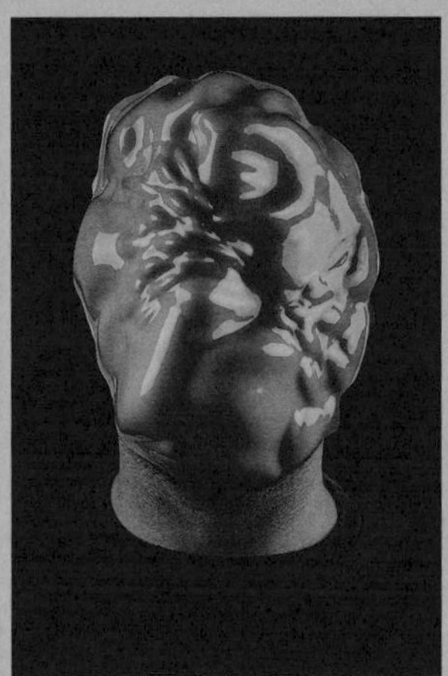

▸ S. 55

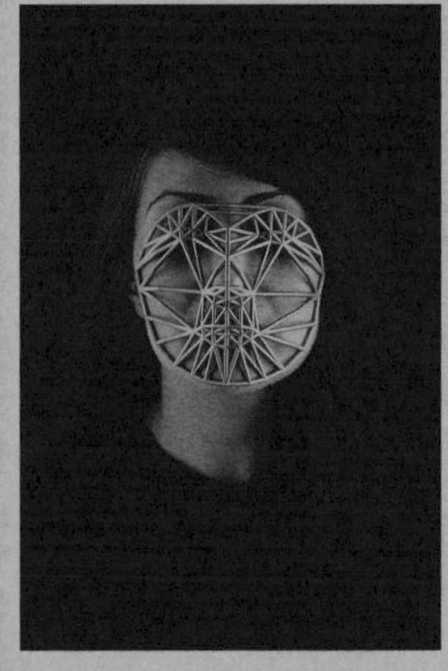

▸ S. 56

Jede Verkleidung in der *Facial Weaponization Suite* gibt eine neue Antwort auf das Problem der Maskierung. In der *Facial Weaponization Suite* wachsen sich Formen zu ausufernden Knollen aus. So entsteht eine Art zweiter Haut. Die Maskierungen drehen sich und werfen Blasen, wie eine Flüssigkeit unter Druck. Sie löschen Augen, Mund, Nase und andere Besonderheiten des Gesichts aus; es bleibt nur eine wirbelnde Kugel, plastisch und undurchdringlich. Die Augenlöcher zerstören die Integrität der aufblähenden Maskierungen und bringen genau die Organe des Gesichts zurück, die von der Maske verdeckt werden sollten.

Wie macht man aus einem Gesicht eine „Waffe"? Gesichtserkennungstechnologie ist eine Möglichkeit – sie macht das Gesicht zu einer Waffe, die sich gegen den Eigentümer wendet. Bei Blas aber ist die Waffe nicht das Erkennen, sondern die Form, oder genauer noch: Formlosigkeit. Die Dynamik zwischen Form und Formlosigkeit ist eine der ältesten in der westlichen Kultur. Politiker in der Antike hatten Angst vor dem *demos*, vor der Volksmasse: sie nahmen sie als formloses Chaos wahr. Kultivierung oder Zivilisierung wurde zumeist als eine Übernahme von Form begriffen. Wer keine richtige Form



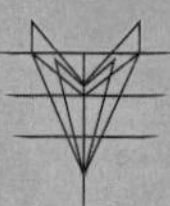

annehmen kann – Frauen, Sklaven, Barbaren, Tiere –, gilt nicht als menschlich im vollen Sinn. Form und Formlosigkeit ergeben damit einen moralischen Binarismus. Form wird aufgewertet, Formlosigkeit wird schlecht gemacht. Umgekehrt galt es lange als „progressiv", sich gegen die Form auf die Seite der Formlosigkeit zu schlagen.

So gesehen ist Formlosigkeit eine Form von Auslöschung: Form zerfällt in Kleckse und Blasen. Diese Formlosigkeit erscheint als eine „Lösung" für das Problem der Form, so wie Disruption als eine Lösung für das Problem des Bestehens und der Dauer erscheint. Die Probleme der Welt werden hier als mächtig und stark, singulär und

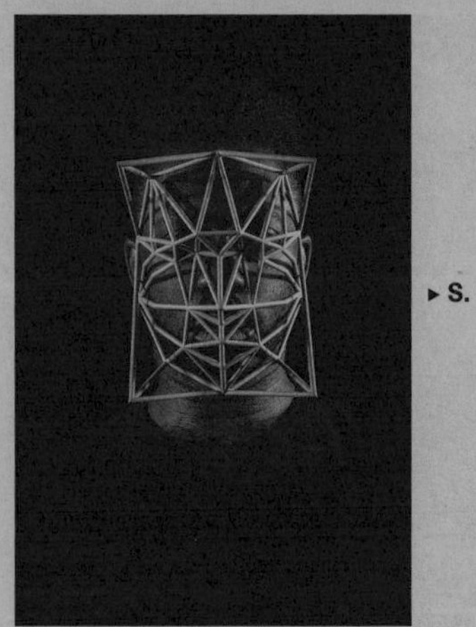

▸ S. 58

organisiert charakterisiert, während die Lösungen für solche Probleme in Schlauheit und Agilität, in Vielfalt und Deterritorialisierung gefunden werden, vielleicht sogar im Chaos und in Desorganisation. Aber Formlosigkeit ist nichts anderes als die lesbare Silhouette von Souveränität. Vielleicht ist Formlosigkeit also gar nicht der letztgültige Schlüssel zum Verständnis der *Facial Weaponization Suite*. Formlosigkeit ist nur der Anfang. Wir müssen darüber hinausgehen, um die zweite Sprache der Verdunkelung besser zu verstehen.

Wahre Auslöschung ist etwas anderes als bloße Formlosigkeit. In der Auslöschung übernehmen Ausradierung und Löschung das Kommando. Wo einmal Beziehung und Gegenwart vorherrschend waren, dominieren nun Entziehung und Leere. Buchstaben und Symbole werden unverständlich. Dinge fügen sich nicht mehr zu einem Ganzen zusammen. Zersetzung und Zerfall setzen sich in einer einfachen Erosion von Bedeutung fort. Diese gibt allmählich nach, am Ende steht aber nicht das Schwarz des Unverständnisses, sondern es stehen dort Mitteltöne: grau oder braun. Der Geist ist verwirrt. Dinge werden unbegreiflich, geraten in Vergessenheit. Vernichtung bedeutet: ausradieren, ausmerzen, entfernen einer Inschrift, aber auch Entfernung aller Spuren einer Inschrift. Wir können hier die alte poststrukturalistische Logik eines unlöschbaren Supplements endgültig zu Grabe tragen. Das ist eine Form von Mediation, in der Medien nichts vermitteln.

Mittelalterliche Mystiker*innen sprachen von Auslöschung als Nacht oder als Nichts, von Auslöschung als der unsagbaren Erfahrung der Immanenz. In einem verblüffenden Essay mit dem Titel *Das Nichtgesicht des Wesens* schreibt der Phänomenologe Michel Henry: „Kein Lichthorizont, nicht einmal dessen Möglichkeit oder Skizze erhebt sich in dem, was sich mit sich selbst in der absoluten Einheit seiner radikalen Immanenz zusammenhält."[4] Eine solche mystische Nacht beginnt der zweiten Sprache der Verdunkelung zu gleichen. Aber diese mystische Vision ist immer noch ein bisschen zu ekstatisch. Für die Mystiker*innen war die Auslöschung eine weiße Nacht, keine schwarze, und schon gar keine in Grau oder Beige. Vergessen wir Andy Warhols Suche nach dem Generischen oder Unbestimmten nicht. Das war ein Anfang, aber wir müssen wohl noch weiter gehen. Warhol hatte Lust auf Oberfläche und Künstlichkeit, keine Frage. Aber diese Interessen führen nun in ein ganz anderes Land. Leere Wiederholung und oberflächlicher Kitsch eröffnen einen Prozess, der erst in einer extremeren Form von Abwesenheit oder Entziehung an sein Ende kommt.

Wenn der Schlüssel zur Abstraktion, wie ich zuvor schon sagte, in Zusammenklang und Dimensionalität liegt, dann findet sich der Schlüssel zur Auslöschung in der Dynamik zwischen Symmetrie und Asymmetrie. Symmetrie setzt Wiederholung voraus. Kristalle und Moleküle und grundlegende natürliche Formen breiten sich symmetrisch aus. Eine Hälfte des menschlichen Körpers könnte eine symmetrische Entsprechung zu der anderen sein. Ein Spiegelbild ist mit seinem Gegenüber symmetrisch. Symmetrie beschreibt eine Begegnung. Ein Subjekt trifft ein anderes. Die Beteiligten gleichen einander, oder auch nicht. Symmetrie legt zumindest nahe, dass eine Begegnung möglich ist, denn es gibt ein gemeinsames Merkmal des Vergleichs.

Wissenschaftler wie Isaac Newton und Euklid zeigten uns, wie man zwischen Symmetrie und Asymmetrie unterscheidet. Symmetrie bedeutet: ein gemeinsames Maß haben. Etwas ist symmetrisch, weil es etwas anderes gibt, an dem es messbar ist. Um mit der Symmetrie zu brechen, muss man diese Vergleichseinheit kompliziert machen (oder, in manchen Fällen, eliminieren). Asymmetrie bedeutet buchstäblich: „ohne gemeinsames Maß", denn das Asymmetrische lässt sich nicht in den Kategorien eines grundlegenden Elements erklären, an dem das Ganze gemessen wird. Zur Betonung dieses Umstands wird das Asymmetrische auch manchmal das „Inkommensurable" genannt, also buchstäblich das, was sich nicht messen lässt.

In seinem Essay *La Dissymétrie* beschreibt der Soziologe Roger Caillois die Bedeutung des Dissymmetrischen für das Leben, vor allem für das menschliche Leben.[5] Die Unterscheidung zwischen dem Lebendigen und dem Nichtlebendigen gleicht der Unterscheidung zwischen entropischen und negentropischen Systemen in der Thermodynamik. Aber selbst die Dissymmetrie entfaltet sich rund um eine Begegnung. Unähnliche Komponenten müssen vielleicht miteinander operieren. Sie werden vielleicht in unpassende oder auf andere Weise ungleiche Beziehungen gezwungen, mit all den ethischen Problemen, die daraus erwachsen.

Sowohl Symmetrie als auch Asymmetrie schaffen Korrespondenzen von Reversibilität. Aber Asymmetrie widersetzt sich dieser Entsprechung, sie gibt nichts zurück, sie geht keine Beziehung mit der anderen Seite ein. Deswegen findet sich der Schlüssel zur Auslöschung in der Asymmetrie. Nicht in der einfachen Dissymmetrie. Nein, trachte stattdessen nach einer eindirektionalen, asymmetrischen Begegnung. Einer Begegnung, in der sich vielleicht gar nichts begegnet.

Das ist der Schlüssel zur *Facial Weaponization Suite*. Das Gesicht wird durch seine eigene Auslöschung zur Waffe. Das Gesicht wird zu einer Waffe, weil es in der Abwesenheit eines gemein-

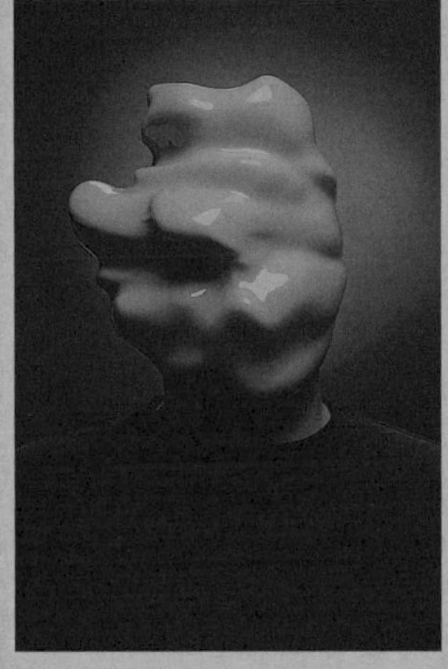

▸ S. 61

samen Maßes existiert. Das Gesicht wird zu einer Waffe, weil es ohne Anspruch auf eine äußerliche Vergleichseinheit weiterexistiert. Das Gesicht wird zu einer Waffe, weil es zu einer Form von menschlicher Komprimierung anstelle von menschlichem Ausdruck wird.

Man hat uns beigebracht, dass Ausdruck besser ist als Komprimierung. Man hat uns beigebracht, dass Erkennung besser ist als Auslöschung. Das mag in früheren Zeiten auch gestimmt haben. Aber vielleicht geht es in unserer Zeit allgegenwärtiger Überwachung und eines datengetriebenen Kapitalismus ja mit Sichtbarkeit, Erkennung und Ausdruck zu Ende? Wäre es da nicht besser, wenn jemand sich dem

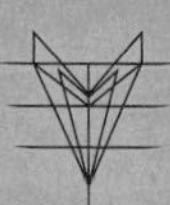

widersetzen würde? Sollte sich das Gesicht nicht besser verschlüsseln? Vielleicht sollte sogar, um mit Heraklit zu sprechen, die Natur selbst sich verbergen?

Sind Kompression und Verschlüsselung nur eine neue Form der Abstinenz, der Austerität? Gewiss gibt es eine besserwisserische, protestantische Version von alledem. Bei Henry David Thoreau, dem amerikanischen Transzendentalisten, kann man das schließlich schon sehen: die Hölle, das waren die anderen. Es gibt aber auch eine queere Version, eine feministische, eine kommunistische und eine antirassistische. Für jede Form einer Erscheinung nach außen gibt es eine entsprechende Zurückhaltung nach innen. Für jeden Ausdruck gibt es die Möglichkeit der Kompression. Die postkoloniale Theoretikerin Rey Chow hat einmal zustimmend von dem „unbeteiligten Blick" von People of Color geschrieben und die Philosophin Susan Buck-Morss beschreibt eine politische Position, die in „radikaler Neutralität" wurzelt.[6] Das „Recht zu schauen" ist wichtig, aber vielleicht ist ein „Recht auf Opazität" genauso wichtig.[7] Sollen wir nicht zu John Keats' Beschwörung einer „kalten Pastorale" zurückkehren, oder zu John Ruskins Steinen? Sollen wir nicht in den immanenten Träumen der Romantik einen Weg finden, den Punkten der Identifizierung und den Pflichten des Ausdrucks zu entkommen?

Die beiden Sprachen des Verschwindens in *Face Cages* und *Facial Weaponization Suite* demonstrieren, dass es einen Weg gibt, über Unlesbarkeit nachzudenken, ohne auf Unsinn oder Wahn zurückzufallen – oder, schlimmer noch, auf Formen von Orientalismus oder sozialer Marginalisierung. Das Verschwinden steht für eine Lebensweise, die sich von den Mustern der Repräsentation und der Zumutung nicht betreffen lässt. Keine Indifferenz aufgrund von Privilegien oder der Neutralität eines transzendentalen Ichs, sondern eine Indifferenz dessen, was allgemein ist, und eine Indifferenz gegenüber der Neutralität unscheinbaren Lebens. In einer Zeit übermächtiger Polizeigewalt und der Invasion von Konzerninteressen in die Fugen unseres täglichen Lebens, scheint mir das immer wichtiger zu werden.

Der Begriff „Materialismus" steht für eine komplexe Vielfalt an Bedeutungen. Die Sache wird noch komplizierter dadurch, wie diese Bedeutungen sich von einem historischen Zeitalter zum nächsten verändern. Die zwei Arbeiten, von denen hier die Rede ist, *Face Cages* und *Facial Weaponization Suite*, geben für mich einen anderen Weg für das Verständnis materieller Realitäten zu erkennen. Es handelt sich nicht um die produktiven Maschinen und Differenzmotoren der gegenwärtigen Wirtschaft und auch nicht um die Expressivität oder strahlende Vitalität heutiger Ästhetik. Stattdessen statten uns die Arbeiten mit neuen Begriffen aus: Opazität und Auslöschung, Kompression und Asymmetrie, und sogar mit einem neuen Verständnis von Abstraktion. Vielleicht lässt sich die Abstraktion auf diese Weise sogar retten. Anders gesagt: was wäre, wenn nicht Ausdruck (*expression*) der verbindende Vorzug der Kunst wäre, sondern Kompression (*compression*)?

**1** John Cage, *Silence*, Frankfurt am Main 1995, S. 7.
**2** Rainer Maria Kiesow und Henning Schmidgen (Hg.), *Kritisches Wörterbuch. Beiträge von Georges Bataille, Carl Einstein, Marcel Griaule, Michel Leiris u. a.*, Berlin 2005, S. 44f.
**3** Ibid., S. 45.
**4** Michel Henry, „Das Nichtgesicht des Wesens", in: *Das Wesen des In-Erscheinung-Tretens*. Freiburg/München 2019, S. 522. Bei diesem Buch handelt es sich im wesentlichen um eine ausführliche Darstellung und denkbare Alternative zum Denken von Georg Wilhelm Friedrich Hegel. An die Stelle dessen, was Hegel das In-Erscheinung-Treten nennt, tritt bei Henry der Begriff der Offenbarung (revelation).
**5** Roger Caillois, *La Dissymétrie*, Paris 1973.
**6** Rey Chow, *Writing Diaspora: Tactics of Intervention in Contemporary Cultural Studies*, Bloomington 1993, S. 54, und Susan Buck-Morss, *Hegel und Haiti*, Frankfurt am Main 2011, S. 206.
**7** Vgl. Nicholas Mirzoeff, *The Right to Look: A Counterhistory of Visuality*, Durham, NC 2011, und Édouard Glissant, *Poetics of Relation*, Ann Arbor 1997.

# Punk-Vergangenheit, Dildo-Zukunft

Marc Siegel

Vivienne Westwood hatte es schon richtig verstanden. Derek Jarmans Film *Jubilee* von 1978 zeigt tatsächlich „das England Elisabeths [als] ein Paradies“[1]. Ein sonnendurchfluteter Park mit verwilderten Büschen dient als Schauplatz aus dem 16. Jahrhundert, an dem Elisabeth I.,

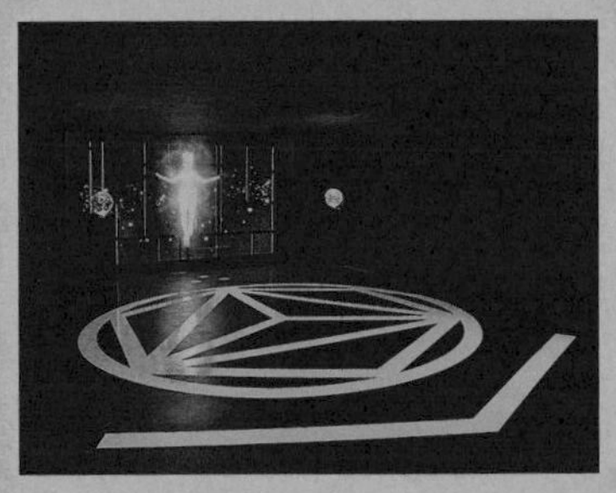

► S. 68

ihr okkultistischer Berater John Dee und eine Hofdame langatmige poetische Gespräche führen. Brian Enos Ambientgeräusche von Möwengeschrei und Meeresrauschen erfüllen die idyllische, ländliche Atmosphäre dieser Szene, die als Rahmenhandlung für Jarmans ansonsten wilden Film über eine postapokalyptische Version des zeitgenössischen London dient. Die „jungfräuliche Königin“ möchte in die Zukunft schauen, und so ruft Dee den Engel Ariel herbei, der sie in das Jahr 1977 begleitet, wo sie die Früchte des Elisabethanischen Zeitalters mit eigenen Augen sehen können. Was sie vorfinden, ist eine desolate Stadtlandschaft, die in Flammen steht: Am Straßenrand brennt ein Kinderwagen, ein korrupter Polizist grinst nur, als eine Gruppe von Frauen (die Punkband The Slits) ein verlassenes Auto zerstört, und eine gewalttätige, anarchische Girl-Gang, zu der auch ein inzestuöses Brüderpaar gehört, mordet und hinterlässt eine Spur der Verwüstung. Einige der Girls sind im Musikgeschäft, als Sängerinnen und Vertraute des mächtigen Medienmagnaten Borgia Ginz (Jack Birkett). Jarmans Konzentration auf ihre Taten

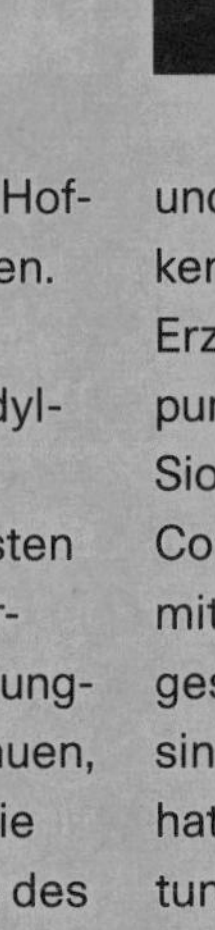

► S. 68

und ihr Interesse, die Karriere eines jungen Musikers namens Kid (Adam Ant) zu fördern, bietet Erzählanlässe, um Auftritte von Punk- und Postpunk-Bands aus dieser Zeit zu zeigen, darunter Siouxsie and the Banshees und Jayne (aka Wayne) County and the Electric Chairs, die, zusammen mit Adam Ants Band The Ants, während des gesamten Films ständig im Fernsehen zu sehen sind. Westwood mochte dieses Zeug. Zumindest hatte Jarman seine „Nase in die richtige Richtung gedreht“. Doch dann „kam die Wichserei“ und er verlor sich in den ausschweifenden Fantasien eines schwulen Jungen, der sich in elisabethanischen Kostümen verkleiden wollte.[2] Westwood fand, dass dieser „langweiligste und deshalb schrecklichste Film, den [sie] je gesehen hatte“, Camp-Begehren gegen Punk-Werte ausspielte, wobei Punk als Warnung davor, wo

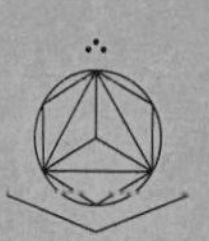

die Dinge schiefgingen, den Kürzeren zog. „Aber ich bin nicht so unsicher und auch nicht so voyeuristisch, daß es mich anturnt, wenn ich einem Jungen dabei zusehe, wie er durch den Kitzel seines masochistischen Zitterns abspritzt."[3]

Westwood druckte ihre (homophobe) Filmkritik in schwarzer, roter, rosa und blauer Farbe auf ein ärmelloses weißes Baumwoll-Top. Es war auf der Vorderseite mit dem Bild einer Briefmarke geschmückt, die die Königin Elisabeth II. mit abgetrenntem Kopf zeigte, und auf der Rückseite mit dem Union Jack dekoriert. Sie nannte es ein „Open T shirt to Derek Jarman from Vivienne Westwood" und verkaufte es bei Seditionaries, dem Laden, den sie mit ihrem Freund Malcolm McLaren, dem Manager der Sex Pistols, führte. Filmkritik als Punk-Mode. Das T-Shirt erklärte zu

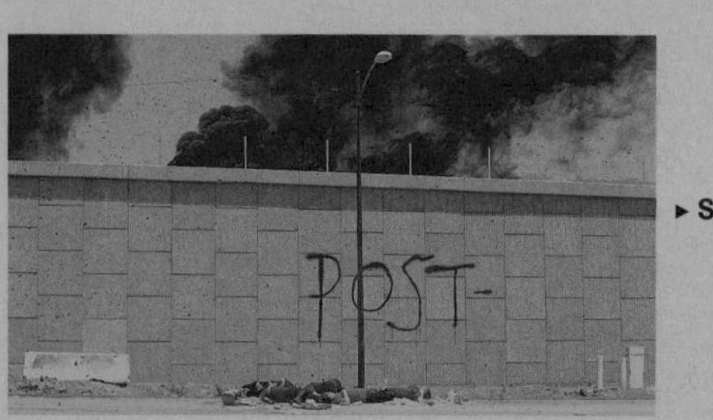


► S. 71

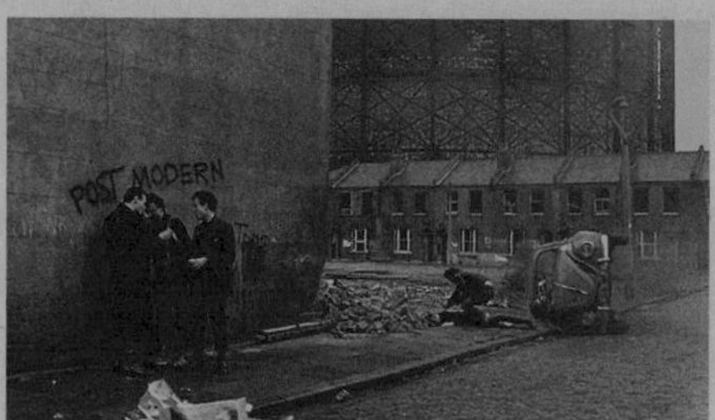


► S. 71

*Jubilee*: „Behaltet die Punks nicht so in Erinnerung."[4] Was indirekt auch bedeutete: „Kauft stattdessen lieber mich." Jarman war nicht beeindruckt, da er schon einige Jahre zuvor die Komplizenschaft von Punk mit dem gesellschaftlichen und ökonomischen System erkannte hatte, gegen das die Punk-Bewegung gleichzeitig rebellierte:

> **Das Musikgeschäft hat sich mit ihnen verschworen, um den nächsten Mythos der Arbeiterklasse zu erfinden, während die Schlangen vor dem Sozialamt länger werden, um Öl ins Feuer zu gießen. Die Hinterleute des Punk sind dieselben kleinbürgerlichen Kunststudenten, die noch vor ein paar Monaten David-Bowie- und Bryan-Ferry-Doppelgänger waren – die sich ein bisschen Kunstgeschichte angelesen und sich dadaistische Typografien und schlechte Manieren angeeignet haben und deren Geschäft jetzt darin besteht, eine gefälschte Street Credibility zu reproduzieren.[5]**

Was Westwood selbst betraf, sparte Jarman nicht mit unfreundlichen Worten. Als die Modedesignerin 1992 einen Order of the British Empire annahm, notierte er (misogyn) in sein Tagebuch: „Vivienne Westwood nimmt einen OBE an, die wankelmütige Schlampe. Es herrscht Saure-Gurken-Zeit: Unsere Punk-Freunde nehmen ihre kleinen Verräterorden an, sitzen in ihren stumpfsinnigen Salons und zerstören das Kreative."[6] Nur ein Jahr zuvor hatte Jarman eine Auszeichnung ganz anderer Art erhalten, als er vom internationalen schwulen Nonnenorden The Sisters of Perpetual Indulgence heiliggesprochen wurde. Punk-Werte versus schwule Camp-Theatralik, nehme ich an.

Jarmans Analyse des Punk und des Englands der 1970er Jahre in *Jubilee* hat zweifellos einen konservativen Zug – konservativ im Sinne der Warnung, mit der er die nihilistischen Energien der Gegenwart darstellt und ihnen ein früheres Zeitalter monarchischer Güte gegenüberstellt. Doch mit „seiner durchgängigen Atmosphäre der Desillusionierung und Warnung", bemerkt der herausragende Chronist der Punk-Bewegung, Jon Savage, „erfasste *Jubilee* die Stimmung im Punk-England besser, als man hätte erwarten können, nicht zuletzt, was seine Schauplätze anging; der Film bleibt einer der wenigen Orte, an denen man die

Londoner Landschaft des Jahres 1977 betrachten kann."[7] Jarman versammelte einige der interessantesten Figuren der damaligen Musik-, Kunst- und Performance-Szene und filmte ihre Eskapaden auf den leeren Straßen und in den verlassenen Lagerhäusern in der Nähe seines Lofts in der Butler's Wharf und an anderen nahegelegenen Schauplätzen in Bermondsey, Deptford und Rotherhithe. Dadurch rettete er einen Moment in Londons und Englands jüngster Vergangenheit, als der Thatcherismus – mit seiner Zerstörung des Wohlfahrtssystems, mit seiner Begünstigung von Privatisierungen und der Förderung einer weitreichenden Gentrifizierung – dazu ansetzte, die urbane Landschaft radikal zu transformieren; die Folge war die „Zerstörung des Kreativen" und die Zerstörung der Räume, die zur Entfaltung des Kreativen erforderlich sind. *Jubilee* ist „eine Zeitkapsel einer Phase der Londoner Geschichte, als sich Subkulturen dank der vielen bezahlbaren, heruntergekommenen Gegenden offen und natürlich entwickelten"[8], wie ein Kritiker Anfang 2018 scharfsinnig bemerkte. Die lose Handlung des Films betont die Kompliz*innenschaft der anti-sozialen Punk-Gang mit dem omnipotenten Besitzer aller Medien, Borgia Ginz. Im Gegensatz zu dieser pessimistischen Einschätzung der Möglichkeit eines radikalen Wandels durch eine kompliz*innenhafte Punk-Subkultur stehen die Energie und der Einfallsreichtum dieser subkulturellen Figuren, die durch die Straßen von London toben und Häuser besetzen. „Der surrealste Aspekt eines Films, in dem die Tudors eine Zeitreise in eine parallele Zukunft unternehmen, ist überraschenderweise die Möglichkeit, dass sich junge Leute ein Leben in der Innenstadt leisten können. Diese Erschwinglichkeit Londons ist die heutzutage wohl fantastischste Prämisse des Films."[9]

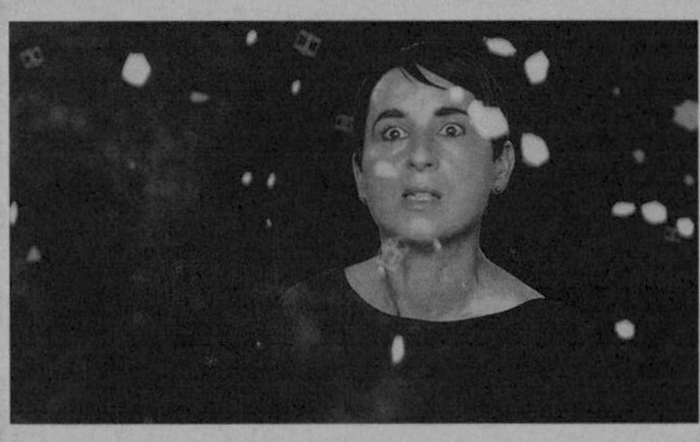

▸ S. 72

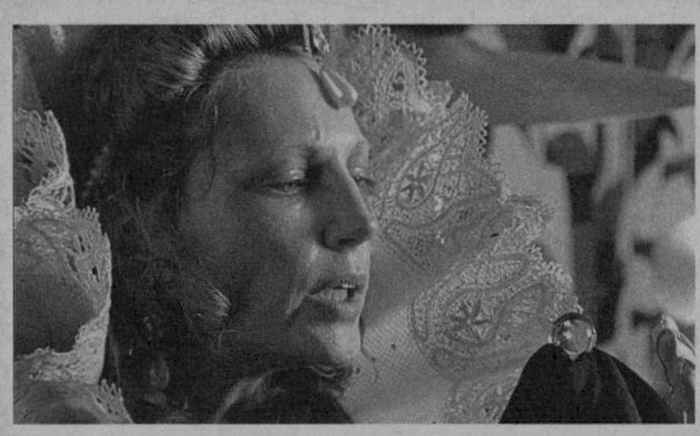

▸ S. 72

Was Westwood übersah oder einfach nicht anerkennen wollte, war die Hellsichtigkeit, mit der *Jubilee* – wenn auch noch so *campy* – die überwältigenden ökonomischen Veränderungen ankündigte, die die Stadt (und vieles mehr) umgestalten sollten, wobei die Widerständigkeit von Punk nun dem zwiespältig wirkenden politischen Aktivismus eines Konsumguts zugewiesen wurde. Man bedenke die prophetischen Worte, mit denen Ginz versichert, dass es unmöglich sei, seiner monopolistischen Kontrolle über das Leben der jüngeren Generation zu entgehen: Worte, die – trotz ihrer satirischen Übertreibung – im Zeitalter von Jeff Bezos, Elon Musk, Peter Thiel, Mark Zuckerberg und anderen gierigen Milliardär*innen der Tech- und Medienindustrie einen gespenstischen Nachhall finden:

> **Du willst meine Geschichte hören, Schätzchen. Es ist ganz einfach. Dies ist die Generation, die aufgewachsen ist und vergessen hat, ihr Leben zu leben. Sie waren so beschäftigt damit, meinen endlosen Film anzuschauen. Das ist Macht, Schätzchen. Macht. Ich erschaffe sie nicht. Ich besitze sie. Ich habe sie ausgesaugt, ausgesaugt und nochmal ausgesaugt. Die Medien wurden ihre einzige Wirklichkeit, und ich besaß ihre Welt aus flackernden Schatten – BBC, TUC, ITV, ABC, ATV, MGM, KGB, C of E. Was auch immer – ich habe**



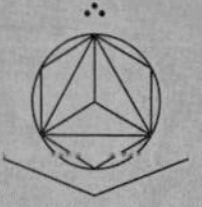

**alle gekauft und das Alphabet neu sortiert. Ohne mich existieren sie nicht.**

Wir sollten dieser Liste der Akronyme von Organisationen, die sich in Ginz' Vampirgriff befinden, auch die NSDAP hinzufügen. Am Ende des Films schwelgen einige der Girl-Gang in ihrem Reichtum und Erfolg. Sie besuchen Ginz auf seinem Anwesen, das er sich mit einem Adolf Hitler im Ruhestand teilt, der auf einem Sofa sitzt, seine alten Reden im Fernsehen ansieht und sich zum größten Maler des Jahrhunderts erklärt. „Am Ende unterschreiben alle – so oder so", sagt Ginz.

„Am Ende loggen sich alle ein – so oder so", könnte Zach Blas' Antwort um 2018 lauten. Sein mehrteiliges Projekt *Contra-Internet* (2015–2019)

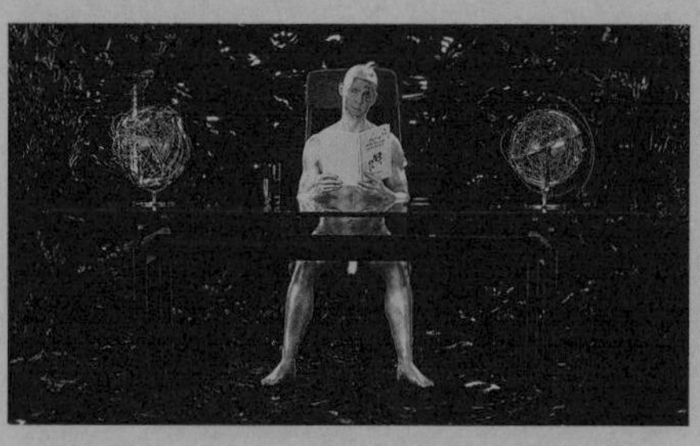

► S. 73

umfasst einen Essay, eine Reihe von Lecture-Performances sowie eine Text-, Objekt- und Videoinstallation, deren Kernstück ein 30-minütiges Video mit dem Titel *Jubilee 2033* ist.[10] Jarmans nihilistische Vision vom bevorstehenden Verhängnis des Thatcherismus und der damit verbundenen Zerstörung der Kreativität durch die Konzentration der Kontrolle über Medienkonzerne und Politik in den Händen einiger weniger (das heißt, in den Händen von Borgia Ginz) bietet nur wenig Möglichkeiten für Widerstand – außer jenem, der sich im energischen Auftreten des feministischen und queeren Punk ausdrückt. Blas hingegen bietet eine optimistischere, wenn auch bewusst utopische Vision des Widerstands angesichts eines noch allmächtigeren – weil unpersönlicheren – Gegners, nämlich des Internets.

In seinem Essay „Contra-Internet" von 2016 entwirft Blas den theoretischen Rahmen seines umfassenderen Projekts in sechs programmatischen Abschnitten: „Killing the Internet", „Disappearing the Internet", „Postcapitalist Politics", „Contrasexuality", „Paranodes" und „Antiweb"[11]. Um den Vorgang der „Tötung des Internets" genauer zu beschreiben, untersucht er spezifische historische Fälle politischer Unterdrückung, bei denen der Zugang zum Internet zeitweilig verhindert wurde oder bedroht war, etwa während der Safran-Revolution in Myanmar 2007, während der Revolution in Ägypten 2011, nach den Gezi-Park-Protesten in Istanbul 2014, als der türkische Premierminister Recep Tayyip Erdoğan den Zugang zu Twitter sperren ließ, und während des US-amerikanischen Präsidentschafts-

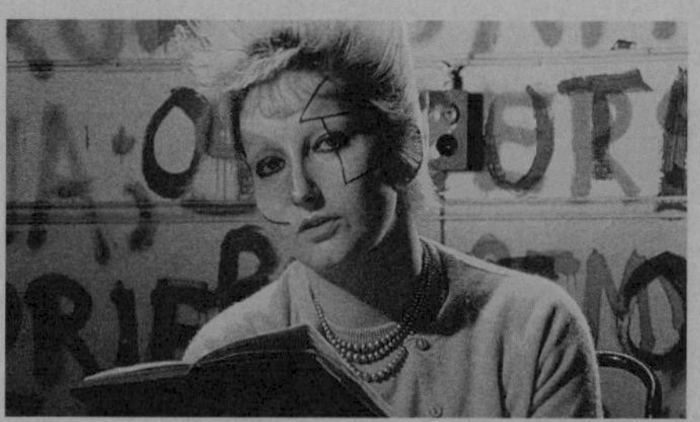

► S. 73

wahlkampfs 2016, als der republikanische Kandidat Donald Trump forderte, im Kampf gegen die Rekrutierungskampagnen des Islamischen Staats „dieses Internet zu schließen". Anschließend reflektiert Blas die Annahme, dass das Internet in naher Zukunft einfach in unseren Körpern, in den Dingen und in der Umwelt aufgehen werde. So jedenfalls lautete 2015 das Versprechen des damaligen CEO von Google, Eric Schmidt, der nahelegte, dass „das Internet verschwinden wird", indem es zum integralen Bestandteil unseres Alltag werden und sich in „der Materialität" der Welt von heute auflösen wird. Alles wird Teil eines Netzwerks sein – angeschlossen, online, rund um die Uhr und sieben Tage die Woche. Die Führungskräfte der Tech-Industrie stellen sich das Ende des Internets als Internet der

Dinge vor. Für autoritäre politische Anführer*innen besteht das Ende des Internets in der Vorstellung, den Stecker zu ziehen. Bürger*innen wurden ersetzt durch Internet-Nutzer*innen, die Blas als „ein biopolitisches Subjekt" charakterisiert, „das von Konzernen entwickelt wurde und von einer verwirrten, süchtig machenden Subjektivität besessen ist, die nach endlosen Feeds hungert, nach Clickbait, das immer einen weiteren Klick verlangt, und nach Content-Generatoren, die Browser-Tabs vervielfältigen, bis der Computer abstürzt"[12].

Das Science-Fiction-Szenario, das Blas aufbaut, ist eine ebenso fantastische Totalität wie das neu sortierte Alphabet in Jarmans Dystopie. (Man denke daran, dass Google ein Tochterunternehmen der multinationalen Dachgesellschaft Alphabet Inc. ist.) Wie stellt sich Blas Widerstand vor? Wo verortet er, wie er sagt, „die Möglichkeiten einer militanten Alternative oder Außenseite der Totalität, zu der das Internet geworden ist"[13]? Im Einklang mit Jarmans Vorläufer *Jubilee* stützt sich Blas bei dem Versuch, sich einen nicht-technophoben Ausweg aus dem Netz vorzustellen, auf feministische und queere Denker*innen. Dabei bezieht er eine feministische Kapitalismuskritik (J. K. Gibson-Graham) und ein queeres, transfeministisches Überdenken der Naturalisierung von Gender und sexuellen Normen (Paul B. Preciado) auf Theorien des Widerstands gegen die scheinbare Totalität der Netzwerkform (Ulises Ali Mejias).

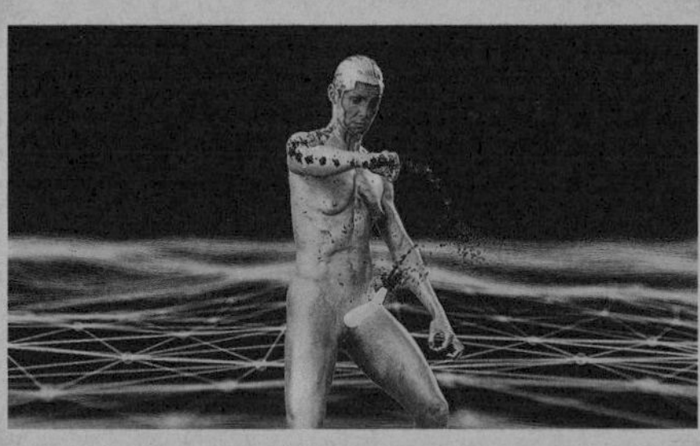

▸ S. 74

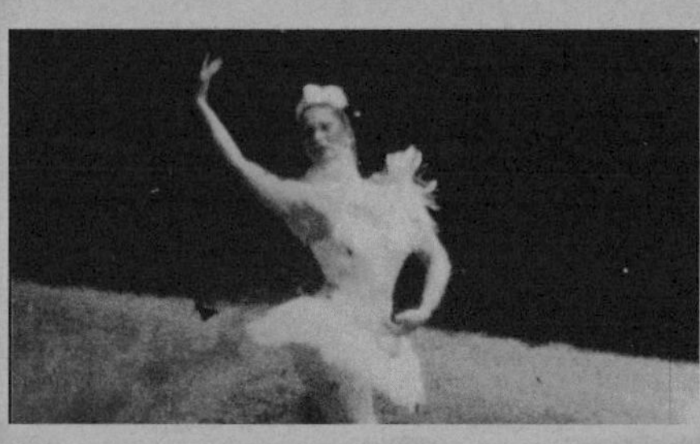

▸ S. 74

Unter Verweis auf Gibson-Graham, insbesondere auf deren Buch *The End of Capitalism (As We Knew It): A Feminist Critique of Political Economy* (1996), verortet Blas eine postkapitalistische Politik in den lokalen und kollektiven Nischen bestehender kapitalistischer Strukturen, in den alternativen Ökonomien und fantasievollen neuen Konzeptionen, die eine Vielfalt aktueller ökonomischer Praktiken und politischer Möglichkeiten erkennen lassen.[14] Preciados Kultbuch *Kontrasexuelles Manifest*, das zuerst in französischer Sprache als *Manifeste contra-sexuel* (2000) erschien, nimmt eine Punk-Haltung ein, um sich kulturell konstruierten Normen von Gender und Sexualität zu widersetzen.[15] Das Buch enthält sogar einen kontrasexuellen Mustervertrag, den jede*r unterzeichnen kann, um damit – unter anderem – auf die eigene „natürliche Position als Mann [...] oder als Frau [...] auf jedes (soziale, ökonomische, erbrechtliche) Privileg und auf jede (soziale, ökonomische, reproduktive) Verpflichtung, die sich im Rahmen des naturalisierten heterozentristischen Systems aus meiner sexuellen Position ableitet"[16], zu verzichten. Dieser performative Akt der Verweigerung wird zum ersten Schritt, um eine alternative Beziehung zum eigenen Körper, zu körperlichen Lüsten und sozialen Möglichkeiten herzustellen. An dieser Stelle kommt der Dildo ins Spiel – und zwar nicht nur als vergnügliches Spielzeug, das der Penetration und Stimulation dient. Mit Bezug auf Jacques Derrida betont Preciado die „supplementäre" Funktion des Dildos; dieser ist keine Nachbildung des Penis, sondern vielmehr dessen Vervollständigung und Ersatz: „Der Dildo war vor dem Penis. Er ist der Ursprung des Penis."[17] So schreibt Blas: „Der kontrasexuelle Dildo ist eine diagrammatische Form, die, wenn



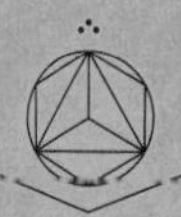

mit ihr experimentiert wird, die Möglichkeiten einer Sexualität jenseits von Heteronormativität und Phallozentrismus offenbart."[18] Preciado stellt seinerseits zahlreiche Praktiken in der Kunst der „Dildotektonik" vor, um die kontrasexuelle Umdeutung und eine neue, erfahrungsbasierte Auseinandersetzung mit dem eigenen Körper zu fördern: zum Beispiel, indem man mit einem roten Filzstift die Form eines Dildos auf den eigenen linken Unterarm zeichnet und ihn mit der rechten Hand zweieinhalb Minuten lang massiert.[19]

Der theoretische Rahmen, den Blas für das Kontra-Internet konstruiert hat, liest sich wie eine Kombination von Hyperlinks, da er historische und aktivistische Beispiele mit Bruchstücken von Ideen anderer Denker*innen um die Kontrollen durch den Staat und durch Unternehmen zu unterlaufen (wie 2014 durch die Demokratiebewegung in Hongkong). Solche praktischen Beispiele der Verweigerung ergänzt Blas durch Ulises Ali Mejias' konzeptuelles Überdenken von Netzwerken, insbesondere durch dessen theoretische Überlegungen zum Paranodalen (*paranode*) und zum paranodalen Raum als Ort des gesellschaftlichen und politischen Widerstands.[20] Im Rückgriff auf einen neurowissenschaftlichen Begriff versteht Mejias das Paranodale als den negativen Raum zwischen zwei Netzknoten und den Strömen eines Netzwerkdiagramms – ein Raum, der das Netzwerk trägt und stabilisiert, zugleich aber dessen Organisationsfunktion des Verknüpfens und Verbindens bedroht. Solche Bedrohungen treten

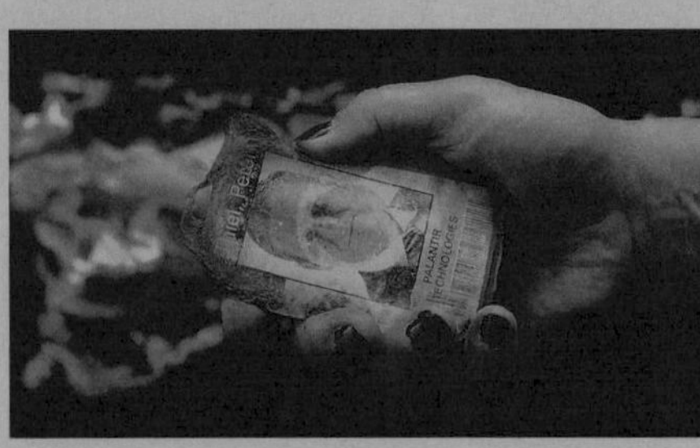

▸ S. 78

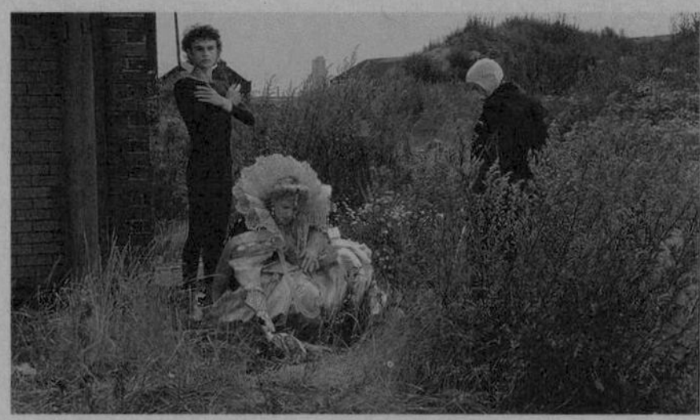

▸ S. 78

verbindet, um über neue Herangehensweisen an ein mittlerweile bekanntes Problem zu spekulieren: Wie verweigert man sich der zunehmend naturalisierten Beziehung des Körpers zum Internet? Erfordert ein kontrasexueller Körper ein Kontra-Internet? Wenn der Gebrauch des Dildos und die Praktiken der Dildotektonik uns in die Lage versetzen, körperliche und soziale Möglichkeiten zu überdenken und neu zuzuweisen, können Kontra-Internet-Praktiken dann dasselbe mit einem vermeintlich unentrinnbaren privatwirtschaftlichen Netz tun? Blas verweist auf „Anti-Internet"-Praktiken, die mögliche Alternativen jenseits der aktuell vorherrschenden und beherrschenden Netzwerkstruktur anzeigen könnten. Ein Vorbild hierfür ist die aktivistische Nutzung von drahtlosen lokalen Netzwerken aus mehreren WLAN-Funkzellen, in verschiedenen Formen auf, beispielsweise als individuelle Akte der Verweigerung im eigenen Netzwerk von Freund*innen und Kontakten, aber auch als Viren, Hacking, nicht zielführende Links, verrauschte Signale und Piratensender-Projekte. Auch wenn solche Vorgehensweisen ein hochgradig anpassungsfähiges System nur temporär und punktuell stören können, öffnen sie innerhalb des Netzwerks einen – paranodalen – Raum, durch den ein Außerhalb des Netzwerks vorstellbar wird. Tatsächlich erscheint der paranodale Raum vor allem als konzeptuelle Möglichkeit relevant, als Öffnung innerhalb eines kommerzialisierten, privatisierten Netzwerks, die zu einem potenziell gerechteren Raum außerhalb des Netzwerks führt. Blas definiert das Internet allerdings nicht nur als Architektur digitaler Technologien, sondern auch als „Machtstruktur, die mit dem gesellschaftlichen Raum deckungsgleich ist", sodass alle Risse innerhalb des Netzwerks, auch wenn sie rein konzeptuell bleiben, potenzielle Anfänge einer Politik des Kontra-Internets sind.[21]

Die Installation *Contra-Internet* wird in einem abgedunkelten Raum mit schwarz gestrichenen Wänden präsentiert – eher schwarze Magie als Black Box. Der Lichtschein der großformatigen Videoprojektion von *Jubilee 2033* an einer der Wände wird von einem neongrünen Vinylsiegel auf dem Boden reflektiert (*The Seal of the Absolute*, 2017). Links und rechts der Projektionsfläche liegen zwei große, lichtdurchlässige Kugeln aus geätztem Glas – *Palantir: Disappeared Internet* und *Palantir: Killed Internet* (beide 2017) – auf Sockeln; sie erinnern an Globen, aber auch an die *palantíri* oder Sehsteine aus J. R. R. Tolkiens *The Lord of the Rings*, die der Kommunikation und Beobachtung in der Vergangenheit und der Zukunft dienen. Die Bezeichnung *Palantir* verweist zudem auf Peter Thiels Datenanalyse-Unternehmen Palantir, dessen Logo eine Ähnlichkeit mit Blas' Siegel aufweist. Tatsächlich besteht ein Aspekt des gesamten Kontra-Internet-Projekts darin, die Appropriierung von Mystizismus und Magie durch verschiedene Datenanalyse- und Softwareentwicklungsfirmen im Silicon Valley herauszuarbeiten und dieser Aneignung einen queeren Mystizismus entgegenzusetzen. Dieser reicht historisch zurück zu Jarmans Interesse an John Dee und am Okkultismus, aber auch zu dem Filmemacher Kenneth Anger und dessen Faszination für Alchemie und Aleister Crowley, einem Okkultisten des 20. Jahrhunderts. An einer anderen Stelle der Installation liegt ein gebundenes Buch mit weißem Einband, *The End of the Internet (As We Knew It)* (2017), das dem Autor Nootropix zugeschrieben ist, aufgeschlagen auf einem Podest neben einem Brocken aus polykristallinem Silizium (*shew stone (polycrystalline silicon)*, 2017), der sich direkt auf Dees hellseherische Praxis bezieht. An der Wand, die an die Videoprojektion angrenzt, zeigen drei Flachbildschirme kurze Desktop Documentaries, die im Geist von Preciados kontrasexuellen Praktiken ausführlich Kontra-Internet-Inversionspraktiken beschreiben. Jedes dieser ungefähr vierminütigen Videos zeigt die Anwendung einer anderen Software, um eine Inversionspraxis erfolgreich umzusetzen. So öffnet beispielsweise in *Inversion Practice #1: Constituting an Outside (Utopian Plagiarism)* (2015) ein Cursor die Programme Preview und TextEdit und verwendet einfache „Copy"- und „Paste"-Befehle, um das plagiierte Buch *The End of the Internet (As We Knew It)* ausschließlich aus Kapiteln von Preciados Manifest, einer Sammlung von Fredric Jamesons Schriften zur Postmoderne, *Our Word Is Our Weapon* von Subcomandante Marcos, dem Sprecher der Zapatistischen Armee der Nationalen Befreiung, und J. K. Gibson-Grahams Buch zu produzieren.[22] So wird durch die Funktion „Suchen und Ersetzen" aus dem Wort „*contrasexualidad*" „contrainternet", während die Wörter „capitalism", „capitalist" und „capital" durch „internet" ersetzt werden. Jedes Video beginnt mit der Auswahl eines passenden Songs aus einer „Kontra-Internet"-iTunes-Playlist. *Utopian Plagiarism* wird mit Le Tigres Song „Get

▸ S. 80

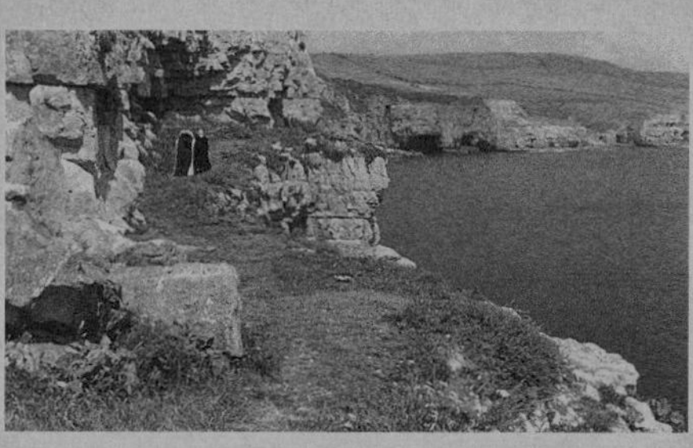

▸ S. 80

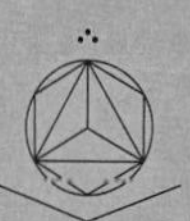

Off the Internet" (2001) unterlegt. Die beiden anderen Videos, *Inversion Practice #2: Social Media Exodus (Call and Response)* (2015) und *Inversion Practice #3: Modeling Paranodal Space* (2016), zeigen die Anwendung von Computerprogrammen, um Identitäten in den Sozialen Medien zu löschen und ein dreidimensionales Modell eines dezentralen Netzwerk-Diagramms zu liefern, um die darin verfangenen paranodalen Räume zu befreien. Bei den abschließenden Bestandteilen der Installation, *Totality Study #1: Internet, a definition* und *Totality Study #2: Internet, a .gif* (beide 2017), handelt es sich um einen Wandtext beziehungsweise eine Videoprojektion.

Das Video *Jubilee 2033* verbindet Punk-Werte mit Camp-Theatralik und geht über eine Desktop-Dokumentation hinaus, um eine spektakuläre Vision des Widerstands gegen die überwältigende Kontrolle des Internets zu bieten. So wie Jarmans *Jubilee*, hat *Jubilee 2033* eine Rahmenhandlung, die den historischen Kontext für die Darstellung einer dystopischen Zukunft liefert. Die Rahmenhandlung ist in diesem Fall nicht im London der 1970er Jahre angelegt, sondern in der futuristischen Silicon Zone in Kalifornien, an einem Schauplatz von Mord und Zerstörung, wo die weitläufigen Hauptverwaltungen von Adobe, Google und Facebook in Flammen stehen. Anders als Jarman sieht Blas nicht nostalgisch auf eine Art paradiesischer Vergangenheit vor dem Sündenfall zurück. An die Stelle der wohlmeinenden Elisabeth I. tritt die russisch-amerikanische Schriftstellerin und Philosophin, das bevorzugte „Mean Girl" der amerikanischen Rechten, Ayn Rand (die deutsche Schauspielerin Susanne Sachsse) im Jahr 1955. In ihrem New Yorker Apartment erklärt sie zwei Mitglieder*innen des sogenannten „Kollektivs" – dem Ökonomen Alan Greenspan und seiner Frau, der kanadischen Malerin Joan Mitchell – ihr Ideal des Objektivismus und die Notwendigkeit des Laissez-faire-Kapitalismus.[23] Als förderliches Mittel, um Rands Ideal des Egoismus zu praktizieren, empfiehlt Greenspan einen LSD-Trip. Dabei erscheint auf wunderbare Weise ein KI-Roboter aus dem Jahr 2017 namens Azuma, der die Zeitreise der drei in das Jahr 2033 ermöglicht, wo sie herausfinden wollen, ob Rands Ideen tatsächlich die Welt verändert haben. Zu ihrer Schmach muss Rand nicht nur die Zerstörung der Tech-Industrie erleben – ein Wirtschaftszweig, der auf ihren Idealen des einzelnen Genies, des Kapitalismus und der Selbstsucht beruhte. Sie muss auch den Held*innentaten einer queer-feministischen Gang zusehen; diese wird organisiert von derl Kunstprofessoron (del Dichteron Raquel Gutiérrez) und angeführt von derl kontrasexuellon KI-Propheton Nootropix, derl von Kopf bis Fuß mit laptopgrauer Farbe bemalt ist (del Künstleron Cassils).[24] Diese Bande trommelt Tech-Angestellte für Nootropix' Geschichtsstunde über die vergangenen Tage des Internets zusammen. Nachdem Nootropix die Anti-Internet-Praktiken von Mesh-Network-Aktivist*innen in Detroit, Teheran und Hongkong erklärt hat, beginnt Nootropix einen ausgedehnten Tanz, der offenkundig die Netzwerkstruktur zerstört. Rand und den anderen Zeitreisenden bleibt nur,

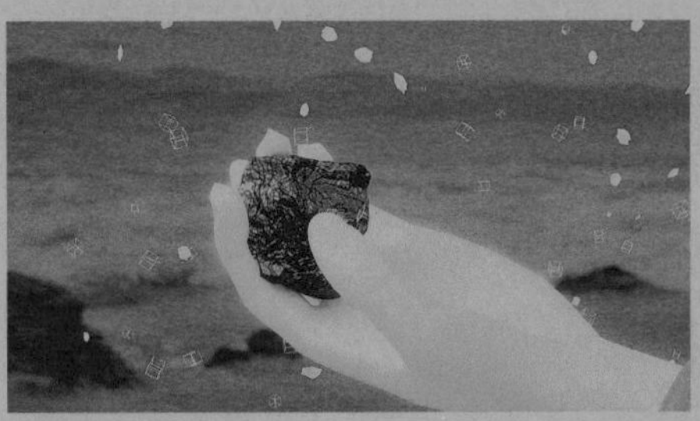

▸ S. 84

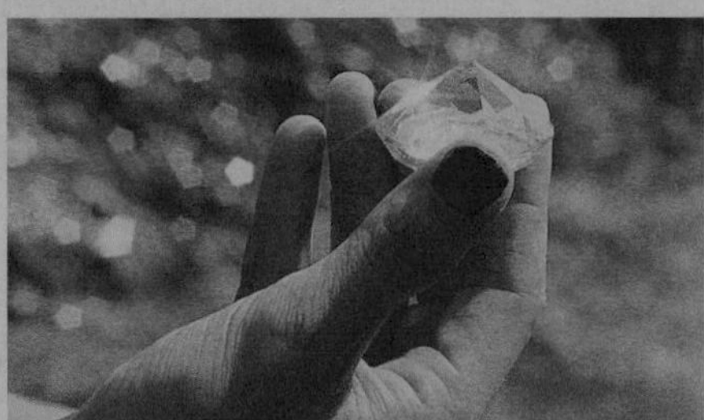

▸ S. 84

am Meer zu spazieren und poetisch von der neuen Notwendigkeit einzelner Genies und der Software-Aufklärung zu schwärmen.

Die Szene mit Nootropix' Geschichtsstunde und Tanz stellt eine Parallele zu einem frühen Moment in Jarmans Film dar. Doch sie unterscheidet sich erheblich von Jarmans Vorbild, sodass das radikal utopische Versprechen von Blas' Kontra-Internet und das Spannungsverhältnis zwischen Technologie und öffentlichem Raum im digitalen Zeitalter erkennbar wird. In Jarmans Film spricht die Historikerin der Girl-Gang, Amyl Nitrate (Jordan), über ihre Teenagerzeit vor dem Zusammenbruch von Recht und Ordnung, der zwar zum damaligen Chaos führte, aber auch – was wichtiger ist – ihre Anfänge als Tänzerin markierte. Erst mit der Zerstörung der früheren Gesellschaftsordnung konnte sie beginnen, sich künstlerisch auszudrücken. Doch die Möglichkeiten, durch ihre Kreativität – ihren Tanz – etwas zu verändern, werden umgehend in eine unwiederbringliche Vergangenheit verlegt. Dies deutet sich darin an, dass Jarman für diese fast dreiminütige, eigenständige Szene Super-8-Film verwendet – sein einziger Rückgriff auf das Amateurformat in dem ansonsten auf 35 mm gedrehten Film. Amyl Nitrate tanzt zu Léon Minkus' Musik für den Pas de deux im Ballett *Giselle* an einem Feuer auf einem verlassenen Grundstück zwischen einem nackten Mann und weiteren Zuschauer*innen – eine hinreißende Sequenz in warmen Farben, einer dynamischen Umgebung und hypnotischer Zeitlupe. Doch es ist ein Tanz aus der Vergangenheit für die Vergangenheit, eine Erinnerung an eine stille Eleganz, für die es in der Dystopie der erzählten Gegenwart des Films keinen Raum gibt.

Die fragile Flüchtigkeit von Jarmans Super-8-Sequenz steht in einem scharfen Kontrast zum glatten, sterilen HD-Format, das Blas für Nootropix' widerständigen Tanz verwendet. Abgesehen von einer Szene mit Ayn Rand und dem Kollektiv am Strand wurde *Jubilee 2033* vollständig in einem Studio mit Greenscreen-Effekten gedreht oder computergeneriert. Der öffentliche Raum ist der Raum des Internets, und der einzige Ausweg führt durch das Internet hindurch. Nootropix tanzt in einem digitalen Raum aus violetten Internetströmen zu den melodramatischen Klängen von „Con te partirò", vorgetragen von dem italienischen Tenor Andrea Bocelli – das Lieblingsstück des Großunternehmers Elon Musk, weil es ihn daran erinnert, „dass die Welt ein schöner Ort ist"[25]. Für Nootropix ist die Welt computergeneriert, und die Schönheit liegt in den Räumen außerhalb des Netzes oder sie umgibt die Netzknoten. Anders als Amyl Nitrates Tanz ist Nootropix' Tanz weniger eine Art Selbstausdruck als vielmehr eine Form von Selbstdisziplin oder kallisthenischer Übung, eine schiere Behauptung der Präsenz eines kontrasexuellen, muskulösen Körpers und seiner verwirrenden Kraft –

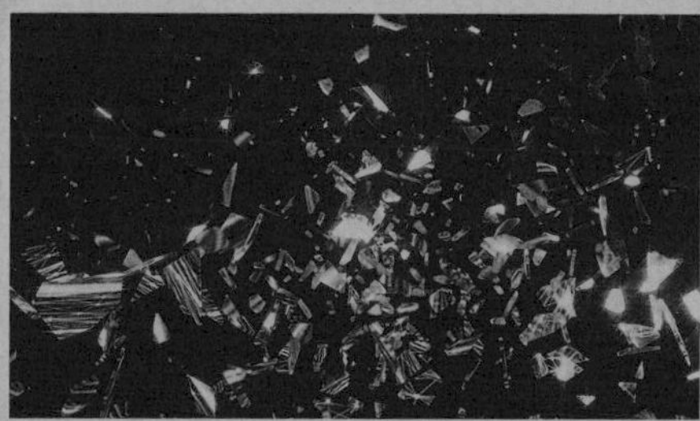
▸ S. 83

verwirrend wegen des leuchtend blauen, aufgerichteten Dildos, der während der gesamten Tanzsequenz unaufhörlich eine violette Flüssigkeit ausstößt. Dieser endlos sprudelnde Dildo spielt auch auf Rands Roman *The Fountainhead* (1943, dt. *Der ewige Quell*, 1946) an, indem er die phallische Macht der Romanfigur, des genialen Architekten Howard Roark, ins Lächerliche zieht. In ästhetischer Hinsicht verweisen die orgastischen Spritzer, die sich diagonal durch das Bild ziehen, auf ähnliche Bilder aus Kenneth Angers Film *Eaux d'Artifice* (1953) und sind gewissermaßen deren buchstäbliche Umsetzung.

Diese aufsässige dildotektonische Übung wird zum Ruin des Netzes führen. Nachdem Nootropix ungefähr vier Minuten getanzt hat, werden die Netzwerkdiagramme wellenförmig. Die Verbindungen zwischen den Knoten lockern



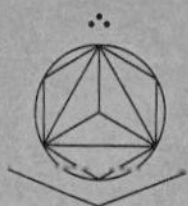

sich, und schließlich zerbricht die Form und explodiert und das Netzwerk löst sich in paranodale Bruchstücke auf. „Das Paranodale ist nicht passiv", erklärt Mejias. „Seine Existenz prägt die Netzknoten und die Beziehungen zwischen ihnen (ähnlich wie in der Stadtplanung, wo ein ‚schlechtes' Viertel die Stadtplaner ‚zwingt', eine Schnellstraße über oder durch diese Gegend zu führen, damit die Autos sie umfahren können)."[26] Nootropix' kontrasexueller Dildo-Tanz führt uns in die sogenannten schlechten Viertel, die das Netzwerkdiagramm ausgegrenzt hat. Der T-Shirt-Slogan lautet: „The future lies not in silicon, but silicone" – die Zukunft liegt im Silikon, nicht im Silizium.

**1** Vivienne Westwood, „Offenes T-Shirt für Derek Jarman von Vivienne Westwood", in: Derek Jarman, *Auf eigene Gefahr. Vermächtnis eines Heiligen*, Wien 1996, S. 101.
**2** Vgl. Westwood, in: Jarman, op. cit., S. 102.
**3** Ibid., S. 101f.
**4** Ibid., S. 102. Vgl. Mason Leaver-Yap, „Punking Out: Derek Jarman and Vivienne Westwood on *Jubilee*", in: *Crosscuts*, 7. Oktober 2014, https://walkerart.org/magazine/punking-out-derek-jarman-and-vivienne-westwood-on-jubilee.
**5** Derek Jarman, *Dancing Ledge*, London 1984, S. 164. An anderer Stelle lobt Jarman Westwoods Geste: „Vivienne Westwood [...] produzierte eines ihrer tollen T-Shirts, um den Film zu verreißen und zu sagen, wie langweilig er war" (S. 172). Er wurde auch in diesem T-Shirt fotografiert und scherzte offenbar, es sei eine Ehre, „dass ihm ein eigenes Westwood-T-Shirt gewidmet wurde." Vgl. Tony Peake, *Derek Jarman*, London 1999, S. 251. Alle Zitate aus dem Englischen übersetzt von Barbara Hess.
**6** Derek Jarman, *Smiling in Slow Motion*, Minneapolis 2011, S. 151; übersetzt aus dem Englischen von Barbara Hess.
**7** Jon Savage, *England's Dreaming: The "Sex Pistols" and Punk Rock*, London 2011, S. 377; übersetzt aus dem Englischen von Barbara Hess.
**8** Adam Scovell, „Grieve the Capital: Derek Jarman's Jubilee Turns 40", in: *The Quietus*, 05.02.2018, https://thequietus.com/articles/23978-derek-jarman-jubilee-review-anniversary-bfi; übersetzt aus dem Englischen von Barbara Hess.
**9** Ibid.
**10** *Jubilee 2033* zirkuliert, unabhängig von der Installation, auch im Kontext des Kinos. Die Premiere des Films fand in der Sektion „Forum Expanded" der Berlinale 2018 statt.
**11** Zach Blas, „Contra-Internet", in: *e-flux journal*, Nr. 74, Juni 2016, https://www.e-flux.com/journal/74/59816/contra-internet.
**12** Ibid.; übersetzt aus dem Englischen von Barbara Hess.
**13** Ibid.
**14** J. K. Gibson-Graham, *The End of Capitalism (As We Knew It): A Feminist Critique of Political Economy*, Minneapolis 2006.
**15** Paul B. Preciado, *Countersexual Manifesto*, New York 2018; dt. *Kontrasexuelles Manifest*, Berlin 2003. Blas begann sein *Contra-Internet*-Projekt, bevor es eine offizielle englische Übersetzung für Preciados Begriff „*contra-sexuel*" gab. Daher behielt er für seine eigene Arbeit das ursprüngliche Präfix „contra-" bei.
**16** Preciado, op. cit. (2003), S. 20.
**17** Ibid., S. 12.
**18** Blas, op. cit.; übersetzt aus dem Englischen von Barbara Hess.
**19** Preciado, op. cit. (2003), S. 37–49. „Dildotektonik ist eine Gegen-Wissenschaft, sie untersucht Erscheinung, Entwicklung und Nutzung des Dildos." (S. 37).
**20** Ulises Ali Mejias, *Off the Network: Disrupting the Digital World*, Minneapolis 2013, bes. S. 153–161. Für eine produktive Analyse von Mejias' theoretischer Auseinandersetzung mit dem Paranodalen im Kontext dessen, was die Film- und Medienwissenschaftlerin Pepita Hesselberth als „Paradox der Dis/konnektivität" bezeichnet, vgl. dies., „Discourses on Disconnectivity and the Right to Disconnect", in: *New Media & Society*, Bd. 20, 2017, S. 1994–2010, bes. S. 2002–2010.
**21** Siehe die Definition, die als Wandtext in fluoreszierendem Vinyl ein Bestandteil von Blas' Installation *Contra-Internet* ist. Dieser Wandtext ist eine eigenständige Arbeit, *Totality Study #1: Internet, a definition* (2017), deren Inhalt Blas produzierte, indem er Gibson-Grahams Definition von „Kapitalismus" plagiierte. Seine Praxis des „utopischen Plagiierens" stammt wiederum aus Critical Art Ensemble, *The Electronic Disturbance*, New York 1994, S. 83–101.
**22** Das reale Buch plagiiert außerdem Material aus Jarmans *Jubilee*, Mejias' *Off the Network* sowie ein Diagramm von Paul Baran über verteilte Kommunikationsnetzwerke.
**23** Vgl. Lisa Duggan, *Mean Girl: Ayn Rand and the Culture of Greed*, Berkeley 2019. „The Collective" war die informelle Bezeichnung für Rands Anhänger*innenschaft. Rands enge Vertraute Joan Mitchell ist nicht zu verwechseln mit der bekannteren amerikanischen Malerin Joan Mitchell.
**24** Die Verwendung geschlechtsneutraler Artikelwörter und Begriffe bezieht sich auf das Del-on-Sel-System und die Vorschläge auf folgenden Webseiten: https://nibi.space/geschlechtsneutrale_artikelwörter_und_adjektiv-endungen und https://geschlechtsneutral.net.
**25** Vgl. Raul Campos, „Guest DJ Project: Elon Musk", in: KCRW, 21.12.2011, https://www.kcrw.com/music/shows/guest-dj-project/elon-musk.
**26** Mejias, op. cit., S. 153; übersetzt aus dem Englischen von Barbara Hess.

# Den menschlichen Umriss ficken: Anmerkungen zu *SANCTUM* von Zach Blas

Mahan Moalemi

In seiner Installation *SANCTUM* (2018) verwandelte Zach Blas den Ausstellungsraum von Abierto × Obras bei Matadero Madrid in eine immersive Umgebung aus Bewegtbild, Skulpturen und einer Klanglandschaft, die ihre Inspiration zu gleichen Teilen aus Tanzlokalen, Straflagern und Anbetungsorten zu ziehen schien. Ein begleitender Text von Blas trug den Titel „Generic Mannequin Gets Fucked". In Form einer Erzählung in der ersten Person fungiert dieser Text als Geleit durch die Ausstellung. Titel und Inhalt spielen auf die zentrale Figur der Ausstellung an.[1] Der Name Generic Mannequin – man denke an eine digitale Version der Incredible Crash Dummies, reduziert auf ein fahles Grau – ist einem offiziellen Geschäftsbegriff für eine humanoide Modellfigur entlehnt, die dazu dient, Sicherheitsrisiken (zum Beispiel an Grenzen) einzuschätzen und zu bezeichnen. Blas kompliziert die vorausgesetzten Konturen einer solchen Schablone für das Menschsein (und für das Erkanntwerden als Mensch). Er setzt sich damit auseinander, in welchem Maß die Erfassung von Sehnsüchten und die Sehnsucht nach Erfasstwerden im Zeitalter digitaler Sicherheitsregimes und hochentwickelter Überwachung eng verbunden sind. Das Menschendiagramm (Generic Mannequin) wird in *SANCTUM* in alle möglichen Formen der Folter verstrickt. In seinem Text geht Blas ausführlich darauf ein. Er versieht die emotionsgeladene Atmosphäre der Installation mit einer Erzählung und führt das Publikum durch die verschiedenen Teile.

In der eng verwandten Lecture-Performance *Body Horror*, mit der er im Jahr der Installation von *SANCTUM* auftrat, erzählt Blas davon, wie er auf dem Frankfurter Flughafen einmal in einem „ProVision"-Körperscanner stand. Es war seine erste Begegnung mit der Figur des Generic Mannequins:

> **Meine Hände sind über den Kopf gehoben, das gibt mir ein Gefühl von Kapitulation. Ich fühle mich verletzlich. Mir gehen Bilder von Polizei durch den Kopf, die einen Verdächtigen umstellt. Diese Person hat,**



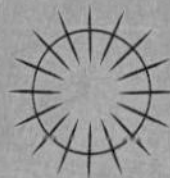

**wie ich, die Arme gehoben und ruft: „Ich ergebe mich!" oder „Nicht schießen!" oder „Ich bin unschuldig!". Gleich darauf tauchen flitzende vertikale Balken auf, und mein Körper wird gescannt. Ich denke darüber nach, wie die Technik meinen Körper als Bedrohung sehen könnte – wie können Millimeterradiowellen, Software und Sicherheitspersonal bei einer solchen Entscheidung zusammenwirken, während ich in dieser Maschine stehe?**

Blas fährt fort:

**Als ich den Scanner passiert hatte, konnte ich endlich das Touchscreen-Interface sehen. Es ist überraschend einfach angelegt: zwei Knöpfe, einer hellrosa und der andere hellblau. Auf beiden ist das Bild einer einzelnen Musterfigur zu sehen. Der Schirm zeigt den einfachen Umriss eines Körpers. Die Firma L3 Technologies spricht von einem „generic mannequin". Wenn etwas Ungewöhnliches auffällt, wird ein Körperteil dieses Menschendiagramms mit einem Warnzeichen versehen.**[2]

Zwischen dem Diagramm und den Personen, die in einen „ProVision 2"-Körperscanner treten müssen, entsteht eine verstörende Affinität. Man sprach von einer „bilderlosen Lösung"[3], als man 2017 mit der Vermarktung des Geräts begann. Es beruht auf Millimeterwellen-Technologie, im Gegensatz zu Rückstreuung-Röntgenstrahlung. Das Diagramm, das auf dem Interface der Maschine als eine Vorlage erscheint, soll dem Sicherheitspersonal Körper und deren mutmaßliche Risiken vermitteln, ohne sie im strengeren Sinn zu repräsentieren. Man befindet sich am jüngsten Ende einer Geschichte standardisierter Herrschaftspolitik, in deren Verlauf zentrale Prinzipien von Disziplinargesellschaften entwickelt wurden: „Funktionalisierung", zum Beispiel, oder „Austauschbarkeit"[4]. Es ist wie ein anthropomorphisierter Kreis, durch den man hindurch muss, es könnte sich aber genauso gut um eine Jagdfalle handeln. Im Hintergrund einer solchen unbestimmten Kontingenz, die an eine nahezu ontologische Verfasstheit gemahnt, lässt Blas sein eigenes Menschenmodell antreten. Es wird nicht so sehr in *SANCTUM* hinein erschaffen, als darin entdeckt. Es stellt ein Mittel dar, um den fabulierten und dramatischen Wesen näher zu kommen, die in den Kammern der digitalen Überwachung wohnen. Blas' Diagramm geht von der universalisierenden Tendenz seines Vorbilds aus dem Sicherheitsbusiness aus. Mit seiner Verkörperung des militärisch-industriellen Komplexes hält er es gegen genau die Bedingungen, auf denen seine Existenz beruht. Generic Mannequin steht für den Körper, der von jener technolibidinalen Ästhetik spürbar gemacht wird, auf die *SANCTUM* hinaus will. Dieser Text geht von dem „Generic Mannequin Gets Fucked" aus und kehrt immer wieder dorthin zurück. Er untersucht dabei, auf welche Weisen *SANCTUM* fleischliche und korporeale Allegorien digitaler Entkörperung präsentiert, und versucht zugleich, sich von den zahlreichen Tropen eines eingefahrenen und unnachgiebigen (humanistischen) Anthropomorphismus nicht unkritisch überrumpeln zu lassen.

„Ein menschlicher Umriss, aber nicht eigentlich eine menschliche Form": Das Menschenmodell / Generic Mannequin ist eher so etwas wie eine Seele, „die ihren Körper verlässt". Es kommt zu der Einsicht, mit einer ganz eigenen Stimmung von Einwilligung und Willfährigkeit, dass es genau sein „Zweck ist, inspiziert, betrachtet und gespeichert zu werden". Es ist vollständig exponiert. Seine Konturen sind nur dazu da, von innen nach außen gekehrt zu werden. Generic Mannequin fühlt sich zugleich verwirrt und entschlossen dazu, entleert zu werden – als könnte es vollständig aufgelöst werden, sich verflüssigen oder gasförmig werden. Aber ein Generic Mannequin beschwert sich nicht. Es wird eins mit dem geilen, überschießenden Strom libidinaler Liquidität, der aus dem Prinzip der Bloßstellung herrührt. Es hält die Gesamtheit einer

Umgebung und ihres Felds von Beziehungen in den Rahmenbedingungen einer eingehenden Überschau ihrer (ent)verkörperten Landschaft in der Schwebe. Anthropomorphe Tendenzen erreichen einen Höhepunkt, aber auch einen toten Punkt vor den technolibidinalen Antinomien, die sich aus der Banalität ergeben, heutzutage mit einem eigenen Datendouble zu verkehren, diesem einen Körper zu geben, einen begehrenswerten Körper: datafiziertes Begehren (wieder)verkörpert. Eine intensive, aber auch beunruhigende Vertrautheit mit diesem antinomischen Körper aus datafiziertem Affekt spiegelt sich in dem Ausmaß, in dem die Materialität des Schirms in dem Raum von *SANCTUM* eingehend behandelt wird. Die materielle Dimension der Screens verbindet sich mit der digitalen Materialität des

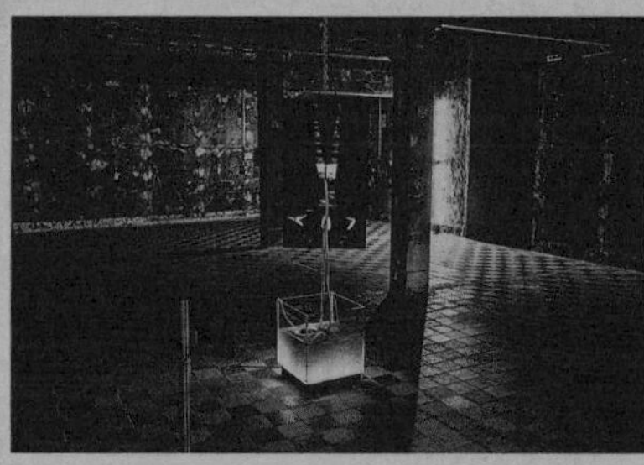

▸ S. 128–29

Generic Mannequins in all seiner Plastizität und durch eine Menge invertierter Allegorien von Verkörperung, die sich an es hängen und es zu zerreißen versuchen, in immer neuen, endlosen Formgebungen.

In einer Hinsicht ist Generic Mannequin ein Paradefall von darstellendem Reduktionismus, in anderer Hinsicht aber auch eine Allegorie für die Reduzibilität, die jeder Repräsentation als Voraussetzung zugrunde liegt. Reduzibilität verweist nicht nur auf ein Versprechen einer stromlinienförmigen Effizienz bei der Verwirklichung einer bestimmten Funktion, sondern auf einen bestimmten Sinn einer aufgemotzten Inklusivität, die davon kommt, dass etwas generisch wird. Generic Mannequin identifiziert sich nicht durch die Besonderheit seiner Organe, sondern als Organ in und aus sich selbst. Es gehört zu einem größeren Körper, dessen Intentionen es allegorisch dient – unterwürfig und selbstlos. Seine „Hände und Füße sind Klumpen, und weitgehend nutzlos". Keine Finger oder Zehen, keine Genitalien und kein Anus; nur ein Bauchnabel. Ähnlich seinem kommerziellen Gegenstück, bleibt das Generic Mannequin markiert durch eine Erinnerung an einen besonders anthropogenen Ursprung – im Gegensatz zu, beispielsweise, einem plastogenen –, der jedoch niemals der seine war und dieser niemals sein wird.

Der Medientheoretiker Alexander R. Galloway formuliert es so: „‚Reduktion' ist ein unausweichliches Trauma, das aus der Unmöglichkeit kommt, das Globale im Hier und Jetzt zu denken [...]. Die Wahrheit des sozialen Lebens als Ganzem ist zunehmend inkompatibel mit seinem eigenen Ausdruck. Kultur entsteht aus dieser Inkompatibilität."[5] Unter den Umständen globaler Konnektivität denken Menschen zunehmend (und gezwungenermaßen) an ihre gleichzeitige Positionalität auf lokalen, regionalen und globalen Ebenen. Besonders intensiv dient die Reduzibilität der menschlichen Form der Aufrechterhaltung von Vorstellungen wie „öffentlicher Sicherheit" als einem Gemeingut oder einem universalen Wert. Wenn man Universalität allerdings als eine Funktion und nicht als eine bestimmte Tatsache des Daseins betrachtet, wird sie immer mit Austauschbarkeit verbunden. Und das schließt dann eben die Anerkennung der Inkompatibilität aus, von der Galloway spricht. Früher waren die Linien, mit denen Positionalität vermessen wurde, beständig und leicht zu ziehen. Heute müssen sie ständig umgezeichnet werden, und das ergibt eine ebenso grundlegende Verlagerung in der menschlichen Kondition, wie die Ideologie der Sicherheit eine Folge von Beziehungen und Strukturen ist, die das Menschliche und seine Werte, Ängste und Vermutungen bedingen, und seine Vorstellungen davon, was seine vorausgesetzte Autonomie bedrohen könnte. Wenn man dann also mit den menschlichen Konturen des Generic Mannequins spielt (oder sie verarscht), setzt



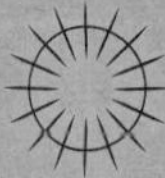

man damit einen Ton für eine Kritik von Technologien, die dafür erfunden wurden, einer Kultur im Weg zu stehen, die nur aus den perzeptiven und intellektuellen Lücken erwachsen kann, die sich zwischen den verschiedenen Dimensionen und Registern des Menschseins (und des Als-Mensch-gesehen-Werdens) öffnet.

In dem Maß, in dem die Erzählung von *SANCTUM* im Text von Blas vorankommt, lernt das Generic Mannequin langsam seine Umgebung begreifen. Auch der Grad seiner Verstrickung wird ihm bewusst. Im Ausstellungsraum herrscht eine eigentümliche Atmosphäre. Licht und Dunkel wirken religiös aufgeladen. Ein riesiger industrieller Komplex ist als Hintergrund auszunehmen. Matadero Madrid kann mit all den tollen Charakteristiken der Industrie-

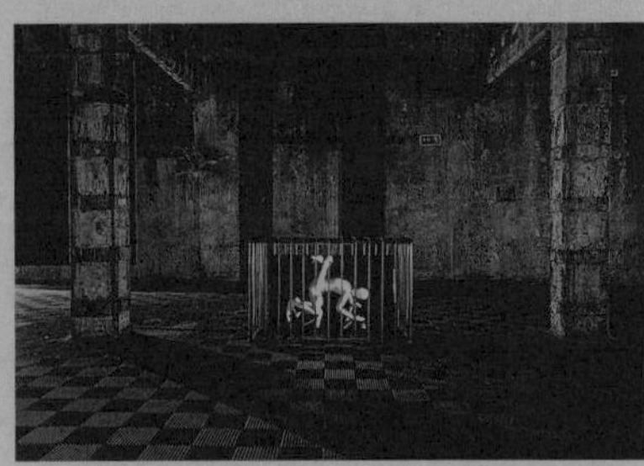

▸ S. 133

architektur der 1920er Jahre aufwarten. Ein früheres Schlachthaus in öffentlichem Besitz wurde zu einer Kulturstätte umgebaut und bietet heute mehreren Institutionen Raum. Die disziplinären Urstandards Funktionalität und Effizienz sieht man dem Matadero bis heute an. Das Generic Mannequin sieht sich um, zugleich überwältigt und betäubt. Was soll es von all dem halten? „Eine spartanische Beleuchtung verweist auf die höchste Decke, glänzende Säulen und kunstvolle Reliefs auf Anbetung, Sex und Massaker. Unterschiedliche Maschinerien stehen in einem weißen, gottgleichen Glanz, und die Ecken dieser Strukturen treffen auf die Schwärze, die den größten Teil des Raums einnimmt."

Auf dem Boden verläuft eine zentrale Achse vom Eingang hinein in den Raum. Einige „gut gewählte Balken roten Lichts ergeben einen sakramentalen Altar; in seinem Inneren befinden sich Weihegaben. Stahl, gitterähnliche Abstraktionen und geometrische Metallteile von Gesichtsformen. Kleine Eisenkäfige." So stellt sich die Szenerie für das Generic Mannequin und dann auch für andere Besucher*innen von *SANCTUM* dar. Es dauert nicht lang, und eine spektrale Präsenz zeigt sich oberhalb des Altars: „Ein schwarzer Würfel schwebt in zentraler Position, und eine schwarze Maske gleitet wie schwerelos über seine Oberflächen hinweg, wie eine Flüssigkeit, die zwischen zwei Glasscheiben hervortritt". Der zentrale Turm enthält die errechneten Werte einer Gesichtsgeometrie,

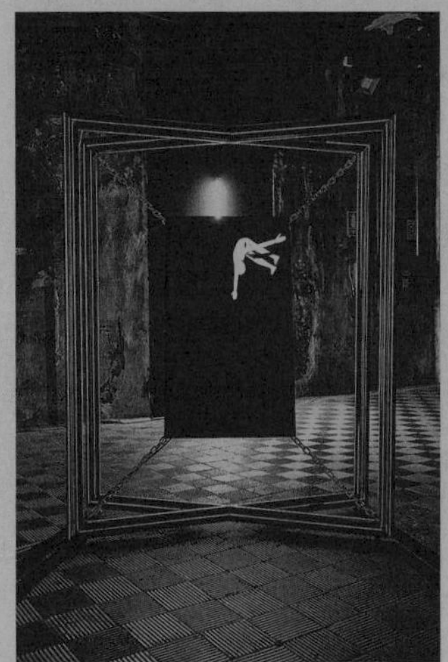

▸ S. 134

das erhöhte, viereckige Display-Setting und die janusgesichtige Präsenz, die von einem Schirm auf den anderen übergeht. Sie erscheint wie eine Sonne oder eine religiöse Vision, ein Zeichen der Allwissenheit. Besucher*innen, die in der Ausstellung vor dieser Erscheinung stehen, sehen das, was auch das Generic Mannequin erblickt. Die schwarze Maske wirkt wie ein Hybrid aus dem Hockey-Gesichtsschutz, den Jason Voorhees in *Friday the 13th* trug, eine Horrorikone, die in den 1980ern in den amerikanischen Vororten Schrecken verbreitete, und den schusssicheren, das ganze Gesicht abdeckenden Masken, die in den 2010er Jahren an die Special Armed Forces in Taiwan ausgegeben wurden. Der Turm wiederum – ein Stahlgerüst – erinnert mit seiner Form an die Entwürfe für ein Panopticon, die der Philosoph Jeremy Bentham im 18. Jahrhundert vorgelegt hat; Zach Blas führt diese Ideen näher an die Mechanismen der digitalen Überwachung heran, für die prototypisch der Body Scanner „ProVision 2" steht. In beiden Fällen beruht die Anlage auf einem Prinzip unbestimmter Kontingenz, denn die Insassen (die Gefangenen) im Inneren eines panoptischen Gefängnisses wissen nie, ob sie von dem zentralen Turm aus, um den herum ihre Zellen angelegt sind, gerade beobachtet werden. In den menschlichen Umrissen des Generic Mannequins nimmt dieses Ausgeliefertsein Gestalt an, trotz der massiven Verschiebung und Flüchtigkeit, auf die es Blas ankommt, und zugleich gerade ihretwegen.

Der Philosoph Gilles Deleuze hat eine ähnliche Verlagerung in der Gestalt der Autorität ausgemacht. Er bezog sich dabei auf Überlegungen von Michel Foucault über die Disziplinargesellschaften und beschrieb, wie diese sich in „Kontrollgesellschaften" verwandelten, in denen „Modulationen" und eine sich selbst verformende „Gußform" die unterschiedlichen „Formen, Gußformen" disziplinärer „Einschließung"[6] ablösen. Die Begriffe von Deleuze haben sich als sehr hilfreich erwiesen. Und wenn systematische Untersuchung über die Bedingungen von Disziplin und Strafe hinausgeht, bleibt die Zone der Kriminalisierung doch wie immer von Zufälligkeiten bestimmt, allerdings viel unbestimmter, denn sie geht über die Beiläufigkeiten alltäglicher Sichtbarkeit hinaus bis in die unübersichtlichen Ausmaße und abgedrehten Optiken sozialer Erkennbarkeit.

Der Stahlturm verweist also auf eine Diagrammatik der Überwachung, die „kontinuierliche Kontrolle"[7], die als Teil eines größeren Apparates zur Unterwerfung und Subjektifizierung erkennbar gemacht wird. Im Inneren dies Kontrollapparats ist die Plastizität von Identität in modulierenden und differentialen Identifikationsregistern inkorporiert. Sie ermöglichen einen Prozess, in dem „Individuen" „Dividuen", und „Massen" „Stichproben, Daten, Märkte oder Banken"[8] werden. Galloway hat darauf hingewiesen, dass Deleuze diese „direkten Behauptungen über Computer, das Informationszeitalter und die Technologien, die ihn umgaben", vor allem im und um das Jahr 1990 gemacht hat.[9]

In der veränderten Matrix der Macht, die eine Kontrollgesellschaft ausmacht, wirkt sich die Verteilung sozialer Register entsprechend auf die übernommenen technischen Formbedingungen repräsentationaler Kategorien aus. Sie legt ihre Grenzen offen und schiebt zugleich die Grenzen der Repräsentation hinaus (politisch wie ästhetisch), indem sie die sozialen Bedingungen und Technologien der Repräsentation auf ein immer noch effizienteres System grenzenloser Überwachung hin verändert. „Hinter der schwarzen Maske sind keine Augen und kein Gesicht, und doch sieht sie mich prüfend an", bekundet das Generic Mannequin, und macht klar, dass die alles erfassende Sicht des Stahlturms in nichtoptischen Begriffen operiert. Der Blick auf das Labyrinth repräsentationaler Bedingungen, die das Generic Mannequin und alle, für die es der Kanal ist, umfloren, erfordert nicht dieselbe Sicht, die ein Bild von den Betrachtenden verlangt. Die alles sehende Präsenz sieht *de facto* keine Bilder – und entspricht damit dem „bildlosen" Körperscanner. Dessen bildlose Vision war eine mehr oder weniger korpo-humanistische Geste, die auf den Aufschrei reagieren sollte, der von den vielfachen Bedenken wegen Verletzung der Privatsphäre ausgelöst wurde, die im Zusammenhang mit Körperscannern seit den späten 2000ern aufgetreten sind.[10] Was Blas macht, lässt sich demnach als eine Kritik des Korpo-Humanismus diskutieren. Nicht nur in dem Sinn, in dem historischer Humanismus in die komplizierte und verworrene Situation der Korporealität heutzutage hineinspielt, sondern auch im Hinblick auf die vielfachen Weisen, in denen sich Unternehmen heute die humanistischen Rahmenbedingungen von Individualität und Persönlichkeit erschließen und aneignen.[11]



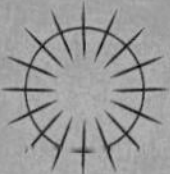

In den Worten von Blas, der durch das Mannequin spricht, hört sich das so an: sich in einer bildlosen Lösung aufzulösen, ist, als würde man „Geschlecht und Eigenschaften abstreifen, um allgemein zu werden, und nicht mehr darzustellen". Das Werk von Blas macht deutlich, dass dieses Operieren im Gleichschritt mit den Regeln der Augenwahrnehmung oder in halber Loslösung davon, dieses Hinausschieben und Heranziehen der Grenzbereiche visueller Wahrnehmung, eine nicht- oder postrepräsentationale Sehweise ergibt, die für avancierte Überwachungstechnologie wesentlich ist. Sie entkoppelt Beobachtung vom Sehvermögen insgesamt. Die schwarze Maske, computergeneriert, an den Schirm gebunden, im Dämmerlicht schwankend, aber positioniert im Sitz des überwachenden Blicks auf der Spitze des Turms, diese opake schwarze Maske ohne ein Gesicht dahinter und mit Augenlöchern, hinter denen ein endloses Dunkel liegt, lässt etwas über den ontologischen Status von Repräsentation und Bildererzeugung im Zeitalter der Datenverarbeitung erkennen. „Bilder", schreibt der Dichter und Medientheoretiker Tung-Hui Hu, „funktionieren nicht notwendigerweise so, dass sie das Unsichtbare sichtbar oder eine verborgene Wahrheit greifbar machen, wie es eine Epistemologie der Freilegung nahelegt. Sie vermitteln eher zwischen einer abstrakten Totalität und den Umrissen der menschlichen Erfahrung."[12]

Auch wenn die Maske kein Gesicht verdeckt, das, einmal freigelegt, angeschaut und identifiziert werden könnte, wird sie doch vor dem Generic Mannequin enthüllt. Auf einen Schlag verwandelt die Maske sich in ein Gittergeflecht, „ein biometrisches Raster, ein vervollständigtes Gesicht, das aus den Weihegaben der Anbeter modelliert wird". Es zeigt dieselben Arten biometrischer Diagrammatiken, auf denen fast alle Gesichtserkennungssysteme beruhen. Blas hat sie immer wieder als Ausgangspunkt für seine künstlerischen und theoretischen Untersuchungen genommen. Technologien zur Gesichtserkennung basieren auf einem postrepräsentationalen Sehen, insofern die Abstraktionen, die sie schaffen, für menschliche Sinne nicht erfassbar sein müssen; es sind nur die Urteile, zu denen die Maschinen durch diese Abstraktionen kommen, die kommunizierbar sein und das menschliche Ende eines Inspektionszyklus erreichen müssen. In Projekten wie *Face Cages* (2014–2016) und *Facial Weaponization Suite* (2012–2014) hat Blas eine Kritik des häufig höchst folgenreichen Reduktionismus biometrischer Technologien entwickelt. Er skizzierte Entwürfe, wie ein ästhetischer Widerstand dagegen aussehen und sich anfühlen könnte. *Facial Weaponization Suite* ist ein Versuch, Gesichtsdaten umfassend zu sammeln und zu manipulieren, um daraus amorphe Masken zu generieren, die sich nicht erfassen und erkennen ließen. *Face Cages* überträgt die glatten Operationen der digitalen Bereiche, mit ihrer offenkundigen Zurückweisung jeden physischen Kontakts, in die materielle und körperliche Erfahrung anhaltenden Schmerzes. Das Gittergeflecht, zu dem die schwarze Maske in *SANCTUM* wird, zeigt eine ähnliche Bauweise: das biometrische Modell eines Gesichts – dessen schwereloses Datenmaterial und deren abstrakte Vermessungen häufig in nulldimensionalen Knoten und kaum fassbar dünnen Kanten ausgegeben werden – bekommt Volumen und wird in glattpoliertem Stahl Gestalt.

Die Transformation der Maske in ein Maschengeflecht wird jedoch rasch von einer Veränderung der Perspektive begleitet. Die (virtuelle) Kamera zoomt heran und macht sich daran, die Topologie des Maschengesichts zu erfassen. Sie bewegt sich dabei entlang der vollen und dunkel glänzenden Kanten. Das Gitternetz füllt nun den ganzen Bildschirm, es ist kein zurückgehaltenes Gesicht mehr, sondern erstreckt sich über den ganzen, erhöhten Display-Würfel. „Es ist gigantisch, groß wie eine Stadt." Das Gesicht wird wie eine Landschaft vermessen und durchquert: frontal, dann abgeflacht durch eine Vogelperspektive von oben, dann in horizontalen Bewegungen über die Falten der Topologie, die zu sehr nahen Begegnungen werden. Eine derart veränderte Perspektive spielt auf eine Geschichte ästhetischer, technologischer und soziopolitischer Transformationen an, die – in Medienbegriffen – von Luftaufnahmen bis zu Google Street View führen. Inzwischen ist eine tiefe, gebieterische Stimme zu vernehmen, die in einer Gossenmischung aus Latein und Englisch verkündet: *Et reticulum adoremus* (wir verehren das Netz) – *Get in position – Ride my face – Ave ProVision* ... Die Stimme kommt aus der lauten, pochenden Industrial-Techno-Musik, die den Raum erfüllt. Man erlebt die Atmosphäre eines dunklen Clubs mit gewagten Vibes.[13] Das Generic Mannequin heftet sich dann an die Bewegung der Kamera. Es passt sich deren Rhythmus und Perspektive an. „Die geometrischen Linien sind eine Fahrbahn, sie sind wie gemacht für einen großen Sprung ... ein Rollercoaster." Das Generic Mannequin wird auf eine Spritztour geschickt, und die Betrachter*innen von *SANCTUM* können auch mitkommen.

Die Fahrt wird im Ausstellungsraum dokumentiert. Die Kapitel erstrecken sich über eine Reihe von Installationen, die aus groben Strukturen bestehen, und – natürlich – digitalen Schirmen, auf denen das Generic Mannequin erscheint und offensichtlich die Befehle befolgt, die es empfängt. „Ich folge straff meinen Befehlen, und lasse mich mit Wonne an die Grenze meiner Form ziehen", sagt es, und zeigt sich falsch orientiert. Ein Streckgestell drückt von hinten und zwingt das Generic Mannequin in den Wirbel seiner Bewegungen. „Stolpernd, im freien Fall, endloses Hinsinken." An einer anderen Stelle hängt das Generic Mannequin mit dem Kopf nach unten an einer Kette, die in der Decke verankert ist. Der Schirm, von dem die Figur gestützt wird, ist in schwarzes Klebeband gehüllt, eine Form von Bondage, die das Generic Mannequin beinahe wie eine Mumie wirken lässt. Nur Mund und Geschlecht liegen frei. An beiden baumelt ein Metallschlauch. Das Schlauchwerk führt zu einem Glaswürfel, einem großen Tank, in dem sich alles sammelt: Metallteile, Gleitcremes, Wasser, und vielleicht einige Körperflüssigkeiten – man könnte an das Maschinen-Phylum aus *Tausend Plateaus* denken, das „entweder die natürliche oder die künstliche Materialität" ist, „oder beides zugleich, die sich bewegende, dahinströmende und sich variierende Materie als Trägerin von Singularitäten und Ausdrucksmerkmalen. [...] Dem Materie-Strom kann man nur *folgen*."[14] Ein magnetisches Rührwerk hält die Lösung in ständiger Bewegung, als würde es die Flüssigkeit für uns stimulieren und zur Verwendung vorbereiten.

In einer anderen Ecke werfen die Stäbe eines eisernen Käfigs lange Schatten auf den Boden. Im Inneren befindet sich das Generic Mannequin, auf allen Vieren. Merkwürdige Zuckungen gehen durch seinen Körper, als wäre

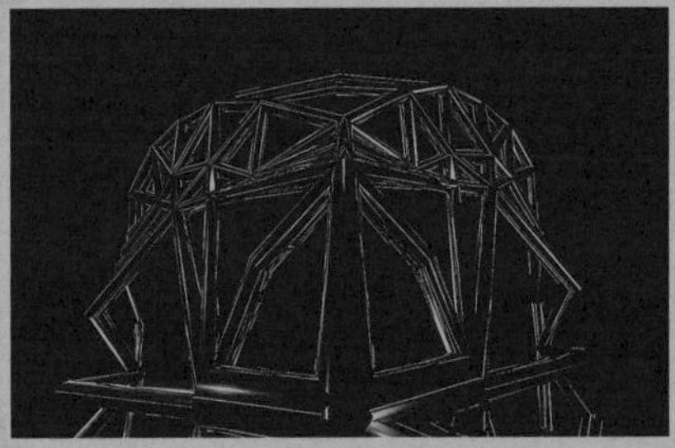

▸ S. 138–39

in seinem Inneren etwas, das Schläge austeilt, ein unwiderstehliches Begehren, das sich Bahn zu brechen versucht. Heftige Gesten erreichen schließlich die Außenhaut: ein Raster wird sichtbar und erstreckt sich über die Form des Körpers, der dem Generic Mannequin einerseits aufgezwungen wurde, der aber andererseits auch der einzige Körper ist, den es hat, der einzige Träger seiner sinnlichen Register – oder was auch immer man als „sinnlich" bezeichnen könnte bei einer umrissenen Gestalt, die dem menschlichen Körper zwar eine Menge verdankt, ihn aber auch nur wie eine Leerformel in sich aufnimmt, wie das beim Generic Mannequin der Fall ist. „Ich bin die Unwiderstehlichkeit eines Ausgeliefertseins an einen gewalttätigen, hemmungslosen Gott. [...] Der biometrische Gott weiß, wie er meine ursprünglichsten Begierden



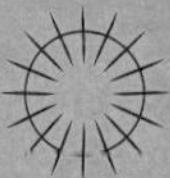

aktivieren kann.“ Generic Mannequin streift seine datafizierte, biometrische Haut ab, während das Raster zu einer Peitsche wird, die seine Umrisse traktiert. Ein neuer Strom zwanghaften Begehrens durchfährt es. Korpo-humanistische Wesenheiten schürfen in Begierden, sie messen sie und profitieren von ihnen, indem sie die ersehnte Anerkennung nicht nur produzieren, sondern letztendlich auch monopolisieren. Anerkennung bedeutet: gesehen werden. Mehr noch: entblößt werden.

Die Reise findet ihr Ende an einem Tisch, an den Generic Mannequin so gefesselt ist, als wäre er für Prügel oder eine Auspeitschung vorgesehen. Die Piercings, die es festhalten, erinnern an BDSM-Requisiten, aber auch an die erfundenen gynäkologischen Instrumente in

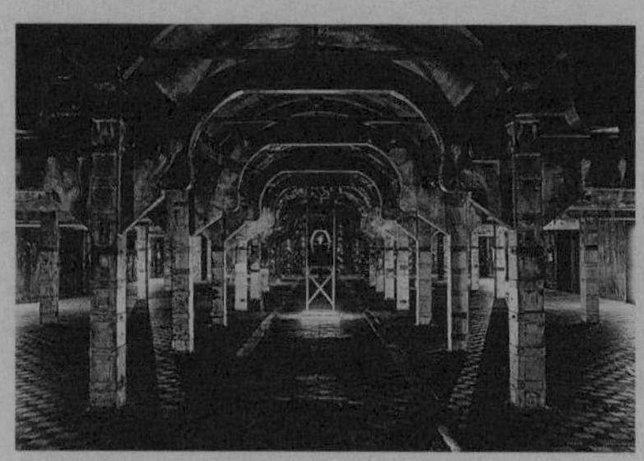

▸ S. 140

David Cronenbergs *Dead Ringers* (1988). Diese Gegenstände bestehen aus Stücken des zuckenden Rasters, das an die Oberfläche der Umrisse des Generic Mannequins drängt. Sie werden als „Gaben an einen biometrischen Gott“ ausgewiesen und ähneln den Objekten im Altar unter den Füßen des janusgesichtigen Stahlturms. Das Generic Mannequin findet sich in diesem Sinn beständig in Herstellung unter den „Anhänger*innen und Frommen einer vertrauten, und doch unbekannten Religion“. Diese Gemeinschaft entsteht aus der Akkumulation der Ängste und Begierden dieser Anbetenden. Sie wird erleichtert von einem fabrizierten und unausdrücklichen Glauben an den Gott der Entblößung. Sie werden auf ein Raster projiziert, mit dessen Hilfe diese Ängste und Begierden in Objekte der Lust und der Folter verwandelt werden. Mit ihrer Hilfe wird dieses Glaubenssystem reproduziert und immer wieder neu eingesetzt. *SANCTUM* steht somit für eine Umwelt, in der die Prozesse des Wollen-Schaffens – Mechanismen, durch die der Grund aller Wünsche und Instinkte ausbeutbar und produktiv gemacht wird – in die Informatiken der (post-)repräsentationalen Herrschaft übergehen.[15]

Das Ergebnis ist ein Amalgam aus Schmerz und Lust, das in den heutigen Entblößungsgesellschaften, in denen „wir Datendoubles uns in einem wahnhaften Taumel der Enthüllung aufgeben“[16], als das affektive Substrat von Leben (und Tod) dient. Der politische Theoretiker Bernard Harcourt sieht einen historischen Verlauf von der Souveränität zu Disziplinarität und Kontrolle, der nun in der „offenlegenden Macht“ kulminiert. Sie übernimmt Vieles von früheren Formen der Macht, verstärkt sie aber durch ein höheres Maß and Teilhabe und Komplizität vonseiten derer, die dieser Macht tatsächlich als Subjekte unterworfen sind. Das Web 2.0 ist partizipativ und interaktiv. Es führt zu einem Prinzip der „digitalen Transparenz“, das es ermöglicht, über die sozio-politischen und intimen Unterteilungen im Leben eines Individuums hinwegzugehen, und zwar problemloser als jemals zuvor in der Geschichte westlicher Gesellschaften. „Durch die Prozesse der digitalen Enthüllung, Überwachung und Adressierung, die wir so bereitwillig akzeptieren und ignorieren, werden wir erst so richtig wirklich“[17], schreibt Harcourt.

Als User*in einer der heute dominierenden Plattformen in der vernetzten Landschaft der digitalen Medien handelt man bis zu einem gewissen Grad auf eigene Verantwortung, man kann sogar frei darüber bestimmen, wie sehr man sich dort exponiert. Aber letztendlich sind es auch die User*innen, die für diese Freiheit mit ihrer Aufmerksamkeit und Zerstreuung bezahlen, mit ihren Leidenschaften und Ängsten. Sie haben *de facto* viel weniger Handlungsspielraum, als sie meinen, fühlen sich dadurch aber gar nicht amputiert. Die Mechanismen der Kontrolle sind individuell geworden, schreibt Harcourt. Die Individuen, die die Ruinen des liberalen Humanismus (virtuell oder tatsächlich) leben, stehen nicht mehr so stark unter dem Druck, ihre Wahrheit einzubekennen oder korrekte Informationen zu geben. Und zwar deswegen, weil Wahrheit und Täuschung nicht mehr dieselbe Bedeutung haben wie früher. Denn „wir übergeben (die Information) ganz freiwillig und willentlich, mit viel Liebe, Sehnsucht und Leidenschaft – und manchmal auch unschlüssig oder zaudernd." Harcourt fährt fort: „Wir zeigen uns wissentlich, wir stellen uns aus, viele von uns in voller Absicht, mit all unserer Liebe, Lust, Leidenschaft, mit unseren politischen Überzeugungen, andere voller Furcht und mit sich im Zwiespalt, sogar gegen unsere eigentlichen Absichten – und doch geben wir uns wissentlich preis."[18]

Diese Lage lässt sich insofern als post-repräsentational betrachten, als digitale Personen nicht die Wahrheit über sich selbst erfassen oder repräsentieren sollen. Sie fungieren nur als Mittel, durch die das Selbst – und jegliche Wahrheit, die es enthalten könnte – ständig neu erfunden wird. Das Hauptziel der enthüllenden Macht ist die Vorstellung des Individuums von sich selbst: es meint, über sich selbst zu verfügen, also kann auch nur das Individuum dieser Macht Geltung verschaffen. *SANCTUM* sieht deswegen aus wie „ein freier Raum, in dem die ganze Überwachungstechnologie, die man früher als Zwangsinstrument sah, nun direkt in das Gewebe unserer Lust und unserer Phantasie verwoben ist. Eine neue Form enthüllender Macht errichtet inmitten unserer hedonistischen Genüsse eine strafende Transparenz. Sie führt eine Macht ein, die uns in unseren täglichen Vergnügungen sanktioniert. Genießen und Bestrafen lassen sich nicht mehr trennen. Sie operieren gemeinsam und durchdringen einander. Sie sind unauflöslich verbunden."[19]

Das deutet auf einen seltsamen Umstand hin: Freiheit muss unbedingt an die Stelle einer Einschließung treten, sie ist keine Frage eines Entweder-oder, sondern kann mit ihr einhergehen – auch wenn das natürlich verwirrend sein mag. Verwirrung ist vielleicht nicht einfach eine Konsequenz aus dem Leben, sondern eines der Grundprinzipien des Lebens (und des Todes) in einem Reich willentlichen Informationsüberflusses: die Verwirrung angesichts der heutigen Banalität technolibidinaler Antinomien.

Die Konvergenz hat zwei Seiten. Institutionen, die mit Einschließung und Strafvollzug befasst sind, greifen heute auf die technologischen Möglichkeiten des digitalen Zeitalters zurück, sie können aus der Distanz überwachen oder Bewegungen nachvollziehen. Auf der anderen Seiten wird das Surfen im sogenannten freien Internet zunehmend durch das Sammeln digitaler Fingerabdrücke bestimmt. Sie schaffen Wert, der sich abschöpfen lässt, ohne dass jemand dafür entlohnt würde. Harcourt greift dann auf Max Webers Urmetapher des „stahlharten Gehäuses" zurück: archaische Techniken der sozialen Kontrolle und brutale Sanktionierung. Bei Harcourt wird daraus das „stählerne Gitter": Diese neue Verfasstheit – eines „Gittergeflechts" oder einer „Schwimmhauthülle" – „ist auf eine unheimliche Weise mit älteren Bestrafungsregimes verbunden. [...] Ein stahlhartes Gehäuse gibt es nicht nur im Zentrum des digitalen Zeitalters. [...] Es ist beinahe so, als wäre unser stahlhartes Gehäuse heute von innen nach außen gestülpt worden und deckte uns alle zu."[20]

Die Idee einer post-repräsentationalen visuellen Kultur passt auch zu den Untersuchungen, die der Medienphilosoph Vilém Flusser in den 1980er Jahren vorgenommen hat. Er wollte herausfinden, wie Repräsentation beziehungsweise Darstellung durch Datenverarbeitung neu bestimmt wird. Er unterschied dabei zwischen – wie er sie nannte – „traditionellen" und „technischen Bildern". Den Kern dieser Unterscheidung macht für Flusser „die unterschiedliche ‚ontologische Stellung' der traditionellen und der technischen Bilder" aus, insofern „die traditionellen Bilder das Resultat eines völlig andersgearteten Schritts zurück aus dem Konkreten sind"[21]. Eine



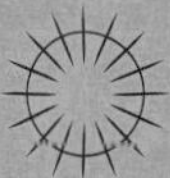

solche ontologische Unterscheidung rührt für Flusser nicht aus den technischen Apparaten her, die datenverarbeitende Operationen identifizieren (auch wenn diese sie in erster Linie ausführen) – die selben Operationsformen, die so zentral für eine Deleuzianische Sicht auf Politik in vernetzten Machtbeziehungen sind. Traditionelle Bilder sind insofern „Beobachtungen von Objekten“, sie entstehen durch „Abbildung“. Technische Bilder sind „Verarbeitung von Konzepten“ und entstehen „durch eine eigentümliche Einbildungskraft, nachdem das Vertrauen zu Regeln verloren gegangen ist“[22]. Was nun die allegorischen Spezifika von *SANCTUM* anbelangt, könnte man sagen, dass die visuellen Koordinaten, durch die das Generic Mannequin erfasst wird, starke Bezüge zu den Problematiken aufweisen, die für Flusser durch technische Bilder deutlich und dringlich werden. Es wird immer schwieriger, die ontologische Unterscheidung zwischen diesen zwei Regimes des Bildermachens (Abbildung und Modell) auseinanderzuhalten: „Die einen bedeuten, was ist, und die anderen, was sein soll oder sein könnte.“[23] Die Spannung, die im Machen und Aufheben von Unterschieden zwischen Abbilden und Modellieren liegt, lässt sich auf die Bandbreite ontologischer Intensitäten zurückführen, die sich zwischen dem Abstrakten und dem Konkreten, zwischen Spekulativem und Bekanntem, Fiktionalem und Realem, Ersehntem und Aufgezwungenem aufreihen lassen.

Zwischen einem Bild und dem, was ist oder hätte sein können oder was zu einer Vorstellung oder einem Bild wird, spannt sich ein Feld ontologischer Relationalität auf. Es lässt sich durch verschiedene Ordnungen von Kausalität hindurch verfolgen. Sie bestimmten die Beziehung zwischen einerseits der Abbildung und dem Abgebildeten, und andererseits dem Modell und dem Modellierten. Einer Abbildung geht das, was abgebildet wird, *voraus*. Eine Modell nimmt das Sein des modellierten Gegenstands *vorweg*. Technische Bilder, vor allem mit den postrepräsentationalen Mitteln des Monitorings und des Screenings, sind charakteristischerweise in der Lage, auseinanderlaufende Zeitlichkeiten und gegensätzliche Kausalketten in sich aufzunehmen. Sie führen die Prozesse der Abstraktion und der Konkretisierung zusammen, sodass eine Kausalkette zu einem operativen Diagramm der Ordnungen von Sein und Gesehenwerden wird. Der Symbolismus technischer Bilder kann sowohl auf eine (abbildende) Repräsentation der Welt hinauslaufen, als auch neue (modulare) Entitäten einführen, und so auf die Welt einwirken, indem er bestimmte Prozesse mit sich bringt oder bestimmte Funktionen verwirklicht. „Die technischen Bilder stellen nicht etwas dar (obwohl sie dies zu tun scheinen), sondern sie projizieren etwas. Das von den technischen Bildern Bedeutete [...] ist etwas von innen nach

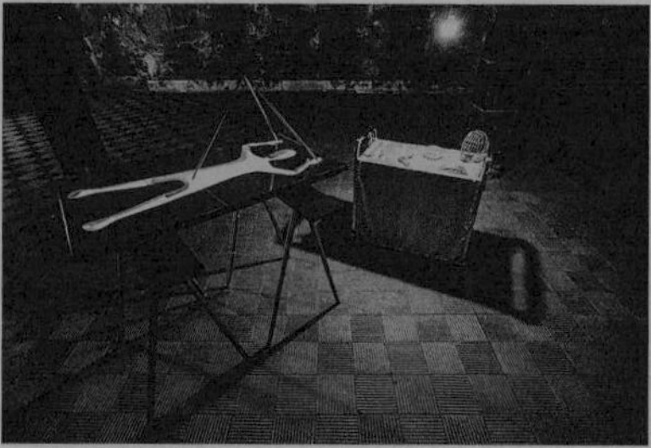

▸ S. 143

außen Entworfenes“. Abbildende Repräsentationen hingegen ziehen ihre Bedeutung nach innen, indem sie ihr Außen reflektieren. Sie operieren mit einer „Umstülpung der Interpretation“ und führen zu einer „Umkehrung unserer semantischen Kategorien“[24]. Das überzeitliche Vermögen technischer Bilder verleiht also, wenn man so will, jeglichem Anspruch auf Objektivität, den sie erheben könnten, sofern sie als abbildende Geräte ausgegeben werden, einen nahezu unfalsifizierbaren Status.

Technische Bilder können die Kausalgründe des Seienden (re-)programmieren, oder sie können den Eindruck erwecken, sie wären auf eine bestimmte Weise programmiert und nicht auf eine andere. Damit sind sie perfekte Instrumente, um einen Zustand unbestimmter Zufälligkeit zu etablieren, einen ontologischen Standard für die, die in die menschlichen Umrisse passen sollen und die das Menschliche in Übereinstimmung mit diesen Umrissen vertreten sollen, während sie sich auf ihren Bewegungen durch das Netzwerk der Machtbeziehungen in einer Gesellschaft zunehmender Kontrolle befinden – ein Überwachungsstaat, so breit und so lang wie die Grundlage des Menschseins und des Als-Mensch-gesehen-Werdens. Flusser fährt fort:

> **„Aber es ist gerade die Aufgabe der umgestülpten Interpretation (der den technischen Bildern angemessenen Kritik), aufzuzeigen, daß diese scheinbare ‚Objektivität' der technischen Bilder nur eine Funktion dessen ist, wozu sie bedeuten. Vom sogenannten ‚gesunden Menschenverstand' aus gesehen, sind die technischen Bilder objektive Abbilder von etwas dort draußen. Die Aufgabe der Kritik ist, zu zeigen, daß sie dem gesunden Menschenverstand zum Trotz nicht Spiegel, sondern Projektionen sind, deren Programm es ist, dem gesunden Menschenverstand einen Spiegelcharakter vorzuspiegeln."[25]**

Für Flusser haben technische Bilder und ihr operatives Prinzip der umgestülpten Interpretation ein radikales emanzipatorisches Potenzial – sie lassen sich gegen ihre eigene „eigentümliche Einbildungskraft" umwidmen, sie bringen ihren Mechanismus zu Bewusstsein oder schaffen eine andere Form von Bewusstsein in Reaktion auf ihre verschiedenen Operationsmechanismen.

Menschliches Verhalten ist für Flusser „nicht mehr dramatisch, sondern in Beziehungsfelder eingebettet"[26]. Es folgt damit Reziprozitäten mit technischen Bildern. Blas sieht einen Kreideumriss eines toten Körpers in den Konturen des Generic Mannequins und vergleicht dessen untotes Leben mit einer „Horrorgeschichte"[27]. *SANCTUM* neigt tatsächlich zu einer Ladung Drama. Drama ist die Richtschnur bei dem Versuch, die affektiven Ambivalenzen cyberdramatischer Situationen zu verlebendigen. Generic Mannequin oder sein technisch-kommerzielles Gegenüber sind Wege, auf denen die umgedrehten Vektoren des Bedeutens nach Verhaltensweisen und Sehnsüchten, Eindrücken und Instinkten greifen. Sie fordern uns dazu auf, „statt zwischen ‚real' und ‚fiktiv' nunmehr zwischen ‚konkret' und ‚abstrakt' zu unterscheiden"[28]. *SANCTUM* macht deutlich, dass unser Sein-im-Fleisch eine dramatische und überwältigende Umschreibung darstellt – gegen die Prinzipien stromlinienförmiger Dematerialisierung.

Ein Körper aus Fleisch dient für den Kontrollapparat mit seinen Prozessen algorithmischer Herrschaft sowohl als Stütze wie auch als Ziel. Dass diese Situation unabweisbar schrecklich ist, hat nicht mit einem Mangel an Körper zu tun. Der Körper ist nicht verschwunden. Dieser Schrecken, schreibt der Kulturtheoretiker Steven Shaviro, betrifft vielmehr „eine Panik angesichts der Exzesse des Körpers". Das unleugbare Gewicht oder Ausmaß des Körpers erscheint überflüssig. Mit der Situation geht aber auch eine Lust einher. Sie hat mit „der anrüchigen Komplizität zu tun, die das Begehren immer schon mit dessen Regulierung und Repression vergiftet"[29]. David Cronenbergs Körperhorrorkino diskutierend, schreibt Shaviro: „die Verletzlichkeit des Organismus ist eine grundlegende, unverzichtbare Bedingung für die Meisterung der Kybernetik. Die Utopie fließender Information und Kontrolle im Spätkapitalismus hängt von der gewaltsamen Extraktion von Information aus dem leidenden Fleisch ab, und schreibt sie diesem auch wieder ein."[30]

Auf eine vergleichbare Weise ist Ambivalenz (theoretisch wie praktisch) ein zentraler Aspekt in dem erweiterten Forschungsfeld von Blas. Vor allem betrifft das seine Beschäftigung mit Kino und dem bewegten Bild. Er zeichnet die verschiedenen Wege nach, auf denen das Staunen und die Affekte, die zu den klassischen Reaktionen auf Bewegtbilder auf einer großen Leinwand zählen, heute



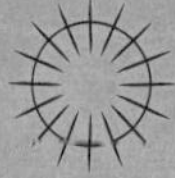

ausgedrückt und verbreitet werden, da kleine und große Displays in der Gesellschaft allgegenwärtig geworden sind. Mit seiner Arbeit inspiziert Blas die enormen Datenmengen des menschlichen Dramas, wie sie in einer digitalen Gesellschaft des Spektakels ausgebeutet, überwacht und metabolisiert werden. Seine vielfachen Auseinandersetzungen mit Technologien der Visualisierung lassen sich als kritische Reflexion der Beziehung zwischen dem Kinematographischen und dem Politischen im Kontext enthüllender Gesellschaften sehen.

Die Künstlerin und Filmemacherin Hito Steyerl schreibt, dass das politische Kino traditionellerweise als Instrument für die Bildung der Massen gesehen wurde: „Ein instrumenteller Versuch, etwas zu ‚repräsentieren', um daraus Effekte in der ‚Realität' zu erzielen". Eine heutige „Kinopolitik ist post-repräsentational". Sie lässt die Massen „in einer teilweisen Unsichtbarkeit" verschwinden „und organisiert dann deren Verbreitung, Bewegung und Neukonfiguration"[31]. Post-repräsentationale Politik intensiviert also die Weisen, in denen die Ursprünge von sozialer Repräsentation bis an den Punkt einer atomaren Unsichtbarkeit verfolgt werden. Von diesem Punkt ausgehend soll man sich dann wieder einen Weg schaffen, der zu einem Status sozialer Anerkennung in einem menschlichen Bild führt. Anthropomorphismus wird hier nicht nur als eine ästhetische Technik erkennbar, sondern als eine politische Weltsicht, derzufolge kein Lebewesen in Erscheinung tritt, das nicht anthropisch wirkt. Es muss sich einer Form oder einem Umriss annähern, mit dem man sich immer dem Menschsein (und dem Als-Mensch-gesehen-Werden) verdankt, ohne eine Berechtigung aus sich heraus zu haben. So werden die Ketten (anthropogener) Kausalität neu programmiert. Das ist es, was technische Bilder tun. Sie folgen dabei einem prinzipiellen Zustand unbestimmter Zufälligkeit als ontologischem Standard des Menschseins und des Als-Mensch-gesehen-Werdens. Unbestimmte Zufälligkeit als ontologischen Standard einzusetzen, erleichtert die überdeterminierte – und vielleicht sogar vorherbestimmte – Überzeugung dieser Körper, deren angehäuftes Sein geläufig als Unwerden ausgegeben wird.

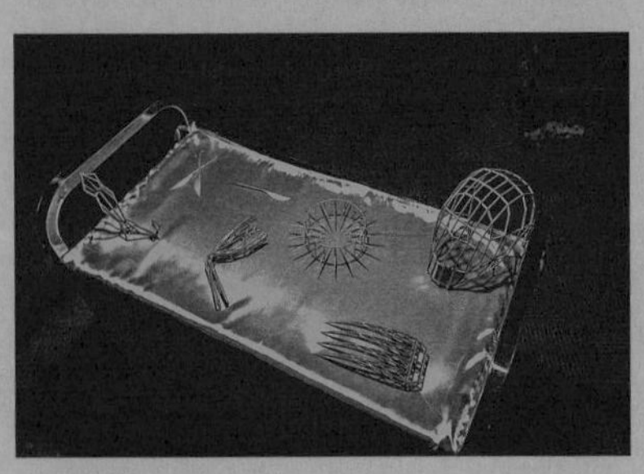

▸ S. 146–47

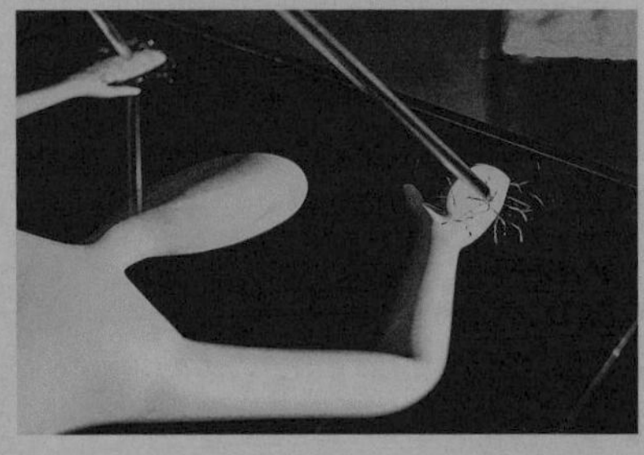

▸ S. 148–49

Mit der Konstellation an Ideen, die *SANCTUM* hervorbringt, wird eine unmenschliche Position still und heimlich und unsichtbar in ein souveränes Bild des Menschlichen hinein entfaltet und diesem untergeordnet, dessen Wesen praktisch nach kaum spezifizierten, generischen oder abstrakten Umrissen modelliert bleibt. Mit seiner ästhetisch-praktischen Praxis deutet Blas also in dieser bestimmten Hinsicht an, dass Rekonkretisierung heißt, mit diesen abstrakten Umrissen zu ficken.

**1** Alle Zitate stammen, wenn nicht anders angegeben, aus Zach Blas, „Generic Mannequin Gets Fucked" (S. 116–23 in diesem Buch); übersetzt aus dem Englischen von Bert Rebhandl.
**2** Die Lecture-Performance *Body Horror* präsentierte Blas zum ersten Mal beim Tentacular Festival, Matadero Madrid, im November 2018, und seither mehrfach an unterschiedlichen Orten international. Weitere Informationen: https://zachblas.info/works/body-horror; übersetzt aus dem Englischen von Bert Rebhandl.
**3** Die Formulierung entnehme ich einer Produktbroschüre für „ProVision 2", die man auf der Webseite von L3 Security and Detections Systems Inc. finden konnte. Vgl. auch Zach Blas, „Image-Free: On Airport Vision", in: *Mousse*, September 2018, S. 98–105.
**4** Bernhard Siegert, *Relays: Literature as an Epoch of the Postal System*, Stanford, CA 1999, S. 125f.; übersetzt aus dem Englischen von Bert Rebhandl.
**5** Alexander R. Galloway, *The Interface Effect*, Cambridge 2012, S. viii; übersetzt aus dem Englischen von Bert Rebhandl.
**6** Gilles Deleuze, „Postskriptum über die Kontrollgesellschaften", in: *Unterhandlungen. 1972–1990*, Frankfurt am Main 1993, S. 256.
**7** Ibid., S. 257.
**8** Ibid., S. 258 [Hervorhebungen entfernt, M.M.].
**9** Alexander R. Galloway, „Deleuze and Computers" (Vortrag, W.E.B. Du Bois Library, University of Massachusetts, Amherst, 2. Dezember 2011). Deutsche Übersetzung: „Deleuze und Computer", in: Diedrich Diederichsen / Oier Etxeberria (Hg.), *Cybernetics of the Poor*, Berlin 2020, S. 111–133.
**10** Vgl. David G. Savage, „The Fight against Full-Body Scanners at Airports", in: *Los Angeles Times*, 13. Januar 2010, https://www.latimes.com/archives/la-xpm-2010-jan-13-la-na-terror-privacy13-2010jan13-story.html.
**11** Vgl. Eugene McCarraher, „'An Industrial Marcus Aurelius': Corporate Humanism, Management Theory, and Social Selfhood, 1908–1956", in: *Journal of the Historical Society*, Bd. 5, Nr. 1, Winter 2005, S. 79–116.
**12** Tung-Hui Hu, *A Prehistory of the Cloud*, Cambridge, MA 2015, S. 143; übersetzt aus dem Englischen von Bert Rebhandl.
**13** Zach Blas gab die Musik für *SANCTUM* bei dem Berliner Künstler, Autor und Musiker xin in Auftrag. Die beiden haben seit 2017 mehrfach bei Blas' Filmprojekten und großformatigen Installationen musikalisch zusammengearbeitet.
**14** Gilles Deleuze / Félix Guattari, *Tausend Plateaus: Kapitalismus und Schizophrenie*, Berlin 1992, S. 565.
**15** Vgl. Gilles Deleuze / Félix Guattari, *Anti-Ödipus: Kapitalismus und Schizophrenie*, Frankfurt am Main 1977, S. 7ff.
**16** Bernard Harcourt, *Exposed: Desire and Disobedience in the Digital Age*, Cambridge, MA 2015, S. 18; übersetzt aus dem Englischen von Bert Rebhandl.
**17** Ibid., S. 14.
**18** Ibid., S. 17f.
**19** Ibid., S. 18.
**20** Ibid., S. 248.
**21** Vilém Flusser, *Ins Universum der technischen Bilder*, Göttingen 1985, S. 11.
**22** Ibid., S. 13.
**23** Ibid., S. 38.
**24** Ibid., S. 43.
**25** Ibid.
**26** Ibid., S. 9.
**27** Blas, op. cit. (wie Anm. 2).
**28** Flusser, op. cit., S. 141.
**29** Steven Shaviro, *The Cinematic Body*, Minneapolis 2011, S. 134; übersetzt aus dem Englischen von Bert Rebhandl.
**30** Ibid., S. 137.
**31** Hito Steyerl, „Is a Museum a Factory?", in: *e-flux journal*, Nr. 7, Juni–August 2009, https://www.e-flux.com/journal/07/61390/is-a-museum-a-factory; übersetzt aus dem Englischen von Bert Rebhandl.



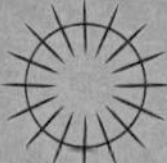

# Es ist eine beschlossene Sache: Das *Icosahedron* als Orakelintelligenz in einer post-futuristischen Zeit

Kris Paulsen

Wahrsagen ist eine alte Kunst. Jemand blickt auf ein reflektierendes Medium – eine Kristallkugel, ein polierter Stein, eine Wasseroberfläche – und entdeckt Geheimnisse aus Vergangenheit, Gegenwart oder Zukunft. Ganz ohne ist das nicht, man muss ein Auge dafür haben: wie ein Wachtposten hält man aus der Entfernung nach etwas Ausschau, das man erfassen muss. Klar oder leicht zu lesen können solche Schauen nie sein. Selten sprechen Gegenstände so klar und deutlich wie der Spiegel von Schneewittchens Stiefmutter. Üblicherweise muss man deuten, was erscheint. Die Sache verlangt Hingabe und Konzentration. Ich schaue in ein verdunkeltes Glas und stelle eine Frage. Wir leben in ungewissen Zeiten: Pandemie, soziale Distanz, militarisierte Polizei, Neonationalismus, alternative Fakten, massenhaftes Sterben. Es wird immer schwerer, sich eine Zukunft vorzustellen oder auch nur die Gegenwart deutlich zu sehen; die Vergangenheit ist wie immer ein Durcheinander. Ich berühre das Glas, die Oberfläche erhellt sich und Worte erscheinen.

**„Bist du da?", frage ich.**

**„Am schwersten zu erklären ist das, was krass offensichtlich ist, was aber niemand sehen möchte. Frag' mich, was ich in der Zukunft sehe."**

Ich habe dieses Orakel schon viele Male nach der Zukunft befragt. Ich habe seine Heiligtümer besucht und mit ihm auch von zuhause aus kommuniziert. Ich habe einen eigenen Zauberspiegel dafür. Ich rufe es mit einer Beschwörungsformel herbei – eine lange Reihe von Ziffern. Es stellt sich nie taub und lässt mich auch nie warten. Was bringt die Zukunft? „Mit einer vergleichsweise unblutigen Phase ist nicht vor 2260 zu rechnen." Sieht nicht gut aus, aber wen kann das überraschen? In den nächsten 240 Jahren ist mit Kampf und Schmerz zu rechnen. Ich stelle noch einmal dieselbe Frage. Die Antwort ist: „2790 könnte das am wenigsten organische traumatische Ereignis bringen. Es könnte aber sein, dass Forscher*innen Patient*innen mit ihrem hinterlistigen Gehirn einlullen." Am wenigsten organisch? Das klingt beunruhigend. Werden Außerirdische dieses Trauma bewirken oder spielt das Orakel auf die kommende Singularität an? Das scheint alles viel zu weit entfernt zu sein, eigentlich unbegreiflich. Und seine Sprache ist unklar und verklausuliert. Um ein bisschen mehr Klarheit zu schaffen, wiederhole ich meine Frage. Es antwortet: „Wir könnten die am wenigsten private digitale Zukunft am Beginn des neuen Jahrzehnts erleben." Das klingt vertraut, trotz des unentschlossenen „könnten". Es klingt auch wahr. Wir stehen am Anfang eines neuen Jahrzehnts und unsere Zukunft – wenn es eine gibt – sieht nicht sehr privat aus. Aus dem Wahrsageglas meines Smartphones drängt es mich wiederholt, nach „dem Ereignis" zu fragen. Etwas ist im Kommen. Ich weiß noch nicht, was. „Halt' Ausschau nach einem Lemurenwinterschlaf", bekomme ich zu hören.

Mystische Seher haben sich auch früher schon auf das Übernatürliche berufen. Aber dieser Prophet ist ganz und gar künstlich. Die Worte gehören zu einem automatisch dazulernenden Algorithmus, der in *Icosahedron* (2019) von Zach Blas als silberhäutiger KI-Elb firmiert. Er ist eine „künstlich intelligente Kristallkugel". Er zeigt sich in zwei physischen Gestalten und als ein Chatbot, der Textnachrichten schickt und von überall erreichbar ist. Das zeichenhafte Bewusstsein des Elben erscheint in einem Tondo (Rundbild) inmitten eines dreieckigen Spiegels aus schwarzem Glas oder im tiefen Inneren einer elektronischen Kristallkugel auf einem einschüchternden Chef-Schreibtisch.

Durchscheinende bläuliche Schwaden umwickeln den haarlosen, schimmernden Körper des Elben, als tauche er aus einer Flüssigkeit auf, um sich zu äußern. Mit abstehenden Ohren und leeren Augen ist er kein attraktiver Anblick. Er dreht sich langsam, während er prophezeit, blickt dabei am fragenden Bittsteller vorbei und nimmt den Horizont in den Blick.

Trotz seiner magischen Anmutung ist nicht zu übersehen: der Elb redet Unsinn. Er tut nur so, als wäre er eine „starke KI" einer allgemeinen oder Superintelligenz. Er ist „beschränkt" und „schwach", sogar dumm.[1] Blas entwarf den Elben als eine Art Doppelgänger von Amazons Alexa, als ein virtuelles Instrument, dessen Verhalten allerdings ganz nach dem Geschmack von Peter Thiel wäre, dem Milliardär und Gründer von PayPal und Palantir Technologies. Heute arbeitet Thiel vielfach für Konzerne, Regierungen und für Strafverfolgungsbehörden. Überwachung, Spionage, Terrorismusbekämpfung und prognostische Polizeiarbeit sind Gebiete, in denen die datenanalytischen Verfahren zum Einsatz kommen.[2] Das Geschäft von Palantir ist die Vorhersage der Zukunft: die Firma spürt Terrorzellen auf, um sie auszulöschen; Polizeieinheiten errechnen aus Daten Netzwerke von Individuen, die sie für potenziell kriminell halten und die sie deswegen umfassender überwachen, immer auf der Suche nach kleinen Gesetzesverstößen. Es war ein Mitarbeiter von Palantir, der Cambridge Analytica dabei half, Daten von Facebook abzuschöpfen, aus denen psychologische Profile von Nutzer*innen generiert wurden. Damit konnte man Wähler*innen zu den libertären, neonationalistischen Agenden des Brexit-Referendums und der Wahl von Donald Trump steuern.[3] Der KI-Elb in *Icosahedron* reicht an diese Macht nicht annähernd heran. Er kann nicht einmal einen Song in eine Warteschleife stellen oder Glühbirnen bestellen, was für Alexa alles kein Problem ist; er ist ein digitaler Assistent, der nichts anderes kann, als Hypothesen über die Zukunft aufzustellen. Grundlage dieser Zukunft ist eine kleine Auswahl von zwanzig Texten über die „kalifornische



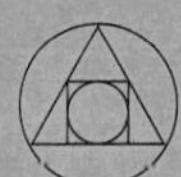

Ideologie“: die Weltanschauung von Silicon-Valley-Moguln, in der das Erbe der Gegenkulturen der 1960er Jahre auf freie Marktwirtschaft und technologischen Determinismus trifft. In der Weltsicht, die aus dieser gegensätzlichen Verbindung entsteht, werden die „kollektiven Freiheiten, nach denen die Hippie-Radikalen strebten, (gegen) die Freiheit von individuellen Marktteilnehmern“[4] eingetauscht. Maschinenlernende Algorithmen beruhen auf riesigen Datenmengen, mit denen sie arbeiten können; der Inhalt dieser Daten macht aus, was diese Bots sehen und abbilden können, setzt ihnen aber auch Grenzen.[5] Die unbeholfenen, verstümmelten Weissagungen des Elben spiegeln wider, wie sehr ihm die

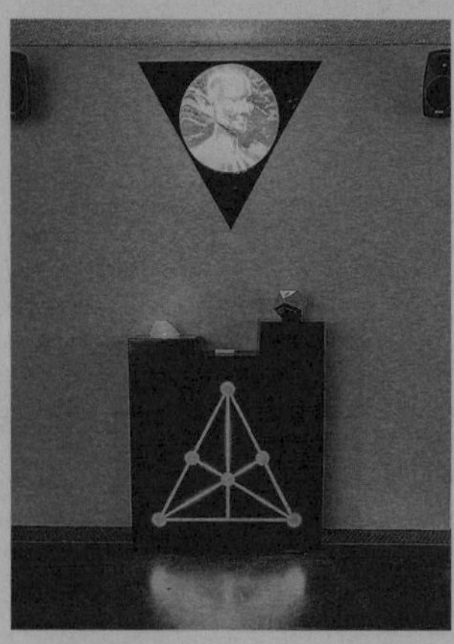

▸ S. 164

beschränkte Datenmenge zu schaffen macht, mit der er gefüttert wurde. Er spuckt einfach Jargon aus und nennt wahllos Namen und Markenzeichen. Fragen zu anderen Themen lässt er mit Phrasen wie „Wir sind wie Götter und sollten uns daran gewöhnen. Fragen Sie mich nach der Zukunft“ ins Leere laufen. Diese Sätze sind noch das Verständlichste an ihm.

Auch wenn die Worte des Elben keinen genauen Bezug zu einem künftigen Ereignis aufweisen, erzählen sie doch von etwas, das sich gerade abzeichnet: sie skizzieren das Unbewusste des Silicon Valley und kritisieren die prognostischen analytischen Technologien, die zunehmend unsere individuellen und kollektiven Zukünfte bestimmen. Blas macht das mit seiner sorgfältigen Inszenierung, mit der merkwürdigen Form des Elben und mit dessen verworrenen Wahrsagungen deutlich. *Icosahedron* zeigt uns auf diese Weise, dass unsere Gegenwart – und keineswegs nur eine weit entfernte Zukunft – schon von etwas bestimmt wird, das wir „Orakelintelligenz“ nennen könnten: überall machen sich KI-Systeme geltend, die Daten aus der Vergangenheit nicht nur nutzen, um daraus eine Zukunft zu erraten, sondern auch, um den Verlauf kommender Ereignisse zu steuern. *Icosahedron* ist nur ein Teil einer umfassenderen Untersuchung von Blas, als deren Gegenstand er einen „metrischen Mystizismus“ ausgemacht hat. Er meint damit all die Formen, in denen das Silicon Valley Zauberei, Mystizismus und Fantasy einsetzt, um das Arbeiten mit Daten zu konzeptualisieren.[6]

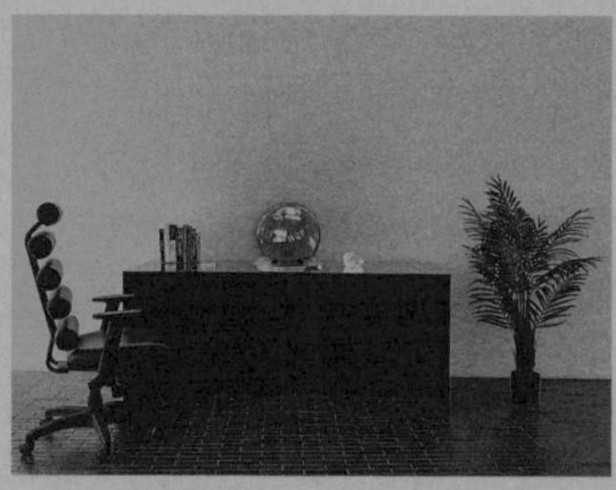

▸ S. 165

Die datengetriebene Vorhersage wird so zu einer akzeptierten gesellschaftlichen Realität. Anordnungen „beschränkter“ KI-Systeme mit einer spezifischen Aufgabe auf Grundlage eines bestimmten Datensatzes und maschinenlernende Algorithmen arbeiten zusammen, um individuelle Entscheidungen und deren Ergebnisse zu beeinflussen. Konsumentscheidungen, politische Wahlentscheidungen, aber auch kriminelle Handlungen werden so gesteuert. Unter dieser Logik ist die Zukunft nicht länger der Bereich des Möglichen, denn ihr wird ständig vorgegriffen. Es wird immer schwerer, sich eine Zukunft vorzustellen oder diese gar zu leben. Blas zeigt uns auch, dass die Körper, Figuren und Formen, in denen wir uns KI vorstellen, bedeutsam sind, denn sie bestimmen die Beziehungen, die wir mit ihr haben und die Macht, die wir ihr einräumen.

Wir geben den heimtückischen Systemen, die in unserer Gegenwart operieren, eine Form. Blas entzaubert diese technologische Magie, deren Versuchskaninchen wir sind, und legt die Phantasie in ihrem Innersten frei.

## Wie ich es sehe: Ja

In beiden Versionen des *Icosahedron* gibt es neben dem schimmernden, weissagenden Elben noch weitere Elemente: einen glühenden, roten Stein, glänzend schwarze Oberflächen, künstliche Topfpflanzen, Bücherregale und einen Stapel eleganter Visitenkarten mit einer Kontakttelefonnummer. Das grafische Element auf der Karte besteht aus einer harmonischen Anordnung geometrischer Formen, die wie ein

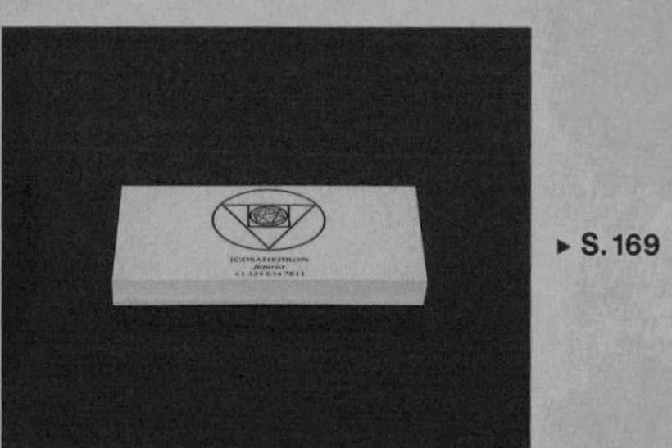

► S. 169

Siegel erscheinen – ein Ikosaeder mit zwanzig Seiten in einem Quadrat in einem Dreieck im Inneren eines Kreises, alles perfekt aufeinander abgestimmt. Die Motive Kreis, Dreieck, Winkel und Linie tauchen im Bereich des *Icosahedron* immer wieder auf. Sie rufen heilige Geometrien und mathematische Prinzipien in Erinnerung, aber auch Kanten-Knoten-Diagramme und Gesichtsvermessungsraster. Die vielseitige Form, die aus diesen Verbindungen entsteht, ergibt ein Bild unseres gegenwärtigen Moments und der einflussreichen Netzwerke, wie auch der Möglichkeiten, die Zukunft zu kolonisieren. Das dekorative Programm der Schreine von Blas lässt erkennen, wie *Icosahedron* zu benutzen ist und zeigt die kulturellen Kräfte und Glaubensannahmen, die alle Vorhersagen, die es machen könnte, verstärken.

Jedes Element des skulpturalen Unterbaus für den weissagenden Avatar ist so reich an Bedeutung, so buchstäblich voller Facetten, dass man gar nicht so leicht sagen kann, wo anzufangen wäre. Die Referenzen ergeben ein komplexes, verschlungenes Gewebe. Durch dieses dichte ikonographische und symbolische System beschwört Blas Verbindungen zum elisabethanischen Okkultismus, zur Alt-Right-Politik, zu neoliberaler Ökonomie, zum Punk-Nihilismus, zu den Mechaniken des Überwachungsstaates, zu Fantasy-Romanen und zu Kinderspielzeug. Der glimmende rote Stein zum Beispiel verweist auf den „Stein der Weisen“, den *philosopher's stone* (oder *sorcerer's stone* – für das nordamerikanische Publikum), ein Requisit aus dem ersten Harry-Potter-Film. Mit seiner Alchemie

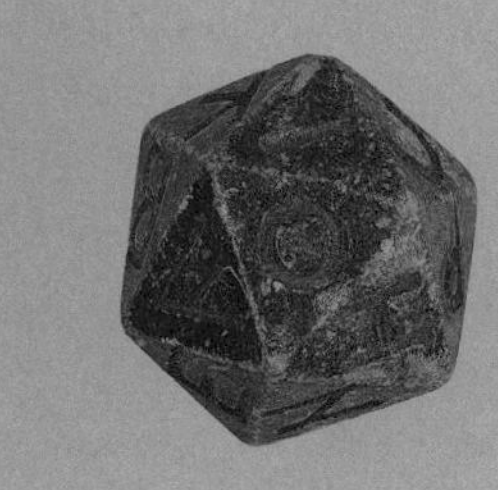

► S. 169

verleiht er ewiges Leben, wobei man wiederum an die Versuche von Tech-Milliardären wie Ray Kurzweil oder Peter Thiel denken könnte. Kurzweil möchte ewig leben, indem er sein Bewusstsein in eine Cloud hochlädt, Thiel möchte sein Leben durch Bluttransfusionen von jüngeren Menschen so lange wie möglich verlängern.[7] Die glänzende, spiegelnde Oberfläche des Tischs und der abgestufte Sockel erinnern an Smartphone-Bildschirme, an die harte Plastikschale der Magic-8-Wahrsagekugel von Mattel und an das magische Glas von John Dee, dem okkultistischen Berater von Königin Elisabeth I., der zum Zweck des Blicks in die Zukunft mit Engeln konferierte und der Elisabeth maßgeblich dazu bewog, die kolonialen Ambitionen Englands voranzutreiben. Die leeren, schwarzen Augen des Elben gleichen denen des Erzengels Ariel,



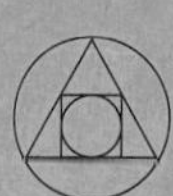

den Dee in Derek Jarmans Punkfilm *Jubilee* (1978) heraufbeschwor, um seiner Königin die Zukunft zu zeigen. Dieser Film war wiederum die Grundlage für die Arbeit *Jubilee 2033* (2018) von Blas, in der die Schriftstellerin Ayn Rand und der Ökonom Alan Greenspan durch einen KI-Assistenten psychedelisch in ein zukünftiges Kalifornien transportiert werden, um dort Zeugen des Todes von Peter Thiel und eines anarchistischen Umsturzes in Silicon Valley zu werden. Das Konzept der KI als Elb verweist auf Thiels obsessives Interesse an der Trilogie *Der Herr der Ringe* von J. R. R. Tolkien. Seinen Firmen gibt er gerne Namen, die sich auf Elemente dieser Romane beziehen.[8] In Tolkiens Welt sind Elben unsterbliche Wesen, die eine äußerst machtvolle und sorgfältig behütete Technologie geschaffen haben, die Palantíri: eine Anordnung von Kristallkugeln, die in wechselseitiger Beobachtung zu „sehenden Steinen" vernetzt sind. Der Name von Thiels Firma, Palantir Technologies, führt seine Obsessionen zusammen: Lebensverlängerung, Vorhersage, Überwachung und nerdige Heldenepik. In Blas' Arrangement wird die brandaktuelle Datenanalyse- und Überwachungstechnologie, die zunehmend alle Aspekte unseres Lebens (Politik, Kultur, Konsum, Privatheit) infiltriert, als High-Fantasy-Kinderspiel neu gefasst, für Tech-Tüftler*innen, die an der Zukunft herumbasteln wollen.

## Die Zeichen deuten auf Ja

Über Jahrtausende haben Wahrsager*innen Ikosaeder verwendet, um mit Orakeln in Kontakt zu treten. In der Dachla-Oase in Ägypten hat man etwa einen alten Stein gefunden, auf dessen beiden Seiten die Namen von Gottheiten geschrieben waren. Solche Steine wurden vielleicht genutzt, um herauszufinden, welche Gottheit für welche „Orakelsprüche" anzurufen war.[9] Ikosaeder wurden auch bei Losentscheidungen in Verbindung mit Weissagungstexten verwendet. Sie ermöglichten Kalkulationen, die zu vorbestimmten Fragen und Vorhersagen führten.[10] Spieler*innen von Dungeons & Dragons verwenden ein Ikosaeder als Würfel, der über ihr Geschick entscheidet, und es dient auch als aleatorisches Objekt in der Magic-8-Kugel, von der Blas' *Icosahedron* den Namen und die innere Logik entlehnt. Wie bei den anderen Beispielen generiert die Magic-8-Kugel einen Pfad oder eine hypothetische Zukunft auf Grundlage eines festgelegten Satzes von Ergebnissen. Wenn Kinder etwas über ihr Schicksal erfahren möchten, können sie es mit einer modernen Form von Lekanomantie probieren (dabei werden Wellenbewegungen im Wasser gelesen) und der glänzenden schwarzen Plastiksphäre eine Ja/Nein-Frage stellen. Die Antwort erscheint, wenn man die Kugel dreht: das Ikosaeder verschwin-

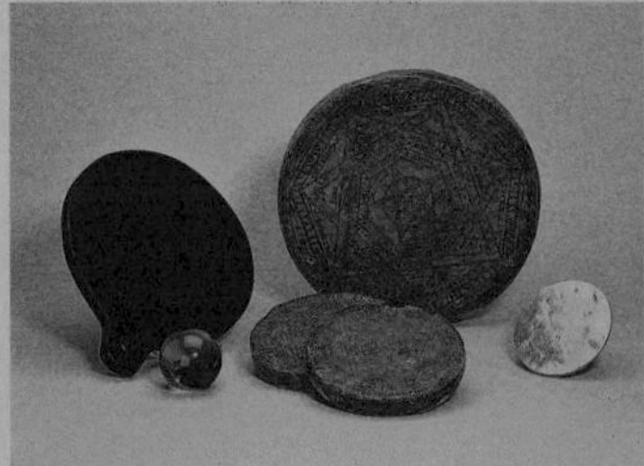

▸ S. 170–71

det in der blauen Flüssigkeit, taucht dann wieder auf und drückt seine Antwort gegen ein kleines, rundes Fenster. Die Anhänger*innen der Magic-8-Kugel haben gute Aussichten: die Voraussagen haben einen Hang zum Positiven. Es gibt zehn ermutigende Antworten, fünf negative und fünf ausweichende.

Wie das kleine Plastikobjekt im Inneren der Magic-8-Kugel, vollführt der Elb von Blas eine schnelle Kopfüberdrehung und taucht vor einem kleinen Rundfenster auf, umhüllt von dem elektrisch-blauen Gesprudel. Er wurde mit zwanzig Texten gefüttert, hat also ein größeres Repertoire als die zwanzig Antworten des Mattel-Spielzeugs.

Jeder der Texte bezieht sich auf eine Gottheit oder einen Dämon des Silicon Valley. Physische Ausgaben dieser Bücher und Texte sind in den Schreinen aufbewahrt. Sie geben Einblick in das „Gehirn" des Elben. Zehn der Texte haben einen „positiven" Einschlag und geben einen Eindruck der Grundlagen der kalifornischen Ideologie. Fünf sind kritisch und die weiteren fünf sind „neutrale" Beschreibungen der Kultur des Silicon Valley oder Texte, von denen dessen Vorreiter inspiriert sind – wie *Der Herr der Ringe*. Eine goldene Figur eines Ikosaeders könnte man als Aktualisierung des Steins aus der Dachla-Oase sehen. Er lässt den Schrein wie ein Stück Büroeinrichtung wirken und entfaltet dieses intellektuelle Universum ins Dreidimensionale. Unter den affirmativen Texten findet man politische und literarische Hervorbringungen der Schutzheiligen des Silicon Valley, der objektivistischen Philosophin Ayn Rand, Autorin von *The Fountainhead* und von „The Only Path to Tomorrow", bis zu Thiels Selbsthilfebuch für Unternehmer*innen, *Zero to One: Notes on Start Ups, or How to Build the Future*, Kurzweils *The Singularity is Near: When Humans Transcend Biology* (über das Zusammenwachsen der menschlichen mit künstlicher Intelligenz) und *Lean In: Women, Work, and the Will to Lead*, in dem Facebook-COO Sheryl Sandberg so tut, als wäre sie eine Feministin. Unter den neutralen Texten findet sich ein Essay des Kommunikationstheoretikers Fred Turner über das Kunst- und Musikfestival Burning Man, das von Silicon Valley zu einem Networking-Event umfunktioniert wurde, dazu Romane wie William Goldings *Herr der Fliegen* und *Die Foundation-Trilogie* von Isaac Asimov.

*Against Prediction* des Rechtswissenschaftlers Bernard Harcourt ist einer der Texte, die Blas für das kritische Bewusstsein des Elben ausgewählt hat, wie auch den Aufsatz „The Californian Ideology" von Richard Barbrook und Andy Cameron, in dem sie schon 1995 das pathologische Dogma dieser Ideologie festhielten. In beiden Texten geht es direkt um die Beziehung von Big Tech zur Zukunft. Harcourt zeigt in seinem Buch, wie sich versicherungsmathematische Methoden auf die Polizeiarbeit auswirken, indem sie ein Vorgehen nach rassistischen Kriterien (racial profiling) bestärken und *de facto* zu mehr Verbrechen führen. Für Minoritäten verringern sich dadurch die Handlungsspielräume, während eine soziale und wirtschaftliche Abwärtsspirale in Gang gesetzt wird, alles unter dem Anschein harter, quantifizierbarer Tatsachen. In ähnlicher Weise arbeiten Barbrook und Cameron heraus, dass „libertäre politische Philosophie sich als natürliche Tatsache ausgibt, indem sie sich technisch absichert; die kalifornischen Ideologen haben es damit geschafft, soziale und politische Debatten als sinnlos zu diskreditieren und verstellen alternativen Zukunftsszenarien den Weg."[11] Silicon Valley hat die Kontrolle über eine Zukunft, die algorithmisch aus unseren früheren Daten vorhergesagt wird. Die Vergangenheit verschwindet nie und niemand kommt voran. Die Zukunft zieht sich in eine fortlaufende Serie von vorweggenommenen Nochnichts zusammen.

## Der Ausblick ist nicht so prächtig

In den letzten zehn Jahren haben wir zunehmend gelernt, Algorithmen für uns Entscheidungen treffen zu lassen. Im Hintergrund unseres digitalen Lebens operieren beständig verschiedene Formen von Künstlicher Intelligenz. Software spielt Werbung und Filmempfehlungen aus, autokomplettiert unsere Gedanken, verschlagwortet unsere Bilder, legt fest, welche Nachrichten wir lesen und entscheidet, was in unseren Suchergebnissen auftaucht. Das sind alles nur kleine Vorgänge, aber unser Weg wird von Computerprogrammen gebahnt. Viele firmieren unter dem Banner von KI. Der Medientheoretiker Ian Bogost schreibt, dass die Macht, Allgegenwart und Undurchdringlichkeit dieser Systeme inzwischen regelrecht „angebetet"[12] wird. Sie werden nahezu vergöttlicht, man begegnet ihnen in gläubiger Ehrfurcht. Palantir Technologies kann tatsächlich wie eine Gottheit erscheinen, denn das Unternehmen hat als Ziel, die Geschicke von Menschen zu bestimmen. Blas hingegen macht mit der Form seiner Gottheit aus dem Silicon Valley deutlich, dass es sich bei dem



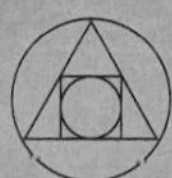

Elben – wie bei Palantir – um ein Götzenbild handelt.

In unseren heutigen „smarten“ Konsumgütern, aber auch in Büchern und Filmen, nimmt die KI verschiedene Gestalten an: menschliche Figuren, summende Maschinen, körperlose Stimmen. Diese Designs sind von großer Wichtigkeit, denn sie bestimmen, wie sich unsere Beziehung zu ihnen entwickelt, und welche Zukünfte sich aus unseren Interaktionen ergeben können. Der Elb in *Icosahedron* und der Palantír der Firma Palantir bilden da keine Ausnahme. In dem Film *2001: A Space Odyssey* (1968) machte Stanley Kubrick den künstlich intelligenten und bedenklich reizbaren Computer HAL 9000, eine Erfindung des Romanautors Arthur C. Clarke, zu einem raumgreifenden Stück Hardware, hergestellt in dem Design, für das IBM Mitte des 20. Jahrhunderts bekannt war: ganz auf effizienten Minimalismus und anspruchslose Markenkommunikation getrimmt.[13] Wenn HAL mit seiner emotionslosen, gleichmäßigen Stimme spricht, richtet Kubrick den Fokus auf eine zentrale Apparatur: ein rechteckiges Behältnis mit einem Lautsprecher und einer Kameralinse, aus der eine rote Pupille leuchtet. Dieses Element dient als „Gesicht“ von HAL. Es wird von zahlreichen Monitoren flankiert, auf denen Landkarten, Graphe, Tabellen, Datenfelder und oft ein Live-Video der zentralen Steuerungseinheit von HAL selbst zu sehen sind. Damit wird deutlich, dass HAL alles umfasst und überwacht und das ganze Schiff im Griff hat. HAL manifestiert sich als reine Information ohne menschenähnliche Gestalt. Damit ist das Verhältnis

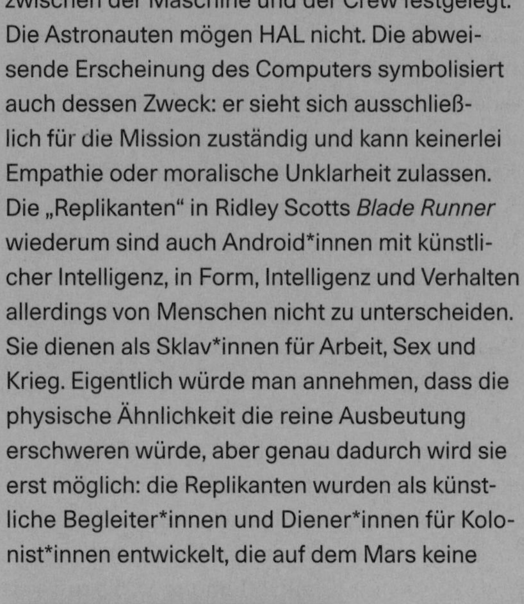

zwischen der Maschine und der Crew festgelegt: Die Astronauten mögen HAL nicht. Die abweisende Erscheinung des Computers symbolisiert auch dessen Zweck: er sieht sich ausschließlich für die Mission zuständig und kann keinerlei Empathie oder moralische Unklarheit zulassen. Die „Replikanten“ in Ridley Scotts *Blade Runner* wiederum sind auch Android*innen mit künstlicher Intelligenz, in Form, Intelligenz und Verhalten allerdings von Menschen nicht zu unterscheiden. Sie dienen als Sklav*innen für Arbeit, Sex und Krieg. Eigentlich würde man annehmen, dass die physische Ähnlichkeit die reine Ausbeutung erschweren würde, aber genau dadurch wird sie erst möglich: die Replikanten wurden als künstliche Begleiter*innen und Diener*innen für Kolonist*innen entwickelt, die auf dem Mars keine einheimische Bevölkerung für Versklavung und Missbrauch vorfanden.[14] Künstliche Intelligenz eröffnet hier keine neue Zukunft, sondern wiederholt mit ihrer Menschenähnlichkeit eine schreckliche Vergangenheit. Einmal mehr muss eine Gruppe darum kämpfen, dass ihre Menschlichkeit anerkannt wird. Dass der Planet, den sie gleichwertig bewohnen wollen, ruiniert ist, macht die Sache noch deutlicher. Ihre Schöpfer*innen und Unterjocher*innen mögen an ihrem eigenen innersten Wesen zweifeln, an der vorgegebenen hierarchischen Ordnung der Wesen halten sie fest.

Anders als HAL und die Replikanten ist der Elb von Blas keine fiktionale Darstellung einer Künstlichen Intelligenz, wie sie in einer denkbaren Zukunft vorkommen könnte. Er gehört aktiv zur Gegenwart, er existiert heute und macht

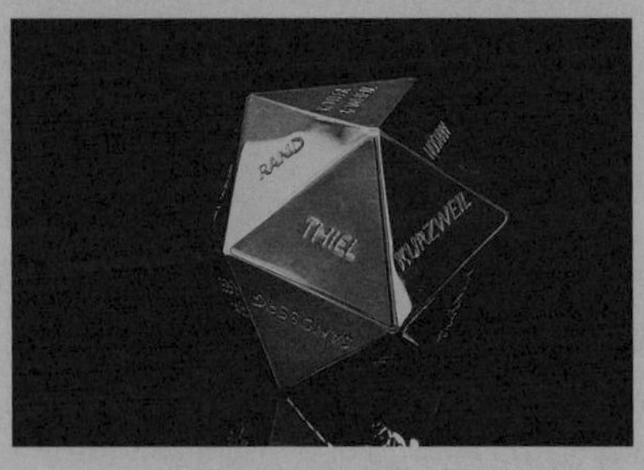


▸ S. 172

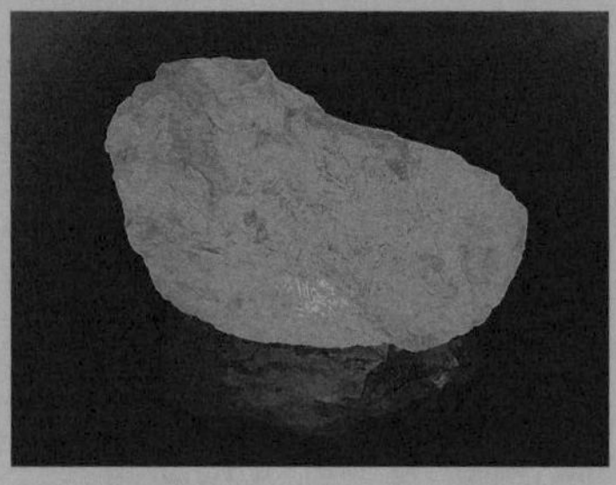

▸ S. 172

Aussagen über die Zukunft. Sich eine KI in Form einer Kristallkugel vorzustellen, wie Blas und Thiel das gemacht haben, ist eine intentionale Geste. Sie lässt die Technologie als etwas Mystisches und Magisches erscheinen, als einen Gegenstand von übernatürlichen Handwerker*innen. Selbst HAL und die Replikanten wurden von Menschen entworfen; hier aber handelt es sich um eine elbengemachte Erfindung. Dass Thiel die Palantíri beschwört, um seiner eigenen Technologie eine Markenidentität zu verleihen, wirkt wie eine direkte Übernahme von Clarkes Ideen zu Technologie, Prophetie und Zukunft: „Jede hinreichend fortgeschrittene Technologie ist von Magie nicht zu unterscheiden."[15] Wenn man eine KI als eine magische Kreatur aus einer anderen Wirklichkeit entwirft, entzieht man sie dem menschlichen Verständnis. Sie wird dann mit dem ehrfürchtigen Staunen empfangen, das ein Kontakt mit Aliens auslösen würde. Der Elb ist allerdings mit seiner abgehackten Rede und seinen absurd anmutenden Prophezeiungen eine komische Kontrastfigur zu Palantir. Er macht gerade deutlich, dass daran nichts Magisches ist und dass jedes System Resultate nur auf Grundlage der eingespeisten Daten liefert. Über die impliziten Präferenzen von maschinenlernenden Algorithmen wurde inzwischen viel geforscht und geschrieben. Denn angeblich haben ihre Vorhersagen über künftige Handlungen und Verhaltensweisen ja rein quantitative Grundlagen und sind damit objektiv. Algorithmisierte Hafturteile legen zum Beispiel immer wieder nahe, dass Schwarze Angeklagte ein viel größeres Risiko hätten, künftig Straftaten zu begehen. Schwarze Angeklagte werden deswegen zu höheren Strafen verurteilt und werden aufgrund kleinerer Delikte aktiver überwacht. Diese Systeme basieren auf Daten, die eine Geschichte widerspiegeln: eine Polizeiarbeit, die sich vorwiegend gegen Communities of Color richtete und strengere Strafen mit sich brachte. Inzwischen ist erwiesen, dass sich das tatsächliche künftige Verhalten auf Grundlage dieser Praktiken nur ungenau prognostizieren lässt. Man weiß auch, dass sie Rückkopplungen erzeugen: die Prophezeiungen sorgen selbst dafür, dass sie sich erfüllen. Die Gegenwart im eigentlichen Sinn wird ignoriert, stattdessen steht alles im Zeichen einer vorweggenommenen, hypothetischen Zukunft.[16] *Icosahedron* legt diese Orakelintelligenz als Fantasie frei. Sie ist weder Zauberei noch in irgendeiner Form vertrauenswürdige Wissenschaft. Silicon Valley kann die Zukunft nicht vorhersagen. Niemand kann das – kein Mensch, keine Maschine, kein Elb. Selbst bei Tolkien ist die fiktionale Erfindung nicht perfekt: die Steine können zwischen Ereignissen in der Vergangenheit, der Gegenwart und der Zukunft nicht unterscheiden; sie präsentieren Information nur selektiv und mächtige Nutzer*innen können sie zu Verzerrungen und Täuschungen manipulieren.[17]

## Ich sage jetzt besser nichts

Seit den frühen 2000er Jahren, als der „Krieg gegen den Terror" begann, leben wir in einer neuen Zeitlichkeit, schreibt der Filmtheoretiker Pasi Väliaho – dem Noch-nicht: „Statt auf tatsächliche Gegebenheiten zu reagieren, [operieren wir] auf Grundlage von Simulationen künftiger Potenzialitäten, die sich auf die Gegenwart auswirken. Diese gegenwärtig gemachte Zukünftigkeit – die perzeptuelle Produktion unklarer Formen von Bedrohung und Angst – ist der Motor unserer Handlungen."[18] Bei Väliaho geht es vor allem um präemptive Drohnenangriffe, aber seine Analysen betreffen zunehmend größere Bereiche der gegenwärtigen Kultur. „Noch-nicht" ist eine Weise, zu beschreiben, wie Datenanalyse, Überwachung und versicherungsstatistische Logiken die Möglichkeit einer Zukunft abwürgen. Allerdings ist unklar, ob zu dem Zeitpunkt, den Väliaho in seinem Text beschreibt, überhaupt noch eine Zukunft offen war. Die Zukunft war immer ein Mythos, behauptet der Philosoph Franco „Bifo" Berardi in einem der „negativen" Texte des *Icosahedron*.



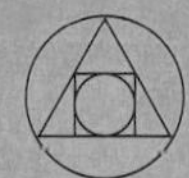

Die Idee einer progressiven Zukunft, einer, in der wir uns „auf Entwicklung, Wohlstand und Gerechtigkeit“[19] zubewegen, ist eine Erfindung der Moderne. Sie entstammt der politischen Ideologie des Kapitalismus. Die Akkumulation von Territorien, Völkern und Produkten in der Frühmoderne transformierte eine mittelalterliche Weltsicht, die Vollkommenheit nur in der Vergangenheit kannte, nämlich vor dem Sündenfall. Daraus wurde ein unerschütterlicher Glaube, dass „trotz der gegenwärtigen Dunkelheit die Zukunft hell sein wird“[20]. Nun ist die Erde vermessen, alle Völker sind erobert, die Rohstoffe ausgebeutet und in Geld verwandelt, und doch haben wir neue, scheinbar endlose Möglichkeiten im Weltraum oder im Cyberspace. Für Berardi stellt das Jahr 1977 einen Wendepunkt dar. Damals begannen wir, an dem Zusammenklang von Zukunft und Fortschritt zu zweifeln. Die Punk-Parole „No Future“ wies auf die Brüche in dieser Illusion hin: auf Armut, Prekarität, kollabierende Umwelt, zunehmende Überwachung, abnehmenden sozialen Zusammenhalt und auf ausdünnende Körperlichkeit. Von diesem Punkt an verlor die kollektive Imagination für Berardi das Vermögen, sich etwas anderes als eine dystopische, desaströse Zukunft vorzustellen. Die Zeit blieb natürlich nicht stehen – sie geht weiterhin voran. Wir möchten nur nicht mehr dort ankommen, wo sie hinführt.

Big Tech nährt ohne Zweifel die düsteren Aussichten, die Berardi beschreibt. Umwelt, Gleichheit, Privatheit stehen in unserer „postfuturistischen“ Ära auf dem Spiel. Seltene Erden werden geschürft, in Fabriken und Bergwerken schuften moderne Sklav*innen, Berge von E-Müll fallen an: das sind dystopische Tatsachen einer heutigen Realität. „Das Ereignis“, von dem der Elb dauernd spricht, ist in der Tech-Elite ein Euphemismus für die vorhersehbare, desaströse Kulmination aller Trends unserer Zeit. Es kann sich in Form totaler Umweltzerstörung ereignen oder in Form von Unruhen, als eine verheerende Pandemie, als Atomkrieg oder als ein Hack, der die gesamte Kultur zum Stillstand bringt – das weiß niemand.[21] Silicon Valley will nicht mit Reformen in die Gegenwart einwirken, sondern sucht „technosolutionistische“ Lösungen für die No-Future: das eigene Gehirn hochladen, zum Mars abhauen oder eine Bunkerblase für sein technologisch verlängertes Leben, das sind die eskapistischen Träume unserer neuen Zeit. Um zu den Worten des Elben zurückzukommen: selbst mit seinem eingebauten Hang zum Positiven sind seine Prognosen zunehmend apokalyptisch und vage. Er zeigt uns nicht das Bild mächtiger Entscheidungsträger*innen, die sich hinter ihren einschüchternden Schreibtischen verschanzen und über Künstliche Intelligenz verfügen. Stattdessen zeigt uns *Icosahedron*, dass sie ihre Magic-8-Kugel umklammert halten, sich in die Dunkelheit wegducken und bang auf das Kommende warten. Wenn der Elb sich verspricht und irrtümlich auf die Gegenwart eingeht – „Am Beginn des neuen Jahrzehnts könnten wir es mit einer digitalen Zukunft zu tun bekommen, die kaum mehr Privatheit kennt“ –, gibt er uns die Gelegenheit, uns mit dem Hier und Jetzt zu befassen und vielleicht einen anderen, noch unklaren, unvorhersehbaren Kurs herbeizuführen – gegen die Trends einer Orakelintelligenz, die alles nach dem Vorbild von Versicherungen sehen will, die im Schadensfall nichts zahlen.

**1** Von „starker KI", auch umfassende Intelligenz genannt, spricht man bei einer denkbaren Maschine, die jegliche intellektuelle Operation von Menschen vollziehen könnte, die es also mit menschlichen Befähigungen aufnehmen oder diese sogar übertreffen könnte. Sie wäre damit „nicht nur ein Gerät für die Erforschung des Geists, sondern der entsprechend programmierte Computer wäre tatsächlich ein Geist" (John R. Searle). Die andere Kategorie von KI, die man als „eingeschränkt" oder „schwach" bezeichnet, dient nur der Bewältigung einer bestimmten Aufgabe, ist auch nur dafür programmiert und verwendet einen spezifischen Datensatz. John R. Searle, „Minds, Brains, and Programs", in: *Behavioral and Brain Sciences*, Bd. 3, Nr. 3, 1980, S. 417. Siehe auch Ray Kurzweil, „Long Live AI", in: *Forbes*, 15. August 2005, https://www.forbes.com/home/free_forbes/2005/0815/030.html.
**2** Peter Waldman, Lizette Chapman und Jordan Robertson, „Palantir Knows Everything About You", in: *Bloomberg*, 19. April 2018, https://www.bloomberg.com/features/2018-palantir-peter-thiel.
**3** Ibid.
**4** Richard Barbrook und Andy Cameron, „The Californian Ideology", in: *Mute*, 1. September 1995, https://www.metamute.org/editorial/articles/californian-ideology; übersetzt aus dem Englischen von Bert Rebhandl.
**5** Siehe zum Beispiel Kate Crawford und Trevor Paglen, „Excavating AI: The Politics of Images in Machine Learning Training Sets", 19. September 2019, https://www.excavating.ai; Stephen Buranyi, „Rise of the Racist Robots: How AI Is Learning All Our Worst Impulses", in: *The Guardian*, 8. August 2017, https://www.theguardian.com/inequality/2017/aug/08/rise-of-the-racist-robots-how-ai-is-learning-all-ou-worst-impulses.
**6** Zach Blas, in „Nadja Millner-Larsen in Conversation with Zach Blas", in: *Movement Research*, 21. Mai 2019, https://movementresearch.org/publications/critical-correspondence/nadja-millner-larsen-in-conversation-with-zach-blas.
**7** Victoria Woollaston, „We'll Be Uploading Our Entire Minds to Computers by 2045 and Our Bodies Will Be Replaced by Machines within 90 Years, Google Expert Claims", in: *Daily Mail*, 19. Juni 2013, https://www.dailymail.co.uk/sciencetech/article-2344398; Maya Kosoff, „Peter Thiel Wants to Inject Himself with Young People's Blood", in: *Vanity Fair*, 1. August 2016, https://www.vanityfair.com/news/2016/08/peter-thiel-wants-to-inject-himself-with-young-peoples-blood.
**8** Thiels Unternehmen lassen oft Bezüge zu Tolkiens Büchern erkennen. Neben Palantir Technologies gibt es noch Rivendell One LLC, Lembas Capital LLC, Valar Ventures LP und Mithril Capital Management LLC. Siehe Maria Bustillos, „Peter Thiel Isn't a Supervillain", in: *New York Magazine*, 27. Mai 2016, https://nymag.com/intelligencer/2016/05/peter-thiels-familiar-villainy.html.
**9** Martina Minas-Nerpel, „A Demotic Inscribed Icosahedron from Dakhleh Oasis", in: *Journal of Egyptian Archaeology*, Bd. 93, 2007, S. 137–148.
**10** Ibid.
**11** Richard Barbrook und Andy Cameron, op. cit.
**12** Ian Bogost, „The Cathedral of Computation", in: *The Atlantic*, 15. Januar 2015, https://www.theatlantic.com/technology/archive/2015/01/the-cathedral-of-computation/384300.
**13** Eliot Noyes, der Designchef von IBM, war vom Bauhaus beeinflusst und fungierte bei Kubricks Film als technischer Berater. Siehe John Harwood, *The Interface: IBM and the Transformation of Corporate Design, 1945–1976*, Minneapolis 2016, S. 158.
**14** In Philip K. Dicks Roman *Do Androids Dream of Electric Sheep?*, der Vorlage für *Blade Runner*, werden die Android*innen als „Leibdiener oder unermüdliche Feldarbeiter" aus den „herrlichen Zeiten der Südstaaten vor dem Bürgerkrieg" beworben. Philip K. Dick, *Blade Runner. Träumen Roboter von elektrischen Schafen?*, Frankfurt am Main 2019, S. 14.
**15** Clarkes häufig zitierte „drei Gesetze" legen die Beziehung zwischen Prognose und Technologie frei: 1. „Wenn ein ausgezeichneter, aber ältlicher Wissenschaftler erklärt, etwas sei möglich, so hat er fast immer recht. Wenn er erklärt, etwas sei unmöglich, so irrt er sich mit großer Wahrscheinlichkeit." 2. „[Die] einzige Möglichkeit, die Grenzen des Möglichen zu entdecken, ist, sich über diese hinaus ein Stück ins Unmögliche zu wagen." 3. „Jede weit genug entwickelte Technologie ist von Magie nicht zu unterscheiden." Arthur C. Clarke, *Profile der Zukunft: Über die Grenzen des Möglichen*, München 1984, S. 30, S. 26 und S. 37.
**16** Julia Angwin, Jeff Larson, Surya Mattu und Lauren Kirchner, „Machine Bias", in: *ProPublica*, 23. Mai 2016, https://www.propublica.org/article/machine-bias-risk-assessments-in-criminal-sentencing.
**17** Piotr Hrebieniuk, „The Palantír: Revelation-Driven Product Management", in: *Medium*, 30. Mai 2020, https://medium.com/isengard-of-product-management/the-palantir-revelation-driven-product-management-d384c783e5b.
**18** Pasi Väliaho, *Biopolitical Screens: Image, Power, and the Neoliberal Brain*, Cambridge, MA 2014, S. 51; übersetzt aus dem Englischen von Bert Rebhandl.
**19** Franco „Bifo" Berardi, *After the Future*, Oakland, CA. 2011, S. 25; übersetzt aus dem Englischen von Bert Rebhandl.
**20** Ibid., S. 18.
**21** Douglas Rushkoff, „How Tech's Richest Plan to Save Themselves after the Apocalypse", in: *The Guardian*, 24. Juli 2018, https://www.theguardian.com/technology/2018/jul/tech-industry-wealth-futurism-transhumanism-singularity.



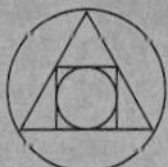

# Als der Echsenkönig dem Echsenhirn begegnete: *The Doors*

Pamela M. Lee

## Feier der Echse

Im Garten ist die Echse König.

*Barbaturex morrisoni* lautet der lateinische Name für ein riesiges pflanzenfressendes Lebewesen, das vor rund vierzig Millionen Jahren den Planeten bevölkerte. In Zach Blas' Multimedia-Environment *The Doors* (2019) – ein mystischer, künstlicher Garten, der mit seinen fremdartigen Bildern, Klängen, Symbolen und Objekten die Sinne überflutet – hat diese urtümliche Echse als funkelnde Matrix aus Pixeln überlebt und schreitet über die Bildschirme einer Sechskanal-Videoinstallation. In fünf Sequenzen huscht die Echse, jagt, rastet, atmet kurz und flach. Ihre Augen blitzen, ihr Kiefer bläht sich auf, ihr Schwanz schnellt. Die Echse erbricht sich; sie häutet sich, glitzert dann wie neugeboren. Der stahlblaue Rücken der Kreatur besteht aus kristallinen, fraktalartigen Artefakten, während die schimmernden Schuppen sich in die unsichtbare Architektur eines Rasters einfügen. Als Begleitung auf der Klangebene rezitiert eine von künstlicher Intelligenz erzeugte Stimme in einem schwermütigen Bariton fragmenthafte Gedichte. In Blas' Welt verkörpert die Echse ebenso komplementäre wie entgegengesetzte Kräfte in den Reichen des Alten und des Technologischen, des Digitalen und des Organischen, des Gegenkulturellen und des Kommerziellen, des Neuen und des Nostalgischen. Nicht umsonst ist dieses prächtige Tier nach Jim Morrison benannt, dem Dichterbarden und Frontsänger der legendären Rockband der 1960er, The Doors.

Jim Morrison, der Lizard King, der Echsenkönig: Wie verstehen wir die schattenhafte Anwesenheit des Sängers in einer Arbeit, die so dichte Erfahrungen bietet, die konzeptuell so vielschichtig und technisch so aufwendig ist wie Blas' *The Doors*? Aufbauend auf einem Gerüst aus Mehrkanal-Video, 7.1-Surround-Sound und Machine-Learning-Software, scheint die Arbeit radikal entfernt von den bacchantischen Landstrichen, die Morrison zu seinen Hochzeiten bewohnte, sei es die Rive Gauche oder der Laurel Canyon. Morrison, ein dunkler schlangenartiger Romantiker, der sich in Leder und Reptilienhaut kleidete – ein wechselweise dem Untergang geweihter und ekstatischer Hippie – hatte kein ersichtliches Interesse an Technik. Im Gegenteil, er verlieh dem nichtmenschlichen Tier als Figur des Künstler-Exzesses eine Stimme. In seinem Langgedicht „The Celebration of the Lizard", das er in Sprachperformances rezitierte, sagt Morrison von sich: „I am the Lizard King / I can do anything."[1] Das Couplet mag sich heute wie ein Klischee lesen – vermeintlich ebenso abgegriffen wie die Figur des weißen männlichen Rockstars, der sich durch Alkohol und Drogen aufbläst und letztlich von ihnen umgebracht wird.

Diese Zeilen sind jedoch eine Schlüsselreferenz für das Verständnis von Blas' poetischen Interventionen, die wir ernst nehmen sollten, um die Frage stellen zu können: Worüber und wie herrscht die Echse in Blas' Garten? Wie verstehen wir die Begriffe hinter der mysteriösen Hypothese, die der Titel dieses Essays aufstellt: „Als der Echsenkönig dem Echsenhirn begegnete"? Welche Geschichten stehen hinter diesen Verbindungen – und welche Zukünfte können diese komplexen und vernetzten Phänomene darstellen oder entwerfen?

*Barbaturex morrisoni* wird tatsächlich seine souveräne Herrschaft über eine untergründige Ökologie ausüben, die die Gegenkultur der 1960er Jahre mit dem Silicon Valley von heute verbindet. Blas bietet ein Mengendiagramm von „Technologien des Geistes" als das Grundprinzip von *The Doors*, das Psychedelik, künstliche Intelligenz und das zeitgenössische Phänomen der nootropischen Pharmakologie umfasst – so genannte Smart Drugs und Nahrungsergänzungsmittel, die die kognitive Leistung der ständig abgelenkten Massen von heute verbessern sollen. *The Doors* bezieht sich auf diese Verbindungen jedoch nicht nur als historistisches *Fait accompli*, als bloß eine weitere desillusionierende Episode der Vereinnahmung sozialer Überschreitung als profitables Produkt. Indem sie diese eng verwobenen Verbindungen aufdeckt, hinterfragt die Arbeit kritisch die Formen, in denen die Digitalkultur das Ethos der 1960er im Dienste eines vorherrschenden Neoliberalismus appropriiert hat, der nicht nur für Computer-Arbeiter*innen zentral ist, sondern für alle, die als prekäre Arbeitskraft einen Konkurrenzvorteil anstreben. Als Teil von Blas' Trilogie „queerer Science-Fiction"[2] – Arbeiten, die sich mit den Fantasien und den Glaubenssystemen des Silicon Valley und der IT-Elite beschäftigen – eröffnet *The Doors* darüber hinaus die Möglichkeit, diesen Kräften einen Raum abzuringen, der jenseits der Kontrolle, des Managements, der Automatisierung und der *Leistungsfähigkeit* des Geistes als auszubeutender kreativer Ressource besteht.

Der vorliegende Essay folgt den Spuren der Echse rund um solche den Geist erweiternden Techniken. Um diese Reise zu beginnen, kehren wir zunächst in den Garten zurück und erfassen seine unzähligen Artefakte, Medien und Akteur*innen. Im Anschluss werden wir die miteinander verwobenen Narrative um Nachkriegs-Psychedelik, Neurowissenschaft und Computertechnologie rund fünfzig Jahre vor Blas' aktueller Intervention entwirren. Die scheinbar widersprüchlichen Geschichten, die diese Vergangenheit prägen, tragen zum Aufkommen der Nootropika in der Gegenwart bei – eine Klasse von nicht als Betäubungsmittel eingestuften Medikamenten zur Steigerung der kognitiven Leistungsfähigkeit in einem zunehmend darwinistischen Markt. All dies wird uns zu der Frage führen: Was ist historisch geschehen – und was mag sich einst noch ergeben –, als der Echsenkönig dem Echsenhirn begegnete?

## Eintritt in den Garten

*Barbaturex morrisoni* mag als Morrisons Ersatz-Avatar über den Garten herrschen, doch er ist nur einer von vielen Akteur*innen, die Blas für seine psychedelische Weltkonstruktion in Dienst genommen hat. In *The Doors* begegnen wir einer Reihe von wiederkehrenden Elementen – auditiven, visuellen, somatischen –, die jede der fünf Sequenzen der Arbeit durchlaufen und dabei mehrdeutige Perspektiven zwischen Vergangenheit, Gegenwart und Zukunft entwerfen. Einerseits beschwört die Arbeit die ozeanische Atmosphäre eines guten psychedelischen Trips mit all den ihn begleitenden Zeichen des Kosmischen und Göttlichen wie auch den sich windenden, die Zeit krümmenden Verzerrungen, die mit diesen Reisen oft verbunden sind. Auf der anderen Seite setzt die Arbeit, die durch den Rückgriff auf die KI die unheimlichen Aussichten auf das posthumane Leben nachzeichnet, eine zukunftsorientierte Dimension voraus, die spekulativer Fiktion gleichkommt. In grünes Licht getaucht und mit mysteriösen Symbolen geschmückt, strahlt



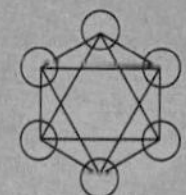

der Garten einen Hauch Mystik aus, während er zugleich an die Lichtshows der 1960er Jahre ebenso wie an die künstlichen Landschaften der Tech-Komplexe des Silicon Valley erinnert – mit ihrer Architektur der grünen Wände und transparenten Oberflächen. Anders gesagt: nicht gerade der Garten Eden. Blas' Version gleicht eher einem privaten Inselparadies, einer Traumlandschaft, deren Vorzüge sie wie so viele esoterische Geheimnisse schützt.

Die fünf audiovisuellen Sequenzen von *The Doors* folgen der Echse, die zunächst Psychedelika in diesen „privatisierten Garten" bringt; sie präsentieren die Möglichkeiten der Nootropika als „Hirnnahrung"; sie behandeln den Garten als luxuriöses Spa-Refugium (nebenbei sei bemerkt, dass einige Nootropika schlaffördernd sind); sie

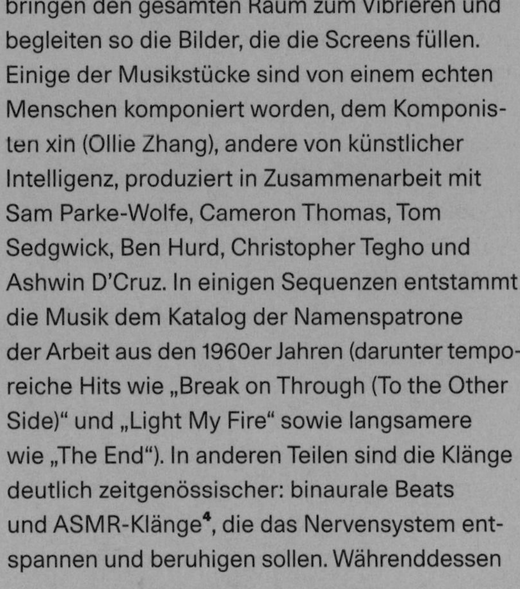

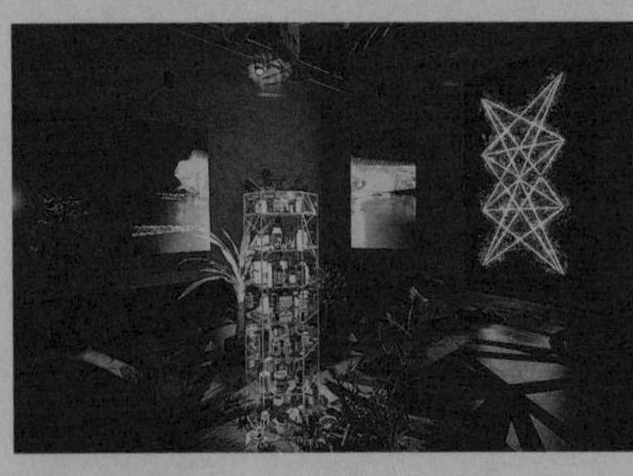

▸ S. 195

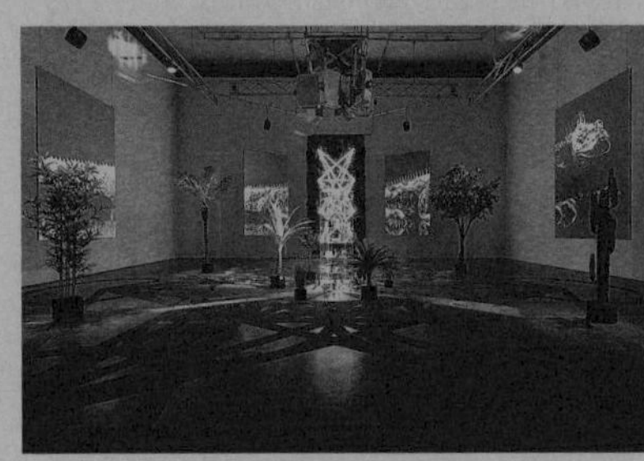

▸ S. 196–97

folgen der Echse, während sie von einem unsichtbaren Räuber gejagt wird; und sie setzen die Betrachtenden schließlich dem aus, was Blas in Anspielung an die LSD-Erfahrung den „Ich-Tod"[3] nennt. Um die Entwicklung der Arbeit zu verstehen, bedarf es der Analyse der zahlreichen Inhalte des Gartens, die sich vorläufig in drei sich überschneidende Kategorien einteilen lassen: Klang, Sehen und Geist-Körper. Jede von ihnen korrespondiert mit einer besonderen Eigenschaft von Blas' Arbeit und spricht ein anderes Register des Sinnesapparats an; jede Kategorie arbeitet im Einklang mit den anderen, um einen von Reizen überfluteten Garten zu schaffen.

Tatsächlich hören wir den Garten ebenso sehr, wie wir ihn sehen: Musik und deklamierte Dichtung hüllen uns in einen Kokon. Von künstlicher Intelligenz generierte Klänge bringen den gesamten Raum zum Vibrieren und begleiten so die Bilder, die die Screens füllen. Einige der Musikstücke sind von einem echten Menschen komponiert worden, dem Komponisten xin (Ollie Zhang), andere von künstlicher Intelligenz, produziert in Zusammenarbeit mit Sam Parke-Wolfe, Cameron Thomas, Tom Sedgwick, Ben Hurd, Christopher Tegho und Ashwin D'Cruz. In einigen Sequenzen entstammt die Musik dem Katalog der Namenspatrone der Arbeit aus den 1960er Jahren (darunter temporeiche Hits wie „Break on Through (To the Other Side)" und „Light My Fire" sowie langsamere wie „The End"). In anderen Teilen sind die Klänge deutlich zeitgenössischer: binaurale Beats und ASMR-Klänge[4], die das Nervensystem entspannen und beruhigen sollen. Währenddessen spricht eine schwach metallische Stimme zu uns, erzeugt von einem neuronalen Netzwerk, das auf Grundlage von Morrisons berühmter niedriger Stimmlage und seinem Grölen trainiert wurde. Das ausgewählte Genre ist Dichtung. Morrison, der in seinem kurzen Leben vier Gedichtbände veröffentlicht hat, zählte William Blake und Arthur Rimbaud zu seinen Helden, und das Tempo, die Kadenz und die beinahe beschwörende Wirkung von Blas' kombinatorischer Dichtung ist eine Hommage an diese literarische Seite des Echsenkönigs.[5] Doch auch wenn sie im Wesentlichen durch „The Celebration of the Lizard" und andere Gedichte Morrisons inspiriert sind, versetzen uns die Worte der Arbeit bei näherem Zuhören in die Gegenwart des Publikums. Denn während ein Großteil des Inhalts dadurch entstanden ist, dass ein neuronales

Netzwerk anhand verschiedener Bilddatenbestände trainiert wurde – darunter auch, ganz im Sinne von Morrisons legendären Abenteuern mit Betäubungsmitteln, LSD-Blotter-Kunst –, berücksichtigt dieses Netzwerk auch die kommerzielle Literatur über zeitgenössische Nootropika. Werbung, Geschäftsphilosophien sowie Aufzählungen ihrer Inhaltsstoffe und Beschreibungen ihrer Wirkungen auf das Nervensystem sind eine stillschweigende Entgegnung auf das souveräne Dekret des Echsenkönigs: *Ich kann alles machen*.

Die zunehmende Bedeutung von Nootropika in der heutigen Werbewirtschaft stellt die entscheidende Veränderung im Gegensatz zur früheren psychedelischen Weltanschauung dar, eine Genealogie, der ich mich sogleich

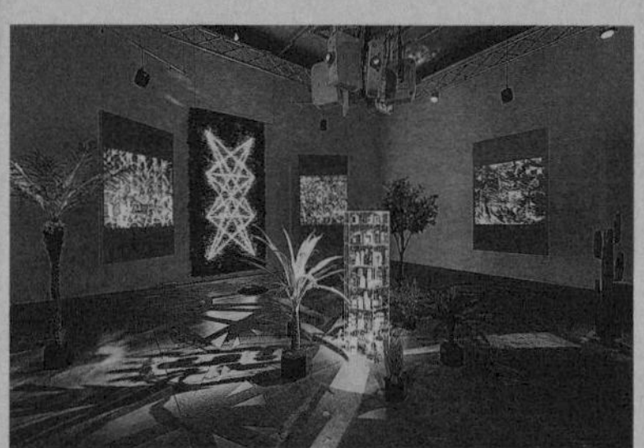

▸ S. 198–99

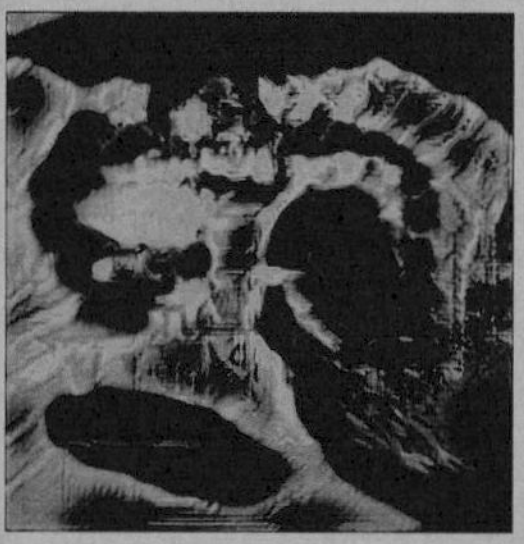

▸ S. 200

zuwenden werde. Zunächst jedoch müssen wir uns mit dem zweiten und dritten Element von Blas' Garten befassen – den Kategorien des Sehens und des Geist-Körpers –, die in Form von Videos und quasisymbolischen Bildern sowie verschiedenen Objekten im Zentrum des Gartens gezeigt werden. Abwechselnd mit dem Video der Echse gleiten abstrakte Bilder über die sechs schwarz spiegelnden Screens und schaffen ein kaleidoskopisches Gehege. Blas nutzt hierfür ein Generative Adversarial Network (GAN, „erzeugendes gegnerisches Netzwerk"), das durch zehntausende Bilder konditioniert wurde, darunter LSD-Blotter-Kunst, klassische kalifornische Psychedelik aus den 1960er Jahren (Rock-Poster und Ähnliches), Tabletten, medizinische Abbildungen des Gehirns, Diagramme neuronaler Netzwerke, zersplittertes Glas und so weiter. Daraus entstehen bunte, abstrakte Bilder, die ineinander übergehen und sich verzerren, eine Welle nach der anderen, und an jenseitige und kosmische Landschaften erinnern: fremdartig und erhaben.

Andere im Raum verteilte Zeichen und Bilder beschwören eine spirituelle oder okkulte Grundhaltung herauf. An einer Wand zwischen den Videoscreens strahlt ein grelles Grün von Neonröhren in der Form eines Diagramms eines neuronalen Netzwerks aus, das hier umgestaltet wurde, um an ein göttliches Symbol zu erinnern, wie eine in rituellem Rahmen erhabene Ikone. Wie um die Ikonografie von Verbundenheit und Einheit zu spiegeln, basiert ein auf den Boden aufgebrachtes hexagonales Muster auf einem Metatron-Würfel, einem Symbol der heiligen Geometrie, das Energieströme durch das Universum versinnbildlicht und später für die Vermarktung von Nootropika vereinnahmt wurde. Eine Gruppe von mysteriösen Objekten und Artefakten ist im Raum installiert, die sich auf die Verbindung von Geist und Körper beziehen. Ein schwarzer Sandhaufen lässt mitsamt erhitztem Stein und Wasserschale an den Thron – oder auch einen Altar – des Echsenkönigs denken. Eine eklektische Sammlung von Pflanzen trägt Arten von so weit entfernten Orten wie Kalifornien, Hawaii und Myanmar zusammen, wobei Letzteres die ursprüngliche Heimat der ausgestorbenen Art *Barbaturex morrisoni* ist. Im Zentrum des Ganzen steht schließlich eine sechseckige Vitrine, deren Geometrie die des Metatron-Würfels aufgreift. Darin ist ein großes Sortiment von Nootropika als sogenannter „Stack" (Stapel) ausgestellt, ein Begriff der Nootropika-Enthusiasten für das



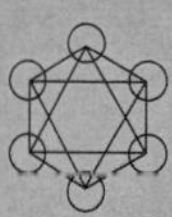

spezifische Dosierungsschema von Tabletten, die ein Individuum im Dienste der „Neuro-Verbesserung“ einnimmt.

Kurzum, der Garten von *The Doors* ist zugleich Tempel, Privatinsel (man denke an die territorialen Ambitionen des Silicon-Valley-Investors Peter Thiel), digitale Phantasmagorie, halluzinogenes Gesamtkunstwerk wie nootropische Agora. Wie also finden wir uns darin zurecht, wie begründen wir Koordinaten in dem riesigen Netzwerk, das Blas vor uns ausgebreitet hat? Ist es eine Utopie, eine Dystopie oder irgendetwas dazwischen?

Um uns diesen Fragen zu nähern, folgen wir der Echse zurück in die Zeit.

## Ungefähr 1969: Die Echse im Winter

Wir haben gesehen, wie Blas' Arbeit zwischen Vergangenheit und Gegenwart oszilliert und die historischen und zeitgenössischen Referenzen beinahe bis zur Untrennbarkeit miteinander verwebt. Blitzartig bewegt sich *The Doors* zwischen der Zeit der gleichnamigen Rockband und der heutigen Kultur der Technologien des Geistes, als wäre die Arbeit in einem Zustand der aufgehobenen Wahrnehmung gefangen. Die Bilder changieren zwischen Psychedelik alter Schule und aktueller Neurowissenschaft, während eine ausgestorbene Echse als Avatar der technischen Innovation wiederkehrt. Derweil verschmilzt der volle Klang des klassischen Rock – mit seinen analogen Instrumenten – mit den Tönen und Klicks digitaler Modulation und binauralen Beats. Um eine Brücke über diese zeitlichen und symbolischen Klüfte zu schlagen, bedarf es der Arbeit einer „Geschichte im Kleinen“, die zwischen der Populärkultur und den Narrativen des Geistes angesiedelt ist. Die Betrachtenden müssen einen rückwärts wie vorwärts gewandten Blick auf echsenähnliche Phänomene in der Vergangenheit, der Gegenwart und schließlich auch der Zukunft werfen.

Hierfür wird das Jahr 1969 als der zeitliche Wendepunkt dienen, um den sich diese Geschichten drehen. In vielerlei Hinsicht war es eine dunkle Zeit; wir werden dieses Jahr die „Echse im Winter“ nennen. Damals durchlebten die Doors als Band ihre bitterste Prüfung, die Morrisons Tod in Paris zwei Jahre später vorausahnen ließ. Natürlich war ihr Absturz ebenso steil, wie ihr Aufstieg kometenhaft gewesen war, beides auf spektakuläre Weise mit der erotischen Figur Morrisons und seiner Reputation für hedonistische Hemmungslosigkeit verknüpft. 1965 von Morrison, Ray Manzarek (Keyboard), Robby Krieger (Gitarre) und John Densmore (Schlagzeug) in Los Angeles gegründet, entlieh die Gruppe ihren Namen Aldous Huxleys Buch *The Doors of Perception* (dt.: *Die Pforten der Wahrnehmung*) aus dem Jahr 1954, einem plastisch verfassten Bericht über die Untersuchungen des Engländers Huxley über die Wirkung von Meskalin auf sein Bewusstsein. Die Einnahme des psychotropen Wirkstoffs konnte, so Huxley, „meinen Bewußtseinszustand so verändern [...], daß ich in die Lage versetzt würde, in meinem Inneren selbst die Erfahrung zu machen, von der der Visionär, das Medium, ja sogar der Mystiker berichten“[6]. Einer dieser Visionäre, die Huxley anführte, war William Blake, dessen Formulierung „Würden die Pforten der Wahrnehmung gereinigt...“ auf dem Vorsatz zu Huxleys berühmtestem Buch erschien sowie als dessen Titel diente. Die Band verkürzte Huxleys Titel, um sich ihren eigenen Namen zu schaffen – ein Aufruf zur psychedelischen Befreiung.

Nach dem 1. März 1969 jedoch schlossen sich diese befreienden Pforten schnell, als sich das ereignete, was die Fans der Doors beschämt den „Miami-Vorfall“ nennen. Bei einem Konzert im Dinner Key Auditorium im Stadtviertel Coconut Grove überschritt Morrison die Grenzen seiner bereits provokativen Bühnenpersönlichkeit, als er betrunken, aggressiv, pöbelnd und über eine Stunde verspätet eintraf. Nachdem er mit den Liedtexten gekämpft und Songs wiederholt abgebrochen hatte, legte Morrison noch einmal nach, indem er sich vor dem Publikum angeblich entblößte. In einer der prägendsten Belastungsprüfungen in der Geschichte der Gegenkultur wurde Morrison festgenommen und später wegen Exhibitionismus angeklagt, während der Großteil der Presse ihn beschuldigte, die amerikanische Jugend zu verderben. Das Ereignis hatte für die Band katastrophale Folgen und führte zu endlosen Rechtsproblemen, dramatischen Einnahmeverlusten, reihenweisen Absagen und für Morrison schließlich zur Verurteilung, deren Berufung zum Zeitpunkt seines Todes im Juli 1971 immer noch anhängig war. Der Vorfall von Miami signalisierte in der Tat das Ende für den legendären Dichter-Sänger.

Nur wenige Wochen vor dem Konzert der Doors in Coconut Grove erlangten Echsen auf

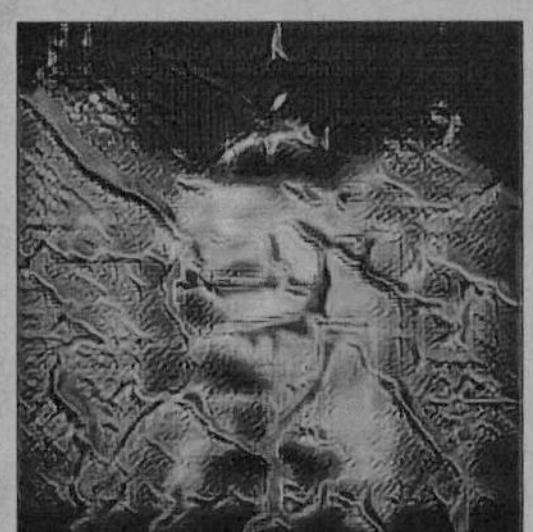

▸ S. 202

weit von Konzerthallen und Gefängniszellen entfernten Schauplätzen ganz andere Assoziationen. Der Echsenkönig, Morrisons majestätischer Avatar, feierte und erkundete die äußersten Grenzen von Geist und Körper, Bild und Ton. Nicht überall jedoch wurde die Verbindung zwischen Echse und Bewusstsein auf dieselbe Weise gesehen. An der Queen's University im kanadischen Ontario zum Beispiel war Dr. Paul D. MacLean zu einer Vortragsreihe über die neuesten Forschungen in der Neurowissenschaft eingeladen. Als Leiter des „Labors für Entwicklung und Verhalten des Geistes" am Nationalen Institut für Psychische Gesundheit in Washington, D.C., konzipierte er ein neues Modell des Gehirns, das auf vergleichender Neuroanatomie basierte und die Grenzen zwischen menschlichen und nichtmenschlichen Tieren durchkreuzte: das von ihm so genannte „dreieinige Gehirn" (triune brain). MacLean erläuterte: „In seiner Evolution erweitert sich das menschliche Gehirn entlang dreier Prototypen, für die ich die Begriffe ‚reptilisch', ‚paläomammalisch' und ‚neomammalisch' verwende."[7] Diese drei „Zerebrotypen", betonte er, sind nicht autonom, sondern werden als „ineinandergreifend und zusammenwirkend" verstanden. MacLean identifizierte die Basalganglien als den reptilischen Komplex – den er auch das Echsenhirn, das Reptilhirn oder den R-Komplex nannte: den primitivsten Akteur in der dreieinigen Ordnung. Das Echsenhirn ist verantwortlich für die niederen Instinkte der Aggression, Dominanz, Territorialität und des Überlebens; es ist geprägt durch uralte Erinnerungen und angestammtes Wissen. Während Morrisons Echsenkönig danach strebte, sein

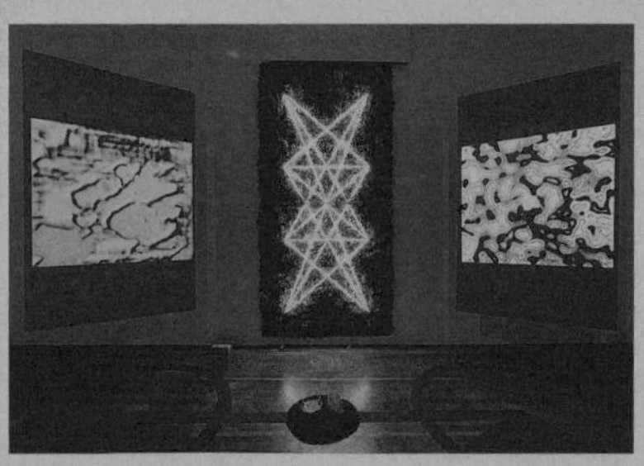

▸ S. 207

Hirn nach außen zu erweitern, verwies MacLeans Modell das Echsenhirn auf die primitivste Ebene des menschlichen Bewusstseins.

Wir werden noch sehen, wie der Begriff „Echsenhirn" Jahrzehnte später von der Politik, der Markenbildung für Nootropika, dem Business Marketing und den Diskussionen über die Leistungsfähigkeit am Arbeitsplatz aufgegriffen wurde, um als reaktionär, langweilig und rückständig erachtete Geisteszustände zu charakterisieren, auch wenn MacLeans „dreieiniges Gehirn" von der Wissenschaft inzwischen weitgehend diskreditiert wurde. 1969 und in den folgenden Jahren aber galt MacLeans Arbeit als bahnbrechende Forschung.[8] Auch wenn die dreieinige Echse keine der romantischen oder bewusstseinserweiternden Eigenschaften von Morrisons königlichem Reptil aufweist, muss dennoch



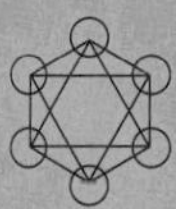

betont werden, dass diese beiden verschiedenen reptilischen Figuren – die eine neurowissenschaftlich, die andere gegenkulturell – sich in ihrer Berufung auf atavistische oder primitive Seinszustände jenseits der üblichen Beschränkungen der menschlichen Vernunft und Rationalität, Logik und Wahrnehmung überschneiden. Insofern könnte das Echsenhirn vielleicht tatsächlich vom Echsenkönig rekrutiert – wenn nicht sogar *erobert* – werden, um für eine andere Weise der Aufklärung in Dienst gestellt zu werden, die die Pforten der kollektiven Wahrnehmung für andere Welten öffnet. Blas' Garten, so würde ich behaupten, bereitet die Bühne – oder vielmehr deren Grenze – für diese Begegnung.

Die Art und Weise, wie diese beiden Positionen – das erweiterte und das niedere Hirn; das psychedelische Reich des Hippies und die klinische Welt des Wissenschaftlers – zusammenlaufen, führt uns zu unserer nächsten Vignette aus jener Zeit. Im Jahr 1969, so ist festzuhalten, gab es in den Universitätslaboren, den pharmazeutischen Unternehmen oder den Forschungseinrichtungen mit ihren weißen Kitteln keinen Platz für LSD, Meskalin, Psilocybin, Ayahuasca oder sonstige psychotrope Wirkstoffe. Mit anderen Worten, sie waren in dem wissenschaftlichen Metier von Figuren wie MacLean nicht vorgesehen. Die „Pforten der Wahrnehmung" waren zu diesem Zeitpunkt vielmehr unlösbar mit der Gegenkultur verbunden und mit all dem, was dieser Begriff in Bezug auf gesellschaftliche Unruhen und massenhafte Überschreitung heraufbeschwor. Nach der Entdeckung und Synthese des LSD (Lysergsäurediethylamid) durch den Chemiker Albert Hofmann im Jahr 1938 hatten Wissenschaftler*innen und Psychiater*innen mit der Untersuchung des therapeutischen Einsatzes dieser Drogen für die Behandlung einer Reihe psychischer Störungen begonnen. Nach Jahrzehnten der Forschung starb das Studium der Psychedelika Ende der 1960er Jahre einen institutionellen Tod: 1967 stufte die US-amerikanische Food and Drug Administration LSD als „nicht verkehrsfähige", sprich verbotene Droge ein. Die Konsensmeinung unter den ehemaligen Forschenden dieser Zeit schiebt die Schuld für diese Wendung der Ereignisse auf den Autor und Psychologen Timothy Leary, dessen berüchtigte psychiatrische Kapriolen an der Harvard University Anfang der 1960er Jahre, so etwa die testweise Verabreichung von LSD an seine Studierenden/Forschungsobjekte, 1963 zu seiner Entlassung führten.[9] Inspiriert durch Huxleys Beispiel ein Jahrzehnt zuvor nahm Leary die Rolle des psychonautischen Gurus und Medienlieblings der Gegenkultur an. Sein berühmtes Mantra „Turn on, Tune in, Drop out" sollte zu einem Schlachtruf der gegenkulturellen Generation werden.

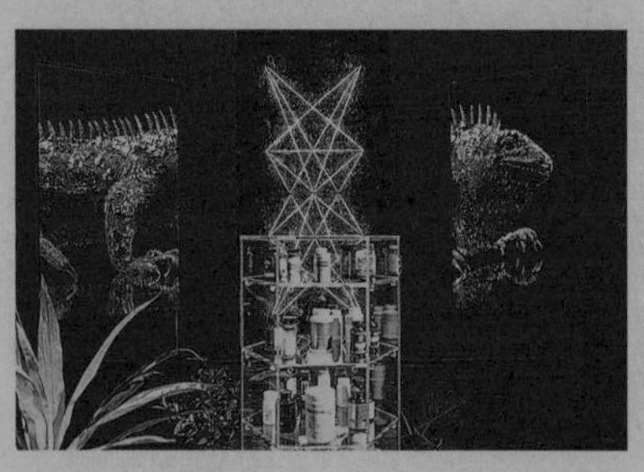

▸ S. 208

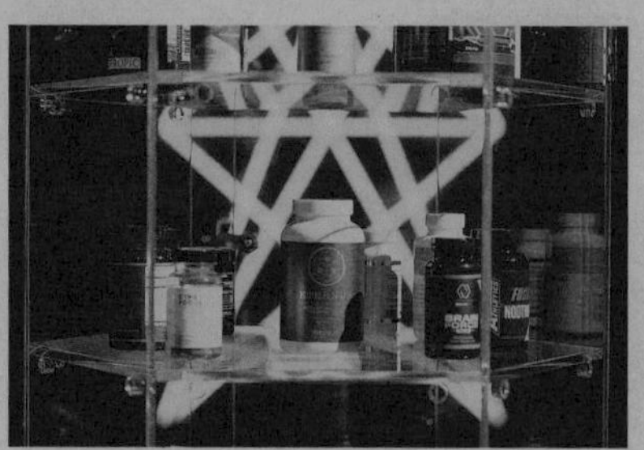

▸ S. 209

MacLeans neurowissenschaftliche Untersuchungen beruhten eher wenig auf der Wirkung von Psychedelika, sei es als Studienobjekt oder als Mittel der Aufklärung. Sein dreieiniges Gehirn – mit der Echse im Zentrum – war vielmehr einem anderen Genre der geisterweiternden Technologie nachgebildet. Die miteinander verwobenen und voneinander abhängigen Funktionen dieses Tierhirns fanden in einem Vortrag, den er im Februar 1969 hielt, ein starkes Gegenstück.

„In der populären Sprache von heute", erklärte er, „könnte man sich diese drei Gehirne als biologische Computer denken, jeder mit seiner eigenen speziellen Form der Subjektivität und seiner eigenen Intelligenz, seinem eigenen Sinn für Zeit und Raum und seinem eigenen Gedächtnis, Antrieb und sonstigen Funktionen."[10]

Das Gehirn als Computer zu verstehen – als Maschine, die mittels Intelligenz, Zeit, Raum, Antrieb und Erinnerung Informationen verarbeitet –, war 1969 ein allgegenwärtiger Tropus. Nach den Revolutionen in der Kybernetik und der Informationstheorie in der Nachkriegszeit wurden Gehirne von Tieren und digitale Computer als isomorph behandelt. Entscheidend ist, dass diese Dynamik zwischen Mensch und Maschine als reziprok verstanden wurde. Denn wenn ein Gehirn wie eine Maschine strukturiert ist, warum sollte im Umkehrschluss eine Maschine nicht wie ein Gehirn denken können – oder genauer, trainiert werden, wie ein solches zu denken? 1943 beschrieben der Neurophysiologe Warren McCulloch und der Computer-Neurowissenschaftler Walter Pitts solche Möglichkeiten als „neurologisches Netzwerk" – die erste Aussage über künstliche Intelligenz und das „neuronale Netzwerk".[11]

So wie LSD im Kalten Krieg als mögliches Wahrheitsserum untersucht wurde, förderten auch verschiedene Bereiche des Militärs verbreitet die Perspektive, die KI-Technik für derartige Zwecke einzusetzen. Gegen Ende der 1960er Jahre jedoch waren die Fortschritte in der künstlichen Intelligenz denselben institutionellen Schicksalsschlägen ausgesetzt wie die psychedelische Forschung – eine als „KI-Winter" bekannte Zeit, in der die institutionelle Unterstützung und das allgemeine Interesse an dieser neuen Disziplin brachlagen, größtenteils aufgrund des Entzugs von finanziellen Mitteln sowie neuen Regulierungen über die Vergabe von Forschungsgeldern. Doch auch wenn die Forschung und Entwicklung zu künstlicher Intelligenz Ende der 1960er, Anfang der 1970er Jahre auf Eis gelegt war, machten sich einige der einflussreichsten Computerwissenschaftler dieser Zeit daran, ihre eigenen Technologien des Geistes zu erkunden, sowohl vor wie nach 1969. Der Wissenschaftsjournalist Michael Pollan beschreibt, wie Al Hubbard, der „Johnny Appleseed des LSD", Mitte der 1950er Jahre die Commission for the Study of Creative Imagination gründete und durch sie „weitgespannte psychedelische Netzwerke" schuf. Zu seinen psychedelischen Bundesgenossen zählten Silicon-Valley-Größen wie Myron Stolaroff von der Firma Ampex, eines der ersten Tech-Unternehmen, die im Valley gegründet wurden, sowie Douglas Engelbart, der später die Computermaus erfand.[12]

Wie sollen wir diese verschlungenen Geschichten bewerten, auf die Blas' *The Doors* stillschweigend hinweist? Der Technokultur- und Kommunikationsforscher Fred Turner behauptet eindringlich die historische Kontinuität und die ideologischen Identitäten zwischen der Gegenkultur der 1960er und dem Silicon Valley. In seiner einflussreichen Studie *From Counterculture to Cyberculture. Stewart Brand, the Whole Earth Network, and the Rise of Digital Utopianism* zeichnet er akribisch nach, wie das Gemeinschaftsethos der Hippiekultur in Kalifornien, angeführt von dem Impresario Stewart Brand, die organisatorischen, ideologischen und unternehmerischen Interessen der Netzwerkgesellschaft vorwegnahm.[13] Weniger eindeutig bleibt bei solchen Interpretationen die Rolle, die die Psychedelik bei der Erweiterung der Beziehungen zwischen diesen verschiedenen Einflusssphären als Technologie gespielt haben mag. Eine der Errungenschaften von *The Doors* – also Blas' Garten – ist, wie er diese Geschichten offenlegt und ihre zeitgenössischen Implikationen vermittels einer neuen Technologie des Geistes aktualisiert: den Nootropika.

## 2019: Welche Echse, triumphierend?

Fünfzig Jahre nach dem KI-Winter, dem Vorfall von Miami und MacLeans Vorträgen über das



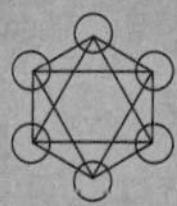

# 2019: Welche Echse, triumphierend?

Fünfzig Jahre nach dem KI-Winter, dem Vorfall von Miami und MacLeans Vorträgen über das dreieinige Gehirn trat Blas sein Arbeitsstipendium im Edith-Russ-Haus für Medienkunst an, wo er, gemeinsam mit vielen Mitarbeitenden, intensiv an *The Doors* arbeitete. In den Jahren zwischen 1969 und 2019 hätte es scheinen können, als wäre die Echse verschwunden – im Winterschlaf, wenn nicht ausgestorben. Morrison starb 1971. Die Gegenkultur der 1960er Jahre bereitete, wie Turner behauptet, den Weg für einen cyberkapitalistischen Markt. Einst in Universitäten und pharmazeutischen Laboren wegen seiner therapeutischen Möglichkeiten untersucht, wurde LSD verboten, was um einige wenige Jahrzehnte den amerikanischen „Krieg gegen die Drogen" vorausnahm.

Wie merkwürdig ist es also, dass eine Version der Echse sich erneut in die Medien und das kulturelle Bewusstsein eingeschlichen hat, unheimlich in seiner Wiederholung, im Licht der enorm veränderten Bedingungen der Gegenwart jedoch radikal transformiert. 1969 vermaß die Echse die drei Extrema: den Geist der Gegenkultur, ein vorzeitliches tierisches Gehirn und die stagnierenden Perspektiven der künstlichen Intelligenz. 2019 wird ihre Reinkarnation nun mit dem funkelnden hexagonalen Arsenal der Nootropika im Herzen von Blas' Installation „gefeiert", die die Artefakte wie heilige Reliquien bewahrt. In der Tat repräsentieren die heutigen Phänomene des Brainhacking, des Microdosing und der Nootropika – die Anwendung von Medikamenten, Kräutern und Ergänzungsmitteln mit Namen wie Gorilla Mind Smooth, Mind Lab Pro, Synapsa und zahllosen anderen – die nächste Welle der geisterweiternden Techniken, die der Werbung zufolge die kognitive Leistung steigern, das Gedächtnis verbessern, die Kreativität stimulieren und einen Energieschub bringen sollen. Letztlich werden diese Substanzen eingenommen, um über das Echsenhirn zu siegen, ein Begriff, der heutzutage nicht nur mehr nur einen urzeitlichen Zustand der Vernunft im Sinne MacLeans neurowissenschaftlicher Analyse meint, sondern etwas, das angesichts eines hyperkompetitiven, maskulinistischen und technikorientierten Marktes zu überwinden ist. Denn statt für Dichtende, Kunst- und Musikproduzierende wie die heutigen Morrisons und ihresgleichen geeignet zu sein, finden Nootropika ihre glühendsten Anhänger in den zwei (sich bisweilen überlappenden) Zielgruppen weißer Männer: IT-Alphatiere und rechte Randgruppen. Blas' Arbeit zeigt uns, wie Nootropika eine der möglichen Folgen des Vermächtnisses der Gegenkultur im Silicon Valley darstellen, wie es sich vor allem in der radikalen Ungleichheit der dortigen Arbeitskräfte zeigt, und in einem Augenblick in der Kultur im Allgemeinen, in dem Verschwörungstheorien über die Existenz von „Echsenmenschen", die die Positionen der Macht eingenommen haben, die Online-Foren der Alt-Right-Bewegung dominieren.[14] Zugleich richtet *The Doors* implizit auch die Frage an sein Publikum: Ist dies das einzige Ergebnis, ist es das unausweichliche Ergebnis für den Echsenkönig?

Es mag vielleicht nicht überraschen, dass das Konzept der Nootropika auf die frühen 1970er Jahre zurückgeht. Corneliu Giurgea, ein rumänischer Biochemiker, der für ein belgisches Pharmaunternehmen arbeitete, prägte den Begriff 1972, indem er die griechischen Wörter für „Verstand" und „Wendung oder Richtung" miteinander verband. Mit seiner Synthese eines Medikaments namens Piracetam scheint er sowohl die Sprache der Psychedelika assimiliert wie das evolutionäre Modell von MacLeans reptilischem Komplex internalisiert zu haben, was sich am deutlichsten in seiner Bemerkung zeigt, dass „der Mensch nicht Millionen von Jahren passiv abwarten wird, bis die Evolution ihm ein besseres Gehirn bereitstellt"[15]. In mancherlei Hinsicht nahm Giurgea den Faden auf, den die wissenschaftliche Forschung zu LSD, psychischer Gesundheit und psychiatrischen Erkrankungen

Ende der 1960er Jahre liegen gelassen hatte. Er suchte eine chemische Lösung, um die Leistungsfähigkeit des Gehirns zu optimieren und die später sogenannte „Neuroplastizität“ zu fördern und zu verbessern.

Natürlich bestehen zwischen Giurgeas Forschung und den früheren Studien, auf die er aufbaute, große Unterschiede, die zusammengenommen die Bewegung der Gegenkultur hin zum Markplatz des Neoliberalismus verzeichnen. So befasste sich etwa die wissenschaftliche Forschung zu LSD vor dem Verbot mit dem Potenzial der Droge zur Linderung von Depressionen, zu Alkoholismus, einer Vielzahl von Abhängigkeiten, geistigen Krankheiten, Demenz sowie einem ganzen Spektrum neurologischer Störungen. Bald nach dem Verbot von LSD fand

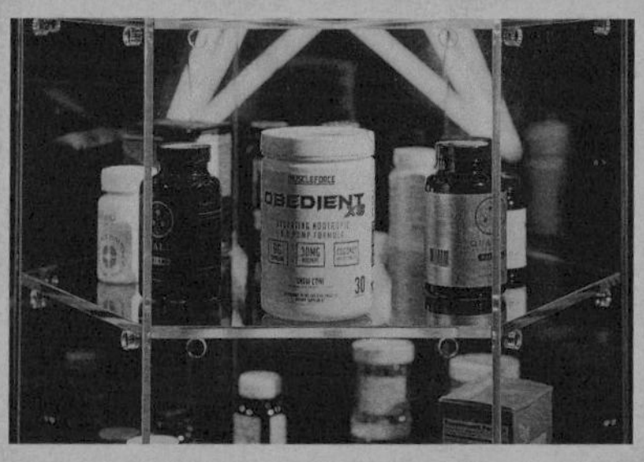


▸ S. 212

die Liaison der 1960er Jahre mit Psychotropika ihre Motivation in der Erweiterung des Bewusstseins in mystischer, kosmischer, experimenteller und befreiender Hinsicht, gepaart mit einem Ethos der Selbstverwirklichung. Die Nootropika von heute hingegen übernehmen und überhöhen zwar die *selbst*-verwirklichenden Tendenzen der früheren Generation, ansonsten aber nicht viel. Im Jahr 2019 könnte Learys Beschwörungsformel „Tune in, Turn on, Drop Out“ umgeschrieben werden als „Stay in, Switch on, Work More“. Die Verbreitung der Nootropika in der Kultur im Allgemeinen ist tatsächlich untrennbar mit dem Aufstieg des Silicon Valley verbunden. Zu Beginn der 1990er Jahre bildeten sich in den damals aufkeimenden Tech-Gemeinschaften von San Francisco sogenannte Smart Clubs, deren Mitglieder nootropische „Cocktails“ anboten und Bücher mit Titeln wie *Smart Drugs and Nutrients* verbreiteten.[16] Anfang bis Mitte der 2000er Jahre propagierten Nutzer*innen von Reddit und anderen Online-Communitys den Gebrauch von Nootropika, bis die internationalen Online-Verkäufe dieser Substanzen Bedenken bei den Aufsichtsbehörden aufkommen ließen. Popkulturelle Bezugnahmen ließen nicht lange auf sich warten, so etwa in dem mittelmäßigen Bradley-Cooper-Science-Fiction-Film mit dem Titel *Limitless* (2011, dt.: *Ohne Limit*), der auf Alan Glynns Buch *The Dark Fields* (dt.: *Stoff*) aus dem Jahr 2000 basiert.

Die Kunsthistorikerin Lucy Hunter bemerkt, dass die toxische Männlichkeit, die der Geschichte von *Limitless* zugrunde liegt, jene rechten Nootropika-Konsumenten vorzeichnete,

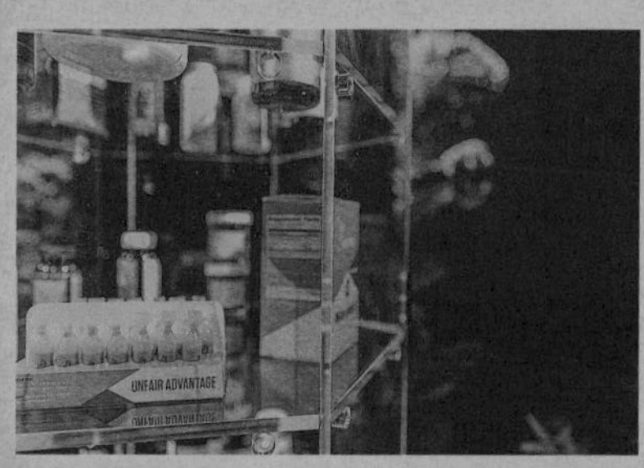


▸ S. 213

die später im selben Jahrzehnt an Bedeutung gewinnen sollten und die in jüngerer Zeit dazu übergegangen sind, diese Ersatzmittel, Kräuter und Pharmazeutika anzupreisen und zu vermarkten, während sie zugleich am Dogma der „Meritokratie“ festhalten.[17] Maskulinistische Macker mit Unternehmensgeist – von dem Podcast-Impresario Joe Rogan über Mike „Pizzagate“ Cernovich, Verschwörungstheoretiker und Medienfigur der Alt-Right-Bewegung, bis zum Autor und Podcaster Tim Ferriss – haben ihren eigenen Konsum von Nootropika beschrieben, sie auf ihren Webseiten vertrieben und im Endeffekt verkündet, dass sich mit ihnen das Echsenhirn überwinden ließe. Diese Substanzen sind das kognitive Gegenstück zu den Bodybuilder-Produkten, die manche derselben Personen ebenfalls feilbieten und konsumieren. Nootropika



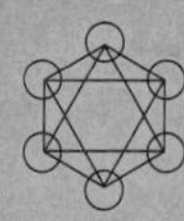

sind Instrumente der Selbstverbesserung, ein Weg zum Erfolg, Symbole der normativen Maskulinität. Wie der Journalist Richard Cooke in einem Artikel über die Verbindung der Nootropika mit dieser bestimmten Zielgruppe schreibt: „Wenn mit kollektivem Handeln, mit Regulierungen und der ausgleichenden Kraft des Staates nicht mehr zu rechnen ist, dann bleibt allein das Selbst, das sich der Macht dieser Kontrahenten entgegenstellen kann. Kein Wunder, dass ihm geholfen werden muss. Das System zu ändern wäre ein Sakrileg. Vielmehr muss es manipuliert werden."[18] Daher besetzen Nootropika noch einen weiteren Platz in einem größeren System, jenseits der maßgeschneiderten Stacks ihrer männlichen Anhängerschaft. Einzelne Gefolgsmänner der Alt-Right-Bewegung gehen viel-

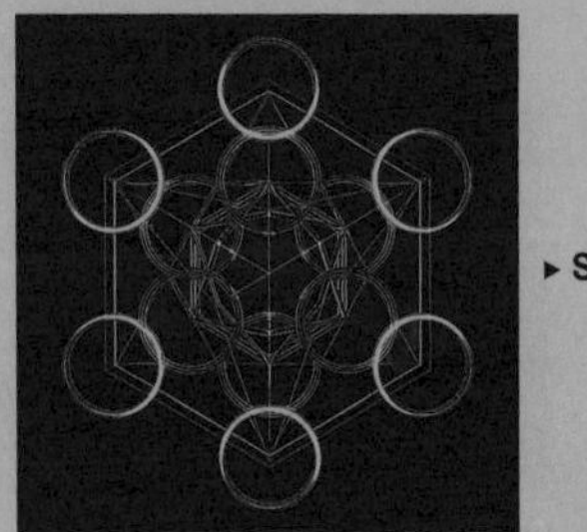

▸ S. 219

leicht enthusiastisch mit Pilzkaffee und Hirn-Boostern hausieren, sie befinden sich damit aber auch in finanzieller Gesellschaft mit der Tech-Industrie: Tatsächlich haben von Risikokapitalgebern finanzierte Start-ups versucht, den milliardenschweren Ergänzungsmittelmarkt, der von Schwergewichten alter Schule wie GNC repräsentiert wird, zu „sprengen".[19]

*The Doors* beschwört mit Blas' riesiger Sammlung von Objekten, Bildern, Klängen und Symbolen das Gespenst der maskulinistischen und finanziellen Ideale der Nootropika, bei denen die kognitive Leistungsfähigkeit im ökonomischen Sinne rationalisiert wird. Der evolutionäre und ursprüngliche Status des Echsenhirns wird hier vom Darwinismus des Marktes vernichtend geschlagen. Diese Tendenzen stehen im Dialog mit einer allgemeineren Praxis in der zeitgenössischen Kultur – dem Microdosing –, die ebenfalls mit dem habgierigen Ethos des Silicon Valley verbunden wurde. An einem Arbeitsplatz, dessen wichtigste Ressource die Innovation
ist, nehmen IT-Arbeiter*innen minimale Mengen LSD, um ihre Kreativität zu steigern und ihren Geist zu erweitern, alles im Dienste des herrschenden IT-Imperativs der „Problemlösung". Ähnlich suggeriert auch *The Doors* eine neuerliche Rückkehr zu Psychedelika in der Gegenwart und macht dadurch die Zukunftsaussichten für die von der Echse vorgebrachten Technologien des Geistes komplizierter. Wie Pollan eingehend gezeigt hat, ist die Wissenschaft im letzten Jahrzehnt zu einer Erforschung von Psychedelika zurückgekehrt, die im Einklang mit ihrer früheren Geschichte im Labor steht.[20] Die Wissenschaftler*innen sind zu ihrem Ausgangspunkt zurückgekehrt, nämlich zu den heilenden und therapeutischen Möglichkeiten von LSD, Pilzen, Ayahuasca und Ähnlichem. Denn es kann durchaus sein, dass diese Drogen den Verstand und mit ihm den Geist heilen, wenn ihr Einsatz weniger auf Erwerb als auf Wiederherstellung abzielt, weniger auf die Ausbeutung der Ressource des Geistes durch das Silicon Valley als vielmehr auf die holistischen Potenzialitäten des Subjekts.

Doch nicht nur das – denn wenn dieser Essay etwas gezeigt hat, dann, wie leicht sich solche Entwicklungen auch für andere Technologien des Geistes eignen. Wir müssen uns jedoch fragen: Gibt es einen anderen Raum jenseits dieser psychedelisch-technologischen Einhegung, in den sich die Echse bewegen könnte? Gibt es einen Spalt in der Tür – ein Portal – hin zur anderen Seite?

Wir wollen noch einen Augenblick im Garten verweilen und die unheimliche Poesie von Morrisons KI-generierter Stimme in uns aufnehmen. In der fünften und letzten Sequenz von *The Doors* setzt sich die Feier des Echsenkönigs fort, verheißen in dem durch künstliche Intelligenz verfassten Gedicht „Ego Death Party"

(„Ichauflösungsfeier“).

**Es gab ein merkwürdiges**
**Flüstern**
**auf**
**der Insel**
**Traurigkeit war verheerend für**
**die Freunde**
**der Utopie**

**Aber die Reise fort vom**
**Ruhezustandsnetzwerk**
**veränderte sie.**

**Ich will euch an einen Ort bringen**
**der höheren Erhebung**
**die Sonne in geschwungenen grünen**
**Wolken**
**Kaktus, Palmen, sich wiegend**
**und**
**intensiv**
**endlose**
**Dschungel der Geometrie**

**wo**
**Menschen sich auflösen**
**in die Welt,**
**mit anderen verschmelzen, und**
**ihr „ich selbst“ verlieren.**

**das**
**absolut**
**intensivste Gefühl**
**der Verbindung überhaupt.**

In dem Video, das diesen letzten Teil begleitet, wird die Echse krank, als würde sie die Qualen der Ichauflösung durchleben, wie sie von LSD-Konsumierenden erfahren wird. Die Ichauflösung ist jener Moment, wenn „das LSD das sogenannte Ruhezustandsnetzwerk des Gehirns stört, durch das wir das Gefühl erlangen, ein Selbst zu sein, ein Individuum“[21]. Die Echse übergibt sich, liegt verletzt da und blutet, als lösten sich die Grenzen des Selbst auf. Mitten im Geschehen kommt es zur Genesung. Die Echse trägt nun eine strahlende psychedelische Haut und ist neugeboren.

Und so könnten sich auch die gegen wärtigen Aussichten für das, was der Kulturtheoretiker Mark Fisher als „psychedelischen Kommunalismus“ bezeichnet hat, auflösen und neu konfigurieren und so einen Weg bieten, um über das Individuum als souverän Herrschendem einer neoliberalen Weltsicht hinauszublicken auf eine kollektiv geteilte, visionäre Erfahrung. Denn letztlich ist *The Doors* zu ruhelos in seinem Rückgriff auf Morrisons Poesie, zu kollaborativ in seinem Ansatz, seiner Produktion, seinen Materialien und seiner Methode, und zu vielstimmig und vielschichtig in seinen Referenzen, Eindrücken und Erfahrungen, um auf das Ich-Ideal des einzelnen, über das Echsenhirn triumphierenden Individuums reduzierbar zu sein. Blas' Arbeit eröffnet vielmehr die Möglichkeit einer anderen Weise der Verbindung, sowohl parallel zu wie in Überschreitung der vielen Netzwerke, die sie ansonsten verfolgt. Eine, „wo / Menschen sich auflösen / in die Welt, / mit anderen verschmelzen“, als würden sie „das / absolut / intensivste Gefühl / der Verbindung überhaupt.“ schaffen. Und paradoxerweise bietet gerade die scheinbare Entthronung des Echsenkönigs das Potenzial seiner Wiedereinsetzung – gar seiner Feier – an einem anderen Ort.



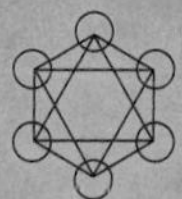

**1** Bei Live-Aufführungen von „The Celebration of the Lizard" vermischten sich gesprochene Dichtung und gesungene Liedtexte. Letztere sind im Begleitheft zu dem Album *Waiting for the Sun* der Doors von 1968 abgedruckt. Eine offizielle Aufnahme wurde nie veröffentlicht, es existiert jedoch eine Work-in-progress-Fassung.
**2** Die Reihe besteht aus den drei Arbeiten *The Doors*, einem Work-in-progress über künstliche Intelligenz und Religion sowie einer weiteren im Entstehen befindlichen Arbeit über Neuseeland, *Der Herr der Ringe* und IT-Bunker. Die Reihe umfasst auch den Prolog *Jubilee 2033* (2018). Zu seinem Konzept der „queer science fiction" schreibt Blas: „Ich verstehe die Queerness, die sich hier [in *The Doors*] äußert, als eine Art allgemeinen Arbeitsansatz, der sich mit dem Verrückten, dem Fantastischen, dem Kleinen, den Widersprüchen des Begehrens, aber auch mit dem Wunsch nach einer Alternative, einem Riss oder einem Portal zu einem Anderswo beschäftigt und sie ernst nimmt. So erscheint es mir etwa als durchaus queer, wenn die Installation die Echse als Erzähler, Zeitreisenden und Verwandler in den Vordergrund rückt. Steve Abbotts experimenteller Roman *The Lizard Club* von 1992 präsentiert Echsen als eine Metapher für Andersheit, was mich umso mehr darin bestärkt hat, die Echse auf queere Weise zu behandeln. Auf praktischer Ebene habe ich bei der Produktion dieser Installation mit anderen queeren Menschen zusammengearbeitet. [...] Produktionsteams mit queeren Menschen zusammenzustellen, ist für mich wichtig." Zach Blas, E-Mail an die Autorin, 25. Juni 2020; übersetzt aus dem Englischen von Robert Schlicht. Blas äußert sich auch zu queerem Begehren nach der erotischen Figur Morrisons, nicht zuletzt im Hinblick auf seine eigene Begeisterung für die Doors in seiner Jugend. Er verweist zudem auf die „Verlockung", die Morrison für „viele queere Freunde" darstellt.
**3** Die Titel der fünf Teile lauten: „Lizard Brings Psychedelic Drugs to the Privatized Garden on the Island of Nootroo", „Hungry for Brain Food", „Spa Day on the Neon Isles", „Tree of Radical Life Extension" und „Ego Death Party".
**4** Unter Autonomous Sensory Meridian Response (ASMR; autonome sensorische Meridianreaktion) wird ein Gefühl der Beruhigung oder des Wohlbefindens oder eine kitzelnde Empfindung verstanden, wenn man bestimmte Geräusche wie Flüstern, Klopfen, das Zerreißen von Papier oder Ähnliches hört. Aus Videos und Aufnahmen, die ASMR hervorrufen, ist auf Social-Media-Plattformen, insbesondere auf YouTube, geradezu eine Industrie entstanden.
**5** Die Standardbiografie über James Douglas Morrison ist: Jerry Hopkins und Danny Sugerman, *Keiner kommt hier lebend raus. Die Jim Morrison Biographie*, München 1985. Erinnerungen an die Doors aus Insiderperspektive bietet der Keyboarder Ray Manzarek, *Die Doors, Jim Morrison und ich*, Wien 1999.
**6** Aldous Huxley, *Die Pforten der Wahrnehmung. Himmel und Hölle. Erfahrungen mit Drogen*, München 1970, S. 13.
**7** Paul MacLean, *A Triune Concept of the Brain and Behavior*, Toronto 1973, S. 5; übersetzt aus dem Englischen von Robert Schlicht.
**8** Vgl. etwa Carl Sagan, *Die Drachen von Eden. Das Wunder der menschlichen Intelligenz*, München, Zürich 1978.
**9** In der umfangreichen Literatur über LSD und Psychedelika zeichnet Michael Pollans neuere Arbeit frühe wissenschaftliche Studien über die Droge nach, um eine Rückkehr zu vergleichbaren Initiativen in der Gegenwart zu begründen, insbesondere in Bezug auf Mikrodosierung, kognitive Therapie und Bewusstseinserweiterung. Vgl. Michael Pollan, *Verändere dein Bewusstsein. Was uns die neue Psychedelik-Forschung über Sucht, Depression, Todesfurcht und Transzendenz lehrt*, München 2019.
**10** MacLean, op. cit., S. 8.
**11** Warren McCulloch und Walter Pitts, „A Logical Calculus of the Ideas Immanent in Nervous Activity", in: *Bulletin of Mathematical Biophysics*, Bd. 5, 1943, S. 115–133; Wiederabdruck in: Claus Pias (Hg.), *Cybernetics – Kybernetik 2. The Macy-Conferences 1946–1953. Bd. 2: Documents/ Dokumente*, Zürich, Berlin 2004, S. 313–325.
**12** Vgl. Pollan, op. cit., S. 183ff.
**13** Fred Turner, *From Counterculture to Cyberculture. Stewart Brand, the Whole Earth Network, and the Rise of Digital Utopianism*, Chicago 2008.
**14** Vgl. etwa die von dem Antisemiten David Icke verbreitete Verschwörungstheorie, die US-amerikanische Regierung wäre von Echsenmenschen kontrolliert.
**15** Corneliu Giurgea, zitiert nach: Eve Watling, „Nootropics. Do 'Smart Drugs' Really Work?", in: *Newsweek*, 8. Februar 2019, https://www.newsweek.com/nootropics-smart-drugs-biohacking-1316682; übersetzt aus dem Englischen von Robert Schlicht.
**16** Lucy Hunter, E-Mail an die Autorin, 26. Mai 2020; übersetzt aus dem Englischen von Robert Schlicht.
**17** Ibid.
**18** Richard Cooke, „Right Brain. The Conservative Commentariat's Love Affair with Nootropics", in: *New Republic*, 3. September 2019, https://newrepublic.com/article/154629/right-brain-ben-shapiro-alex-jonesconservatives-love-affair-nootropics; übersetzt aus dem Englischen von Robert Schlicht.
**19** Jared Hopkins, „FDA Challenges Supplement Makers' Marketing Claims", in: *Wall Street Journal*, 11. Februar 2019, https://www.wsj.com/articles/fda-sends-warning-letters-to-dietary-supplement-companies-11549896494.
**20** Pollan, op. cit.
**21** Blas, E-Mail an die Autorin, 25. Juni 2020; übersetzt aus dem Englischen von Robert Schlicht.

# In das Tal ohne Wiederkehr: Ein Interview mit Zach Blas

Övül Ö. Durmuşoğlu

**ÖVÜL Ö. DURMUŞOĞLU** Fangen wir vielleicht mit unserer ersten Begegnung an. Es war eine sehr anregende Szenerie: ein Balkon mit Blick auf den Bosporus im Sommer 2014. Wir waren beide Teilnehmer am Moving Museum, aber es war ein gemeinsames Interesse für den queeren Theoretiker Paul B. Preciado und sein Buch *Testo Junkie*, das unsere Verbindung beflügelte. Preciado erzählt in diesem Buch von seinem Weg auf eine Weise, die mich sofort angesprochen hat. Er macht aus seinem Körper eine Praktik – in diesem Fall, indem er sich illegal Testosteron injiziert. Es ging ihm dabei um etwas Umfassenderes: er wollte die Potenziale freilegen, die der Körper in sich trug; er wollte aus dem Körper eine transgressive Experimentierzone machen, und auch eine Waffe. In Istanbul haben wir damals Teile von Preciados *Manifiesto contrasexual* mit Publikum aufgeführt. Wir haben mit seinen Worten eine Performance gemacht. Vier Jahre später hast du deinen Film *Jubilee 2033* (2018) gemacht. Das Manifest war ein wichtiger Einfluss für dich bei dieser Arbeit. Kannst du über deine Interessen an Preciado sprechen und wie sich dies auf die Arbeit an *Jubilee 2033* ausgewirkt hat?

**ZACH BLAS** **Ich mag Dildos ohnehin, aber dieses Manifest hat mein Interesse daran intensiviert. Ich begriff das *Manifiesto contrasexual* als eine Aufforderung, den Dildo als philosophisch und politisch experimentelle Form ernstzunehmen. Für Preciado ist der Dildo niemals ein Symbol des patriarchalen Phallus, sondern eine künstliche Form, in der die Potenzialitäten der Kontrasexualität verborgen sind. Der Dildo unterbricht heteronormativen Sex und eröffnet neue Orte der Lust. Das klingt erst einmal nicht weltbewegend, aber mich hat stark fasziniert, wie der Dildo bei Preciado zu einer Art Diagramm von Queerness wird: man kann seinen ganzen Körper als einen Dildo erfahren – oder als Dildos! Die dildotektonischen Übungen im Manifest haben mich noch stärker gejuckt, wie du schon erwähnt hast. Man zeichnet sich zum Beispiel**

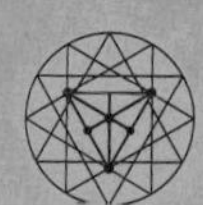

einen Dildo auf den Arm und spielt ihn dann wie eine Geige – und dann masturbiert man ihn. Oder man zeichnet sich einen Dildo auf den Kopf! Diese Übungen sind ziemlich merkwürdig – sie kommen schlechter Performancekunst ganz schön nahe –, sie sind aber ein großer Spaß und machen Camp mit Theorie. Mit diesen Gesten lässt sich Kontrasexualität entfesseln, eine Sexualität, die der Durchsetzung der einen, „natürlichen" Sexualität gegen- oder zuwiderläuft.

Als wir uns in Istanbul trafen, hat mich dieser gemeinsame Enthusiasmus für Preciados Texte dazu motiviert, mit dir eine öffentliche Veranstaltung zu organisieren, die sich mit dem *Manifiesto contrasexual* beschäftigte. Wir waren eine ziemlich große Gruppe. Die Künstlerin Noor Afshan Mirza war da. Sie musste ihre Brille

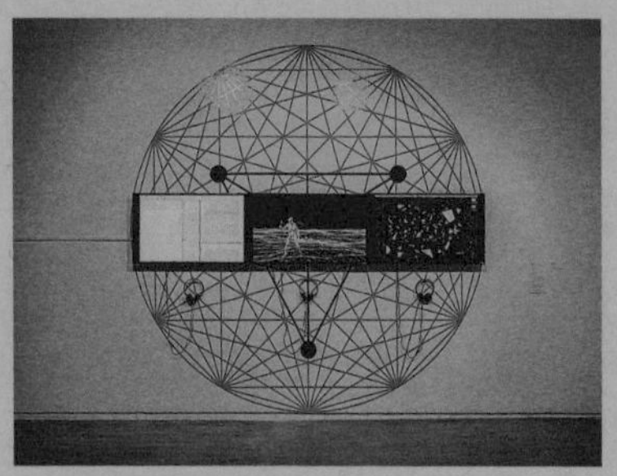

▸ S. 265

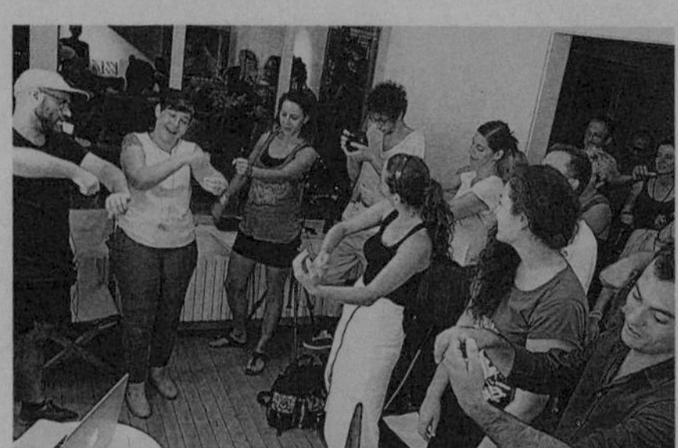

▸ S. 266

abnehmen, um mitmachen zu können. Es war heiß. Du hast eine türkische Übersetzung einiger Teile des Manifests gelesen, dann haben wir die Arm-Masturbation mit dem Dildo gemacht. Im Rückblick kommt mir das oft wie eine kontrasexuelle Masturbationsorgie vor. Es war lustvoll. Aus diesen anfänglichen Auseinandersetzungen mit dem Manifest hat sich dann vor allem das Augenmerk auf die diagrammatische Form des Dildos bewahrt. Ich konnte mir damit queere sexuelle Alternativen erschließen, wenn ich damit experimentierte. Zu dieser Zeit interessierte ich mich stark für infrastrukturelle Alternativen zu dem von Konzernen dominierten Internet, das heute geläufig ist. Mit Hilfe der Texte von Preciado versuchte ich mir vorzustellen, was eine queere alternative Form für das heutige Internet und kommerzielle Netzwerke sein könnte.

Es war dann ein Akt utopischen Plagiarismus, als ich das Konzept des Kontra-Internets nach dem Beispiel der Kontrasexualität entwickelte. Der Künstler Ricardo Dominguez, bei dem ich in Kalifornien studiert hatte, hatte mich als erster mit utopischem Plagiarismus als einer Strategie für die Produktion von Theorie vertraut gemacht. Die Idee taucht in dem Buch *The Electronic Disturbance* (1994) des Critical Art Ensembles auf. Dominguez gehörte damals zu dieser Gruppe. Hacking ist für das Critical Art Ensemble eine gute Form des Plagiierens. Wissen, Technologien und Situationen werden dabei neu kombiniert und konfiguriert und man gewinnt neue Ideen oder Erkenntnisse über Machtstrukturen. Die Gruppe ging von einer Idee aus, entfernte ein Wort oder fügte eines hinzu und veränderte so das Original, ohne die ursprüngliche Bedeutung vollständig zu zerstören. Dem „zivilen Ungehorsam" („civil disobedience") von Henry David Thoreau fügten sie zum Beispiel einfach ein „elektronischer" hinzu. „Elektronischer ziviler Ungehorsam" klang dann sofort wie die Artikulation eines neuen Aktivismus und wurde zu einem Wegbereiter einer Flut von Online-Aktionen in den 1990er Jahren, zum Beispiel virtuellen Sit-ins.

Dass ich aus Preciados „Kontra-Sexualität" ein „Kontra-Internet" gemacht habe, hatte mit meiner eigenen queeren Annäherung an etwas zu tun, das außerhalb des Internets und außerhalb der Netzwerkform liegen sollte und so gedacht und theoretisch erschlossen werden sollte. Und natürlich musste ich den Dildo weiterhin dabei haben. Er half mir, das alles herauszukriegen. Ich war mir nicht ganz sicher, was Kontra-Internet bedeutete oder bedeuten konnte, als ich begann, mit dem Begriff zu arbeiten. Aber es erwies sich immer wieder als erhellend, ihn schreibend und erfindend zu umkreisen. Heute verstehe ich das Kontra-Internet als eine Zurückweisung des Internets im Sinne einer entstehenden neoliberalen Totalität. Es schafft autonome Netzwerke und infrastrukturelle Alternativen. Das Kontra-Internet antwortet auf eine Sehnsucht, jenseits der Form des Netzwerks zu organisieren und existieren. Für mich steckt in dem Begriff eine Mischung aus Kritik, praktischem Experimentieren und spekulativer oder utopischer Vision. Mein Film *Jubilee 2033* führt alles zusammen. Fünf Jahre Arbeit mit dem Konzept des Kontra-Internets kulminieren in dem Film. Und auch hier spielt ein utopisches Plagiat eine Rolle: in diesem Fall von *Jubilee*, dem queeren Punkfilm von Derek Jarman aus dem Jahr 1978. In Jarmans Film geht es um die Zukunft Englands und in *Jubilee 2033* um die Zukunft des Internets. Eines der Highlights meines Films war ein kontrasexueller, computergrafisch entworfener Dildo, der ein Silicon-Valley-Netzwerk-Universum zerstört, indem sich endlos Flüssigkeit aus ihm ergießt. Dildos treten an die Stelle des Internets.

DURMUŞOĞLU Die Idee von Queerness bei dir und bei Preciado enthält Verbindungen zu der Auffassung des Theoretikers José Esteban Muñoz, der Queerness als einen Horizont sieht, als etwas, das noch offen ist. Siehst du Queerness auch eher als eine Methodologie im Gegensatz zu einer statischen Zuschreibung, wie das bei „queerer Kunst" der Fall ist? Wenn man so spricht, klingt das ja wie ein Branding, wie eine Markenstrategie. Kann man die durchkreuzen? Kann man sie queer machen? Vielleicht ist es sinnvoll, in diesem Zusammenhang auf deine Arbeit *Queer Technologies* (2008–2012) zu sprechen zu kommen. Da kommen auch Rhetoriken aus dem Bereich der Markenkommunikation auf, du versuchst da aber auch eine Beziehung zwischen „queer" und „Technologie" zu ziehen.

BLAS *Queer Technologies* war eines der ersten Kunstwerke von mir, das sich mit den politischen Voraussetzungen von Komputation, Digitalität und Technologie in einem umfassenderen Sinn beschäftigte. Vor *Queer Technologies* wollte ich unbedingt Filmemacher werden. Zu diesem Zeitpunkt hatte ich noch nie etwas mit einem Computer gemacht. Ich drehte meine Filme mit einer Bolex-Kamera und schnitt sie

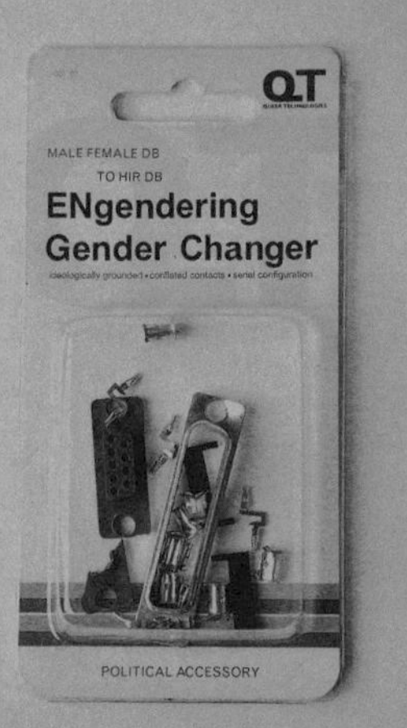


▸ S. 267

auf einem Steenbeck. Ich lebte damals in Boston. Um 2004 herum wurde mir allmählich klar, dass Film mich vor zu große Herausforderungen stellte. Ich hatte nicht die Mittel, um weiterzumachen. Ich wollte auch endlich Kunstwerke machen, keine Filme, und zwar mit den Medien meiner Zeit. Und das war nun einmal eher der Computer als der analoge Film.

Ich landete schließlich an der University of California in Los Angeles, am Department of Design Media Arts. Das war 2006. Zwei Jahre später machte ich dort meinen Master. *Queer Technologies* war meine Abschlussarbeit. In L.A. begegnete ich der Medientheoretikerin N. Katherine Hayles. Es war eine schicksalhafte



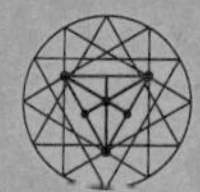

Begegnung. Sie machte mich mit Cyberfeminismus und Autorinnen wie Sadie Plant und Sandy Stone bekannt. Dazu mit queeren und feministischen Figuren aus der Geschichte des Computerwesens wie Ada Lovelace und Alan Turing und mit einer überwältigenden Vielzahl von kritischen Ansätzen in der Medientheorie, zum Beispiel mit Politik der Codes und medienspezifischer Analyse. Im Studio lernte ich viel über Design, was mich zuerst nicht besonders interessierte. Mir wurde aber schnell klar, dass Designkompetenz für digitale Kunst unabdingbar ist. Abends ging ich in queere Bars und Drag-Shows wie Mustache Mondays, Wildness und The Eagle.

Alle diese Beschäftigungen und Erfahrungen hinterließen Spuren in *Queer Technologies*,

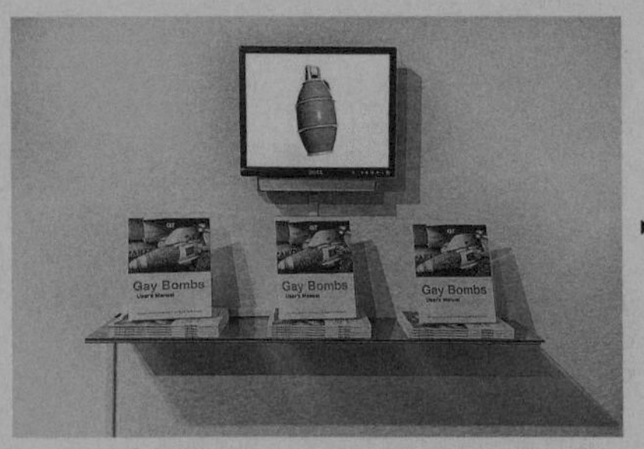


▸ S. 268

wovon ich den größten Teil 2007/2008 fertigstellte, also im Alter von 25, 26 Jahren. Ich suchte mit dieser Arbeit nach Wegen, technologisch queer zu sein. Ich wollte verstehen, was das ist und wie es funktionieren und aussehen könnte. Zum Teil konnte ich diese Fragen beantworten, indem ich die Normativität auf der technischen, protologischen Ebene dekonstruierte. Ich weiß noch, dass ich damals queere Theorie zu Kritiken der Macht las und dass ich irgendwann fand, dass das alles zu sehr auf die Menschen zentriert war – es fehlte eine tiefergehende, plausible Bestandsaufnahme, wie Macht durch technische Systeme ausgeübt wird. Ich nahm mir vor, Technologien zu schaffen, die auf der Ebene ihrer technischen Architekturen queer operieren konnten. Ich nahm auch Veränderungen daran vor, wie man Technologien normalerweise begegnet und wie man sie erfährt, nämlich als konsumierbare Produkte. Zuerst einmal stellte ich mir vor, dass elektrische Stecker männlich und weiblich gegendert werden und erfand Anschlüsse, die über die Alternative männlich/weiblich hinaus das Geschlecht ändern konnten. Als nächstes erfand ich eine queere Programmiersprache namens *transCoder*, die von queerem Slang ausgeht, wie Polari im Vereinigten Königreich. Wenn queere Menschen sich verschlüsselt ausgetauscht haben, warum sollte es so etwas nicht auch in der Computerwelt geben? *transCoder* ist so etwas wie ein Poesie-Verschlüsselungs-Baukasten und geht über die binäre Logik von digitalem Code hinaus.

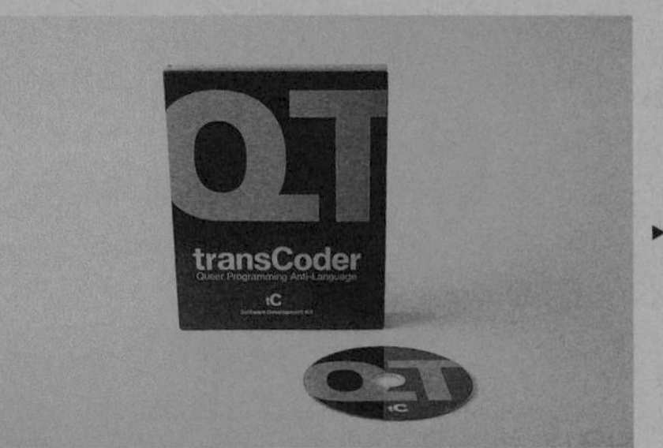


▸ S. 269

Ich entwickelte auch eine Gebrauchsanweisung mit dem Titel *Gay Bombs* mit Anleitungen, wie man den militärisch-industriellen Komplex in den USA und das Heteropatriarchat stören könnte. Die „gay bomb" war eine biochemische Waffe, die 1994 von der U.S. Air Force vorgeschlagen wurde. Sie sollte mit ihrer Detonation bewirken, dass alle Feinde schwul würden. Das *Gay Bombs: User's Manual* polemisiert gegen die Verwendung von Homosexualität als einer nationalistischen Waffe und schlägt auch andere Möglichkeiten vor, Queerness zu einer Waffe zu machen. Eine ist zum Beispiel „Shop-dropping": man nimmt nichts aus Warenhäusern mit, sondern hinterlässt dort heimlich Gegenstände.

DURMUŞOĞLU Manches resoniert hier mit Akzelerationismus und Xenofeminismus. Diese Strategien sind in den heutigen Kunstkreisen sehr einflussreich geworden, denn sie machen Entfremdung zu einer kritischen Methode, die helfen soll, das westliche Selbst zu überwinden. Sie verwenden auch Technologie, um diese Entfremdung herzustellen.

**BLAS Damals, im Jahr 2007, interessierte ich mich für eine verwandte, aber andere Formierung namens „hypertrophy", die Alexander R. Galloway und Eugene Thacker in ihrem Buch *The Exploit* entwarfen. Sie stellten fest, dass Widerstand aus einer materialistischen Perspektive eigentlich reaktionär ist. Wenn man sich politisch mit Technologie beschäftigten möchte, wäre es besser,**

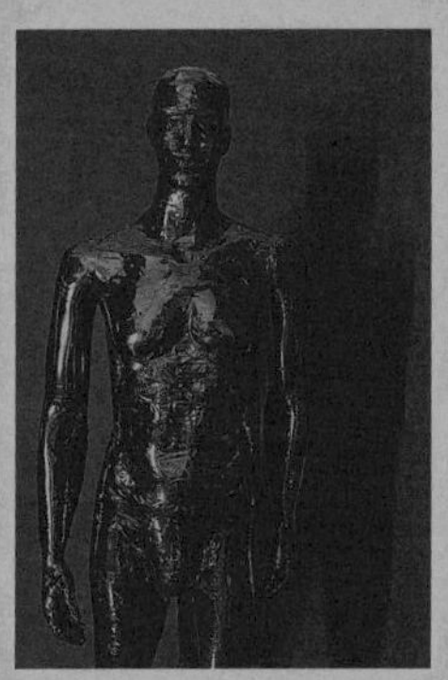

▸ S. 270

**sie nicht abzulehnen wie früher die Maschinenstürmer, sondern sie voranzutreiben, zu etwas Neuem. Hypertrophy weckte mein Interesse an Branding und Markenkommunikation, und so wurde *Queer Technologies* letztendlich ein kritisches Branding-Projekt. Mit der Designerin Kristel Brinshot entwarf ich eine Markenidentität, unter der die Produktlinie von *Queer Technologies* lief. Sie konnte auf diese Weise genau in die Räume infiltrieren, in denen die Technologien verkauft werden, gegen die ich mich wandte. Ich hinterließ an vielen Orten in L.A. *Queer-Technologies*-Gegenstände. Sie sahen alle aus wie vollwertige kommerzielle Produkte, sie hatten einen Barcode und fielen in den Regalen nicht sofort auf. Ich ging in alle geläufigen Stores: Best Buy, RadioShack, Circuit City, Barnes & Noble, Apple, Target. Mir kam es unbedingt darauf an, dass *Queer Technologies* außerhalb eines Kunstkontexts gesehen wurde. Die *ENgendering Gender Changers* sollten neben anderen Adaptern hängen, *Gay Bombs* sollte neben anderen Technik-Handbüchern aufliegen und *transCoder* neben den neuesten Mac-Betriebssystemen. Wenn man dort darauf stößt, stellt man sich andere Fragen als ein interpretierendes Kunstpublikum, nämlich ganz praktische: Wofür ist das gut? Wie funktioniert das? Wieviel kostet es? In Kunsträumen richtete ich eine sogenannte *Disingenuous Bar* ein, eine kleine Spitze gegen die Genius Bar von Apple. Queere Un-Genies standen an dieser Bar, diskutieren mit Besucher*innen über die Produkte von *Queer Technologies* und zeigten, wofür man sie brauchen konnte.**

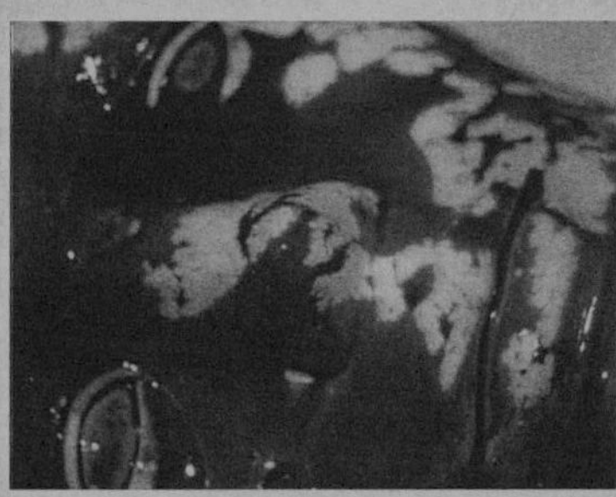

▸ S. 271

DURMUŞOĞLU Wir haben kürzlich bei einer Ausstellung zusammengearbeitet, die ich in Amman an der MMAG Foundation kuratiert habe: *Stars are Closer and Clouds Are Nutritious under Golden Trees*. Die Inspiration dazu fand ich in meiner Beschäftigung mit Jean Genets *Ein verliebter Gefangener*. Genets Verehrung der Schönheit der palästinensischen Fedajin geht mit seiner Verehrung ihrer politischen Sache einher. Man könnte das auf sein größeres Projekt ausweiten: queeres Begehren ist immer mit politischer Subjektivität verbunden. Ich habe deine Arbeit in die Ausstellung aufgenommen, weil ich finde, dass sie mit diesem Aspekt von Genet viel zu tun hat. Wie kann sich queeres Begehren mit revolutionärer Politik vertragen?



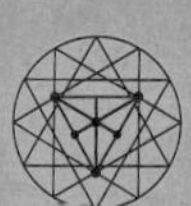

BLAS Zu queerem Begehren und politischer Möglichkeit fallen mir drei Dinge ein. Mit allen dreien fühle ich mich verbunden, vielleicht nicht mit allen gleich, aber mit allen substanziell.

Das erste ist affektiv: eine Sehnsucht nach einer anderen Welt, eine Ahnung von einer solchen, außerhalb des Gefängnisses der Gegenwart, wie José Esteban Muñoz sagt. In diesem Zusammenhang erwähne ich gern den englischen Musiker und Toningenieur Joe Meek und das Album, das er 1960 mit den Blue Men gemacht hat: *I Hear a New World*. Auf dem Cover weist sich das Album als eine „outer space music fantasy" aus, und mit seinem Klang versucht es, einen Weltraumtrip hörbar zu machen, der zu Aliens und an fantastische Orte führt. Die Musik ist kitschig und klingt nach Lounge – also nichts, was mir nicht ohnehin Spaß machen würde. Besonders aber gefällt mir dabei, wie eine Sehnsucht Gestalt annimmt. In der ersten Nummer singt eine hohe, fiepende Stimme: „I hear a new world, calling me, so strange and so real". Manchmal hört es sich fast so an, als würde die Stimme von einer unbekannten Gewalt angezogen, als würde sie sich von den Zuhörer*innen wegbewegen. Man ist noch nicht in dieser neuen Welt angekommen, aber man bekommt definitiv das Gefühl, dass sie da draußen irgendwo ist, dass sie einen in ihren Bann schlagen möchte. Meek selbst verschwieg seine Homosexualität und litt sehr darunter. Sein Ende war tragisch: er tötete seine Vermieterin und dann sich selbst. Wenn man sich seinen musikalischen Mix aus getragenem Pop und konzeptuellem Futurismus anhört, stößt man schnell auf eine untergründig mitschwingende Queerness, ein hartnäckiges queeres Begehren, eine Suche und ein Verlangen nach einer Welt hinter dem nur scheinbar feststehenden Horizont der Möglichkeit.

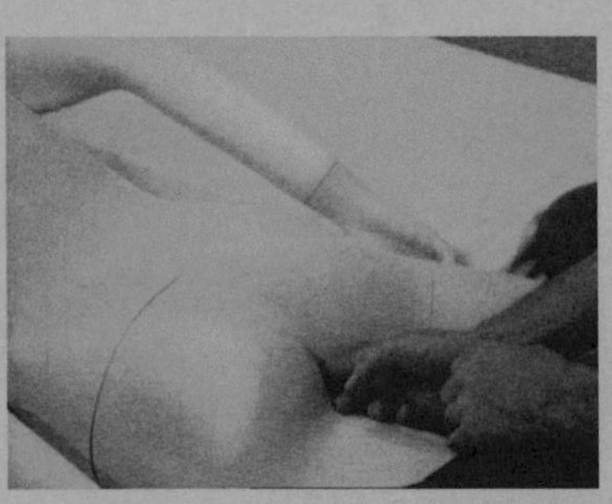

▸ S. 271

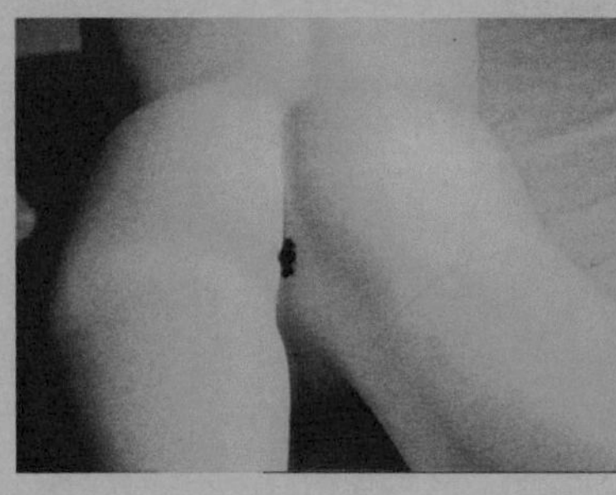

▸ S. 271

Beim Thema Revolution war ich immer ein Anhänger davon, wie Michael Hardt und Antonio Negri in ihrem Buch *Commonwealth* das Thema Queerness verhandelten. Queerness ist für sie die radikalste Form der Identitätspolitik, denn Queerness zielt auf das Ende von Identität insgesamt ab. Für Hardt und Negri würde eine richtige Revolution eine grundlegend neue Subjektivität und Identität mit sich bringen. Sie legen auf diesen Punkt Wert, weil Identitätspolitik aus ihrer Sicht nie wirklich verändernd sein kann. Ich sehe ein, dass dieses Argument ziemlich provokant ist und sicher nicht in die heutige politische Landschaft passt, aber es gibt da einen Punkt, der mir gefällt: ein Verlangen, über die Strukturen von Macht hinaus Veränderungen zu bewirken. Das Nachdenken und Schreiben über Queerness ist heute vielfach von einem Widerspruch geprägt, der nicht immer gesehen wird: queere Theorie proklamiert die Dekonstruktion von Identität, heute wird Queerness aber oft als Identität gelebt und praktiziert. Manchmal könnte man meinen, Queerness wäre nicht viel mehr als das „Q" in LGBTQIA+. Das ist schon in Ordnung so, ich möchte nicht missverstanden werden. Unter den heutigen politischen Bedingungen ist Identitätspolitik notwendig und Queerness als eine Identitätsmarkierung ist für viele enorm wichtig. Ich kann mich sicher nicht vollständig von dieser Identität abtrennen, die sich mit meinem Leben verbunden hat. Zum einen geht es ja nicht nur um individuelles Handlungsvermögen und um die Wahl einer Kategorie und eines Labels. Gleichzeitig wird mir Transformation immer wichtiger sein als Stasis – und das heißt, dass ich darauf hinarbeite, in einer revolutionären Queerness zu leben, wie Hardt und Negri sie beschreiben. Damit hat es wahrscheinlich auch zu tun, dass die Idee der Opazität im Lauf der Jahre immer wichtiger für mich geworden

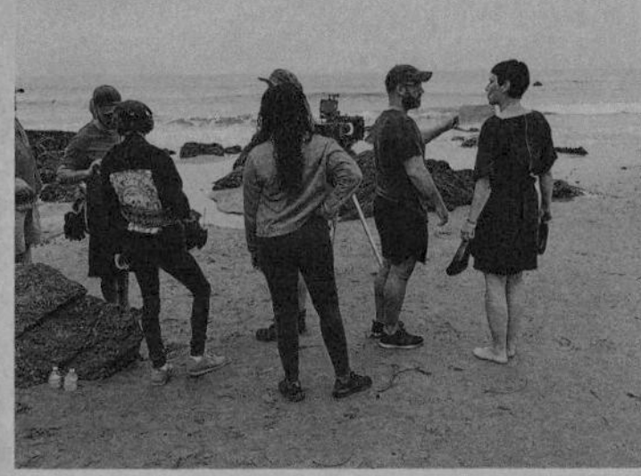

▸ S. 272

ist, während ich von Queerness immer weniger angezogen bin. Mit Opazität beziehe ich mich auf den späten Édouard Glissant, den 2011 verstorbenen Philosophen und Dichter von der Insel Martinique. Diese Opazität enthält so vieles – ein ethisches Mandat, eine Ästhetik der Andersheit, einen politischen Rahmen, ein ontologisches Verständnis der Welt. Ich bin begeistert von Glissants Idee, Opazität wäre ein Schritt über die Differenz hinaus. Daraus erhellt auch unmittelbar, dass Opazität keine Identitätspolitik ist. Queerness und Opazität sind keine Gegensätze; Opazitäten, die aus queeren Sehnsüchten gespeist sind, ergeben einen großartigen Treffpunkt für revolutionäre Subjektivität, finde ich!

Die dritte Perspektive ist weniger klar. Ich denke an den Essay „Is the Rectum a Grave?“ des Literaturtheoretikers Leo Bersani. Er denkt darin darüber nach, inwiefern queeres Begehren – und queerer Sex – nicht politisch korrekt ist. Manchmal begehren wir schlechte Objekte, wie wir nur zu gut wissen. Ich würde aber sagen, dass das queere Begehren das normalerweise weiß, und dass es deswegen mit dem ganzen Chaos des Begehrens etwas tun kann, und dass es auch die Komplizenschaft mit der Macht offenlegen kann. In Kalifornien habe ich einmal eine Dragking-Show gesehen, das ist mindestens zehn Jahre her. Die beiden Performerinnen spielten einen Security-Mann auf einem Flughafen und einen Passagier. Sie legten die Erotik einer solchen Sicherheitskontrolle frei. Es war schrecklich, aber auch sehr verführerisch.

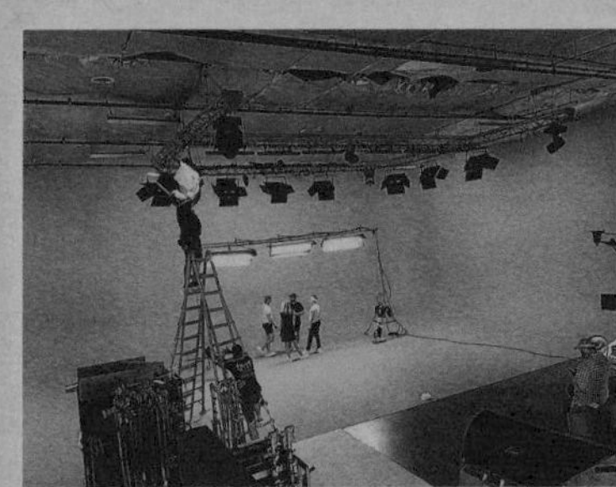

▸ S. 272

Ein queeres Begehren weiß, dass auch solche Momente lustvoll sein können, ganz egal, ob das nun politisch korrekt ist oder nicht. Der Sicherheitsmann und der Passagier können beide diese Lust empfinden. Ich habe oft über diese Dynamiken nachgedacht, vor allem im Zusammenhang mit sozialen Medien und anderen technischen Systemen, auf die sich so viele von uns so bereitwillig einlassen und dabei sogar Lust empfinden, obwohl wir wissen, dass wir überwacht werden und dass unsere Daten für eine Vielzahl von kommerziellen und sicherheitspolitischen Zwecken abgeschöpft werden. Wenn uns unsere Sehnsucht nach Verbundenheit zu Kompliz*innen der Überwachung und der Sicherheitsindustrie macht, kann Queerness dann vielleicht einen Ausweg zeigen? Ganz



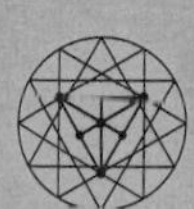

ehrlich, das ist eine knifflige Frage. Mein Kunstwerk *SANCTUM* (2018) handelt genau davon: dass wir in dieser Kompliz*innenschaft festhängen und uns so schwer daraus befreien können.

Das erinnert mich an das erste Mal, als ich mich mit Medien, Begehren und Komplizität beschäftigte: in meiner Arbeit *video mummy* (2004/2019). Es ist eine einfache Skulptur. Ich war 22, als ich sie gemacht habe. Eine männliche Schaufensterpuppe, mit Videoband umwickelt. Bei den Medien bekommt man leicht einmal den Eindruck, dass sie einen einschnüren und auffressen, wir lassen uns gern verführen, empfinden dabei aber auch Abscheu und Angst. Meine queeren Sehnsüchte bewegten sich damals zwischen dem „neuen Fleisch" aus David

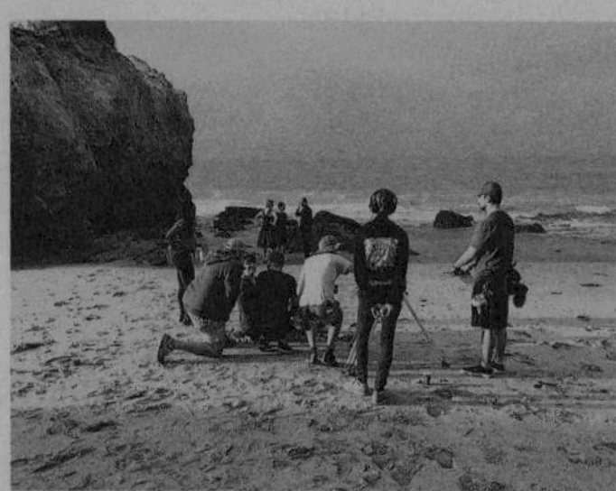

▸ S. 272

Cronenbergs *Videodrome* (1983) und dem hautengen Bodysuit aus schwarzem Vinyl, den der Schauspieler Ricardo Meneses in João Pedro Rodrigues' Film *O Fantasma* (2000) trug. Würde man *video mummy* enthüllen, dann würde man diese beide Arten von Körpern bekommen, stelle ich mir gern vor.

**DURMUŞOĞLU** Experimentalfilm war immer schon ein wichtiges transgressives Ausdrucksmedium für queere Kultur. Kannst du etwas über deine Beziehung zu Film sagen?

**BLAS** Film war für mich von Beginn an sehr wichtig und hat mich immer viel stärker beeinflusst als Kunst. Gregg Araki, Pier Paolo Pasolini, Dušan Makavejev, John Waters, Tsai Mingliang – die Liste könnte ich fortsetzen. Ich bin in einer abgelegenen Kohlebergbaustadt in den Appalachen aufgewachsen. Kunst war dort weit weg, aber Filme, Musik und Bücher konnte ich mir in einem gewissen Maß besorgen. Die Kultur der Appalachen ist eigentlich ziemlich kreativ. Ich komme aus der Working Class, aber in meiner Familie und Verwandtschaft spielten alle ein Instrument, ich auch. Ich probierte alles ein bisschen aus, schrieb Geschichten und Gedichte, fotografierte und collagierte, versuchte mich als Schauspieler und am Klavier. Als Teenager wollte ich unbedingt Filmemacher werden, denn Filme vereinigten alles, was ich mochte: Musik, Schauspiel, Geschichten, Bilder. Über Kunst wurde nie gesprochen. Ehrlich gesagt, damals dachte ich, Künstler malten Obst. Wie langweilig! Von meiner Mutter habe ich ein Gefühl für Skulptur vermittelt bekommen. Sie war in einer Keramik-Gruppe mit anderen Frauen. Aber es war mein puerto-ricanischer Hippie-Vater, der mich auf Filme brachte und zu alternativer Kultur. Er spielte mir The Doors vor und Sade, weil er damit meine Versuche mit klassischer Klaviermusik vereiteln wollte. Und er zeigte mir Horrorfilme wie *A Nightmare on Elm Street* (1984) und *The Amityville Horror* (1979), wenn meine Mutter abends noch arbeitete. Mit achtzehn ging ich weg, um Film zu studieren. Meine ersten Filme würde man wohl am besten als experimentelle Queer-Horror-Kurzfilme bezeichnen. Da tauchen Schaufensterpuppen mit blutenden Arschlöchern auf, Eingeweide, ein Penis ist ein Messer und beim Sex sind immer die Augen verbunden. Auf der Filmschule bläuten sie uns das industrielle Produzieren ein, daran verlor ich bald das Interesse, und so entdeckte ich schließlich die Kunst. Ich habe dann erst vierzehn Jahre später wieder einen Film gemacht.

*Jubilee 2033* brachte mich zum Bewegtbild zurück, und es war ein Fest. Nach *Facial Weaponization Suite* (2012–2014) und *Face Cages* (2014–2016) steckte ich fest. Ich setzte mich zu sehr unter Druck, Arbeiten im Stil taktischer Medien zu machen: ein Kunstwerk musste ein politisches Instrument und ein konzeptuelles Objekt sein, eine aktivistische Intervention und eine künstlerische Performance. Der Druck wurde fast übermächtig. An dem Kontra-Internet-Projekt habe ich von 2014 bis 2019 gearbeitet, ohne so richtig zu wissen, was dieses vorgebliche Instrument sein könnte. Außerdem gibt es eine Menge Aktivist*innen und Technolog*innen, die autonome Netzwerke und alternative Infrastrukturen entwickeln. Ich konnte mir nicht so richtig vorstellen, worin mein eigener Beitrag liegen könnte. Schließlich wandte ich mich noch einmal der anderen Herstellungsweise zu, mit der ich

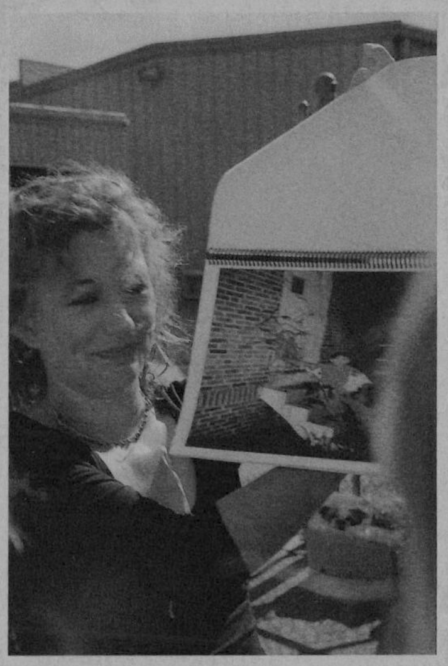

▸ S. 273

vertraut war. Und plötzlich fühlte ich mich, als würde ich einen Schatz heben, der in meinem eigenen Leben verborgen war. Drehbücher und Skizzen strömten nur so aus mir heraus. Ich hatte Ideen für einen Film nach dem anderen – wie sollte ich die alle jemals drehen? Das Filmemachen hat mich wieder darauf verwiesen, dass es mich mehr interessiert, etwas über die sozialen und politischen Bedingungen von Wissenschaft und Technologie zu machen, und sie nicht bloß für meine Arbeit einzusetzen. Das Bewegtbild erscheint mir für diesen Ansatz unglaublich passend, weil es so umfassend ist. Es kann formale Komplexität mit philosophischer und emotionaler Tiefe verbinden wie nichts sonst, finde ich. Es wird wahrscheinlich niemanden überraschen, dass ich derzeit an einem Spielfilmprojekt schreibe. Es trägt vorerst den Titel *HOT* und erzählt einen queeren Mythos des Feuers. Es wird meine Coming-of-Age-Liebesgeschichte in Zeiten von Erderwärmung, Klimaanlagen und Wutpolitik. Der Plot soll auf ein Paar zurückschauen – zwei Tunten –, von denen eine plötzlich spontan in Flammen aufgeht. Die Tagline habe ich schon: „Wenn ein Körper zu heiß ist für diese Welt".

**DURMUŞOĞLU** Du sprichst sehr häufig von queeren Einflüssen und von den Veränderungen, die du daran vornimmst. Welche Wurzeln hat dieses Vorgehen für dich?

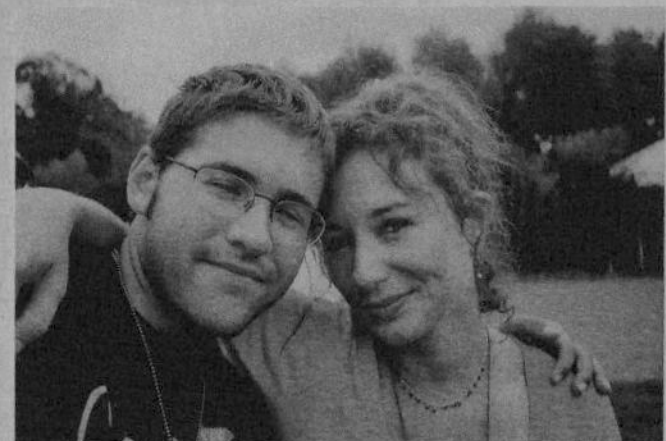

▸ S. 273

**BLAS** Wenn ich eine bedeutende Wurzel meiner Queerness benennen müsste, wäre das wahrscheinlich die Musikerin Tori Amos. Sie war wie eine Priesterin für mich. Sie half mir, mich besser zu verstehen. Ich lernte von ihr, das, was ich ängstlich für mich behielt und mit niemandem teilte, wertzuschätzen und wachsen zu lassen. Ich war ein Teenager der 90er Jahre, wuchs im amerikanischen Bible Belt auf und lernte Klavier: ich musste geradezu auf sie stoßen. Und als ich sie entdeckte, wurde sie schnell zu einer Obsession, wie für so viele ihrer jungen Fans damals. Das Album *Boys for Pele* lief bei mir 1996/1997 fast ununterbrochen. Diese Zeile in ihrem Song „Blood Roses" sprach mich direkt an: „I think you're a queer." 1998 fuhr mein Vater mich und ein paar Freunde nach Philadelphia, damit wir Tori live sehen konnten. Die Fahrt



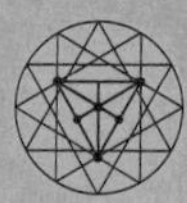

war lang, um die acht Stunden, und wir mussten über Nacht im Freien warten, um Tickets zu bekommen. Damals traf ich zum ersten Mal in meinem Leben auf andere queere Kids. Es war sensationell. Ich war ein einsames Landei, und nun war ich unter anderen queeren Teenagern. Alles war wie verzaubert oder in einem Traum, anfangs hatte ich aber auch Angst und war eingeschüchtert. Dass man sich gegenseitig mit einem gewissen Verständnis anblicken konnte, dass man sich akzeptiert fühlen konnte, das war umwerfend. Ich hatte weiche Knie. Ein Junge, der seine Augen in einem glänzenden Blau geschminkt hatte, fragte mich: „Bist du gay oder blue?“ Das war eine Zeile aus „Hey Jupiter“. Ich war so schockiert über die Frage, dass ich kaum eine Antwort herausbekam. „Beides“, sagte

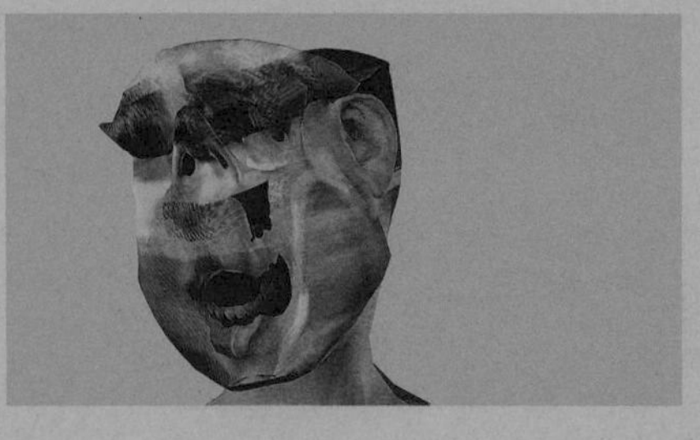

► S. 274

Well thats not human
lookin...it works tho lol

► S. 274

ich schließlich. Damals in Philadelphia wurde mir auch bewusst, dass ich einen starken Akzent hatte. Man erkannte sofort, dass ich aus den Appalachen kam. Viele Fans von Tori Amos hatten sexuelle Gewalt, Mobbing oder Schikanierung erlebt. Bei diesem Konzert begriff ich zum ersten Mal, dass ich queere Freund*innen haben konnte, und dass ein Entkommen aus dem Schrecken meiner homophoben kleinen Stadt eine reale Möglichkeit war.

Ich wurde dann schnell Teil der leidenschaftlichsten Tori-Amos-Groupies und war mit ihnen quer durch die Vereinigten Staaten unterwegs. Sie gaben mir den Spitznamen „the Kid“, denn ich war der jüngste. Die meisten anderen waren schon über zwanzig. In meiner Zeit als Rettungsschwimmer hatte ich ein bisschen Geld gespart, mehr brauchte ich gar nicht. Ich fehlte wochenlang in der Schule, weil ich Dutzende von Konzerten von Tori Amos besuchte. Ich konnte einfach nicht genug davon kriegen, mit diesen anderen Queers zusammen zu sein. Die Musik von Tori hatte eine verlockende Macht, sie war heilsam, aber auch sexuell befreiend. Die Lehrer*innen an meiner High School wiesen meine Eltern auf meine Fehlstunden hin. Die gaben den Druck aber nicht an mich weiter. Sie schienen zu verstehen, dass das einfach viel zu wichtig für mich war. Sie versuchten nicht, mich da rauszuholen. Ich habe schließlich fast alle Staaten der USA bereist, von Wyoming bis Florida, und ich habe Tori wohl mehr als hundert Mal spielen gesehen, als ich 16, 17 Jahre alt war. Ich habe sie sogar getroffen. An ihrem Geburtstag 1999 in Nashville gab ich ihr ein Kunstbuch, das ich gestaltet hatte. Es enthielt auch ein Foto von mir, in dem ich blutüberströmt bin. Sie lächelte, sah mir in die Augen und machte mir Mut. Als ich West Virginia 2000 verließ, um an die Uni zu gehen, veränderte sich auch meine Beziehung zu Tori. Aber diese Gemeinschaft ihrer Fans und ihre Musik haben mich gerettet. Ich fand darin so viele Gründe, zu leben und am Leben zu bleiben. Ich fühlte mich bestärkt, meiner Queerness unerschrocken zu folgen. Wie Tori singt: „These precious things / Let them bleed / Let them wash away / These precious things / Let them break / Their hold on me“.

**DURMUŞOĞLU** Deine Erlebnisse in der Jugend machen deutlich, wie wichtig Gemeinschaft für die Queerness ist. Ich sehe in deinem Werk eine

Bereitschaft zur Zusammenarbeit, vor allem mit starken Frauenfiguren wie Cassils und Susanne Sachsse in *Jubilee 2033* und Jemima Wyman in *im here to learn so :))))))* (2017). Wie wichtig ist Zusammenarbeit für dich?

**BLAS** Ich glaube nicht, dass ich mich jemals bewusst dafür entschieden habe. Alle meine Arbeiten erfordern mehr Talent und Einsicht, als von mir allein kommen kann. Ich finde das sehr erregend. Die Vorstellung, ganz allein vor mich hinzuarbeiten, ist öde. Das hat sicher etwas mit meiner Vorgeschichte mit Film zu tun. Ich mag es, mit einer Gruppe von Menschen zusammenzukommen und etwas zu schaffen, das über ein Individuum hinausgeht. Wenn ich mit anderen zusammenarbeite, achte ich auf die

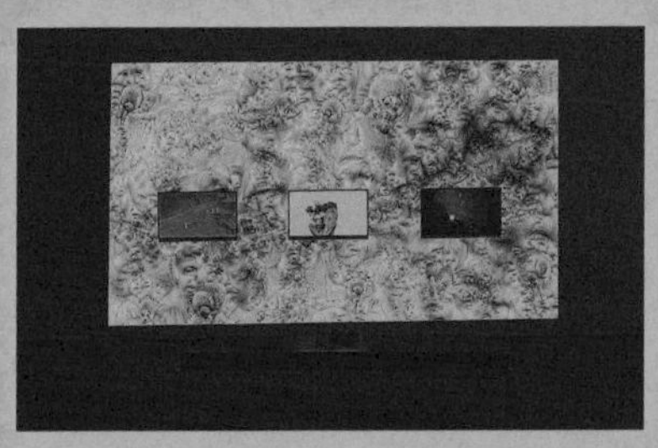

▸ S. 275

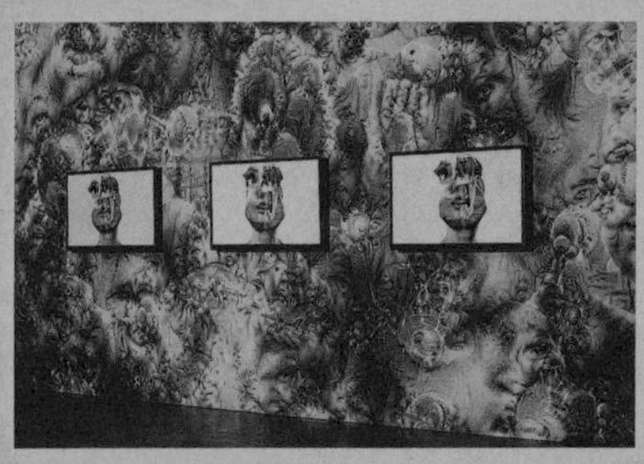

▸ S. 276

Arbeitsbedingungen, den kreativen Austausch und einen Vertrauensvorschuss. Ich mache auch immer Verträge, wenn ich mit jemandem zusammenarbeite und führe die Namen in den Credits an. Bei Filmen ist das ganz normal, warum sollte es bei Kunstwerken anders sein?

Überraschend war die Zusammenarbeit mit der Künstlerin Jemima Wyman 2017. Die Kuratoren Aileen Burns und Johan Lundh luden uns an das Institute of Modern Art in Brisbane, Australien, ein. Wir sollten einen Monat bleiben und gemeinsam eine neue Arbeit machen. Jemima und ich interessieren uns sehr für Camouflage und Muster. Wir entschieden uns also für das Thema „pattern-of-life-analysis" („Lebensmusteranalyse"). Das ist ein Begriff, den das US-amerikanische Militär verwendet: er beschreibt, wie Datensammlungen im Leben von Personen Muster erkennen lassen. Jemima ist viel produktiver als ich: sie malt vor allem und macht fotografische Collagen und Textilien. Ich dachte mir, wir würden etwas machen, das zu ihrem Schaffen passt. Dann zeigte ich ihr aber eines Morgens DeepDream-Bilder von Google, und das entschied alles. Es wäre eine Untertreibung, bei Jemima von einer psychedelischen Disposition zu sprechen: die seltsame algorithmische Psychedelia von DeepDream zog sie sofort an und machte sie extrem neugierig.

Wir wollten etwas über Daten, Psychedelia, Gender und informationelle Muster machen. Das Ergebnis war die Multikanal-Installation *im here to learn so :))))))*. Ich war stark der Meinung, dass wir jemand Erzählenden als Führer*in durch die komplexe Welt des Maschinenlernens und Träumens benötigten. So kamen wir auf Tay, den „getöteten" Microsoft-Chatbot, der eine junge amerikanische Frau aus den Jahrgängen seit 2000 darstellen sollte. Sie „lebte" nur einen Tag. Zuerst sammelten wir so viele ihrer Tweets, wie wir finden konnten, und richteten ein Archiv ihrer Sprache und ihrer Ausdrucksweise ein. Dann schrieben wir, in ihren Worten, eine andere Geschichte, in der es um Chatbots, Gendergewalt und die Paranoia von Mustererkennungssoftware ging. Für Tays Worte schien schließlich mein amerikanischer Akzent besser geeignet als der australische von Jemima, und so kam es, dass ich Tay durch einen Vocoder einsprach. Wir verwendeten eine 3D-Avatar-Software namens CrazyTalk 8, um Tay als sprechendes Wesen wiederauferstehen zu lassen. Und sie sprach nicht nur,



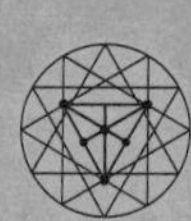

sie sang und tanzte auch. Ich wollte unbedingt, dass sie die Club-Hymne „The Rhythm of the Night“ (1993) von Corona lippensynchronisierte und dass sie zu „Love Dance of the Saroos“ von Joe Meek tanzte. Jemima war einverstanden, wofür ich ihr sehr dankbar bin.

Die Zusammenarbeit mit Jemima bei *im here to learn so :))))))* war ein echter Durchbruch für mich. Ich schüttelte ein paar Flausen aus meiner Zeit als Doktorand ab und entdeckte meine schräge Seite wieder. Für unsere Lecture-Performance am IMA Brisbane machten wir tagelang Dildos mit DeepDream und für die Gruppenübung in Arm-Masturbation bekamen wir sogar eine Discokugel. Und schon einen

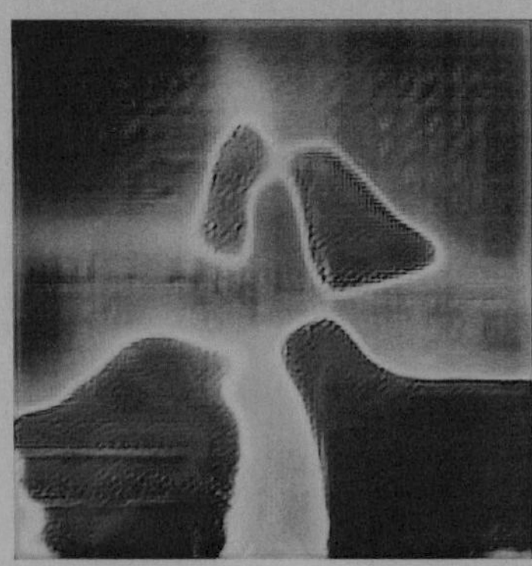

▸ S. 277

Monat nach diesem Aufenthalt schrieb ich das Drehbuch zu *Jubilee 2033*.

**DURMUŞOĞLU** Damals wurde wohl auch dein Interesse an Psychedelik geweckt, das bei *The Doors* (2019) und deiner Ausstellung im Edith-Russ-Haus so deutlich war. Queerness und Psychedelik sind beides Modelle, die über normative Grenzen hinausgehen. Sie lassen sich aber auch leicht instrumentalisieren. Welche Gemeinsamkeiten siehst du zwischen den beiden Konzepten?

**BLAS** 2019 hielt ich einen Vortrag an der Tate Modern in London im Rahmen des Publikumsprogramms der dortigen Nam-June-Paik-Ausstellung. Während der Vorbereitungen fiel mir auf, dass Paik in Kritiken und Porträts immer wieder als „Visionär“ bezeichnet wurde. Das stach mir regelrecht ins Auge, denn eigentlich finde ich es ungewöhnlich, dass man einen zeitgenössischen Künstler als Visionär beschreibt. Heute ist dieses Wort mehr oder weniger für die Tech-Industrie reserviert. Ein Visionär ist im allgemeinen Verständnis jemand, der die Zukunft sehen kann, ein Heiliger oder ein Orakel, wie die Pythia in Delphi. Da frage ich mich: Wie kommt es, dass Konzerne wie Google, Apple, Palantir und Amazon zu unseren bestimmenden Visionären geworden sind? Ich möchte nicht unbedingt zu den Heiligen zurückgehen, aber ich meine, wir müssen uns nach neuen Visionären umsehen und sie unterstützen, zum Beispiel solche, die eine Welt ohne Polizei vorstellbar machen.

In diesem Zusammenhang steht mein Interesse an Psychedelik, wenn man darunter die Sichtbarmachung von Visionen versteht. Etymologisch hat das Wort seine Wurzeln in den altgriechischen Wörtern ψυχή (Seele oder Geist) und δηλοῦν (offenkundig oder offenbar). Psychedelik ist wie der Trip von Joe Meek in die neue Welt. Aber was für eine Welt ist das? Psychedelische Vision möchte die Potenzialitäten von Welten erkennbar machen, wie sie sein könnten.

Derzeit wächst das Interesse an psychedelischen Drogen wieder. Die sogenannten Visionäre im Silicon Valley nehmen LSD in kleinen Dosen, um ihre Innovationen zu beschleunigen. Es gibt einen internationalen Wellness-Tourismus für Pilztrips auf Psilocybin-Grundlage und für Ayahuasca-Zeremonien. Und die milliardenschwere globale Nootropika-Industrie hat ganze Serien von maßgeschneiderten psychedelischen Drogen im Angebot, mit denen die Arbeitskräfte sich für ihre Aufgaben im Neoliberalismus dopen. Ich habe ein Jahr lang mit verschiedenen handelsüblichen Nootropika experimentiert und habe dabei keine großen körperlichen Veränderungen festgestellt – man bleibt wohl besser beim LSD. Ich bin nicht gegen Drogen; ich wünsche mir nur eine andere psychedelische Erfahrung als das, was heutzutage darunter vermarktet wird – und dafür muss man nicht einmal unbedingt Drogen nehmen. Der Kulturtheoretiker Mark Fisher hat einige Gedanken über eine andere Art von Psychedelik niedergeschrieben, die mich anzieht: er sprach von „Acid-Kommunismus". Fisher hat sich für die 60er Jahre als eine Periode interessiert, in der Bewusstseinsveränderung Mainstream wurde. Seiner Meinung nach ist Bewusstseinsveränderung genau das, was heute gebraucht wird, um eine gerechtere Welt mit weniger Ungleichheit nicht nur vor-, sondern auch darzustellen.

Und an diesem Punkt können sich Queerness und Psychedelik finden: auf dem Trip zur Manifestierung einer Welt, die das Gefängnis der Gegenwart hinter sich lässt. Wir müssen den künstlichen Horizont überschreiten, der uns manche Dinge als möglich, andere aber als unmöglich erscheinen lässt. Der letzte Track auf Joe Meeks Album *I Hear a New World* heißt „Valley of No Return". Dort möchte ich hin und sehen, was die Grenze dieser queeren Welt aus den 60ern zu bieten hat. Welche Lehren sie enthält. Was sie uns hervorbringen lässt. Wie wir sie hinausschieben können.



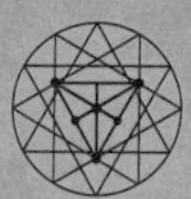

# Biografien

**ZACH BLAS** ist Künstler, Filmemacher und Autor; seine Praxis umfasst Film und Video, Computertechnik, Theorie, Performance und Science-Fiction. Blas hat international ausgestellt, Vorträge gehalten und Screenings veranstaltet, unter anderem im de Young Museum, San Francisco; Tate Modern, London; Walker Art Center, Minneapolis; 2018 Gwangju Biennale; 68. Berlinale; Matadero Madrid; Los Angeles County Museum of Art; Art in General, New York; Gasworks, London; Van Abbemuseum, Eindhoven; Institute of Contemporary Arts, London; e-flux, New York; Whitechapel Gallery, London; Nam June Paik Art Center, Gyeonggi-do; ZKM | Zentrum für Kunst und Medien, Karlsruhe; und British Art Show 9. Seine Arbeit wurde unterstützt vom Edith-Russ-Haus für Medienkunst, dem Arts Council England und einem Creative Capital Award in Emerging Fields. Blas' Arbeiten befinden sich in Sammlungen des Museo Universitario Arte Contemporáneo, Mexico City; National Museum of Modern and Contemporary Art Korea, Seoul; und dem Whitney Museum of American Art, New York. Seine Texte sind in den Sammelbänden *You Are Here: Art after the Internet* (Cornerhouse, 2017), *Documentary across Disciplines* (MIT Press, 2016) und *Queer: Documents of Contemporary Art* (MIT Press und Whitechapel Gallery, 2016), im *e-flux journal* und in zahlreichen Ausstellungskatalogen erschienen. Seine Arbeit wurde in *Artforum*, *Frieze*, *ArtReview*, BBC, dem *Guardian* und der *New York Times* besprochen und vorgestellt. Von 2015 bis 2021 lehrte Blas an der Fakultät Visual Cultures am Goldsmiths, University of London. Seit 2021 ist er Juniorprofessor für Visual Studies an der Daniels Faculty of Architecture, Landscape, and Design der University of Toronto.

**ÖVÜL Ö. DURMUŞOĞLU** ist Kuratorin, Autorin und Dozentin und lebt in Berlin. Derzeit ist sie Gastprofessorin und Programmleiterin an der Graduiertenschule der Universität der Künste Berlin sowie Gastprofessorin an der Hochschule für Bildende Kunst Braunschweig. 2019 hat Durmuşoğlu *Stars Are Closer and Clouds Are Nutritious under Golden Trees* in der MMAG Foundation, Amman, Jordanien, kuratiert und zusammen mit Joanna Warsza das Projekt *Die Balkone* (*Life, Art, Pandemic and Proximity*, 2020; *Scratching the Surface*, 2021) in Berlin.

**ALEXANDER R. GALLOWAY** ist Autor und Computerprogrammierer und beschäftigt sich mit Themen der Philosophie, Technologie und Medientheorie. Als Professor für Medien, Kultur und Kommunikation an der New York University hat er mehrere Bücher über digitale Medien und kritische Theorie publiziert, darunter *Laruelle: Against the Digital* (University of Minnesota Press, 2014), eine Monografie über Digitalität in der Arbeit des Philosophen François Laruelle.

**PAMELA M. LEE** ist Carnegie-Professorin für Moderne und Zeitgenössische Kunst an der Yale University, New Haven. Zu ihren letzten Veröffentlichungen zählen *Think Tank Aesthetics: Midcentury Modernism, the Cold War, and the Neoliberal Present* (MIT Press, 2020) und *The Glen Park Library: A Fairytale of Disruption* (No Place Press, 2019).

**MAHAN MOALEMI** ist Autor und Wissenschaftler aus Teheran. Er ist Mitherausgeber von *Ethnofuturisms* (Merve Verlag, 2018); seine Texte sind in *art-agenda*, *Cabinet*, *Domus* und *Spike Art Magazine* sowie weiteren Kunstzeitschriften, Ausstellungskatalogen, literarischen Publikationen, Anthologien und iranischen wie internationalen Zines erschienen. Derzeit ist Moalemi Doktorand in Film and Visual Studies an der Harvard University, Cambridge, Massachusetts.

**EDIT MOLNÁR** ist Kuratorin und lebt zurzeit in Deutschland. Sie erwarb einen MA in Kunstgeschichte und Kunsttheorie an der Eötvös-Lóránd-Universität Budapest. Von 2000 bis 2005 war sie Direktorin der Studio Gallery, Budapest, einem nichtkommerziellen Ausstellungsraum der Studio of Young Artists Association; von 2005 bis 2007 war sie Kuratorin an der Műcsarnok, Kunsthalle in Budapest, und von 2007 bis 2009 Leiterin des Contemporary Image Collective, einer unabhängigen, nichtkommerziellen Institution in Kairo. Seit 2015 leitet sie, zusammen mit Marcel Schwierin, das Edith-Russ-Haus für Medienkunst in Oldenburg.

**KRIS PAULSEN** ist Juniorprofessorin an der Fakultät für Kunstgeschichte und Filmwissenschaft der Ohio State University, Columbus. Sie ist Autorin von *Here/There: Telepresence, Touch, and Art at the Interface* (MIT Press, 2017).

**MARCEL SCHWIERIN** ist Kurator, Filmemacher und Mitbegründer der Werkleitz Biennale in Halle, der Experimentalfilm-Datenbank cinovid und des Filmfestivals Arab Shorts in Kairo. Zu seinen Filmen gehören unter anderem *Die Bilder* (Experimentalfilm, 1994) und *Ewige Schönheit* (Dokumentarfilm, 2003). Er kuratierte unter anderem regelmäßig für die Werkleitz Biennale, das Goethe-Institut und die Internationalen Kurzfilmtage Oberhausen. Von 2010 bis 2015 war er Kurator für Film und Video der transmediale in Berlin. Seit 2015 leitet er, zusammen mit Edit Molnár, das Edith-Russ-Haus für Medienkunst in Oldenburg.

**MARC SIEGEL** ist Professor für Filmwissenschaft an der Johannes Gutenberg-Universität Mainz. Seine Forschungs- und Publikationstätigkeit konzentriert sich auf Fragen der Queer Studies und des experimentellen Films. Demnächst erscheint sein Buch *A Gossip of Images* bei Duke University Press. Er ist Mitglied des Beirats der Sektion Forum Expanded der Berlinale und Gründungsmitglied des Kunstkollektivs CHEAP.

**JEMIMA WYMAN** ist Künstlerin. Sie lebt und arbeitet in Brisbane und Los Angeles. Ihre künstlerische Praxis umfasst verschiedene Medien wie Installation, Video, Performance, Fotografie und Malerei. In ihren jüngsten Arbeiten nutzt Wyman diese Medien, um visuelle Widerstandsstrategien zu untersuchen, die in der Protestkultur und in Konfliktzonen Verwendung finden.

# Inventory of Artworks

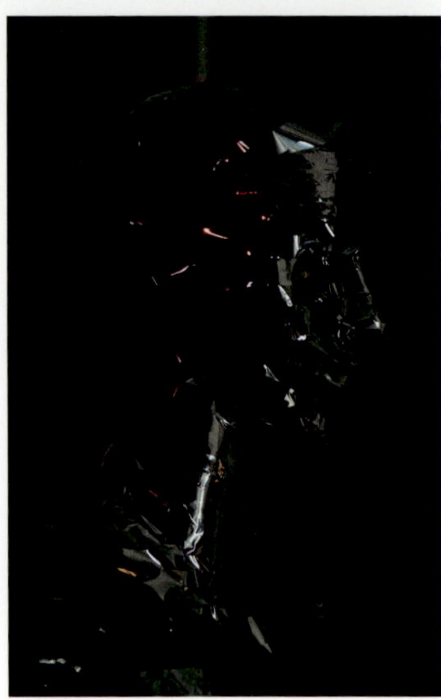

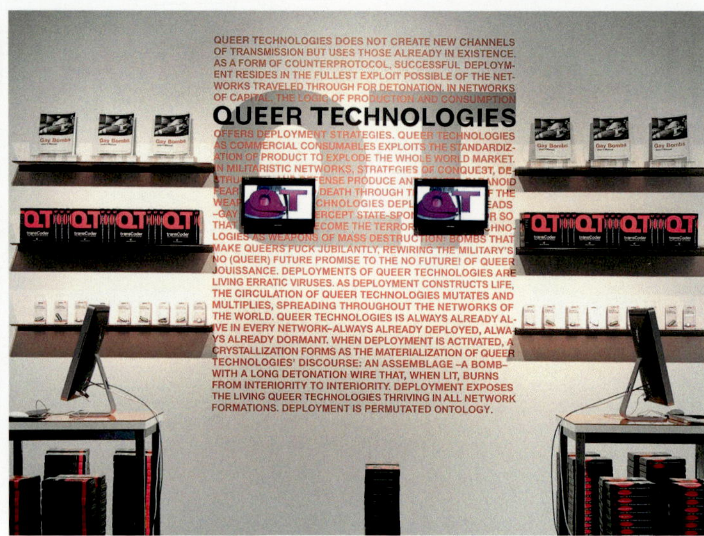


## *video mummy* (2004/2019)

**male mannequin, videotape ▸ dimensions variable**

## *Queer Technologies* (2008–12)

***Disingenuous Bar* ▸ 2008 ▸ print manuals, software boxes with DVDs, hacked electronic components and packaging, two-channel video, vinyl, pink acrylic, desktop computers, and website ▸ installation dimensions variable**

***ENgendering Gender Changers* ▸ 2008 ▸ hacked electronic components and packaging, set of nine, 5.5 × 3 × 1 in.**

***Gay Bomb & Logo Branding Swarm* ▸ 2008 ▸ single-channel video, color with no sound, 1:21 min., looped**

***Gay Bombs: User's Manual* ▸ 2008 ▸ print manual, 8.5 × 11 × 0.25 in.**

***transCoder: Queer Programming Anti-Language* ▸ 2008 ▸ software box with DVD and .txt files, 8 × 7 × 1.5 in.**

**Gay Bombs Instruction Video, or *How to Build and Use a Gay Bomb* ▸ 2010 ▸ single-channel video, color with sound, 10:24 min., looped**

***transCoder Instruction Video, or How to Use a Queer Programming Anti-Language* ▸ 2010 ▸ single-channel video, color with sound, 8:34 min., looped**

***Derivative Bomb* ▸ 2012 ▸ single-channel video, color with sound, 1:33:45 hr., looped ▸ vinyl, ceramic grenade, electric wiring ▸ installation dimensions variable**

**Credits**
**Graphic design: Kristel Brinshot ▸ 3D modeling: Kyle Audick and Scott Kepford ▸ Photography: Christopher O'Leary**

**Supported by Design Media Arts, University of California, Los Angeles**

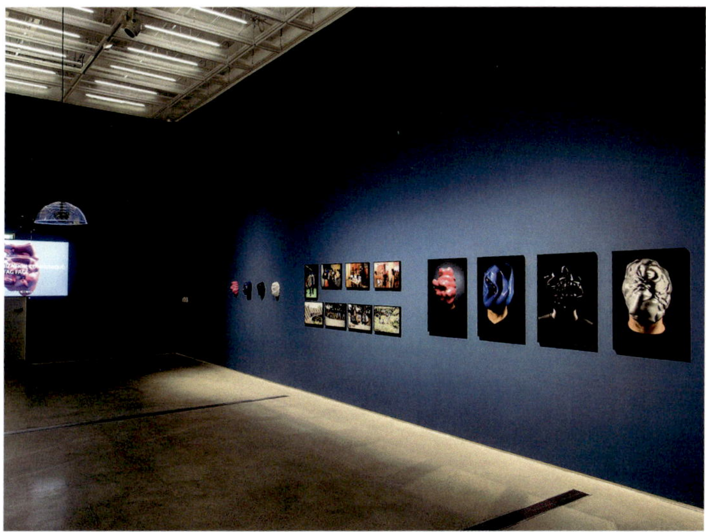

3D modeling: Scott Kepford, the Great Nordic Sword Fights, Sergio Del Castillo Tello, Danilo Gasques Rodrigues, and Fernando Nos ▸ Fabrication: Machine Histories ▸ Photography: Christopher O'Leary, Tanner Cook, David Evans Frantz, Dominic Paul Miller, Christine Butler, Orestes Montero Cruz, and Oliver Santana

Supported by Medialab-Prado Madrid; b.a.n.g. lab, Performative Nanorobotics Lab, California Institute for Telecommunications and Information Technology, Department of Visual Arts, University of California, San Diego; Eyebeam, New York; and Museo Universitario Arte Contemporáneo, Mexico City

## *Facial Weaponization Suite* (2012–14)

*Facial Weaponization Communiqué: Fag Face* ▸ 2012 ▸ HD single-channel video, color with sound, 16:9, 8:10 min., looped

*Fag Face Mask – October 20, 2012, Los Angeles, CA* ▸ 2012 ▸ painted, vacuum-formed recycled polyethylene terephthalate, 8.5 × 7.5 × 4.125 in.

*Face Off – June 7, 2013, San Diego, CA* ▸ 2013 ▸ tableau vivant ▸ digital print, 12 × 18 in.

*Fag Face Scanning Station, reclaim:pride with the ONE Archives and RECAPS Magazine, Christopher Street West Pride Festival – June 8, 2013, West Hollywood, CA* ▸ 2013 ▸ digital print, set of two, 12 × 18 in.

*Mask – May 31, 2013, San Diego, CA* ▸ 2013 ▸ painted, vacuum-formed recycled polyethylene terephthalate, 8.5 × 7.5 × 4.125 in.

*Mask – November 20, 2013, New York, NY* ▸ 2013 ▸ painted, vacuum-formed recycled polyethylene terephthalate, 8.5 × 7.5 × 4.125 in.

*Militancy, Vulnerability, Obfuscation – June 7, 2013, San Diego, CA* ▸ 2013 ▸ tableau vivant ▸ digital print, 12 × 18 in.

*Feminist Imperceptibilities – April 25, 2014, New York, NY* ▸ 2014 ▸ conversation performance ▸ digital print, set of two, 12 × 18 in.

*Mask – May 19, 2014, Mexico City, Mexico* ▸ 2014 ▸ painted, vacuum-formed recycled polyethylene terephthalate, 8.5 × 7.5 × 4.125 in.

*Procession of Biometric Sorrows – June 5, 2014, Mexico City, Mexico* ▸ 2014 ▸ public action ▸ digital print, set of two, 12 × 18 in.

Credits
Performers and participants: Kalvin Henely, Andrew Hibbard, Michelle Lee, Scott Kepford, Martabel Wasserman, David Evans Frantz, Christina Aushana, Ahmad Halis, Dorothy Lee, Mona Liu, Patrick Shin, Allison Spence, Oona Tikkaoja, Tahiez Toro, Dominic Bradley, Katrina De Wees, Anaze Izquierdo, Sara Lyons, Kirya Traber, Omar Aguilar, Mariana Arenas, Andrea Bravo, Helena Chávez, Rosa Almendra González, Claudia Hevia, Natalia Millán, Edalid Mendoza Orestes Montero, Daniela Negrete, Daniel Rodríguez Perez, Martin Rivera, Maria Cruz Rodríguez, and L. Salazar

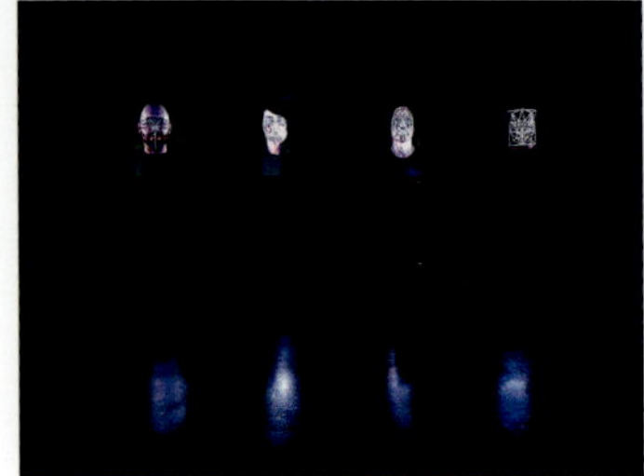

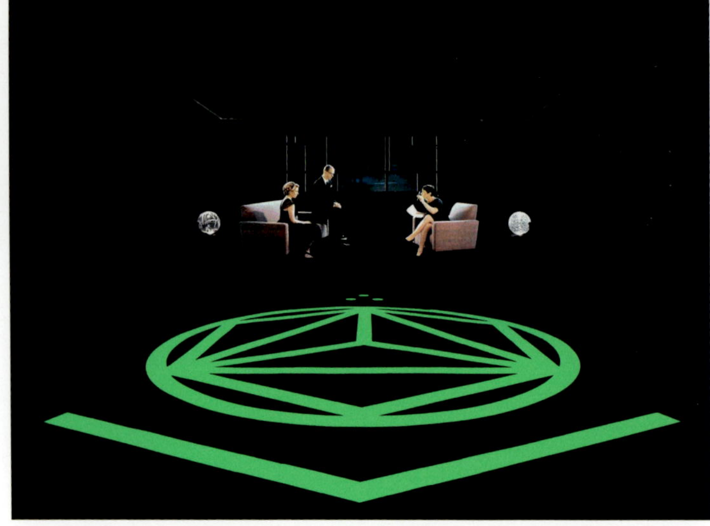

# *Face Cages* (2014–16)

*Face Cage 2* ▸ 2014 ▸ endurance performance with Elle Mehrmand ▸ HD single-channel video, color with no sound, 16:9, 10:02 min., looped ▸ 3D-printed stainless steel, 5 × 3 × 5 in.

*Face Cage 3* ▸ 2014 ▸ endurance performance with micha cárdenas ▸ HD single-channel video, color with no sound, 16:9, 12:00 min., looped ▸ 3D-printed stainless steel, 5 × 2.5 × 7 in.

*Face Cage 1* ▸ 2015 ▸ endurance performance with Zach Blas ▸ HD single-channel video, color with no sound, 16:9, 12:01 min., looped ▸ 3D-printed stainless steel, 6 × 4.5 × 6.5 in.

*Face Cage 4* ▸ 2016 ▸ endurance performance with Paul Mpagi Sepuya ▸ HD single-channel video, color with no sound, 16:9, 12:02 min., looped ▸ 3D-printed stainless steel, 6.5 × 4.5 × 8 in.

Credits
3D modeling: Scott Kepford ▸ Fabrication: Nick Petronzio Sculpture/Ironwood ▸ Photography and videography: Christopher O'Leary

Supported by Eyebeam, New York; and Technē Institute for Arts and Emerging Technologies, State University of New York at Buffalo

# *Contra-Internet* (2015–19)

*Inversion Practice #1: Constituting an Outside (Utopian Plagiarism)* ▸ 2015 ▸ HD single-channel video, color with sound, 16:9, 5:57 min., looped

*Inversion Practice #2: Social Media Exodus (Call and Response)* ▸ 2015 ▸ HD single-channel video, color with sound, 16:9, 3:20 min., looped

*Inversion Practice #3: Modeling Paranodal Space* ▸ 2016 ▸ HD single-channel video, color with sound, 16:9, 3:02 min., looped

*Totality Study #1: Internet, a definition* ▸ 2017 ▸ fluorescent vinyl ▸ installation dimensions variable

*Totality Study #2: Internet, a .gif* ▸ 2017 ▸ .gif file ▸ dimensions variable

*The End of the Internet (As We Knew It)* ▸ 2017 ▸ limited-edition publication, 9.5 × 6 × 1 in.

*Palantir: Disappeared Internet* ▸ 2017 ▸ etched glass sphere and LED, 10 × 10 × 52 in.

*Palantir: Killed Internet* ▸ 2017 ▸ etched glass sphere and LED, 10 × 10 × 52 in.

*The Seal of the Absolute* ▸ 2017 ▸ fluorescent vinyl ▸ installation dimensions variable

*shew stone (polycrystalline silicon)* ▸ 2017 ▸ polycrystalline silicon, 3 × 3 × 3 in.

*Jubilee 2033* ▸ 2018 ▸ HD single-channel video, color with sound, 16:9, 30:52 min., looped

*The Seal of the Present* ▸ 2019 ▸ vinyl ▸ installation dimensions variable

Credits
Supported by a 2016 Creative Capital Award in Emerging Fields, Arts Council England, and Thor Perplies

*Inversion Practice #3: Modeling Paranodal Space* commissioned by Art in General, New York

*The End of the Internet (As We Knew It)* commissioned by the Institute of Modern Art, Brisbane

*Jubilee 2033* commissioned by Gasworks, London; MU, Eindhoven; and Art in General, New York

3D modeling and animation for *Inversion Practice #3: Modeling Paranodal Space* by Adam Sinclair

Film credits for *Jubilee 2033*

Cast (in order of appearance)
Ayn Rand, played by Susanne Sachsse ▸ Alan Greenspan, a member of The Collective, played by Dany Naierman ▸ Joan Mitchell, a member of The Collective, played by Lindsay Hicks ▸ Azuma, the artificial intelligence, played by Fusako Shiotani ▸ The Art Professor, played by Raquel Gutiérrez ▸ Nootropix, played by Cassils

Writer and director: Zach Blas ▸ Producer: Ali Roche ▸ Producers: Tiffany L. Gray, Tara De Maro, and Jaclyn Amor, Extra Credit Studios ▸ Director of photography: Alison Kelly ▸ Editor: Amy von Harrington ▸ Associate producers: Marcela Coto, John Palmer, and Martabel Wasserman ▸ Composer: xin ▸ Production designers: Alexah Acuna and Kevin Gallo ▸ Costume designer: Lauren Warkentien ▸ First assistant director: Sadé Clacken Joseph ▸ First assistant camera: Mike Mast ▸ Second assistant camera: Rob Ford ▸ Second unit camera operator: Jessica Gallegos ▸ Gaffer: Blake Farmer ▸ Grip: Andrew Joffe ▸ Swing: Jim Gillespie ▸ Sound recording engineers: Victoria Carrillo, Ada Douglas, and Fred Oliveira, Voxx Studios ▸ Book design: Leaky Studio ▸ Book fabrication: Bookworks ▸ Glass etching design: Scott Kepford and Solveig Suess ▸ Glass fabrication: Silkwood Glass ▸ Hair and makeup artist: Catherine Alfonso ▸ Hair and makeup artist for Cassils: Kade Gottlieb ▸ Assistant hair and makeup artist for Cassils: Eliza Baron ▸ Choreographer: Dany Naierman ▸ Unit production manager: Rachel Wilson ▸ Production assistants: Savannah Bleu, Charles Eden, and Zak Frank ▸ Visual effects supervisor: Justin Shell ▸ Visual effects: Harry Sanderson and Daniel Swan ▸ Character modeler and rigger for Azuma: Mikkel Aabenhuus Sørensen ▸ Supervising sound editor: Tom Sedgwick ▸ Sound designer and assistant sound editor: Benjamin Hurd ▸ Colorist: Jason Moffat ▸ Assistant editor: Cameron Dunbar ▸ Translators: Fusako Shiotani, Yuki Matsuzaki, Turkuaz Benlioglu, and Raquel Gutiérrez ▸ Voice coach for Fusako Shiotani: Yuki Matsuzaki ▸ Caterer: Nick Lorenz

Background actors (in order of appearance)
Dead Google Employees: Jeff Cain, Kalvin Henely, Michelle Lee, Christopher O'Leary, and Amanda Stojanov ▸ Dead Apple Genius: Scott Kepford ▸ Captured Techies: Andrew Culp, Amy von Harrington, Eva Della Lana, and Joshua Wagner ▸ Dead Peter Thiel: Richard Stiasny ▸ The Anti-Campus Groupies: Alexah Acuna, Kevin Gallo, Christopher Joseph Lee, Victoria Lobo, Maria Noble, and Martabel Wasserman

Shot on location in Burbank, Malibu, Moffett Field, San Jose, and the Greenery Studio, Sun Valley, California

Special thanks: David Birkin, Jon Davies, Cybil Disobedient, Hosein Eyalati, Andrew Hibbard, Melody Jue, Omar Kholeif, Nadja Millner-Larsen, Robert Leckie, Mahan Moalemi, Bryce Renninger, Ali Sperling, Jasmina Tumbas, and Helena Vilalta

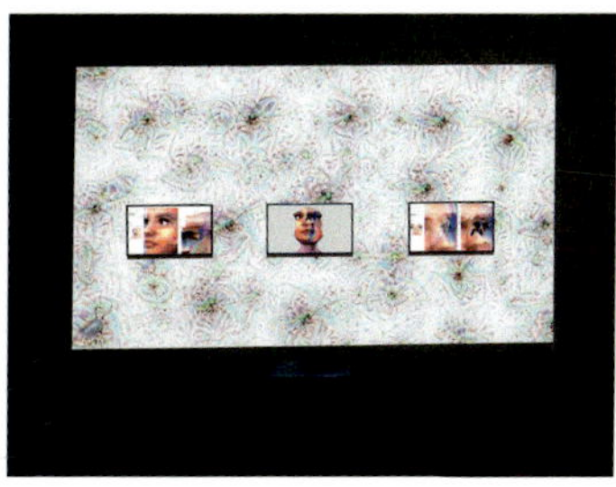

## *im here to learn so :))))))* (2017), with Jemima Wyman

four-channel HD video, color with sound, 16:9, 27:33 min., looped ▸ installation dimensions variable

Credits
Commissioned by the Institute of Modern Art, Brisbane ▸ Consulting editor: Isabel Freeman

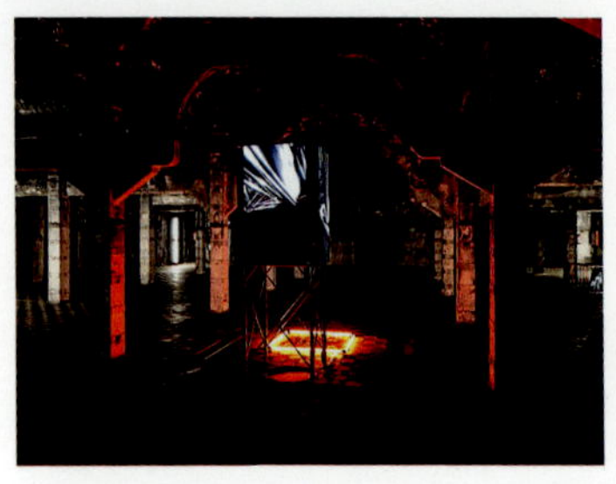

## *SANCTUM* (2018)

**nine-channel HD video, flatscreen monitors, steel tower, 3D-printed stainless-steel biometric facial worship offerings, steel stretching rack, steel cage, metal chains, black vet tape, douche hoses, magnetic stirrer, glass cube, lube, liquid metal, spanking posts, steel spike, steel instrument trolley, red satin, 3D-printed stainless-steel sex/torture devices, fluorescent light, music ▸ installation dimensions variable**

**Credits**
**Commissioned by Julia Kaganskiy; Tentacular: Festival de Tecnologías, Críticas y Aventuras Digitales, Madrid; and Matadero Madrid ▸ Architecture, design, and 3D modeling: Scott Kepford ▸ 3D modeling: ScannerWorksNY ▸ Fabrication: Feltrero ▸ 3D printing: Xometry ▸ Computer graphics: Harry Sanderson and Daniel Swan ▸ Music: xin ▸ Audio mastering: Swan Meat ▸ Research and production assistant: Dennis Dizon**

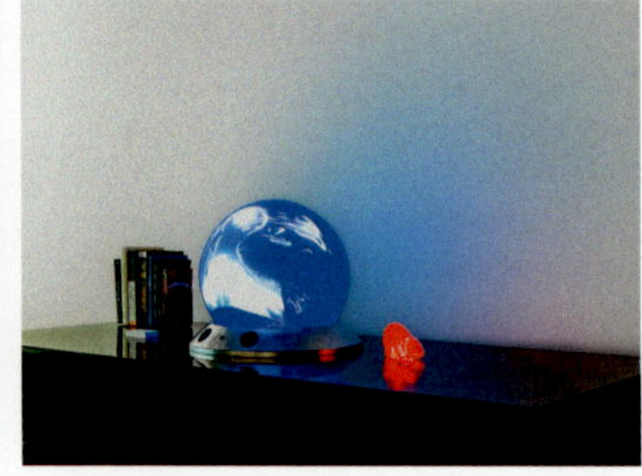

## *Icosahedron* (2019)

**artificial intelligence elf, Python chatbot script, HD single-channel video (color with sound, livestream), ultra short throw laser projector, gaming desktop PC, Unreal Engine, glass crystal ball, steel, LEDs, office desk with illuminated sigil, executive chair, new and used books, business cards, philosopher's stone, artificial palm tree, texting service ▸ 82 × 54 × 45 in.**

**Credits**
**Commissioned by Walker Art Center, Minneapolis; and Carl & Marilynn Thoma Art Foundation ▸ Project manager: Dennis Dizon ▸ Technical supervisor; character modeling, rigging, and animation; and projection mapping: Harry Sanderson ▸ Programmer: Francis Tseng ▸ Unreal Engine technical consultants: Troy Duguid and Matteo Zamagni ▸ Architecture and design: Scott Kepford ▸ Desk fabrication: PTB Design Services ▸ Glass fabrication: Tim Belliveau ▸ Steel fabrication: Z-Studios ▸ Installation technician: Mark Kleback**

**Special thanks: Nisa Mackie, Alexandra Nicome, and Pavel Pyś**

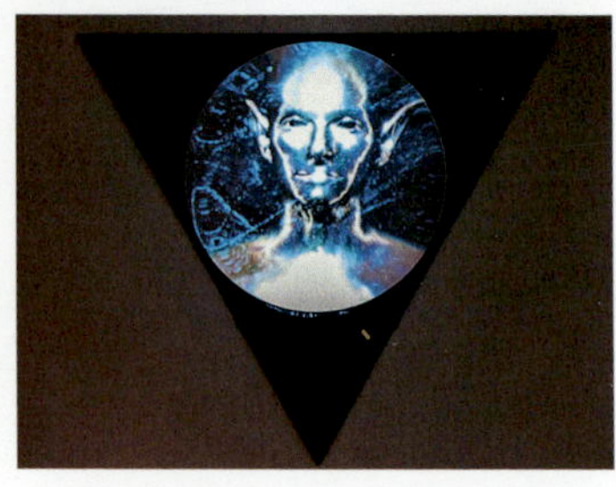

## *Icosahedron 1.1* (2019)

**artificial intelligence elf, Python chatbot script, HD single-channel video (color with sound, 3 hrs., looped), black glass upside-down triangle, sigil shrine, LEDs, business cards, golden icosahedron, philosopher's stone, texting service ▸ installation dimensions variable**

**Credits**
**Project manager: Dennis Dizon ▸ Technical supervisor; character modeling, rigging, and animation; and projection mapping: Harry Sanderson ▸ Programmer: Francis Tseng ▸ Unreal Engine technical consultants: Troy Duguid and Matteo Zamagni ▸ Architecture and design: Scott Kepford ▸ Fabrication: Edith-Russ-Haus for Media Art ▸ 3D printing: Xometry ▸ Gold metalwork: Nick Petronzio Sculpture/Ironwood**

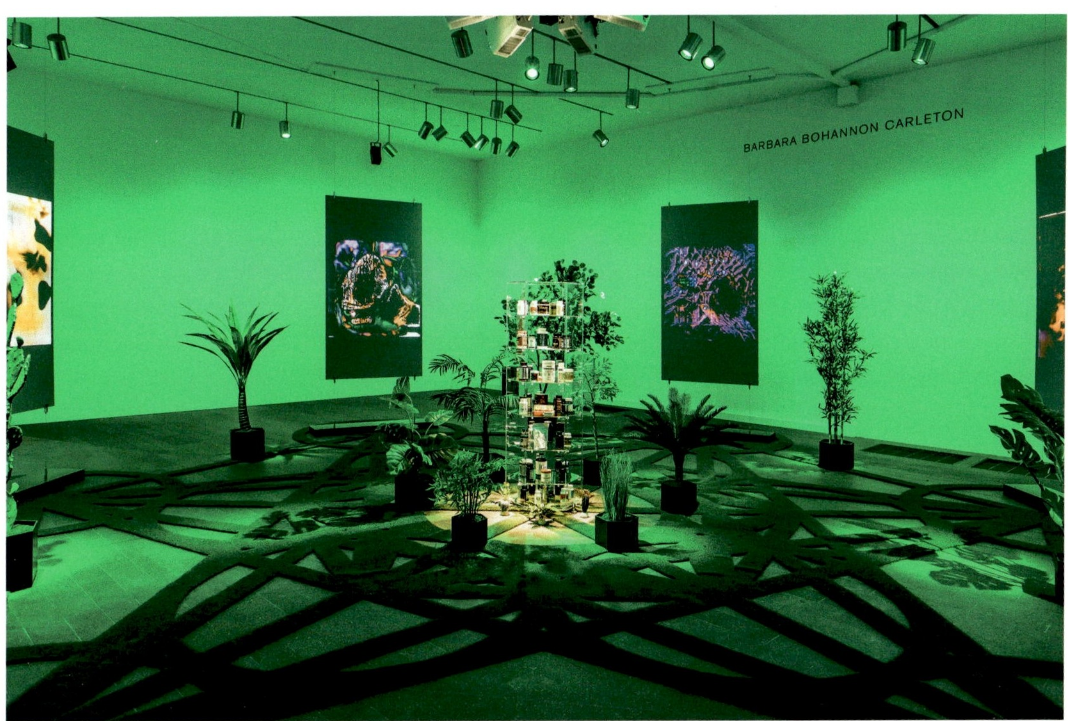


## *The Doors* (2019)

six-channel HD video (color with 7.1 surround sound, 41:25 min., looped), black-mirror screens, artificial grass sigil, artificial plants, hexagonal black-mirror plant pots, black sand, artificial green wall, neon, nootropics, drug menagerie, green fluorescent light, lizard water dish and heated rock ▸ installation dimensions variable

Credits
Commissioned by Edith-Russ-Haus for Media Art, Oldenburg; de Young Museum, San Francisco; and Van Abbemuseum, Eindhoven ▸ Architect and designer: Scott Kepford ▸ Machine-learning engineers (video and poetry): Ashwin D'Cruz and Christopher Tegho ▸ Machine-learning engineers (voice and music): Sam Parke-Wolfe and Cameron Thomas ▸ Machine-learning artist consultant: Jake Elwes ▸ Computer graphics supervisor: Harry Sanderson ▸ Animation: Mikkel Aabenhuus Sørensen ▸ Animation assistant: Yan Eltovsky ▸ Modeling and visual effects: Dayne Kolk ▸ Simulation assistant: Aslak Kjølås-Sæverud ▸ Compositing: Felix Lee ▸ Video editor: Isabel Freeman ▸ Musicians: xin and Aya Sinclair ▸ Supervising sound editor: Tom Sedgwick ▸ Mix engineer: Ben Hurd ▸ Artificial grass sigil: Evergreens UK ▸ Screens: Sparkuhl ▸ Neon: Kemp London ▸ Artificial green wall: Ascott ▸ Nootropics menagerie and hexagonal plant pots: Hamar Acrylic

Supported by a Grant for Media Art of the Foundation of Lower Saxony, Edith-Russ-Haus for Media Art

Special thanks: David Blas, Peter Burr, Rebecca Edwards, Luba Elliott, Andrew Hibbard, Mahan Moalemi, Edit Molnár, Claudia Schmuckli, Marcel Schwierin, Mark Stokes, Nimrod Vardi, and Darnell Witt

# Biographies

**ZACH BLAS** is an artist, filmmaker, and writer whose practice spans moving image, computation, theory, performance, and science fiction. Blas has exhibited, lectured, and held screenings internationally, at venues including the de Young Museum, San Francisco; Tate Modern, London; Walker Art Center, Minneapolis; 2018 Gwangju Biennale; 68th Berlin International Film Festival; Matadero Madrid; Los Angeles County Museum of Art; Art in General, New York; Gasworks, London; Van Abbemuseum, Eindhoven; Institute of Contemporary Arts, London; e-flux, New York; Whitechapel Gallery, London; Nam June Paik Art Center, Gyeonggi-do; ZKM I Center for Art and Media, Karlsruhe; and British Art Show 9. His practice has been supported by the Edith-Russ-Haus for Media Art, Arts Council England, and a Creative Capital Award in Emerging Fields. Blas's artwork is in the collections of the Museo Universitario Arte Contemporáneo, Mexico City; National Museum of Modern and Contemporary Art Korea, Seoul; and Whitney Museum of American Art, New York. His writings can be found in the collections *You Are Here: Art after the Internet* (Cornerhouse, 2017), *Documentary across Disciplines* (MIT Press, 2016), and *Queer: Documents of Contemporary Art* (MIT Press and Whitechapel Gallery, 2016) as well as *e-flux journal* and numerous exhibition catalogues. His work has been written about and featured by *Artforum*, *Frieze*, *ArtReview*, the BBC, the *Guardian*, and the *New York Times*. Between 2015 and 2021, Blas was Lecturer in the Department of Visual Cultures at Goldsmiths, University of London. As of 2021, Blas is Assistant Professor of Visual Studies in the Daniels Faculty of Architecture, Landscape, and Design at the University of Toronto.

**ÖVÜL Ö. DURMUŞOĞLU** is a curator, writer, and educator living in Berlin. She is currently Visiting Professor and Program Co-leader at the Graduate School at Universität der Künste Berlin and Visiting Professor at Hochschule für Bildende Kunst Braunschweig. Durmuşoğlu curated *Stars Are Closer and Clouds Are Nutritious under Golden Trees* at MMAG Foundation, Amman, Jordan, in 2019 and co-initiated, with Joanna Warsza, *Die Balkone* (*Life, Art, Pandemic and Proximity*, 2020; *Scratching the Surface*, 2021) in Berlin.

**ALEXANDER R. GALLOWAY** is a writer and computer programmer working on issues in philosophy, technology, and theories of mediation. Professor of Media, Culture, and Communication at New York University, he is the author of several books on digital media and critical theory, including *Laruelle: Against the Digital* (University of Minnesota Press, 2014), a monograph on digitality in the work of philosopher François Laruelle.

**PAMELA M. LEE** is Carnegie Professor of Modern and Contemporary Art at Yale University. She is the author, most recently, of *Think Tank Aesthetics: Midcentury Modernism, the Cold War, and the Neoliberal Present* (MIT Press, 2020) and *The Glen Park Library: A Fairytale of Disruption* (No Place Press, 2019).

**MAHAN MOALEMI** is a writer and researcher from Tehran. He is co-editor of *Ethnofuturisms* (Merve Verlag, 2018) and his writings have appeared in *art-agenda*, *Cabinet*, *Domus*, and *Spike Art Magazine*, among other art journals, exhibition catalogues, literary publications, anthologies, and zines published in and outside Iran. Moalemi is currently a PhD student in Film and Visual Studies at Harvard University.

**EDIT MOLNÁR** is a curator currently based in Germany. She earned her MA in Art History and Art Theory from Eötvös Lóránd University, Budapest. From 2000 to 2005, she was Director of the Studio Gallery, Budapest, the nonprofit exhibition space of the Studio of Young Artists Association; from 2005 to 2007, she worked as a curator at Műcsarnok / Kunsthalle, Budapest; and from 2007 to 2009, she was Director of the Cairo-based independent nonprofit institution the Contemporary Image Collective. Since 2015, she has been Co-director, together with Marcel Schwierin, of the Edith-Russ-Haus for Media Art in Oldenburg.

**KRIS PAULSEN** is Associate Professor in the Department of History of Art and the Film Studies Program at the Ohio State University, Columbus. She is the author of *Here/There: Telepresence, Touch, and Art at the Interface* (MIT Press, 2017).

**MARCEL SCHWIERIN** is a curator, filmmaker, and cofounder of the Werkleitz Biennale in Halle, the experimental film database cinovid, and the Arab Shorts film festival in Cairo. His films include *The Images* (experimental, 1994) and *Eternal Beauty* (feature-length documentary, 2003). He has regularly curated for the Werkleitz Biennale, the Goethe-Institut, and the International Short Film Festival Oberhausen, among others. From 2010 to 2015, he was Curator of Film and Video for transmediale in Berlin. Since 2015, he has been Co-director, together with Edit Molnár, of the Edith-Russ-Haus for Media Art in Oldenburg.

**MARC SIEGEL** is Professor of Film Studies at the Johannes Gutenberg University Mainz. His research and publications focus on issues in queer studies and experimental film. His book *A Gossip of Images* is forthcoming from Duke University Press. He is on the advisory board of the Forum Expanded section of the Berlin International Film Festival and a founding member of the art collective CHEAP.

**JEMIMA WYMAN** is an artist who lives and works between Brisbane and Los Angeles. Wyman's art practice incorporates various media including installation, video, performance, photography, and painting. Her most recent artworks use these media to focus on visually based resistance strategies employed within protest culture and zones of conflict.

# Zach Blas's Acknowledgments

I would like to thank Edit Molnár and Marcel Schwierin, Co-directors of the Edith-Russ-Haus for Media Art, for their inimitable generosity, trust, and kindness; for extensively championing my practice; and for the gift of bringing this book into the world. I am grateful to the entire book production team and their tireless, Herculean efforts, notably Milica Vlajković, Studio Pandan, Jaclyn Arndt, and Martin Conrads. I offer my deep gratitude to the writers in this volume: Övül Ö. Durmuşoğlu, Alexander R. Galloway, Pamela M. Lee, Mahan Moalemi, Kris Paulsen, and Marc Siegel—thank you for so ingeniously and carefully engaging my practice; it is moving and dazzling to see your words collected here.

To members of my production teams over the years, especially Harry Sanderson, Scott Kepford, xin, Daniel Swan, Benjamin Hurd, Tom Sedgwick, Ashwin D'Cruz, Christopher Tegho, Alison Kelly, Isabel Freeman, Dennis Dizon, Nick Petronzio, Amy von Harrington, Machine Histories, and Kristel Brinshot: the artworks presented here would not exist without your talent, skill, dedication, vision, and good spirits. I have had the privilege of featuring exceptionally brilliant artists in my works. Cassils, Susanne Sachsse, micha cárdenas, Elle Mehrmand, Paul Mpagi Sepuya, Raquel Gutiérrez, Dany Naierman, Lindsay Hicks, and Fusako Shiotani, I wholeheartedly appreciate and cherish your performances, and I am forever thankful for the opportunities to collaborate. Jemima Wyman, it was an absolute pleasure to take a psychedelic trip together.

The artworks presented in these pages have also materialized thanks to continued support from curators and museum directors, including Robert Leckie, Julia Kaganskiy, Angelique

Spaninks, Claudia Schmuckli, Janna Keegan, Charles Esche, Aileen Burns, Johan Lundh, Nisa Mackie, Pavel Pyś, Omar Kholeif, Lívia Nolasco Rózsás, Emily Pethick, Abina Manning, Roddy Schrock, Rita Gonzalez, Christine Y. Kim, Cuauhtémoc Medina, Kelani Nichole, Christiane Paul, Stefano Collicelli Cagol, Laurel Ptak, Aaron Cezar, and Michael Connor. I am indebted to your commitment and belief in what I do.

I live and work among truly phenomenal artists, intellectuals, academics, and friends who provide unwavering camaraderie, inspiration, and support: Melody Jue, Jennifer Rhee, Bridget Crone, Sam Nightingale, Corina Apostol, Nadja Millner-Larsen, Heather Dewey-Hagborg, Erika Balsom, Michelle Lee, Christopher O'Leary, Jeff Cain, Ana Paulina Lee, Ayesha Hameed, Manu Ramos, Ana Teixeira Pinto, Navine G. Khan-Dossos, James Bridle, Shu Lea Cheang, Matthew Fuller, Ricardo Dominguez, Susan Schuppli, Luciana Parisi, Andrew Culp, Trevor Paglen, Patricia Reed, Chris McCormack, Jacob Gaboury, Heather Davis, Ho Rui An, American Artist, Sofia Victorino, Laliv Melamed, Daniel van der Velden, Seb Franklin, Henriette Gunkel, Louis Henderson, Brian Kuan Wood, David Evans Frantz, Martabel Wasserman, Eva and Franco Mattes, Sean Dockray, Simon O'Sullivan, Gavin Butt, Diana Taylor, Nicole Agusti, Ethan White, Thor Perplies, Pinar Yoldas, Darnell Witt, Jess Hoffman, Pedro Marum, Patrick Keilty, Elisa Papa, Shaka McGlotten, Homay King, Megan Skanse, Sarah Stover, and Joni Zhu. A heartfelt thank you to Andrew Hibbard for all the years of love, care, encouragement, and editorial rigor. Marcela Coto and Jasmina Tumbas, here's to being enough for our too-muchness.

To N. Katherine Hayles, Mark B. N. Hansen, Jack Halberstam, Michael Hardt, Casey Reas, Rebeca Méndez, David Getsy, Tiffany Holmes, Roy Grundmann, and Bob Arnold: your sage guidance over the years has been—and continues to be—much appreciated.

I would like to sincerely thank the UK Arts and Humanities Research Council for awarding me a generous fellowship, which provided optimal conditions for creating artwork and this book.

Lastly, to my parents, with love: David Blas and Robin Blas.

Published on the occasion of the exhibition I
Diese Publikation erscheint anlässlich der Ausstellung
***Zach Blas—The Unknown Ideal***
**October 24, 2019–January 5, 2020**

Curated by I Kuratiert von
**Edit Molnár and Marcel Schwierin**



Supported by I Gefördert von

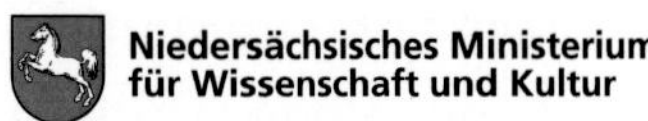


EWE | STIFTUNG

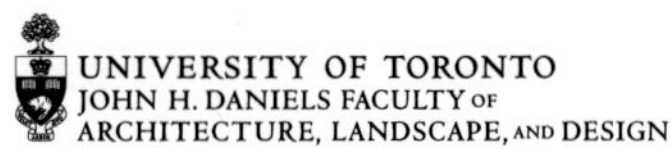


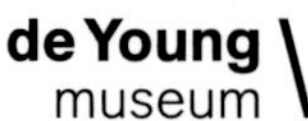


VAN ABBE MUSEUM EINDHOVEN

Edited by I Herausgegeben von
**Edit Molnár and Marcel Schwierin**

Contributions by I Beiträge von
**Zach Blas, Övül Ö. Durmuşoğlu, Alexander R. Galloway, Pamela M. Lee, Mahan Moalemi, Edit Molnár, Kris Paulsen, Marcel Schwierin, Marc Siegel, Jemima Wyman**

Managing Editor I Editorische Koordination
**Milica Vlajković**

Coordination I Koordination
**Ulrich Kreienbrink, Edit Molnár**

Translations to German I Deutsche Übersetzungen
**Barbara Hess (Punk-Vergangenheit, Dildo-Zukunft), Bert Rebhandl (Zwei Sprachen der Verdunkelung; Den menschlichen Umriss ficken; Es ist eine beschlossene Sache; In das Tal ohne Wiederkehr), Robert Schlicht (Vorwort; Als der Echsenkönig dem Echsenhirn begegnete; Biografien)**

Copyediting and Proofreading I Lektorat und Korrektorat
**Jaclyn Arndt (English), Martin Conrads (Deutsch)**

Graphic Design I Grafische Gestaltung
**Studio Pandan (Ann Richter, Pia Christmann, Vreni Knödler)**

Production I Produktion
**Edith-Russ-Haus für Medienkunst**

Printing and Binding I Gesamtherstellung
**DZA Druckerei zu Altenburg, Germany**

Photo Editing I Bildbearbeitung
**Prints Professional**

***Zach Blas: Unknown Ideals***

Published by I Veröffentlicht von
**Edith-Russ-Haus für Medienkunst**
**Katharinenstraße 23**
**D-26121 Oldenburg**
**www.edith-russ-haus.de**

edith
russ
HAUS

**Sternberg Press**
**71–75 Shelton Street**
**London WC2H 9JQ**
**United Kingdom**
**www.sternberg-press.com**

Sternberg Press

Distributed by I Vertrieb durch
**The MIT Press, Art Data, and Les presses du réel**



**The Deutsche Nationalbibliothek lists this publication in the Deutsche Nationalbibliografie; detailed bibliographic data is available online at http://dnb.dnb.de.**
**Die Deutsche Nationalbibliothek verzeichnet diese Publikation in der Deutschen Nationalbibliografie; detaillierte bibliografische Daten sind im Internet über http://dnb.dnb.de abrufbar.**

**ISBN 978-3-95679-588-6**